SEEKING JUSTICE
IN AND OUT OF COURT

STUDIA HELLENISTICA

STUDIA HELLENISTICA

62

SEEKING JUSTICE IN AND OUT OF COURT

DISPUTE RESOLUTION IN GRECO-ROMAN AND LATE ANTIQUE EGYPT

edited by

Sofie WAEBENS, Katelijn VANDORPE
and Nick VANEERDEWEGH

PEETERS
LEUVEN - PARIS - BRISTOL, CT
2023

A catalogue record for this book is available from the Library of Congress.

D/2023/0602/38
ISBN 978-90-429-4878-5
eISBN 978-90-429-4879-2

TABLE OF CONTENTS

ROMAN AND LATE ANTIQUE EGYPT

ABBREVIATIONS

For abbreviations of papyrological sources and instrumenta (*P.*, *O.*, *BL*, etc.), see J.F. Oates, R.S. Bagnall, S.J. Clackson, A.A. O'Brien, J.D. Sosin, T.G. Wilfong, and K.A. Worp, *Checklist of Greek, Latin, Demotic and Coptic Papyri, Ostraca and Tablets*, fifth ed. (BASP Suppl. 9), Oakville & Oxford 2001, regularly updated in the online version at http://www.papyri.info/docs/checklist.

For abbreviations of inscriptional sources (*I.*, *CIL*, *SEG*, etc.), see http://www.antiquite.ens.fr/IMG/file/pdf_guide_epi/abreviations_guide.pdf.

References to papyrological and epigraphical sources are accompanied by the Trismegistos number (TM #) (http://www.trismegistos.org).

Titles of journals are referenced using the standard scholarly abbreviations (a list can be found online at http://www.archeo.ens.fr/IMG/pdf/annee_philologique_abrev_revues.pdf).

Other abbreviations are as follows:

ACO:	E. Schwartz e.a., *Acta conciliorum œcomenicorum*, Berlin 1914ff.
CAPInv. #:	Copenhagen Associations Project, Inventory of Ancient Associations, followed by identification number of the association, see https://ancientassociations.ku.dk/
LÄ:	*Lexikon der Ägyptologie*, Wiesbaden 1975-1992.
PCBE:	*Prosopographie chrétienne du Bas-Empire*, Paris 1982ff.
PLRE:	*The Prosopography of the Later Roman Empire*, Cambridge 1971ff.
Pros. Ptol.:	W. Peremans e.a., *Prosopographia Ptolemaica*, 10 vol., Leuven 1950ff.
TM:	Trismegistos: An Interdisciplinary Portal of the Ancient World, see http://www.trismegistos.org/
TM #:	TM Texts, followed by identification number of the text, see https://www.trismegistos.org/tm/
TM Arch #:	TM Archives, followed by identification number of the archive, see https://www.trismegistos.org/arch/
TM Geo #:	TM Places, followed by identification number of the place, see https://www.trismegistos.org/geo/
TM Per #:	TM People, followed by identification number of the person, see https://www.trismegistos.org/ref/

INTRODUCTION

Family squabbles, fights over real estate, disputes over money transactions and assault cases were no less complex to resolve in Antiquity than they are in the modern world. The unique evidence from Egypt (more than 59,000 papyri and 44,000 ostraca) shows a wide variety of mechanisms that could be used to settle interpersonal disputes and to maintain social order within the country. Most of the evidence comes from petitions, official correspondence, and reports of court proceedings, which have been the subject of renewed attention in recent years and which give us primarily insight into the day-to-day operation of the legal system and the experiences of the people involved with it. Despite this wealth of information, papyri only offer us snapshots of the disputing process: though some legal documents record previous decisions made by officials or actions taken by victims, the outcome of a dispute is seldom known. This raises several questions concerning the prevailing legal procedures, the length of time that passed before a final decision was reached, the government's ability to enforce legal decisions, and the subversive ways in which the legal system could be used.

The legal system, however, represents only one mechanism of dispute resolution: in addition to the delivery of justice by the state courts, the papyri show that attempts were made to settle disputes privately, with no involvement of officials, mainly through coercion, negotiation, and mediation. These private processes of dispute resolution, which are also referred to as "self-help", "personal justice", or "alternative dispute resolution (ADR)", are more difficult to discern, because they are not systematically documented in juristic papyri, which constitute the majority of the evidence from Egypt. Documents such as petitions, private correspondence, temple oaths, oracle questions, and curse tablets nevertheless offer a rich data set for studying — at least partially — disputing processes that took place "in the shadow of the law" and the institutions that underpinned and strengthened these processes (such as social norms, religion, family values ...).

The present volume gathers the contributions of several participants of the international conference "Two Sides of the Same Coin – Dispute Resolution in Greco-Roman and Late Antique Egypt", organized by the Research Group Ancient History at KU Leuven and held at the Faculty of Arts in Leuven and the Royal Flemish Academy of Belgium for Sciences and the Arts in Brussels from June 29 to July 1, 2016. The aim of this conference was to bring together scholars working on dispute resolution from different perspectives (petitioning, law, religion, law enforcement, social norms ...) and different fields (papyrology, legal history, sociology, linguistics ...) to study the phenomenon of "social control" in Egypt,[1] with a particular focus on the transformation of the disputing process between the age of the Ptolemies and the Theodosians. Keynote lectures were given by Prof. Dr. Benjamin Kelly (York University), Prof. Dr. Joseph G. Manning (Yale University), Prof. Dr. Bernhard Palme (Institut für Alte Geschichte und Altertumskunde, Papyrologie und Epigraphik, Universität Wien), and Prof. Dr. Anne-Emmanuelle Veïsse (Université Paris 1 Panthéon-Sorbonne/Université Gustave Eiffel). The conference was organized with the financial support of the Research Foundation – Flanders (FWO – Vlaanderen), the Doctoral School Humanities and Social Sciences of KU Leuven (YouReCa), and the Royal Flemish Academy of Belgium for Sciences and the Arts (Koninklijke Vlaamse Academie van België voor Wetenschappen en Kunsten), for which we express our gratitude.

*

* *

The contributions in this volume address formal and private processes of dispute resolution both in general and in specific documents, and cases or actors involved in the disputing process in Greco-Roman and Late Antique Egypt.

---

[1] The term "social control" was introduced by B. Kelly in his 2011 study on petitions, litigation and social control in Roman Egypt to study the social role of petitioning and litigation: KELLY 2011, p. 16-18. Taken from the field of sociology, social control is defined as all those resources available by which the government attempted to maintain law and order and by which people attempted to resolve conflicts and to assure the norm-conforming behaviour of others.

Four contributions focus on formal dispute resolution under the Ptolemies, who were confronted with a broad range of challenges inherent to a new multicultural society. Anne-Emmanuelle VEÏSSE's paper (*Dispute Resolution in Alexandria and in the Chora in Third-Century BC Egypt*) examines early Ptolemaic evidence for the regulation of violence by comparing normative texts from Alexandria (the so-called *Dikaiomata*) with practice-related documents from the *chora*. For both the civic and non-civic milieus there was a need for a precise description of the violent acts and in both milieus acts of violence were taken seriously, resulting in people's trust in the government to protect their physical integrity.

The focus of Joseph G. MANNING's paper (*Courts, Justice and Culture in Ptolemaic Law: or the Rise of the Egyptian Jurists*) is the well-known trial proceeding report from Siut (Asyut, *P. BM Siut* p. 3-12 no. 10591 ro), testifying to the highly formal justice system of the Egyptian temple courts, including petitions and written pleadings before the trial. The text belongs to a group of texts that are traditionally considered part of a family archive, but Manning puts forward the hypothesis that the connection between the archival texts may be an advocate, engaged in legal affairs at Ptolemais, the seat of the high court and the administrative center of Upper Egypt at that time. He further discusses the reasons for the appearance of professional legal advocates in the Ptolemaic period.

The paper by Valérie WYNS (*Ptolemaic Government Ideology on Dispute Resolution*) studies the impact of ancient pharaonic and Greek cultural traditions on Ptolemaic ideology on dispute resolution. Drawing on sources from the ancient pharaonic, Greek and specifically Ptolemaic context, she concludes that Ptolemaic ideology presents no ruptures with either pharaonic Egyptian or Hellenistic philosophical thought. The most important elements in all three ideologies on officials in their judicial and administrative capacity is protecting the weak, showing leniency when sitting in judgement, emphasizing the application of the law, and being impartial.

The paper by Katelijn VANDORPE and Valérie WYNS (*Access to Justice in Ptolemaic Egypt. Assessing the Judiciary through Three Case Studies from the Thebaid*) seeks to find out to what extent the Ptolemies achieved their general objectives concerning dispute resolution. The role of the judiciary in dispute resolution is assessed in the second-century BC Thebaid through three case studies where the judicial procedures can be followed over a longer period: the Siut, the *Erbstreit* and the Hermias trials. The USIP's (United States Institute of Peace) guidelines offer an interesting framework for the assessment of ancient justice systems. Although the overall assessment is positive, a weak link in the judiciary system was undoubtedly the enforcement of verdicts.

Three contributions deal with private or extrajudicial channels of dispute resolution under the Ptolemies. The paper by Christine HUE-ARCÉ (*The Resolution of Interpersonal Violence through Extrajudicial Channels in the Demotic Documents*), which complements Veïsse's paper, studies the regulation of interpersonal violence through non-legal channels, as attested in the Demotic documents mainly from the Ptolemaic period. While the recourse to divinities and associations followed specific procedures, kinship was a popular informal channel that did not observe established procedures or rules. This article studies the functioning of these extrajudicial channels employed in the resolution of interpersonal violence, points to the role of orality and tries to understand how the non-legal instances worked together and complementary to the legal system.

The other two papers focus on the informal recourse to divinities and associations, respectively. Edward O.D. LOVE's paper (*Beyond Earthly Justice – Petitioning Deities and Divine Judgement in the "Letters to Gods"*) starts from a corpus of at least 41, mainly Demotic "Letters to Gods" from Late to Roman Period Egypt, which succeed a millennia-and-a-half-old tradition of "Letters to the Dead". While they may have been recited and/or accompanied by a practiced ritual, they were ultimately deposited in the catacombs and cemeteries of sacred animals or in temple sanctuaries. They encompass themes from "conducting a case" concerning embezzlement, robbery or loan defaults, to passing "judgement" on family disputes, and even entreaties for children or healing.

Finally, the paper by Mario C.D. PAGANINI (*Keep it for Yourself: Private Associations and Internal Dispute Resolution in Ptolemaic Egypt*) investigates the role private associations played in dispute resolution in Ptolemaic Egypt. The Demotic and Greek evidence shows that associations were a successful first port of call for settling discords between members in order to maintain their outward image of trustworthy and well-ordered institutions. They expected their members to renounce their right to seek legal justice in front of the authority for quarrels with fellow members, and members put a great deal of trust in the association's ability to provide a more informal, speedier, less expensive, and ultimately more satisfactory solution to their troubles.

Seven papers have their main focus on Roman & Late Antique Egypt. Two contributions discuss aspects of formal dispute resolution in Roman Egypt, touching upon fundamental questions such as access to justice and corruption among law enforcement officials and on neglected topics such as the role of police officials in dispute resolution. Benjamin KELLY's paper (*Accessing Justice in Roman Egypt: Quantitative Methods and their Limitations*) shows the possibilities, but also the limitations of using quantitative methods to understand the overall numbers of those seeking to access justice in Roman Egypt, illustrated by three case studies, dealing with (1) the fundamental question about litigation rates, (2) the topic of the fate of cases once they entered the system and the kind of justice litigants received, and (3) onomastic patterns amongst petitioners and plaintiffs. These onomastic patterns can be studied by using a quantitative approach, which suggests that the greater the wealth and economic engagement of a group, the more likely its members were to attempt to access justice.

The paper by Sofie WAEBENS (*Measuring Police Effectiveness in Roman Egypt: A Comparative Perspective*) focuses on the largely ignored topic of the impact of Roman rule on the role of police officials in maintaining social order in Roman Egypt. With the coming of Roman rule, profound changes were made to the police system: new types of (local) police officials were created, but the lion's share of law enforcement fell to Roman soldiers, who are generally depicted as violent and abusive in the sources. The major focus of the paper is the question whether Roman soldiers were therefore an imperfect instrument of law enforcement, as has been assumed in modern scholarship. To answer this question, the paper demonstrates how police effectiveness in an ancient society such as Roman Egypt might be assessed on the basis of insights taken from the fields of criminology and sociology.

Informal processes of dispute resolution in Roman Egypt, already touched upon in the papers of Hue-Arcé and Love for the Ptolemaic period, are investigated in the contribution by Marianna THOMA on various marital conflicts (*Dispute Resolution between Husband and Wife in Roman Egypt. Legal Mechanisms and Familial Strategies*). The paper illuminates not only the available legal mechanisms of resolution, but also private settlements of disputes between couples and the family strategies developed to ensure marital *concordia*. Particular attention is paid to the involvement of family members in the dispute resolution and the impact of the victim's sex on obtaining justice. By the end of the fourth century, under the influence of Christianity, local church officials were involved in the mediation of marital disputes.

In the paper *Predictably Unpredictable: Water Rights, Community, and Conflict in Fayyum Irrigation*, Brendan HAUG shows how fair access to the commons was possible and conflicts could be avoided for more than six centuries without the artificial certainty promised by externally-assigned rights in water. Contrary to the traditional narrative of the Fayyum's late antique difficulties, the paper argues that the water conflicts attested in the fourth century were not the result of external regulatory failures which, in turn, triggered the collapse of otherwise healthy communities. Drawing on comparative evidence from the medieval and modern periods, Haug argues in favour of the absence of externally-regulated water entitlements in the Greco-Roman period, which should be considered a feature of irrigation practice along the edges of the Fayyum depression rather than a failure.

The last four contributions deal with Late Antique dispute resolution in a period of stricter imperial control and Christianization of the country. The paper by Matthias STERN (*Disputing Public Authority in the Late Roman Countryside.* P. Cair. Masp. *I 67002 Revisited*) reviews *P. Cair. Masp.* I 67002, a petition composed by the well-known sixth-century poet and notary Dioskoros in which he complains of misconduct on the part of the local aristocrat Menas, thereby providing a better understanding of how power relations in the countryside were negotiated. The petition and its narrative were probably aimed at creating a case for social cohesion amid internal factionalism, which may echo larger developments, in the course of which increasingly empowered rural communities in parts of the late Roman empire found themselves confronted by more rigid imperial control.

The focus of Bruno MARIEN's paper (*Judicial Interventions in Late Antique Recommendation Letters: a Way of Seeking Justice?*) is a dossier of four papyri from the archive of Dioskoros including the intervention letter *SB* IV 7438, which shares several characteristics with recommendation letters from late antique epistolographers (Augustine, Symmachus, Gregory of Nazianzus, Basil, Synesius and Libanius). These examples show that judicial intervention was a widespread practice in Late Antiquity, taking many forms and occurring at different stages of the procedure.

The contribution by Luise Marion FRENKEL (*Roman Elements of Religious Dispute Resolutions in the Theodosian Age*) studies the suitability of religious leaders such as Christian bishops for dispute resolution based on a set of texts of the Theodosian age, ranging from discourses highlighting their role to rulings circumscribing episcopal legal jurisdiction. The examples point to religious hierarchies in the fourth and fifth century similar to Roman structures of authority, and associate an increased awareness of Roman institutions and regulations with a monk's, bishop's or rabbi's greater authority to arbitrate.

Nicholas VENABLE's paper (*Holy Men, Roman Legal Practice, and Social Memory in Late Antique Egypt*) examines evidence for the involvement of clergy in legal disputes in both discourse (Coptic hagiography) and practice (Late Antique papyrus documents) in fifth and sixth-century Egypt. Although monks and clergy became new figures of authority when handling legal disputes, they frequently acted through Roman officials or used methods of reproducing social memory originating in Roman legal practice. The social prestige of Roman law in Christian documents, and the gradual adaptation of legal institutions to include Christian elements, would persist as monasteries became central to the practice of Roman law in Egypt in the seventh and eighth centuries.

*

* *

Given the focus on both public and private dispute resolution mechanisms in Egypt — which contribute to the same goal and can therefore be considered two sides of the same coin — and the interdisciplinary approach taken to dispute resolution, this volume provides a unique insight into the various ways in which conflicts were regulated in ancient Egypt. It illuminates in particular the functioning of the legal system, the role of private associations, religion and social norms as an alternative form of dispute resolution, and the methodological problems related to the study of petitions, which form the core of the evidence for dispute resolution in Egypt. Covering almost 1000 years of Egyptian history, starting with the liberation of Egypt from Persian rule by Alexander the Great in 332 BC and ending with the start of Arab rule in AD 642, this volume sheds light on some of the changes that the disputing process underwent under (late) Roman rule. Although it is difficult to obtain a complete and coherent picture of the transformation of the disputing process in Greco-Roman and Late Antique Egypt,[2] the papyrological evidence suggests that certain private mechanisms of dispute resolution were discouraged in favour of state adjudication under early Roman rule, resulting in the disappearance of documents such as Demotic temple oaths. From the fourth century AD onwards, however, private mechanisms of dispute resolution are well attested, while the evidence for state adjudication becomes scarce, even to the point that some scholars believe that private means of dispute resolution almost entirely came to replace state adjudication. The extent to which alternative dispute resolution gained importance over state adjudication after Justinian, however, remains a matter of dispute.[3] Though diverse in both topic and scope, the contributions in this volume show that private means of settling disputes without the involvement of the state no longer take place "in the shadow of the law", but were recognized as a means of easing the administrative burden on the judicial system. This change in the disputing process should be placed against the background of the administrative changes that took place in Egypt under Roman rule. The administration reached its peak of systematization under Roman rule, because "Everybody and everything were counted and recorded".[4] The strict procedures and official status categories imposed on the population required an enormous bureaucratic effort from both officials and private individuals, hindering an efficient working of the administration. This is perhaps best illustrated by the famous Nestnephis lawsuit archive (TM Arch 151), which documents a long and bitter dispute between

---

[2] For a broad overview of the changes in government, administration, society and religious life that occurred in Greco-Roman and Late Antique Egypt, see VANDORPE 2019.

[3] These conflicting views were to some extent reflected in the papers presented at the DR Egypt conference by Bernhard Palme ('Courts and Legal Proceedings in Late Roman Egypt') and Marzena Wojtczak ('Private Dispute Resolution in Late Antiquity – An Alternative to State Jurisdiction?'), which are not included in this volume. For further discussion of the scholarly debate on the relevance of the bias in the papyrological evidence towards private forms of dispute resolution, see WOJTCZAK 2012, p. 354-355 n. 5; for discussion of the possible reasons for people to turn away from institutionalized courts in favour of settlements of claims and arbitration, see URBANIK 2007.

[4] ROWLANDSON 1998, p. 13.

Nestnephis and Satabous over the ownership of some empty plots of land in the village of Soknopaiou Nesos, situated in the Fayum. Satabous claimed to have bought them in AD 11, but a search of the archive at Alexandria in AD 15 did not produce the sale contract. Since local notaries had apparently failed to register the contract at the central record office, it had no legal value, and Satabous was forced to pay a large sum of money to become the legitimate owner of the land. Starting from the early third century AD, efforts were made to improve the bureaucratic efficiency and continuity, but the transformation of the administration was not complete until the reign of Diocletian.[5] By the late fourth century, under the influence of Christianity, monks and clergy became increasingly involved in the mediation of disputes. The gradual adaptation of legal institutions to include Christian elements continued under the Byzantine emperors and culminated in the seventh and eighth centuries AD, when monasteries became central to the practice of Roman law in Egypt.

Given the focus on both formal and informal methods of dispute resolution in Egypt, this volume should be considered complementary to the conference volume *Recht haben und Recht bekommen im Imperium Romanum. Das Gerichtswesen der römischen Kaiserzeit und seine dokumentarische Evidenz*, edited by R. Haensch in 2016.[6] It provides a detailed overview of the large amount of epigraphical and papyrological documents published during the last century that provide insight on Roman and post-Roman administration of justice from the Principate until Late Antiquity, illuminating both its weaknesses and strengths. Nevertheless, it should be noted that there are still important gaps in our knowledge of dispute resolution in Egypt, in particular with regard to the effectiveness of public and private justice, other methods of alternative dispute resolution, and the interaction between public and private forms of

---

[5] Particularly interesting is that a similar trend can be observed in modern law: over the past 40 years, there has been a significant growth in and use of alternative forms of dispute resolution, which are recognized as a means to ensure access to "simple, efficient, fast and low-cost ways of resolving disputes", not only at national level, but also within the EU. For the legal framework of alternative dispute resolution, see European Law Institute (ELI), *The Relationship between Formal and Informal Justice: The Courts and Alternative Dispute Resolution. Report of the European Law Institute and of the European Network of Councils for the Judiciary*, Vienna 2018.

[6] Haensch 2016.

dispute resolution. We hope therefore that this volume will stimulate further research into all resources available for the delivery of justice, both in and out of the court.

To conclude, we would like to extend warm thanks to the keynote speakers, the members of the scientific committee (Prof. Dr. Joseph Manning, Prof. Dr. Anne-Emmanuelle Veïsse, Prof. Dr. Jakub Urbanik, Prof. Dr. Alain Delattre and Prof. Dr. Paul Erdkamp), and all participants of the DR Egypt 2016 conference, who came from many different disciplines, each bringing his or her own particular expertise in dispute resolution, and many different countries. Not all speakers have contributed to this volume, but we thank all those present for their stimulating papers and comments in the discussions afterwards. Thanks are also due to our colleagues of the Research Group Ancient History at KU Leuven, in particular Valérie Wyns and Gert Baetens, who have provided invaluable assistance in organizing this three-day international conference in Leuven and Brussels and have contributed to making it a wonderful experience for all those involved, in true *amicitia papyrologorum*-style. Last but not least, we would like to thank Willy Clarysse, Peter Van Dessel and Nick Vaneerdewegh for their help in editing this volume.

Leuven, December 3, 2021
Sofie Waebens and Katelijn Vandorpe

PTOLEMAIC EGYPT

DISPUTE RESOLUTION IN ALEXANDRIA AND IN THE *CHORA* IN THIRD-CENTURY BC EGYPT*

Anne-Emmanuelle VEÏSSE
(Université Gustave Eiffel)

Abstract: The issue of dispute resolution constitutes one of the few instances of common ground, in terms of documentation, between Alexandria and the *chora* in the third century BC. The so-called Alexandrian "Dikaiomata", indeed, contain several sections concerning the regulation of violence in the city; meanwhile, dozens of documents written in the *chora* during the same century refer to acts of violence that have been denounced, investigated and, sometimes, also resolved.

The present article aims at comparing the normative, Alexandrian texts with these practice-related documents, and showing how they might enlighten each other. The study first examines the types of violence that are documented in both categories of sources, and then highlights the various reactions to the acts of violence in civic and non-civic contexts.

INTRODUCTION

While the political and social realities of the Greek city of Alexandria are generally difficult to connect to those of the *chora*, the issue of dispute resolution offers a welcome exception thanks to the Alexandrian *Dikaiomata*. This collection of Alexandrian laws contains several sections about how acts of violence were dealt with in the city. Comparisons may be made to dozens of practice-related documents written in the *chora* which refer to actual acts of violence. The so-called *Dikaiomata* are known from the papyrus *P. Hal.* 1 (TM 5876), which for palaeographical reasons belongs in the third century; however, neither its provenance nor

* I thank K. VANDORPE and S. WAEBENS, the organizers of the conference, and the anonymous reader of this article for their valuable corrections and suggestions.

its purpose have been clearly established.[1] According to the editors, a lawyer (*sunegoros*) gathered the documents for a court case[2] – hence the name of *Dikaiomata*, i.e. "supporting documents", "proof-texts", duly applied to the whole papyrus.[3] This hypothesis has been challenged by Alessandro Hirata, who suggested that the *P. Hal.* 1 was a compilation made to meet an official's needs.[4] The various legal traditions from which Alexandrian city laws were borrowed remain debatable as well,[5] as does the extent of royal involvement in elaborating them. In principle, city law, explicitly referred to as "*politikos nomos*" in one of the sections,[6] is not identical with royal edicts and did not apply beyond the city limits. In particular, as shown by Joseph Mélèze-Modrzejewski, it should not be confused with the *politikoi nomoi* alluded to in some papyri: those were the "common laws" of the Greeks living in the *chora*, which were applicable by the local courts in the absence of a royal disposition.[7] However,

---

[1] The papyrus was edited in 1913 by the members of the GRAECA HALENSIS (F. Bechtel, O. Kern, K. Praechter, C. Robert, E. von Stern, U. Wilcken, G Wissowa). A general presentation was provided by FRASER 1972, p. 109-112, and more recently by HIRATA 2010, p. 39-50; see also HIRATA 2008, p. 675-681, and KEENAN, MANNING & YIFTACH-FIRANKO 2014, p. 449-450. For a presentation of the sections concerning violence, see TAUBENSCHLAG 1955, p. 435-436 (with a comparison with documents from the *chora* p. 436-440). The study of VÉLISSAROPOULOS 1981 is available in modern Greek only. The quotations of the text given in this article are borrowed from the translation by BAGNALL & DEROW 2004, text no. 124.

[2] *P. Hal.* 1, p. 26-33.

[3] The term *dikaiomata* is applied in col. ii, l. 38, in the section about perjury: "the proof-texts of a case (τὰ δὲ δικαιώ[μα]τα τῆ<ς> δίκης), in which someone is challenging testimonies, shall be produced, *etc*." See BAGNALL & DEROW's definition of *dikaiomata*: "the legal texts called upon to support one side".

[4] See HIRATA 2010, p. 40: "Es spricht viel mehr dafür, dass es sich um eine Zusammenstellung für den behördlichen Gebrauch handelte; vielleicht für bestimmte Beamte der alexandrinischen Verwaltung". According to the GRAECA HALENSIS editors, the papyrus, which is not fully preserved, was written by at least six different hands; furthermore, the original order of the different sections was probably altered in some places, including the sections concerning cases of violence (*P. Hal.* 1, p. 8 and p. 109).

[5] Parallels can be drawn with the laws of Athens in the first place, but with other cities such as Rhodes as well. See *P. Hal.* 1, p. 174-177; FRASER 1972, p. 110-112; HIRATA 2010.

[6] Col. iv, l. 79 (about planting and building). Perhaps also col. v, l. 106 within the same section.

[7] MÉLÈZE-MODRZEJEWSKI 2014a, p. 151-169.

three sections of *P. Hal.* 1 make explicit reference to a royal *diagramma*,[8] and another certainly derives from royal legislation (about perjury).[9] Considering the relationship between kings and cities in the Hellenistic world in general, and in the Ptolemaic Empire in particular (the *diagramma* of Cyrene may well come to mind), one may assume that there was at least some sort of royal approval for the other dispositions.[10]

In terms of dispute resolution, the Alexandrian *Dikaiomata* are interesting because of their normative character. Among many other items — such as actions for perjury, construction law, or royal oath — they prescribe how different cases of violence should be litigated, and the applicable penalties.[11] On the other hand, about sixty documents written in the *chora* during the third century BC refer to acts of violence that were in fact denounced, investigated, and, sometimes, also resolved. Although they were all drafted in Greek, these documents concern not

[8] Col. ii, l. 46 (about filing a complaint for perjury "according to the *diagramma*"), col. iii, l. 59-60 and 67, and col. vii, l. 165 (exaction of damages by the *praktor* "according to the *diagramma*"). About the exaction by the *praktor*, which is also mentioned in col. iii, l. 53-55 and col. v, l. 115-119, see MÉLÈZE-MODRZEJEWSKI 2014a, p. 202, n. 17: "l'exécution des sentences des tribunaux alexandrins appartient aux agents royaux, la règlementation de la procédure est donc l'œuvre du roi". Also WOLFF 1970, p. 26, n. 22. In another city law collection from the third century (presumably from Naucratis, or Ptolemais), preserved on the papyrus *P. Lille* I 29 = *C. Ptol. Sklav.* I 1 (TM 3231), a royal *diagramma* about proceedings against slaves is also referred to twice (l. 11-12 and l. 36-37).

[9] The disposition is also found in *SB* X 10494 (third century BC; TM 5937), among other extracts of royal laws, which were obviously relevant both for Alexandria and for the *chora*: see WOLFF 1970, p. 24-27; KALTSAS' introduction to *P. Heid.* VIII 412, p. 11-12; MÉLÈZE-MODRZEJEWSKI 2014a, p. 203 and n. 25. The various texts contained in *P. Hal. 1* also include a letter from King Ptolemy Philadelphus (col. viii, l. 166-185 = *C. Ord. Ptol.* 24; about the billeting of soldiers in the Edfu nome) and another letter from the *dioiketes* Apollonios (col. xi, l. 260-265; about exemptions from the salt-tax / *halike* for the professionals of Greek culture). It is generally considered that these two letters that both bore royal decisions supplemented existing city laws; however, the hypothesis of HIRATA (see above, n. 4) opens up other possible interpretations.

[10] See MÉLÈZE-MODRZEJEWSKI 2014a, p. 99-102 and p. 203. On the *diagramma* of Cyrene: BENCIVENNI 2003, p. 105-149; BERTHELOT 2015.

[11] Due to this normative character, the arrangements made to regulate acts of violence in the *Dikaiomata* are also worth comparing to the Demotic rules of religious associations in the *chora*, in particular *P. Lille Dem.* 1 29 (TM 2784), which also dates to the third century (223 BC). On these associations, see DE CÉNIVAL 1972; MONSON 2006; HUE-ARCÉ 2020, and her contribution in the present volume.

only Greek, but also Egyptian people. More than half of these are petitions submitted to the king (*enteuxeis*) or to his agents (*hupomnemata*)[12], reporting either acts of violence exclusively, or acts of violence alongside another prejudice. Other categories of documents can be added to these petitions: complaints submitted to individuals whose official position is more questionable such as Zenon, or Kleon the engineer; disclosures to law and enforcement (*prosangelmata*[13]); court records; witness-declarations; and some other papyri pertaining to violence cases.[14] In order to compare how violence was dealt with in Alexandria and in the *chora*, we will first investigate the types of violence that the *Dikaiomata* and these practice-related documents describe, and then the various reactions to the acts of violence in civic and non-civic contexts.

---

[12] On Ptolemaic petitions, see now BAETENS 2020a.

[13] The caracterisation of this category of documents is discussed by BAETENS 2020a, p. 197-218.

[14] **Petitions**: *BGU* III 1007 (TM 5552), *BGU* VI 1244 (TM 4405), *BGU* X 1903 (TM 8299), *P. Enteux.* 12 (TM 3289), *P. Enteux.* 18 (TM 3295), *P. Enteux.* 25 (TM 3300), *P. Enteux.* 72 (TM 3347), *P. Enteux.* 73 (TM 3348), *P. Enteux.* 74 (TM 3349), *P. Enteux.* 75 (TM 3350), *P. Enteux.* 76 (TM 3351), *P. Enteux.* 78 (TM 3353), *P. Enteux.* 79 (TM 3354), *P. Enteux.* 80 (TM 3355), *P. Enteux.* 81 (TM 3356), *P. Enteux.* 82 (TM 3357), *P. Enteux.* 83 (TM 3358), *P. Enteux.* 111 (TM 3361), *P. Köln* III 140 (TM 3174), *P. Köln* VI 272 (TM 3202), *P. Lond.* VII 2039 (TM 1601), *P. Petr.* III 22a (TM 7395), *P. Petr.* III 27 Ro (TM 7405), *P. Petr.* III 28e Ro (TM 7410), *P. Petr.* III 32c (TM 7424), *P. Petr.* III 32g Rob (TM 7699), *P. Sorb.* III 103 (TM 121855), *P. Sorb.* III 112 (TM 121859), *SB* X 10271 Ro (TM 5801), *SB* XX 14999 (TM 8121), *SB* XX 15001 (TM 8123), *UPZ* II 151 (TM 2975), P. TCD Pap. Gr. env. 86/87 Ro (TM 8832). ***Prosangelmata***: *P. Col.* IV 92 + *P. Cair. Zen.* IV 59659 (TM 1290), *P. Gur.* 8 (TM 5871), *SB* VI 9068 (TM 6195; a *prosangelma* or a *hupomnema* ? see BAETENS 2020a, p. 199, n. 321), *SB* XVI 12671 (TM 4141). **Complaints to Zenon**: *P. Cair. Zen.* I 59080 + *P. Mich.* I 19 (TM 735), *P. Cair. Zen.* II 59281 (TM 925), *P. Cair. Zen.* III 59443 (TM 1083), *P. Cair. Zen.* III 59454 Ro (TM 1093), *P. Cair. Zen.* III 59462 (TM 1100), *P. Col.* III 6 (TM 1728), *P. Lond.* VII 2009 (TM 1571), *P. Ryl.* IV 570 (= *P. Cair. Zen.* III 59395; TM 2426), *P. Cair. Zen.* V 59830 (TM 1454). **Complaints to Kleon**: *P. Petrie Kleon* 54 (TM 7646). **Witness-declarations**: *P. Hamb.* I 105 (TM 2311), *P. Hib.* II 200 (TM 5184), *P. Petr.* III 22d (TM 7398), *P. Petr.* III 22e (TM 7399), *P. Petr.* III 23 (TM 7401). **Court reports**: *P. Gur.* 2 (TM 5865), *P. Petr.* III 21d, l. 1-4 (TM 2990). **Other documents**: *P. Col.* III 34 (TM 1753), *P. Eleph. Wagner* 1, III (TM 78215), *P. Hib.* I 111 (TM 8241), *P. Tebt.* III.1 821 (TM 5397), *PSI* IV 380 (TM 2064). Only the documents that unambiguously refer to physical assault or verbal abuse were taken into consideration.

1. Types of violence

1.1. *Threats*

Several sections concerning cases of violence against individuals are listed in the Alexandrian *Dikaiomata*. The first one deals with a specific category of verbal violence, i.e. making an armed threat (*epantasis*): "Threatening with iron ([σι]δήρου ἐπαντάσεως). If a freeman threatens a freeman with iron or copper or stone or [...] or wood, *etc.*" (col. viii, l. 186-192).[15] Although this case has no exact equivalent in the practice-related documents, threats could be reported in petitions as support for the legitimacy of the request. For instance, the Egyptian petitioner Tetosiris of *P. Enteux.* 86 (TM 3386) reports that she was threatened, along with her witnesses, with being beaten and expelled from the village by the man against whom she was currently on trail;[16] nonetheless she does not seek redressal on that point, but is merely asking that her witnesses be allowed to testify.[17]

1.2. *Physical assault*

The subsequent three sections of the *Dikaiomata* concern physical assaults.[18] The first deals with bodily harm done in drunkenness, or by

---

[15] "Threatening with iron ([σι]δήρου ἐπαντάσεως). If a freeman threatens a freeman with iron or copper or stone or [...] or wood, he shall forfeit a hundred drachmas, if he is defeated in the suit. But if a male slave or a female slave does any of these things to a freeman or a freewoman, they shall receive no less than [a hundred] stripes, or else the master of the offender, if he is defeated in the suit, shall forfeit to the injured party twice the amount of the penalty which is prescribed for a freeman" (col. viii, l. 186-192).

[16] This man, Apollonios, threatened to subject Tetosiris and her witnesses to the torture of *apotumpanismos*; on this term, see Balamoshev 2011. With this threat, Apollodoros terrorized the witnesses: he made them "bristling with fear" (ἀνεσόβησεν πάντας, l. 6), so that they did not dare to give their testimony.

[17] In *P. Cair. Zen.* III 59462 (TM 1100), Kriton complains to Zenon that a man, whose name is lost, tried to steal his sow and threatened to hamstring the beast. In another complaint addressed to Zenon, a Philadelphia pub-owner reports having been assaulted by night by two thirsty men who intimated him into open his shop, and then "set out to force the entrance, levering open the door with their knives and sticks" (*P. Lond.* VII 2009; TM 1571, transl. Clarysse 2001, p. 163). The owner now asks for justice, without saying, however, if the request relates to any material damage done to the door or indeed to threats.

[18] Physical assaults are also referred to in col. v, l. 115-119, where penalties for a defeated accuser are discussed ("If anyone [after bringing suit for ...] or blows (ἢ πληγῶν) is

night, or in a temple, or in a market-place, that is to say violence committed under aggravating circumstances: "Injuries done in drunkenness (μεθύοντος ἀδικιῶν). Whoever commits an injury to the person (τῶν εἰς τὸ σῶ[μ]α ἀδικημάτ[ων]) in drunkenness or by night or in a temple or in the market-place shall forfeit twice the amount of the prescribed penalty" (col. ix, l. 193-195). The second section concerns blows (*plegai*) inflicted on a freeman by a slave (col. ix l. 196-202) and the third section deals with blows occurring between freemen (col. ix, l. 203-209). In the latter, a distinction is made between striking one blow, striking "more than one blow" (πλείονας πληγῆς μιᾶ[ς]), and striking a magistrate on duty. Similarly, almost all cases of violence reported in the practice-related documents are physical assaults. Some of these documents also stress that the acts were committed under circumstances considered aggravating according to the Alexandrian code: in a temple, at night, or in drunkenness.[19] There are no examples of blows inflicted either by a slave or, for obvious reasons, against a city magistrate; meanwhile, the complaints filed *by* royal agents in the *chora* regarding acts of violence are rare and none of these belong in the third century BC. By contrast, the documents from the *chora* cover a wider spectrum of physical violence, including burning, biting and spitting.[20] In addition, three refer to homicide, which is not mentioned in the sections of the city laws compiled in the *P. Hal.* 1. Two out of the three cases are *hupomnemata*. The first one probably concerns involuntary homicide: a woman has died after having been dragged out of her house and struck in the chest (*P. Köln* VI 272; TM 3202).[21] The second is more ambiguous (*BGU* VI 1244; TM 4405): the brewer Tkollousis refers to the proceedings brought against her before the chrematists (the royal judges) when she was accused

defeated, he shall pay [to the winner] an additional tenth of the value of the suit" (...) "Anyone who after bringing suit for [... or] bodily harm? ([αἰκι(?)]σμοῦ) is defeated shall pay to the winner an additional fifth of the [value of the suit])".

[19] In a temple: *P. Enteux.* 80 (TM 3355), and probably also *P. Enteux.* 78 (TM 3353), cf. l. 11 ἐπὶ τὸν βωμόν. By night and in a drunken state: *P. Lond.* VII 2009. On this document, see CLARYSSE 2001, p. 163, who notices that "the word, μεθυόντων 'being drunk', has been inserted between the lines, apparently to aggravate the case".

[20] Burning: *P. Enteux.* 82 (TM 3357); biting: *SB* X 10271 (TM 5801). Spitting (*P. Enteux.* 79 [TM 3354], *P. Gur.* 2 [TM 5865]) might be considered as physical violence or as *hubris* (see below).

[21] For the l. 1-5, see CLARYSSE 2009, p. 243.

for the murder (*phonos*) of an infant; however, she qualifies the charges as being "unfounded" (*agenetos*) denying any responsibility.[22] The third document, a *prosangelma*, concerns in all likelihood a voluntary homicide considering the fact that the murdered man had previously written a *prosangelma* denouncing acts committed by his murderer (*SB* XVI 12671; TM 4141).[23]

1.3. *Hubris*

The last section concerning personal attacks in the *Dikaiomata* deals with acts of *hubris*, which is a more problematic term:

> *Hubris*: If any person commits against another an act of *hubris* not provided for in the code (...) (ὕβρεως. ἐάν τις καθυβρίσηι ἕτερος ἑτέρου τ[ῶ]ν ἀγράφων, ...) (col. ix, l. 210).

Here, *hubris* is defined not objectively, but relatively, as being an offense other than those already mentioned in the law.[24] In modern research, the term is often translated by "outrage", in accordance with its meaning in the legal texts of classical Athens and of Aristotle's definition:[25] "*Hubris* is doing or saying things at which the victim incurs shame, not in order that one might achieve anything other than what is done but simply to get pleasure from it" (*Rhet.* 1378b23-29).[26] Accordingly, in Athens *hubris* was prosecuted by means of a *graphe hubreos*: this "public action for *hubris*" theoretically permitted one to sue for various sorts of physical assault as well as verbal abuse, even though there are no enduring excerpts of speeches given during a trial for *hubris*.[27] From the perspective of Alexandrian law, given the penalties that applied, *hubris* was a major crime: as we shall further discuss, it belonged to the categories

---

[22] On this document, see BAUSCHATZ 2013, p. 85-86, and *infra* p. 23.

[23] For the l. 4-5 see CLARYSSE 2008, p. 55.

[24] On *hubris* in the papyri, see TAUBENSCHLAG 1955, p. 435-442; HELMIS 1986, p. 21-22; RUPPRECHT 1993; HUE-ARCÉ 2020, p. 37-38. On the relationship between the category of *hubris* in the *Dikaiomata* and the *actio iniuriarum* of the Romans, see TAUBENSCHLAG 1955, p. 436; HIRATA 2008.

[25] See FISHER 1992; OMITOWOJU 2002, p. 29-50; DEMONT 2006; RIESS 2012.

[26] Trad. FISHER 1992, p. 8.

[27] See OMITOWOJU 2002, p. 31: "In fact we have no speech which comes from a case where someone is being tried for *hubris*, but we find texts in which it is threatened as an alternative form of procedure, or in which references are made to actions for *hubris* which were brought, or non-legal texts in which a suit is threatened".

of offences for which the victim had to assess the compensation himself, as in the case of "striking several blows", and (probably) "striking a magistrate on duty", which stands in contrast with the offences for which a set penalty was predefined, namely "striking one blow" and "threatening with weapons".

In the Ptolemaic documentation, the term *hubris* first appears in the marriage contract of Elephantine from 310 BC (*P. Eleph.* 1; TM 5836). It refers to the husband bringing home another woman, or in other words, an instance of a moral outrage:

> It shall not be permitted for Herakleides to bring home another wife in insult of Demetria (ἐφ' ὕβρει Δημητρίας) or to have children by another woman (*P. Eleph.* 1, l. 8-9).[28]

By contrast, from *P. Giss.* I 2 (TM 2796), more than a century later (173 BC), the verb *hubrizein* is used in marriage contracts within a more generic and more ambiguous expression: "it shall not be permitted (to the husband) to cast out (*ekballein*), or to outrage (*hubrizein*) or to abuse (*kakouchein*) (his wife)".[29] The noun *hubris* or the verb *hubrizein* also appear in 18 papyri referring to conflicts between individuals in the third-century BC (petitions and other sorts of documents).[30] In most cases we do not know what specific acts were committed, but some are more

[28] The same expression is found in *P. Cair. Zen.* III 59462 (TM 1100) (see above, n. 17), a complaint addressed to Zenon about attempted theft and threatening behaviour, but no physical violence.

[29] This formula is to be found in two other Ptolemaic contracts drawn up in the *chora* and in seven Alexandrian contracts dating from the beginning of the Roman period. *Chora*: *P. Gen.* I² 21 = *Chrest. Mitt.* 284 (TM 44544; second century BC), *P. Tebt.* I 104 (TM 3740; 92 BC). Alexandria: *BGU* IV 1050 (TM 18493; 12/11 BC), *BGU* IV 1051 (TM 18494, 30 BC-14 AD), *BGU* IV 1052 (TM 18495; 14/3 BC), *BGU* IV 1099 (TM 18537; 30 BC-14 AD), *BGU* IV 1100 (TM 18538; 30 BC-14 AD), *BGU* IV 1101 (TM 18539; 13 BC), *SB* XXIV 16072 = 16073 (TM 79295 and 79296; 12 BC); probably also *BGU* IV 1098 (TM 18536; 19-15 BC), in spite of the lacuna.

[30] *BGU* X 1903 (TM 8299), *P. Cair. Zen.* I 59080 (TM 735), *P. Cair. Zen.* II 59281 (TM 925), *P. Cair. Zen.* III 59454 Ro (TM 1093), *P. Cair. Zen.* III 59462 (TM 1100), *P. Col.* III 6 (TM 1728), *P. Eleph. Wagner* 1, III (TM 78215), *P. Enteux.* 73 (TM 3348), *P. Enteux.* 74 (TM 3349), *P. Enteux.* 75 (TM 3350), *P. Enteux.* 78 (TM 3353), *P. Enteux.* 79 (TM 3354), *P. Gur.* 2 (TM 5865), *P. Hib.* I 32 (TM 7815), *P. Petr.* III 22a (TM 7395), *P. Ryl.* IV 570 (= *P. Cair. Zen.* III 59395; TM 2426), *P. Sorb.* III 112 (TM 121859), *P. Tebt.* III.1 821 (TM 5397). In *P. Hamb.* II 182 (TM 4336), which is an official letter, the term *hubris* is used to describe the abuse of the oil-merchants.

informative. In five cases at least, *hubris* pertains to physical violence. The plaintiff of *P. Enteux.* 74 (TM 3349), whose name is lost, gives a particularly detailed account of how he was beaten up by a man called Peithias after an argument, and consequently he "assesses (the damages caused by the) *hubris*" to be a certain amount (which is lost because of lacuna).[31] In *P. Enteux.* 75 (TM 3350), the Macedonian Crateuas denounces both damages caused to pastures by the shepherds of Alabanthis, and the fact that he was assaulted: first, the shepherds struck him, then they took his coat, stripping him bare (*gumnos*), a point he strongly insists upon: "I went [to the village? and showed] Herodotos the *epistates* the blows, and how I was naked because of them".[32] The request itself has two parts: the first one concerns the damage to the pastures, for which he probably asks financial compensation, and the second is the assault, qualified as *hubris*, whose judgment is entrusted to the *strategos*: "[if it appears that the sheep] grazed, that the men treated me with *hubris* (ὑβρικότες) and stripped (ἐγδεδυκότες) (me), [they must pay the damage done to] the pastures; as for the *hubris*, Diophanes shall decide".[33] In *P. Sorb.* III 112 (TM 121859), three Greek plaintiffs use both the verb *hubrizein* and the noun *hubris* to qualify the ambush that allowed four Egyptians — with whom they had a dispute about the sale of a donkey — to take hold of one of them and to have him imprisoned.[34]

Hubris and physical violence are also unambiguously connected in two complaints addressed to Zenon. In the first one, the weaver (*huphantes*) Iollas reports that he was whipped by five "Egyptian whip-bearers" (*mastigophoroi*) and treated with *hubris* (*P. Cair. Zen.* I 59080 + *P. Mich.* I 19 = *C. Ptol. Sklav.* II 205; TM 735).[35] Many things remain ill-defined in

---

[31] L. 12-13: "consequently, I assess the *hubris*", διὸ τ[ι]μῶμαι τὴν ὕβριν.

[32] L. 6-8: ἐμοῦ δ' ἐλθόντος [...*c. 15 letters*...καὶ ἐπιδείξαντός] μου τὰς πληγὰς Ἡροδότωι τῶι ἐπιστάτηι καὶ ὡς ἤμην γυμνὸς ὑπ' αὐ[τῶν].

[33] L. 14: [ἐὰν φαίνωνται τάς τε νομὰς κα]ταβεβοσκηκότ̣ε̣ς καὶ καμὲ (l. ἐμὲ) ὑβρικότες καὶ ἐγδεδυκότες, τῶν μὲν νομῶν [...*c. 27 letters*...] περὶ δὲ τῆς ὕβρεως Διοφάνην διαγνῶναι.

[34] L. 8-9: "using violence [...] they treated us with *hubris*", οἱ δὲ τῆι βίαι χρησάμ[ενοι καὶ . . .]οντες ἡμ̣ε̣ῖ̣ν ῦ̣β̣ρ̣ιζον and l. 17: "we assess the *hubris* for each of the two to 200 drachmas", τ̣ι̣μ̣ώ̣μεθα τὴν ὕβριν ἑκάτερον αὐτῶν (δραχμῶν) σ.

[35] Iollas: *Pros. Ptol.* V 12765; CLARYSSE in PESTMAN 1981, vol. 1, p. 348. On this document, see GOUDRIAAN 1988, p. 107 and 139 (doc. 102) and BIEZUNSKA-MALOWIST 1974, p. 67.

the narrative but we can infer from the docket on the verso that the mistreatment was ordered by Addaios, otherwise known as an agent of the *dioiketes* Apollionios:[36] "Iollas the weaver about Addaios and how they have treated him with *hubris*": [Ἰό]λλας ὑφάντης περὶ Ἀδδαίου καὶ ὡ[ς] ἐξυβρίκασιν αὐτόν. However, Iollas himself designates a woman, the aptly named Bia, as being "the one who commits *hubris* [...]. For she makes herself master of us and of that man" (Βία γάρ ἐστιν ἡ ὑβρίζου[-σα...*c. 15 letters*...]υτη γὰρ καὶ ἡμῶν καὶ κακείνου[37] δεσπόζει, l. 8).[38] This woman is referred to as a weaver in another document (*P. Mich.* I 16 = *C. Ptol. Sklav.* II 204; TM 1921) and the whole affair is connected with Apollonios' textile factory in Memphis.[39] Here, the context makes it clear that the flogging was not the result of a private dispute but rather given as some sort of punishment. As flogging was typically a punishment for slaves,[40] it has been argued that Iollas himself was a slave.[41] However, he could well have been a freeman-apprentice: the document makes clear that he had to obey a person named Zenodoros who is referred to as a teacher in the art of weaving in *PSI* VII 854 = *C. Ptol. Sklav.* II 202 (TM 2279). The case could thus be compared with *P. Col.* III 6 (TM 1728), in which a woman called Simale complains to Zenon about severe mistreatments inflicted by Olympichos on her son Herophantos, who was part of Apollonios' retinue.[42] Having heard that her boy had been

---

[36] Addaios: *Pros. Ptol.* I 58; CLARYSSE in PESTMAN 1981, vol. 1, p. 277; R. Scholl, commentary to *C. Ptol. Sklav.* II 202.

[37] L. ἐκείνου.

[38] Bia: *Pros. Ptol.* V 12742; CLARYSSE in PESTMAN 1981, vol. 1, p. 308.

[39] See LOFTUS 2000; THOMPSON 2012, p. 48-49.

[40] As is shown by the *Dikaiomata* (col. ix, l. 196-197), as well as by the *P. Lille* I 29 = *C. Ptol. Sklav.* I 1 (TM 3231), l. 33-35 (supra, note 8). See SCHOLL's commentary to *C. Ptol. Sklav.* I 1 and SCHOLL in KEENAN, MANNING & YIFTACH-FIRANKO 2014, p. 447-448.

[41] BIEZUNSKA-MALOWIST 1974, p. 67 states the following with some reservation: "la peine corporelle semble indiquer qu'il était esclave, mais il arrivait qu'on traitait de cette façon un indigène libre". SCHOLL, commentary to *C. Ptol. Sklav.* II 205, p. 810 convincingly argues for Iollas being a freeman: "Die Z. 4 ist m. E. nur oder zumindest bessen zu verstehen, wenn Iollas ein freier Grieche ist. Wenn dann nämlich im Text gesagt wird, dass Iollas von fünf Männern, und zwar Ägyptern, ausgepeitscht wird, so kommt zu dem körperlichen Schmerz noch die psychische Erniedrigung und Beleidigung hinzu, dass er von sozial niedriger stehenden Angehörigen eines eroberten Volkes, geschlagen wird, womöglich noch vor vielen Zeugen".

[42] Olympichos: *Pros. Ptol.* V 14237; CLARYSSE in PESTMAN 1981, vol. 1, p. 379.

"mistreated and rather badly" (ἠνωχλῆσθαί μου τ[ὸ παι]δάριον καὶ σφοδρότερον), she came to see him and found him "lying down in a hardly laughable state" (μάλ' ἀγελοίως δ[ι]ακείμενον). Upon arrival, Olympichos himself acknowledged that "by beating (the boy) rotten (αὐτὸ[ν] τύπτων σαπρόν) he would make him — or that he had already made him — as someone who was already nearly decent".[43] The mother now asks Zenon to report to Apollonios in which way his child has been continuously "treated with *hubris*" (ὑβριζόμενον) by Olympichos.

By contrast, in two other cases *hubris* applies to acts that show a minimal degree of physical violence. Both documents are famous: the first one is the *enteuxis* of the Greek Herakleides against the Egyptian Psenobastis (*P. Enteux.* 79; TM 3354), the second is the *enklema* of the Jew Dositheos against the Jewess Herakleia, enclosed in the official minutes of the hearing held in front of the *dikasterion* of Crocodilopolis in the summer of 226 (*P. Gur.* 2 = *C. Pap. Jud.* I 19; TM 5865).[44] In his petition, Herakleides describes precisely four acts committed by Psenobastis: when he went past the front of her house in the village of Psya, she poured urine on his clothes, then she insulted him, she ripped his coat, "resulting in laying (his) chest bare", and she spat in his face. Then he adds: "everything I accuse her of, she did so while committing an act of *hubris* against me" (ἃ δ' ἐγκαλῶ ἔπραξεν ὑβρίζουσά με, l. 7). The docket on the verso summarizes the facts as being "about *hubris*", περὶ ὕβρεως. Similarly, in his *enklema* against Herakleia, Dositheos claims that the woman insulted him, spat, and then gripped his coat.[45] Once again, the whole offense is characterized as *hubris*: "Wherefore I bring an action of *hubris* against you" (διὸ δικάζομαί σοι κατα[... *c. 12 letters*... ὕ]βριν) (l. 26-27).[46]

These examples confirm to begin with that, as was the case in the Alexandrian *Dikaiomata*, the term *hubris* did not apply to a specific category of violence, but it referred to a wide variety of acts. Four of the

---

[43] The translation of the passages is borrowed from BAGNALL & CRIBIORE 2006, p. 100.

[44] The court report is known by two fragmentary copies, *P. Petr.* III 21 g (= *Chrest. Mitt.* 21, TM 2992) and *P. Gur.* 2 (TM 5865). Some parts of the text, which are given in square brackets in the edition of *P. Gur.* 2, are preserved in *P. Petr.* III 21 g.

[45] Cf. l. 21, καὶ λαβομένη μου τῆς ἀναβολῆς τοῦ ἱματίου...: "and, having gripped the loop of my coat, ...".

[46] Also, in a fragmentary context, σὺ ὑβρίζουσα (l. 25); ὑβρισ[μένος ?] (l. 27).

documents present interesting particularities as well, wherein plaintiffs denounce instances of having been: *spat at* (Crateuas and Dositheos), *stripped bare* (Crateuas, Herakleides, probably also Dositheos), or *whipped* (Iollas). Furthermore, these documents provide the only two known examples of men making complaints referring to assault committed by women (Herakleides, Dositheos) or instigated by a woman (Iollas), and they also constitute two of the rare cases in which Greek plaintiffs qualify the offenders as "Egyptians".[47] In the case of Herakleides, we can be sure that it was not a neutral piece of information considering the way he presents his request: "I beg you, having been treated with no reason with *hubris* by an Egyptian woman, I, being Greek and foreigner"[48] (that is to say, foreign to the village where the assault took place). Herakleides obviously wanted to emphasize the importance of the outrage committed against him. Given the scarcity of such ethnic labelling, it is tempting to attribute the same intentionality to Iollas when he indicates that he was flogged by five "Egyptian whip-bearers", also using the term *anthropos* in a contemptuous sense when referring to them: πέντε ἀνθρώπους Αἰγυπτίους μαστιγοφόρ[ους].[49] These four examples fit in well with the Aristotelian definition of *hubris*, focusing on outrage upon personal dignity. Surely, it remains possible that, in other documents *hubris* would simply have had the general meaning of "violence". But, obviously, it was also an adequate term used by the victims to express a feeling of humiliation, and by the lawgiver to stress the intention of the perpetrator.

To conclude this section, it is worth noticing two types of violence that are neither alluded to in the *Dikaiomata* nor in the practice-related documents: insults and sexual violence. The preserved sections of the *Dikaiomata* only encompass one particular type of verbal violence: armed threats. Similarly, we know of no complaint or court case in the *chora* concerning insults alone. At first glance, this is a clear-cut difference with the Demotic rules of religious associations, which proscribe beating *and* insulting another member of the association, and provide for a fine in

---

[47] The direct opponent in the case of Herakleides, the authors of the physical violence on account of third parties (Addaios and Bia) in Iollas' case. The only comparable documents are *P. Lond.* III 887 (TM 78481) and *P. Lond.* VII 1954 (TM 1517): see GOUDRIAAN 1988, p. 130 (doc. 103) and p. 141-142 (doc. 110).

[48] L. 8-10: δέομαι οὖν σου, βασιλεῦ, εἴ σοι δοκεῖ, [μὴ περιιδεῖν με οὕ]τως ἀλόγως ὑπὸ Αἰγυ[πτίας ὑβρισμέ]νον, Ἕλλην[α ὄν]τα καὶ ξένον.

[49] See SCHOLL, commentary to *C. Ptol. Sklav.* II 205 (supra, note 41).

each case.[50] In Athens, verbal insults were prosecuted by means of a special private legal action, *dike kakegorias*. Nevertheless, it happens that complaints or witness-declarations report both physical assault and verbal abuse, generally referred to with the verb *loidorein*.[51] This suggests that insults were not considered worthy of filing a complaint, but that they were perceived of as aggravating elements. The case of sexual violence may be different because there is no univocal term in Greek used to define rape. Thus, even though we can reasonably think that there was a reluctance to report such crimes, it remains possible that in some documents sexual violence is referred to in terms that do not allow us to distinguish them from other types of violence.[52]

2. Responding to violence

2.1. *Sub-judicial level*

Whereas the *Dikaiomata* only address how repression of acts of violence was dealt with in courts, the documents from the *chora* shed some light on how conflicts between individuals could be settled at a sub-judicial level. Firstly, some papyri show ongoing violence being stopped thanks to a third party. In a complaint addressed to the chief engineer Kleon, Demetrios reports how he was assaulted while distributing bread

[50] See *P. Lille Dem.* 1 29 (TM 2784), l. 13-14, *P. Cairo* 2 30606 (TM 2775), l. 19; *P. Cairo* 2 31179 (TM 3056), l. 24; *P. Cairo* 2 30605 (TM 2774), l. 20; *P. Prag.* (TM 2928), l. 14-15. The *P. Lille Dem.* 1 29 (TM 2784), dated third century BC, extends the ban to instances of slander (calling someone a leper). On this point, see F. de Cénival 1972, p. 203: "les maladies de peau comptaient parmi les interdits rituels observés par les prêtres égyptiens; l'accusé pouvait se voir privé de la possibilité d'exercer sa fonction dans le temple, et par conséquent privé de son revenu". Slander as a category of verbal abuse does not appear in Greek practice-related documents, nor in the *Dikaiomata*.

[51] See, taking into consideration third century documents only, *P. Enteux.* 25 (TM 3300), *P. Enteux.* 79 (TM 3354), *P. Enteux.* 86 (TM 3386), *P. Gur.* 2 (TM 5865), P. TCD Pap. Gr. env. 86/87 Ro (TM 8832). In *P. Enteux.* 79 and *P. Gur.* 2, the reciprocity of the insults exchanged between the plaintiffs (both men) and the accused (both women) is expressed by means of association λοιδορεῖν and ἀντιλοιδορεῖν: "she insulted me / I insulted her back". The terms *paroinein* and *paroinia*, which also appear in a number of documents, are more ambiguous, because they are susceptible to refer to physical violence as well as verbal abuse.

[52] See Hue-Arcé 2020, p. 48-62.

to the quarrymen: things calmed down only when the *presbuteroi* intervened: "he (i.e. one Hephaistion) attacked me and laid hands on me, until Pempsas and the elders who were standing by separated (us)"[53] (*P. Petrie Kleon* 54; TM 7646). In *UPZ* II 151 (TM 2975) the rower Areus complains that a certain Kephalon forced his way into his *stathmos*, beat him and tried to drag him out. Refusing to leave, he called the neighbours for help and "as a number of them ran up and blamed (the aggressor) (ἐπιτιμώντων αὐτῶι), he went away". Similarly, in *P. Enteux.* 79 (TM 3354), the Greek Herakleides reports that the woman who harassed him turned back after being blamed (ἐπιτιμηθεῖσα) by people who were at the scene. The same verb, *epitimao*, is probably to be supplemented in *P. Enteux.* 80 (TM 3355) as is the case in the *enklema* of the Jew Dositheos against the Jewess Herakleia (*P. Gur.* 2; TM 5865). Like the rower Areus, the *isionomos* Amenneus was violently assaulted, as were his wife and children, in his *isieion*, and they were ultimately saved when third parties arrived: "I called people (ἀ<ν>θρώπους) for help. Some people came and blamed our aggressors ([ἐπιτιμών]των αὐτοῖς), who left us and went away" (*P. Enteux.* 80). The aggression against Dositheos took place in the presence of witnesses who blamed the woman and the man who was with her ([τῶν δὲ παρ]όντων [ἐπιτιμ]ώντων σοί τε καὶ Καλλίππωι) (*P. Gur.* 2). The author of *BGU* III 1007 (TM 5552) also called people for help, among them one blamed the aggressors (l. 9, ἐπετίμησεν αὐτοῖς). [54]

Violent cases could also be solved by means of private arbitration in the *chora*, in Greek as well in Egyptian context. The Demotic rules of religious associations endeavoured to settle disputes between members of the association internally.[55] Other documents refer to private settlement of disputes, e.g. *P. Tebt.* III.1 821 (= *C. Pap. Hengstl* 46; TM 5397).[56] The

[53] Trad. Van Beek. The *P. Petrie Kleon* 58 (TM 7658), another letter to Kleon by Demetrios, probably relates to the same case.

[54] The same scenario (interposition and blame from third party) is probably to be found in the fragmentary witness-declaration *P. Petr.* III 23 = *P. Petr.* II 18 (2a-b) (TM 7401), l. 16-17. In *P. Lond.* VII 2009 (TM 1571), the threat of third party intervention made the attackers leave (the pub-owner, who took refuge on the roof, called for help).

[55] See DE CENIVAL 1977, p. 192; MONSON 2006, p. 236 and 238; HUE-ARCÉ 2020, p. 127-128.

[56] On private arbitration in Ptolemaic Egypt, see MÉLÈZE-MODRZEJEWSKI 1952; ROEBUCK 2001, p. 300-343; HUE-ARCÉ 2020, p. 111-129.

document is a *cheirographon*, a private arrangement, whereby a certain Histieia withdraws the accusation of *hubris* she had previously made against a certain Taouthes:

> Histieia daughter of Histieios, Macedonian, to Taouthes daughter of Marres, greeting. In regard to the accusation which I have made against you before the *archeion* of Aristoboulos (περὶ ὧν σοι ἐνκέκληκα ἐπὶ τοῦ Ἀριστοβούλου ἀρχείου[57]), I am reconciled to you and make no accusation in regard to the matters whereon I have accused you and the fair men decided against you (καὶ περὶ ὧν σοι οἱ κοινοί[58] σου κατέγνωσαν). And if I proceed against you for the *hubris* (ὑπὲρ τῆς ὕβρε[ως]), or any people of mine, I will forfeit to you 3000 drachmas. Goodbye. Year 13, Pachon 7. Menekles wrote this on behalf of Histieia, since she affirmed that she was illiterate (*P. Tebt.* III.1 821[59]).

This is one of the documents in which we do not know to what the term *hubris* alludes exactly. According to the agreement, Histieia had brought an accusation before the "*archeion* of Aristoboulos". At first sight, the expression is somewhat enigmatic, but the editors already connected this *archeion* with an official's dealing.[60] The section of the *Dikaiomata* concerning summons to testimony supports this interpretation: "the person summoned shall testify before the *arche* and court (ἐ[π]ὶ [τῆ]ι ἀρχῆι καὶ ἐπὶ τ[ῶι] δικαστηρίωι) to the things at which he was present or of which he knows" (col. x, l. 225-226). As the *Graeca Halensis* editors have already pointed out, in this passage the term *arche* obviously refers to the magistrate investigating the case,[61] and there is little doubt that this also applies to the "*archeion* of Aristoboulos" even if the exact translation remains problematical: "tribunal", "office", or simply "authority". Be that as it may, this dispute was not solved by Aristoboulos himself, but by other people qualified as οἱ κοινοί. The editors of *P. Tebt.* called them "assessors",[62] but thanks to the parallels provided by other documents, such as *P. Enteux.* 59 (TM 3334; 222 BC) and *BGU* VIII 1818

[57] Corr. ex. ἀρχήου.

[58] Corr. ex. σωι ωἱ κοινωί.

[59] Transl. A.S. HUNT & J.G. SMYLY, slightly modified.

[60] HUNT & SMYLY, comments about *P. Tebt.* III.1, 821.

[61] Commentary to *P. Hal.* 1, p. 128-129. See also KALTSAS, introduction to *P. Heid.* VIII 413-416, p. 55.

[62] "I am reconciled to you and make no accusation in regard to the matters whereon I have accused you and your assessors decided against you".

(TM 4897; 60/59 BC),[63] we can safely define the terms more precisely: "fair men", "impartial men".[64] In *P. Enteux.* 59 and *BGU* VIII 1818, these men acted as private arbitrators, and no doubt the same holds true in this case too. This type of private arbitration differs from the conciliation hearings organized by the *epistates* at the *strategos*' order, upon receipt of an *enteuxis*.[65] After initially having lodged an official complaint against Taouthes with Aristoboulos, Histieia obviously agreed to a private arrangement through the "impartial men".[66] However, due to the nature of the sources, private dispute resolutions such as these are less well documented than would be an official dispute resolution at the judicial level.

2.2. *Judicial level*

For people who wanted to obtain reparation by official judgment, naturally, the first step was to report it properly to competent authorities. We do not know precisely how things worked in Alexandria, and whether the plaintiffs had to bring the matter before a magistrate, as in Athens, or if they could go to the courts directly. But in the *chora* the most common method was to provide the officials with a written denunciation, either in the form of *prosangelma* or petition. The *prosangelmata* are usually short and succinct documents; by contrast, the way the facts of a violent act are reported in petitions (*enteuxeis* and *hupomnemata*) deserves closer attention. On the one hand, these petitions contain various elements of narrative *topos* that reveal the role of professionals and how models were used to draft the documents. The most striking fact is probably the use of the expression εἰς ὃ ἂν τύχοι μέρος τοῦ σώματος "(beating me) on all parts of my body that he could reach", which is

---

[63] The marriage contract *P. Eleph.* 1 (TM 5836) and the *prosangelmata P. Lond.* VII 1980-1981 (TM 1543 – TM 2502) probably allude to the same private, arbitral commission of three men.

[64] See GUERAUD, commentary to *P. Enteux.* 59 (TM 3334); MÉLÈZE-MODRZEJEWSKI 1952, p. 247; HENGSTL's commentary to *C. Pap. Hengstl.* 46, p. 130; ROEBUCK 2001, p. 310 and 318 ("common arbitrators").

[65] This is the most frequent instruction given by the *strategos* to the *epistates*: "If possible, reconcile them. But if not, send them to me" (or "send them so that they may be judged in the appropriate court", or "send them so that they may have justice according to the laws").

[66] One can assume that it was not without financial compensation, see HENGSTL, *C. Pap. Hengstl.* 46, p. 130.

given in an almost identical manner in twelve petitions from the third century, plus a witness-statement, referring to acts of violence, not to mention subsequent documents.[67] But on the other hand, the plaintiffs also frequently provide precise information about how violence was inflicted on them, and about the parts of the body that were affected. Thus, for instance, the petitioner of *P. Enteux.* 74 (TM 3349) relates that his aggressor hit him "with the right hand" and "the right leg" on such and such parts of his body (details are missing due to the lacuna), Thaesis indicates that Herieus "hit (her) with both hands", then "bit (her) on her left shoulder" and even "tore a piece of (her) flesh" (*SB* X 10271; TM 5801), Apollonios was struck in the face and on the body (*P. Petr.* III 32c; TM 7424), and Philista was scalded "on the abdomen and the left thigh, up to the knee" (*P. Enteux.* 82; TM 3357).[68]

Once again, the reason for providing such detail is best understood if we turn back to the *Dikaiomata*, and in particular to the provisions concerning how cases of *hubris* should be pursued in court:

> the injured party shall himself assess the damage in bringing the suit, but he shall further state specifically in what manner [he claims] to have been outraged (προσγρα[ψά]σθω δὲ ὀνομαστί, τ[ί ἂν φῆι] ὑβρισθ[ῆ]ναι) and when[69] he was outraged (καὶ τὸν χρόνον ἐν ὧι ὑβρίσθη) (col. ix, l. 210-212).

Based on this section, the Alexandrian courts deemed the element important enough to be appraised under the exact circumstances of each act of aggression. This is consistent with the distinction made in the previous sections between "striking with one blow" and "striking with several blows" (col. ix, l. 203-207), as well as with the provision concerning

[67] Third century: *BGU* X 1903 (TM 8299), *P. Enteux.* 72 (TM 3347), *P. Enteux.* 74 (TM 3349), *P. Enteux.* 76 (TM 3351), *P. Enteux.* 80 (TM 3355), *P. Enteux.* 81 (TM 3356), *P. Enteux.* 83 (TM 3358), *P. Gur.* 8 (TM 5871), *P. Köln* III 140 (TM 3174), *P. Petr.* III 23 (TM 7401, witness-statement), *SB* X 10271 (TM 5801), *SB* XX 15001 (TM 8123), P. TCD Pap. Gr. env. 86/87 Ro (TM 8832). Second and first centuries: *BGU* VI 1247 (TM 4538), *BGU* X 1908 (TM 8302), *P. Heid.* II 217 (TM 6229), *P. Diosk.* 7 (TM 44723), *P. Grenf.* I 38 (TM 262), *P. Hels.* I 2 (TM 5139), *P. Ryl.* II 68 (TM 5286), *P. Tebt.* II 283 (TM 42986), *PSI* III 167 (TM 5544), *PSI* V 542 (TM 2164), *SB* XXVI 16800 (TM 44707).

[68] In *P. Enteux.* 79 (TM 3354), Herakleides specifies that Psenobastis grabbed his coat "with her right hand".

[69] "When he was outraged" in BAGNALL & DEROW 1981, rather than "the date on which he was outraged" in BAGNALL & DEROW 2004.

aggravating circumstances such as drunkenness or assault by night (col. ix, l. 193-195).[70] Likewise, one may assume that the details the petitioners from the *chora* gave were not only intended to arouse sympathy,[71] but that they fulfilled a practical need: the aim being to prove that the aggression was real and to establish its degree of seriousness in view of future compensation. In this regard, complaints for violence can be compared with complaints for theft and with theft reports (in the case of *prosangelmata*): just as victims of theft would provide a list of the stolen goods, the victims of violence would specify injured parts of the body. The fact that injuries served as proof can be clearly seen in the petition of Crateuas, who, after being beaten by the shepherds of Alabanthis, went to the *epistates* to "show him the blows" (*P. Enteux.* 75; TM 3350).

The same practical reasons explain why victims of violence call upon witnesses, far more often than with any other petition. This is the case in nine third-century petitions, along with two complaints to Zenon and one *enklema*, where victims state the aggression was committed in front of witnesses (*martures*),[72] some of whom also acted as mediators. Correspondingly, the major part of the known Ptolemaic witness-declarations

---

[70] This section (col. ix, l. 193-195) helps us to understand the expression τὸν χρόνον ἐν ὧι ὑβρίσθη in the *hubris*-section as referring not to the date, but to the time of day the act of aggression occurred.

[71] On this point see BRYEN's analysis of similar details provided in petitions from the Roman period: "A narrative — however mediated and however imperfect — has two purposes: one is to communicate pain and pathos. The other is to place this pain on display, and in so doing to rouse the sympathies of other" (BRYEN 2013, p. 125).

[72] *BGU* X 1903 (TM 8299), *SB* X 10271 (TM 5801), *P. Enteux.* 72 (TM 3347), *P.Enteux.* 74 (TM 3349), *P. Enteux.* 78 (TM 3353), *P. Enteux.* 79 (TM 3354), *P. Enteux.* 81 (TM 3356), *P. Petr.* III 22a (TM 7395; on this document, see below, note 74), *UPZ* II 151 (TM 2975); *P. Cair. Zen.* III 59443 (TM 1083), *P. Cair. Zen.* V 59830 (TM 1454) (two complaints to Zenon); *P. Gur.* 2 (TM 5865) (*enklema*). Other documents suggest the presence of witnesses, as is the case of *P. Köln* VI 272 (TM 3202): because the woman on the behalf of whom the present petition is written died instantly, the details that are given can only come from people who were present at the scene. The other third-century petitions which explicitly refer to witnesses are *P. Cair. Zen.* IV 59620-59621 (TM 1252-1253) (ownership dispute), *P. Enteux.* 43 (TM 3318) (loan contract), *P. Enteux.* 86 (ownership dispute) and *P. Enteux.* 65 (TM 3340) (damages to a vineyard). Witnesses were probably also called upon in *P. Enteux.* 4 (TM 3282), (breach on contract terms), see Vo, l. 10-11.

concern cases of violence.[73] Those documents introduce the same tension between narrative *topos* and specific details, which had probably been given by the plaintiffs in their own petitions. For example, in *P. Petr.* III 23 (TM 7401) the witness testifies that the victim of the aggression, one Serambos, was beaten by Apollodoros "on all parts of his body that he could reach" but particularly "on his throat" (or neck: κατὰ τοῦ τραχή-λου); according to *P. Hib.* II 200 (TM 5184), Athenaïs struck Chrysis "with her left hand", then "struck her on the face with both hands"; in *P. Hamb.* I 105 (= *C. Ptol. Sklav.* II 229; TM 2311) and *P. Petr.* III 22e (TM 7399), which are fragmentary, the blows were given with "both hands" and "with the fist", respectively. These details can even be given in "negative" testimonies as well, wherein witnesses deny having seen anything. Thus, the witness in *P. Petr.* III 22d (TM 7398) attests that he was not present during any act of violence committed "with both hands".[74] In sum, the *Dikaiomata* and the practice-related documents both show how important words are when it comes to violence. In possible situations where no incriminating evidence was available — such as, in cases of theft, the discovery of stolen goods, or, in the event of an ownership dispute, the actual occupation of the disputed property — the statements made by the victims and witnesses played an essential role in providing real proof with regards to an act of aggression and establishing its degree of seriousness in view of future compensation.[75]

Another issue is who was supposed to judge the cases of violence and establish appropriate compensation. The cases provided for by the *Dikaiomata* fell within the competence of the courts of law. Judging by

---

[73] On Ptolemaic witness-declarations, see KALTSAS' introduction to *P. Heid.* VIII 413-416, p. 45-68, with a list of documents p. 45-46; KRAMER & SANCHEZ-MORENO ELLART, *P. Trier* I, p. 75-108.

[74] *P. Petr.* III 22d and e (TM 7398 and 7399) belong with *P. Petr.* III 22a, b, c and f (TM 7395, 7396, 7397, 7400) in the "Archive of Lamiske, wife of Parmeniskos" (TM Arch 401). The *P. Petr.* III 22a is a fragmentary *enteuxis* in which a man, whose name is lost, denies having committed an act of *hubris* against Lamiske in front of witnesses. The *P. Petr.* III 22 b-f are witness statements possibly referring to the same affair, even though the connection between the different documents is difficult to establish, see STOLK 2011 and KALTSAS' introduction to *P. Heid.* VIII 413-416, p. 64-65.

[75] The same holds true for the Demotic petitions, as shown by the *P. Oxf. Griffith* 38 (TM 48879, 159 BC), a *mqmq* addressed to the *lesonis* of the temple of Soknopaiou Nesos, which denounces a physical aggression; the document contains a list of five witnesses. See BAETENS 2014, p. 41, n. 49 and p. 43, HUE-ARCÉ 2020, p. 128-129.

the sections about blows and *hubris*, those courts were the *dikasteria* (cf. τὸ δικαστήριον, col. ix, l. 201-202, l. 206, l. 213). However, the *Graeca Halensis* editors suggested that the term *dikasterion* only means "court" in those sections, including the *kriteria* therefore — which Hans Julius Wolff suggested ought to be identified with royal courts, and the *diaitetai* — who, unlike in Athens, do not seem to have been only "arbitrators".[76] The situation is even less clear in the *chora*, where officials were also entrusted with judicial powers.[77] A number of petitions concerning all sorts of matters ask the *strategos* for a judgement, as is the case, for instance, for both P. TCD env. 86/87 Ro (TM 8832) about blows, and for *P. Enteux.* 79 (TM 3354), about *hubris*:

> I beg you, king (...) if it seems good to you, to order to Aphthonetos the strategos to write to whom it concerns to investigate these things and, if my story is true, to grant me justice in the way the strategos will decide ([...] μ̣ο̣ι τὸ δίκαιον καθότ̣[ι ἄ]ν̣ συγκ̣ρίνηι ὁ στρ̣α̣τ̣η̣γ̣ό̣ς̣) (P. TCD env. 86/87 Ṙo, l. 7-9; TM 8832).[78]
> I therefore beg you, king (...) to order Diophanes the *strategos* (...) to write to Sogenes the epistate to send Psenobastis to him so that she may be tried in adversary proceedings on these facts ([ὅπως διακρι]θῆι πρός [μ]ε περὶ το[ύτων) and, [if what I write] in (my) *enteuxis* [is true], that she may have the punishment that the strategos will decide (τύχηι ζημίας ἧς ἂν ὁ στρατηγὸς συνκρ[ίνηι]) (*P. Enteux.* 79, l. 8-13).

As is almost always the case with the petitions, we cannot say how those two disputes were ultimately settled, and if the *strategos* judged the case by himself or referred it to a court.[79] However, we know of cases of violence settled by courts in the *chora* in the third century. The *P. Petr.*

[76] *P. Hal.* 1, p. 52-53; WOLFF 1970, p. 33 and p. 34-35; MÉLÈZE-MODRZEJEWSKI 2014a, p. 202: "tout ce que l'on peut dire à propos de ces derniers [the *diaitetai*], c'est qu'ils paraissent fonctionner comme un tribunal ordinaire, prononçant des sentences qui jouissent de l'autorité de la chose jugée, plutôt que de former un collège d'arbitres publics comme l'institution athénienne homonyme".

[77] WOLFF 1970, p. 113-193 makes a clear distinction between the courts and the "Beamtenjustiz" of the officials in the *chora* (see also MÉLÈZE-MODRZEJEWSKI 2014a, p. 207: "les fonctionnaires royaux que nous voyons dans nos sources se livrer à des activités de caractère juridictionnel n'exercent pas une justice à proprement parler, mais seulement un pouvoir coercitif"). It is far from certain, though, that the two were perceived by the litigants themselves as being fundamentally different.

[78] BAETENS & CLARYSSE 2016, p. 400.

[79] See above, n. 65.

III 21d, l. 1-4 (TM 2990) is an extract of a judgment *in absentia* (*dike eremos*) delivered by the local *dikasterion* of Crocodilopolis in 227 BC on a case involving blows, and *P. Gur.* 2 (TM 5865) contains the complete minutes of the trial concerning the *hubris*-action of the Jew Dositheos against the Jewess Herakleia in 226 BC. Besides this, three witness-declarations at least, that refer to acts of violence, were probably produced for a trial before a *dikasterion*:[80] *P. Hamb.* I 105 = *C. Ptol. Sklav.* II 229 (TM 2311), *P. Petr.* III 22e (TM 7399), and *P. Petr.* III 22d (TM 7398).[81] In all those five cases, the parties were Greeks (Hellenes), as could be expected; one may assume that similar cases involving Egyptians were judged in the *laokritai* court. We also have an indirect reference to a case tried in the chrematists court, the royal judges, in the *BGU* VI 1244 (TM 4405), as previously mentioned. In this *hupomnema*, addressed to an *oikonomos*, the brewer Tkollousis alludes to the trial previously brought before the chrematists following the accusations made by one Pasis against her for the murder (*phonos*) of an infant:[82]

> I had a trial before the chrematists who judge matters concerning the (royal) revenues, against Pasis and (?) (ἐνεστηκυίας [μ]οι κρίσεως ἐπὶ τῶν τὰ πρ[οσο]δικὰ κρινόντων [χρ]ηματιστῶν πρ[ὸς] Πᾶσιν καὶ̣ . σ̣ θ̣έαν [τ]ὴν μητέ<ρ>α ? αὐτῶν), about the unfounded charge of the murder of a fifteen day old baby (φόνου ἀγενήτου παιδίου πεντεκαιδεχημέρου)[83] (*BGU* VI 1244, l. 7-16).

Although Tkollousis and Pasis bear Egyptian names the case was not judged by the *laokritai*, so that one may wonder if homicide and murder cases were considered part of the chrematists' area of competence.[84]

---

80 See KALTSAS, introduction to *P. Heid.* VIII 413-416, in particular p. 54 and p. 64.

81 On *P. Petr.* III 22e and d (TM 7399 and 7398), see above, n. 74.

82 On this document, see BAUSCHATZ 2013, p. 85-87.

83 That is how we understand the group παιδίου πεντεκαιδεχημέρου; BAUSCHATZ 2013, p. 86 translates "the murder of a slave fifteen days ago". Was Tkollousis the infant's wet-nurse?

84 The Verso of P. TCD Pap. Gr. env. 86/87 (TM 8831) seemingly pertains to the summons, before the *strategos* Aphthonetos, of a man accused of murder (*phonos*), without our being able to say, however, if the *strategos* was entitled to judge the case by himself. The same question applies to *BGU* VIII 1857 (TM 4936), a petition about a murder, which was probably submitted to the *strategos* of the Herackleopolite nome (first century BC).

2.3. *Penalties*

A last element of comparison between the *Dikaiomata* and the documents from the *chora* are the penalties to which the perpetrators of violence were liable. On this issue, the *Dikaiomata* provide much more detailed information than the practice-related documents because penalties are predefined in a full range of cases, as in the Demotic rules of religious associations. The summary chart below (Fig. 1) shows that the penalties depended both upon the nature of the act committed (one blow / several blows / *hubris*) and upon the status of the assailant and the victim (magistrate on duty / freeman or freewoman). Whereas flogging was the lot of slaves — except if the master agreed to compensate the victim financially — the punishment of the freeman or freewoman always consisted of a financial penalty.[85] In some cases, a fixed penalty was prescribed; in the others, damages were subjected to an assessment by the plaintiff himself, but also, apparently, by the court.[86] The assessment was obviously reserved for the most serious cases, striking more than one blow, *hubris*, and presumably also striking a magistrate on duty:[87]

Slave striking a freeman (δούλωι ἐλεύθερον πατάξαντι):

> (...) for a greater number of blows (the plaintiff) shall himself assess (the injury) when he brings the suit, and whatever assessment [is fixed] by the court, (the master) shall forfeit three times that amount (περ[ὶ δὲ] πλειόνων πληγῶν τιμησάμενος δικασάσθω, ὅτι δ' ἂν τὸ δικαστ[ήριον τιμήσηι,] τοῦτο τριπλοῦν ἀποτεισάτω) (col. ix, l. 200-201).

Blows between freemen (πληγῆς ἐλευθέροις):

> (...) if they strike more than one blow, (the plaintiff) in bringing the suit shall himself assess (the damage caused by) the blows, and whatever assessment is fixed by the court, (the accused) shall forfeit [twice] that amount

[85] See HELMIS 1986, p. 211-213.

[86] Judges in Athens were not supposed to assess the damage themselves, and the Demotic rules of religious associations do not provide for assessment either.

[87] The passage concerning the magistrates (col. ix, l. 207-209) is elliptic. One may assume that the penalties were trebled compared to all previously exposed cases: for instance, 300 drachmas in cases of beating using "one blow" or 600 drachmas for the same act committed in a market-place, and three times the amount set by the court in instances involving several blows.

(ἐὰν δὲ πλείονας πληγῆς μιᾶ[ς] πατάξηι, τιμησάμ[ενος τὰς] πληγὰ[ς δι]κασάσθω, ὁπόσου δ' ἂν τιμήσηι τὸ δικαστήριον, τοῦτ[ο διπλοῦν] ἀποτεισ[άτ]ω). And if anyone strikes one of the magistrates while executing the administrative duties prescribed for the magistracy, he shall pay the penalties trebled, if he is defeated [in the suit] (ἐὰν δέ τίς τινα τῶν ἀρχόντ[ων π]ατάξηι τάσσοντ[α, ὧν τῆι] ἀρχῆι γέ[γ]ραπται τάσσειν, τριπλάσια τὰ ἐ[πι]τίμια ἀποτεισάτ[ω, ἐὰν δίκηι] νικηθῆι) (l. 205-209).

Hubris:

If any person commits against another an act of *hubris* not provided for in the code, (the injured party) shall himself assess the damage in bringing the suit (ἐάν τις καθυβρίσηι ἕτερος ἑτέρου τ[ῶ]ν ἀγράφων, ὁ τα .[. . . . . .] μενος τιμησάμενος δικασάσθω) (...) And the offender if condemned shall pay twice the amount of the assessment fixed by the court (ὁ δ[ὲ] ὀφλὼν διπλοῦν ἀπ[οτεισάτω,] ὃ ἂν τὸ δικαστήριον τιμήσηι) (l. 210-213).

The practice-related documents provide only two confirmed cases of an actual sentence passed for acts of violence in the *chora* during the third century. *P. Hib.* I 32 (TM 7815) is an official notification of judgement given by an unknown judicial authority: a man called Neoptolemos was sentenced *in absentia* to pay 200 drachmas, for *hubris* (πρὸς καταδίκην ἔρημον ὕβρεως πρὸς (δραχμὰς) σ, l. 7-9). An "extra tenth" (*epidekaton*) is added to the fine suggesting, by comparison with the *Dikaiomata*, that at the beginning of the case Neoptolemos was not the defendant, but the plaintiff, and that he has since been defeated.[88] In *P. Petr.* III 21d, l. 1-4 (TM 2990) a man was sentenced to 1000 drachmas, for blows (*plegon*) according to a judgment delivered by the *dikasterion* of Crocodilopolis.[89] As for the petitions, they give us information

[88] According to the *Dikaiomata*, whoever has brought an action for violence, if defeated, shall pay to the winner an additional tenth (in case of "[...] or blows", *plegai*) or an additional fifth of the value of the suit (in case of "[...] or bodily harm", *aikismos*) (*P. Hal.* 1, col. v, l. 115-119).

[89] The *P. Hib.* I 111 (TM 8241) is a more intriguing document, which contains a list of fines that were either paid or would be paid. According to the editors, this record was kept "by some official connected with the judicial administration". The l. 1-4 concern a case of violence (*bia*): "At Takona: the case against Melanthios for violence to Demetria (τὰ πρὸς Μελάνθιον περὶ τῆς βίας ἐπὶ Δημητρίαν), 7 drachmae 2 ½ obols". The amount is not commensurate to the penalties imposed in *P. Hib.* I 32 and *P. Petr.* III 21d, nor is it to the penalties requested in the petitions (see below). Conversely, it is comparable to the level of fine applicable in the Demotic rules of religious associations in case of verbal

about the reparations claimed by the victims of violence. In most cases however, it is difficult to see what the latter wanted exactly, because their appeal to justice is conventional and general, or else because acts of violence are denounced together with other prejudices such as theft or damage to property.[90] However, we see a close parallel here with the *Dikaiomata* in six documents in which the plaintiffs assess the damage precisely, consisting of blows (*plegai*) (*P. Enteux.* 72; TM 3347) or *hubris* (*P. Enteux.* 73; TM 3348, *P. Enteux.* 74; TM 3349, *P. Sorb.* III 112; TM 121859, *P. Gur.* 2; TM 5865), or blows and *hubris* (*BGU* X 1903; TM 8299).[91] The vocabulary matches that used in the *Dikaiomata*: with either the verb *timao* or the noun *timema*. The amount of the assessment has been preserved in four cases: in three of these, it is valued at 200 drachmas (*P. Enteux.* 72, *P. Sorb* III 112, *P. Gur.* 2), as in the judgment reported in *P. Hib.* I 32. In the last one (*P. Enteux.* 73) it amounts to 1000 drachmas, as in the sentence handed down by the *dikasterion* of Crocodilopolis (*P. Petr.* III 21d, l. 1-4). One wonders if this particularly large amount might have included compensation for material damages as well. But on the other hand, judging by the *Dikaiomata*, the amount of compensation could rise rapidly in cases of beatings.

We should take note at last that the penalties mentioned both in the *Dikaiomata* and in the practice-related documents were considered private, just as the trials were private as well: in other words, they were *dikai* and not *graphai*. The question remains as to whether all acts of violence, up to murder, were punished by means of private financial compensation, but it is not possible to go further given the scarcity of information about

or physical violence (between 2 and 10 *kite*, namely between 4 and 20 drachmas in *P. Lille Dem.* 1 29; TM 2784).

[90] Nevertheless, in some cases, the plaintiffs clearly separate the compensation for acts of violence from what is intended for another prejudice. This is the case with Crateuas in *P. Enteux.* 75 (TM 3350) and Thamounis in *P. Enteux.* 83 (TM 3358): "[let the shepherds be forced to pay the damages] to the pastures. As for the *hubris*, Diophanes shall decide (περὶ δὲ τῆς ὕβρεως Διοφάνην διαγνῶναι)" (*P. Enteux.* 75); "have (her) be forced to give me back my coat, or the 30 drachmas it is worth; as for what she did to me, Diophanes shall decide (περὶ δὲ ὧν συντετέλεσται εἴς μ[ε Δι]οφάνην διαγνῶναι)" (*P. Enteux.* 83).

[91] See also *P. Eleph. Wagner* 1, III (TM 78215), a fragmentary letter in which someone mentions a penalty (τὸ ἐπίτιμον, l. 9-10) in relation with a charge of *hubris*. See WAGNER's comment, *P. Eleph. Wagner* 1, III, p. 27: "Comprendre ces lignes ainsi: '…je t'accuse de violence [*hubris*], si je t'accuse, ou bien tu paies l'amende' …".

the Ptolemaic repression of homicide.[92] In any case, some documents show that special provisions were prescribed if the life of the victim was in danger, until the final outcome was known.[93] In *P. Enteux.* 81 (TM 3356) in particular the plaintiff, a woman, refers to the fact that her aggressor will be punished differently according to whether she dies or she recovers.

CONCLUSION

Obviously, there is no exact superposition between the prescriptive dispositions of the Alexandrian *Dikaiomata* and the practice-related documents from the *chora*. This is the case even when we take only those that concern Greek plaintiffs or Greek litigants into consideration. In this respect, the study confirms that the *politikos nomos* of Alexandria is not to be equated with the *politikoi nomoi* of the Greeks living in the *chora*. Nevertheless, both clearly belong to the same social and legal world wherein there is a need for a precise description of the facts of violence; as well as an established principle set for the victim's assessment of the prejudice; and financial compensation for most acts of violence (except if the accused is a slave; the question of homicide remains inconclusive). The two categories of documents also show that acts of violence were taken seriously by the authorities, both in the city itself and in the *chora*. Various forms of violence and various ways of filing a suit due to acts of violence are carefully detailed in the *Dikaiomata*. In the *chora*, despite the existence of private settlement of disputes, of which the present study only gives an imperfect glimpse, it would appear that people turned to authorities even regarding affairs with a minimal degree of physical violence, and that such affairs were susceptible to end up before the local courts. With very few exceptions, the nature of the documentation we have does not permit to know how the cases were ultimately

---

[92] See TAUBENSCHLAG 1955, p. 431-434; HELMIS 1986, p. 147-153; MÉLÈZE-MODRZEJEWSKI 2011, p. 224-230. Following HELMIS, MÉLÈZE-MODRZEJEWSKI goes so far as (too far, in our view) to speak of the "deliberate disinterest" that royal power showed with regards to homicide (p. 226).

[93] See GUÉRAUD's comment on *P. Enteux.* 81 (TM 3356), p. 197-198; TAUBENSCHLAG 1955, p. 439.

settled, nor to assess the efficiency of the system. But the fact that people continued to submit petitions throughout the three centuries of Ptolemaic rule does at least show that they continued to believe in the ability of the state — in the broadest meaning of the term — to solve their problems. And, as far as violence is concerned, that they trust it to protect the most intimate element of their social personality: their physical integrity. One may assume that — even relatively speaking — this trust in the authorities is one of the reasons for the longevity of Ptolemaic rule over Egypt.[94]

[94] For a reassessment of trust in authorities and wellbeing in Ptolemaic Egypt, see VANDORPE 2013, and her contribution in the present volume, and WYNS 2019, and her contribution in the present volume.

Table 1. The penalties prescribed for violence acts in the *Dikaiomata*

Nature of the injury / Identity of the offender	Injuries under aggravating circumstances	Threat with a weapon	Striking one blow	Striking more than one blow	Striking a magistrate on duty	*Hubris*
	twice the amount of the prescribed penalty					
Freeman or freewoman		100 drachmas without assessment	100 drachmas without assessment	assessment of the damage by the plaintiff assessment by the court the offender shall forfeit twice the amount of the assessment fixed by the court	assessment by the plaintiff (?) assessment by the court (?) the offender shall pay trebled penalty	assessment by the plaintiff assessment by the court the offender shall forfeit twice the amount of the assessment fixed by the court
Male slave or female slave		not less than 100 stripes or 200 drachmas to be paid by the master	not less than 100 stripes or 200 drachmas to be paid by the master 300 drachmas if the master is defeated after challenging the accusation	assessment of the damage by the plaintiff assessment by the court the master shall forfeit three times the assessment fixed by the court		

COURTS, JUSTICE AND CULTURE IN PTOLEMAIC LAW: OR THE RISE OF THE EGYPTIAN JURISTS*

Joseph G. MANNING
(Yale University)

Abstract: In this paper I discuss the well-known trial proceeding report from Asyut, *P. BM Siut* p. 3-12 no. 10591 ro, part of a demotic Egyptian archive published by Herbert Thompson in 1934. It was published as a family archive from Siut (Asyut) and has been understood as such ever since the *editio princeps*. But in this paper, I discuss the possibility that it was neither a family archive nor from Asyut. Rather, because other matters gleamed from the verso of the main text suggest that the connection between the family dispute over land, certainly concerned with a family and land in Asyut, and a dispute about land ownership of priests at Aswan may well be an advocate who advised both cases and who seems to be engaged in legal affairs at Ptolemais, the seat of the high court and the administrative center of Upper Egypt under the Ptolemies. I discuss why it was that professional legal advocates appear in the Ptolemaic period under conditions of institutional complexity and change brought about by the interaction of the Ptolemaic bureaucracy and ancient legal traditions.

* I thank the audience in Vienna at the conference *Administration, Law, and Administrative Law*. Second International Conference of the NFN Imperium et Officium, for their comments, as well as audiences in Brussels, at UCL in London, the University of Colorado-Boulder, CUNY in New York City, the Whitney Humanities Center at Yale University, and Yale and Harvard Law Schools. I am most grateful to Ari BRYEN, Mark DEPAUW, Cary MARTIN, Katelijn VANDORPE, Steve VINSON, and to the students in an earlier seminar at Yale on Demotic documents, Alissa ABRAMS, Maria GUTIERREZ, Andy HOGAN, and François GERARDIN, for offering their comments on early versions of this paper. An important article by BAETENS & DEPAUW subsequently appeared (2015). In part it is a response to the working paper that I had prepared for the conference in Vienna, which is cited therein as "Manning, in Baker, Jursa and Täuber (eds.), *Administration, Law, and Administrative Law*."

INTRODUCTION

I discuss in this paper one of the most famous demotic Egyptian archives from Ptolemaic Egypt, *The Archive of Tefhape*.[1] Tefhape was the winning party in a trial that adjudicated a private dispute over the inheritance of land. The texts were purchased by the British Museum in 1923, and total fifteen documents, including the lengthy and impressive report of the trial itself measuring nearly three meters in length, although it is now divided into six plates for reasons of storage. Herbert Thompson published the *editio princeps* in 1934. Two documents later recognized as being part of the archive were published in 1959.[2] It is noteworthy that there are no Greek documents in the archive.[3] Thompson noted that the actual provenance of the texts is unknown, although most of the internal evidence in the papyri strongly suggests that the origin of the archive is the town of Siut (Asyut) in Middle Egypt where the family served as priests and where the trial before the priest-judges of the temple of the god Wepwawet, the local *laokritai*-court, sat.

Tefhape provides some of the most detailed information about the relationship between the mature Ptolemaic bureaucracy of the second century BCE and Egyptian legal institutions. At the core of the family dispute are property rights that were established through marriage agreements and in the context of Egyptian inheritance law.[4] Because it dates to the second century BCE, a period that is often thought of, generally following Polybius' account of the later Ptolemies, as one of decline in Ptolemaic state capacity, seemingly "on the verge of collapse" in 170-169

---

[1] THOMPSON 1934; https://www.trismegistos.org/arch/detail.php?arch_id=237. Subsequent comments on the archive are extensive. For an orientation and the basic literature, see VLEEMING 1989; MANNING 2003, p. 201-205; QUACK 2011; BAETENS & DEPAUW 2015.

[2] SHORE & SMITH 1959.

[3] Herbert THOMPSON is an interesting figure in British Egyptology. He was originally trained as a lawyer, but being bored, turned to medicine, where he found the use of the microscope caused him eye problems. He turned to Egyptology at the age of forty! The publication of the Siut archive, one of his last, thus, came when he was 75. The review by Battiscombe GUNN, *JEA* 20 (1934), p. 223-228, is important, as are the corrections collected in A.A. DEN BRINKER et al., *A Berichtigungsliste of Demotic Documents. Papyrus Editions*, Leuven 2005. For more on his career, see BIERBRIER 2012, p. 540. BAETENS 2020b has published a Greek petition from Rifeh involving a dispute over funerary concessions related to descendants of the main actors in the Siut trial.

[4] A pioneering work on the Ptolemaic bureaucracy using the archive is JOHNSON 1987.

BCE as one modern historian has said, the archive offers valuable insights on the continuing functioning of legal administration in a period of political crisis.[5] Bagnall and Derow noted in the introduction to their translation of *UPZ* II 162 (Thebes 117 BCE, TM 3563), that in this report of a trial (the so-called Hermias dispute) "when the bureaucracy is supposed to have been badly out of order, it appears here to good effect."[6] The same appears to apply to our text some half a century earlier but also at a time of great crisis. *Tefhape* is also important in providing information about the ways in which the Ptolemaic state continued ancient legal traditions within a new bureaucratic framework. This documentation, indeed, suggests that a hierarchical, rules-based system of justice administered by a stratified bureaucracy continued to function despite political chaos and confusion in the capital and elsewhere.

It is generally assumed that Ptolemaic state building did not substantially change the underlying Egyptian legal system, but merely expanded it by accommodating Greek language agreements and Greek courts.[7] But in this paper I argue that the Ptolemaic state and its Greek language based bureaucracy, in fact, also helped to shape Egyptian law and the organization of justice in new ways at the same time as the underlying local institutional structures, including how and when Demotic Egyptian texts were used, continued to evolve. These changes are especially apparent in the relationship between the bureaucracy and the courts.[8] All of this created a *greater complexity* to the legal regime of Ptolemaic Egypt which might have given rise to the need for advocates who were skilled at negotiating this larger, bilingual bureaucratic system.[9] By complexity, I mean that a more formal relationship arose between the bilingual bureaucratic environment, its procedural rules, the courts, and the Egyptian legal tradition.

---

[5] THONEMANN 2016, p. 423. This is also explored in GORRE & WACKENIER 2020. Evidence from this text, and, for example, new military settlements founded AFTER the great Theban revolt post 186 BCE, suggest, indeed, considerable state capacity. On the new garrisons, see FISCHER-BOVET 2014, p. 269-295. On the idea of "decline" in Polybius, see WALBANK 2002.

[6] BAGNALL & DEROW 2004, text no. 132.

[7] See e.g. ALLAM 2008.

[8] The classic, highly formalist, account of the Ptolemaic legal system is WOLFF 1970.

[9] For the already highly developed legal system in the Ramesside period, see DAVID 2010.

1. Narrative of the dispute

The drama of the *Tefhape* dispute came to a head in June 170 BCE in Siut.[10] The text of the trial proceeding, written on the recto of *P. BM Siut* 10591 (TM 43343), is in fact a "copy", and it is generally assumed that it was issued to Tefhape, the defendant, as the winning party after the trial.[11] The record of the trial proceeding documents both parties' oral responses to their written pleadings to Ptolemaic officials, and marked, in theory, the resolution of the family dispute, with the judges giving their reason for their decision and their command to the *eisagogeus*, a state representative, to execute their order at the end of the proceeding.[12]

Both plaintiff and defendant retell their version of events that led up to the trial with vivid and often violent episodes of kidnapping, beatings, imprisonment, sibling rivalry, intrigue, fraud, and coerced agreements. It is the story of a minor family and what must have been a very common type of dispute, but the *Tefhape* trial came at a dramatic turning point in the history of the Ptolemaic Egypt and the entire Mediterranean world, on the eve of the Sixth Syrian War and the first invasion of Egypt by Antiochus IV.[13] Despite the rather out of the way location, and the insignificance of the dispute, the story of the family dispute ends with the plaintiff appearing before one of the most famous men in Ptolemaic bureaucratic and diplomatic history, Noumenios, the *stratêgos* of the Thebaid, who would be, less than two years later, the lead Ptolemaic ambassador to Rome in the aftermath of the Roman expulsion of Antiochus IV from Egypt.[14]

---

[10] Baetens 2020b summarizes texts that derive from the town.

[11] It is not certain why we have a copy, but there are other copies of reports of trial proceedings, e.g. P. Mallawi inv. 620/10 (TM 47352). Was it issued to the winning party or to an advocate at their request? Some third-century BCE Greek proceedings of trials from Krokodilopolis (Fayyum) were recorded in two copies. See Mélèze-Modrzejewski 2011, p. 123, n. 39.

[12] I follow the reconstruction of Thompson 1934, p. xiv, closely.

[13] The family dispute over land contained in the so-called *Erbstreit* papyri from mid-second-century Pathyris offers instructive parallels. Therein, the dispute was resolved by the *chrematistai*. See Vandorpe & Vleeming 2017.

[14] = *Pros. Ptol.* 196; Thomas 1975, p. 35-36; Huss 2001, p. 579. Noumenios also appears in the archive of Hor, the dream interpreter at Saqqara, and in Polybius 30.16. See the comments of Ray 1976, p. 128, and further the recent study by Smith 2018. But

The sole focus of the dispute was the control of ten arouras of land (roughly six American acres), although shares of priestly offices among other property were involved in the inheritance. Petetum, a priest in the local temple who had married twice and had a son and daughter by each marriage, was near death in 181 BCE. He divided his property, by two separate "deeds of division", between his two sons, half-brothers, with two-thirds going to the elder (by at least ten years by Thompson's estimation) and one-third to the younger son. Tuot, the elder son, and his wife Chratianch had married around 185 BCE, regnal year 21 of Ptolemy VI, the year in which he made a "deed of endowment" for her.[15] This was decisive, at least in Chratianch's mind, since she had married, and been endowed with her husband's property as guarantee, *before* the younger brother married his wife.

The first dispute came in 173 BCE when the younger brother wanted to have the one-third share of the land fully in his control. A petition to the *stratêgos* of the Theban region to divide the land was sent that resulted in a "deed of division" being made by his older brother. Importantly, this was confirmed by the older brother's wife Chratianch, who would be the plaintiff in the trial. The land remained controlled by both brothers, as a joint lease made in 172 BCE shows. In the following year, Tefhape, the younger brother and heir to one-third of the family land, leased out the one-third on his own while Tuot leased his two-thirds.[16] Tefhape had claimed that his elder brother Tuot had defrauded him in the joint leasing of the land.

In 170 BCE, Tefhape made a petition to a Ptolemaic official, the *epistates*, claiming fraud and requesting a real division of the land. Chratianch had also written a petition to have her own claim heard when the official in charge of the Theban region, the *stratêgos*, changed from one man, Theomnestos, to another, Noumenios, and asked that all action be stopped in the previous dispute. The occasion for this request and new petition is not clear, but she may have felt that the previous official was biased against her. After all, she claimed, the uncles of Tefhape were the ones who arrested her husband and forced him to sign

note that, *contra* SMITH (2018, p. 226), Noumenios is indeed mentioned outside of the Hor archive.

[15] THOMPSON 1934, p. xii.

[16] Interestingly, in both cases the land was leased to soldiers.

the division of property. The older brother claimed, it is said in the trial, that he was unable to go to the registration office with the younger brother to cede one-third of the land. Chratianch stated in the trial that her husband had been arrested and forced to sign over his share of the property by two uncles of Tefhape the defendant, referred to by Chratianch as a "herdsman" and a "camel herder".

The trial in Siut was the third attempt at a resolution (the first two being through regional and local Ptolemaic officials). One might imagine, as with the family dispute documented in the Erbstreit papyri, that initial resolution was attempted at the local level before the involvement of state officials and the *laokritai*.[17] The parties to the suit were associated with the temple, and the land in dispute was located within the temple estate. Despite the written petitions to Ptolemaic officials to have the dispute resolved by them, the case was turned over to the court of the local temple to decide. Were petitioners required in the first instance to go to Ptolemaic officials for resolution, or were Tefhape and then his wife "forum shopping", seeking a decision by a neutral party outside of their town? We cannot answer that with certainty, but it seems to me that petitions to state officials were a regular part of seeking justice.[18]

The trial presumably took place in front of the main temple gate, the traditional location of trials in Egyptian law.[19] The court was composed of three priests and an *eisagogeus*, a Ptolemaic official who introduced the case before the judges and acted as an official representative of the state and, apparently, the enforcer of the judges' decision.[20] The two parties appear before them, the plaintiff beginning with her main claim, all the land belongs to her and through her to her children. To support her claim, she cited a passage (partial as it turns out) from what is termed the "law of year 21" concerning the rights of children of a first marriage to inherit. That "law" has frequently been noted as an example of an

---

[17] VANDORPE & VLEEMING 2017.

[18] BAETENS 2020a.

[19] On "justice at the (temple) gate", see the survey in MANNING 2012. See also the contribution by VANDORPE & WYNS, n. 26.

[20] The official has a Greek name, but by no means is it clear in second-century BCE context that this official was ethnically Greek. The Greek word for the institution tells, us, however, that the person is functioning within the Ptolemaic state system in an official capacity. Whether this function has an ancient precedent in Egypt is debatable. For the argument in favor, see ALLAM 2008.

actual broad statutory provision, taking "year 21" to refer to a royal decree promulgated in a specific regnal year of a king. She also claimed that her husband had been forced to cede one-third of the land. Tefhape then responded, at length, denying the claims and producing documents proving his claim. Her husband, no doubt was indeed compelled, but probably by state officials to enforce the agreement to divide the property. The plaintiff then responded, and in turn a second response by the defendant Tefhape followed.

The pleadings were then read out by a scribe in front of the parties. The judges asked each party if they agreed to what they have said. Then documents were produced that supported each party's claims. The judges summarized the main legal points of each argument, and quoted the "law of year 21", the same law cited by the plaintiff. Importantly, however, the judges cited a fuller version, observing that the children of a first marriage have priority to the father's property *unless they have agreed to assigning shares to other siblings*. And that was what happened in our case. Chratianch's husband had agreed to the cession of one-third of the land to his half-brother and she had also agreed.[21] The judges found for the defendant on this basis and affirmed their decision with their signatures at the end of the document. A scribe called "one of the scribes who write in the presence of the judges of the priests of Wepwawet and the gods who dwell with him," a different scribe wrote the copy of the proceeding, also signed the decision. But this final decision by the judges did not bring the matter to an end. There is a petition in the archive made in 169 BCE by Tefhape requesting that his brother be prevented from access to his part of the land. And several months later Chratianch appeared before the high court in Ptolemais appealing the decision of the *laokritai*.

2. Analysis

The perseverance of Chratianch in the face of bureaucratic obstacles is reminiscent both of the Middle Kingdom *Story of the Eloquent Peasant* and of the Chinese novel by Chen Yuanbin, *The Wan Family lawsuit*, later made into a popular movie directed by Zhang Yimou, *The Story of*

[21] PESTMAN 1961, p. 135.

Qiu Ju (1992). The basis of the Chinese story is a woman seeking justice for the assault of her husband by a local official, behind which lies a land dispute. Both stories lionize the everyday heroism of rural people seeking justice in the face of a massive, slow-moving, corrupt and abusive bureaucracy. But unlike the Chinese story, we are left to wonder about the fate of Chratianch. Did she in fact have a legal claim or was she simply exasperated by the four-year process with its twists and turns? We are unable, sadly, to investigate Chratianch's claims that Tuot's uncles, the herder and the camel herder, arrested and forced Tefhape to sign over control of his portion of the land. On balance this claim appears unlikely. From what emerges in the trial proceedings, Ptolemaic officials appear in this case as diligent and honest arbiters of justice, determining that the proper forum to resolve the disputed family was the local Egyptian temple and its priest-judges where the land was located, described as being "within the divine endowment of Wepwawet" (the local god). How are we to understand Chratianch's persistence before what must have been an intimidating tribunal? Are we missing some key elements of the story?

What very clearly comes through in the court judgment at the end of the text is that the authority of the Egyptian court continued to have enormous influence upon the local community, confirming what Diodorus tells us.[22] He may well have had Ptolemaic law in his mind

[22] Cf. Diod. Sic. 1.75: "In their administration of justice the Egyptians also showed no merely casual interest, holding that the decisions of the courts exercise the greatest influence upon community life, and this in each of their two aspects. For it was evident to them that if the offenders against the law should be punished and the injured parties should be afforded succour there would be an ideal correction of wrongdoing; but if, on the other hand, the fear which wrongdoers have of the judgments of the courts should be brought to naught by bribery or favour, they saw that the break-up of community life would follow. Consequently, by appointing the best men from the most important cities as judges over the whole land they did not fall short of the end which they had in mind. For from Heliopolis and Thebes and Memphis they used to choose ten judges from each, and this court was regarded as in no way inferior to that composed of the Areopagites at Athens or of the Elders at Sparta. And when the thirty assembled they chose the best one of their number and made him chief justice, and in his stead the city sent another judge. Allowances to provide for their needs were supplied by the king, to the judges sufficient for their maintenance, and many times as much to the chief justice. The latter regularly wore suspended from his neck by a golden chain a small image made of precious stones, which they called Truth; the hearings of the pleas commenced whenever the chief justice

when he was describing "Egyptian" practice. And yet the firm conclusion of the judges, the awarding of Tefhape's share of the land, and the order to the *eisagogeus* to execute the court order did not deter Chratianch. It is interesting to note in passing that Diodorus also suggests that "advocates" were not allowed to speak in court, fearing that eloquence of a professional would provide advantages and echoing not only earlier Greek commentary on legal rhetoric but indeed the very ancient Egyptian fears of obtaining justice in the *absence* of unusual eloquence.[23] While *Tefhape* does not confirm the presence of an advocate at the trial itself, there is good evidence that advocates appeared in courts to make extended and technical legal arguments in the Hermias case dated some fifty years later (*UPZ* II 162).

Three aspects of this family archive are important in understanding the relationship between the Ptolemaic bureaucracy and local law. First, the local dispute over control of family land, and the subsequent complaint brought by the wife of one of the parties to the dispute, was initiated by a petition written in Egyptian (presumably at some stage translated into Greek?) and addressed to Ptolemaic officials.[24] Both the *epistates* and the *stratêgos* were involved. Eventually the dispute was returned by these Greek officials to the local Egyptian court to find the facts and resolve it. This local court had an official representative of the state, the *eisagogeus*, present. Finally, the proceedings of the trial and the decision of the judges were recorded in full.

---

put on the image of Truth. The entire body of the laws was written down in eight volumes which lay before the judges, and the custom was that the accuser should present in writing the particulars of his complaint, namely, the charge, how the thing happened, and the amount of injury or damage done, whereupon the defendant would take the document submitted by his opponents in the suit and reply in writing to each charge, to the effect either that he did not commit the deed, or, if he did, that he was not guilty of wrongdoing, or, if he was guilty of wrongdoing, that he should receive a lighter penalty. After that, the law required that the accuser should reply to this in writing and that the defendant should offer a rebuttal. And after both parties had twice presented their statements in writing to the judges, it was the duty of the thirty at once to declare their opinions among themselves and of the chief justice to place the image of Truth upon one or the other of the two pleas which had been presented." Translation by C.H. OLDFATHER, *Diodorus Siculus* I (Loeb Classical Library), Cambridge 1933.

[23] Diod. Sic. 1.76. I am referring of course to the *Tale of the Eloquent Peasant*, a Middle Kingdom text set in the First Intermediate Period. See PARKINSON 1991.

[24] On petitions in general, see BAETENS 2020a.

The dispute went back to a dying man's division of family property to his two sons by different wives. The plaintiff was the wife of the elder son, and the defendant was the younger son. I will not be able to resolve here whether such bureaucratic reporting of a trial is a new feature of the Ptolemaic bureaucracy or a continuation from earlier times.[25] While earlier Egyptian law was based on principles of custom and equity, later law, certainly seen in Late Period and in Ptolemaic law, was based on the evidence of written legal instruments.[26]

The fact that we have before us a complete record of a trial proceeding and the decision of the judges with their legal reasoning that stood behind their judgment is important enough.[27] Reports of trials from Roman Egypt were roughly organized in the same way: (1) the introduction of the judges, (2) the pleadings and responses by the parties to the suit, (3) the decision and reasoning of the judges.[28] Were such reports normative in the Ptolemaic legal bureaucracy, or only produced at the request of the winning party, or were such texts written for other reasons?[29] Answers are not easy to come by.

Chratianch, the plaintiff, who had lost before the Egyptian priests, appeared several months later before Ptolemaic officials in Ptolemais, the great Ptolemaic administrative city of southern Egypt.[30] The first three columns on the verso of the report of the proceeding contain two documents, the first a petition to Noumenios, the *stratêgos* of the

---

[25] The famous trial of Mes, dating to ca. 1250 BCE, involving disputed land ownership and stressing written evidence, bears some resemblance to our trial, but there are sufficient differences between the two trials in terms of structure and procedure, and between the two document themselves, one recorded in a tomb, the other on papyrus, and more than one thousand years separating them, to warrant caution in comparing them too closely. On earlier Egyptian law and trials, see EYRE 2004.

[26] EYRE 2004; MARTIN forthcoming.

[27] For earlier records of trials, see MÉLÈZE-MODRZEJEWSKI 2011, p. 123-128.

[28] See e.g. *P. Fam. Tebt.* 24 (TM 47332, AD 124). On Roman court proceedings in Egypt, see PALME 2014.

[29] Consider, for example, *P. Yale* I 61 (TM 13738, AD 210), which records a *conventus* of the Roman prefect, taking place over three days. There were 1804 cases. Of course, with the Ptolemaic text we are dealing with a trial before an Egyptian court, and all such disputes were resolved before such a tribunal or, as in the case of the Erbstreit and Hermias trails, before the *chrematistai*. Nevertheless, the volume of disputes that ended up before such courts would not have been negligible, and would have produced mountains of texts if such documents of legal proceedings were normative.

[30] On Ptolemais, see VANDORPE 1995, p. 210; MANNING 2010, p. 104-113.

Thebaid, by priests of Isis at Aswan about ownership of a vineyard that they claim had been illegally seized by two men.[31] The petition records a complaint of the priests of Isis at Aswan against two individuals who had seized temple vineyards. In the petition by the Isis priests, a certain Tuot, the son of Petihor, acted as an intermediary between them and the high court at Ptolemais that held ultimate legal authority over the whole of the Thebaid region.[32]

There are two striking things about this. First, why would a seemingly unrelated petition appear on the verso of this copy of a trial proceeding? The second astonishing thing here is the mention of Noumenios, whose son and grandson would both attain very high rank as well. The second document on the verso is a document from Tuot son of Petihor to the Egyptian judges from Anhour near Ptolemais who may be functioning as advisors on Egyptian law to the Ptolemaic bureaucrats in Ptolemais.[33] The last text of the verso, column four, is a real oddity.[34] It seems to be a rather garbled draft summary of the family dispute, with Chratianch, the plaintiff, apparently present, "here" the text says, in Ptolemais, in the Autumn of 169 BC. And that is where our knowledge of events ends, in between the two invasions of Antiochus, a time when it now appears that Egypt has been officially annexed to the Seleukid kingdom, when "Egypt divorced itself (from Alexandria)" and letter writers could refer to the age as "times such as these".[35]

3. Emotions and the law

Both parties in the dispute tell emotional stories about the family drama and remind us of the importance of narrative in trials and in

---

[31] *P. BM Siut* p. 49-50 no. 10591 vo, col. i-ii (TM 53821) and *P. BM Siut* p. 52 no. 10591 vo, col. iii (TM 53822). See Baetens & Depauw 2015.

[32] Vandorpe & Vleeming 2017, p. 41.

[33] Baetens & Depauw (2015, p. 205) propose the attractive hypothesis that there may have been a cult of Onuris at Ptolemais.

[34] Quack 2011.

[35] Ray 1976, p. 126; Thompson 1999. On the invasions of Antiochus and the resulting political chaos, see Huss 2001, p. 544-567. Tensions among the priestly families at Siut do in fact continue, as the recently published Greek petition of Petophois, Chratianch's son, demonstrates. See Baetens 2020b.

petitions.[36] It is perhaps no accident that such real-world legal drama took center stage in one of the most famous stories from the period, the story of Setne and Tabubu.[37] The author of the text had a strong interest in Egyptian law, perhaps buttressed by the underlying role of the god Thoth in the story.[38] The dramatization of Egyptian legal rules in the story reinforces that in the real world of Egyptian towns and villages, and indeed everywhere, inheritance, particularly of land, was a source of great tension. That tension derives from two main sources: (1) intra-generational control of land, in this case the two half-brothers, and (2) inter-generational claims to inheritance.

The story, "embedded" within a framing story, is known as *Setne I*. Setne Khaemwaset, to give him his full name in the story, was an actual historical figure, the fourth son of Ramses II of Dynasty 19 and the high priest in the temple of Ptah at Memphis, the ancient capital of Egypt and a city of continued great importance in the Ptolemaic period.[39] In the Ptolemaic story, the framing narrative tells the tale of a quest for a magical book written by the great god of knowledge and wisdom Thoth himself that contained great powers. This book had been discovered by a prince long before Setne, and he had taken it to his grave, a victim of suicide after hearing that his wife and son were killed by divine vengeance. Thoth, whose book of magic it was, claimed that his property rights had been violated, and he demanded revenge from the sun god Re (often called, as here, Pre in later Egyptian texts). And so divine justice was done.

---

[36] BRYEN 2013. On emotions in the context of the writing of wills and disinheritance in Roman law, see CHAMPLIN 1991.

[37] The story is preserved in *P. Cairo* II 30646 descr. (TM 55857), which is generally dated to the early Ptolemaic period on the basis of the text's paleography. For the dating, see VINSON 2008, p. 309. For an excellent new edition of the text, see GOLDBRUNNER 2006. For an English translation, see RITNER in SIMPSON e.a. 2003, p. 453-469, therein called "The Romance of Setna Khaemuas and the mummies". Published comments on the text are numerous. For an introduction to the literature, see RITNER in SIMPSON e.a. 2003, p. 582-584. See also QUACK 2009, p. 32-35; VINSON 2011, and now the extensive commentary by VINSON 2018.

[38] JASNOW 2001, p. 77.

[39] On Ptolemaic Memphis, see THOMPSON 2012. Setne is used as part of the personal name, but is in fact a priestly title, deriving from the Demotic priestly title *Sem*. For the name, see GOZZOLI 2006, p. 262.

Later in the story, Setne happened upon the tomb of the magician, and asked for the book. The ghost of the tomb owner challenged him to a game of chance. He was losing the game when, by way of his own magic, he managed to steal the book and ran off. Then Setne, wandering around the temple of Ptah, caught sight of the most beautiful woman he had ever seen, bejeweled, and so dazzling that Setne became lovesick on the spot.[40] She was Tabubu, the daughter of an important priest, and Setne would, we would find out, do anything to have her.

There follows the key part of the story. Setne, a married man, at least a man with children, attempted to convey his property in order to win the heart (and body) of Tabubu, first by writing an annuity contract and a sale contract that transferred his property to her.[41] "If it happens that you wish to do what you desire with me," Tabubu exhorts, "you will make for me a deed of financial support, together with a document of sale regarding everything and all movable property belonging to you in its entirety."[42] Setne commanded that a scribe be brought to draw up the legal instruments to transfer his property to her. When that did not satisfy Tabubu, Setne forced his children to agree to the property transfer. "Do not leave them to contest with my children for your property," Tabubu exclaimed. So, finally Setne's children are murdered in front of his eyes, their bodies thrown through a window to the streets below to be devoured by dogs and cats. Just when Setne was about to touch the woman, he wakens, naked, from this horrible dream.

The Setne story is essentially one of forbidden desire (running in parallel to forbidden knowledge); certain areas of knowledge belong to the gods alone, and there are dire consequences for those who violate this principle. The consequence for Setne is the nightmare of signing over all of his property and losing his children because of his lust. We do not know about an oral tradition of stories such as Setne and Tabubu, although it has been suggested that one of the Setne tales was picked up by Herodotus (2.141).[43] The Setne Romance, in any case, was surely part of a wider world of stories, perhaps in part in response to Greek novelistic tales, that must have had a larger audience than just the scribes who

[40] See RITNER in SIMPSON e.a. 2003, p. 463, n. 26, on the lovesickness of Setne.

[41] I have learned much from VINSON's magisterial 2018 study.

[42] Translations of the Setne passages are from RITNER in SIMPSON 2003.

[43] But see the cautionary remarks by VINSON 2008, p. 308, n. 16.

wrote them down. Such stories, among other things, would have served as cautionary lessons in the collective memory of countless families through the ages who dwelled along the Nile.

Beyond the stories of forbidden knowledge and magic, there is an important legal principle that is highlighted, and one that we know was crucial in the context of Egyptian family control of property. This is the concept of the "right of expectation" (German *Anwartschaftsrecht*). Children held the expectation that they would inherit their parents' property, and they had to give their assent to any conveyance of property in which they had an interest.[44] This inter-generational tension dramatically ended in the Setne story in murder. One wonders if it ever did in the real world.[45]

The anxiety reflected a deep concern in Egyptian society, and it would have resonated with any Egyptian who held property and was contemplating marriage and children. Ancient Egypt's partible inheritance system meant that all children expected to inherit property. The potential to fragment family property, especially real property, was a serious problem.[46] As we see in the Siut dispute, the general preference appears to have been that family land was kept whole and jointly worked or leased out, but we can also see the problems with this. In Egyptian marriage law, the woman was protected by a "maintenance", or annuity, contract by which the man pledged his property to guarantee her maintenance.[47] To complicate matters, divorce and remarriage were apparently as common as property disputes between family members.

In the Setne story, the Ptolemaic bureaucracy and law courts are entirely missing. Yet Setne does go through some of the legal formalities, drawing up a maintenance document and a sale document to transfer his possessions to Tabubu. Rather than risk a legal dispute that could lead to a trial, the children were murdered.

---

[44] On Egyptian inheritance law and the familial expectations, see PESTMAN 1969.

[45] It is fascinating to read Hamid AMMAR's *Growing up in an Egyptian Village, Silwa, Province of Aswan* (1954, and supplemented by a 1988 PhD dissertation at the University of Florida by his son) that details the family tension over control of land in a village in Upper Egypt in the 1950s.

[46] MANNING 2003, p. 221-225; MUHS 2005.

[47] On these annuity contracts and their role in marriage agreements, see JOHNSON 1994 and SMITH 1995.

Ptolemaic Egypt was a bilingual society, and Ptolemaic governance created political and social tensions. The dominant administrative language, established gradually over the course of the third century BC, was Greek, but the local language of most of the population remained Demotic Egyptian. Among other things, the situation created the need for bilingual scribes, interpreters, and translators.[48]

One of the outcomes of early Ptolemaic state building project was, I suggest, both new kinds of legal procedure and, for the first time apparently, the use of advocates or legal advisors in trials.[49] *Tefhape* also provides a textbook illustration of Egyptian marriage, inheritance law, and the technical aspects of the Egyptian solution to the problem of multiple claims to family property. The process appears to have been well ordered. The complaints addressed in petitions to local and regional Ptolemaic officials were resolved, in theory, through the authority of a local Egyptian court but critically with the involvement of the Ptolemaic state as well.

4. The emergence of advocates

Among the more noteworthy aspect of the technical details revealed in the Siut trial is the complexity of the Ptolemaic legal system. That complexity was caused by two main factors. First, the bureaucratic system, including both the legal and the fiscal systems, operated in two languages (Greek and Demotic) at several administrative levels. Greek, or at least officials with Greek names, dominated state administrative offices (e.g. the *epistates*, the *stratêgoi*) while Egyptians, and the Egyptian language, dominated local temple administration. The second more basic element of complexity is the diversity of the population in Ptolemaic Egypt. There may be a third element here to consider and that is the

[48] Mairs 2012. See also the survey of bilingual archives by Clarysse 2010. For the translation of Demotic legal texts into Greek for the purposes of adjudication before Greek officials, see *P. Berlin* inv. 3098 + 5507 (TM 43627), and *P. Leiden* 413 (TM 3578) (Thebes, 136 BCE) and the important observation by Mairs & Martin 2008/9; *P. Erbstreit*, App. II, p. 177-181.

[49] Advocates were explicitly involved in the Hermias dispute over ownership of a house in Thebes between a Ptolemaic high-ranking soldier and funerary priests known as choachytes in 117 BCE, *UPZ* II 162 (*P. Survey* 48; *P. Tor. Choach.* 12; TM 3563) a Greek language trial proceeding.

general historical legal milieu of the second century BCE, a period during which advocates also emerge in Roman sources.[50]

In the Tefhape dispute, petitions were written in Demotic. These must have been translated for the Ptolemaic officials, at least those who were based in Ptolemais. That was also the reason, presumably, that priests of Anhour were involved with Ptolemaic officials in Ptolemais.[51] Secondly, the variety of legal sources cited to support the case of each party was extensive. "The law of year 21", the "sixth law", "the eighth tablet", are cited by both parties. [52] Such citation of various laws appears highly technical and would probably be knowledge outside of the bounds of everyday life. The case turns on the fact that the defendant could produce legally complete and witnessed documents that proved that the older brother agreed to the division by their father of family property between both brothers. Standing in parallel to the written Egyptian legal tradition and the local tribunal were Ptolemaic officials from Siut as well as Ptolemais.

It is all of this complexity that I think provides us with one of the most interesting historical facts coming from this archive. At the end of the proceedings, the judges asked Chratianch, the plaintiff: "Is there a man who speaks for you?" A man, Ouertes (Bartas), a non-Egyptian name (with a "foreign" determinative to prove it), appears to answer a few technical points on behalf of the plaintiff.[53] Might he have been an advocate? He certainly was not a guardian of Chratianch (or a *kurios* in the Greek sense) because he would have been identified as such, as Thompson argued and which I think is correct.[54] On the unrelated petition and legal opinion on the verso, Tuot son of Petihor clearly appears as a legal expert, and one wonders if he also in some way served as a kind of advisor for Chratianch, a collector of facts, and perhaps even a man who knew how to get things done in the hurly-burly world of Ptolemais in 169 BC.

---

50 See DOLGANOV 2018 (chapter 4) and 2020.

51 BAETENS & DEPAUW (2015, p. 18) argue that the "priests of Anhour" were the *laokritai* court at Ptolemais.

52 Cf. Diod. Sic. 1.75.6. See further MARTIN forthcoming.

53 *Demotisches Namenbuch* 1.2, 122.

54 THOMPSON 1934, p. xvii.

In a famous section of his *Economy and Society*, Max Weber sought to explain the emergence of advocates, legal "Honoratiores" (as distinct from lawyers[55]), in Medieval French and English law.[56] There, out of the need for precision in the spoken word in the courts, "judgment finders" would be appointed by the court upon the request for one of the parties to "speak for" them in the case. We know very little about such advocates in pharaonic Egyptian trials.[57] But the context of Ptolemaic law, with its a bilingual environment, with an ancient system of complex written documents, a new, Greek language based bureaucratic system with interconnected local and regional levels, produced new institutional complexities.

Many questions remain. First, why was the husband of Chratianch, who apparently was alive, not involved at the trial. Secondly, was the appearance of advocates merely the result of the complexities of the Ptolemaic system, or did it develop under Greek influence? Finally, what role did Ouertes and Tuot son of Petihor play? It seems clear that such reports of trials and the use of advocates, although better documented from the Roman period, have their origin in the Ptolemaic bureaucratic administration of trials. Most scholars have stressed continuity between ancient and Ptolemaic Egyptian institutions, particularly in scribal habits.[58] But in its size and complexity, its bilingual language environment, its fiscal system, and in its apparent systemization of Egyptian law, the administration of justice under the Ptolemies had evolved from earlier practice.

---

[55] On the distinction, see RHEINSTEIN 1954, p. 198, n. 3. Weber (RHEINSTEIN 1954, p. 199) elaborates on this distinction as follows: "Originally, the advocate stood before the court next to the party litigating. His position was thus quite different from that of the attorney (*avoué*, *Anwalt*, *procurator*, *solicitor*), who assumed the technical tasks of preparing the case and obtaining the evidence." To be sure we know very little about the training, whether this was an exclusive function or merely a part of a broader administrative function, or whether fees were collected by these advocates who appear in the papyri.

[56] Chapter 7 in RHEINSTEIN 1954.

[57] That advocates were involved in Ptolemaic trials is certain. The clearest example comes from the well-known second-century BCE Greek papyrus *UPZ* II 162 (Thebes, 117 BCE). Translated in BAGNALL & DEROW 2004, text no. 132.

[58] See *inter alia* JOHNSON 1987; ALLAM 2008.

Conclusion

The Tefhape archive is one of the most intriguing collections of documents from Ptolemaic Egypt. It tells a dramatic family story set at a turning point in Mediterranean history. We could hardly ask for more. The procedure of the pre-trial process, with petitions and written pleadings before the trial, the apparent short length of time between the pleadings and the trial (thirty days), suggests a highly formal system. Emphasis was placed on written documentation of property, a formal procedure for assigning property rights to children from different marriages, and above all, on the Ptolemaic bureaucratic administration of these ancient institutions. Importantly, it also reveals how complicated the bilingual nature of the Ptolemaic bureaucracy was. Ever since Thompson's *editio princeps*, the documents, although purchased, have been understood to derive from the ancient town of Siut (Thompson 1934, p. ix) and that the collection of texts must be a family archive.

Yet a close examination of the documents *in toto* might suggest an alternative. What connects the main trial text of the recto to the petition of the Aswan priests, and the note in the fourth column of the verso, is a man named Tuot, son of Petihor. Although unnamed in the main document, he is involved in the petition on the verso (columns i and ii), and appears before judges at Ptolemais. These judges, interestingly, included both Ptolemaic officials and the "priests of Anhour" i.e. the town of Thinis a very ancient town near Ptolemais.[59] These priests may have served as a kind of Egyptian tribunal of legal advisors to the Greek bureaucracy for Egyptian cases heard at Ptolemais itself. Column iii is a response from Tuot son of Petihor on the matter of the controlling Egyptian law in the Isis priests' petition. The text of the fourth column, a kind of draft final decree, is an oddity, which, as Thompson said himself (p. 53) makes no sense in the context of a private text. If my speculation is correct, and the archive would be the (partial) archive of an advocate (namely Tuot son of Petihor mentioned in the petition of the

[59] If we follow Baetens & Depauw (2015, p. 205) there may have been a cult of Onuris in Ptolemais itself. On the Egyptian cult of *Pꜣ-sꜣy-hw* at Ptolemais, see the fascinating texts found at Qasr Ibrim in Nubia but clearly related to the Ptolemaic city published by Ray 2005, and esp. p. 23-24.

priests of Isis in Aswan) who participated in the proceedings on behalf of two parties, Tefhape at Siut, and the priests of Isis at Aswan.[60]

Secondly, one may well wonder about the origins of the documents themselves. It has been the universal assumption that the archive comes from "Asyut or its immediate neighborhood".[61] This is a natural assumption based on the fact that the parties to the lawsuit, the land disputed, and the trial itself took place there. But in my brief account here we have seen that the dispute itself involved several locations including the important city of Ptolemais, where royal judges and regional bureaucratic officials sat.

Could, then, this archive originate from Ptolemais itself rather than Siut?[62] The additional British Museum documents published in 1959 (above, n. 3) have nothing to do with the trial itself. This might militate against this suggestion. As Baetens and Depauw also point out, there are some documents in the archive, the marriage contract of Tefhape's sister for example, that do not appear to be immediately connected to the dispute.[63] But if the archive is part of the private archive of the winning party to the trial the archive, and thus a family archive, the petition and curious notes on the verso of the trial transcript remain to be explained. If, on the other hand, it can be demonstrated that the archive derives from Ptolemais, they would be some of the very first documents from this important Greek city and, perhaps, one of the earliest advocate's archives in legal history. Whatever can be decided about the nature of this archive, however, it provides us with precious evidence for the later Ptolemaic bureaucracy and the administration of law, and surely is one of the most significant corpora in the history of ancient law.

---

[60] THOMPSON (1934, p. 51, n. 30) thought that he may have been the *lesonis* of the temple of Wepwawet at Siut. BAETENS & DEPAUW (2015) suggest that he was a scribe of the *laokritai* court at Ptolemais.

[61] SHORE & SMITH 1959, p. 52.

[62] BAETENS & DEPAUW (2015, p. 213 n. 85) argue that because the archive also involves the "inheritance and marriage of Tefhape's sister and the private property of his mother", it must have been a family archive related to Tefhape. They further argue, p. 213, that what may unite both the main trial text and the verso texts is their common subject matter, property law and dispute resolution. But this brings us back, to my mind, to the world of advocates and court proceedings.

[63] BAETENS & DEPAUW 2015, p. 213, n. 85. The marriage contract is *P. BM Siut* p. 70-71 no. 10594 (*P. Ehevertr.* 34; TM 2742, 172 BCE).

The administration of law and the adjudication of private disputes is an important part of the larger subject of studying the complex historical relationship between state and local institutions. Ptolemaic law was a new legal order established in Egypt over the course of the early third century BCE from which emerged the development of parallel courts and a bureaucracy designed, among other things, to adjudicate disputes. This new legal regime presents many seeming paradoxes between state bureaucracy and the authority of local communities and courts, between custom, tradition and continuity on one hand, and a new legal order, and a new state authority with its new bureaucratic structure conducted in a new language, Greek, and a centralizing ideology on the other.[64] One of the outcomes of this new legal order created by Ptolemaic rule was, I have argued, the rise of professional advocates.

In some respects, Ptolemaic law and its administration illustrates similar institutional tensions described by Haley (1991, p. 3-4) in his analysis of Japanese law: deep historical continuity with change brought about by outside political influence, a strong sense of identity along with a respect for authority by the governing power, and a tension between centralized and diffuse political control. Ptolemaic law consisted of several legal traditions (Egyptian, Greek, Jewish being the three main ones), and bureaucratic rules administered by Greek officials at various levels, and community elders. Above all of this stood the king, whose decrees, in theory, always and everywhere had authority.[65] For all of the fancy legal instruments that existed, though, the complex procedural rules, the clear definition of property rights, and the use of advocates, claims to the ownership of land remained highly contested, and the enforcement of judgements difficult.

---

[64] On Ptolemaic state building and law, see MANNING 2010, p. 165-201, with the earlier literature cited therein.

[65] On Ptolemaic law, see WOLFF 1960; MANNING 2010; MÉLÈZE-MODRZEJEWSKI 2011; 2014b; GROTKAMP 2018. *P. Gurob* 2 (*CPJ* I 19; *Sel. Pap.* II 256; TM 5865, 226 BCE) specifically sets out a hierarchy of legal authority in response to a petition to the king by a complainant. Authority flowed from the king to the local *stratêgos* thence to a court assembled to adjudicate the dispute who would follow "the regulations (*diagrammata*) of King Ptolemy, in accordance with the regulations; and on all points not dealt with in the regulations, but in the civic laws (*politikoi nomoi*), in accordance with these laws; and on all other points to follow the most equitable view (*gnome dikaiotatê*)." See MÉLÈZE-MODRZEJEWSKI 2011, p. 123-125; 2014, p. 475-476. Trans. MÉLÈZE-MODRZEJEWSKI 2014b, p. 476.

PTOLEMAIC GOVERNMENT IDEOLOGY ON DISPUTE RESOLUTION*

Valérie WYNS
(KU Leuven)

Abstract: The Ptolemaic dynasty of Egypt (332-30 BC) propagated a complex image, or rather a complex series of images, of itself to the outside world. Sources such as the walls of the great temples display the Ptolemaic pharaos as representatives of ancient Egyptian ideals of kingship, while Alexandrian poetry paints them as examples of the new Hellenistic *basileus*. Definitively assigning the Ptolemaic rulers to one category or the other would neglect the historical reality of Egyptian society at that time. Closely related to images of kingship, the royal ideology propagated by the Ptolemaic kings cannot be interpreted in the light of just one cultural tradition either. I have previously discussed the wider ideology on 'the good king' as present in Egypt during the last three decades BC (Wyns 2017). This paper however, zooms in on the Ptolemaic ideology on dispute resolution, by examining sources from the ancient pharaonic, Greek and specifically Ptolemaic context, as a way to identify the impact of these cultural traditions on the ideology displayed by the Macedonian kings of Egypt, at home and abroad.

INTRODUCTION

Research on Ptolemaic ideology has produced many and sometimes contradicting views on how the Ptolemies wished to be seen by both their subjects and the outside (Greek) world.[1] As part of the KU Leuven project "Burdened by taxes, but trustful of government? The balance

* The author would like to thank Katelijn VANDORPE, Stefan SCHORN, Willy CLARYSSE and Sofie REMIJSEN for their helpful advice and suggestions.

[1] While HAZZARD 2000 argues a dominance of portraying an ideology mainly fixed on Greek ideology aimed at a Greek public, scholars such as MANNING 2010 describe the Ptolemaic interest in interaction with Egyptians as a cornerstone of the dynasty's succes.

between tax burden and well-being in Hellenistic Egypt (332-30 BC)",[2] an analysis of Ptolemaic, contemporary Hellenistic and ancient pharaonic sources rendered new insights into the ideologies held by the rulers of Egypt in the last three centuries BC. The aforementioned project aims to evaluate the performance of the Ptolemaic state through determinants derived from social sciences, more specifically happiness studies. Evaluating people's actual state of subjective well-being (sometimes designated as happiness) in the past is impossible, since this would involve surveys. However, we can verify whether the Ptolemies or any other government invested in determinants that are proven to promote well-being in any culture, such as shelter, sufficient food stores, health, education, and many more. Governmental actions or lack of actions can positively or negatively influence the presence and quality of these determinants. Pilot studies by Jordan (1993, 1996, 2009, 2010) and Ostroot & Snyder (1996), studying people's well-being in Victorian Great-Britain and 16th-19th century France respectively, demonstrated the feasibility and interesting outcomes of such projects. They also pointed to the need for the development of a specific index for each region and period of time, not only because of cultural differences, but also because of available source material. To accommodate these findings, the Ptolemaic Quality of Life-Index (PtolQLI) was developed specifically for the study of the link between well-being and state performance in Ptolemaic Egypt.[3]

Before the actual performance of the Ptolemaic monarchy and its bureaucracy is evaluated, it is deemed logical to first research what this same government claimed to desire for its subjects. The main question is whether Ptolemaic ideology was predominantly Hellenistic (Greco-Macedonian), or whether a stronger pharaonic Egyptian influence can be traced. Study of source texts such as *P. Tebt.* III 703 (TM 5315) and *UPZ* I 110 (TM 3502) has typically been performed relying on a strongly Hellenistically coloured interpretation by modern scholarship.[4] However, a possible relationship between Ptolemaic ideology and ancient pharaonic wisdom has already been suggested by, among others, Claire Préaux

[2] Research project supported by the Onderzoeksraad KU Leuven, supervision K. VANDORPE.

[3] See WYNS 2016, 2018 and 2019.

[4] See e.g. SCHUBART 1937; CRAWFORD 1976; HUSS 1980; GEHRKE 1982; SAMUEL 1993; GRUEN 1996; BARBANTANI 2010; SCHORN 2016.

(1939), Dorothy J. Crawford (1976) and Werner Huss (1980), but was never researched systematically. The Ptolemies probably wished to distance themselves explicitly from the unpopular former Persian rule. As a consequence, they adopted elements of pharaonic kingship, even if only for outward appearance.[5] Moreover, elements of pharaonic wisdom were still present in Egypt's administration, especially in the lower eschelons of Egyptian bureaucracy. Even after Ptolemy II's reform, lower officials of Egyptian origin remained in place mainly at the toparchy and village level, and were trained in the tradition of the scribal schools. Old en new Egyptian wisdom compositions continued to be copied and studied in these scribal schools and temples well into the Roman Period, and contributed to the spread and influence of Egyptian ideology.

In this contribution to the theme of dispute resolution, we will focus on the ruling attitudes among Ptolemaic kings and officials concerning their intervention in both private and public disputes, and analyse the origins of certain ideological notions where possible. First, we examine the attitudes from the two cultural influences that are deemed most influential on Ptolemaic thought, ancient pharaonic Egypt and Greek philosophy. Of course, other influences, such as Persian,[6] can be detected, but are of minor importance to our purpose.

1. Egyptian instruction texts

Egyptian wisdom, more precisely Egyptian instruction texts ranging in composition dates from the Middle (probably even the Old) Kingdom up to Roman times, was one of the most popular genres in ancient Egypt, as testified by the relatively high number of transmissions.[7] The ancient wisdom texts held instructions for life for a wide array of people, ranging from fatherly advice to a son to the pharaoh himself instructing his vizier. Older compositions, such as the *Teaching for Ka-Gemni* or the *Teaching of Ani* were passed on, changing in form and character with the rise of Demotic as a literary language. Identifying the author of separate texts presents an almost impossible task, since sentences or whole

[5] Manning 2010, p. 91-94; Legras 2012, p. 74; Hölbl 2015, p. 109-117; Legras 2019.

[6] Gruen 1996, p. 116-118.

[7] Hagen 2012, p. 35.

paragraphs from one text were copied into another without reference, resulting in 'copy-paste' texts without clear authorship. Wisdom texts influenced and in turn were influenced by external philosophies, resulting for instance in the strong resemblance between Egyptian wisdom and the biblical *Book of Proverbs*.[8] Debate on the exact extent of mutual influence is still ongoing.[9] Instructions such as the *Teaching of Anqscheshonqy* or *P. Insinger* (TM 55918) were composed under the Ptolemies, attesting the continuous renewal of the genre and its continued popularity.

Before starting the study of ideology on dispute resolution in ancient pharaonic wisdom, we selected 16 representative examples of wisdom texts with composition dates from the Middle (or Old) Kingdom to the Ptolemaic Period,[10] as represented in Table 1. Three of the texts concern instructions for the pharaos, the other 13 deal with men all involved in some way with public offices. Selection was based on completeness of the text and number of topics that could be identified. The texts were analysed and every type of behaviour or attitude that was recommended or discouraged was marked. A certain bias because of the random text transmission was taken into account.

Our close reading of the selected works reveal which ways of conduct were important for public persons in ancient Egypt. The most important one is humility, including knowing your place, found in 10 out of the 16 texts, although it (perhaps understandably) never occurs in wisdom concerning the pharaoh. Another important topic is the responsibilities a man carries when performing duties and wielding power. Most prominently present are the care to avoid negligence and the protection of the

---

[8] SIMPSON 1973, p. 241.

[9] See LICHTHEIM 1983; BURKES 1999; QUACK 2002; THISSEN 2002; GOFF 2005; QUACK 2009[2]; HAGEN 2012; JAY 2016; LAZARIDIS 2016.

[10] These are, in probable chronological order: *The Instruction of Ptahhotep*; *The Teaching for Ka-Gemni*; *Admonitions of an Egyptian Sage*; *The Loyalist Instruction*; *The Instruction of Amenemhat*; *The Teaching for Merikare*; *The Satire on the Trades, or The Instruction for Dua-Khety*; *The Teachings of Ani*; *The Teachings of Aamethu*; *The Instruction of Amun-Akhte*; *The Instruction of Amenemope*; *The Duties of the Vizier*; *The Installation of the Vizier*; *The Appointment of Two Judges*; *An Unknown Instruction from P. Brooklyn 47.218.135* (TM 56077); *The Instruction of Anqscheshonqy*; *The Instruction of P3-wr-dl*; *An unknown instruction from P. Insinger* (TM 55918).

	Teaching of Ptahhotep (OK or MK)	Teaching for Ka-Gemni (OK or MK)	Admonitions of an Egyptian Sage (1st IMP)	The Loyalist instruction (12th D)	Instruction of Amenemhat for his son Sesostris (12th D)	Teaching for Merikare (MK)	The satire on the trades (MK): The instruction of Dua-Khety	Teachings of Ani (18th D)	Teachings of Aamethu (for the vizier User-Amun (18th D)	The instruction of Amunakhte (18th D)	Instruction of Amenemope (NK)	Duties of the vizier (NK)	The installation of the vizier (NK)	Appointment of two judges (19th D)	P. Brooklyn 47.218.135 (LP)	The instruction of Anqscheshonqi (Late Period/Ptolemaic)	The instruction of P3-wr-di (P. Louvre N 2414) (2nd century BC)	P. Insinger (Late Ptolemies)	Total (16)
Justice general	x					x		x	x				x	x					6
Prudence with justice		x				x		x						x					4
Do not act according to your own will where the law is known	x												x						2
See that all is done according to the law	x												x	x					3
Importance of impartiality	x					x							x	x		x			5
Do not pass over petitioners before they have been heard (neglect)	x								x			x	x						4
Protect those who are weak and be lenient	x					x			x		x				x	x		x	7
Always speak the truth	x		x			x					x					x		x	6
Be free and clear of any instance of negligence	x	x		x			x							x	x			x	7
Do not interfeer in conflict	x							x								x		x	4
Do not argue with an argumentative man		x					x				x							x	4
Know when to be silent	x						x			x	x					x		x	6
Strike down who's actions cannot be controlled						x												x	2
Punish those who wish to bribe									x		x								2

Table 1. Common themes in dispute resolution in Egyptian wisdom literature.

weak (both 7 out of 16 texts).[11] The importance of most values remained largely the same over centuries of wisdom texts. Some exceptions can be spotted, such as the importance of eloquence diminishing after the New Kingdom, and the increasing importance of refuting slander[12] from the early Ptolemaic period onward.

In more specific instructions on dispute resolution some general attitudes can be detected. First of all, the importance of impartiality is regularly emphasized. An example from the Tomb of Rekhmire (*The Installation of the Vizier*, New Kingdom, l. 41) reads:

> The God abhors partiality.
> Regard him whom you know like him whom you do not know,
> him who is near you like him who is far from you.[13]

Neither the pharaoh or his subordinates are allowed to show favour in any aspect of their public lives. It is not just incorrect behaviour, it directly offends the gods. A second recurring topic is the duty to protect those who are weak, and showing leniency. Every person with authority is warned to beware of punishing too harshly, since this would negatively affect the official's own judgement in the afterlife. An example from the *Teaching for Merikare* (Middle Kingdom, l. 45-50), son of the pharaoh, illustrates the importance of this admonition even to men in the highest of places:

> Calm the weeper, do not oppress the widow, do not oust a man from his father's property, do not degrade magnates from their seats.
> Beware of punishing wrongfully, do not kill (...), excepting only the rebel who has conspired.[14]

One last recurring element in Egyptian instructions is the admonition not to interfere or engage in conflict, as is shown by the following examples:

---

[11] For further results of the study of these 16 instructions, see WYNS 2017.

[12] Also attested in petitions such as *P. Polit. Iud.* 1 (TM 44617, 135 BC).

[13] Translation FAULKNER 1955.

[14] Translation SIMPSON 1973, p. 183.

From the *Instruction of Amenemope* (New Kingdom, V, l. 10; XVIII, l. 1):

> Do not argue with an argumentative man, do not encourage him with words.
> If you catch someone cheating, at a distance you must pass him by.[15]

From the *Instruction of Anqscheshonqy* (Ptolemaic, XIX, l. 11-12):

> When two brothers quarrel, do not come between them.
> He who comes between two brothers when they quarrel will be placed between them when they are reconciled.[16]

Although these warnings might seem counterintuitive for an official wielding judicial powers, they are not as odd as they might appear. The admonition not to engage in conflict does appear in texts addressing all kinds of officials, but never in a context where they are expected to actively wield the powers of their office. The *Duties of the Vizier* for instance, which explicitly describe the responsibilities and tasks attached to the position of the vizier, do not contain these warnings. Officials were expected to fulfill their duties diligently, and a judge running away from conflict would not have fitted this description. However, officials are expected not to engage in disputes as private persons, which is also part of the pharaonic ideal of self-control. The following example nuances the aformentioned admonitions even further:

From the *Teaching for Merikare* (Middle Kingdom, l. 110-115):

> Be inactive about the violent man who destroys altars, for God will attack him who rebels against the temples.[17]

Not only is avoiding conflict only part of an official's life where his private dealings are concerned, a religious motive comes into play as well. Merikare, who is Egypt's crown prince, is also told not to go out of his way to punish men who commit sacrilege, since the gods or god will ultimately see to it that every man receives proper punishment or reward for the actions he undertook during their lifetime.[18]

---

[15] Translation SIMPSON 1973, p. 245 and 256.

[16] Translation LICHTHEIM 1983, p. 84.

[17] Translation SIMPSON 1973, p. 189.

[18] See Table 1 for an overview of topics in the 16 selected texts concerning dispute resolution.

The endurance of the pharaonic ideology is illustrated by the autobiographies of a number of Egyptian priests from the Ptolemaic period on as described by Quaegebeur.[19] One of his examples is the extensive biography of the priest Khenemibre-men from Karnak,[20] which reveals the characteristics the priestly elite considered most important. In the performance of his sacerdotal duties, Khenemibre-men displayed elements that strongly resemble the ideals from the pharaonic wisdom texts: he walks calmly but strongly, and observes silence. When the priest serves in a judicial capacity, his actions also recall Egyptian wisdom, mentioning his own impartiality three times in this relatively short text:

> J'ai passé une longue vie sur terre. J'ai marché sur le chemin de mon dieu local. Je suis juste de cœur, exempt de partialité. Je suis correct, appliquant la justice. Je suis celui qui a la connaissance de sa ville, sans partialité. Les juges s'appuient sur ce que je dis (litt. il dit), celui dont la venue est attendue dans le tribunal du fait de l'importance de ses discours excellents. J'ai dénoncé l'insolence dans le tribunal. Je n'ai pas montré de partialité (ni envers) un humble, (ni) envers son noble. J'ai le cœur apaisé en entendant prononcer une sentence (à) ma plainte. J'ai renvoyé personne, (si on est) venu vers (litt. à côté de) moi. Je suis quelqu'un qui (ne) dit que ce qui est excellent, (ne) répète que ce qui est le plus utile, quelqu'un dont les propos mauvais ne sortent pas des lèvres. Si on cherchait à l'interieur de moi-même (litt. mon corps), on n'y trouverait pas de défection. J'ai réalisé cela (parce que) mon cœur étant équitable, je savais que je rejoindrais Dieu au jour de la mort.[21]

2. Greek philosophical texts

We now turn to Greek philosophy to examine the most essential ideals on kings and officials dealing with dispute resolution. For this analysis, we rely mainly on fourth-century BC writers, most importantly Isocrates and Xenophon, and to a lesser degree Plato and Aristotle. The genre of the Περὶ βασιλείας will also be examined, although these compositions have only survived fragmentarily.

From the fourth century BC onwards, Greek philosophers developed an interest into the behaviour and education of the ideal king. This

[19] Quaegebeur 1993.

[20] El-Sayed 1984.

[21] Translation El-Sayed 1984.

timing was not coincidental, since not only did contemporary political developments bring kings to the forefront of the societal stage, philosophers were also actively deployed by the new monarchs as diplomats and councillors. Moreover, the rising Hellenistic dynasties often assumed patronage over philosophical schools. Although Isocrates and Xenophon were active just before the actual rise of the new monarchies, their writings later turned out to be a foreboding of the ideology held by the Hellenistic monarchies.[22] Most influential are Isocrates' *To Nicocles*; *Nicocles, or the Cyprians*; and *Euagoras*; and Xenophon's *Cyropaedia*. Plato and Aristotle on the other hand, although in turn an influence on more practical writings for kings, wrote in such an abstract way on kingship that application of their ideals would have proved all the more difficult. Their ideas on kingship are scattered throughout their works, but a focus can be found in Plato's *Nomoi* and Aristotle's *Pambasileia* (book III of his *Politics*). Compositions written in the genre of the Περὶ βασιλείας lastly, would have made an interesting addition to our analysis. Unfortunately, these works 'On Kingship' did not stand the test of time, and no full text is available. Oswyn Murray's unpublished PhD-thesis did however reconstruct the typical content and conventional values that would have been present in these works, and determined that they must have strongly resembled the contents of the works by Isocrates and Xenophon.[23] Material on the expected behaviour of the king's officials is largely lacking, since they were expected to act as a mirror image of the monarch they served.[24]

We will point out the most fundamental elements of Hellenistic ideology by presenting a few representative examples. The first ideal on dispute resolution is the importance of impartiality, just as it was in pharaonic Egypt. This is illustrated by the following quote from Isocrates' *To Nicocles* 18:

> In pronouncing on matters about which there is mutual dispute, do not render decisions which exhibit favouritism or inconsistency, but let your verdicts on the same issues be always the same.[25]

[22] Thus SCHARR 1919, p. 299; SINCLAIR 1951, p. 287; FARBER 1979, p. 497.

[23] MURRAY 1971.

[24] SCHORN 2016.

[25] Translation NORLIN 2009.

Consistency in pronouncing verdicts is also deemed essential for the rule of just kings. Justice is one of the key themes in Greek royal ideology, and the justice of the king ought to reflect or imitate the supreme justice of the gods.

A second parallell with Egyptian thought can be found in the next virtue of the good king concerning dispute resolution, which is reflected in Xenophon's *Agesilaos* 1.22:

> Again, he arranged that prisoners of war who were too old to accompany the army were to be looked after, that they might not fall a prey to dogs or wolves.[26]

Those who are weak are spared, and although Agesilaos was in his right to leave prisoners behind over whom he had no responsibility, he decided to care for men who fought opposite him in the war. This is not a unique attestation of mercy and protection for the weak, or a display of leniency. Hellenistic kings were generally celebrated for their generous and merciful treatment of their enemies. Whether these celebrations reflected actual practice, is a different matter.

The third ideal presents a distinctly Greek feature: an emphasis on fair and just laws. Although pharaonic Egypt did recognize the importance of the presence of law, justice emanated from the responsible officials and convention rather than a canonized corpus of legal texts. For Greek philosophers, the drawing up and application of the law are at the core of state ideology, even in monarchies, as demonstrated by Isocrates' *To Nicocles* 17:

> Seek laws that are altogether just and expedient and consistent with each other and, moreover, bring about the speediest possible settlement for your citizens.[27]

The idea that applying the law to appropriate cases automatically leads to correct judgement is in accord with the Greek notion of the sanctity of law. Whether the king is subject to the law or is the physical embodiment of justice, remained a subject for discussion among Greek philosophers.

---

[26] Translation Bowersock 1925.

[27] Translation Norlin 2009.

3. Ptolemaic sources

Now that both pharaonic Egyptian and Greek ideology on dispute resolution have been examined, we turn to Ptolemaic sources for information on the ideals held by both monarchs and their officials. Source material on this subject differs from that of the two aforementioned cultures. Ptolemaic Egypt does not provide us with written statements that explicitly and systematically treat state ideology. However, documentary sources from the royal bureaucracy and decrees from the country's religious sphere do inform us about how the goverment wished to appear before Egypt's inhabitants. Instructions to subordinates, letters of rebuke, employment oaths and ordinances hold a number of implicit or explicit references to common ideology, and texts from the religious context are especially useful in providing elements of royal ideology and the benefactions that were deemed important for the pharaos to display publically.[28] Petitions[29] are more difficult to include, because they convey the expectations the public held towards the ruling powers, rather than the image these powers wished to display towards the population. It can be assumed that petitioners would appeal to characteristics they knew officals would appreciate, but there is no way of determining which of these were part of official ideology.

A general study of characteristics in these texts, and a comparison with pharaonic Egyptian wisdom and Greek philosophy revealed a few interesting finds. Firstly, as mentioned briefly before, a strong overlap between Greek and Egyptian ideology is apparent, although the degree of emphasis on certain elements can differ. Secondly, the figure of the king is less restricted in Ptolemaic Egypt compared to the Greek ideal, most importantly when it comes to enjoying and displaying luxury and opulence. However, some elements of Ptolemaic royal ideology are distinctly Greek in nature. The good breeding of the king (εὐγένεια) for instance, is of

[28] Crawford addressed the ideology of Ptolemaic Egypt thoroughly in her 1976 article, examining a large corpus of papyrological material. Our approach differs in that we excluded petitions, which form a large part of her main body of texts. Moreover, we included a study of earlier Egyptian material to trace the origins of certain elements of Ptolemaic ideology, which Crawford already hinted at on page 196 of the 1976 study.

[29] For an overview of petitioning under the Ptolemies, see Baetens 2014 and 2020a.

far greater importance to the Ptolemies than their pharaonic predecessors.[30]

As in pharaonic Egyptian and Greek ideology, the importance of impartiality recurs in Ptolemaic sources. However, a different emphasis is placed, shifting from not favouring one side in a dispute to an admonition not to abuse the power of one's own office to force a settlement in one's own private disputes, as illustrated by *C. Ord. Ptol.* 34 (TM 2229, 186 BC):

> No-one among the *strategoi*, *epistateis*, *epimeleteis*, collectors of debt, *chrematistai*, ... nor among the other officials who handle the business of the king, the cities, and the temples, will stop no-one for debt or private crime; and because of personal hate, they will not detain free men in houses or other places; but they will make them appear before...[31]

Ptolemaic officials were expected to hand over cases in which they were involved themselves to another official to avoid abuse and impartiality. Several of these warnings are attested, suggesting that this rule was not always obeyed by those wielding power throughout Egypt.

A strong parallel to both Egyptian and Hellenistic ideology is presented by admonitions to protect those who are weak and the importance of leniency. Although the Ptolemaic legal system was less prominently religiously coloured, religious interference was tolerated, as shown by the legal value of temple oaths and the official character of the *laokritai*, Egyptian judges-priests. The concern for subjects' well-being is demonstrated in a passage from the well-known *P. Tebt.* III 703 (end of the third century BC):

> In your tours of inspection try going from place to place to cheer everybody up and to put them in better heart; and not only should you do this by words but also, if any of them complain of the *kommogrammateus* or the komarchs about any matter touching agricultural work, you should make inquiry and put a stop to such doings as far as possible.[32]

Although a certain economic concern shines through in the words of the official who wrote the letter, wishing to keep workers happy so they would continue to produce sufficiently, it testifies at the same time to a concern for the well-being of the population. The extent of Ptolemaic

---

[30] An extended version of this analysis can be found in WYNS 2017.

[31] Author's own translation.

[32] Translation BAGNALL & DEROW 1981.

government's leniency does however have its limits. The following excerpt designates who is excluded from the general amnesty in *P. Tebt.* I 5 (TM 2938, 118 BC):

> (...) except to persons guilty of willful murder or sacrilege.[33]

Excluding murderers and those who defaced or destroyed the temples of the gods is a common tendency in Ptolemaic amnesty.

A Greek element in Ptolemaic ideology is illustrated by the following inscription (*OGIS* I 48, TM 6372, third century BC):

> (Names of magistrates) have governed the city in a fine and worthy manner, and observing that some of the citizens were behaving badly, and were causing exceptional trouble in the councils and assemblies, and especially in the elections, proceeding [as far as violence and] impiety, the *prytaneis* acted against this wrong-doing, [and punished them with] the penalties prescribed by law; as a result of which it happened that the city became [more orderly].[34]

The text honours magistrates who restored order to the city by adhering to the law, which has a distinct Greek ring to it. One has to keep in mind that this honorary stele from the city of Ptolemais came from a thoroughly Hellenized context. Honorary stelae for government officials outside the funerary sphere are rare in the Egyptian context, which has led some scholars to believe inhabitants of Egypt didn't have much to celebrate. However, we have to keep in mind Claire Préaux's keen observation that "Mais il ne faut pas oublier que les bons fonctionnaires ne font pas parler d'eux, dans ce pays qui n'a pas eu, comme les villes grecques, la manie des décrets honorifiques".[35]

The following letter from dioecetes Herodes to a certain Onias (an *oikonomos*?) concerns mistakes by Dorion, a subordinate, which need to be remedied as soon as possible. In his description of the necessary actions, Herodes mentions several types of behaviour expected of a Ptolemaic official, such as care, precaution and zeal. From *UPZ* I 110 (164 BC):

> (...) please apply all zeal and take all precaution, in order neither that those who are unable to work in the fields be impressed nor that those who are

---

[33] Translation Bagnall & Derow 1981, no. 54.

[34] Translation Austin 2006.

[35] Préaux 1939, p. 566.

able to be protected on any pretext whatever; but that each thing be completed according to the manner in which it was indicated in our memorandum which was sent to you.[36]

Conclusion

A strong overlap can be detected between pharaonic Egyptian, Greek philosophical and Ptolemaic ideology on officials in their judicial and administrative capacity. Most of these similarities simply originate from human common sense. The characteristics that are deemed important by the three studied cultural spheres, are traits that we still desire today in an official dealing with disputes. We like them to be unbiased and incorruptible, and able to show leniency where possible. Only the Egyptian "silent man" who doesn't engage in conflict is a pharaonic specificity. An overview of the similarities and differences between the three traditions is represented in Table 2.[37]

	Ancient Egypt	**Hellenism**	**Ptolemaic Egypt**
Suppress Anger	♛ ★	★	★
Know When To Be Silent	★		★
Protect the Weak	♛ ★	★	♛ ★
Be Mild in Punishment	♛ ★	♛ ★	★
Be impartial	♛ ★	★	★

♛ = characteristic specific to the king
★ = characteristic specific to officials

Table 2. Ideal characteristics of the king and his officials concerning dispute resolution.

The difference in source materials used for this analysis should be noted, since no one-on-one analysis was possible, and some desired characteristics might have become over- or underemphasized.

---

[36] Translation White 1986, p. 68.

[37] An extended version of this table is published in Wyns 2017.

The ideology of Ptolemaic Egypt on dispute resolution presents no ruptures with either pharaonic Egyptian or Hellenistic philosophical thought. The most important elements in Ptolemaic ideology are the protection of the weak and being lenient, which was especially prominently present in earlier pharaonic ideology. Another important ideal that was more Hellenistically inspired was the emphasis on the application of the law, especially in the three Greek cities of Egypt. Lastly, impartiality was also deemed of tantamount importance, an attitude inherited from both pharaonic as Hellenistic ideals, and implied a ban on abusing power of one's office for personal gain.

ACCESS TO JUSTICE IN PTOLEMAIC EGYPT. ASSESSING THE JUDICIARY THROUGH THREE CASE STUDIES FROM THE THEBAID*

Katelijn VANDORPE and Valérie WYNS
(KU Leuven)

Abstract: The Ptolemies were confronted with a broad range of challenges inherent in a new multicultural society, including in the domain of jurisdiction. This paper assesses the judiciary in the second-century BC Thebaid, starting from three case studies where the judicial procedures can be followed over a longer period and using the USIP's guidelines which offer an interesting framework for the assessment of antique justice systems. The paper discusses the integration of local traditions of justice, the provision of legal aid & professionalization of justice personnel, language, geographical & financial barriers, and the enforcement of court verdicts. Although the overall assessment is a positive one, a weak link in the judiciary system was undoubtedly the enforcement of verdicts.

INTRODUCTION

The preceding paper by Valérie Wyns has shown that the most significant elements of Ptolemaic ideology on dispute resolution are the protection of the weak, showing leniency when sitting in judgement, emphasizing the application of the law, and being impartial. Did the Ptolemies manage to concretize these general objectives? For this paper we turn to the United States Institute of Peace (USIP),[1] founded in 1984, which works to prevent and resolve violent conflict around the world. When one wants to prevent conflicts in a newly organized society, it is vital to strengthen the rule of law and provide access to justice. According to the USIP

* We are most grateful to Gert BAETENS for his many suggestions.

[1] See http://www.usip.org/about-usip, last accessed in September 2021.

> Access to justice is more than improving an individual's access to courts or guaranteeing legal representation. Access to justice is defined as the ability of people to seek and obtain a remedy through formal or informal institutions of justice for grievances in compliance with human rights standards. There is no access to justice where citizens (especially marginalized groups) fear the system, see it as alien, and do not access it; where the justice system is financially inaccessible; where individuals have no lawyers; where they do not have information or knowledge of rights; or where there is a weak justice system. Access to justice involves normative legal protection, legal awareness, legal aid and counsel, adjudication, enforcement, and civil society oversight.[2]

The USIP's guidelines to organize access to justice are applicable to contexts that lack the amenities of First World countries, and offer an interesting framework for the functioning of antique justice systems. To this aim, we depart from three second-century BC lawsuit dossiers where one can follow the judicial procedures over a longer period, all three originating from the (strongly Egyptian region of the) Thebaid.

In the second-century BC Thebaid, one could file a complaint with and/or cases could be heard by courts:[3] the *laokritai*, the court of Egyptian judges-priests, provided justice for the native population, while the high court of *chrematistai*-judges or "circuit judges" tried fiscal and civic cases over all population groups; by the second century BC this court had become the main state court and was by then sedentary: for Upper Egypt they were based in the Greek city of Ptolemais Hermeiou, sitting also in judgment in Thebes. No appeal was possible after a judgment by the *chrematistai*, who represented the king; anyone who tried to lodge an appeal after their verdict, was fined.[4] It is not clear whether appeal was allowed after a verdict by the *laokritai*.[5] Another new feature of the

---

[2] See https://www.usip.org/guiding-principles-stabilization-and-reconstruction-the-web-version/rule-law/access-justice.

[3] Wolff 1970, p. 37-53, 64-89, 113-193; Seidl 1972, p. 69-84; Lippert 2012, p. 179-188; Manning 2010, p. 181; Grotkamp 2018, p. 11-85; Manning in Vandorpe 2019, p. 114-115.

[4] Seidl 1962, p. 99 with note 5; Grotkamp 2018, p. 136-138.

[5] According to Seidl 1972, p. 99 (but see Lippert 2012, p. 189), appeal was possible after a judgment by the *laokritai*, as following the trial before the *laokritai* in Siut (phase 5), another trial was apparently held before the *laokritai* in Ptolemais after Totoes' wife appealed for a rehearing (phase 6 of the Siut-trials), but the text is difficult to interpret, see *P. BM Siut* p. 54 no. 10591 vo col. iv. In the fragmentary *P. Fordham* inv. 5 a woman writes to the chief judge (*archidikastes*) of the chrematists and the other courts about a case about which she had already complained to the local *laokritai* (*ZPE* 176 [2011],

judicial department, introduced by Ptolemy II, were the *dikasteria*, courts dealing with disputes between Greek-speaking inhabitants and well-attested in the *metropoleis* of Middle Egypt;[6] the *dikasteria* are on the contrary rarely found in the second-century BC Thebaid,[7] and are absent from our case studies having Egyptian and Egyptian-Greek litigants. All these courts (*laokritai*, *chrematistai* and *dikasteria*) were assisted by a clerk and an official representative of the state called *eisagogeus* or "introducer", a "royal functionary cooperating as a liaison man" at various levels of the "judiciary, Egyptian and Greek alike".[8]

On the other hand, people in the second-century Thebaid could petition the king or one of his officials. Not all officials were allowed to preside over a trial or pass judgement: some lower officials were entitled only to bring about a *dialysis*, a "dissolution" or amicable settlement, while higher officials often delegated the case to local representatives or to one of the above-mentioned courts. High officials qualified to preside over a lawsuit, such as the viceroy (*epistrategos*) or nome governors, were assisted by an ad-hoc court:

– in the case of the Erbstreit trials (see below, phase 3), a court of *hegemones* (infantry "commanders") assisted the *epistrategos*;[9]
– in the case of the Hermias trials (see below, phases 5 and 7) the nome governors were assisted by a large number of "judges" from the military and administrative milieu, often bearing court titles and including cavalry and infantry commanders and gymnasiarchs.[10]

p. 213-220, TM 129892; 156-125 BC), but the date may be rather early Roman than Ptolemaic, see DÜTTENHOFER in BAETENS 2020a, p. 91, n. 133. In *P. Hels.* I 1 (TM 5138) someone tried to bring before the chrematists a case that had already been brought before the *laokritai*, although we do not know whether this was successful; here no actual appeal is involved: the court of the *laokritai* had no jurisdiction to rule on matters related to state revenues, hence the petitioner wanted the case to be heard by the competent court, *in casu* the chrematists.

[6] See KALTSAS in *P. Heid.* VIII, p. 3-9; GROTKAMP 2014; ARMONI in *P. Köln* XIV, p. 32-34; KRAMER & SÁNCHEZ-MORENO ELLART 2017; GROTKAMP 2018, p. 24-41.

[7] KRAMER & SÁNCHEZ-MORENO ELLART 2017, p. 27-28.

[8] ALLAM 1991, p. 124-125. See also SEIDL 1962, p. 77; ALLAM 2008; MANNING 2010, p. 169 (with n. 11) and 184; HUSS 2011, p. 111, n. 594; LIPPERT 2012, p. 185; GROTKAMP 2018, p. 19-21.

[9] *P. Erbstreit* (2017), p. 37, with n. 5.

[10] Phase 5: *P. Tor. Choach.* 11bis (TM 3562), col. i, l. 1-4; phase 7: *P. Tor. Choach.* 12 (TM 3563), col. i, l. 1-8.

People were well aware of the wide range of possibilities to petition. In a text of one of our dossiers, one of the parties promised not to complain (*smy*)

> to a commissioner (*sḥn*, corresponding to Greek *-arches* in, e.g., *komarches*), or to a judge (*wpṯ*, i.e. one of the *laokritai*-judges), *dikastes* (i.e. one of the *chrematistai*-judges), *strategos* (title of governor of several nomes in the Thebaid and of the governor of the Thebaid), *epistates* (title of a nome governor in the Thebaid), or also any other man whosoever who is sent on an affair (*md*) of the King.[11]

The three lawsuit dossiers discussed here are the following.

1) **The Siut-trial** (185-169 BC)[12] (see also the contribution by J.G. Manning).

Place: Lykopolis (Siut)
Object of contention: land as part of an inheritance
Parties: half-brothers Totoes (& his wife Chratianch) versus Tefhape
Petitions and/or trials:[13]

(1) 17 May 173 BC, Siut – petition by Tefhape to Theomnestos, the governor of the Thebaid (*strategos*), which led to an investigation by the nome governor
Result: probably no trial, but decision taken by the nome governor resulting in an agreement on 3 June (Tefhape won)

---

[11] *P. Erbstreit* (2017) 17, l. 6 (with commentary on p. 151) = 18, l. 8-10. See also LIPPERT 2012, p. 182-183.

[12] *P. BM Siut* p. 3-12 no. 10591 ro (TM 43343); *P. BM Siut* p. 54 no. 10591 vo col. iv (TM 53823); *P. BM Siut*, p. 57-59 no. 10591 vo col. v-vii (TM 53824); *P. BM Siut* p. 77 no. 10598 (TM 43409); *P. BM Siut* p. 78-79 no. 10599 (TM 48653); *P. BM Siut* p. 79 no. 10600 (TM 44188).

The reconstruction of the different phases of the Siut-trials is problematic, see THOMPSON 1934, p. xii-xviii; VLEEMING 1989; BAETENS & DEPAUW 2015; TM Arch 237. See the bibliography and a translation of *P. BM Siut* p. 3-12 no. 10591 ro in MANNING 2010, Appendix.

[13] For phases 1 to 5, see *P. BM Siut* p. 3-12 no. 10591 ro, and *P. BM Siut* p. 57-59 no. 10591 vo col. v-vii; *P. BM Siut* p. 77 no. 10598; for phase 6, see *P. BM Siut* p. 54 no. 10591 vo col. iv; for phase 7, see *P. BM Siut* p. 78-79 no. 10599 and *P. BM Siut* p. 79 no. 10600.

(2) ?Between June 173 - May 170 BC,[14] Siut – petition by Totoes' wife to Noumenios, the (new) governor of the Thebaid; she requested the case to be handled by the *laokritai* (compare phase 5)
Result unclear
(3) 171/170 BC, Siut – two petitions by Totoes to a royal official and to the nome governor Timarchos, respectively
Result unclear
(4) 170 BC, Siut – petition by Tefhape to a royal official
Result unclear
(5) May-June 170 BC, Siut – petition or complaint by Totoes' wife (probably her petition of phase 2) led to a trial
Result: trial before the *laokritai*-judges, priests of the temple of the god Wepwawet/Ophois in Siut (Tefhape won); the judges ratified the agreement of the first phase of the Siut-trials (when the case was dealt with by the nome governor)
(6) ?After May-June 170 BC, Ptolemais – ?Totoes' wife appealed for a rehearing, also complaining that she had been taken to prison and had been beaten violently after the judgment of the *laokritai* in phase 5
?Result: case probably reheard by the *laokritai* of the city of Ptolemais (not clear who won, but Tefhape probably won given the petitions filed in phase 7)
(7) 16 May 169 BC, Siut – in two petitions addressed to a royal official (*sḥn*) and the *topogrammateus*, respectively, Tefhape complained about his brother Totoes who had prevented him from harvesting the crops on his land. Tefhape referred to the

[14] It is not clear whether the action by Totoes' wife took place shortly after the agreement of phase 1 (agreement of 3 June 173 BC) or was rather the immediate cause of the trial before the *laokritai* in phase 5 (May-June 170 BC). In her plea, Totoes' wife mentions this action immediately after the agreement of phase 1, but her plea may not be chronologically arranged, see *P. BM Siut* p. 3-12 no. 10591 ro, col. ii, l. 3-4. The names of the officials are not helpful to date this phase more precisely: for Theomnestos of phase 1 (TM Per 8946) only one exactly dated attestation is available for him being governor of the Thebaid, that is 17 May 173 BC (*P. BM Siut* p. 3-12 no. 10591 ro, col. iii, l. 13), while for Noumenios of phase 2 (TM Per 10893; MOOREN 1975, pros. 049) equally only one more or less precise date is available for him as governor of the Thebaid, and that is shortly after 30 Sept. 170 BC, see *P. Grenf.* I 38 (TM 262).

agreement of the first phase of the Siut-trials (ratified by the *laokritai* in phase 5)
Result unclear
Evidence: Egyptian Demotic

2) **The Erbstreit-trials** (135-130 BC)[15]
Place: Pathyris, provincial town to the south of Thebes
Object of contention: two large parcels of land as part of an inheritance
Parties: two parties from the same family (aunt & her family versus niece & nephew)
Petitions and/or trials:[16]
(1) 135 BC, Pathyris – petition by the aunt to the mayor of the town of Pathyris
Result: amicable settlement through temple oath (probably in favour of the niece & nephew)
(2) 135/4 BC, Thebes – petition by the aunt to the governor of several nomes, including the Pathyrite nome
Result: probably no trial, but order by the governor resulting in an agreement (aunt won, but agreement not validated)
(3) 134/3 BC, Thebes – petition by niece to the viceroy (*epistrategos*),
Result: preliminary trial before council of the viceroy, resulting in a temporary decision;
final trial before the viceroy and final verdict (niece won)
(4) 133 BC, Thebes – petition by niece & nephew to the *chrematistai*-judges
Result: trial with final agreement (niece & nephew won). No appeal possible

[15] *P. Erbstreit* (2017), abbreviated in this paper as *P. Erbstreit*; see TM Arch 81. *P. Erbstreit* 1 (TM 144), 2+3 (TM 145), 4 (TM 147), 5 (TM 149), 6 (TM 113818), 7 (TM 45846), 8 (TM 151), 9 (TM 152), 10 (TM 113816), 11 (TM 382621), 12 (TM 43363), 13 (TM 5882), 14 (TM 146), 15 (TM 611), 16 (TM 156), 17 (TM 154), 18+19 (TM 113817), 20 (TM 43347).

[16] Compare *P. Erbstreit,* p. 34. Only the series of second contendings are discussed here, for the first contendings (consisting of one phase only), see *P. Erbstreit,* p. 32-33.

3) **The Hermias-trials** (125-117 BC)[17]
Place: Thebes East in the Peritheban nome
Object of contention: house, formerly owned by Hermias' father before the Great Theban revolt (206-186 BC), now in possession of *choachytai*-priests, who stored their mummies in the house, although located in a residential area. The house was claimed by Hermias about 80 years later.
Parties: Hermias, soldier, versus *choachytai*-priests (except phase 1)
Petitions (all submitted by Hermias) and/or trials:[18]

(1) 125 BC, Thebes – petition to the *chrematistai*-judges against Lobais, a previous "onwer", who had "sold" the house to the *choachytai*
Result: trial in Thebes versus Lobais, one of the previous owners plus agreement (Hermias won)

(2) 125/4 BC, Thebes – petition to the governor of the Peritheban nome against the new owners, the *choachytai*
Result: no trial (the *choachytai* withdrew)

(3) 121 BC, Thebes – petition to the governor of several nomes against the *choachytai*
Result: order to give the house to Hermias

(4) 119 BC, Thebes – petition to the governor of the Peritheban nome Herakleides against the *choachytai*
Result: no trial (the *choachytai* withdrew)

(5) 119 BC, Thebes – petition to the governor of the Peritheban nome Ptolemaios against the *choachytai*
Result: trial in Thebes before Ptolemaios and his council (the *choachytai* won)

(6) 117 BC, Thebes & Latopolis – petition to the viceory (*epistrategos*) against the *choachytai*
Result: no trial (the *choachytai* withdrew);
case transferred to the governor of several nomes, who was based in Latopolis; Hermias travelled to Latopolis to submit the petition and to hand over the orders of the viceroy to the governor there; trial planned (the *choachytai* withdrew)

---

[17] *P. Tor. Choach.* 11 (TM 3561), 11bis (TM 3562) and 12 (TM 3563); the documents dealing with the Hermias trials are part of TM Arch 50.

[18] Compare *P. Tor. Choach.*, p. 122.

(7) 117 BC, Thebes & Latopolis – petition to the governor of several nomes against the *choachytai*
Result: when the choachytes did not appear before the governor, the latter went back to his home base Latopolis. The plaintiff Hermias followed him and requested the case to be transferred to the governor of the Peritheban nome Herakleides;
trial before the governor Herakleides and his council in Thebes (the *choachytai* won)

1. Engaging local traditions of justice

The USIP guidelines 7.8.11, entitled *Understand informal justice mechanisms*, and 7.8.12, entitled *Use the local context to determine how and to what extent local practices should be incorporated into the formal legal system,* have:

> These systems [informal justice mechanisms] derive legitimacy from traditional, customary, or religious sources. In these environments, they often help resolve disputes because the formal, state-based system does not reach the entire population, the population views informal mechanisms as more legitimate and effective, and the volume of cases may be too large for the formal system to process. (…) Where these systems are ignored or overridden, the result can be the exclusion of large sectors of society from accessible justice.
> During transitional phases, there will inevitably be overlap and contradictions between formal and informal justice mechanisms. Consider the compatibility of local practices with international norms, whether they can be integrated within the formal justice system or have to stand alongside it, and whether the practices serve to divide society or unite it.

The Ptolemies not only preserved the native Egyptian court system of the *wpṯ.w* or *laokritai*, judges who were associated with temples and had a specific legal training (attested from the 26th dynasty onwards),[19] they also integrated these courts into their judicial system by adding a state representative or *eisagogeus*, and by allowing officials to refer cases to the *laokritai*. In addition, they implemented the Egyptian system of temple

[19] The *wpṯ.w*-judges replaced the previous *qnb.t*-courts from the 26th dynasty onwards, see Massa 2018, p. 63.

oaths,[20] despite the fact that Greek justice was in general deprived from religious connotations. Temple oaths are attested twice in the Erbstreit-trials. Such an oath was imposed a first time in the initial phase of the Erbstreit trials on the local level, probably after one of the parties complained to the *epistates* or mayor of the village. Imposing a decisory temple oath was a frequently used way to reach an amicable settlement in the Egyptian milieu; the oath usually had to be taken by the defendant, especially when the plaintiff could not produce written evidence. The consequences of taking or refusing to swear the oath were laid down in advance by the official in charge.[21] In the Erbstreit case, the aunt claimed that she gave up her share of a (commonly owned) house in exchange for the disputed piece of land, but she could not prove it, so an oath by the other party was necessary, emphasizing that the allegations of the aunt were false.[22]

But not only on the local level or in Egyptian milieus such oaths were sworn, also during the trial before the *chrematistai*-judges, an Egyptian temple oath was imposed, after the same aunt now claimed that she had paid a sum of money for part of the disputed land, but again she could not prove it. The oath had to be sworn by the other party, who firmly denied that money had been paid and won the trial.[23]

The temple oaths of the Erbstreit trials (*P. Erbstreit* 12 and 19) were sworn before the god Suchos/Sobek, surnamed Lord-of-the-Pylon, at his temple which is either to be identified with a(n unknown) chapel of Sobek in Pathyris or rather with the god's temple in nearby Krokodilopolis.[24] Egyptian temple oaths were sworn not inside the sanctuary, as laymen had no access, but in front of a chapel or temple gate where everyone had access to. The oaths sworn by Montu as the Bull-of-Medamud, for instance, were taken at "the gate (*r3*) of Djeme in the temple of Montu-Lord-of-Medamud", identified by D. Devauchelle with

[20] Juridical oaths are attested in Egypt since the early Pharaonic period, see MASSA 2018, p. 23-98.

[21] WILSON 1948; *O. Tempeleide*, p. 28-29; SEIDL 1962, p. 97-98; MASSA 2018, who provides in her PhD an excellent in-depth study of temple oaths in Ptolemaic Egypt.

[22] *P. Erbstreit* 12 and *P. Erbstreit*, p. 34-35.

[23] *P. Erbstreit* 19.

[24] *P. Dryton*, p. 413-414; VANDORPE & WAEBENS 2010, p. 37.

a gate of Djeme belonging to Montu's temple in Medamud.[25] In the case of the Sobek temple, the oath may have been taken in front of the temple pylon, hence maybe Sobek's epithet in the oaths.

Not only oaths were sworn near an Egyptian sanctuary, also the trials before the *laokritai*-judges, and even those before royal officials such as the *strategos*, were held in a religious frame, for instance, at the northern gate (*Premit*) of the local temple in Krokodilopolis (Fayum), or in Eastern Thebes at the propylon of Khons' temple, built by Ptolemy VIII. Many more such "gates of giving justice (*rwt-dy.t-mȝʿ.t*)" have been identified which could take different architectonical forms, from pylons or temple gates to kiosks on the temple *dromos*.[26]

The above examples show that local practices and the religious embedment of justice typical of local culture were embraced and integrated by the Ptolemaic judicial department.

2. Provision of legal aid and professionalization of justice personnel[27]

The USIP guideline 7.8.6 suggests to increase access through provision of legal aid, while guideline 7.8.23 focuses on increasing the knowledge and professionalization of justice personnel to dispense justice.

As argued by J.G. Manning (see his contribution in this volume) one of the outcomes of the new legal order created by the Ptolemies was the rise of professional advocates,[28] although their use was not obligatory.

---

[25] Devauchelle 1997; see also Sambin 1992, p. 166-167, 174-175, 178-184. In the past, scholars assumed that the oaths were sworn in Djeme (Medinet Habu, on the West bank), in front of a shrine near the eastern entrance to the mortuary temple complex of Ramesses III, see Devauchelle 1997, n. 1. Doubted by Varga 2021.

[26] Quaegebeur 1993; see also Traunecker 1992, p. 373-379, including a list of justice gates on p. 374, a discussion of the architectonical forms and the functions of the justice gates; Manning 2012; see especially Massa 2018, p. 198-205.

[27] The professionalization of scribes of petitions is briefly discussed below, section 5.

[28] See Wyns 2019, p. 53: "The only exception to the presence of advocates in court was when the state's finances were concerned. The Ptolemaic government apparently did not wish legal professionals to intervene where its own interests were immediately threatened, and heavy punishments were inflicted on advocates who came into court when a fiscal trial was tried," as established in the royal decree *P. Amh. Gr.* II 33 (*C. Ord. Ptol.* 23, TM 8669).

Whereas trials in Pharaonic times were largely conducted in writing and advocates were not allowed, as already noticed by Diodorus of Sicily (1.75.6-7–76.1-3), in Ptolemaic times advocates became available in all types of courts. They surface in the Egyptian milieu of the *laokritai*-court as shown by the Siut trial, even though the major part of this trial is still conducted in writing: after two sets of written pleas and replies were completed and had been shared, the clerk summoned both parties and the pleas were read aloud; one of the parties, the woman Chratianch, was assisted by an advocate who only added a short, new fact not yet discussed in the pleas and replies.[29] Advocates further surface in the Hermias trials: the latter was not represented by an advocate in the second last trial (while the *choachytai*-priests were, phase 5), but for the last trial (phase 7) he must have changed his mind, and was represented by a professional advocate, although the *choachytai*-priests' advocate was more successful. The well-structured pleas of both advocates and their knowledge of royal decrees and laws of the *chora* (Egyptian law) eye professional.[30] In addition, the advocate of the *choachytai* considered the case from the point of view of both the Egyptian law and the Greek city laws (*politikoi nomoi*);[31] in both cases, the *choachytai* had right on their side, according to their advocate.

In view of the trials, advocates composed a dossier of *dikaiomata* (pieces of evidence, justifications), which were — according to the Hermias trials — deposited before the trial: "Since this was the state of things, the advocates for both parties also argued their cases (...) and proof-texts (*dikaiomata*) deposited by them were read, as selected by each."[32]

In the case of the last Hermias-trial, the dossier of *dikaiomata* of Hermias' advocate consisted among other things of a copy of a previous petition by Hermias, a royal ordinance (*prostagma*), excerpts from Egyptian law, letters and verdicts by other officials in relation to the case. The famous Papyrus Halensis (*P. Hal.* 1, TM 5876) containing selected

---

[29] *P. BM Siut* p. 3-12 no. 10591 ro, col. vi, l. 11-16.

[30] References to royal ordinances: *P. Tor. Choach.* 12, col. iv, l. 13-17; col. v, l. 21-24. References to Egyptian law or "Law of the *chora*": col. iv, l. 17-22; col. vi, l. 31-col. vii, l. 2.

[31] *P. Tor. Choach.* 12, col. vii, l. 2-12.

[32] *P. Tor. Choach.* 12, col. iii, l. 18-21. Translation in BAGNALL & DEROW 2004, text no. 132.

passages of the Alexandrian "civil code" probably also served as written "justifications, supporting documents" for arguments in legal disputes (see the contribution by Anne-Emmanuelle Veïsse in this volume, with her notes 3 and 4).

Not only advocates, also judges acted professionally: they motivated their verdict, sometimes referring to laws, as for instance in the Siut-trial where they refer to the "law of year 21".[33] When necessary, judges consulted officials on the local level to investigate whatever was necessary; higher officials who acted as judge could be assisted by a council. One of the Erbstreit trials was prepared in detail by a council of *hegemones* assisting the *epistrategos*, while the latter gave the final verdict.[34] According to a document on the back of the Siut papyrus, the governor of the Thebaid asked for legal advice about Egyptian law in response to a petition he received: on this occasion the Greek petition was translated into Egyptian and was sent to a scribe of the priest-judges of Onuris of the city of Ptolemais who provided a reply.[35]

The aim of the professionalization of justice personnel is to achieve fairness. The verdicts in our dossiers seem to be fair, based on written evidence, which indicate the winning parties as the rightful owners of the real estate. But how come that in these dossiers so many petitions and trials were necessary, if the written evidence was crucial? The losing parties claimed real estate on the basis of allegations they could not substantiate by written documents, but were taken seriously by the judges. In the Siut-trial, Totoes' wife pretended that she had been coerced to sign a former agreement, while Hermias claimed that the house in Thebes belonged to his father 80 years before, without being able to prove it; the losing party of the Erbstreit-trials allegedly paid a sum of money for part of the disputed land, but they could not prove it either. In the end the written evidence decided it.

[33] This "law of year 21" prohibited children from a second marriage to inherit paternal property without permission of the first wife or the disadvantaged heir (*P. BM Siut* p. 3-12 no. 10591 ro, col. ii, l. 20-23, x, l. 7-9). See also MANNING 2010, p. 196. For other laws referred to in the Siut-trials, see THOMPSON 1934, p. xx-xxi.

[34] *P. Erbstreit*, p. 37-40.

[35] BAETENS & DEPAUW 2015.

3. Addressing language barriers

According to the USIP guideline 7.8.4, entitled *Address barriers to both quantity and quality*, "the justice system should be linguistically accessible with local language proceedings or provision of interpretation."

The Egyptian and Greek inhabitants of the Nile country were able to have their cases brought before the court of their choice; the choice of the court determined the language of communication. The Siut-trial before the Egyptian *laokritai*-judges with Egyptian litigants and Demotic evidence, was conducted in Egyptian. Most of the Erbstreit-trials were held in Greek courts, although the litigants were Egyptians and the evidence, oaths and amicable agreements were written in Demotic. As the Egyptian documents had to be understood and interpreted by the viceroy (*epistrategos*) and his council, and afterwards by the *chrematistai*, these were translated into Greek. Two sets of translations of Demotic pieces of evidence presented in Greek courts are preserved in the Erbstreit dossier: they were needed for the trials before the viceroy and the *chrematistai*-judges.[36] In total, more than 20 Greek translations of Demotic documents are found for Greco-Roman Egypt, usually made in view of a lawsuit before a Greek court or Greek official:[37] the translations found in the early-Roman archive of Satabous, son of Herieus, for instance, were presented as evidence at the Nestnephis lawsuit.[38] Conversely, Greek documents such as petitions could be translated into Egyptian in view of a lawsuit before the *laokritai*, as was apparently the case in the sixth phase of the Siut-trials.[39]

The Ptolemies clearly invested in the training of bilingual interpreters, thus enabling Egyptians to turn to Greek courts; around 134 BC, for instance, at least four different translators were active in Thebes in the judicial departments,[40] but as we have only a small set of evidence,

---

[36] *P. Erbstreit*, App. II, p. 177-181.

[37] See the list in *P. Erbstreit*, p. 180. To be added is now Baetens 2020b (TM 58458), fragm. B+C, col. i(-ii?). The fragmentary *P. Tarich.* 14 (TM 316257) may also be a Greek translation of a Demotic contract, see introduction to *P. Tarich.* 14 and Baetens 2020b, p. 276, n. 14.

[38] *P. Erbstreit*, App. II, p. 180.

[39] *P. BM Siut* p. 54 no. 10591 vo col. iv contains a Demotic translation of (parts of) a Greek petition, embedded in the judgment of a *laokritai*-court.

[40] *P. Erbstreit*, App. II, p. 180.

the real number must have been much higher. The types of mistakes the interpreters made, suggest that they had enjoyed an Egyptian education, before acquiring a decent knowledge of Greek. The style is in line with the fact that "translations for legal or administrative purposes were functional, designed to provide the necessary information, not as an exercise in elegant composition".[41] The Egyptian evidence in the Hermias-trials has also been translated into Greek, as explicitly mentioned in the minutes of the last trials,[42] but the translations are lost. It is not clear whether in case of the Erbstreit-trials the Egyptian litigants were able to follow the proceedings conducted in the Greek language, or whether interpreters were available to them during the court hearings. In the case of the Hermias-trials, the Egyptian litigants (the *choachytai*) were represented by an advocate, who solved the language barrier.

The above-mentioned efforts to overcome the language barrier while at the same time giving the population the chance to turn to the court of their choice, were limited by the law of 118 BC (*C. Ord. Ptol.* 53; *Sel. Pap.* II 210, TM 2938).[43] This royal decree was part of a cluster of 46 prostagmata issued by Ptolemy VIII Euergetes II and the Cleopatras (II and III). Egypt had just emerged from a period of turmoil, and rule of law needed to be reinstated and reaffirmed. Hauben (2016) identifies a twofold goal of the *prostagma* at hand: to protect the population from further legal disorder, and to preserve state institutions from disintegration. Generally, the royal decree determines that the language of written contracts would be the determining factor as to which court was authorized to judge cases about them. This meant in short that Demotic contracts were to be judged by the *laokritai*, Greek contracts by the *chrematistai*.[44] One may wonder how effective this royal decree was, as Demotic

---

[41] MAIRS & MARTIN 2008/9, p. 57.

[42] *P. Tor. Choach.* 12, col. v, l. 4: συγγραφῶν Αἰγυπτίων διηρμηνευμένων δ' Ἑλληνιστί.

[43] For this paragraph, see WYNS 2019, p. 55. See now also GROTKAMP 2018, p. 120-122.

[44] This paragraph is largely copied from Wyns' unpublished PhD (WYNS 2019, p. 55), as is the following note: "The analysis by HAUBEN (2016) further nuances the above rule. Cases between Egyptians about a Greek contract that were pending at the time of the publication of the prostagma, were to be judged by the *laokritai*, and *chrematistai* are explicitly banned from 'seizing' such cases. After the transitional period after publication, these cases were to be tried by the *chrematistai*. In homogenous cases after 118 BC

pieces of evidence were still translated into Greek later on in view of lawsuits.[45]

4. Addressing geographical barriers

According to the USIP guideline 7.8.4, entitled *Enhance physical access*, one should

> bring judges, prosecutors, (…) as well as logistical/security support and public information capacity to areas where the justice system has ceased to function. While mobile courts may be needed in the emergency phase to deal with the most acute needs, they can also provide a long-term solution to endemic access to justice challenges.

When discussing geographical barriers, we should distinguish between people who live in a large city such as Thebes or Siut (Hermias and Siut trials), and inhabitants of provincial towns or villages such as Pathyris (Erbstreit trials). Wherever someone lived, he could always submit a complaint to the local mayor, who pursued an amicable settlement, as in the first phase of the Erbstreit trials. If one wanted to address the courts of the *laokritai* and *chrematistai*, or of the higher officials who were allowed to administer justice, the matter was different. The *laokritai* were not mobile courts, but served in the local, Egyptian temple, as e.g. the temple of Wepwawet/Ophois in Siut. Not all Egyptian temples, however, had a temple court; for Pathyris for instance, a *laokritai*-court is not attested; that may have been one of the reasons why the Erbstreit family never turned to the *laokritai* despite the Egyptian nature of the

(Egyptians versus Egyptians with Egyptian contracts, Greeks versus Greeks with Greek contracts), the decree does not specify which court was supposed to judge, probably because these cases were easily assigned to the *laokritai* and *chrematistai* respectively. It appears that when Greeks filed claims against Greeks about an Egyptian contract (which would not have occurred very often), the *laokritai* were the default judges, except when the plaintiff preferred to have the case brought before the *chrematistai*, in which case the proceedings were transferred. Egyptians that challenged Greeks or vice versa over a Greek contract always were expected to receive a verdict from the *chrematistai*. Apparently, when Greeks challenged Egyptians over an Egyptian contract, or vice versa, defaulted to the *laokritai*, unless the plaintiff wished to appear before the *chrematistai*, in which case the judgement was pronounced by the royal judges."

[45] *P. Erbstreit*, p. 178.

case. The chrematists-judges active in the Thebaid, on the other hand, had their home base in the Greek polis of Ptolemais, but also sat in judgment in the city of Thebes, where both the Erbstreit family and the parties of the first Hermias trial had to appear before them. Higher officials had a permanent home base, but travelled around to administer justice, among other things. Thus, the viceroy, who resided in the Greek city of Ptolemais, judged cases in Thebes (Erbstreit trials). Thebes was often visited by higher officials, including during the period of the major festivals, where they represented the government. The inhabitants could therefore rely on itinerant officials and partly itinerant judges; they had to travel at most 30 km (the distance from Pathyris to Thebes) to attend their trial if they lived in a more remote village.

A peculiar phenomenon is the submission of complaints to the various authorities. Complaints, called petitions in the papyrological jargon, could be lodged with the chrematists through a "vase" (ἀγγεῖον). Hermias deposited his first petition in such a vase, publicly set out (προτεθέν) by the chrematists when they visited Thebes.[46] The petitions filed to officials were delivered in person (or exceptionally through an intermediary), with the petitioner thus having the opportunity to provide orally more detailed information or display courtesies.[47] The choice for a particular official does not always seem logical: in the Erbstreit trials, there seems to be a hierarchical aspect (petition to the governor of several nomes, then to the higher ranking *epistrategos*), but this hierarchical order is lacking in the Siut and Hermias trials (see above). The Siut dossier rather suggests that the choice of the official depended on their availability: when the governor of the Thebaid was in the territory of Siut, Tefhape submitted a petition to him.[48] Also Hermias lodged his complaints with the chrematists and officials when they were present in Thebes.[49]

Geographical barriers seem limited for attending trials and submitting petitions. But if subsequently the official had orders written to a subordinate official at the bottom of the petition, then the plaintiff himself

---

[46] *P. Tor. Choach.* 12, col. iii, l. 23-27.

[47] BAETENS 2020a, p. 219-223.

[48] *P. BM Siut* p. 3-12 no. 10591 ro, col. iii, l. 12-13.

[49] E.g. *P. Tor. Choach.* 11, l. 33-35: "in year 49, when (the governor of several nomes) Hermias went to Thebes and I turned (to him with a petition) about them (the choachytes)".

had to take the petition, including the fresh orders, to the subordinate official himself;[50] Hermias, for example, had to travel with one of his petitions, subscribed with orders by the viceroy, from Thebes to Latopolis (35 km south of Thebes), so he could personally pass on those orders; a trial was planned — in vain — to take place in Latopolis.[51] Geographical barriers were not avoided here, but the advantage of this procedure was that Hermias could keep track of his case and knew at each stage what had been decided.

5. Addressing financial barriers

According to the USIP guideline 7.8.1, "there is no access to justice (...) where the justice system is financially inaccessible."

In Ptolemaic Egypt, people did not face unsurmountable financial barriers to hand in petitions, judging by the large number of petitions filed e.g. in the Siut, Erbstreit and Hermias cases. Of course, if someone was illiterate, he had to ask for help. People could have friends or family members who were able to write Egyptian or Greek.[52] The fixed format of petitions and the uniformity of the Greek formulas[53] in some types of petitions[54] on the other hand suggest that people often appealed to professional writers, who also had the necessary judicial and legal knowledge.[55] These writing services undoubtedly involved costs.[56]

---

[50] Baetens 2020a, p. 223: "Presumably, the petitioners each time had to wait at the office until their petition was returned to them. Sometimes, this could result in long and cumbersome procedures in which many different authorities had to be approached. *UPZ* I 14 [TM 3405] offers a notorious example of the efforts and paperwork that could be involved in this process."

[51] *P. Tor. Choach.* 12, l. 29-35.

[52] For the Thebaid, see e.g. the Greek petition *P. Dryton* 33 and 33bis (TM 253 and 252) by Apollonia and her sisters, written by her husband Dryton, see *P. Dryton*, p. 418.

[53] For the formulas in all types of petitions, see Baetens 2020a.

[54] According to third-century BC *SB* XVIII 13256 (TM 2541) the writing of *enteuxeis*-petitions was the competence of the *monographeion* (*in casu* that of Krokodilopolis in the Arsinoite).

[55] Hengstl 1997, p. 284-287; some petitions even refer to legislation, see ibidem and Hengstl 2002.

[56] On the Ptolemaic feeing policies of scribes of legal documents in general, see Yiftach 2015. There is hardly evidence on fees for scribes of petitions, see maybe P. Heid.

We are scarcely informed about the costs implied when a trial was held.[57] Third and second-century BC texts mention the ἐπιδέκατον (τῆς κρίσεως),[58] "tithe (of the trial)" or ἐπιπεντεκαιδέκατον, a sum to be deposited by plaintiff and defendant before the trial, representing 1/10 or 1/15 of the (estimated) damages done[59] or of the fine.[60] After the verdict, the losing party had to bear these proceedings costs. Accordingly, we read in the amicable agreement of the last Erbstreit trial that the losing party promised to "assume their costs (*hy*) on account of the two parties",[61] "their costs" referring to the costs of the *laokritai*-judges.[62]

Finally, the hiring of an advocate for a trial involved costs as well: a tax called συνηγορικόν had to be paid (per trial), suggesting that the profession and salary of an advocate (συνήγορος) were controlled by the government. The use of an advocate was not obligatory, as shown by the Siut, Erbstreit and Hermias trials.[63] Both the ἐπιδέκατον and συνηγορικόν tax could be farmed by the same person.[64] The, in our view, high trial costs did, however, not prevent the litigants of the Siut, Erbstreit and Hermias cases to sue the opposite party continuously.

6. Enforcing court verdicts

According to the USIP guideline 7.8.17, entitled *Support the enforcement of remedies*, "Remedies are useless if they are not enforced."

Dem. inv. 695 ined. (TM 454), a Demotic settlement of accounts probably of a scribal office of the local temple, also recording fees for the writing of Demotic petitions (called *mqmq* and *ʿn-smy*); we owe the reference to G. Baetens.

[57] On the ἐπιδέκατον, ἐπιπεντεκαιδέκατον and/or συνηγορικόν tax and the papyrological evidence, see *O. Wilck.* I, p. 302-304; *UPZ* II, p. 123-124; Préaux 1939, p. 410-412 ('Les frais de justice'); Huss 2011, p. 232 and 234; Grotkamp 2018, p. 22-24.

[58] ἐπιδέκατον τῆς κρίσεως in *UPZ* II 172 (TM 3573) and *P. Tebt.* III 933 (TM 7828).

[59] E.g. τίμημα in *P. Hal.* I, l. 63 (TM 5876); *P. Tebt.* III 933.

[60] E.g. καταδίκη in *P. Hib.* I 32 (TM 7815).

[61] *P. Erbstreit* 17, l. 12 = 18, l. 20.

[62] Spiegelberg in Gradenwitz, Preisigke & Spiegelberg 1912, p. 56 §xiii; *P. Erbstreit*, p. 154, comment 12 (a).

[63] In the Siut trial, only one party turned to an advocate, in the Erbstreit trials none, and in the Hermias trials Hermias was initially not represented by a lawyer.

[64] *O. Wilck.* II 1537 (TM 44294); *UPZ* II 172.

At the beginning of this paper, we provided an overview of the various judicial actions that the litigants took in the Siut, Erbstreit and Hermias trials; several initiatives were needed to reach a final decision. Clearly, the enforcement of court decisions was a weakness in the Ptolemaic system. Strikingly, in particular the settlement of disputes by civil servants is less successful,[65] although popular (because it was cheaper?). The cases in our files that were handled by the courts, seem to have had the desired effect; especially the trials before the chrematists were successful, after which no further appeal was possible.[66]

The *laokritai* and chrematists courts could rely on the *eisagogeus*: "His functions were to introduce cases before the judges and to take actions in concert with them; and his bailiff was empowered to enforce judicial decisions."[67] In the Siut trial phase 5 the *laokritai* explicitly refer to the bailiff in their verdict: "we have told Harimouthes the bailiff (*pꜣ rd*) of Andromachos, the *eisagogeus*, to put Tefhape (...) in possession of the property which is described (...)".[68] As a result, the opposite party (Totoes' wife) was taken to prison by the bailiff, and was beaten violently, after which she probably filed a new complaint (phase 6).

A crucial document in the *laokritai* and chrematists courts is the agreement that the losing party had to draw up, stating the concessions they made (or had to make) and promising not to litigate further; a large fine had to be paid if the losing party did not stand by the agreement:[69] the agreement of the last Erbstreit trial has: "If it so happens that I have complained (...) I will give real silver evaluated at 25 deben [= 500 drachmas] to the burnt offerings of the Kings$^{\text{l.p.h.}}$, I will give to you other real silver evaluated at 25 deben, in order to complete real silver evaluated at 50 deben [= 1000 drachmas] (...)."[70] Such an agreement was expected from the losing party in the Siut trial before the *laokritai*,[71] as well as in

---

65 Compare WOLFF 1970, p. 159.

66 See above notes 4 and 5.

67 ALLAM 2008, p. 3 and 16; see also above, note 8.

68 *P. BM Siut* p. 3-12 no. 10591 ro, col. x, l. 14.

69 ALLAM 1991, p. 122.

70 *P. Erbstreit* 17, l. 4-8 = *P. Erbstreit* 18, l. 8-14.

71 *P. BM Siut* p. 3-12 no. 10591 ro, col. x, l. 15: "deed of cession/renunciation" (*sẖ n wꜣy*), not a new agreement, but the agreement already presented on an earlier occasion (first Siut phase) and thus ratified by the *laokritai*: the bailiff Harimouthes had "to make this deed of cession a *qnb.t*-deed against the claim" filed (*pace* the translation by

the last Erbstreit trial before the chrematists[72] and the first, chrematist lawsuit of the Hermias trials (Hermias versus Lobais).[73] In the last two cases, the agreement explicitly mentions that it had to be/was presented to the chrematists, who then (according to *P. Merton* II 59)[74] had to accept it and could instruct the bailiff-*praktor* to ensure the agreement was carried out.[75] The agreement ended the discussion about the ownership of the contested property, even though problems could still arise about the crops growing on the land;[76] in the last Erbstreit lawsuit this problem is avoided by negotiating a lease for the losing party.[77]

The cases handled by officials ended with an order or decision, whether or not given after a trial; this decision could be converted into a written agreement of both parties, but the parties were apparently not obliged to do so. Such an agreement was not valid if both parties did not accept it, as in the second phase of the Erbstreit lawsuit.[78] In addition, the losing party could subsequently reverse the written agreement by claiming, as in the Siut process,[79] that the agreement was concluded under duress. If there was no agreement, and only an official order or verdict, the order could in principle be enforced by, for example, informing the mayor (village *epistates*), as we learn from the provisional decision that the council of the viceroy took in the third Erbstreit phase.[80] In

Thompson), that is the deed of cession became a *qnb.t*-deed, immediately subject to actual execution; see also the translation by Manning 2010, p. 216: "(We further order that) he (Harimouthes) give the aformentioned quitclaim deed as proof of title because of the claim made by her". See Lippert 2012, p. 185-186, on the *sẖ n wꜣy*.

[72] *P. Erbstreit* 17, l. 11 = *P. Erbstreit* 18, l. 19-20: "we will give a letter of dissolution (*šꜥ.t (n) bl*) between us to the *dikastai* (chrematists)".

[73] *P. Tor. Choach.* 12, col. ii, l. 11: συνεισέδωκέ μοι συνχώρησιν, "she submitted (to the chrematists-judges) together with me a *synchoresis*". See also *P. Tor. Choach.*, p. 158, "il caso Lobais".

[74] TM 5240; translation in BAGNALL & DEROW 2004, text no. 133.

[75] LIPPERT 2012, p. 188; GROTKAMP 2018, p. 77-83.

[76] In two petitions Tefhape complained about his brother Totoes who had prevented him from harvesting his crops, see phase 7 of the Siut-trials.

[77] *P. Erbstreit* 20.

[78] *P. Erbstreit* 16, col. i, l. 23-24: "an amicable settlement (*synchoresis*) [- -] with which the father did not agree".

[79] *P. BM Siut* p. 3-12 no. 10591 ro, col. i, l. 25 – ii, l. 2: "by reason of force".

[80] *P. Erbstreit* 13G and 13H.

this case, it was the winner who had to pass on the decision to the authorities.

An additional problem with civil servants handling cases is that they could not prevent one of the parties (defendant party) from not showing up. For example, the choachytes (Hermias trials) did not turn up several times. Also in one of the Erbstreit cases (before the council of the viceroy) some of the summoned persons were not present, as explicitly noted in the minutes.[81] When in one of the trials Totoes' wife did not show up because she was menstruating, this was also reported in the minutes (or at least in the draft of the minutes, Siut trials).[82]

Conclusions

The Ptolemies were confronted with a broad range of challenges inherent in a new multicultural society, including in the domain of jurisdiction. We started from three sets of trials from the second century BC where one can follow the judicial procedures over a longer period. These trials all originate from the Thebaid, where fewer Greek immigrants came to live compared to the Delta and Middle Egypt. The strongly Egyptian region must have been an extra challenge for the Greco-Macedonian dynasty. This paper assessed the judicial system in that area with the help of the USIP's guidelines which offer an interesting framework for the functioning of antique justice systems.

The government was making a clear effort towards the local population, who had access to all forms of justice, including courts of Greek judges. In addition, local traditions were respected and even integrated into the judicial system; Greek judges made use of, for example, Egyptian temple oaths, even though Greek jurisprudence had rather been stripped of religious connotations. The court of the Egyptian *laokritai*-judges was integrated into the judiciary and Greek officials could refer cases to them. The *laokritai* were assigned an *eisagogeus* as were the Greek chrematists, a state representative who (arguably) had no predecessor in the Egyptian judicial system.

[81] *P. Erbstreit* 13D, col. ii, l. 51-52, and *P. Erbstreit* 16, col. i, l. 8-9.

[82] *P. BM Siut* p. 54 no. 10591 vo col. iv, l. 22.

The judges faced additional challenges as they were confronted with multiple legal systems, including the royal ordinances, the Greek city laws and the laws of the *chora* (Egyptian law). If the judges felt they did not have the necessary knowledge to pronounce a well-founded verdict, they sought advice with legal advisers. The parties could, if they wanted, be assisted by professional lawyers, who are not attested in pre-Ptolemaic Egyptian society.

Language barriers were avoided: Egyptian documents were accepted by Greek judges and were provided with Greek translations of a fairly high standard. Several interpreters were available to this end in, for example, a city like Thebes. A law of 118 BC tried to change this comfortable situation for the local population, when the language of the evidence determined the choice of the court, but this royal ordinance was apparently not effective as people still appealed to Greek courts to the detriment of the Egyptian *laokritai*. Geographical barriers were avoided as much as possible, thanks to itinerant officials and partly itinerant courts (the chrematists from Ptolemais also administered justice in Thebes). We are not well informed about the financial barriers, but taxes such as the 10% tax to be paid by the losing party and the lawyer's tax did not prevent people from frequently filing petitions.

Although the overall assessment is a positive one, a weak link in the judiciary system was undoubtedly the enforcement of the verdicts. Even though fast-track proceedings were in place, the actual enforcement often left much to be desired, except when the case had been handled by the chrematists court.

THE RESOLUTION OF INTERPERSONAL VIOLENCE THROUGH EXTRAJUDICIAL CHANNELS IN DEMOTIC DOCUMENTS

Christine Hue-Arcé
(Université de Strasbourg, UMR 7044 – Archimède)

Abstract: The study of interpersonal violence in Ancient Egypt is documented by a limited amount of legal texts. Demotic texts witnessing the regulation of violent conflicts through non-legal channels are more numerous than those bearing witness to an involvement of legal instances. This article discusses cases of interpersonal violence regulated outside the legal field, underlining the weight of extrajudicial instances in the treatment of violence. Several channels are attested in the Demotic documents to regulate, denounce, and resolve violent conflicts: divinities, associations, and kinship. While the recourse to divinities and associations is formalized and followed a specific proceeding, kinship is an informal channel that does not observe established procedures or rules. This article endeavors to present the functioning of the extrajudicial channels employed in the resolution of interpersonal violence, and to understand how these instances worked together, and in complementarity with the legal system.

Introduction

Studying interpersonal violence in Ptolemaic Egypt can be seen as a subject of legal history. Yet, the documents available do not always originate from legal instances: in the course of my doctoral dissertation,[1] I have found only two Demotic documentary texts originating from a legal setting,[2] while thirteen were issued in non-legal settings[3] (among

---

[1] Defended at Strasbourg in September 2015, under the title *La violence interpersonnelle dans les documents égyptien du Nouvel Empire et des époques grecque et romaine*, and recently published, cf. Hue-Arcé 2020.

[2] *P. BM Siut* p. 3-12 no. 10591 ro (TM 43343) and *P. BM Siut* p. 54 no. 10591 vo col. iv (TM 53823).

[3] *O. Tempeleide* 224 (TM 50636), *O. Vleem.* 57 (TM 3054), *P. Assoc.* 1 (TM 2784), 3 (TM 2775), 5 (TM 3056), 6 (TM 2774), 7 (TM 2776), 8 (TM 2928), *P. Dodgson* 1 (TM

which seven are association regulation documents). Likewise, the information provided by these texts is not limited to the field of legal history: the study of interpersonal violence can be approached from the point of view of social history.

This paper aims to study the extrajudicial channels through which violence was regulated, as attested in the Demotic documents. It will focus on interpersonal violence, that is physical violence occurring in the framework of social interactions during daily life and seen as reprehensible by the authors of the Egyptian texts reporting it. Interpersonal violence excludes any kind of violence perceived as legitimate, such as military violence or corporal punishments.[4]

Most of the Demotic texts documenting interpersonal violence and the use of non-legal recourses date from the Ptolemaic period. There are, however, a few isolated texts documenting this type of violence in earlier and later periods: *P. Ryl. Dem.* 9, from the Persian period, and an oath dating from the beginning of the Roman rule.

Three main extrajudicial channels are attested in the Demotic evidence: the religious sphere, associations, and kinship. These channels revolve around two essential lines, which structure the present article: formal and informal recourses.

The aim of this paper is not only to present the extrajudicial instances adopted to regulate interpersonal violence, and their functioning, but also to understand how these formal and informal channels worked together, and in complementarity with the legal system.

1. Formal networks

Formal networks are set outside the legal field, yet they are structured channels, with specific procedures to follow. Two formal channels were used in the Demotic documents to resolve and regulate interpersonal violence: the divine sphere, and the associations.

43648), *P. Götterbriefe* 9 (TM 48779), *P. Oxf. Griffith* 38 (TM 48879), *P. Saq.* H5-DP241 (TM 46816), and *P. Vogl. Inv. Dem.* 77 (TM 47204).

[4] Cf. HUE-ARCÉ 2020, p. 43-45.

1.1. *The Divine Sphere*

The intercession of divinities in the daily life was not restricted to matters of religious devotion: individuals had the possibility to turn to religious instances to resolve conflicts in Graeco-Roman Egypt. The Demotic documents witness cases of interpersonal violence regulated through an appeal to divinities. This recourse to the divine sphere to resolve violent disputes occurs in two types of texts: letters to the gods, and temple oaths.

– *Writing to the gods*

In *P. Götterbriefe* 9 (TM 48779),[5] addressed at the end of the Ptolemaic period to "the Ibis, the Falcon and the Baboon", Nepheros and Tsenthotes, the children of Horpakemis, denounce the abuse they suffered from their father, including violence.

Letters to the gods are petitions written to divinities, in an epistolary form.[6] This practice has been seen either as accessible only to a few individuals close to the clerical milieu, or as expressing popular private devotion.[7] Kata Endreffy has shown that an answer can be found between these two opposite views:[8] though many of these letters' authors were involved in religious activities, others — as in *P. Götterbriefe* 9 — do not seem to be linked to the clerical milieu.[9]

According to Edward Love, 40 Demotic letters to the gods are known up to now.[10] The complaints usually revolve around thefts, despoliations, defamations, sickness, or infertility. *P. Götterbriefe* 9 is the only published letter to the gods to report acts of physical violence. The denunciations of the children against their father mainly deal with economic transgressions: the man left them hungry and without resources, and deprived them of their mother's dowry.[11] Yet, besides this economic abuse, Nepheros and Tsenthotes also denounce physical violence: the father

[5] MIGAHID 1987, p. 115-121; HUGHES 1969, p. 43-54.

[6] See the contribution by Love in this volume; see also DEPAUW 2006, p. 307.

[7] ENDREFFY 2010, p. 51.

[8] ENDREFFY 2010, p. 52-53.

[9] On the actual writers of these letters — scribes or the petitioners themselves — see the contribution by Love in this volume.

[10] See the contribution by Love in this volume; DEPAUW 2006, p. 308-309, mentions 37 letters to the gods.

[11] *P. Götterbriefe* 9, l. 9-13.

reportedly incited passers-by to beat his children, and he himself threw dishes at them, whenever they approached his house.[12] The two plaintiffs request justice from the gods, asking them to decide between them and their father.

To make their complaint to the divinities more effective, Nepheros and Tsenthotes emphasize the abuses suffered from their father in the following part of their letter:

> They are too numerous to be written, the papyrus would not receive them, the stringencies, the robberies, the oppressions and the restraints that Horpakemis, the cruel, our father above-mentioned, inflicted to us.[13]

However, the long list of abuses exerted by their father may have been exaggerated by Nepheros and Tsenthotes: the notions of misfortune, destitution, and poverty constitute *topoi* of the letters to the gods, aiming to induce the pity of the divinities.[14]

This letter addressed to the gods is the only one of its kind, to my knowledge, to report physical violence. But violence is here just an additional element to reinforce the claims of Nepheros and Tsenthotes; their claims are otherwise similar to those found in other letters to the gods, which report thefts or despoliation.[15] Reporting the violence is not the main purpose of the complaint against Horpakemis: the children want above all else to claim a roof, something to eat, and most importantly, their mother's dowry.

This complaint against Horpakemis may not have been a simple recourse to a divine authority but could rather have stood beside a lawsuit. Indeed, at the beginning of the letter, Nepheros and Tsenthotes ask the gods to "favor [them] in front of the assembly".[16] Does this "assembly" (*qnb.t*) refer to a divine or earthly court? A later part of *P. Götterbriefe* 9 provides an information that could answer this question: the

---

[12] *wʿ ḏrꜣ.ṯ mḫ=n ḫn pꜣ ḫry iw=f ḏd mḫy=w st bw ir=f ḏd m-ir iw=f nw r-ḥr=n ḥr rꜣ (n) pꜣy=f ʿwy iw=f ḥwy ipy.t m-sꜣ=n*, "May a strong man hit us, he [Horpakemis] says to him 'hit them', he doesn't say 'don't do it'. If he sees us at the door of his house, he throws an *oipe*-jar after us" (*P. Götterbriefe* 9, l. 16-18).

[13] *nꜣ ʿšꜣ.w r sḫ.w r bn ḏmʿ šsp=w nꜣ k.w nꜣ ḥwrʿ.w nꜣ hblꜣ[.w] irm nꜣ ꜣnty.w nty-iw Ḥr(-pa-Kmy) pꜣ whꜣ pꜣy=n it nty ḥry ir n-im=w n=n* (*P. Götterbriefe* 9, l. 20-21).

[14] DEPAUW 2006, p. 312.

[15] See e.g. *P. Götterbriefe* 4 (TM 44002; MIGAHID 1987, p. 56-73).

[16] *mr=tn n m-bꜣḥ tꜣ qnb.t* (*P. Götterbriefe* 9, l. 4).

children ask for their father to take an oath.[17] The swearing of oaths is a common judicial practice in Hellenistic Egypt.[18] The mention of an oath thus supports the hypothesis that this letter may have been written in support to a lawsuit opposing the children and their father.[19] Keeping a copy of the appeal addressed to the divinities could, then, have aimed to keep a proof of the call to the gods for the earthly justice, and particularly of the request that the father should take an oath: this request of an oath could have contrived Horpakemis to swear his innocence in front of the gods, at the temple gate.

– *The Demotic temple oaths*

The swearing of oaths is well known for the Ptolemaic period, thanks to a corpus of copies of the oaths taken at the temple gate,[20] often that of Djeme, according to Didier Devauchelle to be located in Medamud on the Theban East bank, where a gate of Djeme belonged to the temple of Montu-Lord-of-Medamud.[21] Two Demotic oaths sworn at the gate of Djeme report violent behavior: *O. Vleem.* 57 (TM 3054),[22] dating from the mid-second century BC, and *O. Tempeleide* 224 (TM 50636),[23] dating from the early Roman period (8 BC). In both cases, the defendants must swear their innocence in response to an accusation of physical violence. If they decline, they will have to pay a fine:[24] a rejection of the oath may have established the guilt of the defendant. The outcome of the litigation thus depended upon the decision of the accused party to swear or not to swear. If the copies of the oaths taken at the temple gates were mostly written in Demotic, rare examples also exist in Greek: one of these Greek oaths, *O. Wilcken* 1150 (TM 51882),[25] was taken by two brothers accused of having beaten a man.

---

[17] *ỉw=f ỉr pꜣ ʿnḫ ỉ.ỉr ḥr=tn*, "May he take an oath by you" (*P. Götterbriefe* 9, l. 15).

[18] See below.

[19] On the legal validity of the letters to the gods, see HUGHES 1969, p. 43-44; SEIDL 1966, p. 65. Contrary to George R. HUGHES' approach, I think that the legal weight of these documents, particularly their recognition by the judicial system, cannot be rejected.

[20] For the corpus, see KAPLONY-HECKEL 1963.

[21] DEVAUCHELLE 1997.

[22] VLEEMING 1994, p. 129-135.

[23] KAPLONY-HECKEL 1963, p. 207-208.

[24] 200 *deben* in *O. Vleem.* 57, an unspecified amount in *O. Tempeleide* 224.

[25] See VLEEMING 1994, p. 129.

The swearing of an oath to a divinity is part of the jurisdiction performed at the temple gate, a well-known practice in ancient Egypt,[26] particularly in the Ptolemaic period. This type of justice was as much temporal (concerning concrete issues and the social order) as it was spiritual: priests known as the *laokritai* used to meet at the gates of the sanctuaries to perform justice.[27] Some contracts indicate that the swearing of an oath at the temple gate was ordered by the judges,[28] while oaths could also be requested by one of the parties in a private dispute reported to an official, often the village head (*epistates*).[29]

Thus, the Demotic temple oaths do not entirely fall under the divine jurisdiction: they could be ordered by judges or officials, they were sworn in front of witnesses, and copies of them were kept either in the temple archive or in the private archives of (one of) the parties. These documents most certainly enjoyed a legal recognition.[30] In case of a subsequent dispute, the copy of the oath could be referred to in support of a defense or an accusation. The temple oaths illustrate a complementarity between the divine and legal channels in the judicial customs of Ptolemaic Egypt.

– *A complementarity between the divine and legal channels?*

Both the oaths and the letters to the gods witness a recourse to the divine sphere. Yet the oaths were legally recognized, while letters to the gods could be linked to legal proceedings — at least *P. Götterbriefe* 9 may have been written in support of a lawsuit. This observation indicates a complementarity between the legal and religious channels, which were not two compartmentalized instances, but could interact with each other.

Interestingly, the temple gate is involved in the two categories of documents: oaths were taken at this place, while whoever should try to destroy the letter to the gods of *P. Götterbriefe* 9 would have to read it

---

[26] This practice is already known during the New Kingdom: see for example *P. Berlin* 3047 (TM 755046), dating from the reign of Ramesses II (cf. QUAEGEBEUR 1993, p. 201).

[27] QUAEGEBEUR 1993, p. 203-206.

[28] Cf. MATTHA 1975, p. 29; EL-AGUIZY 1996, p. 1.

[29] See for example *P. Enteux.* 46, l. 7 (TM 3321). VLEEMING 1994, p. 129; BRYEN 2013, p. 251; E.g. *P. Erbstreit* (2017), p. 34-35.

[30] The practice of swearing an oath to divinities in the framework of a judicial proceeding is known elsewhere in the Mediterranean, particularly in the ancient Greek law. Cf. PLESCIA 1970, p. 40-43.

at the four entrances of the temple.[31] The temple gate is empowered with a religious value, as it constitutes the crossing point from the profane to the divine world, between the gods and the mortals. Only the clerical personnel and a few privileged persons were able to cross this gate and enter the temple.[32] Yet, the temple gate also carries a judicial value: tribunals of priests were held at the entrance of the place of worship, and the oaths sworn there had a legal recognition. The temple gate, invested of its divine and legal values, was a symbol of the complementarity between the judicial and religious channels.

Thus, the oaths and the letters to the gods contradict the idea, often stated,[33] that the recourse to the divine sphere intervened when the earthly justice was unable to resolve a dispute, or when the central authority was weakened.

However, the use of the religious channels is not a frequent recourse to resolve violent disputes: among 262 Demotic oaths published by Ursula Kaplony-Heckel,[34] and a few others published sporadically in articles,[35] only two documents concern acts of physical violence, while such violence is reported in only one letter to the gods among the 40 currently known. Other extrajudicial frameworks may have been chosen to regulate and resolve interpersonal violence.

1.2. *The Associations*

The regulation and resolution of violent disputes were also operated through the internal justice of religious and professional associations, as is indicated by the rules of these corporate bodies. Within the associations, the regulation of violent conflicts constitutes, above all else, a prevention of the use of violence between members.[36]

---

[31] *P. Götterbriefe* 9, l. 29-30.

[32] On the temple access for people, see DUNAND & ZIVIE-COCHE 1991, p. 118.

[33] See for example TRAUNECKER 1997, p. 46, and ASSMANN 1992, p. 46-47.

[34] 224 Demotic oaths published in KAPLONY-HECKEL 1963, and 40 oaths published in KAPLONY-HECKEL 1968, p. 133-184 (among those, two had already been published in KAPLONY-HECKEL 1963).

[35] See particularly VLEEMING 1994, p. 129-135; KAPLONY-HECKEL 1994, p. 37-45; EL-AGUIZY 1996, p. 1-11.

[36] See also the contribution in this volume by Paganini on private associations in Ptolemaic Egypt. As Paganini points out, the prevention of misbehaviour and violence in the regulations shows that the life was not always peaceful within the associations.

Seven Demotic regulation documents[37] state that if a member of the association beat another member, he had to pay a fine as a punishment. The amount of the fine differed from one association to another, but also according to the period, and to the position of the victim and the aggressor within the association hierarchy: the fine is higher when the aggressor holds a prominent position in the association.[38]

This adjustment of the fines according to the aggressor's status may have aimed at avoiding abuses of authority from individuals in a position of hierarchical superiority. Andrew Monson thought that the heavy fines were purely dissuasive: the aim of these high penalties and of the rules decreed within the associations was to protect and reinforce the "trust network".[39] Yet, in my view, if a member of an association violated the established rules, he definitely had to pay the fine recorded in the regulations. Indeed, for a punishment to be effectively dissuasive, the potential wrongdoers needed to know that if they performed a forbidden action, they would be punished: purely dissuasive fines would not have reached this purpose. Moreover, the actual payment of fines could have been a pecuniary necessity, as they constituted one of the sources of income that assured the financial survival of the association.[40] However, the amounts stated in the regulations may have been indicative, and the fine could have been subjected to a case-by-case assessment, or voted by the assembly of the association.[41] Case-by-case assessments are known through a later, Greek association regulation: *P. Mich.* V 243 (TM 12084), dating from the reign of Tiberius, states that if a member of the association misbehaved, he would have to pay a fine individually decided by the association.[42]

The legal recognition of the association regulations to resolve violence is difficult to establish. However, two requirements of *P. Assoc.* 3

[37] *P. Assoc.* 1 (TM 2784), 3 (TM 2775), 5 (TM 3056), 6 (TM 2774), 7 (TM 2776), 8 (TM 2928) and *P. Vogl. Inv. Dem.* 77 (TM 47204). See DE CENIVAL 1972, and BRESCIANI 1994, p. 46-67.

[38] HUE-ARCÉ 2017a, p. 139-140; HUE-ARCÉ 2017b, p. 179-180. It should be noted that this adjustment of the fines according to the status of the perpetrator is not specific to violence, but is common to all the infractions.

[39] MONSON 2006, p. 230-234.

[40] See the contribution by Paganini in this volume.

[41] On votes within the associations, see PAGANINI 2016, p. 1889-1901.

[42] HUSSELMAN, BOAK & EDGERTON 1944, p. 98-99.

(TM 2775) and *P. Assoc.* 8 (TM 2928) indicate that recourse to the judicial system for the members of associations may have been dissuaded. Complaining to the legal system without a previous recourse to the association was punished by a fine of 25 *deben*;[43] while if a member rejected the judgement handed down by the association, the fine amounted to 75 *deben*.[44] Thus, members of associations were incited to regulate any dispute internally. The aim may have been to protect the "trust network" from state interference.[45]

The association regulations established clear rules to control the behavior of their members.[46] However, the regulation and resolution of violence through their internal system only concerned the members of these corporations, and did not apply outside this framework. Violent dispute resolution through the associations was limited to a small number of wealthy individuals,[47] with a definite profession, and the rules enacted in the regulation documents did not affect the remaining part of Egypt's population.

2. An informal recourse: kinship

While the use of formal extrajudicial channels to resolve violent disputes is attested in the Demotic documents, individuals also turned to an informal channel when violence occurred: kinship.

Kinship needs to be understood in its wider definition, expressed on three levels: the family (individuals related by blood and marriage, including nuclear and extended family); the household (individuals sharing a house or property, including dependents); and finally, the close circle of personal relationship formed outside the last two, including ties of patronage.

---

43 *P. Assoc.* 3, see Monson 2006, p. 235.

44 *P. Assoc.* 8, see Monson 2006, p. 235.

45 Monson 2006, p. 236. See also the contribution by Paganini in this volume, who suggests that the image of the association and of its good order was actually in play here.

46 A parallel can be established with the Jewish *politeumata* (particularly the *politeuma* of Heracleopolis), which had a judicial function: the archons were petitioned to resolve private disputes between Jews, and between Jews and non-Jews. See the contribution by Paganini in this volume; see also Sänger 2013, p. 57-60, and Kayser 2013, p. 138-142.

47 Monson 2006, p. 236-237.

Kinship constitutes an informal channel: this recourse does not observe established procedures or rules, and its choice to deal with a prejudice does not follow a recognized or prescribed path. However, support networks through the ties of kinship could have been the first recourse when violence occurred.

Because of the informality of kinship, the written evidence of this channel to resolve interpersonal violence is not, at first sight, easy to identify: no documents are extant witnessing of a clear and evident recourse to the family to resolve a violent dispute. Yet, several Demotic documents show that kinship is intimately involved in the resolution of interpersonal violence.

In the oath of *O. Vleem.* 57 (TM 3054),[48] Horus son of Meraa must swear that he did not hit Phibis son of Doson. At the end of the document, the wife and son of the defendant have to take an oath as well, swearing Horus's statement of innocence is true. This oath of truth (literally "true oath", *ʿnḫ mȝʿ*) is not an isolated case: the intervention of oath-helpers, who confirm the veracity of the main oath, is present in almost 10% of the temple oaths.[49] An oath of truth is also found in the Greek oath of *O. Wilcken* 1150 (TM 51882),[50] in which the brothers of the two defendants step in as oath-helpers. The oath-helpers are most of the time spouses, children, or siblings of the main swearers. This commitment of members of the close family to the oath of their relatives can be interpreted in different ways: the relatives can be seen as mere eyewitnesses of the scene during which the reproached action was perpetrated;[51] they could also have stood as morality witnesses, pledging the character of their kin, and not his actual behavior relating to the matter at hand. This involvement could be the expression of family solidarity, in which case any perjury of the main swearer would have affected his oath-helpers. This involvement of kinship in the temple oaths nevertheless denotes the suitability of family members to pledge themselves to support their

---

[48] VLEEMING 1994, p. 129-135; cf. *supra*.

[49] On these oaths of truth, see HUE-ARCÉ 2019; KAPLONY-HECKEL 1963, p. 28-29, and SEIDL 1929, p. 26-31. In HUE-ARCÉ 2019, p. 124-125, I have noted the presence of an oath of truth in 23 of the 224 temple oaths published by KAPLONY-HECKEL 1963.

[50] ἀληθῆ τὸν ὅρκον εἶναι. Cf. VLEEMING 1994, p. 129.

[51] Cf. VLEEMING 1994, p. 129-130.

spouses, parents, or siblings, as is the case for the son and wife of Horus son of Meraa in *O. Vleem.* 57.

The oath of *O. Tempeleide* 224 (TM 50636)[52] also witnesses an involvement of kinship: Pakhnoumis son of Polemon has to swear that he did not beat Taesis, the wife of Loulous son of Imouthes. In this procedure, the injured woman, Taesis, is represented by her husband. A similar situation is presented in the Siut archive, documenting the dispute between two half-brothers about the inheritance of their father around 170 BC. Two texts of this archive refer to the use of violence: *P. Siut* 10591 B (TM 43343) and *P. Siut* 10591 verso (TM 53823). They were written in the name of Chered-ankh (Chratianch), the wife of Totoes, the eldest son. Though Totoes is certainly still alive,[53] he is represented by his wife, not only in the texts reporting violence, but in all the documents of the Siut archive. The aim of Chered-ankh was to assure her son's rights, by defending those of her husband to the family inheritance.

In both *O. Tempeleide* 224 and the Siut archive, a spouse is represented by their other half. For similar circumstances, can similar explanations be given? Taesis could have been so injured by the blow she received, that she was not able to carry out the procedure of the oath herself. While in the Siut archive, Totoes could have been put in prison,[54] and thus may not have been able to complain himself to defend his claim and the rights of his son on his father's inheritance.[55] However, the main clue of these documents may not be found in the reasons for the representation of a wife by her husband and of a husband by his wife, but rather in the absence of a justification for it by Loulous and Chered-ankh. Indeed, the plaintiffs do not deem necessary to justify the absence of their spouses, while the instances in front of which they complain do not seem to require a reason for this.

Thus, regardless of the reasons of the absence of these individuals, the temple oath and the Siut archive indicate that when victims of violence were not able to represent themselves, they were not necessarily powerless: their family had the possibility to come to their defence.

---

[52] KAPLONY-HECKEL 1963, p. 207-208.

[53] Cf. THOMPSON 1934, p. xvi.

[54] Cf. THOMPSON 1934, p. xvi-xvii.

[55] See HUE-ARCÉ 2017a.

The study of the support brought by kinship in dispute resolution is also enhanced by the analysis of *P. Ryl. Dem.* 9 (TM 47388). This "chronicle", written during the Persian period, reports the family history of the priest Peteise (III) in El-Hibeh, across three generations.[56] An act of interpersonal violence directed against Peteise and his family proves particularly interesting for us: the murder of the grand-sons of Peteise (I), in 634 BC. The father of the murdered children turns to his father-in-law Peteise (I), who then requests the arrest of the aggressors, and brings them to Pharaoh. Here, the family involvement could seem, at first sight, uncertain: did Peteise (I) intervene as a member of the family, or owing to his position of priest? However, when his grand-sons were killed, Peteise (I) had already retired from his position. Therefore, the father of the children turned to the masculine head of his family, an influential person with a support network, but above all else a family member.

The comparison of the Demotic documentary evidence with the Greek texts from Roman Egypt enlightens the question of the support that could be expected from kinship in violent dispute resolution. In her study of family in Roman Egypt, Sabine Huebner has underlined some features of mutual support between family members.[57] Family played an important role, especially in times of crisis, to bring support in daily life, particularly when a conflict arose.[58] In Roman Egypt, revenge and family vendetta could have been preferred to an official petition: in *P. Oxy.* VI 937 (TM 31326), dating from the third century AD, a man writes that he will get revenge for a violent act against him, while in *P. Mich.* VIII 492 (TM 27102), from the second century AD, a man asks her sister to tell him who injured her, in order to be able to avenge her. Nonetheless, Ari Bryen has underlined that these documents must be weighed against letters in which the authors incite their readers to make use of the judicial apparatus to resolve a violent dispute.[59]

If the evidence of an intervention of the family in violent conflicts is not abundant in the Demotic documents, a thorough analysis of the texts detected several clues of an involvement of kinship; the small number of

---

[56] On *P. Ryl. Dem.* 9, see VITTMANN 1998.

[57] HUEBNER 2013.

[58] HUEBNER 2013, p. 175.

[59] BRYEN 2013, p. 135.

texts is, however, not representative of the place of family as a channel to resolve interpersonal violence in Egyptian society.

The study of mythological texts brings further information on this involvement: in the three main versions of the tale of Horus and Seth, dating from the Old Kingdom, the New Kingdom and the Late Period,[60] kinship is the decisive element to resolve the dispute between Horus and Seth about the inheritance of the throne of Egypt. Marcello Campagno has shown that this role of kinship in the tale of Horus and Seth is one more indicator of its place in daily life, which is anchored at the heart of Egyptian society.[61] Thus, unsurprisingly, the nuclear or extended family may intervene to bring support when a parent — may it be the victim or the aggressor — was involved in a violent conflict.

Conclusions

The Demotic evidence indicates a frequent recourse to extrajudicial instances to resolve violence in Hellenistic Egypt, in various settings: the divine sphere, the associations and ties of kinship were all employed when a violent act occurred. While these channels can be classified between formal and informal ones, they were not strictly compartmentalized: religious channels enjoyed a legal recognition, while kinship had the possibility to step in to bring support during a legal procedure, or in a religious framework, as shown by the Siut archive and the temple oaths.[62] The connections and communications between these channels are strongly intertwined. This observation contradicts the idea that extrajudicial channels may have been turned to when justice had failed to find a solution to a dispute, or when the central authority was weakened.

Hence, the underrepresentation of interpersonal violence in the legal documents can be explained by a wider recourse to extrajudicial instances to resolve these conflicts. Indeed, I think that when a violent act occurred, non-legal channels may have been the first choice, particularly a recourse to ties of kinship;[63] a settlement of violent conflicts in private may have

[60] Campagno 2009, p. 38-43.
[61] Campagno 2006, p. 20-33; Campagno 2009, p. 31-43.
[62] See also Hue-Arcé 2019.
[63] Hue-Arcé 2017a, p. 145-147.

been preferred by the individuals involved. When kinship was unable to resolve the conflict, or when economic aspects were linked to it, then people may have turned to the legal system.

This preference for extrajudicial channels, and particularly for kinship, would explain the lack of texts reporting interpersonal violence: family is a medium that did not produce much written evidence. Orality is attested in legal procedures,[64] but may have been even more significant for an informal channel such as kinship. The weight of orality may explain the limited Demotic evidence for the resolution of violent conflicts; the small number of examples is not representative of the place of interpersonal violence in the society of Hellenistic Egypt.

[64] Cf. THOMPSON 1934, p. xvi.

BEYOND EARTHLY JUSTICE – PETITIONING DEITIES AND DIVINE JUDGEMENT IN THE "LETTERS TO GODS"*

Edward O.D. LOVE
(Julius-Maximilians-Universität Würzburg)

Abstract: From the famous "Curse of Artemisia" to Esrempe's obscurer troubles, women and men from Late to Roman Period Egypt petitioned deities to resolve worldly disputes through writing or commissioning "Letters to Gods". Succeeding a millennia-and-a-half-old tradition of "Letters to the Dead", at least 41 "Letters to Gods" in Demotic (36), Greek (four), and Old Coptic (one) constitute a unique corpus through which disputes were posed to otherworldly, rather than worldly, superiors. These petitions were inscribed upon papyri, linen, limestone and ceramic ostraca, wooden tablets, and ceramic vessels. While they may have been recited and/or accompanied by a practiced ritual, in every case where a secure provenance is known they were ultimately deposited in the catacombs and cemeteries of sacred animals or — for at least one deity without a sacred animal manifestation — in temple sanctuaries. With a diverse terminology from a "letter of lament" (*š῾.t-n-šll*) to a formal "memorandum" (*mḳmḳ*), no single Egyptian term encompasses the entire corpus, but it nevertheless evidences a legitimate institutionalised religious practice, maintained by temple cults along the Nile. Encompassing themes from "conducting a case" (*ỉrỉ ḥp*)

* I am most grateful to Sofie WAEBENS and Katelijn VANDORPE for both organising this conference and the opportunity to contribute to its proceedings. The study presented here also benefitted from stimulating discussions on the topic with Gert BAETENS, as well as other colleagues during my time in Leuven. In addition, I am grateful to Kata ENDREFFY for a fruitful discussion, and for sharing the outline of her own doctoral study on this corpus. My research project during academic year 2015-16, based at the Ruprecht-Karls Universität Heidelberg, Germany, was on the Old Coptic script, and was supported by generous funding from the Leverhulme Trust through a Study Abroad Studentship, enabling me both to attend this conference and produce this study. This contribution was first submitted on 10/10/2017, following that time in Heidelberg but while a doctoral candidate at the University of Oxford, and summarises certain findings of a wider research project into the "Letters to Gods" which was originally envisaged as a doctoral project — see now instead LOVE fc. Throughout, manuscripts are cited with their TM numbers in lieu of comprehensive bibliographies.

concerning embezzlement, robbery or loan defaults, to passing "judgement" (*wpy*) on family disputes, and even entreaties for children or healing, this study provides a summary and selected treatments of a corpus with distinctive insights into the trials and tribulations of Graeco-Roman Egypt's downtrodden, derided, and dispossessed, and the divine interactions which were conceptualised as contributing to the resolution of their disputes.

Introduction

This contribution concerns a bilingual corpus of Egyptian (written in demotic and Old Coptic) and Greek "Letters to Gods" from the Late, Ptolemaic, and Roman Period which provides a unique insight into dispute resolution through petitioning the divine. Ahead of a broader study to be undertaken by the author, this contribution will summarise the corpus and provide selected treatments of representative examples, in order to highlight the media, contexts, and rationale behind these petitions, as well as the mechanism of interaction with manifestations of the divine through which these petitions would have been conceptualised as being efficacious. Through this, insights can be gained into why individuals sought to petition otherworldly, rather than worldly, superiors in order to — among other entreaties — resolve certain disputes.

Before introducing the corpus itself, questions of definition and approach must be raised, and thereby potential limitations acknowledged. This corpus has been most commonly referred to as the "Letters to Gods" by analogy to the earlier Egyptian tradition of "Letters to the Dead" (noted below). This, however, describes principally their format, rather than their overall form and function. Through Mark Depauw's *Demotic Letter* (2006) and Gert Baetens' 'Demotic Petitioning' (2014) and *A Survey of Petitions and Related Documents from Ptolemaic Egypt* (2020a), how far the corpus mirrors that of worldly petitions rather than letters can be considered more closely.[1]

[1] Seidl considered the "Letters to Gods" to be another form of oracle questions, see SEIDL 1966. However, although they share contexts or production and deposition as well as religious conceptions, the "Letters to Gods" do not resemble oracles directly because in an oracle, "a devotee addresses a divinity to ask for information on which he will base his conduct", DEPAUW 2006, p. 301, whereas in a "Letter to a God" a petitioner petitions a deity to intervene directly in their lived experience.

Although select examples of the "Letters to Gods" feature certain epistolary formulae,[2] they are rarely addressed on their verso, nor on their recto,[3] and generally lack the courtesies and closing formulae characteristic of letters. Furthermore, the "Letters to Gods" do not simply communicate information to their addressee, they petition that addressee to intervene in their lived experience, sometimes entreating them that they are (partly/wholly) responsible.[4] Consider *P. Mallawi* 485 (TM 48790), a Saite (664-525 BCE) papyrus from the Ibiotapheion at Hermopolis, in which the petitioner entreats:

> Misery! My great Lord, Oh Thoth, twice-great, Lord of Hermopolis because of Pateêsis, the son of *Ḫr-Ḫnsw*, Thoteus, his son, and Tameneus, his wife." (l. 1-3)
> Misery! My great Lord, Oh Thoth, twice-great, Lord of Hermopolis because of Kasôthês, the son of Tromenêsis. They have stolen from the feeding-place of the ibises. Written by the servant Ithorôth, the son of *P3-tw=s*, before Thoth, twice-great, Lord of Hermopolis, the Great God. (l. 5-8).

This example concerns a dispute and desired outcome, i.e. its resolution, not so dissimilar from that in the petition to a worldly superior of *P. Fitzhugh* D. 1[5] (TM 51408), a second or first-century BCE papyrus from the Fayum, in which Orsenouphis entreats Ameneus regarding

> the feeding-place of the ibises which you have leased to me (l. 4),
> there are men who have already come down to it (i.e. the feeding place) and they have taken from the bean crop to their hearts' content – wrongfully. (l. 6-9).
> That I am giving the memorandum to you is so that you give a copy of it to Paula, the district leaser, besides the rest of the men. (l. 9-12).

[2] For example, while Migahid argued that "a letter to a god contains the same fundamental elements as a secular letter", see MIGAHID 1986, II, p. 11, those "fundamental elements" are essentially a beginning, middle, and end ("Kopf, Corpus und Schluß"). Indeed, in some examples their "epistolary construction" is clear, while in others it is entirely absent.

[3] DEPAUW 2006, p. 311.

[4] Referring to some petitions to Thoth, ENDREFFY noted that "petitioners like to stress both their commitment to the ibises and their own indispensability for their well-being, emphasizing that it is in the god's own interest to act on their behalf", see ENDREFFY 2009, p. 246.

[5] REYMOND 1972, p. 254-260.

> May it happen that you will send to the aforementioned men and have them stay away from the aforementioned feeding place. (l. 12-14)

In the worldly petition, the petitioner can invoke a formal legislative procedure against the accused, requesting directly what is to be done to resolve the dispute. In the otherworldly petition, the example given does not include an address nor any epistolary courtesies, but simply informs Thoth that the accused have stolen from the provisions of the animals sacred to him. Although the resolution goes unspecified, with the petitioner not even entreating Thoth to "conduct the case and enact judgement" as many other petitioners do, the case is entrusted Thoth by nature of his status as "The Lord of Justice" (*pꜣ nb hp*) (*L. Mallawi* 489 (TM 48792) (l. 1).

Thus, when these considerations are compared to the definition of petitions:

> formal communications addressed to the authorities in order to obtain their support in a dispute or other extraordinary circumstances (…) written by individuals or small groups of interrelated individuals who were treated unjustly,[6]

it becomes clear that although "Letters to Gods" communicate information like letters and can exhibit comparable formats to letters, they are directly comparable to petitions. Furthermore, while "letters seem to have served a similar function as petitions did in later periods",[7] another important consideration is that "a clear delineation between civil jurisdiction and oracular jurisdiction probably did not exist".[8] This may help to explain the similarities between worldly and otherworldly petitions, as well as their overlaps with letters.[9] However, "the procedure of addressing a letter was radically different from the procedure of submitting an official petition", with the *mḳmḳ*, ὑπομνήματα, *ʿn-smy*, προσαγγέλματα and ἐντεύξεις "contain[ing] no exterior address", meaning that "they

---

[6] BAETENS 2014, p. 29.

[7] BAETENS 2014, p. 33.

[8] BAETENS 2014, p. 32.

[9] Indeed, MIGAHID concluded that his "investigations of the epistolary formulae clearly demonstrated that worldly court and trial conditions served as a model in the writing of letters", MIGAHID 1986, II, p. 113 — an analysis actually in favour of their identification as petitions or memoranda, rather than letters.

must have been personally handed over to their addressee".[10] Only one of the "Letters to Gods" exhibits an address on the verso,[11] and even this address simply repeats the opening formulae of the recto (treated below),[12] while the "Letters to Gods" — unlike letters — were neither "transported over a long distance nor is a written reply ever expected". As a result, the "Letters to Gods" do not fit the definition of "real" letters,[13] but rather that of petitions.

An important distinction between petitions to worldly rather than otherworldly superiors, however, is that in the former case, "perhaps some petitioners also had the chance to argue their case in an audience", "account[ing] for the fact that most petitions are formatted as relatively short memoranda", with only the main arguments written down — while letters were "less concise and formal".[14] Since there is no such context for the "Letters to Gods", they could at once be "concise and formal" like worldly petitions, and "less concise and formal" like letters — depending on the requirements of that otherworldly petition.

Certain limitations also comprise caveats to any investigation of this corpus. For example, with the majority of the "Letters to Gods" lacking a secure provenance, often little more can be said than that these petitions were written by literate, or commissioned by illiterate, petitioners and deposited in particular contexts. It is ambiguous what proportion of petitioners wrote their own petitions,[15] and whether all petitions were

---

[10] BAETENS 2014, p. 54. For a study of all these types of petition, see now BAETENS 2020a.

[11] The verso of *P. Cairo* 50114 apparently contained an address to "Imhotep, the Great God", but I have been unable to confirm this, see SPIEGELBERG 1904-1932, III, p. 80.

[12] Thus, although MIGAHID argued that because "the letters were handed over by the senders in person", they "did not necessarily require an address", MIGAHID 1986, II, p. 41, the absence of an address on the verso of almost all of the "Letters to Gods" is in fact more reminiscent of petitions than letters.

[13] DEPAUW 2006, p. 313.

[14] BAETENS 2014, p. 54.

[15] Selected opinions include that of MIGAHID, who stated that "the signing of letters does not have to indicate that the addresser wrote it themselves", BAETENS 1986, II, p. 113, and vice versa ZAUZICH, who stated "on the contrary, it may be assumed that they were professional scribes, who drafted and copied the letters to order and in the hope of an appropriate payment", ZAUZICH 1992/93, p. 177, while SMITH argued "that both *sẖ bꜣk* and *sẖ nꜣy* were often used in these documents to indicate that the author had written his own letter or plea", SMITH 2002, p. 374.

produced at the site in which they were deposited. It is also unclear whether the petitioners were local, or travelled from afar, as well as whether they chose to petition a particular deity because they worked within the temple institutions of that particular deity, because they were their local deity,[16] or because the deity's cult centre was a centre of pilgrimage.[17] Uncertain also remains whether the accompanying ritual practice of recitation — implied by a select minority of examples — was representative of the wider corpus, and therefore whether this corpus attests the written manifestation of a much more common oral ritual, which left no evidence in the archaeological record.[18] The question of regionalisation, given that >83% of the published Demotic examples are likely to have come from only two sites, is also important, for it should not be assumed that those examples are in turn representative of the wider tradition throughout Egypt, for which there is regrettably little evidence.

1. Predecessors to the "Letters to Gods" – The Egyptian "Letters to the Dead"

Egyptian conceptions of the living, deceased, and divine — and the relationship between them — is represented in an extract from the second/first century BCE *P. Jumilhac* (TM 56862),[19] in which the *rmṯ.w* "people", i.e. the living/humans, are distinguished from the *nṯr.w* "deities" and *ꜣḫ.w* "transfigured spirits (i.e. of the dead)" — the manifestations of the 'non-human' and therefore divine. This tripartite delineation is maintained through a reciprocal relationship between the living and divine, whereby the living must give offerings to the gods (*ḥtp.w n nṯr.w*) and invocation offerings to the deceased (*pr.t-ḫrw n ꜣḫ.w*).

[16] After all, "the relationship of families to municipality or village deities may well have been largely hereditary or specific to occupation", KESSLER 2005, p. 55.

[17] KESSLER argues between the "Pilgrim" and "Tuna" models in order to inform upon the demographic of the individuals who placed oracle questions or petitions in catacombs or temples, KESSLER 2005, p. 47-53.

[18] While MIGAHID observed that some 'believers' would have 'believed' that a written communication would have been more efficacious than an oral one, MIGAHID 1986, II, p. 14, this implies that exclusively oral petitions were also possible — for which there is little to no evidence —, and that these would therefore have been conceptualised as "less efficacious".

[19] VANDIER 1961/62.

Such a reciprocal relationship was first manipulated through petitioning the deceased, with around 20 "Letters to the Dead" attested during the millennium and a half from the Old Kingdom (2686-2160 BCE) to the Late Period (664-332 BCE). A petitioner would entreat the *3ḫ*, "transfigured spirit", of a deceased individual in order to use the latter's access to the divine tribunal, and thereby intervention (mostly in the form of judgement), to redress grievances or enact justice in the lived sphere. With the majority having been expertly published for nearly a century,[20] a considerable amount of scholarship has been dedicated to them, whether as a phenomenon in their own right,[21] for their materiality, or for their interrelationship with afterlife texts, ancestor worship, domestic religion, and magic.[22] However, although the practice of petitioning deities adapted petitioning the dead, the similarities of the two corpora have only been noted by scholars,[23] while no comparative treatment of the two corpora has ever been undertaken. The latest "Letter to the Dead" known is *P. Brooklyn* 37.1799 E[24] (TM 51144), which — by dating to the seventh century BCE — was produced in a similar temporal, although distinct geographical, frame to the earliest "Letters to Gods".

Several of the "Letters to the Dead" address similar concerns as the "Letters to the Dead", including inheritance, property disputes, healing an illness, and appeals for favour (i.e. not malevolence from the *3ḫ*). The most notable overlap between the rationale behind and mechanics of the two corpora, however, is the example of the healthy conception and birth of a child. In the "Chicago Jar Stand"[25] from the First Intermediate Period (2160-2055 BCE), Idu petitions his deceased father:

> Behold now, this vessel is brought to you over which your mother (i.e. Idu's grandmother) is to judge. May it be agreeable that you should support

[20] For the corpus, see GARDINER & SETHE 1928; GARDINER 1930; PIANKOFF & CLÈRE 1934; SIMPSON 1966; 1970; 1981; WENTE 1975/76; BÜCHBERGER 1991; JASNOW & VITTMANN 1992/93.

[21] See GUILMOT 1966; GRIESHAMMER 1975; PLATER 2001, p. 6-55; EL-LEITHY 2003; VERHOEVEN 2003; DONNAT 2007; 2010; 2014; HARRINGTON 2013, p. 34-37; TROCHE 2018.

[22] For bibliographies to all these aspects, see now those in LOVE fc. §2.1.1.

[23] See BAINES' summary of GRIESHAMMER 1975, p. 860 n. 5, 868-869; BAINES 1987, p. 97, 97 n. 90; and ZAUZICH 1992/93, p. 177-179; RITNER 1993, p. 181 n. 841; BAINES & LACOVARA 2002, p. 27; VERHOEVEN 2003, p. 46.

[24] JASNOW & VITTMANN 1992/93.

[25] GARDINER 1930 (TM 755151).

> her. Cause now that there be born to me a healthy male child. You are an excellent Spirit. (l. 3-4); Moreover, I beg a second healthy male child for your daughter (i.e. Idu's sister). (l. 8a)

The petitioner's reciprocity is then stated:

> As you live for me, the Great one shall praise you, (l. 8) and the face of the Great God shall be kindly disposed towards you; he shall give you pure bread from his two hands. (l. 7-8)

Thus, the desired outcome is pregnancy and birth, and the reciprocity offered is the offerings to the cult of the deceased. By comparison, in *T. Cambridge University Library Michaelidis* x4[26] (TM 48782) from 279/218 BCE, i.e. two millennia later, the father of the god and priest of Amun-Re, the king of the gods, Osoroeris, son of Horos, son of Osoroeris petitions "before his master the royal-scribe Amenhotep-son-of-Hapu, the Great God" (l. 1-3). In this petition, Osoroeris states:

> If it happens that *T3y-pꜥ* becomes pregnant: I will give 1 silver (*ḥḏ*), equivalent to 5 silver staters. If it happens that she gives birth: I will give 1 more silver, equivalent to 5 silver staters. In order to fulfil 2 silver for the expenditure, (on) the day (in) which it will be ordered for me. (l. 3-9)

Thus, once more, the desired outcome is pregnancy and birth, while the reciprocity offered is the donation to the cult of the deity.[27] Of course, neither of these examples appears to concern dispute resolution directly. However, not only are they illustrative of the mechanics by which the desired outcome of the practice was conceptualised as being brought about through human-divine reciprocity, they may also concern the injustice perceived by individuals who were unable to have healthy children, and the resultant disputes this would cause in their lived experience.

2. Contemporaries to the "Letters to Gods"

During the Late, Ptolemaic, and Roman Period, whether through the increased prominence of theophoric names or through the focus on the

---

[26] MALININE 1962.

[27] In his treatment of one example, MALININE expressed surprise in finding the employed priesthood enacting 'bribery' towards the gods, MALININE 1962, p. 37-38. For such "business with the gods", see ENDREFFY 2010.

cults of regional deities,[28] the importance of local deities increases. This is alongside the increased opportunity for interaction with deities outside the institutionalised context of temple-based ritual practices, and even the opportunity to dedicate one's life to the cult of a temple.

In "Documents of Self-Dedication/Servitude",[29] dating to the Ptolemaic Period, the supplicant declares before the god that they will become a servant of that god — and no other —, paying a fixed monthly fee, and thereby receiving protection from both worldly and otherworldly malevolence (in the case of the former, for example, the inability to pay taxes).[30] The close relationship with the deity, expounded in detail in such "Documents of Self-Dedication/Servitude", is comparable to that expressed in the "Letters to Gods", in particular with reference to the individual as the *b3k* "servant" of the deity, who only has one *ḥry* "master", and from whom s/he requires *nḫt* "strength/protection".

Thus, in addition to the corpus of worldly petitions (noted above), also predominantly attested during the Ptolemaic Period, the "Letters to Gods" must be analysed alongside contemporary textual traditions that also concern human-divine interaction in the temple context.

3. THE CORPUS OF "LETTERS TO GODS"[31]

To date, the "Letters to Gods" have been published only sporadically,[32] have received little typological treatment,[33] and are essentially absent from wider works on Egyptian religion. Only one unpublished study has

---

[28] Individuals or their families were binding themselves to specific minor town or villages deities, and these relationships could have become related to familial as well as professional associations, KESSLER 2003, p. 54-55.

[29] For selected examples, see THOMPSON 1940; 1941; DANIEL, GRONEWALD & THISSEN 1986, p. 80-87; RYHOLT 2015; 2018. Kim RYHOLT has identified around 175 in various collections and will publish the corpus — an archive — from Tebtunis in the near future (personal communication).

[30] RYHOLT 2015, p. 340-342.

[31] Building upon that of MIGAHID 1986, II, p. 19-21 and DEPAUW 2006, p. 308-309.

[32] See SPIEGELBERG 1904-32, I; 1904-32, II; HUGHES 1958; 1968; 1969; MALININE 1962; RAY 1975; 2005; BRUNSCH 1982-83; ZAGHLOUL 1985; VITTMANN 1995; MIGAHID & VITTMANN 2003; SMITH in RAY & MARTIN 2011, p. 310-313; 2013, p. 11-16; SMITH & DAVIES 2014.

[33] See ZAUZICH 1992/93, p. 177-179; SMITH 2002; ENDREFFY 2009; 2010.

attempted to compile a corpus,[34] or treat these petitions as a cultural and religious phenomenon,[35] but this work utilised only 13 examples in Demotic. What's more, the "Letters to Gods" in Greek[36] have not been appraised as Greek-language examples of a ritual practice stemming from the Egyptian tradition and, therefore, along with the potential predecessors of this corpus from the New Kingdom written in hieratic,[37] need to be brought into a comprehensive corpus.[38] Although a consideration of the hieratic examples is beyond both the scope of and temporal frame appropriate to this study, the issues stemming from the categorisation of the Greek-language "Letters to Gods" among the "Prayers for Justice" of the Eastern Mediterranean and Europe will be raised where relevant below.[39]

The current corpus of "Letters to Gods" with which I am working numbers 41:[40] 36 in Demotic, four in Greek, and one in Old Coptic.[41] The Egyptian-language examples are attested for perhaps as much as nine centuries, with 17 dating to the Late, six from the Late or Early Ptolemaic, 12 from the Ptolemaic, and two (one of these the Old Coptic example) from the Roman Period. The Greek-language examples are not attested as continuously, with one dating to the fourth century BCE and four dating either to the first or second century CE. Of the 40 "secure" Demotic examples, 24 (66.5%) are on papyrus — in both broad and high

[34] See MIGAHID 1986, I.

[35] See MIGAHID 1986, II.

[36] See WILCKEN 1927, p. 97-104; GALLAZZI 1985; GASCOU 2008.

[37] See SPIEGELBERG 1917; BARNS 1949; ČERNÝ & GARDINER 1957; MCDOWELL 1993, p. 14-15.

[38] The aforementioned doctoral thesis of Kata ENDREFFY will study such a larger corpus.

[39] Otherwise, see further LOVE fc. §2.3; 8.3.

[40] This number comprises the "secure" corpus with which I am currently working, and does not include 10 Demotic manuscripts which have been securely identified as "Letters to Gods" but which remain unpublished (i.e. I have not yet finished editing and therefore cannot yet incorporate into this study), three which have been suggested to be "Letters to Gods" but whose ascription to the corpus cannot be confirmed until their publication, and 11 which also have been suggested to be "Letters to Gods" but are both unpublished and lost (i.e. unpublishable). All of the manuscripts (36+10+3) are surveyed with references in LOVE fc. §2.1.2.

[41] In this study, the entire corpus will not be enumerated. See now instead LOVE fc.

formats depending on period[42] — seven (19.5%) on linen,[43] two (5.5%) on ostraca, two (5.5%) on wooden tablets,[44] and one (2.5%) on a vessel. Of the Greek-language examples, three (75%) are inscribed on ostraca and one (25%) is on papyrus. This corpus exhibits a variation not only in the media utilised, but also in the texts inscribed, with examples ranging from everything from one to 30 lines.[45]

4. Egyptian terms for and in the "Letters to Gods"

A treatment of the terminology exhibited in the "Letters to Gods" reveals that only four terms were used to refer to the documents themselves: *b3k* "document/letter"[46] in two secure cases, *mḳmḳ* "memorandum"[47] once, *ʿn-smy* "report"[48] once, and *šʿ.t n šll* "document of prayer" once.[49] Admittedly, half of the corpus is either not well-preserved enough to tell or does not make a self-reference. Nevertheless, the absence of a clear (set of) self-referential term(s) in Egyptian is notable given the apparent coherence of the corpus to contemporary scholars. Other terms

42 This reflects the letter-like form of many examples, as already noted in MIGAHID 1986, II, p. 35-37 and DEPAUW 2006, p. 313, Late Period examples exhibit a broad format, while Ptolemaic examples exhibit a high format.

43 The significance of linen in the wrapping of mummies relates closely to the utilisation of linen as a medium in the "Letters to Gods", HUGHES 1968, p. 176, not least because six of these seven examples are likely to have come from Hermopolis, and therefore perhaps deposited among or even bound to ibis mummies there. For linen as medium in Egypt, see KOCKELMANN 2014.

44 As already noted by MIGAHID, this choice of medium appears to relate to the deity petitioned, MIGAHID 1986, II, p. 29, i.e. the royal scribe Amenhotep-son-of-Hapu.

45 For the materiality of the "Letters to Gods", see further LOVE fc. §2.2.2.1.

46 The 155 BCE *P. Cairo* 31255 (TM 44002) refers to itself as *p3 b3k* "the document" (l. 3), while the second or first-century BCE *P. BM* EA 10845 (TM 48779) refers to itself likewise (l. 27), as well as perhaps as *wḫ3* "document" (l. 30).

47 The 5 CE *P. Carlsberg* 67 (TM 48778) (l. x+9). For a treatment of the *mḳmḳ*, and its close relationship to the ὑπόμνημα, see BAETENS 2014, p. 35-43. This example is, then, the only *mḳmḳ* to be dated securely to the Roman Period, cf. BAETENS 2014, p. 57. For a study of the *mḳmḳ*, see now BAETENS 2020a.

48 The Late Period *L. BM* EA 73784 (TM 100205) refers to itself as an *ʿn-smy m-b3ḥ ḏḥwty* "report before Thoth" (l. 8-9). For a treatment of the *ʿn-smy*, the "Demotic counterpart of the Greek προσάγγελμα?", see BAETENS 2014, p. 47-49.

49 *P. Cairo* 50110 (TM 48715) (l. 2).

were used to refer to the act of petitioning itself: *smy* "petition" in two secure cases,[50] ⲤⲘⲘⲈ once,[51] comparable to ἐντυγχάνω "petition"[52] and ἱκετήριος "supplication" or ἱκετεύω "supplicate",[53] both once, as well as tbḥ "entreat" in two secure cases,[54] comparable to εὔχομαι "pray"[55] and παρακαλέω "entreat"[56] both once. Other examples refer to themselves as concerning *ʿš* "cry", in two cases,[57] or *šll/šrr* "prayer" once,[58] as well as καταβοή "accusation" once.[59] In other cases, the petitions refer to the fact they concern suffering:[60] seven counts of *hbr/hbl(ꜣ)* "misfortune"[61] are enumerated, which is the opening concern in two examples,[62] as are

[50] For example, the sixth-century BCE *P. Cairo* 31045 (TM 48672), featuring "the petitioner" (*pꜣ nty smy*) (l. 3). "The verb *smy* (basically 'to report') regularly appears in legal documents from the New Kingdom onwards. In a technical sense, it can refer to the act of complaining and even petitioning." The significance of this term in the practice of judicial petitioning is demonstrated by a third-century BCE copy of a legal manual in Demotic, "probably dat[ing] back to the Persian period", which "explains that the rights of a buyer can only be guaranteed if no one reports (*smy*) against him or issues a public protest (*šʿr*) against him for three years", BAETENS 2014, p. 51.

[51] Old Coptic Schmidt Papyrus (TM 92845) = Crum MS XXII. 10 l. a/1, a/3, a/9, and a/10.

[52] In the first/second-century CE *O. Cair.* JdE 38622 (TM 25385) l. 5-6; 14.

[53] In the fourth-century BCE "Curse of Artemisia" *P. Vindob.* G 1 = *PGM* XL (TM 65797) l. 9.

[54] For example, the first-century BCE *P. Cairo* 50114 (TM 44488) l. 8. Demotic memoranda introduced with *tbḥ*, followed mostly by *(iw=f ḫpr) iw=s ḥs* "if it (happens that it) pleases", remind of the Greek petitioning formulae: δέομαι οὖν σου, εἴ σοι δοκεῖ "so I beg you, if it pleases you", BAETENS 2014, p. 40.

[55] *P. Vindob.* G 1 = *PGM* XL (TM 65797) l. 2.

[56] *O. Cair.* JdE 38622 (25385) l. 11. For a study of the ἐντεύξεις, see now BAETENS 2020a.

[57] Consider the "cry of retribution" (*ʿš tbꜣ*) in the 5 CE *P. Carlsberg* 67 (TM 48778) l. x+5.

[58] In the aforementioned Ptolemaic period *P. Cairo* 50110 (TM 48715) l. 9.

[59] *P. Vindob.* G 1 = *PGM* XL (TM 65797) l. 6.

[60] Complaints in Demotic memoranda can be introduced with *gmʿ* "to harm", resembling closely the introduction in Greek ἀδικοῦμαι ὑπὸ τοῦ δεῖνος "I have been wronged by NN", BAETENS 2014, p. 40.

[61] The petitioner of the Ptolemaic period *P. Cairo* 50110 (TM 48715) refers to "misery at night" (⸢*hblꜣ*⸣ ⸢*grḥ*⸣) (l. 7).

[62] For example, at the opening of the 364 BCE papyrus *EES* S. 71/2-DP 146 = *EAS* 5832 (TM 69690), following a regnal year, the petitioner opens with reference to the "Misfortune and Misery, my great lord, O Serapis, at the hand of Teôs" (⸢*h*⸣*br ꜣt pꜣe(=i) nb ʿꜣ i Wsir-ḥp n-tr.ṯ ḏd-ḥr*) (l. 2-3).

15 counts of *ꜣ(ty)t* "misery",[63] which is the opening concern in four examples.[64]

Many petitioners also refer to their petition in its opening lines as the *ḫrw-bꜣk* "voice of the servant"[65] in eight secure cases. But petitions can begin in many different ways, with three examples beginning with a dating formula, as in memoranda. Rather contrary to understanding the "Letters to Gods" as "letters" to an "addressee", only in two cases do they open with a direct address to a deity,[66] and in only two further cases to a supplicatory epithet of a deity.[67] Furthermore, only one example features an address on its recto,[68] and of the three examples which exhibit inscriptions upon the verso, only one of these resembles an address,[69] repeating the opening formula of the recto text.[70]

Most "Letters to Gods" deal with the resolution of disputes, whether economic, work-related, or social — with a small number also concerning healing or the conception and safe delivery of a child. Of the 27 unambiguous cases:[71] around 30% concern (imminent) threat, such as that feared from another, abduction, an illness, or abuse by individuals; around 60% concern (ongoing) injustice, where the petitioners complain

---

[63] The petitioner of the aforementioned Ptolemaic period *P. Cairo* 50110 (TM 48715), subsequent to the reference to "misery at night", refers to "suffering by day" (*ꜣyt n mtry*) (l. 8).

[64] In the first-century BCE *P. Berlin* P 15660 (TM 80872), consider the opening: "Suffering… and Misery of Nekhbet" (⸢*ꜣyt*⸣ … *[hbl]ꜣ* ⸢*nḫb.t*⸣) (l. 1-2) etc. (i.e. to other deities as well).

[65] For references to a discussion of the translation of this term, see BAETENS 2014, p. 44-45 and footnotes. The use of this compound term relates to the fact that "terms such as *ꜥš* 'cry' and *ḫrw* 'voice' may not so much refer to the document itself as rather to its contents", DEPAUW 2006, p. 312.

[66] For example, the Ptolemaic period *P. Cairo* 50015 (TM 44369) opens with "before" (*m-bꜣḥ*) *Ḏd-ḥr-pꜣ-hb* (l. 1).

[67] For example, the Late Period *L. BM* EA 73784 (TM 100205) opens with "My great lord, Oh Thoth, twice-great, lord of Hermopolis" (*pꜣy(=i) nb ꜥꜣ i ḏḥwty ꜥꜣ ꜥꜣ nb ḫmnw*) (l. 1).

[68] The Ptolemaic period *P. Cairo* 50110 (TM 48715), whose first line reads Ἀνουβι "to/for Anubis".

[69] The sixth-century BCE *P. Chicago* 19422 (TM 48777), which has inscribed upon its verso: "Voice of the servant of (the) house of eternity *iw=f-ꜥ(ꜣ).w*, son of *ḥr-nfr-ḫby*, before Thoth, twice-great, lord of Hermopolis. (My)/Oh great lord; Oh may he achieve the lifetime of Pre." (*ḫrw-bꜣk n pr-ḏ.t iw=f-ꜥ(ꜣ).w pa ḥr-nfr-ḫby m-bꜣḥ ḏḥwty ꜥꜣ ꜥꜣ nb ḫmnw pꜣe(=i) nb ꜥꜣ i ir=f pꜣ ꜥḥꜥ n pꜣ-rꜥ*).

[70] Exactly that of the preceding footnote.

[71] Prior typologies of smaller numbers of examples can be found in MIGAHID 1986, II, p. 112 and ENDREFFY 2010, p. 49-51.

about the conduct of other individuals, the embezzlement of workers or of the ibis cult, maltreatment, robbery, an unreturned document, reneged loans, and even the conscription of a petitioner's son; while around 10% express apprehension regarding a future something, such as requiring a guarantee, protection, or ensuring the conception and safe delivery of a child. In order to bring about these desired outcomes, petitioners entreat deities to take certain courses of action, or even demand certain responses in: petitions for protection (*nḫt/nḫṯ*)[72] or efficacy against,[73] mercy (*ḥtp*) regarding,[74] or rescuing from,[75] the aforementioned threat(s); petitions to conduct the case (*hp*) in response to injustice suffered,[76] and/or for judgement (*wpy*);[77] for recognition (*rḫ*) or not to be forsaken (*m-ỉr 3bḫ*);[78] for retribution (*tb3*);[79] and for curses or care.[80]

[72] In *L. BM* EA 73785 (TM 48783) (from the reign of Amasis II or Darius II), the petitioner entreats "Protect me from the evil-one (f.)" (*nḫṯ (-wỉ) n-tr.t n t3 wery*) (l. 7).

[73] In the aforementioned *L. BM* EA 73785 (TM 48783), the petitioner also entreats "Do not let another have power over me" (*m-ỉr ty.t ỉr ge ỉr-sḫy n-ỉm=ỉ*) (l. 10).

[74] In the aforementioned *L. BM* EA 73785 (TM 48783), the petitioner entreats further "Be merciful to me" (*ḥtp n=ỉ*) (5) as well as "Cause them to be merciful to me" (*my ḥtp=w n=ỉ*) (l. 6).

[75] In the aforementioned *L. BM* EA 73785 (TM 48783), the petitioner also entreats further "Rescue me from your fury/rage and wrong" (*nḥm ṯ(=ỉ) r n3e=tn ḫʿry(w) btwe*) (7) as well as "Rescue me from her" (*nḥm ṯ(=ỉ) n-tr.ṯ=s*) (l. 8; 9).

[76] In the 155 BCE *P. Cairo* 31255 (TM 44002), the petitioner entreats the lady *3s.t-n3-nfr.t-ỉr-šy*, the great goddess: "May you (f.) conduct my case and enact judgement for me (literally 'my judgement') with the one who is stronger than me" (*ỉ-ỉr=t ỉr p3e(=ỉ) hp* ⌜*t3e(=ỉ)*⌝ ⌜*wpy*⌝ *ỉrm p3 nty* ⌜*nḫ.ṯ r-ḥr=ỉ*⌝) (l. 13-14).

[77] In the late second/first-century BCE *P. BM* EA 10845 (TM 48779), the petitioners entreat Thoth in his manifestations as the Ibis, Falcon, and Baboon: "May you (pl.) ask (i.e. interrogate) him and may you (pl.) judge between us and the aforementioned man" (*šn=tn -st wpy=tn n=n ỉrm p3 rmṯ rn=f*) (l. 15).

[78] In the aforementioned 219/218 BCE *T. Cambridge University Library Michaelides* x4 (TM 48782), Osoroeris entreats: "Hear my voice. I am your servant, the son of your servant since the beginning. Do not forsake Osoroeris" (*sḏmy.ṯ ḫrw=y ỉ[nk] p3y=k b3k p3 šr p3y=k b3k ṯ3y(-n) t3 ḥ3.t m-ỉr 3bḫ r wsỉr-wr*) (l. 11-14).

[79] In the most comprehensive 'curse' formula of any of the "Letters to Gods" — beyond even that of the "Curse of Artemisia" — the petitioner of the first-century BCE *P. Berlin* P 15660 (TM 80872) invokes: "Retribution against their men. Retribution against their women. Retribution against their children" (⌜*tb3*⌝ *n3y=w ḥ(w)ṯ.w tb3 n3y=w s-ḥm.wt tb3 n3y=w ḫrṯ.w*) (l. 26-28), among *many* other things.

[80] In the third-century BCE *P. BM* EA 10857 (TM 48780), Thotnachthês expresses the hope that "If it happens that Komoapis, your servant, is well, in that he has not died

From the Egyptian terms used to refer to the manuscripts or texts themselves to the concerns or outcomes behind the writing or commissioning of the "Letters to Gods", it has been seen that there is an evident diversity that must be taken into account when making any 'global' statements about the corpus. Emphasising this diversity, what follows highlights the regional differences in the corpus which should also be taken into account — on a 'cult by cult' basis.[81]

5. Regional differences within the "Letters to Gods"

Given the variety in media, text length, concern, and outcome highlighted in the previous sections, how far this diversity is a product of regional differences in the tradition of "Letters to Gods" should also be considered, proceeding on a 'cult by cult' basis. "Letters to Gods" in Demotic are attested from Saqqara to Thebes, and in Greek from Saqqara to Esna. Although this distribution of sources could suggest an Egypt-wide tradition, as with most textual evidence from Egypt inscribed upon movable media, the distribution of the evidence tends to cluster at certain sites. Hence, not only would the 'global' treatment of a corpus which is dominated by sources from only two sites be unrepresentative, it would even disguise the discontinuities between these two sites.

All of the "Letters to Gods" were found at, or can be ascribed to, certain temple institutions — the majority servicing animal cults.[82] 19 (63%) of the 36 "secure" and published Demotic examples certainly or most likely come from Saqqara,[83] relating to the cults of Osiris-Apis (Apis bull), Isis (Mother of Apis cow), Anubis (dog), Thoth (the ibis, falcon, and baboon), and Imhotep — among others — as does one (25%) Greek example. 11 (30.5%) are certainly or are most likely from Hermopolis,

[from] the illness he suffered" (l. 3-5), he will donate 3 kite of silver annually to the cult of the ibis and the gods of Heracleopolis (l. 10-14).

[81] For a study of the desired outcomes of the "Letters to Gods", see further Love fc. §2.2.3.1.

[82] As noted above and applies throughout, see now the corpus established in Love fc. and a study of their contexts in Love fc. §2.2.2.2.

[83] Four "secure" but unpublished examples are also certainly or most likely from Saqqara.

two of which were excavated in the Ibiotapheion itself,[84] relating to the cult of Thoth (the ibis, falcon, and baboon or living ibis). Three (8.25%) Demotic examples are from the Fayum, relating to the cults of *ḏd-ḥr-pꜣ-hb* (oracular baboon) at Theadelphia, Sobek at Tebtunis, and *ꜣs.t-nꜣ-nfr.t-ỉr-šy* et al. at Euhemeria. Two (5.5%) Demotic examples are from Deir el-Bahari, relating to the cult of Amenhotep-son-of-Hapu.[85] Three (75%) Greek examples were excavated at the fish necropolis at Esna. Only one "secure" published and two "secure" unpublished examples are without any clear provenance, while — despite a certain consensus — none were in fact found in tombs.[86]

Notably, only three petitioners at current count have a priestly title, and are therefore individuals who could safely be assumed to have the literacy required to write their own petitions and access to the catacombs in which they most likely deposited.[87] Yet these are not necessarily priests of the deity they petitioned,[88] and in most cases nothing more is known about the petitioner than their name, and the concern or dispute about which they petitioned.

Proceeding on that 'cult by cult' basis, the examples treated in what follows will draw from the content of the petitions themselves, and — where known — their context of discovery and therefore deposition, to

---

[84] Another "secure" but unpublished example was excavated in the Ibiotapheion, ENDREFFY 2010, p. 49 n. 1, and two further "secure" but unpublished are most likely to come from Hermopolis.

[85] Another "secure" but unpublished example, on an ostracon, was in the middle niche in the south wall of the main sanctuary (barque shrine) at Deir el-Bahari, later reused as a chapel for Amenhotep-son-of-Hapu, KARKOWSKI & WINNICKI 1983, p. 102; WYSOCKI 1985, p. 366-367; pl. 2. I am most grateful to Kata ENDREFFY for making me aware of this crucial find.

[86] See the treatment of the examples for which such a provenance has been suggested in LOVE fc. §2.2.2.2.

[87] As elaborated below, this is "most likely" because every single example of a "Letter to a God" that has a secure provenance, except for the unpublished example from Deir el-Bahari (see the preceding footnote), was excavated in a catacomb or cemetery of sacred animals — not to mention a host of internal factors, such as the invocation of "the gods who rest (*ḥtp*)" with named deities, which refers to buried animal mummies, where the "house of rest" (*ʿ.wỉ-ḥtp*) denotes their catacombs.

[88] In the aforementioned 219/218 BCE *T. Cambridge University Library Michaelides* x4 (TM 48782), Osoroeris is both a father of the god and god's servant of Amun-Re, King of the Gods, but nonetheless chooses to petition "his master" (*pꜣy=f ḥry*) the royal-scribe Amenhotep-son-of-Hapu.

elucidate the motivation behind those petitions, the outcome desired of that divine intervention, and how such divine interactions were conceptualised as resolving disputes in the lived experience of those petitioners.

At Saqqara, a perhaps unnamed petitioner[89] petitions against Teôs, the agent (*rd*) of Imhotep, to Osiris-Apis in the first instance, and then Osiris-Apis and Imhotep, son of Ptah, in the second, about the fact that the servants (*b3k*) of Imhotep, son of Ptah, had been reassigned to the service of some "great men" (*rmṯ ˁ3*)[90] — belonging to temple authorities or councils.[91] It is perhaps notable that the petitioner does not specify for which — presumably worldly — purposes or "great men" the servants of Imhotep had been 'embezzled', but three complementary interpretations present themselves. Firstly, the petitioner was presumably of a lower status than Teôs, given that Teôs could — apparently with impunity — 'embezzle' the labour of the servants of Imhotep. Secondly, the idea that divine service is being 'embezzled' for worldly benefit was presumably perceived as being unacceptable to both Osiris-Apis and Imhotep, and therefore Teôs was appealing to the sense that such an action was an 'injustice'. Thirdly, the petitioner perhaps presumed that those gods were simply not aware of Teôs' transgression, with the implication that by making them aware, they would intervene — doing a service for those gods in return for a service from those gods.[92]

Roughly contemporary with this example is the petition to Osiris-Apis by Artemisia — one of several female petitions attested in this corpus.[93] Known as the so-called Curse of Artemisia, the text upon *P. Vindob.* G 1 is not a magical text invoking a curse down upon an individual nor the

[89] Perhaps the "Khaef" who could be read in l. 8.

[90] In the 364/363 BCE papyrus *EES* S. 71/2-DP 146 = *EAS* 5832 (TM 69690).

[91] See the references in DAVIES 2002, p. 81 n. 8.

[92] Consider the judicial associations of "reporting" (*smy*) to a superior, discussed above in the case of P. Cairo 31045.

[93] Consider also *T. BM* EA 50145 (TM 48781) and the Old Coptic Schmidt Papyrus (TM 92845). In other cases, such as the aforementioned 219/218 BCE *T. Cambridge University Library Michaelides* x4 (TM 48782), men wrote or commissioned petitions for women, but not necessarily with their consent. For example, given that Osoroeris wrote or commissioned the petition, it cannot be assumed that *T3y-pˁ* actually wished for a child as Osoroeris apparently did.

flagship example of the putative corpus of "Prayers for Justice",[94] but a "Letter to a God" which happens to be written in the Greek, rather than Egyptian, language. One of the earliest extant Greek-language texts from Egypt, treatments of Artemisia's petition have — almost without exception — been undertaken by scholars from outside of Egyptology who have either been unaware, understated, or decidedly ignored the preceding, contemporary, and succeeding tradition of "Letters to Gods" attested in Egypt from the Late to Roman Period[95] — a tradition that both pre- and post-dates the "Curse of Artemisia" by centuries and is attested by numerous contemporary examples in Demotic from Saqqara.[96] When an Egyptologist finally engaged with this text in writing, it was appraised as "an ancient Egyptian text written in Greek" and one which "can be turned almost word for word into ... demotic".[97]

Artemisia petitions:

> Oh lord Oserapi and <the> gods who sit with Oserapi.[98] I pray to you (pl.),[99] Artemisia, the daughter of Amasis (*ỉʿḥ-ms*), against the father of my

---

[94] For a retreatment of this text among the "Letters to Gods", as well as a deconstruction of its attribution to the putative corpus of "Prayers for Justice", see now LOVE fc. §2.3; 6-8. For VERSNEL's formative thesis on the "Prayers for Justice" in Greek and Latin from the eastern Mediterranean and Europe, of which the "Curse of Artemisia" is the flagship example, see VERSNEL 1991; 2002; 2010.

[95] For a treatment and deconstruction of such philologically hellenocentric approaches, see further LOVE fc. §7.4.

[96] For example, while acknowledging their existence, Versnel does not engage in any way with the "Letters to Gods" — which he, without justification, terms "demotic prayers for justice" (consider the fact numerous examples do not concern dispute resolution) —, implying they are neither of benefit for understanding the Egyptian context of the Greek-language examples nor his putative corpus of "Prayers for Justice", VERSNEL 1991, p. 69 with n. 38.

[97] RAY 1994, p. 55. Although I am not of RAY's judgement that the text is 'completely Egyptian', there are striking parallels that are only apparent when one actually looks at the Egyptian parallels. For semantic parallels to Greek-language curses, which would of course also be expected in a Greek-language text, see further the discussion in LOVE fc. §8.1.

[98] Ὦ δεσποτ' Ὀσερᾶπι κα<ὶ> <οἱ> θεοὶ οἱ μετὰ τοῦ Ὀσερ[άπιο]ς καθ[ήμενοι], i.e. * *ỉ p3y(=ỉ) nb wsỉr-ḥp ỉrm n3 nṯr.w nty ḥtp ỉrm wsỉr-ḥp* (l. 1), where "the gods who sit with" the named deity are buried animal mummies, a term common in dedications and votives across the Sacred Animal Necropolis at Saqqara, see further LOVE fc. §8.1.

[99] [εὔχομ]αι ὑμῖν, i.e. *tw=y smy/šrr/tbḥ r-ḥr=tn* (l. 1).

> daughter, [who] deprived [her] of the grave goods/funerary rituals (κτέρεα) and coffin/tomb (θήκη). (l. 1-3)

After making the case that this was an unjust act,[100] the desired outcome of Artemisia's petition is then stated explicitly as

> May Oserapis and the gods ensure that (he) not receive a coffin from (his) children and that he himself may not bury his very own parents. (l. 4-6)

Thus, by declaring that she has been the victim of an injustice that was quite unprovoked, i.e. that there was no cause for the father of her daughter to deprive her daughter of the grave goods/funerary rituals and coffin/tomb expected or she had expected but not received such, Artemisia petitions Osiris-Apis et al. that he himself suffer such an injustice in turn to render justice.[101] At the most important cult site of the most important city in Egypt during the fourth century BCE, space for votives, dedications, and "Letters to Gods" was not guaranteed in perpetuity.[102] Consequently, given that deposited petitions may not have stayed deposited forever, but may have been replaced by more recent ones, and given the possibility that at least some at Saqqara were hung upon the walls of those catacombs, or perhaps even shrines,[103] where they would not have hung forever, Artemisia then expresses her concern that an officiating priest may remove the deposited petition:

---

[100] "If, then, he did not act justly to me, and (did not act) justly to his own children, as in fact he did act unjustly to me and to his own children" (l. 3-4).

[101] It could even be considered that Artemisia was condemning the father of her daughter to the "Second Death" in the way that he had perhaps almost condemned her daughter to the "Second Death" by depriving her of her grave goods/funerary rituals and coffin/tomb.

[102] For the cursing formulae from Saqqara against those that would erase the names of the benefactors of dedicatory inscriptions and votives, see SMITH, ANDREWS & DAVIES 2011, I, p. 254-255.

[103] Consider the fourth-century BCE H5-1660 [3545] (TM 92339), a petition inscribed upon linen affixed to a wooden bracket. This petition was excavated in the western half of the compound of the Central Temple Enclosure, and Ray interpreted the bracket as "reveal[ing] how it was attached to the shrine wall or gate/door frame", RAY 2005a, p. 171. Thus, "the purpose of this was no doubt to enable the text to be inserted into the mud-brick wall of a shrine or chapel, or into the frame of a gate or door, so that the text would face inwards towards the shrine, where it could be read by the god Osorapis as it fluttered in the breeze", RAY 2005a, p. 175. It is equally possible, if not more likely given the secure provenances of finds in the Ibiotapheion at Hermopolis, that this example was affixed to the wall of a catacomb at Saqqara, but this possibility is not engaged with by RAY.

> So (long as) the accusation lies here, badly may he die, both on land (and) at sea, both he and that which is his, by (the hand) of Oserapis and the gods who sit in Poserapi,[104] and may he not receive the graciousness of Oserapis nor (of) the gods who sit with Oserapis. (l. 5-8) So, whoever should take this document and who may act unjustly (ἀδικεῖν) towards Artemisia the god shall impose judgement. (l. 12-13)

This, in turn, is to ensure the desired outcome of Artemisia's petition, not simply the punishment — "cursing" — of the father of her daughter, but also that they conduct her case (i.e. *ỉr hp*), redressing her grievance and resolving her dispute.

> Artemisia has deposited this supplication, supplicating (before) Oserapis and the gods who sit with Oserapis to judge (δικάζω) the judgement (δίκη) (i.e. decide/adjudicate the lawsuit). (l. 9-10)

Characteristic for the "Letters to Gods", how the dispute is to be resolved is not explicated, with such ambiguity lending itself to the perhaps cynical interpretation that any positive outcome following the petition could be interpreted as a positive divine intervention in favour of the petitioner. In what is preserved of her petition — admittedly, at least one third is missing — this positive outcome would be that Osiris-Apis et al. deem Artemisia's petition to be "just" (l. 3-4) and therefore that the treatment of her daughter was "unjust" and that it would be "just" to punish Amasis through the eye-for-an-eye principle. The explicit nature of the dispute resolution is, however, in the case of Teôs and Artemisia, left up to the petitioned deities, and in the latter case the implication appears to be that retribution through like-for-like suffering constitutes the desired outcome.

The theme of redressing grievances through punishment — retribution through cursing —, rather than resolving disputes, also features in the aforementioned *P. Carlsberg* 67 (TM 48778), a papyrus from the temple of Soknebtunis at Tebtunis, dating to 5 CE. The unnamed petitioner entreats Sobek, Lord of Tebtunis, for "the judgement (*wpy*) of the lord!" and "the retribution (*tbꜣ*) of the Lord!" (l. x+3) because of "suffering at the hand of Tsenêsis" (l. x+6). This suffering — the justification

[104] I.e. *pr-wsỉr-ḥp*, a term not only for the Temple of Osiris-Apis (Serapeum) but also applying to the entire Sacred Animal Necropolis at Saqqara.

for the curse — may be her having done something in falsehood (*ꜣyḏꜣ* < *ʿḏ* ?) (l. x+7). The petitioner precedes to curse her:[105]

> I will give this memorandum to you so that you will conduct my case (and) enact judgement for me (literally 'my judgement') swiftly and you will not delay. You will place harm after her bones (and) illness after her limbs at night as well as at midday. (l. x+8-12)

Similar to Artemisia's petition, this example demonstrates that the redressing of grievances was sometimes more a matter of retribution than resolution. Where the injustice the petitioners have suffered cannot be taken back, and therefore cannot be truly resolved, the only way to redress grievances is to see that such transgressions are acknowledged as unjust by a divine if not worldly superior, and therefore that justice be done through punishment. After all, in some cases, seeing the accused getting away with their transgressions may well have been interpreted as a further injustice.

Arriving at Hermopolis, the Saite (664-525 BCE) *P. Mallawi* 485 (TM 48790), found in the Ibiotapheion — the catacombs of the ibis mummies sacred to Thoth,[106] — is the petition of Ithorôth (*ỉr.t=w-rḏ*) against Padeêsis, Thoteus, his son, and Tameneus, his wife as well as Kasôthês concerning "misery" because "they have stolen from the feeding-place of the ibises" (l. 7). In this case, Ithorôth does not entreat Thoth to conduct his case, nor enact justice and judgement in response to this injustice. Instead, it appears as if Ithorôth aims primarily only to make Thoth aware of this transgression, leaving Thoth to devise an appropriate resolution and/or retribution through punishment accordingly. It is unfortunately unknowable whether Ithorôth is also responsible for the provision of "the feeding-place of the ibises", and therefore would be held partly responsible were the matter not resolved. But, nevertheless, Ithorôth does not appear to prioritise the punishment of the accused over the resolution of the dispute. Given that stealing from the feeding-place of the ibises is a theft directly from Thoth himself — i.e. the embezzlement of his offerings —, it appears that Ithorôth expected Thoth's

---

105 The first editor, by comparison, interpreted this text as a "healing-prayer". The deciding phrases, however, are that the suffering is *at the hand* of, not from, Tsenêsis (*[ỉw] y.t n-tr.ṯ tꜣ-šrỉ.t-ꜣs.t*) (l. x+6) and that harm is to be *placed after* her bones (l. x+10-11), not driven out, contrary to RAY 1975, p. 183.

106 ZAGHLOUL 1985, p. 1.

intervention accordingly.[107] The entrusting of this dispute to Thoth, who is able to make his own judgements, is reflected in the reverence shown for Thoth through the aforementioned epithet as "Lord of Justice" (*pꜣ nb hp*) in *L. Mallawi* 489 (TM 48792), a sizeable linen sheet inscribed in the petition of an unnamed individual, also from Hermopolis.

From a site not so far from Hermopolis is a petition inscribed upon the so-called Old Coptic Schmidt Papyrus. The original papyrus — dating to the first or second century CE — is now lost, and is known only through an image (Crum MS XXII.10) in the archive of the Griffith Institute, Oxford.[108] Having been characterised as a magical text by its original editor,[109] the text itself was not initially identified as the only example among the "Letters to Gods" written in Old Coptic. The manuscript was found inside a sarcophagus upon the lid of the coffin of a corn mummy during the excavations of a cemetery thereof at Tehna.[110] Thus, as with the examples on papyrus and linen found in the Ibiotapheion at Hermopolis or on ostraca excavated at the fish necropolis at Esna, this manuscript was deposited with a medium which would presumably have served as the medium to — and offering for — the petitioned deity. Consequently, it is quite appropriate that Esrmpe petitioned Osiris in Hasrō, a mortuary deity known otherwise only in afterlife texts.[111] Esrmpe petitions (ⲥⲙⲙⲉ) against Hōr saying:

> My Lord Osiris in Hasrō, I petition you. Conduct my case with Hōr, the son of Tanesnēou, concerning what I did to him and what he did to me, because he will not abandon you, whereas I am powerless, since I do not have (the) protection of (a) son, nor do I have (the) help of (a) daughter. I am (thought) barren.[112] there is not the one who will petition on my behalf against him before [... (l. a/1-a/9)

[107] This relates to the "business with the gods" noted above, see ENDREFFY 2010.

[108] For a re-edition and retreatment of this manuscript among the "Letters to Gods", see now LOVE fc., esp. §3-5.

[109] SATZINGER 1975, corrected in SATZINGER 1984, p. 138, but still included as part of a compendium of "magical texts" in MEYER & SMITH 1994, p. 21 #1.

[110] This has apparently been known for decades, see OSING 1998, p. 58; 58 n. 237, clarified recently by ROQUET 2016, p. 663. For a re-edition and retreatment of this manuscript in light of these findings, see now LOVE fc, esp. §3-5.

[111] FRANKFURTER's (2018) erroneous conjecture that Esrmpe deposited her petition in a public "shrine" of "a local spirit" is deconstructed in LOVE fc., esp. §3-5.

[112] While using the word ⲗⲁⲣⲏⲛ (< *ꜣkrn*; *S* ⲗⲁϭⲣⲏⲛ), this does not mean that Esrmpe was indeed barren, but that she thought herself, or was thought, barren — presumably

From this fresh translation,[113] it appears that Esrmpe considers herself not only maltreated by Hōr, but also unable to help/defend herself against him, or find anyone to help/defend her herself due to a lack of immediate family — where a childless old age was the "worst of all fates", with domestic, social, economic, and legal consequences, including that she was unable to find someone who will petition on her behalf.[114] Indeed, Esrmpe challenges Osiris in Hasrō to judge whether what Esrmpe did to him was worse than what Hōr did to her, and consequently conduct her case appropriately. Esrmpe turns to Osiris in Hasrō not only because Hōr will not abandon, i.e. ignore/forsake, that deity or his intervention, but also because she has no worldly individual to turn to. Important to consider is that contrary to the past androcentric interpretations which have seen Esrmpe's petition exclusively as a request for a child,[115] Esrmpe — at least in the preserved sections of the manuscript — does not petition for a child. Such is attested in the corpus of "Letters to Gods", but the structure of such petitions — as has been seen — is considerably different. Indeed, there is nothing in the text itself to suggest that Hōr should even be identified as Esrmpe's husband. Osiris in Hasrō is, after all, a mortuary deity, and so it could even be that Hōr is deceased — whether a deceased husband, brother, father, etc. —, and is being blamed for exerting a malevolent influence upon Esrmpe's life.[116] Ultimately, as is the case with numerous examples among the "Letters to Gods" which tell only part of the story and entrust the rest of their case

---

by nature of never having had any children. If her lack of children was a result of never having conceived (as opposed to never having carried a child to full term), this could just as readily have been a consequence of an impotent partner; in a patriarchal society, however, such a consequence was unlikely to have been acknowledged.

[113] For a refutation of prior readings, including the infamous translation of the *editio princeps*, see now LOVE fc. §3.2.

[114] For this, see HUEBNER 2013, esp. p. 162-175.

[115] SATZINGER 1975, followed by FRANKFURTER 1998, p. 251-252; 2018.

[116] Consider the "Letters to the Dead" of *CG* 25375 (TM 755150) from the early 12th Dynasty in which the deceased is reproached by the petitioner for not having looked after the ill serving-girl, GARDINER & SETHE 1928, p. 7-8, or P. Leiden I 371 (TM 755091) from the 19th Dynasty in which the petitioner entreats the *3ḫ* "transfigured spirit of the deceased" not to be malevolent towards the petitioner, GARDINER & SETHE 1928, p. 8-9. Petitioners in "Letters to Gods" also petitioned concerning malign divine influences, e.g. concerning *t3 wry(.t)* "the evil one", "the demonic being which creates bad fortune for a person", HUGHES 1968, p. 179, in the aforementioned *L. BM* EA 73785 (TM 48783).

to the petitioned deity, there are a host of possible interpretations for both the motivation behind and desired outcome of Esrmpe's petition, all of which are to be considered in a re-edition and retreatment of the Old Coptic Schmidt Papyrus.[117]

Further south of Tehna come the examples from Thebes which petition Amenhotep-son-of-Hapu, one of which is the aforementioned petition for *Tȝy-pꜥ* to become pregnant and bear a child. In this context, it is clear that no animal cult was involved, and the aforementioned unpublished example from Deir el-Bahari suggests that petitioners to that deity were instead deposited in his temple sanctuary. Albeit a small corpus, these examples attest another regional variant in the broader tradition of petitioning deities.

From further south than any Egyptian-language examples with secure provenance are three first/second-century CE Greek-language examples excavated at the fish necropolis sacred to Athena-Neith at Esna.[118] The petition of "Claudius Silvanus and his brothers" inscribed upon an ostracon and directed to "the Lady Athena against Longinus son of Marcus" concerns an accusation that Longinus "against whom we often petition (ἐντυγχάνω) you" has "gone against us, in respect of (our) lives, we having done nothing wrong, being poor. For he having no profit from the deed, attacks evilly — we entreat (παρακαλέω) (you) to exact vengeance (ἐκδικέω)" (*O. Cairo* JdE 38622 l. 4-12). As in several of the preceding examples, Claudius et al. did not think it necessary to specify exactly what they were accusing Longinus of. However, it seems, as with several of the preceding examples, that they were in an inferior position of social power and/or economic privilege with respect to Longinus — as a result of which Longinus was able to get away with his unjust actions. This suggests that it would not have been sensible, or even possible, to go "over his head" with a petition to a worldly superior. Indeed, it appears this had been the case for a considerable amount of time, given their statement that they had already "even petitioned Amun" about him (l. 12), and therefore perhaps had been forsaken time and time again.

---

[117] LOVE fc., esp. §3-5.

[118] *O. Cairo* JdE 38622 (TM 25385); *O. Garstang* 1 (TM 115545); *O. Garstang* 2 (TM 115546), see GALLAZZI 1985; GASCOU 2008. For a retreatment of these examples as "Letters to Gods" in Greek, see now LOVE fc. §2.3.

The preceding treatment of selected examples from this corpus has sought to illustrate not only the diversity of concerns about which individuals petitioned, but also to highlight the complexity of dissimilarities within a corpus that was the product of ritual practices spanning nine centuries, is attested disparately along the length of the Nile, manifested in different forms in differing regionalised contexts, and was utilised differently by a variety of petitioners. The remainder of this study will instead be concerned with how the mechanics of divine interaction within these petitions can be understood, as well as how the mechanics of resolving disputes could have been conceptualised as occurring.

6. Mechanics of divine interaction in the "Letters to Gods"

The aforementioned tripartite distinction presented in *P. Jumilhac* suggests that Egyptians conceptualised manifestations of the divine as the transfigured spirits of the deceased (*3ḫ.w*) and deities (*nṯr.w*). As the living/humans (*rmṯ.w*), they could interact with both these manifestations in order to bring about tangible changes in their lived experience. Consequently, petitioners collaborated or bargained with the dead or deities within the framework of a reciprocal relationship.

This practice of petitioning is illustrated by the Ḥû Bowl[119] (UC 16244), dating to the First Intermediate Period (2160-2055 BCE), from a tomb at Diospolis Parva. Nefersefkhi petitions her "brother" about the maltreatment of her daughter by a man and states that she is

> making invocation offerings (*pr.t-ḫrw*) to the transfigured spirit (*3ḫ*) in return for interceding on behalf of the living. (l. 4-5)

Comparable to the conceptualisation evidenced in the "Letters to the Dead" that the transfigured spirit of the deceased would intercede reciprocally on behalf of the living in return for offerings made are numerous references to offerings among the "Letters to Gods".[120] In addition to Osoroeris offering Amenhotep-son-of-Hapu "money" discussed above, consider, for example, the entreaty by the petitioner of the substantial linen sheet *L. BM* EA 73784 (TM 100205):

[119] Gardiner & Sethe 1928, p. 5 (TM 755148); Donnat 2014, p. 44-48.

[120] Discussed fully in Love fc. §2.2.3.2.

> Oh the living ibis, go to Hermopolis for the offering (*pꜣ ʿḳ ḥtp-nṯr*) again. Report (*ʿn-smy*) before Thoth, twice-great, the lord of Hermopolis (l. 7-8) (because) there is no other man like (me) <in that> he made good things for the Ibis, written by the servant of the Ibis, Horouaphrês. (l. 9-10)

This petition suggests that the service Horouaphrês has given to the cult of the Ibis was conceptualised as being an appropriate inducement for the Ibis to petition Thoth on his behalf. Not to mention that by going to Hermopolis, the living ibis would partake in the offering, tangible reciprocity provided by humanity (*rmṯ.w*) for the gods (*nṯr.w*).

While the provenance of the Ḥû Bowl makes clear that the offerings promised by Nefersefkhi were brought to the tomb, where the mummy of the deceased would have served to transmit the petition, the linen strip, if not itself once part of the wrappings of an ibis mummy, is likely to have been deposited among ibis mummies in the catacombs, which were themselves conceptualised as "gods" (*nṯr.w*) which could transmit the petition.[121] For examples without secure contexts, other potential places of deposition have been proposed. At Saqqara, Smith proposed that the base of a stone structure preserved in the sanctuary of the Central Temple Enclosure at Saqqara was "in all probability" one which "supported a naos for an oracular image of Osiris-Apis or Isis, Mother of Apis, facing out into the main chamber",[122] which is where oracles questions were answered and perhaps even where petitions were deposited. Similarly, the aforementioned example on linen exhibiting a wooden bracket was suggested by Ray to have been affixed to the wall of a sanctuary,[123] but this example could equally have been affixed to the wall of a catacomb. That example was, after all, found in the fill of the Northern Enclosure, adjacent to the Mother of Apis catacombs, which included various objects such as stelae that had clearly been removed from those

[121] Consider the examples found in the Ibiotapheion, noted above, as well as the views of HUGHES 1968, p. 176; MIGAHID 1986, II, p. 26; RAY 2005a, p. 177-178; DEPAUW 2006, p. 313 and ENDREFFY 2010, p. 52. While Migahid also suggests that petitions on linen could also have been deposited upon a human mummy, MIGAHID 1986, II, p. 29, there is no evidence in favour of this suggestion because no examples of "Letters to Gods" were actually found in private tombs, see LOVE fc. §2.2.2.2. For animal mummies as intermediaries, see FITZENREITER 2013, p. 165.

[122] SMITH 2002, p. 369.

[123] RAY 2005a, p. 171; 175.

catacombs.[124] Thus, given the examples found in the Ibiotapheion at Hermopolis, the most parsimonious interpretation is actually that this example was hung up in the catacombs themselves. Nevertheless, although not attested at Saqqara and Hermopolis — the sites from which perhaps as many as 30 (83%) of the 36 "secure" examples stem — a context in which proximity to the cult state of a deity would have meant proximity to a manifestation of the divine, and transmitting medium equivalent to an animal mummy, must be envisaged for cults such as that of Amenhotep-son-of-Hapu, which was not served by any animal cults. This is in turn suggested by the aforementioned unpublished example from Deir el-Bahari following a certain amount of time, after which it was perhaps understood that the deity had either acted upon the petition or had no intention of doing so, deposited petitions — administered by the relevant priesthood — were likely removed in order to make space for new ones.[125] As noted above, this in turn explains the internal evidence for curses against those who would remove not only "Letters to Gods" from their place of deposition, but also who would remove, efface, or rename, votives, stelae, and other dedicatory inscriptions as known from, for example, Saqqara.[126]

7. Mechanics of petitioning in the "Letters to Gods"

A caveat highlighted at the beginning of this study is the difficulty in ascertaining, whether for the entire corpus or for the regionalised practices of a particular site, whether or not the petitions themselves were recited, or whether any other such ritual practice accompanied their production and deposition. The latest extant "Letter to the Dead", the aforementioned Abnormal Hieratic *P. Brooklyn* 37.1799 E (TM 51144), features an inscription on the verso to "recite it at the door of/entrance to the tomb" (*ʿš -sw r3=f (n) t3 ḥw.t*), which has been taken in some cases as representative of both the "Letters to the Dead" and "Letters to

[124] Smith, Andrews & Davies 2011, II, p. 7.

[125] Depauw also considered, following Migahid 1986, II, p. 24-27, whether some manuscripts could not have been "handed over to the priests of the local divinity who may have deposited it in their archive", Depauw 2006, p. 313.

[126] See further a study of these in Love fc. §8.1.

Gods".[127] Among the "Letters to Gods", Migahid has already highlighted that the textual content of the petition inscribed upon *P. BM* EA 10845 (TM 48779), a second or first-century BCE papyrus apparently from Saqqara, implies recitation:[128]

> [Have them make] the aforementioned man [recite it] (at) the south-entrance, the north-entrance, the west-entrance, (and) the east-entrance of the place in which the gods rest.[129]

However, what has been overlooked is that Hughes' suggested reconstruction of this essentially illegible passage is — in his own words — "conjecture only".[130] If the "aforementioned man" were the "cruel father" of the petitioners, it would make very little sense that the accused party would somehow be made to recite the petition against him in the presence of "the Ibis, the Falcon, the Baboon, and the gods who rest with them in the resting-place" (l. 3), i.e. the animal mummy catacombs, presumably at Saqqara. If the "aforementioned man" were instead "any man of the land who will reach this document",[131] this would instead be a priest who would have access to the manuscript who is then instructed not to ignore the plea, but recite it from start to finish after it was submitted to him.[132] Regardless, this example is both ambiguous due to its state of preservation and an outlier in the corpus of "Letters to Gods".

Nevertheless, recitation of a petition at the entrance to a catacomb would perhaps have provided a context in which petitioners who did not name themselves in their written/commissioned petitions were made known to the deity.[133] But this also raises a route of enquiry, which can only be mentioned here, as to which petitions were written and recited by their petitioners, and which were written and recited by priests on

---

[127] In particular FRANKFURTER 1998, p. 252.

[128] MIGAHID 1986, II, p. 102.

[129] *[my ty=w ʿš̌-st] p3 rmṯ rn=f (n) p3 r(3) rsy p3 r(3) mḥt p3 r(3) ỉmnt* ⸢*p3 r(3) ỉ3bt*⸣ *(n) p3 m3ʿ r(ỉw) n3 nṯr.w ḥtp n-ỉm=f* (l. 28-30).

[130] HUGHES 1969, p. 154.

[131] *rmṯ -nb (n) p3 t3 mtw(ntỉ-ỉw)=f (r) pḥ p3y bk | hbl*⸢*3*⸣ (l. 27), Hughes read instead *tk p3y b3k (n) h3ʿ[h]* ⸢*r ẖb*⸣*=f* "set this document on fire ⸢to destroy⸣ it", both very doubtful and very interpretive, given that reading *pḥ* is entirely consistent with the example in l. 28 and *hbl*⸢*3*⸣ with that in l. 22 etc..

[132] *m-ỉr ty.t šm=f r-bl ḥr ẖrw=n | my ʿš̌=f -st (n) ḥ3.t=f r pḥ=f* (l. 28).

[133] For example, as in *P. Cairo* 31045 (TM 48672) from Saqqara and *L. Mallawi* 489 (TM 48792) from Hermopolis.

behalf of commissioning clients. It seems likely, for example, that Patechons "servant (of) the ibises", who wrote the petition inscribed upon *L. Michaelides* (TM 81172), could have recited it himself, but less so regarding the "children" petitioners of *P. BM* EA 10845 (TM 48779).

Although literacy is — in one sense — the only limiting factor in the production and recitation of a petition,[134] the deposition of a petition in a catacomb,[135] cemetery[136] or — in the case of Deir el-Bahari — temple sanctuary,[137] would have required the engagement of a priest — for these were not public places. As a result, it is currently unclear what inductions can be made from isolated examples among the "Letters to Gods" for the 'global' mechanics of petitioning practices. Smith suggested for the case of Saqqara that "pleas, complains and requests for help ... were probably presented or read out to the divine image in much the same manner as oracle questions", but it is also clear that all the examples with a secure provenance were left deposited, and so were not brought out to their clients again as was the case with oracle questions. Further, Smith suggested that the gestures of the movable oracular statues or sacred animals "form[ed] the basis of a positive or negative reply delivered by the *ʿn-wšb* or priest",[138] with Ray also suggesting a petitioner would have received an oral reply from the petitioned deity, but without elaborating on how this would function or is evidenced.[139]

Unlike with oracle questions, which posed binary questions for "yes/no" answers, "Letters to Gods" sought divine intervention in the lived experience of their petitioners, not simply answers about their past or

---

[134] Albeit already refuted by its context of deposition, for a rebuttal to FRANKFURTER's proposition that the Old Coptic Schmidt Papyrus was written in Old Coptic "in order that Esrmpe herself, who presumably could not read Egyptian script but might have been literate in Greek, could read her own plea before the shrine", and that this "*must* have been connected to the custom of reading such letters aloud before tombs and shrines" (emphasis my own), FRANKFURTER 1998, p. 252 n. 43; 252 — reiterated in FRANKFURTER 2000, p. 230; 2018 and taken up by MARTIN 2007, p. 252-261 —, see now LOVE fc. §3.1.

[135] Consider the aforementioned examples found in situ in the Ibiotapheion at Hermopolis.

[136] Consider the aforementioned examples excavated at the fish necropolis at Esna as well as now the Old Coptic Schmidt Papyrus.

[137] Consider now the ostracon found in a niche of the chapel of Amenhotep-son-of-Hapu, noted above.

[138] SMITH 2002, p. 369.

[139] RAY 1975, p. 187.

future. Questioners would act on the answer given by the deity, but petitioners wanted *the deity to act*! Thus, both Smith's and Ray's suggestions that answers to the petitions could be provided by priests does not actually account for the desired divine intervention. At this current point in my research, the pattern of evidence suggests that — just like oracle questions — petitions were mostly commissioned, rather than written by their petitioners, and thereby that they were most likely written by the same priests who would have delivered them to their point of deposition, presumably reciting them before the divine image (whether animal mummies or cult statues) before doing so. Yet how the writing and reciting of "Letters to Gods" was actually conceptualised as resolving disputes can therefore be seen as a separate issue to the mechanics of petitioning itself.

8. Mechanisms of dispute resolution in the "Letters to Gods"

Petitions that concern disputes seem to always concern individuals who, despite their maltreatment and/or hardship, are simply unable to acquire the help of others and consequently entrust their case to deities.[140] Given this latter point, Kata Endreffy considered that petitioning deities "might also have been a complementary solution accompanying a request for an oath, or a civil process",[141] while Karl-Theodor Zauzich even considered suggested that disputes would instead be resolved before the judges in the afterlife.[142]

[140] Zauzich 1992/93, p. 165.

[141] Endreffy 2009, p. 242. Perhaps certain petitioners entreated the petitioned deity that they have no protection other than that deity "because they were unable to prove their right in a given legal dispute", Endreffy 2009, p. 243. Here, there are similarities with the content of many of the petitions typologised as "Prayers for Justice": "once the prayer is inscribed and dedicated it is then envisaged that the god, who is perceived as the ultimate and majestic judicial authority, will help litigants achieve a successful outcome in their litigation or exact retribution if judicial procedures are abused", Papakonstantinou 2008, p. 40.

[142] "A message to the sender is superfluous because the future itself will show how the decision has failed, or because the decision is instead expected in the afterlife court", Zauzich 1992/93, p. 179.

As has been suggested for several of the examples above, however, the power dynamics of the relationships involved seem to explain why petitioners petitioned otherworldly rather than worldly superiors. At this current point in my research, it seems that the petitioners were simply unable to stop those who held higher status, and thus exercised greater social power/status or economic privilege/influence, from abusing their status at the expense of those below them. This seems true in cases of anything from abuses of economic privilege/influence (e.g. being able to get away with embezzling from a cult) to abuses of social power/status (e.g. being able to assault people with impunity). With the worldly authorities turning a blind eye or indeed supporting the accused, divine authorities were instead entrusted to intervene in the lived experience of petitioners and resolve their ongoing disputes, because only they could.

At this current point in my research, I would term the four mechanisms proposed as ways in which to understand how the "Letters to Gods" (as "Prayers for Justice") 'worked' as the (ia) "implicit" and (ib) "explicit" "social" mechanisms, alongside the (iia) "implicit" and (iib) "explicit" "priestly" mechanisms, as well as the (iii) "psychological" and (iv) "attribution" mechanisms.[143] As will be seen, however, these mechanisms are not necessarily mutually exclusive, while their central claims can only be treated here briefly.

The interpretation of curses, petitions, and prayers which has gained the most traction is the first, what I term the implicit social mechanism, in which desired outcomes are argued to have been brought about in a socially discursive way (e.g. through social pressure) that was an *unconscious by-product* of such petitioning. By its principal proponents, this mechanism is, however, assumed to have been predicated on those texts being "publicly displayed", as argued for the "Prayers for Justice" by Henk Versnel in his formative study.[144] Taking Artemisia's petition as the flagship example of that corpus,[145] Versnel concluded that the manuscript was "publicly displayed" because Artemisia curses against those who would remove it, interpreting therefore that anyone had access to

[143] All of which are treated at length now in LOVE fc. §8.3.

[144] Maintained by FARAONE e.a. 2005; FARAONE & RIFE 2007; FARAONE 2011 and subsequently taken up for the "Letters to Gods" by KOTSIFOU 2016 and FRANKFURTER 2018.

[145] VERSNEL 1991.

it, and could potentially remove it.[146] The thesis of "public display" maintains that petitions, such as Artemisia's, were to "be opened and inspected by persons concerned … while attracting attention to the complaint by informing a priest or a neighbour, who then would take care of the circulation of the rumour".[147]

Despite the fact that the majority of "Prayers for Justice" were inscribed upon lead, and/or rolled/folded, and sometimes even pierced like *defixiones*, not to mention deposited in irretrievable places such as springs or wells,[148] Versnel overstated certain outliers to this trend in order to propose that the curses contained in the "Prayers for Justice" were "publicly displayed", read, and resolved through a social mechanism.[149] Versnel's approach to the "Curse of Artemisia" is not only problematic due to its philological hellenocentrism, i.e. in taking a Greek-language text from Egypt and comparing to Greek-language sources from elsewhere while disregarding preceding, contemporary, or succeeding textual traditions from Egypt, but also because it entirely disregards the Egyptian context more concretely.[150] Versnel's interpretation that the "Curse of Artemisia" would have been "publicly displayed" not only neglects to consider that public access to temple enclosures in Egypt

---

[146] VERSNEL 1991, p. 69; 2002, p. 59. Various other explanations for this particular cursing clause were presented above, and are discussed fully in LOVE fc. §8.1; 8.3.

[147] VERSNEL 2002, p. 73. RAY, when publishing the aforementioned petition on linen affixed to a bracket which he interpreted as a means by which to attach it to a wall, contradicted his own earlier conclusion by adding the suggestion that the petition "was mounted somewhere in the great temple enclosure, where the god, and no doubt the neighbours, could be expected to read it". To RAY, the rationale behind the petition for the petitioner was therefore "to bring justice upon his persecutor, in a way that will be so severe and conspicuous that everyone will talk of it", RAY 2005a, p. 177. Such an interpretation is, however, mutually exclusive to his earlier interpretation that "the text would face inwards towards the shrine, where it could be read by the god Osorapis as it fluttered in the breeze", RAY 2005a, p. 175. Temple sanctuaries that contained the cult statues of deities were simply not public places.

[148] For a reconsideration of the archaeological evidence and deconstruction of the consensus that maintains that the "Prayers for Justice" were principally "publicly displayed", see now LOVE fc. §8.3.

[149] Resultantly, see the ensuing conclusion in FRANKFURTER 2018, p. 191.

[150] Not to mention that Artemisia was a Hellenomemphite, a member of a Grecophone community of Greek cultural descent and apparently with contacts to Grecophone communities outside of Egypt, but which was heavily Egyptianised and endemic to Egypt, see the treatment of this community context in LOVE fc. §7.

— like literacy — was heavily proscribed, it is undermined by the fact that all "Letters to Gods" with secure provenances were deposited in places only accessible to priests.

Versnel also bases his entire interpretation — that the manuscript was "undeniably *available*" and "*intended* for inspection"[151] — on an assumption about the meaning of that cursing clause itself. Artemisia specifies in her petition that as long as her petition lay where it lay, the father of her daughter would suffer retribution. This implies directly that the removal of the petition would prevent this from occurring, and hence why anyone who would remove it should be cursed, i.e. to make them think twice about removing it.[152] As noted above, even in places which would have only been accessible to priests and other servants of temple cults, such as temple sanctuaries and the catacombs of sacred animal mummies, curses against those would remove, efface, or rename, votives, stelae, and other dedicatory inscriptions are well attested because Egyptians were cognisant of the fact that everything from temples and tombs to stelae and coffins were usurped or replaced eventually.

As is clear from the survey above, the thesis of "public display" is refuted for the "Letters to Gods" by nature of their contexts of deposition. That is to say, in all cases where a secure provenance is attested, these petitioners were "hidden from human view", and therefore "the matters put forward were thus wholly transferred to the care of the deity addressed" — indeed "writing and transmitting the petition remained a private matter".[153] This refutation does not mean, however, that the implicit social mechanism was not possible, but just that "public display" does not need to be seen as a prerequisite through which such a mechanism can function.

While the context of deposition, and the locus of interaction with the divine being cult statues and the mummies of sacred animals, speaks against the recitation of petitions having been a "public performance", this does not mean that individuals in the families and communities of petitioners were not cognisant of those petitioners having been made — not least given the likelihood that scribes were commissioned to write

---

[151] VERSNEL 2002, p. 59 (emphasis my own).

[152] The removal of texts that curse as well as texts that bless as a means of "disarming" them is a common cross-cultural phenomenon, see now the discussion in LOVE fc. §8.1.

[153] ENDREFFY 2009, p. 246; 2010, p. 52.

them for their petitioners. Furthermore, in the context of Egypt, a ritual practised in a non-public space but which is of public interest and has public consequences is hardly remarkable given that the majority of ritual practised at temple institutions were done so behind closed doors, and yet people must have been cognisant of the fact that they were being practised.

A potential problem with the implicit social mechanism is that it could never account for the resolution of issues that did not involve socially discursive dispute resolution, such as healing and childbirth. Only what I would term the explicit social mechanism — that desired outcomes are argued to have been brought about in a socially discursive way that was a *conscious intention* of such petitioning —, proposed by David Frankfurter, could account for this. In the case of the Old Coptic Schmidt Papyrus, Frankfurter interpreted that Esrmpe's desired outcome was that Hōr have sex with her so she could conceive a child.[154] Frankfurter maintains Esrmpe was *consciously intending* "to solicit social pressure through oblique ritual means", and therefore that her petition is "the deft public maneuver of a woman deliberately engaging the forces of rumor and social pressure".[155] Notwithstanding that Frankfurter's interpretation — including that it was "publicly displayed" — is refuted by the context of deposition, it is nevertheless curious to find such an interpretation. That is, Frankfurter has conflated the etic, rationalist, and functionalist frames of reference utilised in social anthropology that allow contemporary scholars to explain to themselves why they think individuals practiced rituals with the emic, religious frames of reference of the petitioners themselves, and why they thought they practiced their rituals. Frankfurter therefore maintains that these petitions were not the product of a religiously motivated behaviour, where any social mechanism was an *unconscious by-product*, but the product of a socially-strategic behaviour in which a social mechanism was both an *explicit* and *conscious* intention behind such petitioning — petitioners themselves apparently conceptualised their petitioner as "oblique ritual means" through which to bring about their desired outcome by "solitict[ing] social pressure". The possibility that a petitioner actually held a conviction in the potential for divine intervention in their lives apparently does not come into it.

[154] FRANKFURTER 2018, p. 192.

[155] FRANKFURTER 2018, p. 193.

An issue with the social mechanism, whether implicit but especially if explicit, also arises in cases where petitioners clearly conceptualised their petitions as not having 'worked'. Notwithstanding that their petitions were buried with the sacred fish mummies of Neith in a necropolis thereof at Esna — and therefore not "publicly displayed" —, the social mechanism does not address why Claudius et al. would have petitioned Athena subsequent to petitioning Amun. That is, I would challenge the etic, rationalist, and functionalist assumptions and interpretations that implicitly or explicitly suggest that ritual practices only persist if they 'worked'. That Claudius et al. petitioned both Neith and Amun demonstrates that this is simply not the case.

A priestly mechanism has also been proposed, in which "appeals addressed to a god to denounce an injustice were intended in reality to obtain the intervention of his priests".[156] If such an explicit priestly mechanism was *conscious*, as Gallazzi proposed, however, this interpretation exhibits the same issues problematised for the explicit social mechanism. Yet, even if priestly intervention were implicit, an *unconscious by-product* of the petition, how petitioning priestly authorities would have been more effective than petitioning judicial or civil authorities has not been addressed by advocates of the priestly mechanism.

A further possibility is the psychological mechanism, where petitioning provided a "placebo", "catharsis", or a sense of "agency" for the petitioner.[157] The former would, however, have to be understood as an *unconscious by-product*, given that a placebo effect only works when a patient does not know it is a placebo, while such a process would only apply to petitions concerning healing. By comparison, given that many petitioners were in such dire straits — socially, economically, physiologically —, it is rather questionable how far such catharsis would have benefited the petitioner for long. Perhaps, then, a sense of "agency" was regained if coupled with a conviction that the deity is now taking care of the petitioner's concern. Yet, as with catharsis, regaining a sense of agency would not have been enough to actually resolve disputes.

---

[156] GALLAZZI 1985, 105.

[157] "... the letters were perhaps effective from a psychological as opposed to practical perspective: they served to ease their authors' conscience by shifting the weight of the problem and the responsibility of solving it onto the god", ENDREFFY 2009, p. 246; 2010, p. 53.

By comparison, unlike the preceding, the attribution mechanism does not seek to explain how the rituals themselves may have brought about their desired outcome — how they 'worked' at an objective level —, but instead how those rituals could have been conceptualised as bringing them about — how they ended up being conceptualised as having 'worked' at an intersubjective level. On a prior occasion, I have referred to the "causality-attribution", stemming from the basic premise of attribution theory from behavioural and social psychology whereby individuals assign causes to events — apparently a phenomenon universal to human experience. In that context, I suggested how "causality attributions" could occur when the desired outcome of a practised ritual correlated with an event which appeared to be the manifestation of the desired outcome of that ritual.[158] For example, if a ritual was practiced in order to heal someone who subsequently recovered from their illness, causality could be attributed post hoc. Thus, the agentive link in the process of unwell to well is the ritual practice itself (cause) as related to the recovery (event), and divine intervention could indeed be conceptualised as having occurred. After all, if a petitioner did not conceptualise that their action — cause — influenced the outcome — event —, it stands to reason that they would not have undertaken it.

If a "causality attribution" is possible, and not necessarily only a product of 'coincidence' given the variety of considerations from the implicit social mechanism to the placebo effect considered above, should we not in fact take the central claims of the petitioners, that they were consciously petitioning a deity because they conceptualised that that deity could intervene in their lived experience, earnestly? It does not, after all, seem an unreasonable premise that the petitioners genuinely conceptualised their petitions as being received and consulted, and consequently acted upon through divine intervention that resolved their disputes, as well as perhaps that also, like worldly petitions, they could fall on deaf ears. Certainly, in the cases of the conception and safe delivery of a child for *Tȝy-pꜥ*, it seems perfectly reasonable to suppose that the petitioner would have attributed this to divine intervention on the part of Amenhotep-son-of-Hapu, and the same would have likely been true if Thotnachthês' father Komoapis had recovered.

158 See LOVE 2020.

In this vein, in my judgement, identifying "causality attribution" provides a link between the objective phenomena of lived experience — e.g. the outcomes of rituals — and the intersubjective phenomena of lived experience — e.g. how those outcomes were conceptualised as having been brought about — regardless of what the exact ritual practice or desired outcome was. This constructed the intersubjective by which individuals conceptualised that human-divine could bring about desired outcomes in their lived experience, ensuring that such ritual practices persisted as long-lived traditions. That not every petition was acted upon, in the way that not every prayer is answered, evidently does nothing to undermine the strength of that intersubjective framework, as evidenced by Claudius et al.

In the case of dispute resolution, a variety of these mechanisms could be envisaged, especially given they are not mutually exclusive. While it certainly seems unlikely that serious social or economic disputes that had escalated so much that they led a petitioner to petition a deity would have simply resolved themselves overnight, it is also possible that social pressure was exerted by a petitioner, or members of their family and community,[159] or that catharsis and/or a sense of agency with the conviction that the dispute would be resolved eventually was beneficial to a petitioner in a certain way.

Conclusion

On balance, this study's survey of the "Letters to Gods" and treatment of selected examples has demonstrated not only the diversity of these sources and the variety of questions to brought to bear on this rich corpus of social, cultural, and religious history, but also the importance of studying the "Letters to Gods" in their regionalised contexts, as regionalised traditions. This corpus contains a variety of distinct concerns petitioned about, suggests a variety of mechanisms through which the desired outcomes of their petitions could have been conceptualised as having

[159] The crucial distinction between this interpretation and the thesis of "public display" is, however, that the latter maintains that causality was attributed ante hoc, in anticipation of a desired outcome, rather than post hoc, following the desired outcome actually occurring.

been brought about, and was long lived enough to have been transmitted as a bilingual and trigraphic written tradition over a near millennium. While the concluding sections of this study have posed more challenges than they have solved problems, they also demonstrate that while this corpus provides a substantial and unique body of evidence about the trials and tribulations of Graeco-Roman Egypt's downtrodden, derided, and dispossessed, the study of these sources is some way from being able to inform about the exact mechanisms through which these rituals were conceptualised as resolving these disputes, and how these manifested in the lived experience of those individuals as disputes resolved.

KEEP IT FOR YOURSELF: PRIVATE ASSOCIATIONS AND INTERNAL DISPUTE RESOLUTION IN PTOLEMAIC EGYPT*

Mario C.D. PAGANINI
(Austrian Academy of Sciences, Vienna)

Abstract: The present paper investigates the role private associations played for dispute resolution in Ptolemaic Egypt. After accessing the relevant Demotic and Greek evidence, it is argued that associations represented a generally successful first port of call for settling discords between members. In fact, associations strove to maintain order and harmony amongst their members while keeping possible quarrels internal, so that their outward image of trustworthy and well-ordered institutions would not be jeopardized. However, despite best efforts, sometimes things slipped off hands and official procedures (petitions and trials) in front of the authority were started: even in the cases of a fiasco of the group's harmony and of its mechanisms of internal dispute resolution, associations somehow often managed to make the best of the situation, by ultimately asserting their fundamental values of trust and good order.

INTRODUCTION

When someone received a wrong and wanted to obtain redress in Ptolemaic Egypt, they could address the official authorities with a petition or a complaint. The matter was dealt with and solved — in fortunate circumstances — by local officials, at the best of times, or brought to the higher courts (also in Alexandria), if necessary.[1] However,

---

* I am grateful to the organizers and participants of the conference *Two Sides of the Same Coin: Dispute Resolution in Greco-Roman Egypt*, where a preliminary version of this paper was given. The present study was conducted as part of the research activities of the Copenhagen Associations Project, generously funded by the Carlsberg Foundation. Associations are indicated with their CAPInv. #, as found in the *Database of Ancient Associations*: https://ancientassociations.ku.dk/.

[1] The standard work on legal practices in Hellenistic and Roman Egypt is still TAUBENSCHLAG 1955. For a more recent survey, see YIFTACH-FIRANKO 2009. On Ptolemaic

Ptolemaic officials and court judges were not the only agents of justice available: concomitant systems of informal jurisdiction were in fact in place; people probably referred to them (in addition and in conjunction with more formal legal methods) even more often than one may quantify.[2] It is on one of these informal systems that the present contribution focuses: the role of associations in Ptolemaic Egypt for dispute resolution amongst their members. I intend to assess (1) the reasons why private associations decided to implement such a practice; (2) the effectiveness of the procedures put into place by associations and by the same token the effectiveness of associations as agents of dispute resolution; (3) and finally, the role that associations played in local societies thanks to their self-invested position of "source of justice".[3]

1. Ancient associations and "good order"

The values cherished in associations of the ancient world — and to some extent even today — are various, but one above all was considered important: harmony or internal order, which in turn promoted respect and trust. The members of an association gathered because they liked to spend time with one another, because they shared interests, certain values, and agenda. They did so in an ordered manner and they got along nicely and in a friendly way. This is at least in theory and what the jargon

---

Egypt, the reference remains WOLLF 1970, see also MÉLÈZE-MODRZEJEWSKI 1995. For a treatment of the practicalities of petitions, dispute resolution, and general cases of violence in Roman times, see KELLY 2011 and BRYEN 2013; for late antique Egypt, see GAGOS & VAN MINNEN 1994.

[2] On private arbitration in Ptolemaic Egypt, see MÉLÈZE-MODRZEJEWSKI 1952; for private dispute resolution in Roman Egypt see KELLY 2011, p. 244-286 (with his critique of HOBSON 1993 and the remark of a fluid nature of the informal system, by which different formal methods, including petitioning, could be strategically used for private dispute resolution mechanisms).

[3] Bibliography on private associations in the ancient world is vast. For Egypt more specifically, see, for instance, BOAK 1937; SAN NICOLÒ 1972; DE CENIVAL 1972; MUSZYNSKI 1977; MUHS 2001; MONSON 2006; MIGLIARDI ZINGALE 2007; MONSON 2007; VENTICINQUE 2010; GIBBS 2011; GIBBS 2015; VENTICINQUE 2015; LANGELLOTTI 2016; VENTICINQUE 2016; PAGANINI 2017. Internal dispute resolution by associations is also commented on by MONSON 2006, p. 235-236; HAWKINS 2016, p. 118-120 and VENTICINQUE 2016, p. 58-60.

of some passages of association's documents would want us to believe. This is particularly true for the associations' charters: these texts were formally codified in various fashion on stone or on papyrus (in Ptolemaic Egypt, usually as contractual agreements) and regulated the different aspects of the organization and life of associations. Particular attention was of course devoted to financial matters and behaviors. The habit of producing regulations by associations seems to have been universal: not only have we evidence for it in the Greek and Roman worlds, but also in the local Egyptian practice (both in Demotic and in Greek), as well as from societies further afield, such as for instance China and India. This attests to the intrinsic desire — and pragmatic necessity — by associations to have a codified course of action and specific dispositions regarding certain aspects of their life, so that the smooth running of the association's affairs may be guaranteed.[4]

The regulations by associations surviving from Ptolemaic Egypt are mainly written in Demotic (only two regulations in Greek survive, one of them very fragmentary).[5] In Demotic regulations stress is laid on the unanimity of the decisions taken: all members agree in adopting the rules and appointing one of them as president; they will follow his instructions and are all happy to meet together and celebrate in common. In Greek decrees by associations from the Hellenistic world, we find similar expressions of communal understanding and agreement in the passing of decisions: the process is depicted as a smooth discussion with a unanimous vote, in which all members are of one mind and behave impeccably according to the virtue of "good order".

However, things were not as idyllic as they are portrayed. In the text of the regulations themselves, which convey the image of a harmonious group of well-behaved people with one goal and common sentiments, we find signs of the opposite. Punishment for misbehavior is contemplated and in fact codified in a detailed way, clearly showing that things did not always go down in friendly terms. Misconduct in the associations

---

[4] On ancient associations' regulations, see now the papers in GABRIELSEN & PAGANINI 2021.

[5] For the Demotic regulations of associations in Ptolemaic Egypt, the standard work is DE CENIVAL 1972. The only two Greek regulations from Ptolemaic Egypt are *P. Lond.* VII 2193 = *SB* V 7835 (TM 2462; 69-58 BC = CAPInv. 654) and *BGU* XIV 2371 (fragmentary; TM 3991 = CAPInv. 1514).

did in fact occur: whether such a thing was a rare occurrence or not, is hard to say. However, it certainly did happen and touched the heart of the values of the associations, which in fact reputed important to put a stop, punish, and by the same token discourage such behavior. The spectrum of misconduct contemplated in the Demotic regulations of associations, for instance, varies: we go from unruly or rude behavior at meetings and feasts to misconduct of a more moral nature, from shoving in front of somebody else at a banquet in order to get there before the porridge is cold to having a go at a fellow member's wife. There could be disobedience towards the president or his helpers or even violence against fellow members or against the officials of the association: blows, insults, and rows apparently occurred and were punished. Yet another kind of misbehavior was seriously frowned upon; this was in fact the kind that touched associations in one of their softest spots, namely their coffers: members could refuse to pay their annual dues, their contributions, or possible fines imposed on them because of breach of the rules. Such behavior was seriously punished, as it was detrimental to the association's (financial) survival.

Breach of the association's regulations was severely punished and a system of internal justice for such cases is also attested for associations in the Greek world. The late classical *Labyadai* in Delphi, for instance, had an internal court entrusted to some elected judges amongst the members to trial fellow members who had broken some of the association's regulations.[6] In the case of the association of the descendants of Diomedon on fourth/third-century BC Cos, the officials of the association gathered in assembly and passed judgment on those who dared change anything from the established rules.[7] Similarly, in the case of an unnamed association from Piraeus, those who broke the regulations could be sued by any member of the association and brought before the association as a whole, who would judge them and punish them.[8] In all the above-mentioned cases, the association's legal jurisdiction is clearly limited to association's affairs only and more specifically to the breach of the association's regulations by members.

---

[6] *CID* I 9 (TM 813793), C 3-19 (V-IV BC) = CAPInv. 1964.

[7] *IG* XII.4 348, 130-44 (CAPInv. 1919).

[8] *IG* II^2 1275, 14-17 (325-275 BC) = CAPInv. 266.

2. Associations' internal dispute resolution: a new channel for justice

In addition to breaking the association's rules, members could also have personal disagreements with other members, for whatever reasons. These might be deemed irrelevant to the association, since they involved single members in their "private" capacity. However, membership of an association was a whole-encompassing experience which often embraced larger aspects of one's life, beyond what one did in the association itself. In fact, in many associations' rules from Egypt provisions regulate what to do in case of disputes amongst the members. Associations in fact provided internal justice and internal tribunals to judge suits amongst members. Unlike their counterparts in the wider Hellenistic world, the associations of Ptolemaic Egypt seem to have had jurisdiction also on the private affairs of their members and not only on strictly communal matters and in case of breach of the association's regulations.

In fact, the custom by association's officials (or a chosen board of members) to judge disputes could recall the practice of local officials administering justice, the so-called *Beamtenjustiz*: local officials were petitioned and could investigate and judge various cases without referring them to judicial courts, solving disputes by the force of their authority.[9] Associations were thus potentially mirroring this tradition by local officials and perhaps took inspiration from it for their internal practices — the opposite is also theoretically possible: proof for either is absent. The *archontes* of the *politeuma* of the Jews of Heracleopolis, for instance, were called upon to judge private disputes (default in contracts and agreements, violence and abuse) amongst members of the *politeuma* and sometimes even between Jews seemingly non-members of the *politeuma*: they in fact are sometimes called *kritai*, "judges".[10] Furthermore, the *politarches*, head of the *politeuma*, and the (officials of the) *politeuma* seem to have decided about the detainment of prisoners and their release.[11] With the case of the Jewish *politeuma* of Heracleopolis we can see how a private association, gathering military men from Jewish background (and their families), over time acquired more importance and was

---

[9] Wolff 1970, p. 113-193.

[10] Cowey & Maresch 2001, esp. p. 10-18.

[11] *P. Polit. Iud.* 2 and 17 (TM 44618 and TM 44633) = CAPInv. 1370.

invested with a somewhat institutionalized public role and broader jurisdiction.[12]

Beyond issues concerning associational affairs proper (for instance, members' default in paying contributions or breach of regulations), associations in Ptolemaic Egypt also sought to solve members' disputes that went beyond matters strictly relevant to the associations themselves. The rhetoric employed by associations in this respect is interesting. We find explicit reference to the juridical role of associations in the Demotic regulations and the atmosphere evoked from the passages is worth noting.

> The man amongst us who will sue one of us before the military or civil authority or the police, without having first brought his plea in front of those of the house (= the association), his fine will be 50 *deben*. The man amongst us who will sue one of us in front of those of the house, if they judge his case and if he rejects (the decision) in order to appeal in front of the military or civil authority or the police, after judgement (*pꜣ hp*, lit. "law") has been passed for him, his fine will be 75 *deben*.[13]

This is just an example of a standard formula found in other Demotic regulations — and even in a fragmentary passage of a regulation in Greek.[14] Associations discouraged their members from suing other members in front of the authority: they should turn to the association itself instead, to solve their issues there. Moreover, members are expected to be satisfied with the decisions by the association and not to appeal to the civil authorities. Therefore, following the legal channels of justice is discouraged all round. This would hardly seem to us a legitimate practice and resembles more the behavior of illegal organizations rather than that of innocuous associations. Another passage from one of the Demotic regulations adds more information on the matter.

> The man amongst us who will sue one of us before the military authority or the police (?), without having first brought his plea in front of those of

[12] On *politeumata* of Egypt, see HONIGMAN 2003; THOMPSON 2011; SÄNGER 2014; KRUSE 2015; HONIGMAN 2016; SÄNGER 2019.

[13] *P. Assoc.* p. 83-91 = *P. Prague dem*, l. 17-18 (TM 2928) = CAPInv. 1690.

[14] Demotic: *P. Assoc.* p. 3-10, l. 22-5 (TM 2784 = CAPInv. 1689); *P. Assoc.* p. 45-51, l. 18-22 (TM 2775 = CAPInv. 1932); *P. Assoc.* p. 63-68, l. 20-21 (TM 3056 = CAPInv. 1932); *P. Assoc.* p. 73-78, l. 19-20 (TM 2774 = CAPInv. 1932); *P. Assoc.* p. 39-42, A l. 14-15 (fragmentary; TM 3055 = CAPInv. 1971); ARLT & MONSON 2010, l. 4 (TM 129749 = CAPInv. 1686); VITTMANN 2011 = *P. Mainz dem.* 10, l. 7 (TM 133259 = CAPInv. 1688). Greek: *BGU* XIV 2371 (fragmentary; TM 3991 = CAPInv. 1514).

> the house (= association), his fine will be 2 *kite*. The man amongst us who will sue one of us in front of those of the house (= association) and we will pass justice concerning the affair in question, and who will bring his plea in front of the military authority (?), his fine will be 2 *kite*. The man amongst us who will bring his plea in front of those of the house (= association) as per above and to whom justice will be passed and who will say: "Let the case be brought to the judgment (?) of another association, because it has happened that they have not done (?) me justice in this matter", if the judgement of the association in question is in agreement with that of the first association, his fine will be 4 *kite*.[15]

After the indication of the disincentives — if not real prohibition — to follow the established legal channels for justice, a new element is included: judicial collaboration among associations. A member could bring the case against another member to be judged by another association: however, such practice may potentially be detrimental, as a fine (double the amount than the fine for petitioning the authority) is exacted in case the second association passes the same judgment as the first. This procedure of appealing to a second association seems to be applicable only in case of dual membership: although it is possible to imagine that an association could judge a member of another association *pro bono*, as it were, it seems more likely that such a procedure was in place if the members in question belonged to both associations at the same time. This was in fact possible, although cases of dual or multiple membership are only few and often difficult to pinpoint in our evidence.[16]

The option of solving disputes internally might from one angle be interpreted as an advantage, as members would not need to spend money in legal procedures but could make use of their network in order to find a solution to their problems. However, associations did not limit

---

[15] *P. Assoc.* p. 3-10 = *P. Lille dem.* I 29, l. 22-5 (TM 2784 = CAPInv. 1689).

[16] Evidence for the practice may be found, for instance, at second-century BC Rhodes (*IG* XII.1 155 c IV + d I-III = CAPInv. 10, with GABRIELSEN 1994), in second-century BC Piraeus (*IG* II^2 1325 = CAPInv. 235 and *IG* II^{2}1327-8 = CAPInv. 361, with Skaltsa 2016) and at second-century AD Thessalonike (*SEG* 56: 765 (TM 961708) = CAPInv. 756 and CAPInv. 774). In the Greco-Roman world, funerary monuments in which an individual is honored by different associations may also point to membership in — and certainly patronage of — multiple associations: so far, we have no evidence of this kind from Egypt. Although a ban on leaving an association to join another is attested (for instance, the Ptolemaic association of Zeus *Hypsistos* (CAPInv. 654) of *P. Lond.* VII 2193, l. 14: TM 2462) prohibition of concomitant membership in more than one association is not.

themselves to that but forbade their members from following the legal paths of justice, to which they were entitled by right. Here again, the leading associative value of "good order" seems to play a major role: associations did not want to give outsiders the impression that they were formed by people who disagree, are unruly, and sue each other. Any disputes that might rise among members should be dealt with internally and anyone who does not comply should be punished: the image that the association wants to transmit to the local society and the outside world as a whole is one of harmony, reciprocal respect, and civil behavior of their members.[17]

3. Enforcing the system

After establishing directives on various matters, associations had to make sure that rules were respected and procedures followed. The ways in which associations strove to maintain the "good order" were various and are differently recorded in their documents and regulations. Monetary fines occupy a place of paramount importance and represent the principal enforcement method: for nearly every infraction to the rules or codes of conduct a fine is applicable and exacted by the president, styled as "leader" (*hegoumenos*) in Greek and "the representative of the house" (*pꜣ rt pꜣ ꜥ.wy*) in Demotic, or one of his assistants. Fines vary according to the gravity of the transgression and in case of iteration of the crime: through this (sometimes complex) system of fines, associations could levy a fair amount of funds. It is therefore hardly surprising that much emphasis is put on them in the associations' charters.

Physical coercion could also be used in some cases: reference to the practice is rare and not clear. In Demotic regulations, the "representative of the house" is entitled to force a member to comply with the rules or to pay up a fine, without specifying the actual method: some degree of physical force might be expected, alongside verbal persuasion.[18]

[17] See also Venticinque 2016, p. 58-59.

[18] *P. Assoc.* p. 93-97 and 227-229 (TM 2776 = CAPInv. 1970); *P. Assoc.* p. 59-61 and 219-220 (TM 3057 = CAPInv. 1932); *P. Assoc.* p. 83-91 and 225-227 (TM 2928 = CAPInv. 1690); *P. Assoc.* p. 63-68 and 221-222 (TM 3056 = CAPInv. 1932); *P. Assoc.* p. 73-78 and 222-225 (TM 2774 = CAPInv. 1932). Similarly, in case of default members the president of the *apolysimoi* from early Roman Tebtynis (CAPInv. 1409) has the "authority to seize

A fragmentary passage of one of the two Ptolemaic regulations written in Greek may also refer to physical punishment (flogging) for those members who abused verbally or physically other members.[19]

In the case of grave crimes, such as adultery with another member's wife or calumny (calling someone a leper), expulsion from the association is contemplated, together with a pecuniary fine.[20] The harshness of the punishment is no doubt linked to the fact that these two typologies of crime undermined the main value upon which associations lived and based themselves: trust. Members were expelled and excluded from social relations with the other members of the association. The fact basically represented social (and often economic) death.[21]

In the case of associations which were involved in ceremonies with animal gods (crocodiles and falcons), a curse is inflicted on members who fail to take part in specific ceremonies or in the funerary rites of the sacred animals.[22]

Though these are the only enforcement methods mentioned in our documents, others were no doubt put in place too: for instance, a good level of mediation and verbal persuasion must have been employed to settle disputes and unruly behavior, or to solve problems arising from refusal to pay fees or fines. Although they did not leave any trace in our documentation, these (time-consuming) methods were presumably frequently practiced in order to avoid more formal and more unpleasant procedures.

---

him in the main street, or in his house, and hand over him or his slaves" (*P. Mich.* V 244, l. 13-15; TM 12085).

[19] *BGU* XIV 2371, l. 6-7 (TM 3991 = CAPInv. 1514): λοιδορήματος ἢ | ῥαπίσματο[ς] ἢ ....[...]ατος [....] ῥάβδου πληγῆς β αντ[.].[..]ης.

[20] Adultery: *P. Assoc.* p. 3-10 (TM 2784 = CAPInv. 1689); *P. Assoc.* p. 83-91 (TM 2928 = CAPInv. 1690); *P. Assoc.* p. 63-68 (TM 3056 = CAPInv. 1932). Calumny: *P. Assoc.* p. 45-51 (TM 2775 = CAPInv. 1932). Plus a fragmentary passage of the regulations of the *choachytes* (*P. Assoc.* p. 103-131, text A par. 3 l. 14-5: TM 3058 = CAPInv. 1480).

[21] Standard work on the concept of "trust" and "trust networks", especially for their economic implications, is TILLY 2005. Related to it is the concept of "social capital", developed in sociology and institutional economics: see, for instance, COLEMAN 1988 and BURT 2005, with OGILVY 2004.

[22] *P. Assoc.* p. 59-61 (TM 3057 = CAPInv. 1932); *P. Assoc.* p. 63-68 (TM 3056 = CAP-Inv. 1932); *P. Assoc.* p. 73-78 (TM 2774 = CAPInv. 1932); *P. Assoc.* p. 3-10 (TM 2784 = CAPInv. 1689). The enlisting of supernatural powers for dispute resolution has also been object of attention by legal anthropologists: see for instance ROBERTS 1979, p. 63-65.

4. Effectiveness

It is difficult to say how effective the enforcement methods adopted by associations were. The fact that some crimes could be punished with expulsion and exclusion from the association must have worked as a powerful tool of prevention: losing one's face and being cut off from social life in what were often small and certainly tightly knit communities was something no-one could afford. It is on this concept that the association of Amon-Opet of the choachytes of Djeme counted in order to force everyone in the business to join: the members of the association would exclude from social interaction and from funerary ceremonies those choachytes (and the men of their families) who had been in service for some years without joining.[23] With such a prospect before them, it is likely that very few indeed would make the mistake of not complying.

However, what could be done if a member refused to pay? The president or his agents could try to persuade the wrongdoer to pay, processes of mediation could be put in place and even some physical force (or some kind of detention) could be used to convince the recalcitrant member to cooperate. However, if someone did not intend to obey, there was little that could be done to make them — unless, of course, a formal lawsuit, thing which associations apparently abhorred.

In this respect peer-pressure played a paramount role: members often complied with the rules or rectified their behavior for fear of shame in front of their fellow members and the people in their communities. Being a respected member of one's own local community was a big affair, both for social and economic reasons. In fact, in most cases we can suppose that people abided by the rules and respected their enforcement (more or less immediately) because they were expected by their peers to do so.[24]

The different ways in which rules were enforced, internal disputes avoided, solved, or punished and the degree of their effectiveness rest on four interconnected general values or areas of principle:

---

[23] *P. Assoc.* p. 103-131, text A par. 1 l. 2-4 (TM 3058 = CAPInv. 1480). On the choachytes, see Derda 1991, p. 23-26; Pestman 1993; Vleeming 1995.

[24] For a theoretical treatment of esteem and social recognition, including its economic implications, see for instance Brennan & Pettit 2004. For shaming practices in legal anthropology, see for instance Roberts 1979, p. 61-63.

1. *Contractual practice*. The regulations were agreements entered (more or less) voluntarily by the members; in the case of the Demotic regulations, they were indeed presented as contracts that bound together the members. On the basis of the legal force of such a contract, the members were obliged to respect the rules. Otherwise, sanctions typical for contractual default were exacted: fines.

2. *Social norms*. The members of an association had decided to be part of it and promised to comply with certain rules. Peer pressure and social obligations towards each other made sure that everyone felt that it was their duty to behave like the others. Feelings of belonging to a close-knit community contributed to the way in which rules were applied and enforced. In fact, exclusion from the association's networks, as in the case of grave crimes against fellow members and the group's trust (adultery and defamation), or temporary disfavor had serious consequences, which few were willing to face.

3. *Family values*. Beyond feelings of community there were also family values. The rhetoric discourse often employed by associations in fact recalled family bonds: the members were brothers and the whole community theoretically functioned like a family.[25] All their components worked and behaved to the good of the association/family. Besides, actual blood ties between the members made the sense of belonging to a family even stronger: fathers and sons could be members of the same association; in some cases, membership in the association itself was based on membership in specific families (e.g. the choachytes).[26] Examples of the same kind come from other areas of the Hellenistic world and attest a common practice.[27]

---

[25] See also VENTICINQUE 2010.

[26] Some of the *technitai* of Dionysus of the *polis* of Ptolemais in Upper Egypt, for instance, were relatives (CAPInv. 115: *I. Prose* 3 and 6 = TM 6374 and TM 6375), as so were some of the members of the *koinon ton ktiston* of Memphis (CAPInv. 181: *SB* I 681 = TM 6572).

[27] For instance, different family members belonged to the same association in: the *Poseidoniastai* on Delos (CAPInv. 9: *I. Délos* 1520 (TM 768941) and 1772-1796 (TM 769154-769178)); the *Dionysiastai* of Piraeus (CAPInv. 235: *IG* II^2 1325-1326); the *koinon ton symporeuomenon para Dia Hyetion* of Cos (CAPInv. 1879: *IG* XII 4.1 121); the *basilistai* of Lycian Limyra (CAPInv. 1657: WÖRRLE 2015); the *therapeutai tou theou* of Maroneia in Thrace (CAPInv. 739: *I. Thrac. Aeg.* E182-183, E212). Some associations were founded with the specific purpose of gathering members of one family only: for instance, the

4. *Religious values*. Religion occupied an important role in the life and dealings of ancient associations. In some cases, oaths were taken as promise of fulfillment of the regulations; however, no examples of this come from Egypt; as seen before, curses were employed in special cases for those who jeopardized the religious life and trustworthiness of the association.[28] However, even without the necessity of spelling out possible religious consequences in case of misbehavior by members, the fact that associations often undertook religious ceremonies as "private communities", in which each member had a position of importance towards the divinity, probably made members want to comply in order to avoid possible disadvantages of not taking part in those ceremonies.

5. Faulty internal dispute resolution mechanisms?

The regulations of associations in Ptolemaic Egypt give us details of the rules and their enforcement but do not tell us how internal disputes were actually dealt with — besides the obligation to deal with them internally — nor do they provide evidence for their actual occurrence. With one exception. In Heracleopolis we have petitions addressed to the officials of the *politeuma*, who judged private disputes between members of the *politeuma* as well as Jews not belonging to the *politeuma*. These disputes mainly concerned default in contracts and agreements, violence and abuse. In one case only, the prerogatives of the *politeuma* seem to go beyond minor private business: the *archontes* of the *politeuma* had delegated the inquiry over the death of a *paidarion* (child or slave) in a neighboring village to the elders (*kritai*) of the Jewish community of the same village. The elders' job was to decide about the circumstances of the death (accident or murder with possible further legal implications) and produce a verdict (*synkrisis* l. 11, or *hypographe* l. 15, 23) on the matter.[29] However, the affair remains unclear as we do not know all the details of the case. At all events, given the peculiar developments in

koinon of the relatives of Epikteta on Thera (CAPInv. 1645: *IG* XII.3 330 + *IG* XII Suppl. 154, with Wittenburg 1990).

[28] An oath by admittance is required in the association set up by Dionysios at Philadelpheia in Lydia (CAPInv. 348: *TAM* V.3 1539 (TM 877512)).

[29] *P. Polit. Iud.* 6 (TM 44622 = CAPInv. 1370).

the public nature of the competences of this communal body, the case of the *politeuma* of the Jews represents an exceptional instance in the world of ancient associations. In fact, for the "normal" private associations of Egypt we know basically nothing of the practicalities in case of internal disputes beyond what is indicated in the rules, viz. that they should be sorted out internally. Paradoxically, the only actual evidence of internal disputes, disagreements, or non-compliance with the rules is a testimony to the failure of the system of internal dispute resolution by associations, when, against the association's wishes and dispositions, internal cases were brought before the public authority.

Two third-century BC petitions to the King were filed by relatives of two deceased members of two associations — one in Alexandrou Nesos, the other in Kerkethoeris, both villages of the Arsinoite nome — who had been promised a funerary indemnity (*taphikon*) as part of the "package" for their membership in the association.[30] Despite what promised, upon the death of these two people the associations did not pay:[31] in one case the sister and in the other case the sister and husband of the deceased members petitioned the authority in order to seek justice. Presumably, they had approached the associations first in order to have the issue solved internally and informally; since this led nowhere, they turned to official legal channels. Now, the texts do not state that the petitioners were also members of the said associations — this seems unlikely, and even impossible in the case of one of them, namely the husband of one of the diseased members, as his wife belonged to a women-only association. Therefore, as the petitioners were not members of the associations, they did not have to abide by the association's regulations, which in all likelihood discouraged petitioning the authority: thus, the filing of the *enteuxeis* was not in breach of association's regulations but was probably the only (effective) way for the petitioners to obtain what they were entitled to.

Completely different is the case of the *nekrotaphoi* as recorded in a first-century BC judicial proceedings and sentence of the *chrematistai*.[32]

---

[30] *P. Enteux.* 20 and 21 (TM 2981 and TM 3296), respectively.

[31] *P. Enteux.* 20 clearly states that the association had not behaved κα]τὰ [τὸν θιασι]τικὸν νόμον (l. 5), "according to the *thiasos*'s regulations".

[32] On *nekrotaphoi*, see DERDA 1991, p. 26-31 (on p. 28 read 67 BC instead of 57 BC for the date of the text) and UYTTERHOEVEN 2009, esp. p. 330-394 (for Hawara specifically).

> ... all the grave-diggers belonging to the association (οἱ ἐκ τοῦ ἔθνους νεκροτ̣[άφοι) had made an Egyptian contract (Αἰγυπτία συγγραφή), registered in the 19th year, Phamenoth 9, through the record-office of the same city, concerning the division among them of the shares agreed upon, whereby it was provided that any person breaking the agreement or claiming the shares assigned to each should be compelled to pay to the association a fine of ... of copper and the same sum to the Treasury. These and other provisions being contained in the contract, and the petition declaring that Petosiris, Paris, and their supporters, taking no heed whatever of the fixed rules, carried off a number of corpses from them, the details of which will appear in the forthcoming inquiry, they asked that the accused should be ordered to be brought forward and compelled perforce to pay to them the fine fixed as well as the other sums due to the Treasury, and that they should receive also the proper penalty. In these circumstances, Petosiris and the others ... we, seeing (?) that the accused have deserted and are entirely triumphant (?), but those who brought the accusation are still further distracted by their opponents through a long-continued injury, have jointly decided that the provisions of the Egyptian contracts voluntarily made by the parties, and the other rules thereby fixed, shall remain as they are, valid and inviolate. Read: the 14th year, Mecheir 24.[33]

The association of *nekrotaphoi* had signed a Demotic contract, which represented the group's regulations. The document regulated the division of shares of each member in the business of the burial of corpses which had been agreed upon by the members themselves and was registered in the local *grapheion* — probably that of Oxyrhynchus — on 9 Phamenoth of the 19th year of an unmentioned sovereign (probably Ptolemy X Alexander I and Cleopatra Berenice: 23 March 95 BC).[34] Some members did not abide by the shares agreed and refused to pay the relevant fines. Therefore, almost thirty years after the registration of the contract/regulations, on 24 Mecheir of the 14th year of another unmentioned ruler (Ptolemy XII Auletes: 1 March 67 BC), the *ethnos* wrote a petition to the authorities to ask for justice and started a lawsuit against its defaulting members. This goes against the principles clearly stated in the surviving

---

33 *P. Ryl.* II 65; tr. *ed. pr.* (TM 5284).

34 This is similar to what the salt merchants of Tebtynis (CAPInv. 1658) did a little over than a century later, in AD 47: *P. Mich.* V 245 (TM 12086). However, their regulations with dispositions about the sale of salt and gypsum were written in Greek. GABRIELSEN 2016, p. 92-95 argues that the salt merchants were not an association but a business partnership and the document they drew up was not the association's regulations but a business contract.

Demotic regulations, that as we have seen wanted to keep affairs internal at all costs. The fact that the *ethnos* had to petition the authority shows how difficult internal enforcement of the regulations sometimes was: the *nekrotaphoi* spent many years trying to convince the defaulting members to obey and pay their dues (some probably even died in the meantime and were perhaps succeeded by their children), albeit unsuccessfully. As the judicial decision of the *chrematistai* states, the *nekrotaphoi* who petitioned the authority had been vexed by their unruly fellow members for a long period of time. Distressed and unable to force their members to comply, the *nekrotaphoi* had to resort to the official legal channels to obtain justice. The system of the association's internal dispute resolution and rule enforcement had miserably failed.[35]

Another matter regarding money was the reason why an association of soldiers of the Royal Guard in first-century BC Heracleopolite sent a petition to the *grammateus ton dynameon*, the secretary of the troops or quartermaster general of the whole army.[36] Despite the fragmentary state of the papyrus, it appears that some money was due to the association by a soldier, Isidoros son of Isidoros, in service at Alexandria but registered for payment in the Heracleopolite nome. The money had not been returned to the association and a petition was therefore sent in order to request that what was due to the association be withheld from Isidoros's pay towards the debt's extinction. Although this is likely, there is no evidence that the debtor was member of the association: associations could in fact lend money to members and non-members alike. If Isidoros was not a member, petitioning the authorities was not in breach of any associational code of conduct; on the other hand, if Isidoros was indeed

[35] Another example of failure of internal resolution by Ptolemaic associations could be *P. Dryton* 31 (TM 286) = CAPInv. 672: however, incomplete details are preserved to allow any firm conclusions regarding a possible dispute between Dryton and an alleged *synodos*. A parallel case to that of the *nekrotaphoi* in Roman times could be *I. Alex. Imp.* 24 = *I. Prose* 61 (TM 104030 = CAPInv. 1492) from AD 120: copy of a decision of the *Idios Logos* regarding the right to guardianship of tombs, which pertained to the *politeuma* of the Lycians, who went to the authority to seek justice. However, in this case, the problem could not be dealt with internally, as it stemmed from a minor local official (the secretary of the *komogrammateus*). For later times, *P. Oxy.* XVI 1943 (TM 35610) from late fifth-century AD Oxyrhynchus records a suit brought by the association of tow workers against one of their members: see also VENTICINQUE 2016, p. 90-92.

[36] *BGU* IV 1190 (TM 4525) = CAPInv. 302. On the *grammateus ton dynameon*, see MOOREN 1975, no. 0231.

a member, we would have a similar case as for the *nekrotaphoi*: the association had failed to obtain what was due using the other methods and resorted to enlisting the help of a third party (the petition might have also had the simple effect of persuading Isidoros to pay). This association of soldiers was well integrated with a position of influence into the system of the Ptolemaic army hierarchy, as they felt able to obtain that the army officials diverted Isidoros's salary into their own private coffer. One may also suppose that this association was not just a group of some soldiers who gathered for various socio-economic and recreational purposes, but represented a constituent and structured part of the army itself, more or less corresponding to the unit(s) in which the soldiers were serving. More precision on the matter is impossible to achieve, given the fragmentary state of the text.[37]

Although this was against the associations' ideals and represented an occasion for uncovering the ineffectiveness of the associations' enforcement mechanisms, suing the defaulting members also constituted one way by associations to reassert their authority (although via the state legal system) against unruly elements. This had a double consequence: (1) it worked as a warning against other members who might have thought to get away with insubordination and disrespect; and (2) it provided an example to all outsiders that misconduct was not tolerated and disrespectful and untrustworthy people were not harbored within the association.[38] Thus, in spite of the risk of a provisional detriment of the association's image, its values relating to its good name and good order could be ultimately upheld.

Despite the incomplete nature of our evidence, the fact that we only have few attested cases of failure of internal dispute resolution may suggest that in most cases associations managed to solve their disagreements internally and to obtain the respect of their rules by the members. Their enforcement methods, leaning on the four above-mentioned values of contractual practice, social norms, family values, and religion, were probably generally effective, though this cannot be quantified.

[37] On the Ptolemaic army, see FISCHER-BOVET 2014.

[38] On this, also VENTICINQUE 2016, p. 90-92.

6. Social role of associations as sources of justice

What is certain is that associations carved out an important role for themselves in local society. Presenting themselves as respectable and respected institutions, regulated by codified norms and displaying good order in their affairs, associations represented sources of justice for their members. In a socio-political set-up where the usual course of justice could be expensive, long, uncertain, and often perceived as distant, the readiness and potential availability of justice through membership in an association was an important feature for the self-image of associations and a reassurance for their members — at least in theory. This fact may have constituted a further incentive to join a club: in case of quarrels one could hope for a quick and inexpensive solution.[39]

But what was the reaction of the state in front of private institutions presenting themselves as agents for dispute resolution — even more than that, discouraging their members from following the official paths of justice? As in many other cases, the Ptolemaic administration adopted a *laissez faire* attitude. Just as in many petitions, local officials delegated their subordinates to solve the issues themselves in an informal way, thus trying to avoid clogging the over-burdened courts of justice, similarly the state did not mind that associations acted as informal agents of dispute resolution, easing the Ptolemaic administration of the weight of unnecessary legal proceedings.

Conclusion

In conclusion, private associations implemented various practices for internal dispute resolution and even expected their members to renounce their right to seek legal justice in front of the authority for quarrels with fellow members. Associations wanted to "wash their dirty linen" in private: it was of paramount importance for them to build a good reputation and give to outsiders an image of themselves as communities characterized by good order, friendly behavior, and mutual respect. By the same token, their members were being presented as decent, good-natured,

[39] For the vicissitudes of legal control in Roman Egypt (which were similar to those of the Ptolemaic administration), see Kelly 2011, p. 75-122.

upright, and trustworthy people. This increased the association's potential and prestige with positive repercussions for prospective membership and contributed to the creation of a respectable profile in local society, which brought with it social and economic advantages for the association as a group and for the single members as individuals. Although some exceptions occurred, most of the time the procedures put into place by associations to ensure the respect and enforcement of their rules were generally effective: members abided by them, prompted to do so by concomitant values of contractual practice, social norms, family values, and religion. In addition to this, by refraining from suing fellow members in front of the authority and by seeking justice within the association, members put a great deal of trust in the association's ability to provide a more informal, speedier, less expensive, and ultimately more satisfactory solution to their troubles. In this respect, associations proved their general success as "sources of justice": by doing so, they carved for themselves a role of distinguished, respected, and reliable institutions in local societies, while at the same time potentially easing the overloaded state channels for justice. Associations' members understood the advantage of such practices and were generally satisfied with the methods adopted and the values fostered by associations: they reaped various advantages from the profile that associations enjoyed in local society, also thanks to the implementation of mechanisms for dispute resolution. For this reason, people continued to gather in association and pay their dues: this guaranteed the success and the survival of associations.

Thanks to the evidence provided by private associations in Ptolemaic Egypt we are able to catch a glimpse of an area of dispute resolution processes that is most of the time invisible but was probably adopted far more often than we may be willing to concede or able to quantify. Rather than following only the established legal paths, which could be uncertain and aloof, people tried to solve private disputes informally, in associations, often orally, by exploiting their networks and by hinging on their sense of belonging to a group and the reciprocal social pressure that this brought with it.[40]

[40] On how formal legal procedures (i.e. petitions) were often strategically used to ease private dispute resolution in Roman Egypt, see KELLY 2011, p. 244-286. A similar phenomenon may in fact be supposed for Ptolemaic times too.

ROMAN AND LATE ANTIQUE EGYPT

ACCESSING JUSTICE IN ROMAN EGYPT: QUANTITATIVE METHODS AND THEIR LIMITATIONS*

Benjamin KELLY
(York University)

Abstract: This chapter concerns the promises and pitfalls of using quantitative methods to understand the overall numbers and demographic features of those seeking to access justice in Roman Egypt. It focuses on three case studies: (i) *P. Yale* I 61, which shows the prefect receiving 1,804 petitions during a *conventus* stop; (ii) the differing distribution of case-types in petitions and reports of proceedings, which has been taken to show that people complaining about minor, "criminal" disputes failed to access the courts; and (iii) the onomastic patterns amongst petitioners and plaintiffs. It is stressed that statistics need to be contextualized to be meaningful and that attention must be paid to the diverse factors that caused the preservation of different genres of documentary papyri. It is argued that onomastic patterns can be profitably studied, and that these patterns suggest that the greater the wealth and economic engagement of a group, the more likely its members were to attempt to access justice.

INTRODUCTION

Just over fifty years ago, John M. Kelly published a book entitled *Roman Litigation*.[1] In it, he attempted something quite revolutionary by the standards of mid-twentieth century Roman law scholarship: to imagine the processes of Roman litigation from a social history perspective. The picture he painted was bleak: one of poorer litigants constantly frustrated in their quest for justice, especially if their opponents were richer or more powerful. The appearance of Kelly's book prompted a brief

* I am very grateful to the participants at the Leuven conference for their feedback on this paper, and to the Editors and anonymous reviewer of this volume for their astute comments. I am also greatly indebted to Cornelius CHRISTIAN for his kind assistance with statistical methods and calculations. Carly MURDOCH served as research assistant on the project, with her customary precision and efficiency.

[1] KELLY 1966.

and constructive debate, with an especially important contribution from Peter Garnsey.[2]

After this, however, the discussion of access to justice in the Roman empire mostly fell silent, at least as far as the Republic and High Empire were concerned.[3] Since then, the only real advances in understanding the social profile of litigants have come from studies of imperial rescripts, but these necessarily concentrate on the third century and later.[4] The situation in Roman studies can be contrasted with the advances in recent decades in the understanding of early modern European legal cultures.[5] For this later period, there has been extensive discussion of a range of access to justice issues: the overall number of people who engaged in litigation; the social, economic, gender, and ethnic profiles of litigants; the economic and ideological barriers that limited some groups' access; and the different quality of justice received by people of different levels.

With the exception of Serena Connolly's discussion of the rescripts issued by Diocletian as he traveled through the provinces of the lower Danube in AD 293-294, a specifically *provincial* perspective has been lacking in discussions of access to justice in the Roman world. As is often the case, Egypt would seem to be the most promising area of the Empire in which to study the accessibility of the justice process at a provincial level, since the papyri allow us to see in great detail people actually engaging with the organs of adjudication provided by the state. Such a study will not necessarily confirm or invalidate the existing picture of the accessibility of justice at the center of the empire; it will, however, at least bring the peripheries into the discussion, and potentially highlight regional variation.

We face, however, the difficult question of how best to exploit the promising mass of Egyptian documentation. It would clearly be unsound to try to sift through the papyri to find individual cases of demonstrably low-status individuals obtaining (or not obtaining) access to the courts and being heard (un)fairly by them: isolated cases are potentially

---

[2] GARNSEY 1970, p. 181-218. See too CROOK & STONE 1967; FREDERIKSEN 1967.

[3] For a general survey of the question of access to justice in the Roman empire, see KELLY 2021.

[4] HUCHTHAUSEN 1973; 1974; 1976; 1992; CORCORAN 1996, p. 96-114; CONNOLLY 2010, p. 67-83.

[5] For a very useful survey of the literature on access to justice in early modern Europe, see VERMEESCH 2015a.

unrepresentative, and one can produce anecdotes that seem to give diametrically opposed pictures of how welcoming the system really was for the marginalized.[6] Slightly more promising is the use of personal and family archives containing petitions and reports of proceedings to build up a picture of the social level of people who approached the justice system, and this has been attempted elsewhere.[7] But there is still the lingering suspicion that the petitioners and litigants attested in archives are not representative of petitioners and litigants in general, since wealthier individuals with complex financial affairs and property ownership were perhaps more likely to generate personal or family archives. Another productive approach would be to make inferences from the structural features of the institutions of dispute resolution in Roman Egypt about its accessibility, as Katelijn Vandorpe does in this volume for the Ptolemaic period.[8]

But the Holy Grail in the study of access to justice in the Roman period is surely to find a sound way to exploit the petitions and reports of proceedings to come up with useable statistical data. Statistical methods are at the heart of studies on accessibility conducted by legal

[6] Thus, for example, in *P. Mil. Vogl.* I 25.i.4-iv.17 (TM 12345), a report of proceedings, we find a freedman suing over a debt allegedly owed to him by his deceased master. In spite of the defense advocate's somewhat snobbish comments about the plaintiff's low origins, the *strategos* hearing the case gives the freedman fairly even-handed treatment. On the other hand, in *Chrest. Mitt.* 81 = *P. Oxy.* IV 706 (TM 20406), another freedman is involved in litigation with his former master before the prefect, who not only rules against the freedman, but also threatens him with a beating if he challenges his patron again. In *Chrest. Mitt.* 91 = *BGU* II 388 (TM 20156), one also finds freedmen who claim to have been manumitted by a deceased master being treated with clear suspicion by the procurator of the *idios logos*.

[7] Kelly 2011, p. 126-143.

[8] See now the study by Haensch 2015 on the costs of accessing the courts during the Principate, a structural issue that has obvious relevance to the accessibility of justice in Egypt. Such a "structural" approach for the Roman period has been attempted in relation to one access to justice issue, namely the efficiency with which cases were processed between the initial petition and a final adjudication, and the potential for them to drop out of the system (Kelly 2011, p. 75-122). The suggestion that statistical data somehow contradicts the results of this "structural" approach is unconvincing (cf. Ruffini 2013, p. 604). This data relates to nineteen cases scattered over three centuries in which we can calculate the speed with which petitions were processed by their recipients, a sample that is too small to be meaningful. In any case, the processing of a petition was only one step in a multi-stage process, and the speed of that stage is not evidence for what happened at later stages.

historians of more recent societies, and those of contemporary legal sociologists. Can a social historian of Roman Egypt likewise hope to employ such methods? To explore this question, this paper concentrates on three case studies. Firstly, I shall look at whether we have meaningful data about the proportion of the population that petitioned the authorities for assistance in their disputes in any given year. Secondly, I shall examine the question of whether one can see a quantifiable tendency for more minor disputes to be diverted out of the formal justice system, leading to a kind of two-tiered state dispute resolution regime. And thirdly, I shall consider at greater length the onomastics of petitioners, and what this might or might not tell us about their cultural or social profile. I say quite frankly that there are going to be dead ends ahead, but the process of clarifying which avenues are fruitless is an important methodological exercise, and one with broader implications. The journey is often as important as the destination.

1. The rate of petitioning

One of the most fundamental access to justice questions for any legal system is just how often people brought their disputes before state adjudicators. For early modern Europe, there are sufficient records for some jurisdictions to track litigation rates, and even see how these changed with time. This has led to the interesting finding that in many European jurisdictions, there was a decline in the overall volume of litigation between the mid-seventeenth and mid-eighteenth centuries, and that litigation did not return to seventeenth-century levels until the Industrial Revolution greatly increased economic activity. A major cause of the so-called 'great litigation decline' in the eighteenth century is believed to have been the escalating expense of the courts, which was partly the consequence of the increased professionalization of the law.[9]

The barriers to conducting a similar analysis for Roman Egypt are formidable.[10] One cannot simply count up the number of surviving

[9] For literature on the "great litigation decline", see VERMEESCH 2015b, p. 221.

[10] So too for the Roman emperor and the legal petitions with which he had to deal. It is clear from the surviving law codes and documentary sources, as well as from anecdotes in the literary sources, that he received and responded to many petitions, and that this

petitions and reports of proceedings and analyze them chronologically. Any numbers produced in this way would in part reflect the patterns of survival for the papyri containing such documents, rather than the prevalence of petitioning and litigation with time. There is, however, the famous *P.Yale* I 61, an early third-century declaration from the *strategos* of the Arsinoite nome that mentions that during the recent *conventus* stop in the nome metropolis, the prefect of Egypt had received 1,804 petitions in a little over two days.

> Sarapion, also known as Apollonianos, *strategos* of the Themistos and Polemon divisions of the Arsinoite. The most illustrious prefect, Subatianus Aquila, in accordance with his foresight in regard to all things, ordered that the petitions submitted to him in the Arsinoite on the 26th and 27th and part of the 28th of the month of Phamenoth, numbering 1,804, having been publicly displayed also in Alexandria for a sufficient number of days should also be displayed locally for three full days and be made clear to the people in the nome so that those who wish can copy down what pertains to them. It is announced, therefore, to those in each village that if someone has submitted a petition, he may come up to the metropolis and make an extract. I have signed it. [..] year of L. Septimius Severus Pius Pertinax and M. Aurelius Antoninus Pius Augustus and P. Septimius Geta Caesar Augustus, Pachon 27.[11]

The number 1,804 is usually mentioned with hushed awe by papyrologists,[12] and the text is indeed important for understanding the

---

was a crucial mechanism of communication between the emperor and his subjects. We cannot, however, quantify the scale of the phenomenon. On the quantity of petitions with which the emperor had to deal, see MILLAR 1992, esp. p. 6, 11, 244-245.

[11] *P. Yale* I 61 (TM 13738), cf. *BL* VI, p. 204, VII, p. 282, VIII, p. 514: [Σ]ạραπίων ὁ καὶ Ἀπολλων(ιανὸς) στρ(ατηγὸς) Ἀρσι(νοίτου) Θεμ(ίστου) καὶ Πολ(έμωνος) μερίδων. (hand 2) [ὁ λαμπ]ρ̣ότατος ἡγέμων Σουβατιανὸς [Ἀκύλας] κατὰ τὴν εἰς πάντα αὐτοῦ πρόνοιαν ẹ̓κέλευσεν τὰ ἐπιδοθέντα αὐτῷ βιβλίδια \`ἐν Ἀρσ̣ινοί(τῃ)´ τῇ κς καὶ κζ καὶ μέρει τῆς κη τοῦ Φαμενὼθ μηνὸς ἀριθμῷ Αωδ προτεθέντα καὶ ἐν Ἀλεξανδρίᾳ αὐτακερσιν (l. αὐταρκέσιν) ἡμέραις καὶ ἐπὶ τόπ⟦οισ⟧\`ων´ προτεθῆναι ὁλογλήροις (l. ὁλοκλήροις) ἡμέρας (l. ἡμέραις) τρισὶν καὶ δηλωθῆναι τοῖς ἐν τῷ νομῷ ἵνα οἱ βουλούμενοι (l. βουλόμενοι) τὰ διαφέροντα ἑαυτοῖς ἐκλαβῖν (l. ἐκλαβεῖν) δύν⟦ον⟧\`ων´ται. παραγγέλλενται (l. παραγγέλλεται) οὖν τοῖς κατὰ κώμην ὅπως εἰ τυγχάνῃ τις ἐπιδοὺς βιβλίδια \`ἀν´ελθὼν εἰς τὴν μητρόπολιν τὴν ἔκλεμψιν (l. ἔκληψιν) ποιήσ⟦ον⟧\`η´ται. σεσημ(είωμαι). (hand 3) (ἔτους) [..] Λο̣υ̣[κίο]υ̣ Σ̣ε̣π̣τ̣ι̣μίου Σεουήρου Εὐσεβοῦς Περτίνακος [καὶ] Μάρκ̣[ο]υ̣ Α̣ὐ̣[ρ]ηλίου Ἀντω̣νίνου Εὐσεβοῦς Σεβαστῶν κ̣α̣ὶ̣ Π̣ουβλίου Σεπτιμίου Γέτα Καίσαρος Σεβαστοῦ Πάχωνς κζ.

[12] See, for example, LEWIS 1981, p. 121; BRYEN 2013, p. 19. The process need not have been as time-consuming for petitioners as Lewis imagines if the prefect allowed petitions

ways in which petitions were processed by the prefect in this period. But can the number 1,804 be transformed into something that is meaningful for our understanding of the social realities of dispute resolution?

One scholar has recently attempted to make meaning out of this number with an ingenious piece of statistical modeling.[13] His procedure is to contextualize this figure of 1,804 against population figures, taking 44,000 as the notional population of Arsinoe, and 100,000 for the population of the Arsinoite nome. He then divides these figures by 1,804, giving a range of 1 petition to every 22 heads of population to 1 petition to every 55. These numbers are still too high, he suggests, since one has to eliminate all the women and children, something he achieves by dividing his numbers by three, which produces ratios of 1 petition to every 7 men, or 1 petition to every 18. This numerical modeling, he suggests, points to "a very high rate of petitioning indeed".[14]

Such numerical modeling is now an established feature of ancient demographic and economic history, and certainly can be useful, provided that one realizes that it does not generate real numbers, but simply permits us to glimpse the limits of the possible or rough orders of magnitude.[15] But such thought experiments are only as good as their starting premises; if the starting premises are faulty or unstable, then they do not let us glimpse anything useful at all.

In the case of *P. Yale* I 61, the population totals chosen to contextualize the figure of 1,804 petitions can and probably should be revised; the result is a radically different set of parameters for understanding this statistic. The choice of the putative population of Arsinoe — 44,000 — as the minimum dividend is apparently based on an assumption that it was possibly only people living in the metropolis who presented petitions to the prefect during the *conventus*. This was, however, clearly not the case. Indeed, the very text of the document makes it obvious that the prefect had received petitions from villagers. This is in line with what we know of petitions to the prefect generally: of the Roman-era petitions

to be simply deposited in a box, as the Ptolemaic *chrematistai* did (cf. *P. Tor. Choach.* 12.ii.6 = *UPZ* II 162 [TM 3563]). We lack hard data on just what the physical act of submitting a petition entailed in the Roman period.

[13] RUFFINI 2013, p. 610-611.

[14] RUFFINI 2013, p. 611.

[15] This is RUFFINI's stated aim: "to get a sense of the possible range of answers, at least within orders of magnitude." RUFFINI 2013, p. 610.

that can be confidently be assigned to a village or a metropolis, there are 44 petitions addressed to the prefect involving disputes; 27 are from villagers and 18 from inhabitants of metropoleis. Some villagers were therefore clearly willing and able to travel to *conventus* centers or even Alexandria to submit petitions to the prefect.

Moreover, the putative population of the nome — 100,000 — is potentially invalid as the maximum dividend, since it seems to be based on the assumption that the catchment area for the *conventus* stop at Arsinoe was confined to the Arsinoite nome. This might be justified if the prefect stopped at every one of the forty or so nome capitals, yet this does not seem to have been the case.[16] In his fundamental article on the organization of the *conventus* in Egypt, Rudolf Haensch marshaled evidence for ten stops, although not all of these were necessarily annual.[17] Thus, one could suggest that to find the "catchment" for an average *conventus* city, one should divide the population of Egypt by eleven (ten *conventus* centers, plus Alexandria). Here, of course, we run against the problem that we really do not know the population of the country in the Roman period. We can choose from Diodorus' 3 million, Josephus' 7.5 million (excluding Alexandria), or the various estimates of modern scholars, which go as high as 9 million.[18] Thus, if we use eleven as our divisor, the catchment of an average *conventus* stop could be anything between 272,727 and 818,181 people. Divided by 1,804, this would give us a rate between 1 petition per 151 heads of population and 1 per 454 — over eight times the higher number offered by the previous estimate.

Now, if this kind of mathematical thought experiment were to have any sort of value, we would then need to contextualize these hypothetical numbers: just what is a high rate of litigation?[19] Here we need to use comparative data, since there is nothing serviceable from the Roman

[16] Cf. *P. Oxy.* XXII 2342 (TM 22214), where a note on the papyrus indicates that the petitioner, an inhabitant of Oxyrhynchus, submitted the petition to the prefect in Ko in the Herakleopolite nome — or at least planned to do so, since the text is apparently a draft.

[17] HAENSCH 1997, p. 325-329.

[18] Diod. Sic. 1.31.6-9 (ca. 59 BC); Joseph, *BJ* 2.385. For modern literature on the size of the Egyptian population, see SCHEIDEL 2001, p. 57-59.

[19] RUFFINI's solution here is too rooted in a particular time, place, and culture: "we can only think of our own experiences — how many of our friends and family have recently been involved in lawsuits" (2013, p. 611).

empire. There is some such data from early modern societies, and a good deal from modern societies. Legal sociologists typically use the metric of lawsuits per head of population, without trying to confine their analysis to groups that were more likely to sue. A comparative exercise should absolutely not just use the putative number of men in Roman Egypt as the population group. Women and children could and did petition and litigate in this society; they did so at lower rates than adult males, but the same was true of almost all other premodern societies, and is probably true of many modern ones as well.

In Tables 1 and 2 I have collected a range of comparative data. The aim here is simply to sketch something of the range of different litigation rates that scholars have calculated; it would be virtually impossible to present a "representative" or "systematic" collection of historical or contemporary litigation rates. The statistics for modern countries refer to lawsuits commenced in a particular year in all of that country's courts combined. On the other hand, the early modern statistics refer to the cases commenced in a single court, and there were generally other judicial options, since overlapping jurisdictions were a feature of the early modern European legal order. In this regard, these early modern jurisdictions are somewhat more analogous to Roman Egypt, where the same category of dispute could be taken to several different officials, with the prefect being just one of these – albeit the one who was the source of formal jurisdiction.

Table 1: Litigation rates in early modern societies

JURISDICTION	PERIOD	HEADS OF POPULATION PER CASE PER YEAR
Castile, Royal Chancillería of Valladolid (appellate cases only)[20]	16th century	571-666
Bremen, Germany (civil cases only)[21]	1550-1780	23-130
Accomack County, Virginia[22]	1639	4

[20] KAGAN 1981, p. 16-17.
[21] WOLLSCHLÄGER 1990, p. 268.
[22] GALANTER 1983, p. 41.

Westminster, England, Courts of Common Pleas and King's Bench (civil cases; advanced stage only)[23]	1640	89
Leiden, tribunal of the Peacemakers (Vredemakers)[24]	1664-68	10
King's Lynn, England (civil cases only)[25]	1683-86	5
Leiden, tribunal of the Peacemakers (Vredemakers)[26]	1750	50

Table 2: Civil litigation rates in modern societies[27]

JURISDICTION	PERIOD	HEADS OF POPULATION PER CASE PER YEAR
Belgium	1969	36
Canada	1981-82	21
Chile	1957	40
Chile	1970	80
Columbia	1955	73
Columbia	1969	100
Costa Rica	1945	88
Costa Rica	1977	31
Denmark	1970	24
England and Wales	1973	24
France	1975	33
Italy	1973	100
Japan	1978	83
Netherlands	1970	125
New Zealand	1978	19
Norway	1976	50
Spain	1970	333
Sweden	1973	29

[23] MULDREW 1993, p. 30.

[24] VAN MEETEREN 2006, p. 19, 227.

[25] MULDREW 1993, p. 30.

[26] VERMEESCH 2015b, p. 216, 220.

[27] The statistics for Chile, Columbia, and Costa Rica are from CLARK 1990, p. 564; the statistics for the other countries are from GALANTER 1983, p. 52, 56.

United States	1975	c. 23
Western Australia	1975	16
West Germany	1977	43
Yugoslavia	Late 1970s-early 1980s	4.4

If one assumes 151 to 454 heads of population per petition, the comparative evidence might make Egypt look unremarkable in terms of the rates at which people accessed justice. One should also remember that the data for modern and early modern jurisdictions is always for lawsuits, whereas our number of 1,804 is for petitions submitted, and not every petition to the prefect sought a legal hearing. Some asked for the prefect simply to issue a declaration that a certain person enjoyed particular rights or to write to a subordinate official to instruct him to behave; this kind of request was especially common in disputes over liturgies. Other petitions to the prefect did not even arise out of disputed matters. Even if one accepts the higher rate of one petition to every 22 to 55 heads of population that has been proposed, one can find single jurisdictions in the early modern period with much higher rates; the court of the Vredemakers in seventeenth-century Leiden, for example, heard one lawsuit for every ten heads of population.

Should we therefore conclude that litigation rates in Roman Egypt were actually unremarkable by world historical standards? I am not going to express an opinion on this, because I think we have entered the realm of fantasy, and it is now best to leave. As the legal sociologist Marc Galanter argued in a classic article, trying to establish and compare litigation rates in different modern societies is fraught with difficulty, due to differences in record-keeping, the varying nature of jurisdictions, and the ambiguous line between "adjudication" and other forms of dispute-resolution.[28] Moreover, the procedure that one must use to conjure up a figure for litigation rates based on *P. Yale* I 61 is open to all manner of objections: we can only guess at the population of Egypt and nomes within it, and we do not really know how many people outside the Arsinoite nome would have naturally looked to the *conventus* stop there as the closest place to submit a petition to the prefect. Further, we do not

[28] GALANTER 1983, p. 51-61.

know if the year of *P. Yale* I 61 was a typical or extraordinary year; the study of the court records in early modern Bremen, for example, has shown considerable variation between years; could Egypt be similar?[29] We know that there were some years in which there was no *conventus* in the Arsinoite, so there is a chance that the year before *P. Yale* I 61 was one of these, which could have increased the petitions the next year. We also know of years in which prefect made visits to only a few cities; in *P. Oxy.* IV 709 (TM 20410), for instance, we learn that in one year in the mid-first century AD, the prefect held the *conventus* only in Pelusion (for the benefit of nomes in the eastern Delta), in Memphis (for the benefit of the Thebaid, the Heptanomia, and the Arsinoite), and in Alexandria (for the benefit of all the remaining regions). If the year of the Yale papyrus was such a year with only a restricted number of *conventus* stops, and Arsinoe happened to be one of these, this would inflate the number of petitions submitted.

We have reached a dead end here, but the process has been methodologically instructive. Two points emerge. The first is that isolated statistics are rarely of much use in themselves: they need contextualization. For an antique society like Roman Egypt, for which we do not even have reliable population figures, it is often difficult to come up with the numbers needed for such contextualization. A second point relates to numerical modeling. As impressive as such exercises may seem, they are only as strong as their starting assumptions. As we have just seen, if we change our assumptions and use ones that are at least as plausible as the previous estimate, if not more so, the result is a litigation rate several orders of magnitude lower. This kind of shaky modeling has been a feature of much Roman economic history. As Andrew Wilson has recently cautioned, "All attempts to calculate Roman GDP per capita have relied on a battery of different figures as inputs to the calculation of which almost none are actually known. What you get out of such a calculation is entirely a function of the assumptions you put in."[30] Social historians interested in the study of dispute resolution in Roman Egypt would do well to heed this warning.

---

[29] WOLLSCHLÄGER 1990.

[30] WILSON 2014, p. 149.

2. Two tracks for official dispute resolution?

The overall number of people approaching the justice system is just one issue relevant to studying access to justice in Roman Egypt. Let us turn to another: the fate of cases once they entered the system, and the kind of justice litigants received. On this topic, information can potentially be gleaned by comparing the categories of cases that appear in surviving petitions, and those that appear in surviving reports of proceedings. As can be seen in Table 3, there is a noticeable disparity between petitions and reports of proceedings when it comes to petty offenses against the person or property: assaults, thefts, damage to property, and cases in which property had been damaged by errant livestock or in other ways. These kinds of cases feature in many petitions, but are relatively rare in reports of proceedings.

Table 3: Factual claims made in petitions and reports of proceedings[31]

Type of dispute	Number in petitions	Number in reports of proceedings
Debt disputes	90	27
Illegal grazing	20	0
Disputes over liturgies/compulsory public services	53	21
Misconduct by officials	60	7
Other	34	48
Property damage	37	2
Real property	46	24
Inheritance disputes	35	24
Theft	141	8
Violence	133	9
Marital disputes	11	6
Totals	*660*	*176*

A stimulating suggestion has recently been made about the absence of certain kinds of cases from the surviving reports of proceedings: that it is reasonable to see the lack of cases of theft, assault, and property

[31] This table updates Kelly 2011, Table 4.3, p. 163.

damage in the reports of proceedings as evidence for the "lower echelons of the bureaucracy"[32] successfully dealing with these sorts of cases before there was a need to send them to a higher level for a court hearing. In relation to the violence petitions, this scholar senses that "violence was mostly dealt with by lower levels of government and that local officials were mostly successful in letting petitioners blow off steam and satisfying them with their intervention, whatever form that took."[33]

If this is true, then it is important to our understanding of the role of state agents in dispute resolution in Roman Egypt. And as we shall see presently, there is reason to surmise that people of lower economic station were more likely to submit petitions regarding theft and assault than they were to submit petitions on other matters. It would be significant if we could prove that these people were generally being fobbed off with some kind of local rough justice.

It should be said that there is nothing resembling direct evidence for this sort of phenomenon. What one would need are written instructions from higher officials who had received petitions, in which such higher officials order local, village- or town-level officials to try to resolve disputes informally. For the Ptolemaic period, such evidence does exist: to a number of petitions surviving in the third-century BC Magdola archive, the *strategos* Diophanes has added a subscription telling local village *epistatai* to try to reconcile the disputing parties if possible.[34] Such explicit instructions to facilitate informal reconciliations vanish, however, in the Roman period. There is one clear case in which a village *archephodos* plays a dispute-resolution role, but there is nothing to suggest that this was done pursuant to instructions from on high, following a petition.[35]

---

[32] VAN MINNEN 2013, p. 720.

[33] VAN MINNEN 2014, p. 265. Here we have to assume that by "local officials", village-level or town-level officials are meant. Cases were certainly delegated to *strategoi* for hearings by prefects and other high officials, but hearings before *strategoi* were documented in reports of proceedings: some 22.2% of proceedings (35 of 158) in which the judge's position is clear were hearings before *strategoi*. The dispute-resolution activities of the *strategos* therefore do not account for the absence of violence, theft, and property damage cases in reports of proceedings.

[34] E.g. *P. Enteux.* 32 = *P. Lille* II 13 (TM 3307); *P. Enteux.* 60 = *Chrest. Wilck.* 338 = *P. Lille* II 28 (TM 3335); *P. Enteux.* 72 (TM 3347).

[35] *BGU* I 321 = *Chrest. Mitt.* 114 (TM 9053) (duplicate = *P. Berol.* inv. 7081, recto [TM 48207]); *P. Louvre* I 3 = *SB* I 6 (TM 11842) (duplicate = *BGU* I 322 = *Chrest. Mitt.* 124 [TM 9054]), to be read with JÖRDENS, *P. Louvre* I, p. 15-16 and WHITEHORNE 2003.

Can such a scenario be inferred *indirectly* from the numbers in Table 3? The difficulty is that one can suggest other hypotheses to explain why certain categories of cases are noticeably absent from the surviving reports of proceedings. It could be that some petitioners in more minor cases gave up on the legal system, since it was too slow and expensive to litigate a matter of little financial importance. Perhaps others submitted a petition and used the threat of litigation to broker an informal compromise solution without the involvement of any state officials, something that might have happened more readily in cases where the economic interests involved were smaller. One can also imagine that some petitioners submitted the petition as an emotional outlet, without ever having the intention (or the capacity) to take the matter further.[36] And it is conceivable that some matters were indeed dealt with informally by local officials, and that this practice never left a documentary trail.

We can, therefore, develop a number of hypotheses to explain the apparent disparity between the two columns in Table 3, and there might be an element of truth in all of them. But we lack the kind of direct evidence that we need to privilege one hypothesis above the others. Moreover, there is a much more serious problem in using the statistics in Table 3 to provide indirect evidence of a local dispute-resolution regime: it is not at all clear that the figures for reports of proceedings in the second column of Table 3 are truly representative of the range of cases that were heard in courts in Roman Egypt. In the case of the surviving petitions, we can be fairly confident that they reflect with reasonable accuracy the range of cases in which petitions were submitted. Most of the petitions on papyrus that have survived did so because they were copies or drafts of petitions that were submitted, or because they had been submitted, subscribed by an official, and then returned to (or copied out for) a petitioner who lived in an area conducive to the preservation of papyri.

On the other hand, reports of proceedings were mostly preserved in quite different ways. Exactly 100 published reports of proceedings involving disputes are sufficiently complete to infer something about their preservation mechanisms. Of these, only three clearly are part of actual

[36] This possibility is raised by VAN MINNEN 2013, p. 720.

magistrates' *commentarii*.[37] All the rest have been copied out of *commentarii* (and then potentially recopied one or more times) for one of four reasons. Twenty-three were quoted (either in whole or in part) in the text of petitions, either (1) to illustrate a legal point in an analogous matter (at least eleven cases), or (2) to evidence a decision at an earlier stage of the same matter (at least seven cases). (3) Others were copied so that they could be added to a collection of reports illustrating similar points of law; such collections of "precedents" were either presented in court during litigation in like matters, or were used in legal education — it is often difficult to tell with certainty which of the two goals the creator of such a collection had in mind.[38] There are twenty-six discrete reports preserved in such collections.[39] (4) Thirty-seven reports are "freestanding" protocols, without any obvious connection to a petition or a collection of "precedents".[40] One imagines that many of these were copied at the behest of petitioners, either as records of rights for the future arising from decisions, or as records of earlier stages of complex cases with multiple hearings. The fact that some are preserved in the archives of litigants strengthens this supposition.[41] With this said, it is not unthinkable that

[37] A fourth possibly is part of original *commentarii* of a magistrate: *P. Bodl.* I 120 (TM 31928).

[38] On collections, see KATZOFF 1972, p. 282-289.

[39] Nine other reports of proceedings are potentially from 'precedent' collections, but there is not enough context to be certain on the point: *P. Oxy.* XXXVI 2757.i (TM 16547); XXXVI 2757.ii (TM 16548); LI 3614 (TM 15349); *P. Oxy. Hels.* 18.1-10; 18.11-19 (TM 15804); *PSI* IV 281, recto, i.15-23; 281, recto, i.23-25, ii.39-41; 281, recto, ii.41-48 (TM 27850); SCHUBERT 2005, p. 229-230 = *BGU* I 361 = *Chrest. Mitt.* 92 = *FIRA*² III 57 (TM 9085).

[40] There is also a residual category of eleven reports of proceedings that do not fit into the four categories outlined above. These include reports annexed to or quoted in official correspondence (*BGU* XI 2058.13-16 [TM 16913]; *P. Fam. Tebt.* 15.ix.131-146 [TM 10732]; *SB* I 5761 [TM 13999]; 5954 [TM 14002]); reports copied onto papyri containing other documents relating to the same case, probably as part of a record-keeping effort by a party (*P. Mil. Vogl.* I 27.iii [TM 12347]; II 98.i.1 – ii.24 [TM 12370], II 98.ii.25 – iii.64 [TM 12370]; *SB* I 5240.i.1-19 [TM 13987]); reports in miscellaneous collections of documents on the same papyrus (*PSI* V 450, recto, ii.26-47 [TM 27856]; *SB* XXIV 16257.ii [TM 41600]); and one report quoted as a precedent in another report of proceedings in a different matter (*SB* VI 9016.i.5-9 [TM 17842]).

[41] See *P. Mil. Vogl.* I 25.i.4 – iv.17; I 25.iv.18 – v.25 (TM 12345); I 27.iii (TM 12347) (Archive of Patron's descendents); *P. Oxy.* I 37 (TM 20699) (Archive of Tryphon weaver); *P. Sakaon* 31 (TM 13049) (Archive of Aurelius Sakaon).

some individual protocols were actually intended for use by lawyers in arguing like cases.

These mechanisms of preservation are likely to have favored cases of particular kinds: complex ones and ones that raised difficult issues of law. One can see similar processes of selection in relation to rescripts preserved in the late-antique law codes. These were not preserved randomly, but because they illustrated legal rules in complex and difficult areas of the law.[42] Rescripts arising from criminal cases — which tended to turn on matters of fact rather than complex legal arguments — were necessarily underrepresented. I would suggest that a similar process was at work with the reports of proceedings, many of which were also preserved for their relevance to points of legal doctrine. Moreover, simple matters like thefts, minor assaults, and property damage would have been less likely to require multiple hearings. A successful prosecution at most would result in some kind of punishment for the offender or restitution of small amounts of property, and so prosecutors would have less need of a permanent record of the hearing to evidence their rights to land, deceased estates, or liturgical exemptions in the future. Thus, even if cases of theft, assault, and property damage were reasonably common in the courtrooms of Roman Egypt, one would not expect to find them attested frequently in the reports of proceedings that have survived.

In view of all of this, I would suggest that we should resist comparing the statistics in the two columns of Table 3. The two kinds of documents were subject to quite different processes of preservation. And this, I think, raises a broader methodological point for those of us interested in doing the social history of law using papyri. Roger Bagnall has urged papyrologists to engage in taphonomy — that is to study the processes by which objects enter the archaeological record. If historians ignore this issue, they risk mistaking patterns in the deposition of papyri for genuine patterns of social or administrative practice.[43] The absence of reports of proceedings regarding petty matters like theft, assault, and property damage could simply reflect a preservation pattern: the insignificance of their contents meant that these reports were not copied from *commentarii* and taken to areas of Egypt where they had a chance of surviving in the archaeological record.

[42] TURPIN 1991.

[43] BAGNALL 2011, p. 27-74, esp. 28.

3. Onomastic patterns in petitions[44]

3.1. *Methods and data*

My third case study concerns the onomastic patterns visible in petitions and reports of proceedings. Here we can make some rather better progress with a quantitative approach. Unless it is damaged at a critical place, each petition contains the name of the petitioner or petitioners. An examination of the petitions from the Roman period involving disputes yields 472 individual petitioners' names.[45] The reports of proceedings yield rather less onomastic data, but of the 228 reports in my dataset containing clear disputes, 91 give the names of at least one plaintiff, yielding 102 names. Studying the broad onomastic patterns of these names can potentially tell us something about what sort of people attempted to involve the state in their disputes. Most names have an identifiable linguistic origin, so I have divided these into the main linguistic categories used in the Trismegistos database: Egyptian,[46] Greek,

[44] The raw datasets standing behind this section (and the discussion of reports of proceedings above, p. 176-177) are available as Excel spreadsheets that can be downloaded from TM Corpus Data at https://www.trismegistos.org/tmcorpusdata or from York University's YorkSpace institutional repository: http://hdl.handle.net/10315/39454.

[45] To avoid double counting, I have excluded from Tables 4-8 and the discussion relating to them petitions and reports of proceedings involving plaintiffs who appear in earlier petitions or reports of proceedings. Thus, for example, an individual who submitted multiple surviving petitions will be counted only once. I have also omitted altogether *P. Gen.* I² 16 (TM 11214) and *SB* I 4284 (TM 13929), two third-century petitions from Soknopaiou Nesos that relate to the same complaint and are submitted by the same group of over twenty petitioners. Petitions with so many named petitioners are unparalleled, and including these outliers would especially distort the statistics for third-century petitions from villages.

[46] In designating names as "Egyptian" in linguistic origin, I have not separated out the small repertoire of Egyptian-language names regularly used by families that were (as far as we can see) culturally Greek. The overall number of occurrences of these names in the petitions, reports of proceedings, and census declarations is much too small to analyze them separately. This repertoire included the male names Thoonis, Psennesis, and Onnophris, and the female name Termoutis. The male name Thithoetion and the female name Thaubarion, both hybrid Greek derivations of Egyptian names, have also been seen as part of this repertoire. For the phenomenon, see Bingen 1991, p. 328; Rowlandson 2013, p. 224; Broux 2015, p. 153-154, 195.

Latin,[47] and Hybrid. I have also used a residual category ("Other/?") for names that come from other languages (including Semitic languages) or whose origin is unclear. Hybrid names, I should explain, tend to be Egyptian derivations of Greek names[48] or Greek derivations of Egyptian names,[49] but other kinds of hybrids are possible. In studying the names, I have also placed double names (e.g. Σαραπίων ὁ καὶ Ἑρμαῖος) into a separate category. The raw results of this analysis are presented below in Table 4.

Table 4: Onomastic patterns amongst petitioners and plaintiffs in reports of proceedings

	PETITIONERS	PLAINTIFFS IN REPORTS OF PROCEEDINGS
Egyptian	151 (32.0%)	22 (21.6%)
Greek	218 (46.2%)	49 (48.0%)
Latin	44 (9.3%)	13 (12.7%)
Hybrid	10 (2.1%)	3 (2.9%)
Double	47 (10%)	13 (12.7%)
Other/Unknown	2 (0.4%)	2 (2.0%)
Totals	*472*	*102*

By themselves, these figures do not tell us much. The numbers need to be contextualized against onomastic patterns in the population at large to give us a sense of the typicality of petitioners' names. Such contextualization is no straightforward task. No overall study exists of the onomastic patterns visible in the papyri, so we cannot compare the relative frequency of names of particular linguistic origins in petitions to those

[47] I have not, however, classified people in petitions submitted after AD 212 as having Roman names merely because 'M. Aurelius' or 'Aurelia' are affixed to their names. The grant of Roman citizenship by M. Aurellius Severus Antoninus (i.e. Caracalla) meant that a large proportion of the Egyptian population gained the right to add elements derived from that emperor's name to their own — not that the right was consistently exercised.

[48] E.g. Ταμύσθα (appearing in *Chrest. Wilck.* 360, l. 2) (TM 20177), which combines the Egyptian Ta- with the Greek personal name Mysthas: 'the one of Mysthas'.

[49] E.g. Ὡριγένεια (appearing in *SB* X 10537, l. 10) (TM 17426), which combines the name of the Egyptian god Horos with the Greek suffix -geneia: 'born from Horos'. For the phenomenon, see DOGAER 2015.

in the papyri in general. In any case, the onomastic patterns found in documentary papyri in general might not be representative of those in the population at large, since the papyri disproportionately mention people who were part of the administration or whose social level made them likely to be mentioned in wills, marriage agreements, contracts, and other such legal documents. In the alternative, one could look at documents such as the Karanis tax rolls from the 170s or at archives such as that of Petaus, *komogrammateus* of Ptolemais Hormou in the 180s. These, however, have the opposite problem: they are too specific, since they give a snapshot of a single village at a very particular time.

The documentary category most likely to provide something approaching a random cross-section of the population, I would suggest, are the household census declarations, since these were supposed to report people of all social levels.[50] Of the census declarations in Bagnall and Frier's catalogues,[51] 209 have usable onomastic information, yielding a corpus of 712 individuals whose names can be studied with an eye to their linguistic origin and composition.

Not only must the onomastic information in the petitions and reports of proceedings be contextualized, it also needs to be disaggregated in three ways, whenever possible. Firstly, it must be analyzed by century, since the onomastic patterns in most populations will change with time. Secondly, petitions from metropoleis and those from villages must be analyzed separately, since rural naming patterns in Roman Egypt were different from those that prevailed in urban areas. This procedure also circumvents the problem that the census declarations are disproportionately of metropolitan origin, and so could give a skewed sense of general naming patterns unless urban and rural declarations are treated separately. Thirdly, there is the suspicion that naming practices varied with gender. It has been observed that females in families of gymnasial status or belonging to the 6475 *katoikoi* of the Arsinoite nome sometimes had Egyptian-language names when the males of the family had names of

[50] There is, of course, a good chance that the census in Roman Egypt, like all premodern census, missed some parts of the population, especially the very poor (cf. BAGNALL & FRIER 2006, p. 41-42, 47-49). The census returns nevertheless can be reasonably expected to have captured a more representative cross-section of the population than any other genre of documentary papyri.

[51] BAGNALL & FRIER 2006, p. 179-325.

Greek or even Latin origin.[52] The census declarations tend to suggest that this phenomenon was not widespread: in the second century, from which the most census declarations survive, 69.5% of males living in metropoleis had Greek-language names, as opposed to 63.3% of females; in the same period, 8.4% of men in metropoleis had Egyptian-language names, as opposed to 13.3% of females. In the villages in the same period, the difference was virtually non-existent: 67.7% of males in the census declarations have Egyptian names, as do 68.7% of women; the figure for Greek names is 22.2% and 21.3% respectively. Thus, any gender differences that existed across the whole population must have been quite subtle. Nevertheless, even subtle variations could potentially distort our findings, so I have elected to disaggregate according to gender as much as possible.

Disaggregating the data in three different ways has the disadvantage that it reduces some sample sizes to such an extent that they become useless. Thus, for example, there are only three petitions from villages securely dated to the first century submitted by women. Overall, out of the 472 petitioners with legible names, only 65 are female, which is barely a satisfactory sample size, even if one refrains from then disaggregating this data further by century and community type. As for plaintiffs in reports of proceedings, the domicile is virtually never mentioned, so it is impossible to analyze these litigants by community type. In any case, the sample of names in reports of proceedings — 102 names of plaintiffs, of whom 20 are women and 82 men — is too low to examine the onomastic patterns in these documents as an independent question.

In what follows, therefore, the focus will be on onomastic patterns visible amongst male petitioners, since we have the names of over 400 male petitioners from the Roman period. This will not entail ignoring the names of female petitioners altogether, or those of the plaintiffs in reports of proceedings. But the onomastic patterns in these groups will be brought in only when they shed some light on the much more statistically significant patterns visible amongst male petitioners.

Table 5 therefore presents the onomastic patterns for males visible in both petitions and census declarations from villages. Table 6 presents the equivalent data for metropoleis. What we need to find in these tables are statistically significant differences between how often a particular type of

[52] BINGEN 1991.

name occurs in the corpus of petitioners, and how often it occurs amongst people declared in the census returns. To find such statistically significant differences, I have employed a Pearson's chi-square test, the most appropriate test for statistical significance in this context.[53]

This process produces four disparities in naming practices that appear to be statistically significant. Firstly, there is a higher proportion of petitioners with Latin names in petitions from both villages and metropoleis than one might expect on the basis of the census declarations. With the village statistics, the disparity is statistically significant at 99% — i.e. there is a 99% probability that this is not a random variation. The smaller overall number of male petitioners from metropoleis means that certainty is less attainable, but there the probability that the higher number of Roman names amongst metropolitan petitioners is not the result of pure chance is still around 90% (p-value = 0.107); this is short of the 0.05 p-value conventionally used as the threshold for statistical significance in social sciences research, but the result is still suggestive. Latin names are also more common amongst plaintiffs in reports of proceedings than they are amongst people declared in the census declarations: 13 out of 102 (12.7%) the individuals mentioned as plaintiffs have Latin names, as opposed to 14 out of 403 (3.5%) in the census declarations, a disparity that is significant with 99% certainty.

A second pattern also relates to villages: in petitions from villages, names of Egyptian origin are less common than we would expect on the basis of the census declarations. The pattern is especially pronounced for males in the second century, for which there is a disparity of 19.7%, and the third century, which has a 32.9% disparity.[54] There is a 99% chance that these disparities are statistically significant, and not the result of random variation.

[53] The chi-square test checks the probability that the divergence between two sample groups in relation to the prevalence of a particular variable is not the result of chance. Results are expressed as a p-value; for instance, a p-value of 0.05 indicates a 95% certainty that a divergence is not due to chance — or, to use the customary statistical terminology, a p-value of 0.05 indicates a 95% certainty that we should reject the "null hypothesis", namely that the two variables come from the same underlying distribution.

[54] In the reports of proceedings, 19 out of 82 male plaintiffs have Egyptian names (23.5%), as do 3 of 20 (15.0%) of female plaintiffs — although we cannot distinguish between residents of metropoleis and those of villages in these documents.

Thirdly, there appears to be a surfeit of double names in petitions in the metropoleis during the second and third centuries. 20.0% and 28.2% of male metropolitan petitioners in the second and third centuries respectively bear double names, well above the proportions in the census declarations. The second-century sample is large enough to give a 90% probability of statistical significance, although the sample for the third century is too small for similar confidence (p-value = 0.261). The case for an unusually high number of double names is strengthened when the data is analyzed without disaggregation. Overall, 10.0% of petitioners (47 out of 472) have double names; for plaintiffs in reports of proceedings, the proportion is 12.7% (13 out of 102). Yanne Broux has kindly extracted the data on double names from the Trismegistos database for me, which reveals that 4,150 of the 173,162 individuals (i.e. 2.4%) in the first three centuries AD bore double names.[55] The much larger sample sizes allow a confidence of over 99% that the disparity with petitioners and plaintiffs is not due to pure chance.

A final possible pattern — and one probably related to the prevalence of double names, as we shall see — relates to Greek names in the metropolite petitions. There are fewer petitioners with single names of Greek linguistic origin than one might expect. For male petitioners this is most pronounced in the second century documents, where there are 16.2% fewer metropolitan male petitioners with Greek names than males with Greek names in census declarations; the disparity is statistically significant at a confidence level of 90%. There are possible hints of a similar story with female metropolitan petitioners, although the small sample size does not allow a high degree of confidence: 41.2% (7 out of 17) of female petitioners bear Greek names; the proportion of females with Greek names resident in metropoleis is 56.7% (68 out of 120) in the census declarations.

[55] Date of extraction: 20 June 2016.

Table 5: Onomastic patterns amongst male petitioners and males in census declarations from villages

	PETITIONERS TOTAL	CENSUS DECLARATIONS (1st-3rd c.)	PETITIONERS (1st c.)	CENSUS DECLARATIONS (1st c.)	PETITIONERS (2nd c.)	CENSUS DECLARATIONS (2nd c.)	PETITIONERS (3rd c.)	CENSUS DECLARATIONS (3rd c.)
Egyptian	112 (51.4%)	135 (65.2%)	41 (62.1%)	6 (42.9%)	47 (48.0%)	107 (67.7%)	9 (30.0%)	22 (62.9%)
Greek	78 (35.8%)	49 (23.7%)	22 (33.3%)	6 (42.9%)	35 (35.7%)	35 (22.2%)	13 (43.3%)	8 (22.9%)
Latin	15 (6.9%)	1 (0.5%)	0 (0.0%)	0 (0.0%)	8 (8.2%)	1 (0.6%)	7 (23.3%)	0 (0.0%)
Hybrid	3 (1.4%)	10 (4.8%)	1 (1.5%)	1 (7.1%)	1 (1.0%)	9 (5.7%)	1 (3.3%)	0 (0.0%)
Double	10 (4.6%)	8 (3.9%)	2 (3.0%)	1 (7.1%)	7 (7.1%)	4 (2.5%)	0 (0.0%)	3 (8.6%)
Other/?	0 (0.0%)	4 (1.9%)	0 (0.0%)	0 (0.0%)	0 (0.0%)	2 (1.3%)	0 (0.0%)	2 (5.7%)
Totals	*218*	*207*	*66*	*14*	*98*	*158*	*30*	*35*

Table 6: Onomastic patterns amongst male petitioners and males in census declarations from metropoleis

	PETITIONERS TOTAL	CENSUS DECLARATIONS (1st-3rd c.)	PETITIONERS (1st c.)	CENSUS DECLARATIONS (1st c.)	PETITIONERS (2nd c.)	CENSUS DECLARATIONS (2nd c.)	PETITIONERS (3rd c.)	CENSUS DECLARATIONS (3rd c.)
Egyptian	7 (7.9%)	17 (8.7%)	1 (5.6%)	4 (23.5%)	1 (3.3%)	13 (8.4%)	5 (12.8%)	0 (0.0%)
Greek	52 (58.4%)	134 (68.4%)	15 (83.3%)	12 (70.6%)	16 (53.3%)	107 (69.5%)	19 (48.7%)	15 (60.0%)
Latin	11 (12.4%)	13 (6.6%)	2 (11.1%)	0 (0.0%)	6 (20.0%)	12 (7.8%)	3 (7.7%)	1 (4.0%)
Hybrid	1 (1.1%)	12 (6.1%)	0 (0.0%)	0 (0.0%)	1 (3.3%)	8 (5.2%)	0 (0.0%)	4 (16.0%)
Double	17 (19.1%)	17 (8.7%)	0 (0.0%)	0 (0.0%)	6 (20.0%)	13 (8.4%)	11 (28.2%)	4 (16.0%)
Other/?	1 (1.1%)	3 (1.5%)	0 (0.0%)	1 (5.9%)	0 (0.0%)	1 (0.6%)	1 (2.6%)	1 (4.0%)
Totals	*89*	*196*	*18*	*17*	*30*	*154*	*39*	*25*

The challenge now is to explain what these onomastic patterns might tell us about who chose to access state avenues of adjudication, and who stayed away from them. There is rarely an obvious explanation that springs fully formed from cold lists of numbers such as these. Rather, one must formulate hypotheses and see which hypothesis best fits the statistical patterns. As a heuristic exercise, I should like to formulate three hypotheses and then see how they fit the onomastic patterns that we are observing. The first of these relates to the different status groups into which the Roman administration divided the population; a second relates to culture; and the third relates to the disparate economic positions and activities of different segments of the society of the province.

3.2. *Hypothesis 1: legal status*

I begin with legal status, although I think that this is the least likely explanation for the patterns we are seeing. As is well known, the Romans divided the Egyptian population into three status categories: Roman citizens, citizens of the Greek-style *poleis* in the province, and "Egyptians". Within the third category, metropolites were marked off somewhat from the mass of Egyptians in that male metropolites of the taxable age were liable to a lower rate of poll tax. These status demarcations are perhaps the most straightforward of the different types of social divisions existing in Roman Egypt, since they were defined by law. Understandably, they feature very prominently in the modern literature. Should one perhaps hypothesize that people of higher legal status were treated better by the authorities and therefore tended to petition and litigate in higher numbers?

Such a scenario seems plausible, but it is in no way corroborated by our onomastic data. The problem is that names often did not correlate well with an individual's legal status. The bearers of Latin names were not necessarily Roman citizens.[56] Sometimes there is a good chance that they were, for instance if we find the full *tria nomina*. There was, however, apparently a tendency for Latin names to be given to children simply because they sounded prestigious, since one finds such names amongst people who were demonstrably not Roman citizens. Likewise, Greek names did not necessarily correlate with metropolite status. Many of the petitioners bearing Greek names who were residents of metropoleis

[56] Broux 2015, p. 77-79.

were no doubt metropolites, but the same cannot be assumed of a sizeable proportion of petitioners from villages with Greek names: some were perhaps displaced metropolites, but surely not all.

The fact that there is a fairly high proportion of people with double names amongst petitioners and plaintiffs is also unlikely to reflect a bias on the part of administrators and courts towards people of higher legal status: before AD 212, such people were generally metropolites rather than Romans. As far as legal status was concerned, they were not necessarily of higher status than bearers of single names, although there is a possibility that double names were especially prevalent in the gymnasial order.

3.3. *Hypothesis 2: cultural differences*

A second hypothesis links the patterns that we are seeing to culture rather than legal status. The suggestion is that certain groups are found petitioning in higher or lower rates because they found the administrative and legal system to be more or less culturally familiar. The legal system had traits that could conceivably have made it seem alien and unapproachable to some groups in society: legal documents and hearings were in Greek; it was a system that placed considerable emphasis on written documents; the officials receiving petitions and hearing cases would have been culturally Greek (in the case of *strategoi*) or members of cultural groups from elsewhere in the Empire (in the case of the equestrian administrators at the higher levels). The premise behind this hypothesis would be that there was a broad correlation between one's name and the cultural universe one inhabited. This would not require us to go as far as to suggest that linguistically Greek names equaled Greek ethnicity; there is, indeed, some considerable doubt about whether there was a widespread notion in the Roman period of an exclusive "Greek" ethnic identity whose holders differentiated themselves from "Egyptians".[57] However, it does not seem unreasonable to suggest that in general (albeit not in every specific case) people with Egyptian names would have had lower levels of competence with the Greek language and fewer cultural affinities with regional and provincial administrators than was the case with people bearing Greek names.

[57] BAGNALL 1997; ROWLANDSON 2013.

Again, the hypothesis does not seem implausible, but do the onomastic patterns lend any support to it? The confidence that people bearing double names evidently had in approaching the authorities could perhaps be the result of cultural factors. As Yanne Broux has recently shown, double names — and more specifically those connected with the formula ὁ καί or ἡ καί — were especially concentrated in elite metropolitan families during the second and third centuries. Such names correlate strongly with employment in the administration, tenure of metropolitan *archai* and prestigious metropolitan liturgies, membership of the gymnasial order, and (from the start of the third century) membership of town councils.[58] These people would probably have indeed had closer cultural affinities with the provincial and regional administrators than the general run of the population. Doubts arise, however, from Table 7, which correlates onomastic patterns in petitions with the addressees of petitions.

Table 7: Petition addressees and onomastic patterns amongst male Petitioners

	EGYPTIAN	GREEK	LATIN	HYBRID	DOUBLE	OTHER/?
Soldier	12 (10.0%)	19 (12.1%)	7 (21.9%)	1 (20.0%)	1 (2.9%)	0 (0.0%)
Strategos	76 (63.3%)	68 (43.3%)	12 (37.5%)	2 (40.0%)	12 (34.3%)	1 (100%)
Epistrategos	3 (2.5%)	8 (5.1%)	1 (3.1%)	0 (0.0%)	6 (17.1%)	0 (0.0%)
Prefect	12 (10.0%)	27 (17.2%)	2 (6.3%)	1 (20.0%)	10 (28.6%)	0 (0.0%)
Other	17 (14.2%)	35 (22.3%)	10 (31.3%)	1 (20.0%)	6 (17.1%)	0 (0.0%)
Totals	*120*	*157*	*32*	*5*	*35*	*1*

The striking pattern here is that people with double names show no marked preference for approaching the *strategos*: in fact, they are half as likely as people bearing Egyptian names to petition this official.[59] If cultural affinities were at the forefront of the minds of our double-named

[58] BROUX 2015, p. 97-100, 269-285.

[59] The this disparity is significant at 99%.

petitioners, then we would surely expect a strong preference for involving the *strategos* in their disputes: *strategoi* were, after all, recruited from elite metropolitan families in other nomes. On the other hand, bearers of double names appear to have been more likely than other onomastic groups to approach the prefect and the *epistrategos*,[60] officials who were Roman equestrian officials, and who were either ethnically Roman or Italian, or (especially as time went on) drawn from the elites of societies from all around the Empire.

Do the onomastic patterns show any signs of particular groups having a cultural *aversion* to the justice process? If they did, then their aversions must have been quite subtle. There is no secure evidence in Tables 4-6 that cultural affiliations prompted any particular group to avoid state involvement in dispute resolution completely. To be sure, there is only one petition in my corpus submitted by a petitioner who was Jewish.[61] The minimal presence of Jewish names cannot, however, be read as evidence for a tendency on the part of Egyptian Jews to avoid the legal system.[62] In fact, it is precisely what we would expect on the basis of the census declarations: only one of the 706 names of census declarants is Hebrew.[63] The general lack of identifiably Jewish people in documentary papyri is the result of a combination of circumstances. The small number of papyri from Alexandria means that the important Jewish community in that city is hardly represented in the papyrological record. Moreover, Jews in Egypt commonly bore non-Hebrew names, making it hard to

---

[60] The confidence level for the statistical significance of the disparity between the proportion of people with Egyptian names and double names approaching the *epistrategos* and prefect is 99% in both cases. With petitioners approaching the *epistrategos*, the confidence level is 95% for a non-random disparity between Greek and double names, and 90% between Roman and double names. With the prefect, the level is 95% for Roman names vs. double names.

[61] In *CPJ* II 151 (TM 18584), Hellenos, son of Tryphon, bears a Greek name but identifies himself as Jewish. In *CPJ* III 455 (TM 13798), the petitioner's name was initially misread as a Greek-Hebrew hybrid (Isakous), but this has now been corrected to the Greek Isarion: see GONIS, Korr. Tyche 827.

[62] *Pace* KANTOR 2012.

[63] *P. Hamb.* I 60 = *CPJ* III 485 (= 89-Hm-1) (TM 21047): Pascheis (TM Per 362847). *P. Lond.* III 1119a = *CPJ* II 430 (= 103-Ar-6) (TM 11758) is a fragmentary declaration of a daughter of Iesous (TM Per 338415).

identify their ethnicity unless there is some other marker.[64] In the case of petitions, it is difficult to believe that a Jewish petitioner would gratuitously declare his or her ethnicity, in view of the sometimes troubled relations between the Roman administration and the Jewish community of the province. Further, Roman reprisals in the wake of the revolt of AD 115-117 drastically thinned out the Jewish population of Egypt, to judge from the fact that Jews virtually disappear from the papyri at this date.[65] The combination of all of these factors means that the low number of identifiably Jewish petitioners cannot be interpreted as evidence for a tendency to avoid of the justice system on the part of Egyptian Jews.

As for people who were culturally more Egyptian than Greek, there was clearly no wholesale avoidance of the state when it came to dispute resolution: there are too many petitioners with Egyptian-language names to believe this. But could the somewhat lower proportion of petitioners with Egyptian names suggest a weaker, but nevertheless real aversion on the part of people who were culturally Egyptian? The answer to this would seem to be in the negative if one considers Table 8, which correlates the onomastic features of petitioners with the categories of complaints that they make.

The table shows that for some categories of cases, the proportion of petitioners with Egyptian names is quite high: in the same region (or even a little higher) that we would expect on the basis of the census returns. This is especially so in theft cases, where about half of the petitioners bear Egyptian names. Petitions containing complaints of violence also have somewhat higher rates of petitioners with Egyptian names, especially if one considers 'pure' cases of violence, in which allegations of assault are not mixed with allegations of other misdeeds in the petition. On the other hand, in debt disputes and disputes over liturgies, the proportion of Egyptian names is rather lower. Thus, one would have to believe that to people who were culturally Egyptian, the administrative and legal system of the province seemed more or less alien depending on

---

[64] For the use of non-Hebrew names by the Jewish community of Egypt, see TCHERIKOVER & FUKS, *CPJ* I, p. xvii-xix. One can see the widespread adoption of non-Hebrew names by Jews in Egypt already in the Ptolemaic period in the second-century BC archive of the *Politeuma* of the Jews in Herakleopolis, where only two Hebrew names are to be found: see HONIGMAN 2003, p. 99 n. 111.

[65] See SCHAUB 2014, p. 161-162 for evidence and modern literature.

the category of dispute in which they were involved: they were happy to go to the authorities if someone stole money from them, but distinctly less happy to do so if someone refused to repay a loan. This seems unlikely: either the legal process seemed strange and alien to such people, or it did not.

Table 8: Dispute categories and onomastic patterns for male petitioners[66]

	THEFT	DEBT	LITURGICAL DISPUTE	VIOLENCE	'PURE' VIOLENCE	MALE PETITIONERS TOTAL	CENSUS DECLARATIONS (1st-3rd C.)
Egyptian	47 (48.0%)	14 (21.5%)	8 (18.2%)	32 (38.6%)	14 (50.0%)	136 (33.4%)	152 (37.7%)
Greek	44 (44.9%)	31 (47.7%)	25 (56.8%)	40 (48.2%)	10 (35.7%)	187 (45.9%)	183 (45.4%)
Latin	2 (2.0%)	10 (15.4%)	8 (18.2%)	3 (3.6%)	0 (0.0%)	40 (9.8%)	14 (3.5%)
Hybrid	2 (2.0%)	1 (1.5%)	1 (2.3%)	1 (1.2%)	1 (3.6%)	6 (1.5%)	22 (5.5%)
Double	3 (3.1%)	8 (12.3%)	2 (4.5%)	7 (8.4%)	3 (10.7%)	38 (9.3%)	25 (6.2%)
Other/?	0 (0.0%)	1 (1.5%)	0 (0.0%)	0 (0.0%)	0 (0.0%)	0 (0.0%)	7 (1.7%)
Totals	*98*	*65*	*44*	*83*	*28*	*407*	*403*

3.4. *Hypothesis 3: economic position and activity*

It is perhaps time to approach our problem from an entirely different angle, and think in economic terms. The premise from which I start here is that petitions and lawsuits overwhelmingly involved property and economic interests: they involved money or goods stolen; loans not repaid; property that had been damaged; land or real estate whose ownership was in doubt; liturgies that were a drain on time and money; and

[66] Petitions complaining of multiple types of wrongs have been included (except for the 'Pure' Violence category). Only cases where the offence category is clear have been included.

officials who threated economic interests. Even cases of violence often had an economic dimension.[67] My hypothesis is that the onomastic patterns in the petitions reflect the facts that petitioning and litigation were overwhelmingly an extension of economic activity or related to material interests, and that the greater one's wealth and the more complex one's economic affairs, the more opportunities one had to become embroiled in disputes of the sort that might give rise to petitions and lawsuits.

The critical fact in this context is that, although there were doubtless some correlations between names and cultural affiliation in Roman Egypt, there were also correlations between one's name and one's economic status.[68] People with Latin names were sometimes veterans or belonged to veteran families, and were therefore part of an economically privileged stratum of society. Those who gave their children Latin names without having Roman citizenship or connections to the army were clearly of a class that had ambitions of upward mobility. It is scarcely any wonder that Latin names appear in higher frequencies amongst the petitions than amongst the general population, as represented by the census declarations: the bearers of Latin names were more likely to have the level of wealth and economic engagement that gave rise to petitions and lawsuits.

A similar explanation would seem to hold for the relatively high number of double names amongst petitioners and plaintiffs. The bearers of such names were members of a political and cultural elite in their communities,[69] and so they were doubtless also richer than average. As with the bearers of Latin names, they too would be more likely to have occasion to submit petitions and involve themselves in litigation than the general run of the population.

As for Greek names, it is necessary to distinguish between petitioners bearing Greek names in villages and those in the metropoleis. In the villages, there was probably some correlation between wealth and a Greek name. Some such people might have actually been the descendants of military settlers of the Ptolemaic period. Others would have been members of upwardly mobile families for whom Greek names had attractive connotations of prestige and prosperity. Some would have been displaced

---

67 KELLY 2011, p. 163-165.

68 BROUX 2015, p. 71-73.

69 Above, p. 188.

metropolites, living in the villages to better manage the land they held there. It is scarcely any wonder, then, that we find Greek names in somewhat higher proportions than we might expect in petitions from villages, since the economic affairs and material interests of such people were more likely to give rise to disputes of the sort that might result in petitions and lawsuits. The bearers of Egyptian names in villages, being on average of a somewhat lower economic level, are found petitioning at lower rates.

The bearers of single Greek names resident in metropoleis are, I think, a different case, at least in the second and third centuries. Such petitioners appear in lower proportions than we might expect on the basis of the census records. This I would attribute to the fact that during these centuries metropolites with a higher economic position tended to take on double names and Latin names with greater frequency. On average, therefore, bearers of single Greek names in the metropolis would have been somewhat poorer.

I should stress that my third hypothesis is not quite that petitioning and litigation were expensive and this kept poor people away. The cliché that justice is only for the rich does not match the onomastic evidence. In particular, it is contradicted by the data in Table 8, which shows that petitioners in theft and violence cases had Egyptian names in the proportions that one would expect on the basis of the census declarations. Clearly even relatively poor victims of these sorts of wrongs did not regard justice as inaccessible in such cases. With this said, we still have the patterns in Table 7 to account for: people with Egyptian names seem to have shown a stronger tendency to approach the *strategos* rather than the prefect or *epistrategos*. Here the costs of petitioning and litigation in terms of time and money might well have been a factor. Except for the brief period of the *conventus*, the prefect and *epistrategos* were for many geographically distant figures. Petitioning the *strategos*, on the other hand, at most would require a trip to the metropolis, and indeed sometimes *strategoi* visited villages, so a journey would not always have been necessary.

With this economic hypothesis, which I think fits the onomastic evidence better than the other hypotheses, we have come full circle back to John Kelly's *Roman Litigation*. Kelly's analysis was overwhelmingly economic, and presented a bleak picture of the prospects that a poor litigant would face in trying to obtain justice from a richer opponent. The evidence for our one province of the empire would seem to present a different picture, however. Property and economic activity would seem to have been central in determining who submitted petitions and appeared as a plaintiff in litigation. But this was so because those who were more involved in complex transactions and had more material interests to defend were more likely to become embroiled in disputes of the sort worth litigating about. There is rather less of a sign in the onomastic evidence that the costs of petitioning made it entirely off limits for relatively poor people: the *strategos*, at least, seems to have been relatively accessible to sub-elite Egyptians, to judge from the onomastic data. The relatively wealthy are overrepresented in the petitions purely because petitioning and litigation were part of the ebb and flow of economic life in the province, and so those who were more engaged in the economy and were playing for higher stakes had more about which to petition.

Table 9: Onomastic patterns amongst male petitioners and their male opponents

PETITIONER-OPPONENT	CASES	PETITIONER-OPPONENT	CASES
Greek-Greek	49	Double-Latin	1
Greek-Egyptian	18	Double-Mixed	2
Greek-Latin	5	Latin-Latin	3
Greek-Double	4	Latin-Greek	7
Greek-Mixed	8	Latin-Egyptian	1
Egyptian-Egyptian	28	Latin-Double	1
Egyptian-Greek	17	Latin-Mixed	1
Egyptian-Latin	2	Mixed-Mixed	0
Egyptian-Double	1	Mixed-Greek	4
Egyptian-Mixed	12	Mixed-Egyptian	1
Double-Double	3	Mixed-Latin	0
Double-Greek	5	Mixed-Double	0
Double-Egyptian	2		

A final onomastic pattern is relevant here. In Table 9, I have analyzed the linguistic origins and forms of the names of both petitioners and their opponents. Thus, 'Greek-Greek' cases involve a petitioner or group of petitioners with Greek names petitioning against an opponent or opponents with Greek names; 'Egyptian-Greek' cases involve people with Egyptian names petitioning against opponents with Greek names; 'Egyptian-Mixed' cases involve petitioners with Egyptian names petitioning against multiple opponents with names of two or more different linguistic origins.

The data in this table is not compatible with the sort of scenario that John Kelly imagined for elsewhere in the Roman world, whereby poorer litigants were systematically disadvantaged if they were facing richer opponents. It would have been difficult, he argued, to get the rich and powerful into court in the first place, and then judicial bias in favor of people of high socio-economic status would have favored rich defendants. However, people with Egyptian names are found petitioning against individuals with Greek, Latin, or double names, or groups with a mixture of names about as often as against other people with Egyptian names. We should not be seeing this pattern if the system were heavily biased in favor of richer litigants. Rather, we would expect to see people with Egyptian names mostly taking on other people with Egyptian names. The overall numbers in Table 9 are small though, since it is less common that petitions preserve both petitioners' names and those of their opponents. Certainly, however, the table provides no confirmation of a heavy class bias discouraging people from accessing justice in Roman Egypt.

Conclusions

Our road has been long and circuitous, and there have been wrong turns and dead ends. But travelers — to paraphrase a much later Greek of Egypt, Constantine Cavafy — often become rich with all they have gained on the way, and not from their destinations, not from arriving at their Ithacas. Our journey has taught us to be wary of numbers, to be suspicious of their Siren song. Statistics like the one in *P. Yale* I 61 turn out to be meaningless without other numbers to contextualize them, and elaborate attempts to construct mathematical models to do this often rely on data that we simply do not possess. Further, when we create statistics from different genres of papyrus documents, the patterns we detect can often be suspected as reflecting variations in the ways in which papyrus documents were created and preserved.

Even when, with great care and pain, we can produce promising statistics, we must face the fact that the Siren song of numbers, although seductive, is often not very clear. Fervid claims to certainty based on isolated statistics should be recognized for what they are: rhetorical moves not likely to lead to real historical understanding. Instead, I would advocate that we formulate multiple hypotheses to explain our numbers, that we try to discern which one best fits the evidence, but that we recognize that as ancient historians, we are in the business of educated guesses, not mathematical certainties.

MEASURING POLICE EFFECTIVENESS IN ROMAN EGYPT: A COMPARATIVE PERSPECTIVE*

Sofie WAEBENS
(KU Leuven)

Abstract: When Egypt became a Roman province in 30 BC, profound changes were made to the police system that had been in place throughout the nearly 300 years of Ptolemaic rule. New types of police officials were created, but more importantly, Roman soldiers henceforth acted as the strong arm of the law along local officials: they secured public roads, apprehended runaway slaves, fought bandits, investigated crimes, detained offenders, and received petitions from victims of crime. Nevertheless, a substantial number of petitions were filed against soldiers, accusing them of engaging in beatings, unlawful imprisonment, extortion, and unauthorized requisitions of goods and animals. The dominating theme in the sources is in fact the brutal oppression of civilians by soldiers, whom emperors were unable to restrain. According to most scholars, abuse was so widespread that it hindered an efficient working of the criminal justice system and threatened public order. Apart from the widespread corruption within the ranks of the Roman army, however, the impact of Roman rule on the role of police officials in maintaining social order in Egypt has thus far been largely ignored in modern scholarship. This paper will address some of the challenges historians face when studying the complex role of police and army in (Greco-) Roman Egypt, and demonstrate how police effectiveness might be assessed on the basis of insights taken from the fields of criminology and sociology.

---

* Much of the primary evidence discussed in this paper is collected and translated in ADAMS 2013 and CAMPBELL 1994. This paper is based on research conducted while I was a Postdoctoral Fellow of the Research Foundation – Flanders (FWO – Vlaanderen), for which I wish to express my gratitude. I am also indebted to B. Kelly, whose study on petitions, litigation and social control in Roman Egypt has contributed significantly to the development of the methodological framework for my research on police effectiveness in Roman Egypt. An earlier version of this paper has been presented at the European Social Science History Conference, held in Valencia from 30 March to 2 April 2016. I would like to thank all those present for their comments on the material presented on this occasion.

Introduction

Towards the end of the reign of the emperor Tiberius, a farmer named Chairemon, son of Horion, who lived in the village of Euhemeria in the northwestern Fayum, petitioned Sarapion, the *epistates ton phylakiton* (the chief of police of the Fayum), concerning damage to crops caused by grazing sheep, asking him to write to the *archephodos*, the local police official (*SB* XX 15182, TM 14956). The papyrus breaks off at this point, but Chairemon probably requested that the owners of the sheep be brought before him to recompense him for the damage suffered, as the subscription at the base of the document suggests (l. 21): ἀρχε̣(φόδῳ)· ἔκπ[ε]μ̣[ψον] ("To the *archephodos*: send them up").

Although a professional "police" force, as we know it nowadays, only came to exist in the late nineteenth century, documents such as Chairemon's petition show a wide variety of officials policing the Egyptian countryside under Ptolemaic and Roman rule, to whom victims could turn to seek justice for crimes committed against them. Officials from different spheres of government such as the *strategoi* (the chief administrators of the *nomes*, the administrative regions in which Egypt was divided), the *oikonomoi* (the chief financial officials in the *nomes*), and the *machimoi* (soldiers) all performed police duties from time to time,[1] but the lion's share of law enforcement in the Ptolemaic period fell to the *phylakitai*, who were supervised by the *archiphylakitai* at village level and the *epistatai ton phylakiton* at nome level.[2] They investigated crimes, sealed homes, confiscated property, arrested, questioned, and imprisoned offenders, received petitions, provided protection, guarding not only government infrastructure, but also private property, and thus performed what we would call "police duties". We should nevertheless avoid anachronistic thinking, because the duties of these police officials were diverse and not altogether similar to those of our modern police — for instance, they also collected tax revenue for the government and measured out seed and grain to the villagers.[3]

---

[1] BAUSCHATZ 2013, Chapter 2: The Officer Corps II: Civil and Military Police, p. 99-159.

[2] BAUSCHATZ 2013, Chapter 1: The Officer Corps I: The *Phylakitai*, p. 49-98.

[3] BAUSCHATZ 2013, p. 48, Chapter 5: The Strong Arm of the Law: Security and Muscle, p. 281-327.

When Egypt became a Roman province in 30 BC, the police system underwent substantial changes: the *phylakitai* and their superiors were disbanded, new types of police officials such as the *nyktophylakes* (night guards) were created, and other posts became liturgical.[4] But the most profound change was that Roman soldiers henceforth acted as the strong arm of the law alongside local officials:[5] they secured public roads, apprehended runaway slaves, fought bandits, investigated crimes, detained offenders, transferred prisoners, and received petitions from victims of crime, thus replacing the *phylakitai* as Egypt's primary police officials.[6] We know, however, from the literary and documentary evidence of the Empire that Roman soldiers were seen as brutish and abusive and that they were feared by local populations, in particular by the lower classes. Soldiers represented not only Roman imperial power, but they also enjoyed special privileges and treatment in court[7] and often had contact with local people, sometimes in a police capacity; in areas less easily controlled by magistrates, Roman officers such as the *beneficiarii* or *stationarii* were probably the only available source of jurisdiction.[8] The Roman army could also requisition goods or animals from local communities as military supplies, so it is hardly a surprise that soldiers exploited their status, power and their physical force to oppress civilians and to requisition goods and animals, sometimes on their own initiative, sometimes on the orders of higher officials.[9] The large number of papyri preserved from Egypt reveals that a substantial number of complaints were filed against soldiers, accusing them of engaging in beatings, unlawful imprisonment, extortion, and unauthorized requisitions of goods and animals. In *P. Oxy.* XIX 2234 (TM 22184), a petition of AD 31 from Oxyrhynchos, for instance, Hermon, son of Demetrius, complains about

---

[4] FUHRMANN 2012, p. 75 and 77-79; SÄNGER 2011, p. 241-253.

[5] ALSTON 1995, p. 79-101. On the balance between military and civilian policing in late Roman Egypt, see AUBERT 1995, p. 257-265 and BAGNALL 1993, p. 173.

[6] On policing in ancient Rome, see BAUSCHATZ 2013, p. 23-27; FUHRMANN 2012, p. 93-121; NIPPEL 1995; on the role of the Roman army in the provinces, see ADAMS 2013, p. 268-271; FUHRMANN 2012, p. 147-169 and esp. 201-238; CAMPBELL 1994, p. 110-127.

[7] CAMPBELL 1994, p. 160-170.

[8] ADAMS 2013, p. 269; CAMPBELL 1994, p. 170. On the role of high-ranking officers in legal jurisdiction and the (informal) role of soldiers in petitioning and as arbiters in disputes, see PALME 2014, p. 494-495; ADAMS 2013, p. 269; PEACHIN 2007.

[9] ADAMS 2013, p. 262; CAMPBELL 1994, p. 170.

illegal fishing on his property by some local fishermen and their accomplices, as well as the soldier Titius:

> Κυ[ίντ]ω̣ι Καίωι Πάσσερι ἑ̣κατοντάρχηι παρὰ Ἕ̣ρ̣[μ]ωνος τοῦ Δημητρίου. ὑπάρχει μοι περὶ κώμην Τῆιν τῆς Θμοισεφὼι τοπαρχίας τοῦ Ὀξυρυγχείτου παππ̣ικὸς πατρικὸς κλῆρος Δρύου λεγόμενος, ἐν [ῷ]ι δημόσιον χῶμα καὶ λάκκος κατ̣ὰ μέσον τῶν ἡμετέρων καὶ ναύβια καὶ ἕτερα ὑπέρ τ̣ε πάντων τελῶν τὰ καθήκοντα δημόσια, καταβιαζόμενος δὲ καὶ συναρποζόμενος (l. συν|αρπαζόμενος) ὑπ̣ὸ ἁλιέων Παύσιος καὶ {Π} Παψιοῦτ̣ο̣ς καὶ τοῦ ἀδελφοῦ καὶ Καλεοῦς καὶ Μέλανος καὶ Ἀττίνου καὶ Πασόιτος καὶ τῶν σὺν αὐ[τ-]ο̣ῖς οὐκ ὄν̣τ̣ων ὀλίγων. ἐπαγαγόντες καὶ Τίτιον στ̣ρ̣ατιώτην μετὰ πολλῶν λίν̣ων καὶ ξυ̣στρῶν ἐπελθόντες ἐπὶ τὸν ἡμέτ[ε]ρ̣ον λάκκον μετὰ κολλορόβων ἡλίευσαν καὶ ἀνέσπασαν ἰχθ̣[ῦ]ν ἄξιον ἐπὶ τὸ α̣ὐ̣τ̣ὸ̣ [ἀ]ργυρίου (τάλαντον) α, κ[α]ὶ̣ λογοποιουμένου μου [αὐτοῖς] ἔ̣γγισαν (l. ἤγγισαν) με ὡς μέλλοντές με ἐκπ̣ο̣[.]ν̣. ἐπ[ε]ὶ δὲ κατὰ πολλὰ βιάζοντά (l. βιάζοντα<ί>) με, τὴ̣ν ἐπί σε καταφυ̣[γ]ὴν ποιούμενος ἀξιῶ, ἐὰ̣ν φαί̣ν̣ηται, ἀχθῆναι τοὺς ἐγκαλουμ̣έ-νου[ς] ἐ̣πί σε̣, ὅ̣πως ἀπ̣[ο]δῶσί μοι τὴν τιμὴ̣ν τ̣οῦ̣ ἰχθύο̣ς, ὡς προ[είρ]η̣τ̣αι, εἰς δὲ τὸ μέλλον ἀποσχῶνται τῶν ἡμετέρων, ἵν̣' ὦ εὐεργε̣τ̣ημένος. διευτύ-χ(ει). (ἔτους) ιζ Τιβερίου Καίσαρος Σεβαστοῦ Παχὼν ιζ.
>
> To Quintus Gaius Passer, centurion, from Hermon, son of Demetrius. There belongs to me near the village of Teis in the toparchy of Thmoisepho of the Oxyrhynchite nome a plot of land, which I have inherited from my paternal grandfather, called "of the Woodland", in which there is a public dyke and a cistern, which is situated in the middle of my land, along with cubic measures (?) and other things. For all of these I pay the appropriate public taxes. But I am being attacked and plundered by the fishermen Pausis, Papsious and his brother, and Cales, Melas, Attinus, Pasois, and their accomplices, not few in number. They also brought along Titius the soldier and approaching my cistern with many fishing lines and scaling knives, they fished with gaffs and pulled out fish worth 1 silver talent. Moreover, when I remonstrated with them, they came up to me apparently intending to [...] me. Since they are using force against me in many ways, I am taking recourse to you, and I request, if you agree, that you have the accused brought before you so that they may pay me back for the value of the fish, as was mentioned above, and so that in future they may keep away from my property, in order that I may assisted. Farewell. Year 17 of Tiberius Caesar Augustus, 17 Pachon.[10]

This has led some scholars to conclude that "[i]nscriptions and papyri containing the complaints of provincial communities preserve an authentic record of serious, widespread, and persistent abuse, and indicate that in any analysis of the failings of Roman provincial administration,

---

[10] Translation: CAMPBELL 1994, p. 172 no. 286.

soldiers appear as the most intransigent culprits",[11] that "many provincials' experience of the governor, his hangers-on, and soldiers was marked by mistrust and fear of cruelty and exploitation",[12] and that "Rome's soldiers were quite obviously an imperfect instrument of law enforcement".[13] Apart from topics such as the widespread misconduct and corruption within the ranks of the Roman army and the ineffectiveness of the policing system under Roman rule,[14] however, the impact of Roman rule on the role of police officials in maintaining social order in Egypt has thus far been largely ignored in modern scholarship. This is not surprising, because no comprehensive study on law enforcement in Roman Egypt is yet available due to the complexity of the policing system.[15] It should be noted that the term "policing system" is therefore used here as a kind of shorthand for the broad array of officials who carried out functions analogous to those of our modern police, though some of their activities transgressed the occupational domain of what we consider police tasks, overlapping with those of higher-ranking officials in other domains such as administration, finances, and army. As a result, it is sometimes difficult to decide whether an official should be considered as police or not. In what follows, I will address some of the challenges historians face when studying the complex role of police and army in (Greco-)Roman Egypt and demonstrate how police effectiveness might be assessed on the basis of insights taken from the fields of criminology and sociology.

1. Defining "police effectiveness"

A key question that any scholar working on law enforcement should ask himself is: "what constitutes an efficient law enforcement system?". Yet to date there has been no attempt in studies on law enforcement in Egypt — or any other ancient society, for that matter — to define the

[11] Campbell 1994, p. 170.

[12] Fuhrmann 2012, p. 189.

[13] Fuhrmann 2012, p. 237.

[14] Fuhrmann 2012, p. 236-238; Alston 1994; Hobson 1993; Bagnall 1989.

[15] A notable exception is Hirschfeld 1892, but the hundreds of new documents that have been published since its appearance renders this study out of date.

term "police effectiveness", despite the fact that scholars often provide definitions of what they mean when using terms as "police" and "police duties". As a result, opinions on the effectiveness of the policing system and the criminal justice system in maintaining law and order in Egypt under Ptolemaic and Roman rule are divided, ranging from highly efficient[16] to almost non-existent.[17] Both views are based on the same evidence, but as R.S. Bagnall already noted: "Just as different views of the extent of lawlessness arise from the same evidence, so do views of the efficacy of official control of crime."[18] The first challenge lies therefore in defining indicators or "metrics" that can be used to assess police effectiveness in Greco-Roman Egypt in a more objective and meaningful way. When reviewing modern scholarship on law enforcement, it becomes clear that the following arguments are most commonly used within the debate on police effectiveness:

2. Possible indicators of "police effectiveness"

2.1. *Calculating crime rates*

Scholars initially attempted to use complaints to calculate crime rates, drawing on these documents to identify what sorts of crimes were committed and who committed crimes against whom in Greco-Roman Egypt.[19] This "history of crime" approach, however, is now considered useless for indicating overall levels of crime in Egypt. Apart from the limitations posed by the survival patterns of the papyrological evidence,[20] "crime" is a highly problematic area in the papyri, because crime is defined in modern law as the intentional commission of an act deemed

[16] Bauschatz 2013 and, to some extent, Fuhrmann 2012, p. 81-82.

[17] Hobson 1993; Bagnall 1989.

[18] Bagnall 1989, p. 203. For a similar observation, see Fuhrmann 2012, p. 246: "Admirers of Rome will appreciate wide-scale policing as part of Rome's military and administrative grandeur. (...) Rome's admirers cannot ignore the corruption, brutality and failure we often see in policing. There is some evidence for all of these views – each is valid to some degree, because Roman policing was so multifaceted and complicated."

[19] On crime and criminals in Egypt, see Grünewald 1999; Helmis 1986; Davies 1973; Baldwin 1963; on violence in Egypt, see Bryen 2013; McGing 1998; Alston 1994; Bagnall 1989; Helmis 1986.

[20] Kelly 2011, p. 63-73.

socially harmful or dangerous and specifically defined, prohibited and punishable under criminal law. Crime and punishment thus form an indissoluble conceptual unity in modern thought,[21] but although there are some cases preserved from Egypt in which punishment is requested, there is no evidence that a distinction was made between criminal law (which deals with criminal wrongs that are punishable by the state), and tort law (which deals with civil wrongs and provides civil remedies) in the papyri.[22] It is therefore important to avoid anachronistic thinking and eschew the use of the term "crime" in connection with the papyrological evidence. The "history of crime" approach also assumes that reported crimes can provide insight into patterns of actual crimes, but criminologists have long recognized that only a small proportion of crimes are reported to the police or brought before court. Any attempt to study crime on the basis of police reports is therefore useless.[23] Moreover, there is the additional problem that petitions, which are our main evidence for wrongs brought to official attention, are often partisan, formulaic, and highly rhetorical, because they were written to provide a narrative of the events to the legal authorities with the request to intervene in his or her affairs and therefore fell within the boundaries of a certain legal genre. Petitions thus provide a rich but complex and problematic data set for studying crime in Egypt.[24] Petitions and reports of court proceedings therefore cannot be used to analyse patterns of crime or the effectiveness of the police system.

2.2. *Existence of a highly developed and well-organized policing system*

At first glance, a highly developed police system appears to have been in place in (Greco-)Roman Egypt to tend to the needs of victims of crime and the day-to-day requirements of law enforcement, but the papyri may be somewhat misleading. Numerous petitions submitted by victims seeking redress for wrongs (for the most part violence, theft,

---

[21] BAGNALL 1989, p. 203.

[22] KELLY 2011, p. 8; for a discussion of penal law in the papyrological documentation, see ANAGNOSTOU-CANAS 2000; ANAGNOSTOU-CANAS 1991.

[23] KELLY 2011, p. 8-9; see also BAETENS 2020a, p. 185 and BAUSCHATZ 2013, p. 74, who noted that crimes such as murder and rape are almost entirely absent from the papyrological evidence.

[24] BRYEN 2013; BAUSCHATZ 2013, p. 39; KELLY 2011, esp. p. 45-49 and 73-74.

official misconduct or negligence and, in Roman Egypt, debt disputes)[25] do not necessarily signify efficient policing.[26] While the papyrological evidence from (Greco-)Roman Egypt provides us with a picture of a tightly run police state, involving a wide variety of officials authorized by the state to tend to routine law enforcement matters at all geographic and administrative levels,[27] there was no rigid hierarchy of command among police officials, resulting in strong regional variation in the policing system in both Ptolemaic and Roman Egypt. Perhaps as a result of the lack of a strictly organized policing system, the occupational domains of officials involved in policing were not always clearly defined and overlapped from time to time. It has been argued by J. Bauschatz that it was in fact the "lack of rigid organization that made for a self-sufficient, flexible police system" in Ptolemaic Egypt,[28] but the papyrological evidence suggests otherwise. Although Bauschatz claims that victims of crime could seek justice from any of a number of police officers and they knew precisely whom to contact for specific forms of remediation, this statement is contradicted by the many petitions in which the petitioner asked that the right person be contacted.[29] In addition, it is difficult to draw conclusions about the effectiveness of the criminal justice system from the papyrological evidence,[30] because the outcome of a dispute is seldom known. The so-called lawsuit archives suggest, however, that at least in some cases, the legal system was unable to achieve the aim of legal control. The papyri preserved in the Tefhape lawsuit archive (TM Arch 237, 181-169 BC) are mainly related to an inheritance dispute between Tefhape and his half-brother Tuot, which culminated in a trial before the *laokritai* Egyptian judges in the temple of Siut on June 22, 170 BC. Although the judges ruled in favour of Tefhape, he complained in two

---

[25] Roman Egypt: KELLY 2011, p. 163, Table 4.3; Ptolemaic Egypt: BAETENS 2020a, p. 183-185.

[26] For a similar observation, see FUHRMANN 2012, p. 81.

[27] FUHRMANN 2012, p. 81; BAUSCHATZ 2013, p. 279-280.

[28] BAUSCHATZ 2013, p. 111.

[29] BAUSCHATZ 2013, p. 163.

[30] For a similar observation, see FUHRMANN 2012, p. 247: "We cannot even determine for certain if these policing experiments were, on the whole, successful – we have nowhere near the right amount or kind of data for such a conclusion. We can go as far as to say that it was not a total failure (...) Numerous anecdotes and chance documents prove a general, widespread faith in institutional policing."

petitions written on May 16, 169 BC (*P. Siut* 10599 and 10600, TM 48653 and 44188) that his half-brother and his sister-in-law continued to deny him his rights to his inheritance.[31] Similar difficulties are encountered in the *Erbstreit* dossier (TM Arch 81, 186-92 BC), which is composed of written evidence produced by the parties, court minutes, court decisions, copies of temple oaths, and settlements. A similar observation can be made about Roman Egypt, since petitions were sometimes sent to up to three or four different officials at the same time.[32] In addition, the petition below (*P. Mich.* VI 421 of AD 41-54; TM 12260), in which the petitioner reported the theft of two donkeys to the *archephodos* of Karanis, who subsequently set out with him to follow the thieves to the town of Bakchias, situated to the southeast of Karanis, reveals a lack of coordination between village police officials, allowing the culprits to get away with the stolen animals (l. 1-27):

> [-ca.?-] ̣[ ] ̣ἀρο( ) οε ̣νυκτὶ τη[- ca.11 -] τοῦ Φαρμοῦθι τοῦ ἐνεστῶτ[ος . . . .] Κλαυδίου Καίσαρος Σεβαστοῦ Γε[ρμανικοῦ] Αὐτοκράτορος, τινὲς λῃστρικῶι τρόπωι [δ]ι̣ω̣ρυξαν τὴν τῶν ἡμετέρων ὄνων α̣ὐ̣[λ]ὴν καὶ ἔνδον γενόμενοι ἀπήλασάν μο[υ] ὄνους λευκοὺς δύο τελείους τιμηθέντας̣ (δραχμῶν) σϙ καὶ ὑπὲρ τούτων ἐπέδωκα τῷ τῆς <Καρανίδος> ἀρχ[ε-]φόδωι Πανκράτηι ὑπόμνημα κα̣ὶ σὺν τούτωι γεμίσας ἕτερον ὄνον ὕδατους (l. ὕδατος) καὶ τροφῶν ἕτερον ἐξωρμήσαμεν, τοὺς αἰτίους ἰχνοσκοποῦντες ὅθεν εὕρομεν τὴν πορείαν — εἰς τὰ μέρηι τῆς Βακχιάδος γεγονέναι — καὶ πάλιν εἰς τὸ ὄρος. ὁ δὲ τῆς Βακχιάδος ἀρχέφοδος Πασίων καὶ οἱ πρὸς τῇ πύληι ἐκώλυσαν ἡμᾶς ἤδη μελλόντων τοὺς αἰτίους καταλαμβάνειν παρ᾽ ἑαυτοῖς· κατε[ί]χοσαν ἐμέ τε καὶ τὸν τῆς Καρανίδος ἀρχέφοδον καὶ τὰ μὲν ὕδατα κατεάξαντες καὶ τὰς κράνους ἀφαρπάσαντες ἐν συνοχῆι ἐποίησαν ἐφ᾽ ἡμέρας τρεῖς ἕως μὴ δυνασθῶμεν συνλαβεῖν τοὺς αἰτίους. ἔπειτα ἀπενεγκάμενοι ἡμῶν σαγὰς δύο καὶ τοὺς ἄρτους καὶ μηλωτὴν καὶ χιλωκτὰ δύο καὶ καδίκισάν (l. κατῄ|κισάν) με πληγαῖς καὶ εἰπὼν (l. εἰπόντες) ὁ κωμογραμματεὺς καὶ <οἱ> πρεσβύτεροι ἀνήγκασαν (l. ἠνάγκασαν) ἡμᾶς ἀπολυθῆναι. ἀξ(ιῶ) ἀντιλ(ηφθῆναι) ὑπὸ̣ (σοῦ).

> […] On the night of the […] of Pharmouthi of the present […] year of the Emperor Claudius Caesar Augustus Germanicus, certain persons dug their way like thieves into the courtyard where we stable our donkeys and,

[31] For further discussion of the archive, see MANNING 2010, p. 207-216; MANNING 2003, p. 201-205. See also the contributions by MANNING and by VANDORPE and WYNS in this volume.

[32] The best known example of this practice comes from the Nestnephis lawsuit archive (TM Arch 151), which documents a long and bitter dispute between Nestnephis and Satabous over the ownership of some empty plots of land in the village of Soknopaiou Nesos. For further discussion, see KELLY 2011, p. 1-6.

> having effected an entrance, drove off two full-grown white donkeys of mine valued at 280 drachmae; and concerning this matter I submitted a report to the *archephodos* of Karanis, Pankrates. With his help I loaded one donkey with water and another with food, and we set out, tracking the culprits from the place where we picked up their trail. We found that it led into the region of Bakchias and back into the desert, but just as we were on the point of taking the culprits in their own abode, the *archephodos* of Bakchias, Pasion, and the guards stationed at the gate prevented us. They placed both me and the *archephodos* of Karanis under arrest, and after breaking the water jars and seizing our staves they kept us in confinement for three days, until we should be unable to lay hands on the culprits. Then, having carried off our two packsaddles, the bread, a sheepskin, and two fodder bags (?), they also beat me. The village secretary and the elders spoke with them and compelled them to release us. I beg that you come to my assistance.[33]

The archives of certain individuals or families such as the Drusilla lawsuit archive (TM Arch 91) also suggest that the enforcement of legal decisions may have been somewhat problematic. The central character of the so-called Drusilla lawsuit was Tertia Drusilla, the widow of a soldier named Valerius Apollinarius, who lived in Karanis at the beginning of the second century. Between AD 119 and 128, Valerius Apollinarius received various loans from another soldier named Iulius Agrippianus, who also lived in Karanis. To secure these loans, Apollinarius mortgaged several plots of the land he owned in the vicinity of Karanis to Agrippianus, who took possession of the land when Valerius could not repay the loans. After Apollinarius died, which occurred between AD 129 and 135, his widow Drusilla reclaimed the lands from Agrippianus. Proceeding on behalf of both herself and her children, Drusilla's argument for reclaiming her late husband's estate was that some of the plots of land belonged to her dowry, while the other plots were part of her children's legacy. The legal proceedings dragged on for at least fifteen years: when

[33] Translation: *P. Mich.* VI 421. According to FUHRMANN 2012, p. 81-82, the so-called "orders for arrest", containing instructions from higher officials to local police officials to arrange for the appearance of an individual or individuals in court, probably emerged in the first century AD as an institutional means to address intervillage disputes. He then adds: "Matters would not have gone so badly [referring to the beating and imprisonment of the police-led search party in the other village] had the victim first been able to obtain a proper summons from a higher authority". Reports of court proceedings, however, often state that the defendant was summonsed, but failed to appear in court. For these texts, see KEENAN 2014, p. 506-508; KELLY 2011, p. 97-103.

Agrippianus died, Drusilla reclaimed the land from his son, Iulius Agrippinus, a soldier of *legio II Traiana fortis*. To deny Drusilla's claim to the plots of land, Agrippinus' lawyers collected excerpts from records of court proceedings before the prefect of Egypt between AD 119 and 142, attesting that soldiers were not permitted to marry and that soldiers' children born during service were thus illegitimate (*Chrest. Mitt.* 372, also known as *P. Cattaoui*, TM 9923).[34] The archive ends in AD 147/148, when the case was still unsettled.

B. Kelly made a similar observation about the judicial system of Roman Egypt with regard to its capacity to produce final and binding resolutions to disputes. Drawing on a corpus of 568 petitions and 227 records of court proceedings, he concluded: "As noble as the ideals of administrative culture in Roman Egypt may have been, it is nevertheless unlikely that the adjudicative decisions made by the judges of Roman Egypt made a significant contribution to social control in the province."[35] The lack of clear jurisdictional boundaries, the many steps through which a case had to pass before a final judgment was given, and the procedural rules and practices that allowed for hearings to be adjourned for long periods hindered an efficient working of the justice system, allowing individuals to petition several officials at once, ignore unfavourable decisions from officials, or take steps to reopen a case before one adjudicator that had already been decided by another.[36] The judicial system of Roman Egypt was thus, "by modern standards, a very complicated and poorly structured system. The opportunities for parties to hinder and delay the progress of cases deliberately were numerous, and there is persuasive evidence that they sometimes did just that."[37] The question whether the policing system, and thus the justice system, worked efficiently can therefore not be satisfactorily answered given the current state of the papyrological evidence.

2.3. *Police corruption and misconduct*

Corruption and misconduct are often believed to have been so widespread within the ranks of the Roman army that it hindered an efficient

[34] For an extensive discussion of this papyrus, see PHANG 2001, p. 23-34.

[35] KELLY 2011, p. 120.

[36] KELLY 2011, p. 77-119.

[37] KELLY 2011, p. 78.

working of the policing system and threatened to undermine the power of the Roman state.[38] Although there is some evidence that local communities benefitted from the presence of the Roman army, the dominating theme in the sources is the brutal oppression of civilians by soldiers.[39] The literary evidence of the Empire in particular provides us with a picture of abusive and ignorant soldiers, who were inadequately supervised and difficult to bring to trial.[40] In Apuleius' *The Golden Ass*, for instance, the encounter of the hero, who has been turned into an ass and is now in the service of a gardener, with a centurion is described as follows (9.39):

> Nec innoxius ei saltem regressus evenit. Nam quidam procerus et, ut indicabat habitus atque habitudo, miles e legione, factus nobis obvius, superbo atque adroganti sermone percontatur, quorsum vacuum duceret asinum? At meus, adhuc maerore permixtus et alias Latini sermonis ignarus, tacitus praeteribat. Nec miles ille familiarem cohibere quivit insolentiam, sed indignatus silentio eius ut convicio, viti quam tenebat obtundens eum dorso meo proturbat. Tunc hortulanus subplicue respondit sermonis ignorantia se quid ille disceret scire non posse. Ergo igitur Graece subiciens miles: "Vbi" inquit "ducis asinum istum?". Respondit hortulanus petere se civitatem proximam. "Sed mihi" inquit "opera eius opus est; nam de proximo castello sarcinas praesidis nostri cum ceteris iumentis debet advehere"; et iniecta statim manu loro me, quo ducebar, arreptum incipit trahere.

> But our return was not free from trouble. For we encountered a tall legionary soldier, as his dress and appearance indicated, who arrogantly and abusively demanded where he [= the gardener] was taking the unladen ass. But my master, who was still rather perplexed, and ignorant of Latin, passed on without saying anything. The soldier, unable to contain his usual insolence,

---

[38] FUHRMANN 2012, esp. p. 224-237; ISAAC 1991, p. 459; BAGNALL 1989; MACMULLEN 1988. The same correlation between corruption and police effectiveness can be observed in BAUSCHATZ 2013. Given the overall argument of the book that the police system in Ptolemaic Egypt was efficient, effective and largely independent of central government control, it is no surprise that police corruption is only briefly dealt with on p. 36: "The occasional involvement of the Alexandrian administration in town and village law enforcement matters perhaps helps to explain the lack of evidence for corruption among the Ptolemaic police. One imagines that an organization operating as freely as the Ptolemaic law enforcement system did would be plagued by official abuses? Yet there are few indications that police corruption was a serious issue."

[39] Most of the evidence discussed in this section comes from ADAMS 2013, p. 266-268.

[40] For a broad overview of Roman soldiers in Greco-Roman literature, see BRINK 2014, p. 77-82.

> struck him with the vine-wood staff he was holding and shoved him off my back. Then the gardener replied humbly that he could not make out what he had said because he did not understand his language. Then the soldier interjected in Greek: "Where are you taking this ass?" The gardener said that he was making for the next town. The soldier said: "But I need its help, for I have to bring our governor's belongings from the nearby fort with the other baggage animals", and he seized me by the rein and began to take me away by force (...).[41]

A similar picture emerges from the New Testament (Luke 3.14), in which John the Baptist advises two soldiers (probably those of King Herod) "not to extort money from anyone, not to use blackmail, and to be satisfied with their own pay."[42] Other passages in the New Testament reveal that soldiers were likely to exploit their status to claim unjust privileges for themselves, particularly by making illegal financial exactions.[43]

Brutish and abusive soldiers were not just a literary *topos*. Documents, which provide important information about the Roman army and the local populations with which it interacted, also paint an unflattering portrait of soldiers. Epictetus, for instance, warned his audience in his *Discourses* 4.1.79 not to oppose a soldier attempting to requisition one's mule, but to let it go, as holding on to the animal would only result in a beating and the mule being taken anyway. Papyri also indicate that the experiences of many provincials with the Roman army may have been accurately described in the literary sources.[44] Numerous petitions survive from Egypt in which soldiers are accused of engaging in beatings, extortion, unlawful imprisonment, and unauthorized requisitions of goods and animals. Just how common extortion at the hands of soldiers could be, is perhaps best illustrated by a fragmentary private account dating to the second century AD (*SB* VI 9207, TM 27283, l. 4-8):[45]

---

[41] Translation: CAMPBELL 1994, p. 174 no. 291.

[42] Translation: CAMPBELL 1994, p. 178 no. 295. On the literary portrayal of Roman soldiers in Luke-Acts, see BRINK 2014; on the historical value of the New Testament and the negative perception of Roman soldiers in Jewish and later Christian writings, see FUHRMANN 2012, p. 19 and 231-233.

[43] CAMPBELL 1994, p. 178.

[44] ISAAC 1991, p. 459.

[45] CAMPBELL 1994, p. 178 no. 295.

To the soldier on guard duty (*stationarius*)	2 drachmae, 1 obol
Gift	240 drachmae
Suckling pig	24 drachmae
To the guard	20 drachmae
For extortion	2200 drachmae
To two police officials	100 drachmae
To Hermias, police agent	100 drachmae
To the [---]	2574 drachmae, 3 obols

Along with expenses such as 20 drachmae for a suckling pig, entries are made in this account for payments to guards: 100 drachmae to two police officials, an additional 100 drachmae to another police official, and 2200 drachmae for "extortion" (διασεισμός). Apart from one exception, these are by far the most expensive items on the account.

The account of the month Phamenoth shows similar entries and it therefore looks as if payments to police officials and soldiers were routinely made by the owner (l. 8-15):

Second half-year, Pha[menoth]:	
To the soldier at his demand	500 drachmae
Currency exchange	12 drachmae
8 jars of wine at 10 drachmae ⅛ obol	[---]
To the police chief	[---]
Dyke tax	1 drachma
Cattle tax?	1 drachma
To the soldier at his demand	400 drachmae
Currency exchange	15 drachmae

The entries for payments to soldiers "at their demand" are also by far the most expense items on the account of the month Phamenoth: 500 drachmae to a soldier, followed by a 400 drachmae to another soldier. These are very large sums of money: for a house in Karanis with two courtyards, Gaius Iulius Niger, veteran of the *ala veterana Gallica*, paid 800 drachmae in AD 154 (*P. Mich.* VI 428, TM 12266).

The evidence of abusive and violent soldiers acting as agents of imperial administration appears throughout the Roman Empire and in all sources,[46] but if the evidence for abuse and extortion is substantial, so is the evidence for official measures taken against the abuse of civilians by soldiers. The unauthorized requisitioning of transport (known as *vehiculatio*)[47] by soldiers generated numerous complaints to officials, including the emperor, and prompted the imperial administration to take action against soldiers' illegal exactions.[48] We know from the legal sources that edicts and laws were regularly passed to prevent abuse. In *Dig.* 1.18.6.5-6, an extract outlining the duties of provincial governors, the jurist Ulpian wrote:[49]

> Ne quid sub nomine militum, quod ad utilitates eorum in commune non pertinet, a quibusdam propria sibi commoda inique vindicantibus committatur, praeses provinciae provideat.
>
> The governor of the province should ensure that "nothing is done in the name of the soldiers by certain individuals unjustly claiming advantages for themselves.[50]

Imperial responses against soldiers who violated the limitations and regulations of the state transport system often took the form of official instructions to enforce proper state transport rules, as illustrated by an edict of emperor Hadrian concerning regulations of public transport from the province of Asia (*IK* LXIX 412, TM 950308 of AD 129):

> ἀγαθῇ · τύχῃ· Αὐτοκράτωρ Καῖσαρ, θεοῦ Τραϊανοῦ υἱός, θεοῦ Νέρβα υἱωνός, Τραϊανὸς Ἁδριανὸς Σεβαστός, ἀρχιερεὺς μέγιστος, δημαρχικῆς ἐξουσίας τὸ τρισκαιδέκατον, ὕπατος τὸ τρίτον, πατὴρ πατρίδος, ἀνθύπατος, λέγει· κατὰ τὴν ἐπιδημίαν ᾗ ἐπεδήμησα τῷ ἔθνει ὑμῶν ᾐσθόμην τὰς πόλεις καὶ τὰς κώμας πλέον τῶν δικαίων ἐνοχλουμένας ὑπὸ τῶν διοδευόντων στρατιωτῶν· ὡς δὴ ἐντεῦθεν ἐκεῖνοι εἰδεῖεν ὧν ᾗ ἀπ<ο>σχέσθαι αὐτούς, <ὑ>μ<εῖ>ς δὲ ἃ δεῖ τελεῖν καὶ μὴ ἀνέχεσθαι ἀπαιτούμενοι, διατάγματ[ι] ἐδέησέν με <δηλῶσαι>· ὄχημα μόνοις διδόσθω τοῖς δίπλωμα ἔχουσιν· ὁ χρώμενος τῷ ὀχήματ[ι] διδότω τὸ ἐπὶ τοῖς διπλώμασιν τεταγμένον· ὁδηγὸν μηδενὶ ἐξέστω λαμβάνειν οὔτε γὰρ ἐκτρέπεσθαι τῆς δημοσίας ὁδοῦ τοὺς στρατιώτας ἀνανκαῖον, καὶ μὴ ἐκτρεπομένοις οὐδὲν δεῖ τῶν ὁδηγούν[των]· εἰ μέντοι χειόνος ποτὲ μεγάλης ἐπιπεσούσης ἄδηλοι γένοιντο αἱ ὁδοί, τότε μ[ό]νον ἐξέστω λαμβάνειν ὁδηγόν· ἄριστον ἢ δεῖπνον [ἢ] κ[ρ]ειθὰ{ι}ς {κρειθὰς} ἢ χό[ρτ]ον προῖκα μήτε αἰτεῖν ἐξέστω μήτε διδότω

[46] BRINK 2014, p. 74-77.

[47] On requisitioned transport in the Roman Empire, see MITCHELL 1976.

[48] FUHRMANN 2012, p. 159-160.

[49] ADAMS 2013, p. 266.

[50] Translation: CAMPBELL 1994, p. 176 no. 292.

τις αἰτούμενος· ἀλλὰ καταγωγὴν προῖκα μηδενὶ δὲ τῶν καθ' ἑαυτοὺς ὁδοιπορούντων στρατιωτῶν ἔστω λαμβάνειν· εἰ δὲ ὑπὸ σημείων τι<νὲ>ς παρ<ί>οιεν ἢ χρήματα τῆς ἀρχῆς κομίζοντ<ε>ς ἢ δεσμώτας ἄγοντες δὲ ἢ θηρία, τούτοις μόνοις καταλύσεις δημόσια<ι> διδ<ό>σθωσαν καὶ ἀγορὰ τιμῆς ἥτις ἦν πρὸ δέκα ἡμερῶν· καὶ ἄν παρὰ ταῦτα ἀξιώσωσίν τινες ἢ βιάζωνται, [τὰ] τῶν λαμβανόντων ὀνόματα τῷ τοῦ ἔθνο[υς] ἡγουμένῳ πεμπέσθω καὶ τῷ ἐπιτρόπῳ μ[ου] — οὐδὲν δὲ μεικρόν ἐστιν τὸ βοηθῆσον ταῖς πόλεσιν πρὸς τὸ μηδὲν βίαιον παθεῖν — καὶ vac. πρὸς ἐμὲ ἐπιστελλέσθων· vac. vac. πρ[οτ]εθή[τω]. vac.

Good fortune. Imperator Caesar Trajan Hadrian Augustus, son of the divine Trajan, grandchild of Nerva, *pontifex maximus*, *tribunicia potestas* for the thirteenth time, *consul* for the third time, *pater patriae*, *proconsul* says: During the stay which I made among your people, I had become aware that the cities and the villages are being troubled more than the rules allow by the soldiers who are travelling through. In order that they shall know in the future what to keep themselves away from, that you (shall know) what you have to perform and what (you shall) not tolerate even if being requested, I found it necessary <to set forth> (these measures) by an edict: (1) A wagon shall only be given to those who have a diploma. He who uses the wagon shall pay what is fixed in the diplomas. (2) No one shall have the right to take a guide since soldiers do not need to leave the public roads, and since they do not leave they have no need for anyone to show the way. In case the roads become invisible because of a heavy snowfall, only then shall it be allowed to take a guide. (3) It shall not be allowed to demand breakfast, dinner, barley or fodder for free nor should anyone give these when called upon. (4) But free lodging shall not be allowed for any soldier to take while travelling on private business. But if someone is passing through while on duty or if they are bringing the ruling power's money, or transporting prisoners or wild animals, public lodgings shall be given only to them and provisions at the market price which was effective ten days earlier. Then if anyone contrary to this shall make an exaction or use force, the names of those who take shall be sent to the provincial governor and my procurator (nothing is small, i.e. insignificant, which assists the cities for the future so they suffer no harm) and shall be forwarded to me. Let it be posted.[51]

The continuous efforts to prevent the recurrence of illegal and excessive exactions by soldiers and officials reveals serious determination on the part of emperors to prevent abuse of civilians. Since official measures were mainly aimed at preserving the interests of the Roman state, however, they were probably not only motivated by a concern to protect the

[51] Translation: HAUKEN & MALAY 2009, p. 3.

provincial population. *PSI* V 446 (TM 19292), an edict of M. Petronius Mamertinus, prefect of Egypt from AD 133 to 137, forbidding requisitions without certificates (*diplomata*), reveals also some concern over the perception of soldiers as representatives of the state on the part of Roman authorities (l. 8-10):[52] ἐξ οὗ τοῖς μὲν ἰδ̣ιώταις ὕβρις (l. ὕβρεις) τε καὶ ἐπηρείας γείνεσθαι, τὸ δὲ στρατ[ι]ωτικὸν ἐπὶ πλεονεξίᾳ καὶ ἀδικίᾳ διαβά[λλ]εσθαι συνβέβηκε ("Because of this, private persons are subjected to arrogance and abuse and the army has come to be censored for greed and injustice").[53]

Particularly illuminating in this regard is an extract of emperor Domitian's *mandata* or official instructions to a *procurator* on an inscription from Syria (*IGLS* V 1998, TM 761280 of AD 81-96), in which the concerns of the emperor regarding soldiers' illegal exactions are clearly stated (l. 11-12 and 17-30):

> μήτε ὑποζυγίων μισθώσεσιν, μείτε ξέ[νων] ὀχλήσεσιν βαρύνεσθαι τὰς ἐπαρχείας. (…) ἐντέλλομαι δὴ καὶ σοὶ φρον̣τ̣ί[δα] ποιήσασθαι ὅπως μηδεὶς ὑποζύγιον λάβῃ εἰ [μὴ] ὁ ἐμὸν ἔχων δίπλωμα· ἀδικώτατον <γ>άρ ἐστι[ν], ἢ χάριτί τινων ἢ ἀξι<ώσει> τὸ γραφὰς γεινέσθαι, ἃς [μη]δενὶ ἔξεστιν διδόναι ἢ ἐμοί· μηδὲν οὖν γε[νέσ]θω ὃ τὴν ἐμὴν ἐντολὴν καταλύσει καὶ τὴν συμ[φο]ρωτάτην ταῖς πόλεσιν γνώμην φθερεῖ· βοη[θεῖν] γὰρ δίκαιόν ἐστιν ἀτονούσαις ταῖς ἐπαρχε[ίαις] αἳ μόγις τοῖς ἀναγκαίοις ἐξαρκοῦ<σιν>· μηδ[ὲ] βιαζέσθω τις αὐτὰς παρὰ τὴν ἐμὴν βο[ύ]λησιν· ὁδηγόν τε μηδεὶς λαμβανέτω εἰ μ[ὴ] ὁ ἐμὸν ἔχων δίπλωμα· ἐναποσπωμένω[ν] γὰρ τῶν ἀγροίκων, ἀγεώργητοι μενοῦ[σιν] αἱ χῶραι.
>
> Neither by the renting of beasts of burden nor by the distress of lodging should the provinces be burdened. (…) I instruct you to see to it that nobody commandeers a beast of burden unless he has a certificate from me. For it is most unjust that, either by the favour or prestige of certain people, requisitions should take place which nobody but myself can grant. Therefore, let there be nothing which will break my instructions and spoil my intent, which is most advantageous to the cities, for to help the weakened provinces is just, provinces which barely have enough for the necessities of life. Let there be no violence used against them [the civilians] contrary to my wish and let no one commandeer a guide unless he has a certificate from me, for, when farmers are torn from their homes, the fields will remain without their attention.[54]

---

[52] FUHRMANN 2012, p. 234.

[53] Translation: CAMPBELL 1994, p. 176-177 no. 293.

[54] Translation: FUHRMANN 2012, p. 160-161.

Such edicts concerning abuse were thus common throughout the Empire, revealing not only the continuous determination and efforts from the Roman authorities in preventing illegal military exactions, but also their inability to solve the problem. Despite the willingness of the emperors and their officials to prevent abuse, the response was not sufficiently strong or effective to make a lasting difference and measures therefore often had to be repeated.[55]

The evidence for abuse and extortion of civilians by soldier-police is thus widespread, but not unproblematic, because the Roman army was the most visible feature of Roman control and authority, and could therefore be perceived either as a peacekeeping force or an army of occupation, depending on the province and the outlook of particular groups within provinces.[56] The negative perception of soldiers in Jewish and later Christian writings can also — at least in part — be explained by the fact that Jews and Christians were often on the receiving end of Roman hostility. From the evidence it is thus clear that abuse of civilians by soldiers occurred, but not to what extent.[57] In other words: how can the corruption level within the ranks of police be measured? Even in the case of modern societies, this is a difficult question to answer, despite the mass of quantitative data to which scholars have access.[58] For a premodern society such as that of Roman Egypt, for which statistical data are mostly lacking, it is almost impossible to answer this question.

One approach would be to try to manufacture statistics on corruption by calculating the number of times that misconduct occurs out of all offences recorded in petitions. From a preliminary analysis of 650 petitions dating from the late first century BC to the late third century AD it emerges that only 10% concern misconduct by a soldier or official (primarily extortion). Caution is needed, however, because civilians may have been reluctant to file complaints against soldiers, who were entitled to special privileges and treatment in court. According to Juvenal (*Satires*

[55] ADAMS 2013, p. 267; FUHRMANN 2012, p. 234; CAMPBELL 1994, p. 180 no. 301.

[56] ADAMS 2013, p. 264-265.

[57] It should be noted that all societies suffer from corruption to some extent, so a moralizing approach to this issue should be avoided: HOLMES 2015.

[58] The different approaches to measuring corruption are discussed in detail in the Manual on Corruption Surveys (UNODC, UNDP and UNODC-INEGI, 2018, p. 20-29).

16), the outcome of such a case would usually be in the soldier's favor, whether in prosecution or defense. He writes (l. 7-34):

> Commoda tractemus primum communia, quorum haut minimum illud erit, ne te pulsare togatus audeat, immo, etsi pulsetur, dissimulet nec audeat excussos praetori ostendere dentes et nigram in facie tumidis liuoribus offam atque oculum medico nil promittente relictum. Bardaicus iudex datur haec punire uolenti calceus et grandes magna ad subsellia surae legibus antiquis castrorum et more Camilli seruato, miles ne uallum litiget extra et procul a signis. 'iustissima centurionum cognitio est, agitur de milite, nec mihi derit ultio, si iustae defertur causa querellae.' Tota cohors tamen est inimica, omnesque manipli consensu magno efficiunt curabilis ut sit uindicta et grauior quam iniuria. dignum erit ergo declamatoris mulino corde Vagelli, cum duo crura habeas, offendere tot caligas, tot milia clauorum. quis tam procul adsit ab Vrbe praeterea, quis tam Pylades, molem aggeris ultra ut ueniat? Citius falsum producere testem contra paganum possis quam uera loquentem contra fortunam armati contraque pudorem.

> Let us discuss first the benefits shared by all soldiers, of which not the least is that no civilian would dare to beat you up, and if he gets a trashing he will conceal it and will not dare to show the praetor his teeth which have been knocked out, and the black lumps and swelling bruises on his face, and his one remaining eye for which the doctor holds out little hope. If a man seeks to gain redress for this, he is granted a military judge in hobnailed boots and hefty jurors sitting on mighty benches, in accordance with the ancient law of the military camps (...) that a soldier may not be involved in litigation outside the wall of the camp and far from the military standards. Of course the judgment of centurions in the case of soldiers is extremely just, and I am certain to obtain retribution if I lodge a legitimate complaint! But the whole unit is against you, and all the soldiers unite in complete agreement to make sure that your retribution is something that needs medical treatment and is worse than the original offence. So it would be an act of incredible stupidity, since you have two legs, to provoke so many boots and thousands of hobnails. Besides, what witness would dare to come so far from the city? (...) You can more easily find a dishonest witness who will speak out against a civilian, than one prepared to tell the truth against the interests and honour of a soldier."[59]

Other approaches used for measuring corruption in modern societies are perception surveys, which measure perceived levels of corruption rather than the actual occurrence of corruption, and experience-based surveys, which measure actual personal experience of corruption by, for

---

[59] Translation: CAMPBELL 1994, p. 166 no. 275.

example, asking citizens or businesses if they have paid a bribe or were involved in other forms of corruption. Each method has its own limitations: actual occurrences of corruption are difficult to measure, while measurements based on perception surveys are based on perceptions of levels of corruption among citizens, business representatives, civil servants or other stakeholders in a given country. While perception surveys can be useful tools, they cannot be used as a proxy for actual levels of corruption, because they are based on subjective opinions. People's opinions are affected by many factors, and their views on corruption may not be primarily informed by actual experience of corruption. The *Manual on Corruption Surveys* therefore advises that using a variety of corruption methods instead of just one provides a better basis for approximating the truth.

While perception surveys or experienced-based surveys are not possible for obvious reasons, it should be noted that a large number of petitions were submitted to soldiers, as illustrated by the following petition (*P. Mich.* III 175, TM 11981 of AD 193):

> Ἀμμωνίῳ Πατε̣ρνῳ (ἑκατοντάρ)χ(ῃ̣) παρὰ Μέλαγ̣ος Ὡρίω̣νος ἀπὸ κώμης Σοκνοπαίου [Ν]ήσου ἱερέως τοῦ ὄντος ἐν τῇ κώμῃ θε̣[ο]ῦ. ὑπάρχει ἐμοί τε καὶ τοῖς ἀνεψιοῖς μ[ο]υ̣ Φανήσι καὶ Ἁρπαγάθῃ κοινῶς ἐξ ἴσου π̣αππικὸν κατὰ μητέρα ἐν τῇ αὐτῇ κώμῃ ψειλὸς (l. ψιλὸς) τόπος περιτετι̣χισμέν̣ο̣ς (l. περιτετειχισμέ|νος) ἔνθα [ἀ]ποτιθόμεθ[α] (l. [ἀ]ποτιθέμεθ[α]) κ̣ατ᾽ ἔτος̣ ὃν ἔχ̣ομεν χόρτου. τοῦ οὖν ἑνὸς Ἁρπαγάθου ὑπογύως τελευτήσαντος καὶ τοῦ μέρους αὐτοῦ κατα̣ντήσαντος εἰς ἀμφοτέρους ἐξ ἴσου, ἐχθὲ̣ς, ἥτις ἦν κβ, ἐμοῦ ἀποτιθομένου (l. ἀποτιθε|μένου) ἐν τῷ τόπῳ τὸν ἡμέτερον χόρτον ὁ Φανῆσις βιαίως καὶ αὐθάδως ἐπελθὼν ἐκσ̣πετέρισέν (l. ἐσφετέρισέν) μου τὸν χόρτον οὐκ ἐάσας με ἐν τῷ ἡμετέρῳ μέρι (l. μέρει) ἀποτίθεσθαι ἐπι̣-χειρῶν̣ ἐκ τούτου ἀποθεῖν (l. ἀπωθεῖν) με καὶ αὐτὸν μόνον ἀντιποιεῖσθαι τοῦ μοι προσήκοντος οὐ μόνον ἀλλὰ καὶ τὴν ἀνωτάτην μοι ὕβριν παρεῖχεν. ὅθεν ἀξιῶ κελεῦσε (l. κελεῦ|σαι) μεταπεμφθῆναι αὐτὸν ἵνα δυνηθῶ τῆς ἀπὸ [σ]ο̣ῦ ἐπικίας (l. ἐπιεικείας) τυχεῖν. διευτύχει. (2nd hand) (ἔτους) α Π̣ο̣υ̣βλί[ο]υ Ἑλβίου Π̣ε̣ρτίνακος Σεβαστƭο(ῦ) (l. Σεβαστο(ῦ)) Φαρμοῦθι κγ.
>
> To Ammonius Paternus, centurion, from Melas, son of Horion, of the village of Soknopaiou Nesos, priest of the god who is in the village. In the same village there belongs to me and my cousins Phanesis and Harpagathes, held in common and with equal shares as an inheritance from our maternal grandfather, a vacant plot of land, surrounded by a wall, where we deposit every year the hay which we have. Then recently one cousin, Harpagathes, died and although his share was inherited equally by both of us, yesterday, which was the 23rd, while I was stacking my hay, Phanesis attacked me

> boldly and insolently, took my hay, and did not allow me to deposit it in our share, but tried to exclude me from this and to claim for himself alone what belongs to me; in addition to this, he treated me with the most disgraceful viciousness. Therefore I request that you order him to be brought before you so that I may obtain the fair decision that is in your power. Farewell. (Second hand) Year 1 of Publius Helvius Pertinax Augustus, 23 Pharmouthi.[60]

Such petitions may of course have been filed in the mere hope of eventual redress, as has been argued by some scholars, but this documentary behavior shows nonetheless a level of public confidence in the performance of police and other officials that is difficult to reconcile with the "fear and loathing" felt by all "articulate classes in the societies of the Roman Empire toward outposted military police".[61] Graph 1, based on a corpus of 650 petitions dating from the late first century BC to the late third century AD, shows that nearly as many petitions were addressed to soldiers as to other law enforcement officials.

Graph 1: Distribution of petition addressees

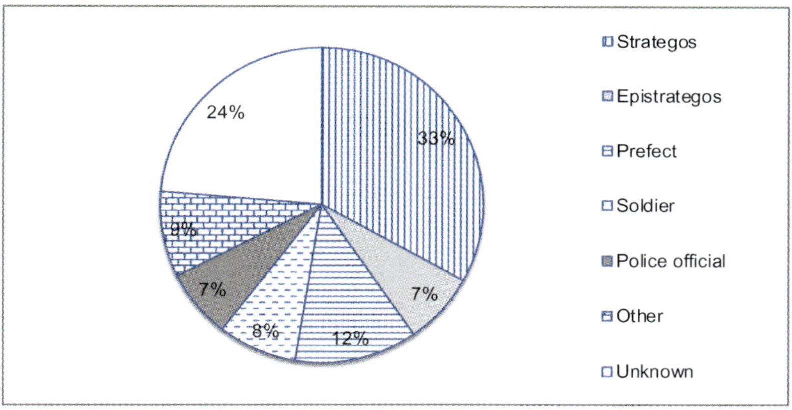

Looking at the chronological distribution of the petition addressees in Graph 2, it is clear that soldiers gradually began to replace law enforcement officials from the late first century onwards. Before this period,

---

[60] Translation: CAMPBELL 1994, p. 173 no. 288.

[61] FUHRMANN 2012, p. 231; for a contrary view, however, see ADAMS 2013, p. 267.

most petitions to police were addressed to the *epistates ton phylakiton,* who disappears from the records after AD 42.

Graph 2: Chronological distribution of petition addressees

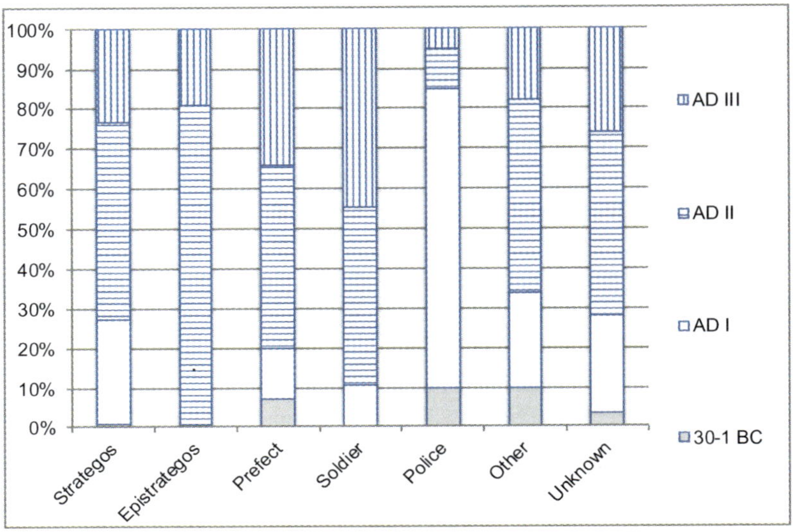

There is thus no evidence that soldiers were more prone to violence and extortion than other persons whose status of power may have allowed them to claim certain privileges for themselves, such as tax collectors and law enforcement officials.

Another approach for measuring corruption levels is used by Transparency International's Corruption Perceptions Index (CPI), which is still the best known and most widely used indicator of corruption despite recent criticism. This approach is summarized in the introductory remarks to the CPI:

> There is no meaningful way to assess absolute levels of corruption in countries or territories on the basis of hard empirical data. Possible attempts to do so, such as by comparing bribes reported, the number of prosecutions brought or studying court cases directly linked to corruption, cannot be taken as definitive indicators of corruption levels. (...) Capturing perceptions of corruption of those in a position to offer assessments of public sector corruption is the most reliable method of comparing relative corruption levels across countries.

While it is therefore not possible to assess the absolute level of corruption of soldiers in Roman Egypt, the number of petitions recording official misconduct by soldiers may be compared with those by law enforcement officials from the Ptolemaic period, which reveals that such abuses were not restricted to the Roman period. Complaints of police misconduct are also known from the Ptolemaic period, and the Ptolemaic kings also issued royal ordinances to prevent abuse, but without much success.[62]

Finally, measurements of corruption are particularly sensitive to the definitions of corruption employed. For example, the understanding of corruption may differ greatly from one country or society to another. Bribery, for instance, cannot always be clearly distinguished from corruption. Additional research on corruption in Greco-Roman Egypt has revealed that, contrary to modern society, the division between bribery and extortion was probably often blurred. L. Bellienus Gemellus, a veteran who lived in the Fayum in the late first and early second centuries AD, for instance, actively sought to cultivate good relations with local officials and wrote in a letter to his son Sabinus (*P. Fay.* 117, TM 10782 of AD 119, l. 1-8):

> Λούκιος Βελλῆνος Γέμελλος Σαβίνωι τῶι υείῶι (l. υἱῶι) χαίρειν καὶ διὰ παντὸς εὐ<τυ>χεῖν. Γείνοσκαι (l. γίγνωσκε) ελ[.]υραν (l. Ἐλου̣ρᾶν) τὸν βασιλεικὸν (l. βασιλικὸν) διαδέχεσθαι̣ τὴν στρατηγείαν Ἐράσου ἐκ (l. ἐξ) ἐπιστολὴν (l. ἐπιστολῆς) τοῦ κρατείστου (l. κρα|τίστου) ἡγεμόνος. αἰάν (l. ἐάν) συ δώξῃ (l. δόξῃ) πέμσαι (l. πέμ|ψαι) αὐτῷ ἐλᾶς (ἀρτάβην) α καὶ εἰκθύδιν (l. ἰχθύδιον) ἐπὶ (l. ἐπεὶ) χρίαν (l. χρείαν) αὐτοῦ ἔχωμον (l. ἔχομεν).
>
> Lucius Bellienus Gemellus to his son Sabinus, greeting and continual good health. You must know that Elouras the royal scribe is to become deputy for the *strategos* Erasos, in accordance with a letter of his highness the prefect. If you think it well, send him an *artaba* of olives and some fish, as we want to make use of him.[63]

Particularly interesting in this regard is that among the payments in the fragmentary private account *SB* VI 9207 (TM 27283), there is an entry of 240 drachmae for a "gift" (θαλλός). Formal dependency relation-

---

[62] For police corruption in Ptolemaic Egypt, see BAUSCHATZ 2007, esp. p. 22. Abuse of official power in Egypt was rejected by official ideology and policy, but difficult to repress in practice; for a general discussion of this conflict, see CRAWFORD 1978.

[63] Translation: ADAMS 2013, p. 266.

ships formed an important part of life in Roman society: the upper strata were connected to the lower strata of society through a dense and complex patronage network, and people often relied on "friends" for support, protection or promotion to a higher social order. The documentation preserved on papyrus, in particular the private correspondence of soldiers, demonstrates that letters of recommendation from influential persons, the use of connections and even money were necessary to rise within the ranks of the Roman army (Davies 1969; Saller 1980). No research has thus far been carried out on how the coming of Roman rule and the introduction of a more rigid social hierarchy transformed interpersonal relations in Egyptian society, but private letters can provide important information on the ways in which people attempted to use the system to their advantage. Further analysis of the papyri for evidence about gift exchange and bribery and its importance for developing strong social ties may therefore contribute to a better understanding of corruption in Ptolemaic and Roman Egypt.

More important, however, for the purposes of this paper is the question whether corruption hindered police effectiveness. According to researchers on police corruption, police corruption undermines the confidence of the public in the police and destroys respect for the law: if law enforcement officers cannot be trusted, most citizens have nowhere else to turn when seeking justice. Leading on from this, if citizens do not trust the police, they are much less likely to cooperate with them, resulting in higher unsolved crime rates. Based on the numerous complaints that continued to be sent to soldiers and police officials, however, police corruption, if widespread, did not drastically alter the perception of people towards the criminal justice system. Based on his analysis of the major features of the judicial system in Roman Egypt, B. Kelly reached a similar conclusion: "The fundamental problem with the [judicial] system was not negligent or corrupt officials, but the poor architecture of the system and the manpower limitations of the ancient state."[64]

3. Litigation versus "self-help" in obtaining justice

Several petitions also record previous actions taken by victims of crime to settle a dispute, leading scholars to conclude that people were reluctant

[64] Kelly 2011, p. 78.

to seek redress from legal authorities and that petitions were only submitted in the final stage of a dispute, when all other means of settling a dispute had been exhausted.[65] The underlying premise is that all societies have various mechanisms at their disposal to settle disputes, and that a distinction should be made between:

(1) formal mechanisms of ensuring social order (= those emanating from the state: essentially the criminal justice system and its three main 'subsystems': police; courts and law; correctional procedures and institutions);
(2) informal mechanisms of control, defined as 'a variety of informal reactions and interventions at non-governmental level', including social norms, religion, ...

Previous studies on law enforcement therefore attempted to assess the role played by law enforcement in maintaining order by examining whether institutional means (the criminal justice system) or non-institutional means (self-help or community regulation) were more effective in preserving social order.[66] In other words, they examine whether the government or the victims themselves were responsible for ensuring that justice was obtained for crimes committed against them. This "social control" approach, however, has been used in a variety of ways by sociologists,[67] and from my own study of the evidence from Roman Egypt I would rather argue in favor of those recently developed in social criminology; namely that social control is maintained by both legal systems and a wide range of social institutions, from religion to family life. A key issue in this approach is the consideration that both forms of control are two-way processes and that top-down and bottom-up perspectives are equally important. This means that people participate in the legal system and help shape it, not only influencing, but occasionally also thwarting the system's formal purpose of providing social control, a consideration that has thus far been largely neglected in the current debate about the effectiveness of the police system in Roman Egypt. To give an example of this interaction between both formal and informal forms of

[65] HOBSON 1993: the petitioning process exists on the perimeter of what is essentially a system of self-help rather than a penal system as we know it; BAGNALL 1989.

[66] FUHRMANN 2012, passim; ALSTON 1994.

[67] DEFLEM 2015 provides an excellent overview of the concept of social control throughout the history of sociology and the related areas of criminology and criminal justice.

seeking justice: in l. 15-17 of *P. Enteux.* 25 (TM 3300), a petition dating to 222 BC in which a father complains that he quarreled with his son about the late repayment of some money he had lent him, the police official is instructed by the *strategos* to insist that father and son first try to sort out their disagreement, and that only if this fails is he allowed to ask for further instructions to end the dispute:

> Πτολεμαίωι. μάλιστα μὲν αὐτὸς σὺ διάλυσον τὸν πατέρα πρὸς τὸν Στρουθόν· ἐὰν δέ τι ἀντιλέγηι, ἀπόστειλον αὐτὸν πρὸς ἡμᾶς, καὶ ὅπως μὴ ἄλλως ἔσται. (ἔτους) κς, Δαισίου κγ, Φαῶφι ε.

Rather exceptionally, the papyrus also informs us about the outcome of the dispute, because at the base an unknown third hand has written that the mediation was successful and that the son agreed to provide his father with 2 drachmae per month as pension. The father, Pappos, is said to have declared himself content with this arrangement.

Finally, it should be noted that the police system is essentially "caught" between two worlds, namely those of the state and people, whose interests do not always coincide with one another. Police officials therefore play a dual role in society, since they are responsible for both governing and protecting people.[68] The Roman army, which was the most visible feature of Roman control and authority, could therefore be perceived either as a peacekeeping force or an army of occupation, depending on the province and the outlook of particular groups within provinces. This may explain to some extent the negative perception of police and army found in the sources. The relations between the army and the provincials is perhaps best summarized by C. Adams, who concluded that "In general, the relationship between the army and the provinces was exploitative, but also provided social and economic opportunities to provincials".[69]

Conclusion

The above shows that it is thus essential to have a clear understanding of what constitutes an efficient law enforcement system when reviewing the papyrological evidence. But how can police performance be measured?

---

[68] Spierenburg 2004.

[69] Adams 2013, p. 264-265.

Nowadays, assessments of police effectiveness are based on statistical data (reports may examine, for instance, crime rates in relation to police and population numbers, though this method is considered unreliable), and, more importantly, on surveys indicating overall levels of public confidence in policing (the PSA 23 survey, for instance, is now used to measure police effectiveness in England and Wales[70]). Yet, even these reports remain cautious, pointing out the various problems associated with the recording of crime.[71] For a pre-modern society such as Roman Egypt, for which we mostly lack statistical data, the question whether the police system achieved its aim of formal control is even more difficult to answer. It is of course tempting to use the large number of surviving petitions and records of court proceedings (1487 texts in all) to manufacture statistics that will shed light on the efficiency of the police system in Roman Egypt, but this is not advisable due to the uneven patterns of survival of the papyrological evidence and the problems associated with the recording of crime. Likewise, surveys as indicators of public confidence in local law enforcement in Roman Egypt are not possible, but the number of petitions submitted to officials may at least suggest a level of public confidence in police efficiency. Petitions were expensive to write, and the relatively large number of petitions surviving from Egypt indicates that people thought it worthwhile to petition officials when seeking justice for crimes committed against them, regardless whether they expected to obtain justice through the legal system.

In conclusion, I hope to have shown that, while previous studies tended to generalize conclusions drawn from particular evidence or from particular police tasks to the policing system as a whole, the insights taken from sociology and criminology provide a more systematic treatment of the social context of the policing system in Egypt. While it is not possible to assess police effectiveness in Roman Egypt in absolute terms due to the nature of the evidence and the problems associated with assessing police efficiency, even in modern societies, this paper argues in favor of a relative approach by comparing a comparable data set (the papyrological documentation) from Late Hellenistic Egypt with Roman Egypt in order to gain insight into the operation of the policing system in Roman Egypt. Petitions, which form the core evidence for policing in

---

70 JACKSON & BRADFORD 2010.

71 For a relatively recent overview, see PRATT 2012.

Greco-Roman Egypt, but have been labeled "unreliable" by some scholars due to their rhetorical motives, may therefore be used in a more methodologically sound way for both periods. While it is therefore not possible to state with certainty that the policing system in Roman Egypt was efficient or not, a preliminary analysis of the papyrological evidence from Late Hellenistic and Roman Egypt reveals that there was no sharp decline in the number of petitions addressed to law enforcement officials (thus: soldiers) in the Roman period. It can therefore be concluded that there are no indications that soldiers were an imperfect instrument of law enforcement or that the policing system in Roman Egypt was less effective in obtaining its aim of ensuring social order than in Late Hellenistic Egypt. There are in fact indications that the petitioning process became standardized under the Romans, since the officials to whom petitions were addressed are much more diverse in the Late Hellenistic than in the Roman period, when complaints were primarily submitted to the office of the *strategos*. Further research, however, should be conducted to assess the impact of this change on the operation of the policing system, and to map the transformation of the policing system in Egypt under Roman rule in the first four centuries AD in detail.

DISPUTE RESOLUTION BETWEEN HUSBAND AND WIFE IN ROMAN EGYPT: LEGAL MECHANISMS AND FAMILIAL STRATEGIES

Marianna THOMA
(University of Athens/University of Vienna)

Abstract: Documentary papyri from Roman Egypt give evidence of various conflicts between husband and wife, about which they requested legal action. Women usually complained to the authorities about bad treatment, marital abandonment and removal of their dowry or parental inheritance. For example, in *PSI* V 463 Athenarion submitted a petition against her husband, who took her dowry, while *P. Tebt.* II 334 preserves Herakleia's petition to the centurion, because her husband carried off to his own house everything her parents bequeathed her after their death. Men's petitions dealt equally with abandonment and property removal by the wife, for example *P. Heid.* III 237, where a husband blamed his wife for deserting him and their child, also taking his farming tools with her. This paper aims to discuss various marital disputes and the available legal mechanisms of resolution, as implied in petitions, letters and other documents from the Roman era. It also investigates the impact of the victim's sex on obtaining justice. Particular attention is paid to the involvement of family members in the legal or private settlement of a dispute between a couple, along with the family strategies developed to ensure marital *concordia*.

INTRODUCTION

While in marriage contracts from Roman Egypt promises of marital faith and respect are given, documentary evidence suggests that many couples ended up fighting. In most cases marital disputes and divorce, especially by mutual consent, were a family matter.[1] However, papyrus documents illustrate many conflicts between husband and wife about which they requested legal action. In this paper I discuss various cases of

[1] For divorce agreements from the Roman era, see for example *P. Lips.* I 27 (TM 11620); *P. Mil. Vogl.* III 185 (TM 12392); *P. Oxy.* XXXVI 2770 (TM 16561); XLIII 3139 (TM 30221); *P. Strasb.* III 142 (TM 13169).

marital disputes and the available social and legal mechanisms of resolution on the basis of petitions, letters and other kinds of documents from the Roman era. Particular emphasis will be given to the involvement of family members in the private or legal settlement of a marital dispute, along with the family strategies developed to ensure marital *concordia*.

Marriage in antiquity made each partner subject to several obligations.[2] The husband was the head of the family and his wife had to obey him.[3] Adultery by a man was considered a sexual offense only in case the woman was not a permissible partner, such as a prostitute or slave, while adultery by a wife was always ground for divorce.[4] On the other hand, the husband should not cast out (ἐκβαλλεῖν) his wife, nor insult (ὑβρίζειν) or ill-treat her (κακουχεῖν).[5] The husband had control of the dowry during the marital union, but several constraints were placed both in the Ptolemaic and Roman era on his ability to dispose of the family assets, including dowry, in order to secure the wife's maintenance.[6] The

---

[2] Greek contracts and contracts drawn up by Romans outline in detail the husband's obligation to maintain his wife and the wife's obligation to be faithful to him. See TAUBENSCHLAG 1944, p. 120. The obligation of the husband to support his wife can also be found in Egyptian marriage contracts. For further details see YIFTACH-FIRANKO 2003, p. 186; RUPPRECHT 1998, p. 63-69; VÉRILHAC & VIAL 1998, p. 267-279. For marriage contracts with joint obligations of the spouses from the Roman period see for example *P. Bon.* 26 (TM 27063); *P. Col.* VIII 227 (TM 27235); *CPR* I 237 (TM 29087); *P. Oxy.* II 265 (TM 20536); *P. Oxy.* III 497 (TM 28355); *SB* XXVIII 17045 (TM 20592).

[3] See for example *P. Giss.* I 2, l. 15-17 (TM 2796): ἔστω [δὲ Ὀλ]υμπιὰς παρὰ Ἀνταίωι πειθαρ/χοῦσα αὐτοῦ ὡς π[ροσῆκόν ἐστιν γυναῖκα ἀ]νδρὶ κυριεύουσα μετ' αὐτοῦ/ κοινῆι τῶν ὑπα[ρχόντων].

[4] TREGGIARI 1991b, p. 264. It is also said that kinsmen, together with the husband, could sentence an adulterous wife to death. A main concern expressed in most marriage documents was any moral misconduct of the wife, which could cause shame to her husband.

[5] See for example *SB* XXVIII 17045, l. 9-10 (TM 20592): μηδ' ἐκβάλλειν μηδ' ὑβρίζειν/ μηδὲ κακουχεῖν αὐτὴν μηδ' ἀποκλεῖν μεδενὸς (l. ἀποκλείειν μηδενὸς) [τῶν ὑπαρχόντων]. For κακουχεῖν see *P. Oxy.* II 265, l. 14 (TM 20536). The term ἐκβαλλεῖν probably denotes a volatile casting out of the wife and is contrasted by ἀποπέμπειν, a lawful termination of marriage by sending her away. *Hybrizein* and *kakouchein* appear together, conjoined in a formula, both in marriage documents and in two of five petitions reporting harassment. For further details see YIFTACH-FIRANKO 2003, p. 187-188.

[6] The dowry had a dual purpose: it was partly a contribution to the expenses of married life and partly the financial basis for the maintenance of the wife after the termination of the marriage. For the woman's dowry in Ptolemaic and Roman times, see HÄGE 1968, p. 33-36; SALLER 1984, p. 195-205.

husband's duties found in marriage agreements included respect for the wife and for her property, her maintenance according to his means and the preservation of mutual love and fidelity. These clauses found in most marriage contracts were characterized by Joseph Mélèze-Modrzejewski as "clauses morales".[7] They were not legal grounds for divorce in the modern technical sense, but they could be regarded as social and legal norms permitting the spouse to dissolve the marriage.[8] Almost all marriages from Roman Egypt include a clause stipulating the duties of the parties in case of divorce, as the dissolution of a marriage was anticipated from the time of its formation.[9] Both Greek and Roman law included provisions for the protection of a wife's dowry after separation. In the older Greek contracts, the husband had to refund the dowry and pay an additional amount: 100% in earlier times and 50% in later times.[10] Later, the divorce penalty disappeared, but the obligation to refund the dowry immediately (παραχρῆμα) was retained. The husband, if not guilty, was granted a reasonable period to restitute the dowry.[11] A wife who abandoned her husband was not subject to any fines, but if she neglected her marital duties, ancient Greek and Alexandrian marriage contracts

---

[7] MÉLÈZE-MODRZEJEWSKI 1984, p. 251.

[8] The marriage documents offered some routine procedures to the spouses who wished to dissolve their marriage. If a partner left the joint household making clear in some way that he or she did not intend to come back for serious reason, the marriage would be considered dissolved. See also ARNAOUTOGLOU 1995, p. 18.

[9] This clause can be seen even in the later Christian period, as in *P. Bal.* II 152 (TM 85497), a Coptic marriage contract of a priest or a priest's son. Dotal contracts naturally took into account the various ways in which marriage could be brought to an end.

[10] See TAUBENSCHLAG 1944, p. 124. Cf. *P. Lond.* II 178 (TM 19960), where Petronia Sarapias confirms having received back a smaller part of her dowry (400 dr.), from her ex-husband Iulius Apolinarios, a soldier. She also retains the right to proceed for the remaining 600 dr. Petronia and Iulius Apolinarios obviously violate the law forbidding soldiers to marry, however, in the end Petronia was lucky, because her husband did not deceive her. A ruling of the prefect M. Rutilius Lupus (*P. Cattaoui* recto, col. 1, l. 5-13, TM 9923) makes it clear that Petronia would not have won the case, if it had ended up in court.

[11] TAUBENSCHLAG 1944, p. 123-124. For example, see *P. Mil. Vogl.* II 85, l. 21 (TM 11574) for a period of sixty days granted to the husband to return the dowry. In most of the cases the extended return period is connected with separation initiated by the wife. See also ARNAOUTOGLOU 1995, p. 20, n. 16.

deprived her of her dowry.[12] As the receipt of the dowry acknowledged the existence of a lawful marriage, its return made it *ipso facto* clear that the marriage was dissolved. In marriage contracts from the Roman period authors avoid pointing the "sending away" of the wife by her husband as an act terminating the marriage. In the early Roman Arsinoites, the term ἀποπομπή signifies an act of divorce initiated by the husband, whereas ἀπαλλαγή[13] signifies a rupture initiated by the wife. The term *apopompe*, as a generic term for any act of divorce, is not attested again before the fourth century AD.[14] In addition, in Roman law the woman's dowry could also be protected via the *actio rei uxoriae*.[15]

Legal anthropologists identify seven stages in a disputing process[16]: lumping,[17] avoidance,[18] coercion,[19] negotiation,[20] mediation,[21] arbitration[22] and adjudication.[23] Papyri testify in marital disputes mainly the

---

[12] TAUBENSCHLAG 1944, p. 121. In Roman law a wife who committed adultery might forfeit one-sixth of her dowry in subsequent judicial proceedings. See Ulpian, *Tit.* 6.9-13.

[13] The husband had the right to ἀποπομπή, while the woman the right to ἀπαλλαγή, corresponding to the Attic ἀπόλειψις.

[14] YIFTACH-FIRANKO 2003, p. 204, n. 32.

[15] Generally, *actio iudiciuma rei uxoriae* was a specific action against the husband for the recovery of the dowry, independently of a particular agreement on the matter. It is not certain whether the action was *bona fide*, but the judge had to consider *ex aequo et bono* the questions connected with the restitution. The rules concerning the restitution made a distinction as to whether the marriage came to an end because of the death of one of the spouses or by divorce, and in case of divorce whether the husband or the wife was at fault or the divorce was mutually agreed. See BERGER 1953, p. 444. If the divorce were due to the fault of the wife or her father, the husband could retain one-sixth for each child up to three.

[16] For the stages of a disputing process see NADER & TODD 1978, p. 9-12; HOBSON 1993, p. 200.

[17] Lumping is the situation where one of the aggrieved parties in a dispute decides to ignore the problem and the dispute ceases without actually having been settled.

[18] Avoidance occurs when one of the parties withdraws from the dispute.

[19] Coercion involves using force or the threat of force to resolve the conflict.

[20] Negotiation describes dispute settlement, where the two parties come to an agreement on the subject at issue without the intervention of a third party.

[21] Mediation describes a situation where the disputing parties agree to have a third party help them settle the disagreement.

[22] In arbitration two disputants agree in advance to abide by the decision of a third party who has been chosen to help the parties involved.

[23] Adjudication, also as arbitration, involves the presence of a third party who has the authority to settle the dispute in whatever way he wants. See also GAGOS & VAN MINNEN 1994, p. 35-46.

stages of arbitration and adjudication, which involved invoking the law as the final stage. The source material from Roman Egypt for dispute resolution between a couple mainly consists of petitions to the authorities and of private letters. A spouse's petition to an official for help is actually the end of the disputing process rather than the beginning, while the private letters reflect the everyday marital problems and the family strategies for compromise between the spouses, without legal recourse. In most letters, a wife complains about her husband's absence from the household or his indifference to the family problems. In *PSI* III 177 (TM 28065) Isidora, who is afraid that her sick child is about to die, blames her absent husband for not supporting them.[24] A mother's involvement in a marital dispute is recorded in *P. Mich.* VIII 514 (TM 30514) from the third century.[25] Isidora plans to visit her daughter Sarapias in order to restore the marital harmony disrupted by a disagreement between the couple due to Sarapias' father. In *SB* VI 9271 (TM 25291), a wife requests her brother's protection against her abusive husband, who even threatened to kill her.

1. Women's petitions

The corpus of petitions is more instructive, as far as the resolution of marital disputes is concerned. Judicial hearings concerning violence were held in front of magistrates according to the *cognitio* procedure.[26] Women usually complain to the authorities about abuse, marital abandonment, removal of their dowry or other kind of property.[27] A wife could claim

---

[24] Bagnall & Cribiore 2006, p. 280-281. Cf. *UPZ* I 59 (TM 3450) from the second century BCE, where Isias accuses her husband Hephaistion, because he has not yet returned from Sarapeion in Memphis and shows indifference to their household problems. Moreover, in *P. Oxy.* IV 744 (TM 20442) in his letter Hilarion reassures his wife Alis who is afraid of being forgotten by him.

[25] Bagnall & Cribiore 2006, p. 269-270.

[26] The magistrate — Roman prefect, *epistrategos* or *strategos* — was presiding official and judge in legal proceedings. As Bryen points out, litigants of all classes would be treated by officials who were more or less legal amateurs. See Bryen 2013, p. 46. *Cognitio* was the examination of a judicial case by a magistrate or a juror. See Berger 1953, p. 393.

[27] Anagnostou-Canas (1984, p. 337-360) has provided a general discussion of cases of women appearing in courts of justice as plaintiffs or defendants.

her property rights against her husband, in spite of her belonging to the weaker sex. An Alexandrian marriage contract in the form of a *synchoresis*, from the end of the first century BCE, provides that if the husband violates his marital obligations, the wife will have the right to exact payment from him by a court judgment.[28] However, in practice this procedure was more complicated. In women's petitions, abuse in the context of a conflict over property is always reported in the same manner: ἐκβαλλεῖν, κακουχεῖν, ὑβρίζειν.[29] In the first half of the first century CE, Syra complains that her husband Sarapion squandered her dowry and maltreated her.[30] They had contracted a marriage *synchoresis*. After her abandonment, she asks the *archidikastes* to force her husband to return to her the φερνή increased by ἡμιολία, a fine of 50% established in the Alexandrian marriage documents for misconduct of the husband.[31] She also proclaims her innocence in lines 12-14: ἀνέγκλητον ἐματὴν (*l.* ἐμαυτὴν) ἐν ἁπᾶσει (*l.* ἁπᾶσι) παρειχό/μην, in order to anticipate a cross-action of her husband, who could state in his defence that he left her due to improper behavior on her part.[32] A woman who invoked the accusation procedure against her husband, while staying with him, could also be accused of living away from his house without his consent, in case she decided to leave him first. If charges were proven, she could lose her dowry according to the terms of the marriage document.[33] But Syra could not be accused, because Sarapion was impoverished and she had received

---

[28] *BGU* IV 1050, l. 18-19 (TM 18493). See also EVANS-GRUBBS 2002, p. 124.

[29] See ARNAOUTOGLOU 1995, p. 23.

[30] *P. Oxy.* II 281 (TM 20552). Cf. *PSI* VIII 944 (TM 17598), where a woman submits a petition to the prefect blaming her husband, because he spent her dowry, while he also had many debts.

[31] Cf. *BGU* IV 1099, l. 19 (TM 18537). *Hemiolia* clauses appear as penalty in marriage instruments of Ptolemaic and early Roman period, when the husband fails to return the dowry within the agreed period of time. See for example *P. Gen.* I² 21 (= *M. Chr.* 284, l. 8-9, 12-14, TM 44544); *BGU* IV 1050 (= *M. Chr.* 286, l. 16-17, TM 18493); *P. Oxy.* III 496 (= *M. Chr.* 287, l. 9, TM 20632).

[32] This claim was allowed according to the marriage *synchoreseis*. For the accusation procedure see HÄGE 1968, p. 68.

[33] See YIFTACH-FIRANKO 2003, p. 199-202. In *P. Gen.* I 21 (TM 44544) from the second century BCE a wife is accorded with an additional mean of bringing about a divorce besides the accusation procedure. The divorce would be set in motion by the *apaitesis*, the demanding back of the dowry. She could get back her dowry in a period of 60 days, with no addition, but without having to prove anything.

him into her parents' house, while their joint life ended with him leaving.[34] In a fourth century case Aurelia Herais, expelled by her husband for no reason, awaited ten years for the resumption of the marriage and then decided to reclaim her property.[35] She explains that she was married to him as a young virgin and that she belonged to an excellent family. Although family members were supposed to get involved in marital conflicts in order to contribute to the dispute resolution, Herais blames her husband's sister for persuading him to abandon her.[36]

If the deserted spouse was pregnant or had children, she might encounter greater financial problems.[37] As a result, many marriage documents provided for the possibility of pregnancy in case of divorce.[38] In

---

[34] Accusing the husband of *enkataleipein* his wife in an uxorilocal marriage, as in the case of Syra, had the same import as accusing him of casting out his wife in a virilocal marriage. See YIFTACH-FIRANKO 2003, p. 199.

[35] *PSI* I 41 (TM 33258).

[36] Lines 13-16: παροξυνόμενος ὑπὸ τ[ῆ]ς ὁμογνησίας αὐτοῦ/[ἀδελφῆς -]ς καὶ συμβουλευόμενος πα[ρ]' αὐτῆς ἐμὲ μ[ὲν] ἐκβαλεῖν, ἔχειν δὲ /[αὐτὴν γυναῖκα - τ]οῦτο ὑπουργῶν τῇ ἰδίᾳ ἀ[δ]ελφῇ καὶ πει[θό]μενος ταῖς συμβουλείαις /[αὐτῆς --]εὶς ἐξέωσέ [μ]ε ἄνευ αἰτίας πρὸ δέκα τούτω[ν ἐνι]αυτῶν εἰς τὴ[ν πα]ροῦσαν / [ἀπορίαν]. A dispute between a wife and her sister-in-law is also described in *BGU* III 970 (TM 9420) from the second century. Tapetheus requests the help of the authorities against her sister-in-law, as she is a helpless woman. After her husband died, his sister and legal heir Helen refused to return to Tapetheus the value of her dowry, or concede her the house that belonged to her husband in Karanis and which had been used as a mortgage to secure the return of the dowry. She issued a counter-statement (*antichresis*). Limnaios had made her an *engraphos asphaleia* providing, among others, for the case that he could not return her dowry. In that case, Tapetheus could take ownership of a part of the house and some of his property. It was also agreed that she would pay a debt of one-hundred drachmas owned by Limnaios to a third party. Although the wife did not have the *kyrieia* on her husband's assets, she had the *protopraxia*, by which she was given priority over other creditors in the exaction of the debt. Tapetheus had probably made repeated recourse to *protopraxia*, as Helene may have placed the property that her brother had given as security for his wife's dowry in the hands of another creditor. For a discussion of models of a wife's security in case of husband's death see YIFTACH-FIRANKO 2003, p. 252-253.

[37] See for example *BGU* VIII 1848 (TM 4927); *P. Oxy.* LIV 3770 (TM 15286); *P. Panop.* 28 (TM 16198); *SB* XIV 11392 (TM 25320).

[38] In a noteworthy *psephisma* of Ptolemais a pregnant woman is granted the right to request alimony from her divorced husband both for herself and her child. See TAUBENSCHLAG 1944, p. 124. If there were children of the marriage and the divorce was the wife's fault, her ex-husband was entitled to receive a share of her dowry, since legitimate children remained in their father's power after divorce. See also EVANS-GRUBBS 1999, p. 227.

one third century CE marriage contract the spouses agree that if at the time of separation the bride is pregnant, the groom should give her 40 drachmas for the expenses of childbirth.[39] Dionysia, living in the first century BCE, complains to the *strategos* that her husband Apollonios deserted her and their baby two years previously, and as a result she had to move into her brother's house.[40] Apollonios went to Alexandria, where he had an affair — either a second marriage or a concubinage — with another woman and a new baby. Dionysia requests that her dowry of 2000 drachmas be returned. However, her husband has spent all of it and then instructed his father to sell some real estate in order to pay back the dowry.[41]

The parents could sometimes prevent a wife's maltreatment by her husband. For instance, in *P. Tebt.* II 334 (TM 13493) Herakleia submits a petition to the centurion claiming that her husband Hermes started harassing her only after the death of her parents. Her basic arguments are that they have two children, and she has never thought of another man. As she was now an orphan and could no longer have recourse to her parents. *P. Lips.* I 41 (TM 33701) of the fourth-century records the courtroom speech of the attorney Nilammon representing the orphan Olympiane. The girl was married with her curator's consent, but the groom could not provide the required bridal gifts and promised to secure the fulfillment of his promises. When the wife requested the gifts with the assistance of her curator, Besarion abandoned the house, taking some of her property with him. The attorney requests the receipt of the gifts

[39] *P. Oxy.* X 1273, l. 33-34 (TM 21791). See also *P. Oxy.* II 267, l. 20-21 (TM 20538); *P. Oxy.* III 496, l. 10-11 (TM 20632); *SPP* 4 p. 115-116, l. 24-26 (= *P. Oxy.* III 603 descr., TM 20694). The corpus of petitions does not include disputes regarding children's custody in case of marital separation. ARNAOUTOGLOU (1995, p. 24) has pointed out that there are two possible reasons for this occurrence: the practice of child-exposure and the custody arrangement in the marriage contracts. In Roman law, children born in legitimate marriage came under their father's power and after divorce he had sole custody.

[40] *BGU* VIII 1848 (TM 4927).

[41] As she has no hopes of saving her marriage, she tries to salvage what she can. In *P. Bon.* 21 (TM 25132) of the first century, another deserted wife wants her dowry recovered from her husband and also asks for the children's maintenance. Cf. *PSI* IX 1075 (TM 17483) from the fifth century, in which a woman complains that her husband sold all the items included in her property.

and the return of the girl's property.[42] He confirms that the girl had obtained the right to divorce her husband. But this statement is not clear, because the document dates back to the time of Constantine, when desertion did not constitute a rightful ground for divorce.[43] Moreover, the lawyer could not have referred to the marriage document, as the couple's union was an *agraphos gamos*. In spite of the husband's misconduct in any given way, Nilammon confirms that if all the things requested were to be accomplished, marital harmony would be restored. The orphan girl may not really wish to divorce her husband, but rather to restore the marital *concordia*. All these petitions exemplify how difficult it was for wives to press charges against their husbands who sometimes reacted violently. As a result, the women may have preferred to maintain the marital union, but on better terms.

Sometimes after a domestic crisis, spouses wish to base their marriage on a new marital arrangement recorded in a special document.[44] A resumption of the marriage after a temporary rupture is recorded in an application concerning a contract of remarriage of uncommon type.[45] Apollonarion, who owned property alongside her dowry, became indebted both to the state and to other creditors. These debts may have been the cause of the couple's separation. Horion paid back to Apollonarion her dowry, without breaking off their relations. He lent her money to pay her dues to the state and then remarried her receiving security for the repayment of her debts, both to himself and to other creditors. In addition, *P. Murabbat* II 115 (TM 16759) preserves a contract of remarriage between two Jewish spouses involving a dowry of

[42] The role of the curator is also important, as he has probably taken the place of the woman's deceased father. If Mitteis was right that the curator also had to give his consent to the girl's divorce, we may be dealing with an application of local rules or possibly the curator was necessary, because the divorce included financial settlements between the two spouses. *Dig.* 24.2.4 excludes such a prerogative, even in the case of the insanity of the ward. For further details see also URBANIK 2014, p. 173-175.

[43] For Constantine's legislation on divorce see later note 57.

[44] Such a contract of remarriage after divorce is preserved in *BGU* IV 1101 (TM 18539) from the first century BCE. Cf. also *PSI* I 64 (TM 78828) from the first or second century BCE, which includes a series of restrictions on sexual and moral behavior of the bride Thais, who may have previously misconducted against her husband.

[45] *P. Oxy.* XII 1473 (TM 21874).

200 denars.[46] Most of the time, a remarriage, as a family strategy resolving the marital dispute, took place when the husband initiated the first divorce. But if the reconciliation was so rapid, did the first separation constitute a true divorce?[47] If we take into consideration that in such cases the dowry was paid back and a new dowry was granted to the bride, in my opinion the first separation should be considered a real divorce.[48]

This paper has already discussed several cases of marital conflict after a wife was abandoned by her husband. A wife who suffered physical abuse could also have recourse to her blood relatives or officials for assistance to initiate a divorce and obtain restoration of property damage, before being abandoned by her husband. In a document from the end of the first century BCE Tryphaine complains to Protarchos, the head of the *kriterion*, that her husband Asklepiades treated her as a slave and stole her dowry.[49] As Tryphaine is still living with him, she should leave him, at the same time proving the accusations made against Asklepiades. Otherwise she would risk being charged with the accusation of an unlawful departure and forfeit her dowry according to the terms of the marriage *synchoresis*.[50] Her main request is the return of the dowry[51] and the enforcement of her departure by a court of law in order to prove that her reasons for divorce were justified.[52] If a court official approved her

[46] This document shows that Jewish matrimonial law was also influenced by Greco-Roman law. Biblical law permitted remarriage provided that the wife had not started a relationship with another man during the separation. For the possible Hellenization of Jewish legal tradition, see also TCHERIKOVER 1945, p. 139.

[47] A temporary interruption of a joint life without intent to divorce was common in Roman Egypt. Cf. *P. Oxy.* VI 903, l. 15-17 (TM 33342); *P. Oxy.* L 3581, l. 9-10 (TM 32313).

[48] Return of the dowry without dissolving the marriage was related to loans that wives gave to their husbands in lieu of a dowry in first-century Oxyrhynchos. For such loans see GAGOS e.a. 1992, p. 181-208.

[49] *BGU* IV 1105 (TM 18546). She uses the same arguments as Syra did in *P. Oxy.* II 281 (TM 20552).

[50] Cf. *BGU* IV 1050, l. 19-21 (TM 18493).

[51] In most of the divorce documents from the Roman era the person who acknowledges the retrieval of the dowry is the ex-wife, especially if she is old enough and legally capable of managing her own affairs. In *P. Fam. Tebt.* 13 (TM 10730) and *P. Lips.* I 27 (TM 11620) the father acknowledges the recovery of the dowry, while in *P. Mil. Vogl.* III 185 (TM 12392) it is the bride's mother who acknowledges it.

[52] She requests that one of Protarchos' employees verifies her proper departure and finalizes the divorce. Tryphaine does not ask for the separation fine of 50%, but rather she requires her husband to balance accounts (διαλογίζεσθαι) with her father for the

departure, it would not be easy for her husband to press charges against her in the same court of law. She also explains that she was at first unwilling to marry Asklepiades, but that he persuaded her parents to approve their marital union. Apparently she is also assisted by her father.[53] Another unwilling bride with an unhappy marriage appears in a petition from the fourth century.[54] Aurelia Attiena blames Paulus for using violence to force her to marry him and then leaving her for another woman, an act she describes as bigamy.[55] Also when some soldiers billeted in their house, Paulus robbed them. After the mediation of the clergy, she took him back and his father acted as his guarantor. But Paulus became even more abusive and after she sent him a deed of divorce, sent a crowd of men to carry her off and imprison her in his house. Although at this period most divorce evidence concerns mutual agreement, Aurelia Attiena states the unilateral repudiation of her husband. She had sent him a *repudium*, "through the *tabellarius* of the city, according to imperial law".[56] Though he could have invoked imperial legislation against unilateral divorce, he preferred to break into the house and assault her.[57] Late Roman law did indeed impose significant restrictions on the right of wives — and, to a lesser extent, of husbands — to repudiate their spouses unilaterally. However, neither Constantine, who introduced strict regulations on divorce, nor any of his successors until Justinian

amount of 66 dr., a sum that is higher than the value of the dowry itself. If she were to lose the case, the consequences would be disastrous both for her reputation and her financial position. See YIFTACH-FIRANKO 2001, p. 1333.

[53] *BGU* IV 1105, l. 21-24 (TM 18546). Her father's presence most probably restrained her husband from counterattacking her.

[54] *P. Oxy.* L 3581 (TM 32313).

[55] See ROWLANDSON 1998, p. 208-209, no. 154.

[56] *Repudium* was the unilateral breaking up of a betrothal. In later empire, it could be considered a legal instrument, new in Egypt, with which the wife requested the dissolution of a marriage and the return of the dowry. See *Dig.* 24.2; BERGER 1953, p. 676. Again, from the fourth century, *P. Lips.* I 39 (= *M. Chr.* 127, TM 22351) also describes that a woman suffered physical abuse by her husband, after sending him a *repudium*.

[57] See URBANIK 2014, p. 169. Constantine introduced regulations in 331 AD on divorce. *CTh* 3.16.1: women were forbidden to send repudiation to their husbands on the pretext that they were drunkards, gamblers or philanderers. Wives could use only homicide, poisoning or tomb destroying as legal grounds. Otherwise, they would be deprived of their property and exiled to an island. A man could claim only adultery, sorcery or procuring on penalty, otherwise he had to restore the wife's dowry and would not be able to remarry. For a further discussion see BAGNALL 1987, p. 42.

declared illegal divorces to be void.[58] Attiena asks to secure the payment of two ounces of gold that were defined in the spouses' agreement as a fine for Paulus' misbehavior with the security of her father-in-law.

The family of the wife not only acted at the early stages of a marital dispute for the restoration of marital harmony, but they also played a role in legal proceedings against the husband, as implied by petitions composed by them on the wife's behalf. In *P. Oxy.* LIV 3770 (TM 15286) of the fourth century Aurelia Ptolema submits a petition to the *syndikos* of Oxyrhynchus on behalf of her daughter Arilla, who is married with Theon and had given birth to a boy, but whose husband did not support any of them and had left them a long time ago.[59] The bride's mother requests her daughter's divorce, while she also blames Theon for asking for the return of the marital gifts (*hedna*) given to Arilla.[60] Ptolema uses as a rhetorical strategy that Theon despised her weakness. Under certain circumstances, especially if the wife was young and financially dependent on her mother, the mother could initiate the rupture without her daughter's explicit consent.[61] The parents of the bride were initially entitled to dissolve their daughter's marriage, but this right was limited by the second century CE.[62] However, if the husband did not care for his family's maintenance after a marital dispute or separation, the bride's family, and mainly the father, were responsible for feeding her and her children, and

---

[58] They were punishable, but nonetheless still effective.

[59] EVANS-GRUBBS 2002, p. 216.

[60] *Hedna*, documented in the papyri from the fourth century, are the presents given by the groom to the father of the bride in anticipation of a marriage.

[61] See YIFTACH-FIRANKO 2001, p. 1336. The father also had this right, but for the restitution of the dowry it was the wife who should initiate the divorce procedure. For further details see also TREGGIARI 1991b, p. 443. It is generally held that by the late Republic women who were independent and not under the husband's control could legally divorce, as simply as their husbands could. On the occasion of a case of mother's intervention into her daughter's divorce, Diocletian remarked that "a daughter's divorce was not in the power of the mother" (*CJ.* 5.17.4).

[62] By the second century AD paternal right was restricted. Fathers were entitled to take this action also in fourth-century BCE Athens. See LEWIS 1982, p. 161-178. Roman officials hearing cases, which dealt with father's attempts to apply this right, predicated it on the daughter's approval. Lawyers representing a daughter maintained that this right was to take effect only if her father was married to her mother in an *agraphos gamos*. Dionysia's case in *P. Oxy.* II 237 (TM 20506) proves that some wives preferred to remain loyal to their husbands involved in disputes with their fathers-in-law. See YIFTACH-FIRANKO 2001, p. 1336.

as a result they were interested in claiming the wife's rights. *P. Ryl.* IV 706 (TM 32785) of the fourth century preserves a part of petition addressed to the prefect by a citizen of Antinoopolis against his son-in-law, who abandoned his daughter together with their child. The father complains about the expenses of feeding them for three years.[63]

In a similar way, a father petitions in *SB* XII 11221 (= *P. Panop.* I 28) (TM 16198) against his son-in-law, who abandoned his daughter with their son, also taking with him the pawns given as security for the dowry. Aurelia Senmoros found refuge in her father's house.[64] In most petitions submitted, mainly by abandoned wives, the couple's offspring are not mentioned, while in a few the offending spouse is said to owe obligations towards the children. In the case of Aurelia Senmoros her father refers to his little grandson's maintenance.[65] It was only after the husband took away his son that the woman and her father decided to send the petition. In Roman times, a father could sue for the return of his daughter's dowry, but only if she consented. In a later document, *P. Oxy.* I 129 (TM 37141), a father informs his son-in-law that the marriage with his daughter, who is under his *patria potestas*, is dissolved. After Euhemeria's maltreatment by her husband, her father sent him a *repudium* through the *defensor civitatis*, requesting that the marriage should be dissolved.[66]

[63] In case of divorce, papyri imply that both in Roman and peregrine law provision is made for the maintenance of the children and among the Romans father had usually this duty. See *Dig.* 25.3.3.1, TAUBENSCHLAG 1944, p. 124.

[64] Lines 9-11: διὸ πρ[οήχθην] δεηθῆναι τῆς σῆς χρηστ̣[ό]τ̣ητος, ἡγεμὼν κ̣ύριε, διά/ τῆσδέ μου τῆς ἀναφορᾶ̣[ς] ἀξιῶν κελεῦσαι διὰ τῆς σῆς κελεύσεως δι' οὗ ἐὰν δοκι/[μάσ]ῃ σου τὸ μεγαλεῖον τοῦτον ἐπαναγκάσαι λυτρωθῆναι τὰ ἐνέχυρα αὐτῆς καὶ ἀποκα[τα-στ]α̣θ̣ῆ̣ν[αί] μ̣ο̣ι καὶ μὴ [ἐνοχ]λεῖσθαί με περ[ὶ] ὀφειλῆς αὐτοῦ.

[65] A divorced wife could leave part of her dowry to her husband, if the children continued to live with their father. Dowry agreements made before marriage sometimes provided for all or part of the wife's dowry to remain with the husband in the event of divorce, if there were children, to contribute to their rearing. See *Dig.* 23.4.2 and *P. Oxy.* II 265, l. 24 (TM 20536) for example. If the divorce was the wife's fault, the husband was entitled to keep one sixth of the dowry for each child up to three children. See Ulpian, *Reg.* 6.9. See also CANTARELLA 2005, p. 35; KRAUSE 2011, p. 633.

[66] The *defensor civitatis* was an official appointed by the emperor for the first time in 362 CE for the defense of the poor classes of the population. See BERGER 1953, p. 428; FRAKES 1994, p. 337-348. In Roman law, if a father gave his son-in-law notice of divorce and the daughter did not agree with his wishes, the marriage continued and her father could not even reclaim the dowry he had given, unless she consented. See TREGGIARI 1991a, p. 34. In addition, in *P. Mich.* V 227 (TM 12068) a Tebtynis petitioner complains

He appears to be interested mainly in his daughter having a happy life. In the third century CE, fathers would try to exercise their traditional rights by using a legal instrument called *interdictum de liberis ducendis*.[67] An enforceable order given to the reluctant spouse allowed the father to take his son or daughter away from the conjugal residence. In fact, in a passage of Ulpian we read that an *exceptio*, i.e. a judicial defense, had been accorded to a husband against his father-in-law, who had used this legal instrument.[68]

Apart from the petitions, an affidavit submitted to the authorities by a wife can also shed some light on everyday marital disputes. Such a document can be found in *P. Oxy.* VI 903 (TM 33342) from the fourth century, which describes the misconduct of an abusive husband during a considerable period of time.[69] The document is a kind of affidavit used in proceedings taken against the husband by the wife. Both parties own a large number of slaves and they may be landowners. Their marriage is based on the Egyptian tradition of unwritten union, later formalized by a contract. The wife accuses her husband of treating their slaves violently and insulting her.[70] Even the mediation of the local bishops could not obtain a resolution in the couple's dispute and the wife had to address the authorities.[71] The document probably comes from a Christian context, but it is not clear if it is a true or a fictional story. The woman did not divorce her abusive husband earlier, probably for financial reasons or because she may have believed that she should tolerate his bad behavior, as a Christian wife should do.

---

on behalf of his sister's daughter, who has apparently suffered abuse by her husband, but unfortunately the document is not clear. In most of these cases a male relative, mainly the father, addresses the authorities to try to safeguard a woman's property rights.

[67] BERGER 1953, p. 510.

[68] *Dig.* 43.30.1.5 = Ulpian *ad edictum* 71. In a papyrus dated to 312 CE (*P. Sakaon* 38 = *P. Flor.* 36 = *M. Chr.* 64, TM 13056) a father, after his wife's death, compelled his daughter to leave her conjugal home, possibly against her will and certainly against her husband's wishes. Her father-in-law asked the local magistrate to intervene in order to bring her back to his son's house. The petition aimed to safeguard the agreement concerning the payment of the gifts and the restoration of his son's marriage. The decision was that the problem should be solved in accordance with the woman's wishes.

[69] See also MONTSERRAT 1996, p. 99-100.

[70] He even stripped his wife's foster-daughter and tormented her with fire (lines 6-7).

[71] She mentions an oath given by her husband in the presence of the bishops declaring that he trusts his wife with the keys of his house. However, after that he continued to maltreat her and even locked her out of the house.

2. Men's complaints against their wives

On the other hand, many husbands complained about their wives' misconduct. *P. Oxy.* III 528 (TM 28368) from the second century preserves an uncommon emotional letter addressed by a husband to a woman who abandoned him. Serenus denies himself the therapeutic effect of a bath as a sign of mourning, since Isidora has left him. It is likely that Isidora abandoned him after some kind of a personal dispute or a dispute over property and she was then in a relationship with another man. Unfortunately, there are many textual difficulties.[72] Serenus does not have recourse to the authorities, but only wants to express his deep feelings for Isidora. She could be his wife, but it has also been suggested that she was his concubine. In *SB* XVIII 14043 (TM 27687) from the second century a husband questions an oracle about his wife's return: whether he should wait for her to come back by herself or make the first move to persuade her. These documents show some emotional aspects of the marital relationship and the husband's abandonment by his wife or concubine.

Men's petitions can shed more light on everyday problems within the household and disputes with wives, which are mainly about abandonment or property removal. In *P. Oxy.* II 282 (TM 20553) of the first century a husband complains, because his wife left their house, taking with her some of his belongings.[73] The use of the verb "carried off" in its plural form may indicate that someone, probably her mother, helped Demetrous to abandon her husband. The weaver Tryphon submits a petition to the *strategos* Alexander claiming the return of his property. His basic argument is that he fulfilled his marital duties, supplying Demetrous everything she needed during their life together. The continuing conflict between Tryphon and Demetrous is the subject of two more petitions submitted by Tryphon to the *strategos* after his divorce.[74] Tryphon may believe that the state was actually concerned with the

[72] See MONTSERRAT 1996, p. 116.

[73] See also WHITEHORNE 1984, p. 1267-1274. Cf. *P. Vindob. Barbara* inv. 34, a Ptolemaic *enteuxis* submitted by a priest to the king accusing his wife of stealing various items from his house. See also the relevant discussion on HARRAUER & PINTAUDI 2012, p. 3-12.

[74] *SB* X 10239 (= *P. Oxy.* II 315 descr., TM 16677); *SB* X 10244 (= *P. Oxy.* II 324 descr., TM 16683). In these petitions, Tryphon complains that his former wife has assaulted both his present wife Saraeus and him.

protection of his individual rights and wished to find a solution to his familial tragedy.[75]

In *P. Heid.* III 237 (TM 31479) from the third century a husband claims that his wife left him δίχα τῆς καλουμένης ἀπ[?αλλαγῆς] (l. 7-8). She deserted him and their child, also taking with her his farming tools. The husband complains that she has already remarried without having formally divorced him and he reports that her new husband "unlawfully abducted" her. In his petition, he demands that his property be restored. Jane Rowlandson alleges that Panetbeus, as a public farmer, stresses that his wife has stolen his farming tools in order to attract the centurion's attention: if he is not able to farm his land, he will be unable to pay his taxes.[76] He may not desire his wife's return, but only needs his tools and assets back. He argues she has not yet returned anything to him, while he still supplies to her the child's maintenance. In *SB* XVI 12505 (TM 16255) of the third century AD a husband complains that his wife sold some common property without his consent.[77] While in marriage contracts the return of the dowry is provided in case of separation, we are not well informed about a husband's claims on his own property against his wife.[78] In Greek contracts, the removal of the husband's property by the wife is treated as theft and the verb used is ἀποφέρειν, while in Roman law an *actio rerum amotarum* was a legal procedure used in cases of theft between spouses.[79] We do not know of any particular penalty or fine imposed on the wife, but the husband could have recourse to the

---

[75] MORRIS 1981, p. 365.

[76] ROWLANDSON 1998, n. 137.

[77] Cf. *P. Oxy.* LXV 4481 (TM 78580) from the second century, where a husband submits a petition against his wife, who has gone off with property, to some or all of which he claims she has no right. He asks the prefect to ensure that his wife will turn up in court, when the case comes up for trial.

[78] In the Gortynian Law Code the removal of a husband's property from his wife is not considered as theft, but as a kind of Roman *actio rerum amotarum*. The same is found in the demotic contracts from Egypt. In the Law of Gortyn, if the wife took away anything else belonging to her husband, she had to pay five staters and restore whatever she took. If she wanted to refute any such action, she had to swear an oath of denial by Artemis. See *Gortyn Code Lex*, col. III, l. 1-9; 43-44; SEIDL 1975, p. 236-238.

[79] See BERGER 1953, p. 344. Some jurists, such as Nerva and Cassius, believe that a wife does not commit a theft since the marriage makes her in a sense an owner of the couple's property. This special lawsuit was introduced, because it was unacceptable to be able to sue a wife for theft.

authorities in order to recover his lost belongings.[80] In a divorce contract from the fourth century, Soulis and Senpsais are separated due to an "evil demon", but they both recover their belongings, as the separation is based on mutual agreement.[81]

The involvement of another mother-in-law in a husband's abandonment by his wife is described in *P. Cair. Preis.* 2 (TM 20209) from 362 AD. The husband complains that his mother-in-law took away his wife Tamounis during his business trip, on the pretext that the wife "had an experience of the devil". She then gave her to another man. The petitioner implies that the divorce was invalid, because it was imposed by the mother, probably without the consent of the daughter.[82] His main arguments are that: 1) he fulfilled the laws of marriage[83] and 2) he lived three years with her. When Serenus married Tamounis six years before, she received bridal gifts. Unfortunately, as the document breaks off before the object of the petition, we do not know whether Serenus requested the recovery of bridal gifts or whether he also wished to bring back his wife to their household.[84] In *P. Lond.* V 1651 (TM 19675) a wife, who also took some of the husband's belongings, is accused of unlawful departure, while requests her arrest before the arrival of the governor of the Thebaid, who will decide on the outcome of the lawsuit. Dios probably wanted an *actio rerum amotarum* to take place. In such petitions, husbands used the notion of unlawful divorce (ἄνομος ἔξοδος) as a rhetorical strategy which could provoke the officials' malevolence towards the wife.[85] Dios appears worried, mainly about the stolen documents,

---

80 ARNAOUTOGLOU 1995, p. 25.

81 *P. Grenf.* II 76 (TM 22632). The husband is paid back the *hedna* and everything bestowed to her and she acknowledges the receipt of her dowry. For divorce-demons see also *P. Lond.* V 1713 (TM 19730). This cause of separation is mainly found in divorce contracts from the fifth and sixth century.

82 For different reconstructions and interpretations of some lines of this document see URBANIK 2014, p. 171-172 (4.2.4).

83 The failure of the husband to provide to his wife anything she needs is considered an injustice (*iniuria*) by the law and the social norms of marriage. See MÉLÈZE-MODRZEJEWSKI 1959, p. 78-79.

84 In a similar way, in *PSI* VIII 893 (TM 13800) a husband blames his father-in-law for taking his wife from their household.

85 Dios' mention may be considered as the only indication of Constantine's norm in practice in such documents. See URBANIK 2014, p. 170.

which constituted proof of ownership, and not about his unsuccessful marriage.[86]

In a complicated family conflict over property from the second century, two spouses and their daughter are involved.[87] Diogenes of Tebtynis is married to his sister Herakleia and has a married daughter named Ptolema. After a quarrel with his wife, he transferred some property to the ownership of his daughter. Then Ptolema applied for a divorce from her husband, so that she would have control over this property. Her father appealed to the *strategos* to restore his *patria potestas* over his daughter and she made a counter appeal to the *archidikastes*. Diogenes appeals to the *archidikastes* to instruct the *strategos* to settle the differences between him and the two women before his daughter's divorce. On the other hand, *P. Oxy.* LIV 3758 (TM 15267) describes a different marital dispute: a married couple still living together, testifies before the *logistes* on opposite sides of a dispute about an inheritance. Sarapion acts against his wife Helen, who also had the *ius trium liberorum*, about some property including gold jewelry bequeathed to her by his mother. The problem is whether the will is considered as a deposit or not. Sarapion believes that after his mother's death, this property belongs to him and he uses the petitionary procedure. In the end, the court decides that the girl can keep the jewelry as her own property.

In all the above-discussed cases, the husband accuses his wife mainly of property removal and abandonment of their home.[88] However, adultery by a wife was the most serious ground for divorce and punishment. *P. Philammon* (*BGU* IV 1024, TM 64373) records a case of adultery in an urban environment, but we cannot be sure if it is a made-up story or a real incident.[89] A husband finds his wife in bed with her lover, who manages to escape from the husband's house. He then kills his wife with the sword intended for the lover. Under Roman law, a man who caught

[86] Documents, such as loans and deeds of sale of a house, constituted proof of ownership which could be transmitted to the new owner in case of sale.

[87] *P. Mil. Vogl.* IV 229 (TM 12417).

[88] In *P. Sakaon* 48 (TM 13067) a strange case of marital tension is recorded. While a man blames some other men for kidnapping his bride Nonna and stealing his property, there are also some accusations for Nonna's conduct. Cf. *P. Sakaon* 38 (TM 13056).

[89] For a discussion on the kind of the document see KANAVOU & PAPATHOMAS 2016, p. 453-469.

his wife in adultery was allowed to kill the lover, but not the wife, if they were caught in his own house.[90]

CONCLUSION

In conclusion, resolution of marital conflicts in Roman Egypt can be examined on the basis of petitions, court proceedings, letters, marriage and divorce contracts which imply the various mechanisms used to settle these disputes.[91] However, mainly in villages, strong ties of kinship undoubtedly maintained social order and marital harmony, in ways which would never have been recorded.[92] The everyday problems between a couple brought to light through the letters and petitions illuminate the social and moral values and standards of behavior in the society of Roman Egypt. The family of the bride was interested in the settlement of disputes, as in case of the wife's desertion or abandonment by her husband, they would provide refuge to the woman and her children.[93] Families on both sides tried to reach a compromise with the opposite side either by mediation or offering security for a new marital agreement. By the end of the fourth century, under the influence of Christianity, local church officials were involved in the mediation of marital disputes. Interestingly, in spite of invoking the weakness of their sex, wives in Roman Egypt took the initiative, alone or with the assistance of their family, to separate from their husband, after they had suffered harassment.[94] In some cases, economic and social circumstances could lead to

[90] See *Dig.* 48.5.43. See also Diod. I.78 about the punishment for consensual adultery and Paul., *Sent.* 2.26.14. See MONTSERRAT 1996, p. 105; KEENAN 1989, p. 15-23. Under Roman law a woman could not be prosecuted for adultery, while still married. Her husband had to divorce her before he or anyone else could bring charges. See also EVANS-GRUBBS 1999, p. 202; TREGGIARI 1991b, p. 284. A woman who had been convicted in court of adultery would suffer the penalty of exile banishment and loss of much of her property. See also CANTARELLA 2005, p. 37.

[91] Divorce documents and petitions against spouses imply behavior considered appropriate for married people in Graeco-Roman Egypt.

[92] HOBSON 1993, p. 200.

[93] For the role played by the wife's relatives in marital disputes see *P. Lips.* I 41 (TM 33701), *P. Oxy.* LIV 3770 (TM 15286), *P. Ryl.* IV 706 (TM 32785), *SB* XII 11221 (TM 16198) already discussed.

[94] BEAUCAMP 1992, p. 155.

attempts at reconciliation and resumption of the marriage, without addressing the authorities. Even if a wife chose to resolve her marital dispute on the basis of legal grounds, she sometimes had to suffer the husband's anger or violence against her about her decision to divorce.

In great contrast to women, men abandoned by their wives did not usually act with familial support, while sometimes the bride's mother played an important role in the dissolution of a marriage.[95] Usually both spouses, and especially the husbands, are more interested in recovering their stolen property rather than in finding a remedy to improve their marital relationship.

For both sexes, the marriage instrument was the legal basis of any claim and the arguments stated in the petitions were based on the moral values of marital fidelity and care.[96] Women were usually satisfied with the return of the dowry or the execution of a court's decision on the husband's property, especially in the case of unjustified abandonment. Men usually succeeded in recovering the property stolen by the wife, when they could prove that they had fulfilled their marital duties.

The petitions against spouses coming from the fourth century are not all clearly dated and, unfortunately, we cannot draw any definite conclusion as to the efficacy of Constantine's reform. It is not clear if these unhappy wives suffered under Constantine's restrictions on unilateral divorce, as many of these cases seem to violate the emperor's legislation. Despite the economic or moral satisfaction of each spouse after the settlement of the dispute, Greco-Roman society tended to consider divorce as a misfortune. A divorced or abandoned woman raising her children alone would encounter various economic, social or even moral issues in her everyday life.[97]

---

[95] Selfhelp is documented in most petitions of husbands against their wives: *P. Heid.* III 237 (TM 31479), *P. Lond.* V 1651 (TM 19675), *P. Oxy.* II 282 (TM 20553), *SB* XVI 12505 (TM 16255).

[96] The petition is usually based on the belief that the rights of the petitioner have been violated in a way which needs to be rectified.

[97] In Roman society, a divorce could also cast doubt on the woman's reputation and suitability as a bride. See TREGGIARI 1991a, p. 41. Cf. Apul., *Apol.* 92.

PREDICTABLY UNPREDICTABLE: WATER RIGHTS, COMMUNITY, AND CONFLICT IN FAYYUM IRRIGATION

Brendan HAUG
(University of Michigan)

Abstract: Papyri from the Graeco-Roman Fayyum's marginal villages preserve no unambiguous evidence for the existence of an externally-regulated system of water rights or quotas in rural irrigation. It has been suggested elsewhere that this underregulation incentivized heavy water use along upstream portions of the Fayyum's canal system, which deprived downstream farmers of water and subsequently contributed to the collapse of marginal villages like Aurelius Sakaon's Theadelphia in the fourth century CE. Utilizing comparative evidence from the medieval and modern periods, this paper argues that the absence of externally-regulated water rights from the papyri was instead a practical adaptation to the unpredictable nature of the water supply at the tail end of the Fayyum's canal system.

INTRODUCTION

> You can argue that the character of a man or woman can be as much formed by genetic and cultural material as by the location of their garden or chile patch along the length of a ditch, toward the beginning where water is plentiful or at the tail where it will always be fitful and scarce. "He's that way because he lives at the bottom of a ditch and never gets any water," is an accepted explanation for even the most aberrant behavior in this valley. The man who lives at the bottom of a ditch is forever expectant, forever disappointed.[1]

ʿAbd al-Hādī was frustrated: there was not enough water to go around, tempers were flaring, patience wearing thin, and violence had become all but inevitable. The trouble had all started some time ago when Egypt's Ministry of Irrigation halved the village's statutory irrigation period from

---

[1] CRAWFORD 1988, p. 23-24.

ten days per month to five. Under the previous ten-day regime, the villagers had been accustomed to transfer water from the public feeder canal to their village's canal network using a single animal-powered waterwheel (*sāqiya*). Although the *sāqiya* lay on ʿAbd al-Hādī's land and was nominally owned by him, the villagers possessed time-shares in it and used it by turns, yoking their respective animals to its axle and directing the water they raised to their own fields. The length of each of these time-shares was fixed, having been assigned in proportion to the amount of money that each had contributed to finance the wheel's construction and then calibrated to the ten-day irrigation period. Unfortunately, this finely-tuned system had been established "when the days of irrigation had been ten, when no one had expected they would ever be less than ten"; it had therefore become obsolete the instant the Ministry reduced the village's irrigation period.

After a period of increasing tension, communal solidarity was suddenly and violently shattered when ʿAbd al-Hādī began taking his own share at the wheel. While walking along the edge of the small canal leading to his field, monitoring the flow of the water he had raised, he discovered that his neighbor Diāb had breached the earthen dyke that separated their plots, thereby diverting ʿAbd al-Hādī's water into his own field and that of his neighbor Masʿūd Abū Qāsim. But when ʿAbd al-Hādī confronted his neighbor about his brazen theft, Diāb spit back:

> Listen to what I'm saying to you ʿAbd al-Hādī… I have one day at the *sāqiya* and my neighbor Masʿūd Abū Qāsim has a day. I'll take water as I like… You say it's your *sāqiya*, do you? Yours!? Well, we each have a day of it, Muḥammad Abū Suweilim has a day, as does Masʿūd Abū Qāsim, and the eastern sector of the village have two days, and you have the rest of the ten days. I'll take our day at the *sāqiya* today! Now c'mon, take your animal off because Masʿūd Abū Qāsim's wife is coming with their animal!

The simultaneous arrival of both Masʿūd Abū Qāsim's wife and a number of farmers from the village's eastern sector only inflamed the situation further since each demanded to begin taking their respective shares of the wheel. ʿAbd al-Hādī attempted to mediate, reminding his fellow irrigators that their previous arrangements were now defunct:

> ʿAbd al-Hādī tried to change their minds: yes, [the eastern sector] may have had two days when the irrigation period was ten, but if they clung fast to these two days, there wouldn't be enough shares in the *sāqiya* left over

> to irrigate other thirsty land... Since the irrigation period was now only five days, their share should now become one day. But both the men and the women raised their voices together in rejection of ʿAbd al-Hādī's proposal... As the sun rose, the conflict grew heated... and each felt that the others were trying to deprive him of life itself!... In the name of defending the life of his land — indeed life itself! — the villagers began to exchange blows without ceasing, each proclaiming their own land's right to water.

The village elders soon intervened but their pleas for an end to the violence went unheard. Only the discovery that Masʿūd Abū Qāsim's buffalo had fallen into the *sāqiya*'s well put an end to the brawl. This disaster required the beaten and bloodied villagers to put aside their enmity, if only temporarily, and work together to lift the animal out. After all, what good was even a full share of the wheel without an animal to turn it?

*

* *

This story is a fiction, a vignette from the Egyptian novelist ʿAbd al-Rahmān al-Sharqāwī's social-realist classic *Al-Arḍ* (1953), which recounts the dissolution of an unnamed Nile Delta village in the 1930s in the face of government oppression.[2] I begin with this slice of twentieth-century Egyptian popular culture because al-Sharqāwī's fiction, based in turn upon his own Delta upbringing, illustrates in vivid detail the social relations of Egyptian irrigation and, in the process, sheds light on the twin subjects of this paper: (1) the difficulties inherent in sharing a substance as variable and unpredictable as flowing water and (2) the conflicts that can erupt when rural water-sharing regimes break down.

At least in theory water apportionment schemes like al-Sharqāwī's imagined *sāqiya* time-shares eliminate competition and conflict between irrigators by reconfiguring common-pool water supplies as private property and granting each user exclusive title to a specific portion of the total supply. This approach, based upon the model of modern Western private property rights, stands in stark contrast to traditional land-based systems

---

[2] The above passages appear on p. 153-155 of AL-SHARQĀWĪ 1968, p. 153-156. Translation by author. My thanks to Usama GAD (Ain Shams, Cairo) for his assistance with Egyptian dialectical difficulties. The novel has been lightly abridged and translated into English by Desmond STEWART as *Egyptian Earth* (Saqi Books, London 1990) and filmed as *Al-Arḍ* by Egyptian director Youssef CHAHINE in 1969.

of apportionment in which the right to benefit from the flow of a public watercourse is generated simply by possessing land abutting and/or irrigated by it (e.g. the common law doctrine of riparian rights).[3]

Convinced of the superiority of private property rights in water, the United Nations' Food and Agriculture Organization has urged developing countries to eliminate such traditional water-sharing practices, arguing that property rights in water will reduce tensions and lead to more efficient and environmentally-sustainable water management.[4] The FAO's enthusiasm is nonetheless tempered by its acknowledgment that water supplies in many parts of the world are variable and insecure, making it impossible to guarantee that every user's water entitlement can forever be fulfilled by the available resources. Al-Sharqāwī's fictional conflict illustrates this conundrum: the stability of his fictional village's system of water entitlements was illusory since it was founded upon an unstable water supply. When the Ministry of Irrigation reapportioned local water resources, the rigid system of shares collapsed in violence and discord, since it was not sufficiently flexible to respond to sudden changes in the resource base.[5]

Scholarship on irrigation and water rights lends credence to the underlying logic of al-Sharqāwī's village melodrama by demonstrating that irrigation communities served by predictably unpredictable water supplies — waters whose arrival and/or volume varies and cannot be predicted in advance — usually avoid assigning water entitlements and instead adopt more flexible distribution practices that can accommodate uncertainty. In spate- and flood canal irrigation systems in particular, where the timing and amount of the annual water supply may vary widely from year to year, water is often shared via a set of guidelines that structure the flow of the common-pool water resources through the community. This flexibility allows irrigators to distribute floodwater in a manner tailored to the unique character of each annual flood. In such systems, rights in water are not assigned from without; instead, a right of access to the common-pool water resources is generated from within by maintaining reciprocal relationships with neighboring canal-sharers

---

[3] SCOTT 2008, p. 63-66.

[4] HODGSON 2006, p. 98 (Modern Water Rights).

[5] On the social effects of reorienting prevailing water flows in contemporary Egyptian irrigation see BARNES 2014.

and by participating in the collective labor of building and repairing communal irrigation infrastructure. "Water rights" in flood- and spate irrigation are therefore best regarded as manifestations of local social relationships. Far from abstract legal entitlements, "water rights... are inseparable from the way water management is organized... [and] part of a bundle of responsibilities to the entire group."[6]

The observations will be brought to bear on a long-standing problem in the scholarship on Graeco-Roman Egypt: the nature of water rights, water sharing, and water conflicts along the flood-canal irrigated margins of the Fayyum depression (the ancient Arsinoite nome). Although Fayyum papyri shed considerable light on various physical and institutional aspects of irrigation in the nome, they provide no evidence that a system of rights or quotas ever governed water sharing between or within villages.[7] This silence is striking, particularly since we possess evidence, albeit limited and scattered, for inter- and intra-village conflicts over water from the Ptolemaic, Roman, and early Islamic periods.[8] In an important article on water rights in the Roman Empire, Dennis Kehoe has critiqued this lack of external regulation, arguing that Rome's "inadequate governance" of the Fayyum's commons created perverse incentives for upstream irrigators to use as much as water as possible, thereby depriving downstream farmers and contributing to the collapse of marginal villages like Aurelius Sakaon's Theadelphia in the fourth century CE,[9] a paradigmatic example of the so-called "tragedies of the commons" famously described by ecologist Garret Hardin.[10]

Yet these purportedly perverse incentives did not suddenly materialize in the fourth century; the durability of this unregulated, farmer-managed irrigation system, attested papyrologically from the third century BCE to the early Islamic period, must therefore be explained. Inspired by the late economist Elinor Ostrom, whose work demonstrated that farmer-managed irrigation systems do not inevitably produce tragedies of the

---

[6] MEHARI e.a. 2007, quote at p. 115. See also OSTROM 1990, p. 69-81; VAN STEENBERGEN 1997; MEINZEN-DICK & NKONYA 2007; CLARKE & MALCOLM 2016.

[7] BONNEAU 1993 remains the best study of these aspects of Egyptian irrigation.

[8] For disputes in the Roman and Ptolemaic periods see, respectively, ANAGNOSTOU-CANAS 1994 and 2001. For the eighth-century CE Islamic Fayyum see texts 16 and 17 (*P. Mich.* inv. 5613B and 5625A, TM 870290 and 870245) in SIJPESTEIJN 2014 at p. 347-356.

[9] KEHOE 2008.

[10] HARDIN 1968.

commons,[11] I suggest that the absence of externally-regulated water entitlements was not a failure but a feature of irrigation practice along the edges of the Fayyum depression, a practical adaptation to predictably unpredictable water supplies of this marginal, near-desert environment. In the absence of firm papyrological testimony, the comparative evidence of Abū ʿUthmān al-Nābulusī's *Villages of the Fayyum* (hereafter *VF*), a fiscal survey of the Fayyum carried out in 1242-3 CE, is indispensable.[12] The text reveals that, at least in the Islamic period, local environmental conditions consistently informed approaches to water apportionment throughout the region. According to al-Nābulusī, only villages with predictable water supplies drawn from the gravity-fed perennial canal system that irrigated the Fayyum's double-cropped central plain possessed firm water rights in the form of an assigned, enforceable water "quota" (*ʿibra*).[13] By contrast, settlements located on higher grounds — i.e. areas poorly served by gravity-fed perennial irrigation and usually watered only by the annual flood — were not assigned a quota and made use of whatever water they received during the inundation. Where water was plentiful and predictable, in other words, apportionment was strictly regulated; where water supplies were variable, unpredictable, and not infrequently scarce, irrigation was less rigidly structured and more opportunistic.

The latter scenario, I argue, obtained along margins of the Fayyum in antiquity. Lying at or near the tail-end of a long canal system and possessing lands on relatively high ground,[14] the water supply to these settlements was susceptible to significant interannual variation influenced by the height of the Nile's flood, changing patterns of upstream water consumption, and even simple conveyance loss.[15] As the number of surviving declarations of unflooded land (ἀβροχία) indicate, the water supply of villages at the end of the canal system was indeed precarious.[16]

[11] Ostrom & Gardner 1993; Ostrom 1990; Ostrom 1999; Ostrom 2002.

[12] The text is edited and translated in Rapoport & Shahar 2018, from which the translations below are drawn.

[13] For the central Fayyum's environment see Haug 2017.

[14] As Theadelphia is described in *P. Sakaon* 35.

[15] The diminution of an irrigation canal's water supply in transit through evaporation, ground seepage, or other unplanned leakage from the system. For the cultural effects of conveyance loss in the modern Fayyum see Price 1995b.

[16] For declarations of ἀβροχία in general see Habermann 1997. The appearance of ἀβροχία-declarations in the latter half of the second century CE is suggestive albeit not

Since this inconsistent hydrological regime was ill-suited to apportionment via fixed water entitlements, it is unsurprising that the water conflicts recorded in the papyri do not revolve around alleged violations of irrigators' private rights in water.[17] Instead, complainants focused their frustrations on physical changes to the canal system that altered its customary flow: modifications of the shared irrigation infrastructure that effectively denied them unhindered access to the commons.

As in contemporary farmer-managed spate- and flood-irrigation systems, maintaining free access to the Fayyum's common water supply will have required significant investments of cooperative, communal labor in order to clean and repair the local canal networks in advance of the arrival of the flood. This much is already well known. But face-to-face personal relationships and collective action, including at times violent confrontations, will also have been necessary to preserve individual and/or communal access to water in the event of any upstream modifications to the canal system that impeded its downstream flow. The sharp decrease in the population of villages like Theadelphia in the western Fayyum — visible in the overwhelming dominance of the formerly thriving village's territory by the estate of Aurelius Appianus in the third century CE[18] and the virtual desertion of the site during the first half of the fourth century CE[19] — significantly reduced the ability of marginal communities to maintain local infrastructure and secure their access to the commons.

The goal of this paper is therefore twofold. It seeks first to advance a socio-environmental account of Fayyum irrigation, depicting it as a dense entanglement of environmental phenomena and adaptive human agency. Second, it attempts to reorient our perspective away from the external regulatory role of the state and toward the internal social organization

dispositive evidence of chronic reductions in flood-height and subsequent water scarcity in this period. The potential that land might be unflooded (ἄβροχος) had always been a threat and could be accounted for, e.g. in leases, in which case the lessee would be absolved of some portion of the rent: e.g. *P. Yale* I 51 (TM 2974, 184 BCE); *P. Tebt.* I 106 (TM 3742, 101 BCE); *SB* XVI 13017 (TM 14698, 24 BCE); *P. Tebt.* II 374 (TM 13530, 131 CE). For the argument of increasing flood instability in later antiquity see the data in McCormick e.a. 2012 and the synthesis in Harper 2017, p. 133-135.

[17] The case of *P. Sakaon* 35 is exceptional and will be discussed below.

[18] Rathbone 1991.

[19] Bagnall 1982.

essential to the continued functioning of this unique socio-natural system. Section 1 examines the flow of water through the Fayyum's canal system highlighting endemic upstream/downstream conflicts and the lack of water quotas or entitlements. Section 2 advances an environmental account of this phenomenon, arguing the approach to irrigation visible in the papyri was an adaptation to specific environmental conditions. Finally, Section 3 argues that significant reserves of social capital were necessary to preserve and defend access to water within this largely unregulated irrigation system, a resource that severely depopulated villages like fourth-century CE Theadelphia sorely lacked. Irresoluble conflicts, eventually fatal to the weaker downstream parties, were the inevitable result.

This account thus reverses the order of cause and effect in the traditional narrative of the Fayyum's late antique difficulties. The water conflicts attested in the fourth century CE were not the result of external regulatory failures that, in turn, triggered the collapse of otherwise healthy communities. Nor were they entirely the product of decaying infrastructure, although it remains possible that damage to major irrigation works upstream from villages like Theadelphia had significant downstream ramifications.[20] Rather, this contribution foregrounds the human element of Fayyum irrigation and argues that the struggles faced by villages like fourth-century Theadelphia were instead symptoms of the breakdown of complex socio-environmental system due to the fraying of the communities that had formerly sustained it.

1. Upstream/downstream

Unlike the Valley and Delta, the Fayyum depression receives water not directly from the main stem of the Nile but from the Baḥr Yūsuf, a long and meandering side channel that branches off from the river over 200 km south of Fayyum near the city of Dairūṭ. Once within the Fayyum's enclosed basin, water is distributed amongst its villages by a complex canal network; agricultural wastewater is then directed to the north

---

[20] Römer 2013 & 2017.

of the Fayyum, collecting in the Birkat Qārūn, a brackish lake that serves as the depression's main drainage sump.[21]

The unique canal-based hydraulics of the region introduced to Egyptian irrigation the problem of upstream/downstream water conflict. As Karl Butzer recognized decades ago, competition for and conflict over water resources had never been a significant problem in the Nile Valley and Delta since settlements within the floodplain had essentially equal access to the waters of the annual flood.[22] In the Fayyum, however, villages shared a radial canal system that delivered water in stages, settlement by settlement, from the head of each canal to its tail. Upstream settlements therefore had the ability to deprive their downstream neighbors of water, e.g., by blocking their shared canal entirely or by drawing from it so heavily that downstream settlements were left with straitened resources.[23] These upstream/downstream tensions remain a fixture of Fayyum agricultural life in the present day and exert a centripetal pull on the farmers at the farthest extremities of the canal system. The downstream position (*taḥt*, "below"), where water is most scarce, is known to be disadvantageous and "everyone wants to be what they call *fowq*, 'above', meaning upstream".[24]

Although contentious upstream/downstream relationships are attested in the Fayyum papyri as early as the Hellenistic archive of Zenon[25] they are most vividly depicted in the fourth-century CE archive of Aurelius Sakaon of Theadelphia. The *locus classicus* is *P. Sakaon* 35 (TM 13053, ca. 332 CE), a courtroom *narratio* outlining the few remaining Theadelphians' complaint against several upstream neighbors (l. 4-15):

> κατὰ τὸν προπέρυσι ἐνιαυτὸν καὶ πέρυσι τῶν ἐδαφῶν [[τῆς ἐδαφῶν]] τῆς κώμης ἡμῶν ἐν ὑψηλοῖς τόποις ὄντων καὶ τῶν ἔγγιστα κωμῶν, Ναρμούθεως καὶ Ἑρμουπόλεως κώμης καὶ Θεοξενίδος, ὑποκλεπτόντων ἡμῶν τὰ ὕδατα καὶ οὐκ ἐπιτρεπόντων ἀρδεύεσθαι ἡμῶν τὴν γῆν, διὰ τὸ ἀρχὴν αὐτῶν εἶναι τῶν πάγων καὶ ἡμᾶς ὑστέρους εἶναι τοῦ πάγου, ἔρημον κώμην

[21] The lake served as the only drainage sump until 1973, after which wastewater from the Fayyum's south has been channeled out of the Fayyum into the Wādī Rayyān depression where it has formed two artificial lakes.

[22] BUTZER 1976, p. 109.

[23] BAGNALL 1993, p. 141-142.

[24] BARNES 2014, p. 124.

[25] *P. Lond.* VII 1967 (TM 1530, 255 BCE).

οἰκοῦντας, ἡ γὰ[ρ] φορολογία τῆς κώμης ἡμῶν συνάγ[ε]ι εἰς πεντακοσίας ἀρούρας τὰς [ἀεὶ] ἀβροχίας τυγχανούσας.

The year before last, as well as last year, since the fields of our village are situated on high grounds and the nearest villages, Narmouthis, Hermoupolis Village, and Theoxenis, steal our water and prevent our land from being irrigated because they are at the front of the pagi and we are the last in the pagus and inhabit a deserted village, the tribute of our village amounts to 500 arouras, consistently unwatered.

On paper the situation is straightforward: the downstream village of Theadelphia lay at the end of a canal and was being deprived of water, allegedly illicitly, by several of its upstream neighbors. Yet the accusation of theft (ὑποκλεπτόντων) introduced here is anomalous, a rhetorical flourish rather than a claim of property rights violated. Indeed, elsewhere in Fayyum papyri, including the remainder of the Sakaon archive, conflicts over water apportionment simply highlight alleged distortions of customary patterns of canal flow.

A paradigmatic example is the Ptolemaic petition *P. Tebt.* I 50 (TM 3686, 112/111 BCE) in which a βασιλικὸς γεωργός in the village of Kerkeosiris complains that his upstream neighbor has blocked up (συνέχωσεν) their shared public canal (a "royal waterway", βασιλικοῦ ὑδραγωγοῦ) for several years in a row thereby denying him multiple opportunities to irrigate from it as he had been long-accustomed to do (e.g. l. 24-25: ἀκολούθως τοῖς ἐθισμοῖς).

Similar complaints are made centuries later in *P. Sakaon* 33 (TM 13051, ca. 320 CE), a fragmentary record of proceedings before one Valerius Tziper, then *praeses* of Aegyptus Herculia.[26] Here the Theadelphians voice two separate but substantively identical grievances. First they allege that the inhabitants of an upstream village named Andromachis "block up the channel and do not allow the waters to flow in easily" (l. 8: προσχώνουσιν τὸ ῥῖθρον καὶ [ο]ὐκ ἐῶσιν εὐμαρῶς εἰσρ̣ιε̣ῖν τὰ ὕδατα). They claim secondly that a certain Manos, his associates, and his brothers, who possess some twenty arourai in the plain (πέδιον) and thus lie upstream (ὑπερκαθήμενοι, "above"[27]) from marginal Theadelphia "block

[26] On Ziper's name see AST 2001.

[27] PARASSOGLOU's (1978) translation of ὑπερκαθήμενοι ἡμῖν in *P. Sakaon* — "Manos' associates and his brothers *are situated on higher ground than ours*" — misconstrues the spatial relationship between the two villages. The translation in HGV renders

up the channel and do now allow the waters to be sent to us" (l. 15-16: ἀποφράσ[σο]υσιν τὸ ῥῖθρον καὶ οὐκ ἐῶσιν εἰς ἡμᾶς πέμπεσθαι τὰ ὕδατα). Again, at issue is not the theft of Theadelphian property *per se* but the allegedly inappropriate obstruction of the flow of the common-pool water resources through public canals. In his judgment in the first case, the *praeses* accordingly orders those who have blocked up the channel should clean it out, "in order that the water be able to have its customary inflow".[28] In the case of Manos and associates, he simply orders that the upstream users draw only the water they need, allowing the remainder to flow downstream.[29] Nowhere is it stated that Theadelphia had any entitlement to a specific share of the canal's water.

On the opposite edge of the Fayyum in 305 CE the κωμάρχαι of Philadelphia leveled a comparable accusation against their upstream neighbor Tanis (*P. Wisc.* I 32 = *Pap. Choix* 27, TM 13708). Although their language is less precise than that of the Sakaon papyri, the Philadelphians likewise lay the blame for their longstanding debt to the treasury upon Tanis (l. 9-10: ὑπὲρ τῆς ἡμετέρας κώμης οὐ μὴν̣ [ἀλλ]ὰ̣ κ̣αὶ ὑπὲρ μέρους Τάνεως) and request that an inspection of a stone channel at Tanis be carried out, "in order now that we, too, are able to acquire the water forthwith and derive benefit [from it] and cultivate all of our land and pay the public taxes due on them and the annona-tax and all kinds of extra charges."[30] Although the Philadelphians do not allege any specific malfeasance on the part of their neighbors, at issue once again is the impairment of the flow of a public canal. Whether through malice, neglect, or accident the Philadelphians claim that Tanis was depriving them of access to the commons and they accordingly requested assistance

ὑπερκαθήμενοι ἡμῖν oddly as "our superiors" based upon a piece of Russian scholarship to which I have no access (see *BL* VIII, p. 300).

[28] L. 23-24: ἵνα τὸ υὕδωρ (*sic*) τὴν συνήθη εἴσροιαν ἔχειν δυνηθῇ. The verdicts in both cases were originally transcribed in Latin and Greek translations were added at the end of the papyrus in a second hand. The Latin text of this first verdict is fragmentary and the original Latin of this excerpt cannot be restored.

[29] L. 18-21: *praepositus pagi prouidebit quatenus hi aduersus quos postulatur percepta sufficiente aqua iuxta terram quam posside\n/t superfluam in terris susceptorum tuorum tradaṇṭ, quo idem quoque possint terras ad se pertinentes inrigare.*

[30] L. 10-12: ὑ(πὲρ) τοῦ οὖν εὐθέως δύνασθαι τὰ ὕδ̣[ατα] κ̣αὶ ἡμᾶς καταλαμβάνιν καὶ ὄνησιν ἔχειν καὶ τοῦ πᾶσαν τ̣ὴ̣ν̣ γῆν ἡμῶν γεωργῖν καὶ δύνασθαι τελῖν τὰ ὑπὲρ αὐτῶν δ̣ημ̣όσια τελέσματα καὶ ἀννωνιακὴ καὶ παντοίας ἐπιβολάς.

"so that we too can benefit from the coming-up of the flax and have potable water and sow the plain of our village and remain in our own territory and derive benefit from our own property."[31]

Although the Philadelphians do not specify the nature of their troubles, *P. Sakaon* 33 clearly alleges the deliberate obstruction of shared canals. The blocking of canals was nonetheless a standard feature of Fayyum irrigation. The use of transverse dykes (ἐμβλήματα) to temporarily dam a feeder canal and allow those below the dyke to redirect all or a portion of the canal's flow onto nearby lands is attested in the papyri and appears to have been a standard feature of Fayyum irrigation.[32] In *P. Prag. Varcl* II 52 (TM 14210), an undated letter of the Heroninos archive, a certain Kopres is ordered to dam up (ἐμβληματίσαι) a canal (διώρυχα) for a day and release it (ἀπολ[υ]θῆ[ν]αι) on the following day.[33] Yet these ἐμβλήματα might become, unsurprisingly, the target of downstream frustrations. Such is the case in *P. Sakaon* 45 (TM 13064, 334 CE), a petition to an εἰρηνάρχης, in which Sakaon complains of the allegedly illicit (ληστρικῷ τρόπῳ) installation of an ἔμβλημα in a canal during the "time of the waters" (τὸν καιρὸν τῶν ὑδάτων) by two men and their respective sons, an action that must have denied Theadelphia access to some portion of the flood. For comparison, the perspective of a beneficiary of an ἔμβλημα is preserved in *P. Ryl.* II 133 (TM 12919, 33 CE). Here, a certain Penneis claims that one Onnophris has assailed a named ἔμβλημα and damaged it. Although the relationship between the two is not specified, it is not implausible, albeit unprovable, that Onnophris was downstream of the dyke and felt disadvantaged by it (l. 6-22):

> τῆι ιζ τοῦ ἐνεστῶτος μηνὸ(ς) Νέου Σεβαστοῦ τοῦ κ (ἔτους) Τιβερίου Καίσαρος Σεβαστοῦ ἐπιβαλὼν Ὀννῶφρις Ὀννώφριος εἰς τὸ λεγόμενον

---

[31] L. 18-20: ἵνα δυνηθῶμεν καὶ ἡμῖς τῆς τοῦ λίνου παροχῆς ἀπọḷαύειν καὶ πότιμον ὕδωρ ἔχειν καὶ τὸ πεδίον τῆς ἡμẹ[τ]ẹρας ḳώμης κατασπίριν καὶ ἐν τῇ ἰδίᾳ στῆναι καὶ ὄνησιν ἔχ̣[ει]ν ṭῶν ἰδίων.

[32] On *emblemata* see BONNEAU 1993, p. 39-44. The technique remains in use in the form of the "ad hoc mud dams" that contemporary Fayyum farmers use to direct water to the desired location. MEHANNA e.a. 1984, p. 92.

[33] RATHBONE 1991, p. 222. l. 2-6: ἐνẹṭιλάμ̣ην οὖν τῷ [Κο]πρῇ πρὸς τὴν μία[ν ἡμέ]ραν ἐμβληματίσαι [τὴν] διώρυχα ὑμῶν [καὶ τῇ] ἑξῆς ἀπολ[υ]θῆ[ν]ạι. The building-up (ἀναβολάς) of ἐμβλήματα is described as one of the yearly tasks (τὰ κατ' ἔτος ἔργα) in the land-lease published as *P. Tebt.* II 378 (TM 13534, 265 CE). On the importance of ἐμβλήματα to a village see *SB* XIV 11478 (TM 14456, 210/11 CE).

Ταορβελλείους ἔμβλημ(α) οἰκοδομήμενον μετὰ δαπάνης οὐκ ὀλίγων κεφαλαίων ἀργυρικῶν αὐθάδως κατέσπασεν ἀπὸ μέρους, ἐξ οὗ κινδυνεύει τῷ ὅλωι ἐξαρθῆνα[ι] καὶ τὰ ὑποκείμενα τούτῳ ἐδάφη οὐκ ὀλίγα εἰς ἄσπορον ἐκτραπῆν[α]ι.

On the 17th of the present month of Neos Sebastos of the 20th year of Tiberius Caesar Augustus, Onnophris son of Onnophris, having attacked the dyke called "of Taorbelles," built at the expense of no small amounts of money, stubbornly pulled it down in part, for which reason the entirety is in danger of being carried away and the fields beneath it, not few, becoming unsown.

In each of these cases, conflict between irrigators was generated by deliberate (or in the case the Philadelphia-Tanis perhaps accidental) upstream modifications of public irrigation infrastructure, which altered prevailing patterns of water flow to the detriment of downstream irrigators. Yet alterations of canal flow and subsequent social disruptions might also arise from the evolution of cultivation patterns upstream. Such a case is attested in an eighth-century Arabic papyrus from the administrative archive of ʿAbd Allāh b. Asʿad recently published by Petra Sijpesteijn. The text is fragmentary but it concerns a water conflict between Narmūda (Greek Narmouthis) and a neighboring settlement.[34] The upstream villagers of Nuwayra have apparently been watering sycamores to the detriment of their downstream neighbors in Narmūda.

In the name of God the Merciful, the Compassionate. From Nājid bin Muslim to ʿAbd Allāh bin Asʿad. Peace be upon you and I praise for you God besides Whom there is no god but He. Further... bin Abi Muslim came to me reminding me that] the one you endorsed of the people of ...] .. [...] water that you intended (?) for Narmūda. [...] of the people of Narmūda... me the sluice to the canal of Nuwayra they watered their land which has on it the sycamore trees which they are not allowed to do and have no permission for (?). So do not allow them the water you intended (?) for Narmūda...[35]

The effects of crop changes on canal flow and upstream/downstream relations are still more clear in al-Nābulusī's *VF*. Here, several villages are

[34] The upstream settlement seems to be a village called Nuwayra, perhaps identical with modern Nawwāra, ca. 8 km NE of the site of Narmouthis/Medīnat Māḍī. How these two settlements would have been connected by canal is, however, unclear.

[35] *P. Mich.* inv. 5613B (TM 870290, ca. 730-50 CE). Trans. SIJPESTEIJN 2014, p. 348-349.

said to have been affected by the recent increase in the cultivation of sugarcane, a notoriously water-intensive crop.[36] Dahmā, a large village southwest of the central capital city of Madīnat al-Fayyum, had abandoned cotton on account of the increase in cane cultivation (*VF* 154):

> Cotton was sown in it before the water was diverted to the sugarcane (*al-aqṣāb*). When the [cultivation of] sugarcane increased, it absorbed the entire amount of water, and the sowing of cotton in the villages was discontinued.

Similar situations are recorded in the large northeastern village of Dhāt al-Ṣafā' (*VF* 155)[37] and in Shidmūh (*VF* 180).[38] The former had recently abandoned rice cultivation in order to allocate water to sugarcane (*li-tawfīr al-māʾ ʿalā-l-aqṣāb*) while the latter had abandoned summer cultivation entirely after sugarcane cultivation increased. Yet the most significant disruptions effected by sugarcane cultivation were at Shāna (*VF* 178), which formerly lay toward the eastern extremities of the Fayyum "at the base of the mountain" (*fī dhail al-jabal*), i.e. close to the high limestone ridge that rings the depression. The inhabitants of "Old" Shāna had recently migrated north and inward toward the Fayyum's plain to found "New" Shāna. Among the several reasons given for this relocation was a "dearth of water, due to the increase in [cultivation of] sugarcane in the Fayyum" (*qillat al-māʾ lammā katharat al-aqṣāb bi-l-Fayyūm*).

In sum, the Fayyum's landscape was highly fluid. Changes in patterns of water flow regularly provoked conflict between upstream settlements

[36] Sugar is by the thirstiest major crop in modern Egypt measured by water consumption per *feddan*. IBRAHIM & IBRAHIM 2003, p. 123.

[37] The only published papyrological attestation of this settlement occurs in the bilingual Greek-Arabic village list *P. Ross. Georg.* V 73 (TM 39737, VIII CE) where its Greek name is given as χώριον Πτολεμαΐδος. Considering the fact that the *P. Ross. Georg.* V 73 includes villages scattered throughout the Fayyum and that al-Nābulusī places Dhāt al-Safā' in the northeast, it is unlikely that this settlement is identical with Ptolemais Hormou at the mouth of the Fayyum, which is in Arabic texts generally referred to as al-Lāhūn, an Arabization of Coptic *Lehone*. As for the precise location of Nābulusī's Dhāt al-Safā' it received water from the homonymous Dhāt al-Safā' canal, which it shared with several other villages, three of which are still extant: Maṭar Ṭāris, Furqus (now Furquṣ), and Sirsinā. All lie NE of the central capital, Maṭar Ṭāris ca. 8 km, Sirsinā ca. 15 km, Furquṣ ca. 19 km. As a result, the Ptolemais of *P. Ross. Georg.* V 73 should not be identified with Ptolemais Hormou, as it is in *Dizionario* IV, p. 213.

[38] Ca. 14.5 km SW of the capital.

and their downstream neighbors and could also prompt reorganizations of cultivation and settlement patterns in the affected areas. This hydraulic instability was and remains an endemic feature of Fayyum agricultural life and did not materialize only in Late Antiquity.[39] Yet as I have argued here, despite the constant threats to their water supply, farmers at the tail-end of the Fayyum's canal system never complained about violations of their legal rights in water; rather, they protested actions that denied them unobstructed access to common-pool resources. The next section suggests that this unregulated approach to water apportionment was not the product of insufficient governance but was instead a necessary adaptation to the unpredictability of the water supplies at the end of the canal system.

2. On high ground: Apportioning unpredictable flows

Rights in water were not entirely absent from Egypt during antiquity. A small collection of fifth-century BCE demotic ostraka from ʿAin Manāwir in the Kharga Oasis preserves evidence for sophisticated rights in water in the form of time-based allotments. The documents refer in various contexts to so-called "days of water", lengths of time marked in full days and fractions of days during which irrigators were permitted to draw water from a specific and occasionally named water source. These "days of water" were inextricably bound to the plot of land they irrigated; when the land was ceded the attached water rights also passed to the new owner.

The hydrology of the Kharga oasis supported this practice since the "days of water" depended upon reliable year-round flows delivered by *qanāt* from the oasis' artesian sources, which could then be collected and distributed.[40] The water of wells, cisterns, and other still-water collection basins are indeed more easily allotted by time or volume since their

---

[39] For contemporary examples see PRICE 1995a and BARNES 2014.

[40] "Days of Water": CHAUVEAU 2001. Kharga hydrology and irrigation in general: WUTTMANN 2001. See BURMIL 2003 for the geology and hydrology of the oases of Egypt's Western Desert. For comparison see the irrigation system at Lamasba in Roman Numidia, whose surviving inscription was famously studied by Brent SHAW (1984). It was likewise fed by underground sources through a foggara permitting time-based allotment. For corrections and updates to Shaw's study see LEONE 2012.

volumes can be quantified with ease. A modern comparandum has been studied in the Yemenī highland valley of al-Aḥjūr, where reliable spring flows are collected in cisterns or dammed basins for later distribution on a rotation cycle throughout the year. One turn in the cycle is "measured at the cistern according to either a defined time unit or a measure of volume". One studied cistern had a 17-day rotation cycle, the smallest unit of irrigation time in which is the *rubʿ* or "quarter" (of a 12-hour day). In other areas, water is distributed only after the volume of a cistern has been measured in "hand widths" (*kufūf*). The irrigator's turn is then allotted in "hand widths", converted into a time unit. Few disputes occur since the aggregate water supply is easily quantifiable and every irrigator knows precisely what he is allotted.[41]

The canal system of the Fayyum presents a hybrid case study, one in which predictable water supplies and precise water quotas coexisted alongside areas with unpredictable water supplies and correspondingly looser approaches to water sharing. The former situation, unparalleled elsewhere in the Nile Valley, attracted the notice of Medieval Egypt's central administration.[42] In the *Kitāb qawānīn al-dawāwīn* ("Book of the Rules of the Ministries"), an administrative survey compiled by one Asʿad Ibn Mammātī (d. 1209 CE), it is claimed that "there are many renowned (*mashūra*), fully-filled (*ʿāmira*), and overflowing (*ghāmira*) canals in the Fayyum… every village has a fixed supply of water (*shurb maʿlūm*) at a known time (*waqt mafhūm*).[43]

Yet the Fayyum of Ibn Mammātī's day occupied only the low-lying, steeply-sloped central plain of the depression, the margins settled in antiquity having been fully abandoned. In much of the plain, reliable perennial irrigation was possible thanks to a constant trickle of water through the Baḥr Yūsuf and seepage from high-lying perched aquifers that kept the canals flowing even after floodwaters had been consumed.[44]

Al-Nābulusī's *VF* confirms Ibn Mammātī's claims by recording the water quotas (*ʿibra*) obtaining in many of the villages described in

---

[41] VARISCO 1983.

[42] And geographers and historians as well: HAUG 2017.

[43] IBN MAMMĀTĪ, *Qawanīn al-Dawāwīn*. Edited by ʿAzīz S. ʿATIYA (Cairo: Royal Agricultural Society 1943), p. 229. See also the translation of COOPER 1974, p. 74.

[44] HAUG 2017. See RATHBONE 1991, p. 222, for distinctions between irrigation in the plain of the Fayyum and the margins at Theadelphia hinted at in the Heroninos archive.

the tenth chapter of his survey, information he includes in the opening few sentences of each village-entry. Translated here are two representative examples. The first is the extinct village of Buljusūq (Coptic Pelgisoq, Greek Kerkesoucha Orous[45]), a settlement from the southern stretches of the Fayyum. The second is the village of Sinnūris (ancient Psenyris[46]), one of the largest and wealthiest villages in the Medieval Fayyum — one of its "brides" (*ʿarāʾis*) — and still extant some 11 km north of the capital.

> Also beginning with the letter *bāʾ*: Buljusūq. One of the hamlets of the Tanabṭawayh Canal.[47] This is a pleasant and large village in southern Fayyum, four hours' ride from Madinat al-Fayyum. It has a few date palms and one sycamore tree... It gets its water from the Tanabṭawayh Canal, from the southern bank. Its [water] quota is 11¼ *qabḍas* (*VF* 131).
>
> ...
>
> Beginning with the letter *sīn*: Sinnūris. This is a large village, one of the famous brides and celebrated villages of the Fayyum. It lies north of Madinat al-Fayyum, and has much water, plentiful orchards, and gardens of date palms, grapes, and abundant fig trees. All the varieties of cereals are cultivated, both winter and summer crops. It is three hours' ride from Madinat al-Fayyum... It gets 19 *qabḍas* of water for the irrigation of winter crops, sugarcane, summer crops and for private estates, out of the total of a canal named after the village [i.e., Sinnūris canal], which branches off from the divisor known as al-Shādhrawān (*VF* 159-160).

The *qabḍa* (pl. *qubaḍ*) is a linear unit of measurement, a "cubit" or "hand width" equal to 15.875 cm and it is thus not immediately apparent to what amounts of water these quotas correspond. Tsugitaka Satō declined to offer an opinion on the problem in his study of rural society in Medieval Islam.[48] More recently Wakako Kumakura has suggested that the unit refers to the length of irrigation channels, an unlikely scenario given the small numbers involved in each case.[49] Yossef Rapoport

---

[45] GALLO in *O. Narm. Dem.* 2, p. LXI. See also BERKES & HAUG 2016, p. 215. Medieval Buljusūq is a descendent of the ancient village, the settlement having migrated to the north away from the high ground of the desert margin and toward the plain of the Fayyum (*VF* 18). Cf. the case of the village of Shāna mentioned above.

[46] BANAJI 2001, p. 247-248.

[47] I.e. the "Tebtynis" canal, the large southern border canal of the ancient *meris* of Polemon.

[48] SATŌ 1997, 223.

[49] KUMAKURA 2017, p. 97.

posits that the figures refer to the size of the opening on a village's offtake from the public feeder canal.[50] A narrower opening would admit less water and a wider opening would admit more, thereby making these *qabḍa*-allotments effectively proportional allotments. This is possible, although in consideration of the reliable perennial flow of the central canal system, these measurements might also refer to canal depth, i.e. each village with a water quota was entitled a draw a continual flow from its feeder canal sufficient to fill the village's own canals to a depth measured in *qubaḍ*.[51] Whatever the case, since water within these "fully-filled and overflowing" canals could be divided so precisely amongst irrigators, complainants in water conflicts were capable of basing their claims upon alleged violations of their legal rights. Kumakura documents just such a dispute in the mid-sixteenth century CE between Ṭāmiya and its upstream neighbor al-Rawḍa, both still extant in the north/northeast of the Fayyum. Although both villages were entitled to 5 *qubaḍ* from their shared canal, an additional ditch leading to Ṭāmiya had been excavated, denying upstream al-Rawḍa its full entitlement. The ditch was therefore stopped up and judgment was rendered that Ṭāmiya was to take only its five-*qubaḍ* share.[52]

As already mentioned above, however, this level of precision was not universal since villages on higher ground were ill-served by gravity-fed perennial canals and thus could not easily be assigned a water quota. Al-Nābulusī explicitly states that a number of villages were "without a quota" (*min ghair ʿibra*) due, e.g., to the elevation of their lands. Other settlements are more simply described as being watered by natural flood-irrigation (*rayy*) like "the countryside" (*al-rīf*, i.e. the Nile's floodplain) and not by the unusual system of perennial canal irrigation (*saqī*) that characterized the Fayyum. This data is collected in the tables below.

---

[50] RAPOPORT 2018, p. 191-192.

[51] Canal-depth is a feature of the modern Fayyum's water apportionment strategy: MEHANNA e.a. 1984.

[52] KUMAKURA 2017, p. 103. Ṭāmiya (Greek Tamauis) is well known. Al-Rawḍa is smaller and lies at a slightly higher altitude just over 5 km SE of Ṭāmiya.

Table 1: Medieval Fayyum villages without water quota

VILLAGE NAME	WATER SUPPLY	REASON FOR LACK OF QUOTA
Bamawayh (*VF* 225-226)	Canal (*baḥr*) without weir (*bi-ghayr binyān*) homonymous with the village itself.	Not stated
Thalāth (*VF* 136)	Canal (*khalīj*) branching from south bank of the Baḥr Yūsuf[53] without weir.	Not stated
Khawr al-Rammād (*VF* 141)	Summer and winter canal (*khalīj*) without weir branching from the northern bank of the Baḥr Yūsuf.	Not stated
Dimūh al-Dāthir (*VF* 152)	Canal (*khalīj*) without quota for winter crops (*al-shatawī*).	On high ground (*min ʿuluww*)
Ṣunūfar (*VF* 182)	Canal (*khalīj*) only for winter crops in the form of a ditch (*misqā*) branching from the northern bank of the Baḥr Yūsuf. Two additional ditches (*masāqī*) without weirs or quota.	"Because of the elevation of the land" (*bi-ḥukmi ʿuluww al-arḍ*).
ʿAnz (*VF* 188)	Canal (*khalīj*) with one sluice-gate (*bāb*) for winter crops branching from the south bank of the Baḥr Yūsuf.	Not stated
Ghābat Baja (*VF* 189)	Two canals (*khalījain*) and one ditch (*misqā*) without weir or quota.	One canal has a lower quota "because of the elevation of its lands" (*bi-ḥukmi ʿuluww arāḍihā*).
Qushūsh (*VF* 202)	Three ditches (*masaqī*) branching from the northern bank of the Baḥr Yūsuf for winter cultivation only.	"Because of the elevation of its land" (*li-ʿuluww arḍihā*).
Abu ʿUsayya (*VF* 205-206)	Ditch (*misqā*) without quota branching from the Baḥr Yūsuf.	"Because of the elevation of its surrounding area" (*li-ʿuluww nāḥīyatihi*).

[53] When al-Nābulusī makes reference to the stretch of the Baḥr Yūsuf interior to the Fayyum, i.e. the portion of the channel beyond the dam at al-Lāhūn he refers to it as the Grand Yūsufī Canal (*al-Baḥr al-Aʿẓām al-Yūsufī*). The portion of the canal exterior to the Fayyum and extending south to Dairūṭ is dubbed the *al-Manhā*.

Minyat al-Dīk, Banī Majnūn, Shalmas (joint settlements, *VF* 228)	Banī Majnūn Canal, one sluice-gate, without weir or quota, for winter crops; ʿAnz Shalmaṣ Canal for winter crops; ditch (*misqā*) without quota for summer crops (*al-saifī*), ditch without quota for orchards; occasional ditch, ca. one *qabḍa*.	Banī Majnūn Canal: "the elevation of its lands" (*ʿuluww arāḍīhā*). Summer ditch: "high [elevation]" (*ʿāl*).

Table 2: Medieval Fayyum villages cultivated like "the countryside" (*al-rīf*)

VILLAGE NAME	IRRIGATION AND CULTIVATION PATTERNS
Al-Ḥammām (*VF* 97)[54]	Watered by a canal fed during the "days of the Nile [flood]" (*ayyām al-Nīl*) from a canal running east from the dam (*bunyān*) at al-Lāhūn, like the countryside (*rayy rīf*).
Al-Lāhūn and Umm al-Nakhārīr (joint settlements, *VF* 95)	Al-Lāhūn: Watered during the flood (*ayyām al-Nīl*) "like the villages of the countryside without [perennial] irrigation after the fashion of the Fayyum" (*uswatan bilād al-kūra min ghair saqī ʿalā ʿadatan al-Fayyūm*). Umm al-Nakhārīr: "Its lands are watered like the villages of the countryside" (*turwā arāḍīhā uswatan bilād al-rīf*).
Babīj Ghaylān and Kawm al-Raml (joint settlements, *VF* 130)	Two flaxes (*kittānain*) and winter cereals (*al-ḥubūb al-shatawī*) are cultivated like the countryside (*rīf*).
Bandīq (*VF* 129)	Watered from the Wardān canal without quota, during the "days of the Nile as the countryside is watered, not like the Fayyum" (*turwā ayyām al-Nīl ka-mā turwā al-rīf ghair al-Fayyūm*).
Dumūshiyya (*VF* 145)	Although it cultivates both winter and summer crops, it possesses one meadow (*marj*) that cultivates flax, cucumber, wheat, and barley "with the water of the Nile [flood] just as the countryside is cultivated". (*bi-māʾ al-Nīl ka-mā tuzraʿ al-rīf*).

[54] The village is exterior to the Fayyum proper, lying northeast of its entrance at al-Lāhūn.

Dimūh al-Dāthir (*VF* 152)	"One of the high villages" (see above, Fig. 1). Some of its lands (*baʿḍ arāḍīhā*) are cultivated like the countryside (*ka-l-rīf*) and partially by perennial irrigation (*saqī*) like the lands of the Fayyum (*k-arāḍī al-Fayyūm*).
Sidmant (*VF* 173)	"Watered by the Nile [flood] and cultivated as the countryside is cultivated" (*turwā min al-Nīl wa tuzraʿ ka-mā yuzraʿ al-rīf*).
Ṭimā (*VF* 183)	Cultivates winter cereals (*al-ḥubūb al-shatawiyya*) and irrigates with the "[flood] irrigation of the countryside from the Nile, not by [perennial] irrigation like the lands of Fayyum" (*tuzraʿ rayy al-rīf min al-Nīl lā min saqī k-arāḍī al-Fayyum*).
Minyat al-Uskuf (*VF* 205)	Irrigated during the days of the Nile (*ayyām al-Nīl*).
Nāmūsatayn (*VF* 234)	Watered by the Nile like the countryside (*rayy al-rīf*).

The entry for the village of Ṭubhār (*VF* 185), a village still extant some 13 km west of the capital, most clearly conveys the difficulties faced by villages on higher ground. Although possessing a water quota of 8 *qabḍas*, Ṭubhār was still faced with shortages after the flood:

> Winter crops (*shatawī*) are sown but nothing else. Its lands are high (*ʿāliya*) and water does not reach them except with difficulty (*bi-kulfa*). [Water] lessens at the burning-up of the water (*iḥtirāq al-māʾ*)[55] and its disappearance may be complete. At this time its people drink from wells (*al-ʾābār*) and water is discharged for it [sc. from alternate sources?] for the need of the vines (*al-kurūm*) during the time of the burning-up.

Each of these atypical settlements lacked full access to the gravity-driven perennial canal system that supported the regime of water-quotas throughout the rest of the Medieval central Fayyum. They may be regarded, I suggest, as analogous to the settlements of the Fayyum's ancient margins. Ensconced on higher grounds along the rim of the depression and lying at or near the ends of the canal system (as Theadelphia is explicitly described in *P. Sakaon* 35[56]), marginal ancient settlements did not possess a reliable, perennial water supply and were instead

[55] I.e. the period of evaporation and lowest water after the flood waters had been consumed.

[56] L. 5-6: τῶν ἐδαφῶν τῆς κώμης ἡμῶν ἐν ὑψηλοῖς τόποις ὄντων and l. 11-12: καὶ ἡμᾶς ὑστέρους εἶναι τοῦ πάγου.

irrigated opportunistically with whatever floodwaters they received, high land (ὑψηλός) being particularly vulnerable to failures in the water supply.[57] It is surely this unique topographical and hydrological situation, rather than any failures of ancient governance, that explains the lack of water entitlements described in the previous section.

Irrigation practices along the Graeco-Roman margins of the Fayyum should thus be regarded not as dangerously under-regulated but as a productive adaptation to specific environmental circumstances. Harder to irrigate by virtue of their location and thus ill-suited to schemes of apportionment by entitlement, "water rights" at the tail-end of the ancient canal network were simply the customary right to access the water of a shared canal during the flood, whatever its quantity, without hindrance or obstruction. Yet this farmer-managed system required communities to pool their energies not only to maintain local infrastructure but also at times to defend their access to the commons against upstream irrigators. The final section describes these communal aspects of irrigation and argues that the water conflicts attested in the fourth century CE resulted from the internal disintegration of the social infrastructure that generated and defended the water rights of these vulnerable downstream communities.

3. Social relations and the maintenance of water rights

Irrigation from a shared canal is an inherently communal activity. As described by Jessica Barnes, an acute observer of contemporary Fayyum irrigation practices, the successful channeling of water through a canal-irrigated settlement is the product of a community's routinized collective engagement with the earth and water upon which it depends:

> [I]t is the community that makes the water flow; a community that is generated not by turning up at a meeting but by everyday practices of

---

[57] High lands are recorded as unflooded (ἄβροχος) in *P. Bagnall* 9 (TM 44543, 199-175 BCE); *SB* XX 14179 (TM 7881, 185/4 BCE); *P. Bagnall* 46 (= *P. Tebt.* IV 1117c, TM 219272; 119 BCE). The account published as *P. Wisc.* II 77 (TM 2455, after March 245 BCE) also references the digging of a canal to irrigate high ground (τὰ ὑψηλά, l. 37). Cattle-breeders are said to retreat to the highest places (τοὺς ὑψηλοτάτους τόπους, l. 172) during the flood in *P. Tebt.* III 703 (TM 5315, 210 BCE).

> blocking, unblocking, digging, and weeding an irrigation ditch. It is a community generated not through a collective imagination but through the shared work of maintaining the flow of water.[58]

Communal social infrastructure is thus intimately entwined with the physical infrastructure of an irrigation system, the dense web of "arteries of ditches and bloodlines" described by writer and irrigation farmer Stanley Crawford in the epigraph above.[59] This is to say that, while gravity may propel the water of a canal system downhill, it is the community of water-users the establishes the ever-changing patterns of its flow: fluid, physical manifestations of the community's shifting social relations continually inscribed and reinscribed on the landscape. In the case of the ancient Fayyum, population shocks such as those precipitated by the Antonine and Cyprian Plagues — epidemics whose devastating effects on the Empire are only now being fully appreciated[60] — will have severely damaged the social infrastructure that maintained established patterns of water flow throughout the Fayyum. Shrunken and weak, the most vulnerable tail-end communities will have been particularly hard-pressed to defend their access to the commons from upstream irrigators.

The Ptolemaic petition *P. Tebt.* I 50 (112-111 BCE), already mentioned above, establishes in microscopic detail the importance of social relationships between irrigators to the maintenance of customary water flows:

> [Μεγχε]ῖ κωμογραμ[ματ]εῖ Κερκεοσίρεως [παρὰ] Πασῖτος το[ῦ Πε]τεσούχου βασιλικοῦ γεωργοῦ τῶν [ἐκ τ]ῆς αὐτῆς. ἔτ[ι ἐκ τ]ῶν ἔμπροσθεν χρόνων [ἐθισ]μοῦ ὄντος π[οτί]ζεσθαι τὴν ὑπάρχουσάν [μοι] περὶ τὴν αὐτὴν κώμην βασιλικὴν γῆν [δι]ὰ τοῦ διείργοντος διὰ τῆς ἐπικειμένης Λύκου τοῦ

58 BARNES 2014, p. 87. Although clouded by nostalgic haze, the late Egyptian president Anwar al-Sādāt's *encomium* to irrigation in his home village of Mīt Abū-l-Kūm in the Nile Delta similarly conveys the importance of collective action to irrigation: [W]e had to leave at dawn for the special canal that filled to overflowing for no more than two weeks, our "statutory" irrigation period, during which all land in the village had to be watered. It was obviously necessary to do it quickly and collectively… The main thing was to ensure that at the end of the "statutory" period all the land in the village was irrigated. That kind of collective work — with and for other men, with no profit or any kind of individual reward in prospect — made me feel that I belonged not merely to my immediate family at home, or even to the big family of the village, but to something vaster and more significant: the land. SĀDĀT 1979, p. 2-3.

59 See epigraph above. CRAWFORD 1988.

60 HARPER 2017.

Ζωπυρίωνος καὶ ἑτέρων βασιλικῆς τε καὶ ἱερᾶς γῆς βασιλικοῦ ὑδραγωγοῦ, ἐν δὲ τῶι β (ἔτει) χωρισθέντος μου εἰς ἀλλοδημίαν περὶ ἀναγκαίων πραγμάτων τῶν Ἀσκ[λ]ηπιάδου τοῦ συγγενοῦς ὁ προγεγραμμένος Λύκος νομίσας καιρὸν εὐφυηι ἔχειν ἐπιβαλὼν συνέχωσεν τὰ ἐν τῆι ἑαυτοῦ γῆι μέρη τοῦ σημαινομένου ὑδραγωγοῦ...

To Menches, village scribe of Kerkeosiris, from Pasis son of Petesouchos, crown-cultivator from the same village. It long been customary for me to water the royal land belonging to me near the same village with the royal canal that passes through the adjacent crown and temple land of Lykos son of Zopyrion, and others. But in the second year while I was abroad on urgent business for Asklepiades kinsman [of the king], the aforementioned Lykos, having thought that he had an ideal opportunity, dammed up the portions of the aforementioned canal [that lie] on his own land...

The complainant Pasis' absence (l. 9: εἰς ἀλλοδημίαν) from the village is the critical issue here. As argued by Elinor Ostrom, face-to-face communication is essential to the successful management of the commons. Personal relationships facilitate trust, foster a sense of collective identity and solidarity, and reinforce the unwritten social norms that govern the use of common resources.[61] As argued above, the marginal Fayyum's environment lacked a system of water rights assigned and enforced by an external authority. Hence, presence on the ground in the fields during irrigation periods was an essential component of successful irrigation. Pasis' absence was therefore an "ideal opportunity" (l. 12: καιρὸν εὐφυῆι) for his upstream neighbor to engage in water-theft. Even in the modern Fayyum where perennial irrigation and water rights are recorded and enforced by a central water bureaucracy, it falls first upon farmers themselves to defend their water rights in the field:

> Everyone gets his fair share of water (more or less) but at the cost of watching not to be cheated, which means that when someone is irrigating, someone else must stay at the branching point on the canal to make sure nobody comes along and diverts the water.[62]

Yet beyond simply monitoring one's neighbors to passively enforce social norms of water sharing, internal management of the commons could also require more aggressive, at times violent, face-to-face encounters. From this perspective, the attack upon the ἔμβλημα already

[61] OSTROM 1998 and OSTROM 1999. See also CASTIGLIONE 2016.

[62] MEHANNA e.a. 1984, p. 109.

discussed above in *P. Ryl.* II 133 may be viewed not as simple malice but as one farmer's aggressive assertion of his rights to the commons. A more graphic example is narrated in Palladius' *Lausiac History* in the life of a holy virgin Piamoun. Palladius writes that the virgin's village was at one time set upon during the flood by its spear- and club-wielding neighbors, "for they fight about the distribution of water" (μάχονται γὰρ εἰς τὰς ὑδριμερίας).[63]

This sort of aggressive collective action is also alluded to in the fragmentary *P. Merton* I 11 (TM 11902, 39-40 CE). The text is badly damaged and cannot be reconstructed in its entirety but its outlines are reasonably clear. A royal farmer by the name of Harpaesis complains that he had been prevented (ἐκ̣ω̣λ̣ύ̣θ̣[ην]) from watering the one hundred arouras of land he possesses by a certain Sambas and a crowd of fifty men (συνόδ̣ο̣υ εἰς λόγον ἀνδ(ρῶν) ν). Although damaged at this crucial point, the sense seems to be that the water was then diverted to Sambas' own plot (αὐτοῦ κλῆρον̣ γ̣[ειτνιῶ(ντα)] ἐμοῦ προκιμένου). The reasons behind the conflict are, unfortunately, unstated and irrecoverable.

Yet the collective, potentially violent, assertions of water rights discussed here are nowhere better attested than the well-known *P. Haun.* III 58 (TM 11456, 439 CE), the latest dated papyrus from Karanis. In this declaration (dubbed both a χείρ and an ἀπόδειξις) a group of men address themselves to the villagers of Karanis and assert their exclusive rights to a named water source (Θανεσαμήν). Any attempt by the villagers to draw water from this source, they continue, will be smashed (συνκλάσομεν), actions for which they will incur no blame whatsoever (οὐκ ἔχομεν μέμψιν παρά τινος τῆς κώμης καὶ διὰ τοῦτω). This text, peppered with unusual vocabulary and unorthodox orthography, has been regarded either as simply perplexing and ambiguous or else as evidence of the collapse of the agricultural regime at Karanis.[64] And yet, although it documents a claim of exclusive and highly localized water rights, perhaps to a reservoir,[65] rather than a defense of the commons, it nonetheless documents behavior common to unregulated farmer-managed

[63] *HL* XXXI. Cited in BAGNALL 1993, p. 138.

[64] VAN MINNEN 1995.

[65] Θανεσαμήν is translated as "The place of the reservoir" in Trismegistos: http://www.trismegistos.org/place/2342. Accessed 3 January 2018.

irrigation communities: the communal defense of water rights against competitors, including the right to "smash" any malefactors.

P. Haun. III 58 and the other, admittedly limited, evidence adduced here suggests that defending access to water at the tail-end of the Fayyum's ancient canal system demanded face-to-face relationships, ranging from watchful presence at the site of irrigation to the mobilization of larger, potentially aggressive groups. The conflicts between fourth-century CE Theadelphia and its neighbors should therefore be understood within a social context in which farmers were regularly active in the defense of their individual and communal water rights. Yet with a male population hovering near twenty-five between the years 312 and 336 CE, a period in which the village might even be nearly deserted in the worst years,[66] Late Antique Theadelphia sorely lacked the social capital necessary to convince (or physically coerce) upstream irrigators to permit it a share of the common-pool resources. Sakaon's series of plaintive appeals to the state are therefore not evidence of its own insufficient governance and the subsequent creation of perverse incentives; indeed, as I have argued here, water distribution in the nome had never been so closely regulated. Rather, these texts document the final stages of an irrigation community's internal decay, the erosion of the human infrastructure that had ensured that water reached the tail-end of a canal.

As a result of this decay, the attempts by the praeses Valerius Tziper in *P. Sakaon* 33 (ca. 320 CE) to resolve Theadelphia's conflicts were futile. Local officials — the *praepositus pagi* and the "dyke inspectors" (χωματεπίκται)[67] — could indeed order upstream irrigators to cease and desist and permit Theadelphia their customary share of the commons. But who was left on the ground in Theadelphia to enforce those judgments after the state's representatives departed? Most of the village's population had already departed permanently, e.g. for the Oxyrhynchite and Kynopolite nomes to the south (*P. Sakaon* 44, TM 13063, ca. 331-332 CE).

Since village irrigation communities are therefore best regarded as complex socio-natural entanglements of human beings and their surrounding environments, we must necessarily regard fourth-century Theadelphia as an irrigation community in name only, one that was at this

[66] BAGNALL 1982.

[67] BONNEAU 1993, p. 160-165.

point merely as a fiscal unit in the Roman state's cadastral accounts. Its physical infrastructure of canals and dykes may still have existed but the collective agency that made water flow through it each year could no longer be generated by its few remaining inhabitants. No amount of external regulation could have replaced this missing human element.

Conclusion

Elinor Ostrom identified three fallacious assumptions at the heart of contemporary critiques of common-pool resource governance:[68]

1) "Resource users are explicitly thought of as norm-free maximizers of immediate gains, who will not cooperate to overcome the perverse incentives of dilemma situations in order to increase their own and others' long-term benefits unless coerced by external authorities."
2) "[D]esigning rules to change the incentives of participants is a relatively simple analytical task best done by objective analysts not intimately related to any specific resource."
3) "[O]rganization itself requires central direction."

In short, critiques of the commons tend to portray human actors as coldly rational and uncooperative utility-seekers concerned only with their own immediate material benefit, their simplistic and predictable behaviors easily molded by regulations imposed and enforced by an external authority. In contrast, this paper has attempted to sketch a picture of a commons successfully organized from within through its users' productive adaptation to predictably unpredictable water supplies. Unlike the irrigation community imagined by ʿAbd al-Rahmān al-Sharqāwī, which was organized around a rigid and brittle system of water-shares ill-adapted to its unstable local water regime, the margins of the Graeco-Roman Fayyum were flexibly adapted to the region's hydrological rhythms and thus better able to withstand the vagaries of the annual flood. It was a durable system, one that ensured fair access to the commons for more than six centuries without the artificial, illusory certainty promised by externally-assigned rights in water. The relative paucity of surviving evidence for water disputes indeed suggests that,

[68] Ostrom 1999, p. 496.

although the Fayyum's marginal villages were not rural utopias immune from conflict, communal relationships within and between villages were sufficient to overcome the tensions and perverse incentives inevitably created by the nature of upstream/downstream water flow in canal systems.

Given sufficient human infrastructure, then, irrigation along the margins of the Fayyum was a relational process of give-and-take, not an all-out competition, a "race to the bottom" by norm-free maximizers in dire need of external regulation.[69] Only when the population declined swiftly and unexpectedly did the internal social structure of the irrigation system begin to break down. Theadelphia's upstream neighbors therefore did not begin to monopolize water resources because local property rights in water were ill-defined or because they were not sufficiently chastised by the state. Rather, as an irrigation community, a collection of relational individuals who worked together to make water flow, Theadelphia no longer existed and its pleas for water could be easily ignored.

[69] *Pace* KEHOE 2008, p. 250.

DISPUTING PUBLIC AUTHORITY IN THE LATE ROMAN COUNTRYSIDE. *P. CAIR. MASP.* I 67002 REVISITED*

Matthias STERN
(LMU München/DAI München)

Abstract: This contribution reviews *P. Cair. Masp.* I 67002, in which petitioners from the village of Aphrodite in the Thebaid take a stand against the notorious pagarch Menas, whom they accuse of violent misconduct. Reading this text in terms of dispute resolution, this paper re-examines the case, its conditions, and its consequences in regard to late Roman politics of social control. It follows the steps of this escalating process as it unfolded before the authorities, from which emerge two interlinked primary arguments: first, rather than illustrating the insubordinate private powers of late antique magnates, the highly stylized petition in fact reflects officially condoned conduct on the part of the pagarch; and second, rather than being directed primarily against the alleged villain, the petition and its narrative were more probably aimed at creating a case for social cohesion amid internal factionalism. Both findings may echo larger developments, in the course of which increasingly empowered and confident rural communities in parts of the late Roman Empire found themselves confronted by stricter imperial control.

INTRODUCTION

Between May and July 567 CE, the inhabitants of the village of Aphrodite filed a petition to the *dux et Augustalis* Athanasios, the provincial governor of the Thebaid.[1] This text, known as *P. Cair. Masp.* I 67002 (TM 18977), was composed by the well-known poet and notary

* This contribution was developed under the auspices of the research project 162963: "Change and Continuities from a Christian to a Muslim Society — Egyptian Society and Economy in the 6th to 8th Centuries," funded by the Swiss National Science Foundation SNSF. Dates of papyri are given by year only if the specific date is not essential to the argument. I owe thanks to Caroline WAZER and Irene SOTO MARÍN for helpful suggestions.

Dioskoros, who put great effort into advancing the case of the "most humble servants and wretched smallholders" in their own voice,[2] and produced "an unparalleled record of misery inflicted upon the villagers", which had long been taken to be a vivid illustration of the once commonly held view of late antiquity as a period of decline, chaos, and widespread corruption.[3] The petition complains of misconduct on the part of the local aristocrat Menas, who is said to have invaded the village with armed forces, imprisoned villagers, seized property, and destroyed the fields, allegedly stealing their harvest, cattle, and large amounts of money.[4] Reading through this document, one is struck by the extent of Menas' acts, which left the villagers with nothing to eat but cattle-fodder, harvest slops, and grains dropped during the transport of the grain tax,[5] and thus one cannot help but admire the courage on display on the part of the poor villagers in pursuing their case against a powerful enemy. Their opponent was not just a ruthless local landlord contesting boundary rights or the like: Menas was also pagarch of the city of Antaiopolis, the central authority in the countryside of the *civitas* that the village of Aphrodite was part of — and therefore had substantial coercive force at his disposal.[6]

---

[1] PALME 2007 provides an overview of the provincial organization of late antique Egypt.

[2] *P. Cair. Masp.* I 67002 praef., l. 2: τῶν ἐλε<ε>ινοτάτων δούλων ὑμῶν καὶ ἀθλίων λεπτοκτητόρων. Dioskoros, his work, and his world have been thoroughly analyzed particularly in MACCOULL 1988, FOURNET 1999, and the various contributions to FOURNET 2008; see also FOURNET 2003, SARRIS 2006, p. 96-114, RUFFINI 2008a, p. 147-197, and VANDERHEYDEN 2012.

[3] Essential earlier scholarship on *P. Cair. Masp.* I 67002 is discussed in KEENAN 2008, p. 172-173 (quote) and listed in RUFFINI 2008a, p. 158, n. 74. The most prominent uses of this text for drafting the narrative of notoriously repressive large landowners have probably been GELZER 1909, p. 92-96, BELL 1917, p. 99-100 (cf. BELL 1944, p. 33-35), and HARDY 1931, p. 137-138. The historiographical context is discussed in KEENAN 1993 and PALME 2013, esp. p. 129-132.

[4] An outline of the main narrative the petition puts forward is provided in KEENAN 2008, p. 174.

[5] *P. Cair. Masp.* I 67002, col. i, l. 10-11: ὅτι ἐν τῷ χειμο[ν]ι (read χειμῶνι) δρόξιμα (read τρώξιμα) καὶ ὀλύρας ἐσθίομεν, τῷ [δὲ] | θέρει τὰ ἀποκαθάρματα ἤτοι ἀποκοσκινήματα καὶ καταστελλματα τῆς ἐμβολῆς ἡμῶν παρ' ἑστίαις ἐδόμενοι. The emotional register of Dioskoros' petitions will be evaluated in PALME forthcoming.

[6] The most comprehensive study on the Byzantine pagarchs so far remains MAZZA 1995 (with earlier literature in n. 1); more recent contributions include LIEBESCHUETZ

The present contribution aims to read the dispute present in *P. Cair. Masp.* I 67002 as a "dispute against an official", and makes the case that this reading enhances our understanding of local relations of power. This paper argues that the dispute in question features several apparent divergences from larger patterns in the petitioning process, which can be subjected to a structural analysis placing emphasis on the interaction between the state and its subjects in the late Roman countryside, on the role of an enforced *fiscalité* in a late antique imperial context, and on how documents like *P. Cair. Masp.* I 67002 negotiated these issues. I will begin by determining what makes the dispute between Menas and the Aphroditans a distinctive "dispute against a public authority". Second, I will review the petitioners' case from the opposite perspective, that of the bureaucrat, as it were, in order to put it into the context of the mechanics of public administration.[7] Third, I will shift the chronological frame backward in time in order to evaluate the conditions and procedures of the dispute that led to the petition preserved in *P. Cair. Masp.* I 67002. Fourth, by extending the frame of view and considering the dispute from an imperial perspective, I will outline probable resolutions of the villagers' case, before concluding with a discussion of the main findings.

1. A DISPUTE AGAINST (A) PUBLIC AUTHORITY?

Considering whether the conflict between the Aphroditans and the pagarch Menas constitutes a dispute against an official authority, it is evident that the case includes a large part of the range of what can possibly be imagined as subjects of disputes, some of which are studied in detail by various contributions in the present volume: debts, seizure or damage of real property, theft, and violence. However, we obviously are not dealing with, say, a squabble between two neighboring landholders. After all, this is, formally, an entire village community collectively taking

---

2001, p. 188-189, BANAJI 2007, chapters 4-6 *passim* (most-pointed on p. 97-100, 140-141, and 148-149), RUFFINI 2008a, p. 187-195, and STERN 2015.

[7] The concept of bureaucracy in a late antique context has most recently been discussed in EICH 2015.

action against Menas,[8] and there are considerable sums of money involved. Furthermore, Menas held the position of pagarch, by that time the backbone of public authority at the nome level in Egypt, and was in charge of tax collection in the territories of the *civitates*. Generally entwined with the local population via their sometimes extensive landholdings, the pagarchs represented one of the instruments with which the late Roman government tried to pull influential families even further into its administrative network, holding them more immediately responsible for the imperial cause on a local level. Though the pagarchs were subordinate to the *dux et Augustalis* (the provincial governor), ultimately the final verdict over their tenure, impeachment, or penalties lay in the hands of the emperor.[9] The pagarchs and their apparatus were therefore — next to the military — the most immediate representation of imperial control in the countryside.

Pagarchs were generally aristocrats from the ranks of the *viri clarissimi* at least, and Menas himself is known to have been part of the bureaucrat elite of the Thebaid.[10] So our petition is, at the very least, a document that relates to a dispute against a member of the elite, who might have just coincidentally been the pagarch. To what extent, however, were there concrete repercussions of the accused being an official authority? To name two particularly influential contributions to the subject of dispute resolution: Deborah Hobson, in her treatment of "The *Impact* of *Law* on Village Life in Roman Egypt", does not appear to consider complaints of misconduct by officials to be a distinct category of dispute, but rather seems to count them among cases of "unacceptable or abusive behavior on the part of someone, usually someone known personally to

[8] Dioskoros stylizes the petition as being conveyed by the village community, consequently using the first person plural; he uses the third person singular in reference to himself and his own misfortunes at the hands of Menas in the first column. The epistemological problem of the petitioners' "tormented voices" being filtered by the hand and mind of Dioskoros is discussed in KEENAN 2008, p. 178-179. It adds to the magnitude of the dispute that the "village" of Aphrodite was considerably larger than most Egyptian villages (see *P. Mich. Aphrod.*, p. 14-15). While it was of course in the petitioners' interest to evoke the involvement of the entire village community, the reality was likely to have been more nuanced, as will be discussed in the final section of this paper.

[9] These regulations are put down in chapters 12 and 25 of Justinian's *Edict* 13 of 539 CE, on which see generally PALME 2013, p. 103-105, with further literature. Penalties could lead as far as the seizure and transfer of the pagarch's estates into others' hands.

[10] On Menas, see RUFFINI 2011, s.n. Menas 13.

the petitioner".[11] Benjamin Kelly, however, in his monograph on *Petitions, Litigation, and Social Control in Roman Egypt*, distinguishes "[m]isconduct by an official" as a particular form of dispute.[12]

In our case, *P. Cair. Masp.* I 67002 yields three observations allowing for more specific categorization of a "dispute against an official". First, when reporting the means of the pagarch's alleged raids, the petition states that he intervened "with military and civil auxiliaries".[13] The role of the military in enforcing tax collection is known particularly from Justinian's *Edict* 13, and in the present case it appears that detachments of the "Macedonian" and the "Scythian" soldiers assisted Menas in his intervention — not under his command, however, but under that of a *vicarius*.[14] Furthermore, parallel evidence from Aphrodite, the Fayum, and — under slightly different conditions — Oxyrhynchos suggests that the pagarch was in charge of smaller detachments of civil guards in villages and in other rural parts of the nome.[15] Consequently, it appears that Menas acted with regular auxiliary forces when coming to the village. Second, the context of the dispute appears to have been essentially one of fiscal debts, which the villagers themselves acknowledge, as will be further discussed below. Third, the petitioners clearly perceive Menas as a public representative and they frequently allude to this role. They claim, for instance, that the pagarch's aggressive form of intervention would ultimately lead to tax shortcomings.[16] Thus, the villagers accuse Menas of being incapable of fulfilling his central service to the state, that is, ensuring the proper operation of the tax collection process — which goes to show that the villagers perceived Menas as an official entity and that they aimed precisely at undermining his official authority. A further

---

[11] HOBSON 1993, p. 204; see also p. 203, n. 4, where the author even appears to contrast the concepts "dispute" and "official".

[12] KELLY 2011, appendices I and III.

[13] *P. Cair. Masp.* I 67002, col. ii, l. 23: μετὰ πολλῆς ληστρικῆς τε καὶ παγανικῆς καὶ [στ]ρ̣α̣τι[ωτ]ικῆς βοηθεί[ας]. On the term παγανικός in similar contexts, see F. MITTHOF in *CPR* XXIII, p. 204-205.

[14] *P. Cair. Masp.* I 67002, col. ii, l. 12: τοῦ βικαρίο(υ) τῶν στρατιωτῶν Σκυθῶν καὶ τῶν Μακεδόνων. On these units, see MITTHOF 2008. The role of the military in collecting taxes has been highlighted by C. ZUCKERMAN in *P. Aphrod. Reg.*, p. 154-155; cf. PALME 2007, p. 256 and see also GREY 2011, p. 125-126 with n. 15.

[15] STERN 2015, p. 133-135.

[16] *P. Cair. Masp.* I 67002, col. iii, l. 18-19: πρὸς λύμην τῶν βασιλικῶν φόρων καὶ σκεδασμὸν τῆς αἰσίας | ἡμῶν ἐμβολῆς.

hint is given by another episode in the same document, in which the petitioners complain of their earlier arrest by a certain Serenos while they were at a cattle-market in the Hermopolite village of Thynis.[17] This man, a local aristocrat addressed inter alia as a *vir magnificentissimus*, who apparently held no current official position, had them assaulted and their cattle stolen. Rather than accusing Serenos, however, the petition here points at Menas, who according to the villagers was ultimately responsible.[18] Apparently, this conflict was not simply about restitution but was also, to a considerable degree, about holding a public authority accountable.

Consequently, we can speak of the present case as a "dispute against an official". And while this was not a challenge of public authority in the sense of regime critique,[19] it probably reflects a deeply rooted belief in the rationality of Roman officials — that there were rules and regulations to be followed, to which these officials could be held accountable.[20]

2. Switching perspective: officials and official maxims

Though we do not have Menas' opinion on the events that *P. Cair. Masp.* I 67002 describes in terms of ravage, destruction, and starvation, we can still balance the petition's tone with three major points: the pagarchs' own involvement in resolving disputes, the literary side of the petition, and the legitimacy of Menas' claim.

First — though this is a more general note to the historiographic tradition of the pagarchs as oppressors of the late antique peasantry — the pagarchs themselves were approached in order to settle disputes, though

---

[17] *P. Cair. Masp.* I 67002, col. ii, l. 1-16. The location is put into context by Keenan 2008, p. 177. There will be more to say about this episode in the third section.

[18] *P. Cair. Masp.* I 67002, col. ii, l. 2.

[19] See on this point the balanced evaluation of Palme 2008, p. 218-219.

[20] Harries 1999, p. 96-98 for late antiquity; Kelly 2011, p. 195 and Ando 2000, p. 380-382 (and 373-374) for the Roman period; Bryen 2013, p. 25 in the context of petitioning. The fact that petitioners frequently appealed to the state's fiscal self-interests, as the Aphroditans did, does not contradict but rather reinforces this perception; the deliberate use of this topos in order to get the state to intervene in private disputes is analyzed in Grey 2011, p. 216-225. Cf. Crawford 1978 for "official standards" in the Ptolemaic period.

the evidence for this is comparatively hard to come by.[21] In one instance, a widow had donated to a monastery land that was now being contested by a man about whom we know no more than his name; in the petition linked to this case, the monks ask the *dux et Augustalis* to order the local pagarch and the *topoteretes* "to keep him away from us".[22] In another petition, another widow complains that she had been assaulted and imprisoned; she goes on to argue that before having turned to the *dux* by means of petitioning, the pagarch had already intervened in her case and ordered her release, which means that she or a confidant of hers must have approached the pagarch beforehand.[23] These instances illustrate that the pagarchy was hardly in itself an institution of oppression.[24]

Second, the extraordinary amount of violence that had allegedly taken place during Menas' intervention in the village must be balanced with the petition's literary character, which according to Jean-Luc Fournet is one "[e]ntre document et littérature":[25] given the tradition of late antique petitions we are well advised to remain critical of the heavy tone in *P. Cair. Masp.* I 67002. Likewise, the text features a variety of topoi that

---

[21] There is more obvious evidence for pagarchs receiving petitions after the Islamic conquest of 642 CE, although using this as an argument would require thoroughly retracing the survival of Byzantine administration in early Islamic Egypt, which I will leave for elsewhere.

[22] *P. Cair. Masp.* I 67003, l. 24-25 (TM 18978: Antinoopolis?; ca. 567): ὅθεν παρακαλοῦμεν τὸ ὕψος ὑμῶν (…) εἰ παρασταίη προστάξαι τῷ παγάρχῃ τῆς Ἀνταίο(υ) καὶ τῷ τοποτηρητῇ ταυτῆς ἀφ' ἡμῶν αὐτὸν ἀποτρέψαι, δέσπο(τα) ὑ̣π̣(ερ)φ̣υ̣ε̣σ̣τ̣α̣(τε). The chronologically closest known pagarchs are Menas himself and Kollouthos, on whom see the following note and n. 64, yet possibly also another, unknown pagarch is addressed here, who would have been a colleague of Menas or Kollouthos, and who may also have been *topoteretes*: it is commonly assumed that the pagarch and the *topoteretes* in this text are two different individuals, but cf. *P. Cair. Masp.* I 67002, col. iii, l. 19: ἔγραψεν (!) γὰρ αὐτῷ ὁ γραμματεὺς καὶ ὁ διακονητής; the link between these two passages was already established in GELZER 1913, p. 361, n. 1.

[23] *P. Cair. Masp.* I 67005, l. 19 (TM 18980: Antinoopolis?; ca. 568): ἐκέλευσεν ὁ δεσπ(ότης) μου ὁ λαμπρ(ότατος) κύριος Κόλλουθος ὁ καγκελλάριος κ(αὶ) παγάρχης ἀπολυθῆναί με. It is elusive why the pagarch's order was apparently ignored.

[24] Cf. *P. Oxy.* XVI 1831 (TM 35593: Oxyrhynchites; late fifth century?), where a village headman evokes the authority of the pagarch(s?) as a threat in order to persuade his opponent into conceding.

[25] See FOURNET 2004 (quote) and FOURNET 2015, p. 256-257; cf. KOVELMAN 1991 for the narrative aspect in these petitions. A list of preserved petitions on papyrus is provided in FOURNET & GASCOU 2004.

were expected in this type of document — such as the mere opposition of a humble community against a powerful outsider.[26] A telling instance may be Dioskoros' own story in *P. Cair. Masp.* I 67002, where he — through the voice of the villagers addressing the *dux* — describes his stay in Antinoopolis essentially as an exile in the wake of Menas' pursuit: "until now the wretched [i.e. Dioskoros], lacking a proper defender, dwells abroad along with his children, begging for your good judgment, o master," implying that he may return as soon as Menas' aggressions are curbed, and much of the modern literature has since followed him.[27] However, his move to Antinoopolis follows a pattern that is suspiciously well-known for provincial bureaucrats, and as a ducal notary Dioskoros was certainly not without opportunity in the provincial capital.[28] Moreover, Dioskoros was already in Antinoopolis when the celebratory effigies arrived for the occasion of Justin II's inauguration.[29] Justin ascended to the throne on November 14, 565, and while it might have taken some time for the news (and the effigies) to reach the Thebaid, this would hardly have taken so long as until May 566, when Menas entered the pagarchy and, according to *P. Cair. Masp.* I 67002, started harassing Dioskoros.[30] So the order of events was probably the other way around and Menas went after Dioskoros' land *because* the poet-notary was out

---

[26] See BAGNALL 1989, p. 211-212 and BRYEN 2013, p. 96-100. In reality, Menas was of course anything but an outsider (RUFFINI 2008a, p. 191-195).

[27] *P. Cair. Masp.* I 67002, col. i, l. 19: ὁ ἄθλιο[ς] ἕως νῦν ἐπὶ ξένης σὺν τέκνοις, αἰτῶν \ῶν καὶ/ ἐκδικίας ἀγαθῆς ὑμῶν τυχεῖν, δέσπο(τα). The most prominent instances are probably H.I. BELL in *P. Lond.* V, p. 56, MACCOULL 1988, p. 24, PALME 2013, p. 128, and FOURNET 2015, p. 265. A more prosaic and probably more compelling interpretation in light of Dioskoros' professional career is given by T. GAGOS and P. VAN MINNEN in *P. Mich. Aphrod.*, p. 21.

[28] See KEENAN 2001, p. 66-68 and 70 for Antinoopolis and cf. p. 72-73 for a similar pattern in Oxyrhynchos, the capital of Arcadia. On Dioskoros' possible connections to the ducal *officium*, see PALME 2008, p. 211.

[29] *P. Aphrod. Lit.* IV 17 (TM 65008). We may thus suppose that Dioskoros was in the city even longer, and that he had been planning to do so for longer still.

[30] *P. Cair. Masp.* I 67002, col. i, l. 10-11: ἀπὸ προοιμίων τῆς ἔναγχος διαδραμο(ύ)σης πεντεκαιδεκάτης ἐπινεμήσεως, ἀφ' ἧς ἀντελάβετο τῆς παγαρχίας | Ἀνταίο(υ), καρποῦται τὰς ἀρούρας τοῦ συναδέλφου ἡμῶν καὶ ἀθλίο(υ) δούλο(υ) τῆς ὑμῶν ἐνδόξο(υ) φιλανθρωπίας Διοσκόρου. For the beginning of the indiction year at that time, see BAGNALL & WORP 2004, p. 30. FOURNET 1999, p. 330-331 (cf. 321) grants that the arrival of these effigies (and thus, he argues, the commencement of Athanasios' tenure as *dux* and Dioskoros' move to Antinoopolis) "doit être datée de l'extrême fin 565 ou du début 566".

of his reach at that point. Also, Dioskoros' return to Aphrodite can hardly be linked to the end of Menas' pagarchy.[31] Naturally, however, taking refuge would make a much better story for him to tell and is — also in the context of "fiscal oppression" — a common topos occurring well before late antiquity.[32]

Third, it has already been said that Menas' intervention was due to tax arrears. The petitioners, naturally, cite this as "pretext",[33] yet they never complain that the pagarch should not have taken money in the first place. Instead, they criticize his failure to issue proper receipts, thereby in fact acknowledging Menas' claim as legitimate.[34] Apparently, the pagarch was entitled or at least expected to intervene in this case in order to ensure the proper collection of taxes.[35] All of these factors suggest that Menas was not the "bad official" that the petition wants us to believe he was, but probably simply doing his job. The government cared about its tax revenues, and this was what Menas was after. We will see in the following section that when we follow the story backward in time, the prologue to *P. Cair. Masp.* I 67002 neatly fits into this interpretation.

Dioskoros apparently dwelled in the village as late as November 7, 565 (*P. Lond.* V 1686 = TM 19703).

[31] Dioskoros returned to Aphrodite at some point between November 570 and the end of 573 (RUFFINI 2008a, p. 158, n. 69). Menas, however, was no longer pagarch by March 14, 570, at the very latest (*P.Lond.* V 1714 = TM 19731; see below n. 63), when he is part of the ducal *officium* in Antinoopolis.

[32] On this topos and its tradition, see ZICHE 2006, p. 128-132.

[33] *P. Cair. Masp.* I 67002, col. ii, l. 17: προφάσει δημοσίων.

[34] *P. Cair. Masp.* I 67002, col. ii, l. 13: οὐδὲ μὴν κατελογίσατο τῷ δημοσίῳ τῆς ἡμῶν κώμης Ἀφροδίτης. See also col. ii, l. 22: ὁ αὐτὸς πάγαρχος ἔλαβεν τὸ δημ[όσι]ον, which goes without further comment by the petitioners; STERN 2015, p. 128.

[35] This view holds even if the extracted 1.017 *solidi* are not a valid representation of Aphrodite's annual tax quota (see KEENAN 2008, p. 175-177 against C. ZUCKERMAN in *P. Aphrod. Reg.*, p. 213-214; cf. BRANSBOURG 2016, p. 332), as the villagers' tendency to present their village as a unity (see below the last section) may obscure the simple solution that Menas was cracking down on numerous individual debtors from the village. A similar reading of this episode as presented above has been proposed already by GERACI 1979, though in a different context. For other "rehabilitations" of Menas, see RÉMONDON 1968, p. 78, 86, and RUFFINI 2008a, p. 193-194.

3. Means of dispute: before the petition

With regard to their history with the fiscal regime, the petitioners argue that "there have been eight pagarchs so far of Antaiopolis and we have never been in arrears with the imperial taxes nor with the grain tax."[36] While this may have been true in a technical sense, it is misleading in so far as we have evidence that this was not the first time the villagers had been in arrears with their *local* taxes. Menas is especially clear in a letter to the village headmen, one of them being Dioskoros himself: "(I have written) in order that you know that if you do not bring me by tomorrow the quota of the city tax and the village tax in full, you will not be delighted about your behavior. Be aware, I have written to warn you!"[37] While this letter most likely predates the events of *P. Cair. Masp.* I 67002, it is still indicative of an apparently recurring problem and thus suggests the dispute before the dispute, as it were: Menas demanding the payment of taxes due.[38] The aforementioned episode that took place in the Hermopolite village of Thynis, where — if we are to believe the petitioners — Menas had apparently arranged the detention of several Aphroditans, also suggests that the village had a lingering problem with its taxes. These events had occurred under the *dux* Kyros, whom Athanasios succeeded as governor around the very end of 565 or in early 566,

---

[36] *P. Cair. Masp.* I 67002, col. ii, l. 18-19. Constantin Zuckerman has argued in *P. Aphrod. Reg.*, p. 213 that this passage refers to the number of incumbent pagarchs since Aphrodite had lost its *autopragia* (see below n. 54) in the early 550s — a hypothesis to which the table provided in Fournet 2000, p. 247 lends much plausibility.

[37] *P. Cair. Masp.* I 67060, l. 4-6 (TM 36803) with *BL* XII 45 (translation adapted from Sarris 2006, p. 110): (…) ἵνα τ̣[ὲ] (read δὲ) μ̣ά̣θ̣η̣τ̣ε̣ ὅτι εἰ μὴ δι̣[ὰ τ]ῆς α̣ὔριον ἐξενέγκητέ μοι | τὸ μέτρον τοῦ τε ἀστικο(ῦ) καὶ κωμητικο(ῦ) ἐπλήρους (read ἐκ πλήρους), ο[ὐ]κ [ἔχετε] ε̣[ὐ]χαριστῆσαι̣ τῷ | πράγματι, ἰδοὺ οὖν, γέγραφα διαμαρτυρο̣(ύ)μενος ὑ̣μ̣[ῖν. Cf. *P. Cair. Masp.* I 67061 (TM 36804), most probably relating to the same events.

[38] Jean-Luc Fournet and Jean Gascou (2002, p. 35, n. 43) suggest to date *P. Cair. Masp.* I 67060 to 553 CE, when Menas is attested as pagarch (*P. Lond.* V 1660 = TM 19677; *P. Lond.* V 1661 = TM 19678) and when Apollos and Dioskoros are known to have been *protokometai* (*P. Cair. Masp.* I 67094 = TM 19021; *P. Lond.* V 1661). However, they acknowledge that other dates are possible, given Menas' second tenure from 566/567 onward and given the lost dates of other letters where Dioskoros and Apollos appear collectively as *protokometai*. On the former prefect Ioulianos who occurs in this text, see the next section. If Ruffini's Ioulianos 1 is the same as Ioulianos 2 (Ruffini 2011, s.n.), he was certainly not pagarch at the time of *P. Cair. Masp.* I 67060, which would then point to a post-553 date.

i.e., months before Menas took office as pagarch in May 566.[39] Menas may have been part of the governor's financial staff at that time,[40] but he may also have wanted to take precautions against a looming threat to his designated pagarchy. However, we have seen that Menas did have a legitimate case; the petitioners' main argument could therefore only concern the amount of violence which had taken place during the pagarch's intervention in the village.

From *P. Cair. Masp.* I 67002 emerge two earlier attempts to deal with this issue, allowing us to locate the petition more firmly within the process of dispute resolution.[41] The first attempt figures in the account of the Thynis episode, where the petitioners claim that they had approached the preceding governor Kyros and that he had ordered their release, "yet we were not released."[42] The passage looks deliberately imprecise, as if it was meant to give the impression that Menas had been ignoring a ducal order which in reality was more probably directed at Antinoopolite authorities or at the *magnificentissimus* Serenos, and which may not have ordered the villagers' release from custody in general, but rather only their release from the Antinoopolite prison or from the jail at Thynis so that this issue would be dealt with where it belonged, that is, in the Antaiopolite.[43] The second attempt occurs later, in the context of Menas' direct intervention in the village, when "the scribe and the deacon wrote

---

[39] *P. Cair. Masp.* I 67002, col. ii, l. 1 (Kyros); for the beginning of Menas' pagarchy, see above n. 30. There remain some chronological problems in the accounts of KEENAN 2008, p. 177 and FOURNET 1999, p. 330-331, but these cannot be dealt with here. At this point it shall suffice to note that the detentions at Thynis took place before Menas stepped into the Antaiopolite pagarchy.

[40] This may be inferred from his constant attribution as *scriniarius*; see below n. 63.

[41] Naturally, self-help was virtually impossible in this context owing to the evident imbalance of coercive power. A conceivable alternative to petitioning may have been *anachoresis*, i.e., to abandon the village and thus to avoid fiscal obligations, as villagers under comparable circumstances threaten to do in *P. Lond.* V 1674, l. 100-105 (TM 19693); on this phenomenon, see KELLY 2011, p. 204-208. However, despite being rhetorically insistent on their poverty, the villagers stylized as the senders of the petition are likely to have been comparatively well-off local players with much to lose, and to whom *anachoresis* was therefore not a realistic option; see, e.g., the long list of signatories in *P. Cair. Masp.* III 67283 (TM 18420, an earlier petition against the pagarch Ioulianos, on whom see the next section) and generally BAGNALL 1993, p. 168 and KELLY 2011, p. 150-167.

[42] *P. Cair. Masp.* I 67002, col. ii, l. 10-11.

[43] STERN 2015, p. 136-138.

to him in the matter, lest he come up to the village and disarray the grain tax."[44] In light of these earlier attempts, *P. Cair. Masp.* I 67002 appears to constitute a "last resort" rather than a "tactic to force settlement".[45] This is a notable divergence from the pattern established by Benjamin Kelly and cannot be explained by Menas' superior standing or coercive power alone, as higher authorities also tended to back off if confronted with the "shadow of the law".[46] Menas, however, felt safe enough to ignore the villagers' threat — and he probably had good reason to, as will be made plausible in the following section, where the likely resolutions of the dispute will be scrutinized, suggesting a benign outcome for Menas.

4. RESOLUTION(S) OF THE DISPUTE: BEYOND THE PETITION

Despite the high emotional register Dioskoros deploys while making his case in *P. Cair. Masp.* I 67002, he must have been aware that the man on the other side, the *dux* Athanasios, was a man of equal learning and would have been able to decipher compositional conventions and rhetorical devices. The account of Menas' conduct is therefore unlikely to have been understood at face value, which begs the question of what the petitioners actually sought to achieve. According to Deborah Hobson, petitions were filed not because of a legal principle, "but because some act of restitution is required."[47] Curiously, though, the petitioners nowhere demand any restitution. Although the text mentions specific amounts of money on several occasions,[48] precise qualifications or

---

[44] *P. Cair. Masp.* I 67002, col. iii, l. 19: ἔγραψεν γὰρ αὐτῷ ὁ γραμματεὺς καὶ ὁ διακονητὴς τούτου χάριν, \το(ῦ)/ μὴ ἀνελθεῖν τὴν κώμην ἀκαίρως καὶ διαστρέψαι τὴν ἐμβολήν. Note as well the role of the deacon as an intermediate of the village to Menas in the aforementioned *P. Cair. Masp.* I 67060, l. 1.

[45] These phrases perhaps best subsume the two widely received models by HOBSON 1993, p. 199-200 (though she does not herself use "last resort") and KELLY 2011, p. 276. Like others, FOURNET 2015, p. 263, takes the petitions against Menas and Ioulianos (on whom see below) as a "dernière solution".

[46] HARRIES 2001b.

[47] HOBSON 1993, p. 205. In fact, the quote occurs in the context of a case study, yet the author's general conclusions are implicit.

[48] Specific amounts occur in *P. Cair. Masp.* I 67002, col. ii, l. 6, 10, 13, and 23.

quantifications of the alleged damage or theft are absent, so in regard to restitutions the evidence is ambiguous. As to the fate of the pagarch, the petition is even more taciturn. According to Justinian's *Edict* 13 from 539 CE, a fraudulent pagarch could be removed from office, with his estates subject to seizure. Although the *dux et Augustalis* was not authorized to do so on his own, he was the one through whom such demands would pass before reaching the emperor.[49] One would be inclined to think that the events of *P. Cair. Masp.* I 67002 provided an exemplary case for applying these regulations, yet the petitioners stick to the demand that Menas "not bother us any longer," although they do request that several of his compliant auxiliaries "be thoroughly destroyed."[50] In terms of the pagarch this request may be seen as a return to the status quo ante, which is particularly remarkable since Benjamin Kelly and Ari Bryen have pointed out that in cases of violence petitioners rather regularly push for punishment.[51]

One might argue that this situation reflects a certain modesty, in the sense that it would be inappropriate to openly demand the punishment of people of high standing. However, a parallel case suggests that the villagers did indeed hope for at least some material compensation, even if they did not go so far as requesting to have Menas removed from the pagarchy. About twenty years earlier, in 547 CE, a certain *magnificentissimus* Theodosios had embezzled an entire installment of Aphrodite's tax payments.[52] Consequently, the provincial authorities charged the village a second time, and the *gloriosissimus* Ioulianos, who at that time was pagarch of Antaiopolis, came to the village in order to collect the arrears by means of coercion.[53] Dioskoros travelled to Constantinople and issued

[49] On *Edict* 13, see above n. 9.

[50] *P. Cair. Masp.* I 67002, col. iii, l. 22-23: (…) προστάξαι τὸν μὲν εἰρημέ(νον) πάγαρχον ἀποπαύ[εσ]θαι ἡμῶν θυμολεοντ[ο]φθόρον: ἔπειτα δὲ καὶ τοὺς ἀλιτηρίο(υ)ς πλείω βαρβάρων κακούργο(υ)ς καὶ ἀ̣ρ̣χιληστὰς μηλονόμους | ἀ̣γ̣αιρεθῆναι σὺν ῥίζαις.

[51] BRYEN 2013, p. 129-135; KELLY 2011, p. 188-194.

[52] For Theodosios and his role in Aphrodite, see RUFFINI 2011, s.n. Theodosios 16.

[53] On the pagarch Ioulianos, see RUFFINI 2011, s.n. Ioulianos 2. The events and the context are outlined in ZUCKERMAN 2004, esp. p. 75-77. For the sake of clarity, the discussion of the Theodosios/Ioulianos episode focusses on documents that refer to the involvement of the pagarch Ioulianos. For a detailed timeline of this episode and the relevant documents, see ZUCKERMAN 2004, esp. at p. 82-83 and 88-90, VAN MINNEN 2003, p. 118-119, PALME 2008, p. 205-208, and FOURNET 2015, p. 259-261.

a petition to the emperor that targeted Theodosios as well as Ioulianos, and the extent of the misconduct of which Ioulianos is accused of in this text is quite comparable to that of Menas: "Without hesitation or mercy he ruined the inhabitants, so that they pledged large parts of their cattle and longed for their untimely death. And thereupon our said estates were torn down to the detriment of the public treasury."[54] In this matter, Dioskoros had already received a rescript from the *curator domus divinae*, which has been preserved and in which the *dux et Augustalis* is told to proceed with litigation "in accordance with justice and the law", but all the same the *curator* demands that Theodosios' reputation be taken into consideration.[55] This latter request — a passing remark at first glance — is significant in our context, and we will see below how it was put into practice. Moreover, this document neither advertises the pagarch's name, nor condemns his collection of the alleged arrears.[56] The empire looked after its own.

This is hardly coincidental, as is apparent from the subsequent events. In 551 CE, Dioskoros travelled a second time to Constantinople and took the draft of an imperial rescript with him, which has been preserved.[57] Consequently, rather than revealing what had actually been decided by the imperial chancery, the document describes what Dioskoros

[54] *P. Cair. Masp.* I 67019 verso, l. 19-22 (TM 18986: 548/549 CE): [ἀό]κ̣ν̣ως̣ καὶ [ἀ]φ\ε/ιδῶς ἀνα̣τ̣ρέπει τοὺς ἐνοικοῦντας | \ὥ̣στε/ μ̣α̣κ̣ρ[ᾶς] τῆς ἑαυτῷ̣ν ζωῆς ὑποκεῖσθαι καὶ ἐπικα̣λ̣ε̣ῖν ἐπὶ [τ]ὸ[ν] \πρὸ καιροῦ τὸν/ | θάνατον, καὶ τὰ εἰρημ[ένα ἡ]μ[ῶ]ν κτήματα ἐκ τούτο(υ) ἀ̣π̣ε̣τράπησαν πρὸς λ\ύ/μην | τ̣ο[ῦ] δ̣η̣[μο]σίου λόγο(υ). The village at that time enjoyed the privilege of *autopragia*, meaning that it was allowed to pay its taxes directly to the provincial authorities without the interference of civic authorities or the pagarch. It appears, however, that the pagarch was still entitled or expected to intervene in cases of irregularities and further evidence suggests that the village had lost its autopract status when *P. Cair. Masp.* I 67002 was written; on this issue see STERN 2015, p. 127-129 and cf. *P. Aphrod. Reg.*, p. 213.

[55] *SB* VI 9102, l. 18-22 (TM 17848: ca. September 548): τοῦτο μὲν | διὰ τὸ δίκαιον καὶ τὸν νόμον, | τοῦτο δὲ καὶ διὰ τὴν ὑπόλημψιν | τοῦ προειρημένου μεγαλοπρεπεστάτου | ἀνδρός; ZUCKERMAN 2004, p. 84. Cf. for the first part ("in accordance with justice and the law") the parallel wording in a passage from the draft of the later imperial rescript mentioned above (*P. Cair. Masp.* I 67024, l. 42-52).

[56] GERACI 1979, p. 203.

[57] This draft is preserved in *P. Cair. Masp.* I 67024 recto (TM 18988 = A), *P. Cair. Masp.* I 67024 verso (TM 18988 [sic] = B), and *P. Cair. Masp.* I 67025 (TM 18989 = C). As long as their differences do not affect the general argument, the text(s) will be quoted simply as *P. Cair. Masp.* I 67024.

considered a beneficial outcome with reasonable chances of being achieved — the maximum demands, as it were. Yet even this text disregards actual adjudication, instead leaving it to the governor to start a formal inquiry and to finally come to a decision.[58] Dioskoros would then take this document back to Egypt in order to start a formal procedure in the case of continued malevolence.[59] As for the pagarch, the text of the rescript draft indeed orders the *dux* to compensate the villagers if their case is just; it is striking, however, that the subordinates of the ducal *officium* are the only parties whose punishment is explicitly mentioned — Ioulianos gets away with it, as it were.[60] Apparently, when Dioskoros composed the rescript draft aiming for a settlement he hoped for at least some material compensation for the village, but did not do so for impeachment proceedings against the pagarch. Because he knew he *could* not hope for it? As Constantin Zuckerman has conscientiously pointed out, the result of the Theodosios/Ioulianos episode was probably only a much-reduced version of what Dioskoros had prepared in the rescript draft, as is apparent from a contract regarding the *exsecutor negotii* who was supposed to hand over the eventual imperial decision and enact the will that spoke from it.[61] In this document, Theodosios and Ioulianos are not even mentioned, but instead the original affairs had been reduced to an internal dispute between two leading village families, the resolution of which was apparently the only charge of the *exsecutor*.

---

[58] *P. Cair. Masp.* I 67024, l. 39-41: θεσπίζομεν τοίνυν τὴν ἐνδοξ(ότητα) τὴν σὴν | ἐξετάσαι τὰ περὶ τούτου \α/ μεθ' ὅσης νόμος ἀκριβείας προστάττει, | καὶ εἰ ταῖς \α/ ἀληθείαις (...); FOURNET 2015, p. 262-263.

[59] ZUCKERMAN 2004, p. 87-88; cf. KEENAN 1975, p. 246.

[60] *P. Cair. Masp.* I 67024, l. 42-52. Notably, when it comes to the question of who is to compensate the villagers, ms. A, in a later correction, next to the officials of the ducal bureau also includes the local officials (l. 46: \τῆς \τε/ σῆς τάξεως καὶ παγανῷν/). However, mss. B and C, of which the latter is arguably the most advanced in terms of redaction, do not any longer refer to them. The ἡμαρτηκότες ("wrong-doers") in l. 51 do apparently not include the pagarch Ioulianos, as they are still part of the passage relating to the ducal staff (cf. l. 47: χρήμασιν καὶ ἐγκλήμασιν with l. 48: χρήματα and l. 49: ἐγκλημάτων).

[61] *P. Cair. Masp.* I 67032 (TM 18996); ZUCKERMAN 2004, p. 85-91; cf. FOURNET 2015, p. 264-265. It is furthermore apparent that the style of the rescript draft (*P. Cair. Masp.* I 67024) is notably wordier and more poetic than the earlier "actual rescript" (*SB* VI 9102), a fact which by itself may reveal how the imperial chancery may have compressed the cause of *P. Cair. Masp.* I 67024 afterward.

We can easily imagine that this was also the line taken in the case of Menas, and that the outcome of the dispute for him, if there was any, was probably rather modest.[62] Indeed, a papyrus from about three years after *P. Cair. Masp.* I 67002 shows Menas attached to the ducal bureau in the provincial capital Antinoopolis, which supposedly means that he was no longer pagarch of Antaiopolis.[63] Moreover, in ca. 568 CE the Antinoite bureaucrat Kollouthos makes his appearance as pagarch apparently in Aphrodite, i.e., in the Antaiopolite.[64] It is, however, unlikely that this situation reflects a removal of Menas from the pagarchy resulting in his "degradation" to a member of the ducal staff: Menas bore the title of *scriniarius* — supposedly a marker of profession referring to an earlier duty — already during his pagarchy, and, furthermore, the papyrus that refers to him as staff of the ducal bureau after this pagarchy also grants him the rank of a *vir clarissimus et spectabilis* instead of the simpler *vir clarissimus* that consistently marks Menas' earlier appearances.

Conclusion and prospect

Two questions remain, the first of which being *why* Menas did not suffer any serious consequences to his standing? It has often been argued that higher authorities refrained from taking concrete actions in many such cases because their economic, political, and social ties were too tightly interwoven.[65] However, the apparent lack of actual consequences against Ioulianos in the rescript draft and also against Menas in *P. Cair. Masp.* I 67002 (that is, in the demands of the petitioners) suggests that structural political considerations are in play as well. It has recently been underlined that late antique aristocratic power was still largely dependent

[62] On the following remarks about Menas' career and the possible links to Kollouthos, see Stern 2020.

[63] *P. Lond.* V 1714, l. 12-13 (TM 19731: Antinoopolis; March 14, 570): τοῦ λαμπροτάτου καὶ περιβλέπτου κυρίου | Μηνᾶ σκρινιαρίου τῆς κατὰ Θηβαΐδα λαμπρᾶς δουκικῆς τάξεως. The governors' *officia* and their staff are analyzed in Palme 1999b.

[64] On the pagarch Kollouthos, see Ruffini 2011, s.n. Kollouthos 36. A short tenure alone would be insufficient to indicate that Menas was removed from the pagarchy, since there is no apparent pattern in the length of the pagarchs' tenure.

[65] Ruffini 2008a, p. 193; Palme 2008, p. 214-215; Fournet 1999, p. 327-329. In the case of the pagarch Ioulianos, who was criticized even before the emperor, the question is who actually handled petitions that went to Constantinople.

on the emperor,[66] and also the pagarchs were part of an environment that seems inconceivable without imperial patronage.[67] Menas was doubtless aware of his importance to the state apparatus — likewise, he must have been aware of his liability: there was always the chance to go broke for anyone involved in tax collection and especially at this level, given the potential sums involved.[68] The villagers' apparently repeated failure to pay their due taxes must have alarmed Menas, who would not tolerate this any longer and opted for confiscation.[69]

That these events escalated into violent clashes is, regardless of rhetoric, beyond doubt.[70] The question, however, is if the state cared all that much, or if it actually relied on this sort of official *mentalité* in order to ensure its tax revenues, and to "remind" its subjects of what it was capable.[71] Menas' position was considered important in this respect and his conduct seems to have been tolerated, which becomes especially plausible if the tax demands of *P. Cair. Masp.* I 67002 reflect imperial policy after the accession of Justin II, who found the empire in a critical financial situation.[72] There was obviously no endorsement of the type of major devastation described in the petition, but how much of that description was embellished by the "literary Dioskoros"? The more important situational aspect to consider was probably whether the machinery of extraction could be kept in running order.[73] In Menas' case, apparently, as in Ioulianos', the balance swung in favor of the pagarch.

---

66 See BEGASS 2018, p. 415-456 and WEISWEILER 2012, arguing against the idea of a "private takeover" of public institutions, which for Byzantine Egypt seems already largely abandoned. See for the fiscal implications in the West already CECCONI 1994.

67 STERN 2020.

68 On liability, see ZICHE 2006, p. 132.

69 Cf. GERACI 1979, p. 205.

70 PALME 2008, p. 217. Though one could argue that detention, as part of law enforcement, "necessarily involved a great deal of violence" (TORALLAS TOVAR 2006, p. 102) in premodern societies.

71 See BAGNALL 1989, p. 209, BELL 2013, p. 270-272, and ZICHE 2006 on such sort of "organized violence"; see also BRYEN 2013, p. 66-68 for some theoretical considerations. Cf. WICKHAM 2005, p. 66-67 and 145.

72 C. ZUCKERMAN in *P. Aphrod. Reg.*, p. 215-216; cf., e.g., *P. Lond.* V 1674 (TM 19693: Antinoopolis; ca. 570). For a connection of the crisis that preceded the "Ioulianos episode" to the Justinian plague of the 540s, see *P. Aphrod. Reg.*, p. 217. On both links see also the meticulously worked analysis in BRANSBOURG 2016, esp. p. 322, 343-344, and 388.

73 Cf. SCHULLER 1982, p. 207-208, BRYEN 2013, p. 48, and BAGNALL 1989, p. 204.

It would appear that it was the villagers who lost in this equation, and therefore the second question becomes the elephant in the room, as it were: if one follows the above explanation without assuming total naivety on the part of Dioskoros and the Aphroditans, what explains the effort of drafting *P. Cair. Masp.* I 67002 — or the investment of considerable resources in comparable cases?[74] A factor may have been the use of the petition as a means to make oneself heard and to have one's place in the public network recognized and acknowledged. Even if the dispute was not really "settled", it was at least "handled",[75] and this is what may have been important: Dioskoros and the villagers of Aphrodite thus would have hoped to find recognition — a particularly compelling interpretation when the normative aspects conveyed by narratives of violence are taken into consideration.[76] Justinian in particular had encouraged his subjects to petition against official misconduct — a strategy which may have been caused in part by his constant problems of legitimation.[77] Thus, petitions against officials served as an important ideological notice of the possibility of holding officials and the state accountable, which the petitioners of *P. Cair. Masp.* I 67002 seem to take advantage of, even if they were apparently aware of the limited possible outcomes. Accordingly, one could argue that even if Menas did not suffer grave consequences, there still existed the chance that he would somehow be brought back in line, perhaps by an internal order of the *dux*.[78] However, the new emperor Justin II had arrived on the scene only about 18 months before the petition had been composed. Two years afterward, in 569 CE, Justin issued *Novel* 149, in which he proclaimed that provincial governors would no longer be appointed by the imperial center, but rather chosen by the provincial nobles themselves. In return, the new emperor in essence rejected any responsibility for their actions and in advance denounced any petition about their official misconduct.[79] Despite

---

[74] See FOURNET 2015, p. 263 and 265-266.

[75] Cf. the general remarks of BAGNALL 1993, p. 161.

[76] On this normative aspect, see BRYEN 2013, p. 84-85 and 139-140.

[77] Encouragement: ZUCKERMAN 2004, p. 90. Problems of legitimation: BELL 2013, p. 267-317.

[78] For an indication of such an internal order, see *P. Lond.* V 1674, l. 96-98, where Athanasios is said to have ordered (Menas?) to collect only the net taxes (on these "net taxes," see *P. Aphrod. Reg.*, p. 214).

[79] *Nov.* 149.3; ZUCKERMAN 2004, p. 90-91.

P. Cair. Masp. I 67002 not being addressed to the emperor, this context makes it even less likely that the regime took extensive action against officials like Menas.

Another probable explanation may be found in the petitioners' frequent assertions of their internal unity and evocations of their social cohesion, which are especially striking given the evident internal conflicts of the Aphroditan community during this period: from the "murder mystery" to the role of Aphrodite's shepherds, who also acted as field guards and are strikingly, perhaps tellingly, absent from *P. Cair. Masp.* I 67002 — while the shepherd-field guards of the neighboring village of Phthla were indeed explicitly involved, though on Menas' side.[80] Earlier still, in the course of the episode around the *magnificentissimus* Theodosios, influential villagers had turned to the village headmen for compensation of the embezzled taxes, leading the way to self-help-like seizure of some of the headmen's estates.[81] Thus it appears possible that we are dealing with an elaborate discourse aiming to establish group solidarity and social cohesion in a community experiencing notorious internal discord, which might have contributed considerably to this conflict in the first place. And Dioskoros, as one party within the village, is trying to turn his faction's case into the villagers' case.

Both the state's strong hand in dealing with the matter and Dioskoros' move for social cohesion amid tensions with Antaiopolite officials yield connections to recent research that has argued for a late antique countryside that emerged as increasingly confident vis-à-vis the authorities of the empire, reacting and adapting to changes in the late antique fiscal system.[82] Are the "smallholders" of Aphrodite to be seen as an Egyptian

---

[80] Social cohesion: KEENAN 2008, p. 178-179; see also the list of subscriptions in *P. Cair. Masp.* III 67283 (on which see *P. Mich. Aphrod.*, p. 10-16; cf. RUFFINI 2008a, p. 177-179), relating to the earlier case against the pagarch Ioulianos. Aphrodite's internal conflicts are most compellingly analyzed in RUFFINI 2008b; see furthermore RUFFINI 2008a, p. 180-184 on the "murder mystery", p. 218-226, on the role of Aphrodite's shepherds, and p. 184-187 and 194-195 on the conflicts with the neighboring, though socially interconnected village of Phthla. Ironically, it is the pagarch Menas who in *P. Lond.* V 1682 (TM 19700) shields Dioskoros against one of these neighboring shepherd-field guards (RUFFINI 2008a, p. 222, where the text number is misspelled in n. 92), though it is unclear whether this text dates to Menas' first or second pagarchy.

[81] *P. Cair. Masp.* I 67024, l. 24-30; ZUCKERMAN 2004, p. 77, 88-89.

[82] See DOSSEY 2010, GREY 2011, and their discussion in WEISWEILER 2014.

expression of the "super-peasants" that John Weisweiler modeled?[83] It would probably be worth pursuing this argument in light of the phenomena that had long been evaluated as evidence for the "quasi-serfdom" of the late antique Egyptian peasantry, but have since been subject to more nuanced analyses, such as the deeds of surety for *coloni*.[84]

This, however, is beyond the scope of this paper, which in accordance with the subject of our conference has set out to investigate *P. Cair. Masp.* I 67002 in terms of dispute resolution. Reading this petition as a dispute against an official, it has demonstrated how this context provides us with a better understanding of how power relations in the countryside were negotiated. It further serves to illustrate how a late antique office like the pagarchy drew elites like Menas more firmly into a public administrative network in an attempt to tighten the imperial hold over the province of Egypt. Ultimately, by understanding this particular dispute as a dispute against an official, we might shed further light on the administrative aspects of social control in the periphery.

[83] WEISWEILER 2014, p. 252. Especially Aphrodite, because of its particular administrative status, could be seen as an interesting fit if DOSSEY (2010, pointedly at 197 and 199-200) is right in attributing major significance to the city-village dichotomy as a driving force of such developments.

[84] A nuanced view on these documents can be found in PALME 1999a.

JUDICIAL INTERVENTIONS IN LATE ANTIQUE RECOMMENDATION LETTERS: A WAY OF SEEKING JUSTICE?*

Bruno MARIEN
(KU Leuven)

Abstract: *SB* IV 7438 shares several characteristics with recommendation letters from late antique epistolographers. Not only *SB* IV 7438 but also examples from different letter writers (Augustine, Symmachus, Gregory of Nazianzus, Basil, Synesius and Libanius) prove that a judicial intervention was a wide-spread practice in Late Antiquity. Regularly, letters writers would directly write to the judge on the case. The intervention could take many forms and occur at different stages of the procedure. Letter writers regularly approached more than one office holder for the same case, when they deemed that the power or influence of only one official was not sufficient for an intervention to be effective. Also, they used some rhetorical strategies to increase the pressure on the addressee. Short letters might point to a lack of engagement. It is very difficult to estimate to which extent legal knowledge played a role in the settlement of a dispute. The letters provide an interesting glimpse of how not only the intervening party, but also the opponent could undertake actions in his own favour. In particular, the dossier of Dioscurus shows that a dispute could last over a certain period.

INTRODUCTION

An interesting, but not always clearly perceived, link exists between recommendation letters and dispute settlement. In a dispute each party has a particular, but frequently unequal, amount of resources to his disposal, such as money, knowledge, expertise and network. Each party might employ one or more resources, in order to (attempt to) exert an influence on the outcome of the dispute. The extent to which a party

* I would like to cordially thank the organisers of the congress, in particular Katelijn VANDORPE and Sofie WAEBENS for providing me the opportunity to present the paper.

can influence a dispute, is not only limited by the means he has at his disposal, but also by the resources the adversary can deploy.

This paper[1] discusses a particular way of influencing an ongoing dispute in antiquity: one of the parties could turn to a more powerful person who, by writing a recommendation letter, tried to influence the dispute in a way that he deemed favourable for his recommendee. Often such an intervention was a reaction to the sway the opponent was exerting at that moment.

Recommendation letters were a common letter type in ancient epistolography.[2] They are found not only in letter collections of ancient epistolographers, but also in documentary papyri.[3] Also, ancient epistolary

---

[1] The translations of Greek and Latin texts are taken from modern English translations, which in some cases have been slightly modified. If no modern English text was available, the translations are my own.

[2] Some direct testimonies point to the recommendation letter as a distinct epistolary category. An early example is *P. Mich.* VIII 468, l. 38-41 (TM 27081), where the writer makes an interesting remark about the value of a recommendation: *Hic a*[*ut*]*ẹm sene aer*[*e*] [*ni*]*hil fiet neque epistulae commạndaticiae nihil valunt nesi si qui sibi aiutaveret* — "But here nothing will be accomplished without money, and letters of recommendation have no value unless a man helps himself." The translation is provided by http://papyri.info/ddbdp/c.ep.lat;;142, accessed on 2 November 2020. COTTON 1981, p. 1: "Recommendation letters undoubtedly formed a well-known and well-established convention, since the letter writer refers to them without further comment or explanation." An example from Late Antiquity is Lib. *Ep.* 61, 7: (…) δι' ὑμῶν δὲ ὡς αὐτὸν ἐλαύνοντι γράμματα δώσεις, ταυτὶ δὲ οὐκ ἀσθενέστερα παρουσίας — "Should he pass through on his journey to court, you will give him letters of introduction. These are no less effective than your personal intervention" (translation Norman).

[3] I identified more than 100 recommendations, dating from the third century BC to the beginning of the fifth century AD. These papyri are:

(i) third century BC: *P. Horak* 26; *P. Cairo Zen.* I 59042; *P. Cairo Zen.* V 59805; *P. Cairo Zen.* I 59002; *P. Zen. Pestm.* 42; *P. Mich.* I 6; *P. Lond.* VII 1946 + *P. Zaki Aly* 15 b; *P. Lond.* VII 1945; *P. Cairo Zen.* I 59045; *P. Cairo Zen.* I 59046; *P. Cairo Zen.* III 59474; *P. Cairo Zen.* II 59192; *P. Mich.* I 33; *P. Col. Zen.* I 41; *P. Zen. Pestm.* 67; *P. XV. Congr.* 5; *P. Cairo Zen.* II 59284; *P. Cairo Zen.* V 59853; *PSI* V 520; *Pap. Lugd. Bat.* 20 Suppl. D; *P. Cairo Zen.* III 59342; *P. Cairo Zen.* IV 59590; *SB* XXII 15278; *P. Mich.* I 82; *Chrest. Mitt.* 22; *P. Cairo Zen.* III 59397; *P. Lond.* VII 2026; *SB* XXVI 16636; *P. XV. Congr.* 6; *P. XV. Congr.* 7; *SB* XVIII 13616; *P. Col. Zen.* II 111; *P. Col. Zen.* II 112; *P. Petr.* III 43 (4) = *P. Petrie Kleon* 83; *UPZ* II 159; *P. Lond.* VII 2027;

(ii) second century BC: *P. Mich.* XVIII 770; *P. Cair. Goodspeed* 4; *P. Tebt.* I 20; *P. Köln* IX 365;

(iii) first century BC: *BGU* VIII 1871; *BGU* XVI 2623; *BGU* XVI 2647; *BGU* XVI 2654; *PSI* XV 1539; *SB* VI 9564;

theory theorised about the recommendation letter.[4] Except for examples in letters on papyrus dating to the third and second centuries BC, the recommendation seems to have been practised more in Late Antiquity than in earlier periods. Conspicuous examples from the fourth century AD are Symmachus and Libanius.

In general terms, a recommendation letter is a request which is addressed to someone belonging to the writer's network on behalf of a third person (the recommendee), who is normally of lower status.[5] A recommendation letter can be considered a means of bridging a physical,

---

(iv) first century AD: *P. NYU* II 18; *P. Merton* II 62; *P. Col.* VIII 211; *P. Oxy.* IV 787; *P. Oxy.* IV 746; *P. Oxy.* II 292; *ChLA* X 424; *ChLA* XI 493; *P. Herm.* 1;

(v) first-second century AD: *P. Ryl.* IV 608;

(vi) second century AD: *P. Giss.* I 71; *P. Giss.* I 88; *P. Brem.* 7; *P. Brem.* 8; *P. Brem.* 9; *P. Brem.* 5; *P. Brem.* 6; *P. Oxy.* XX 2265; *SB* VI 9636; *P. Hib.* II 276; *SB* V 8005; *P. Oslo* II 51; *P. Oslo* II 55; *P. Graux* II 22; *P. Oxy.* LI 3643; *ChLA* IV 267; *ChLA* XXVIII 841; *BASP* XLVIII (2011) p. 54; *Tyche* XXVI (2011) p. 36;

(vii) second-third century AD: *P. Strasb.* IV 174; *P. Oxy.* XIV 1663;

(viii) third century AD: *P. Oxy.* IX 1219; *CPR* XXV 2; *P. Gen.* I (2e éd.) 75; *PSI* IX 1041; *SB* XVI 12304; *P. Alex.* 29; *P. Oxy.* XXXVI 2785; *PSI* III 208;

(ix) third-fourth century AD: *P. Got.* 11; *PSI* XV 1560; *P. Col.* XI 298;

(x) fourth century AD: *P. Oxy.* XXXI 2602; *P. Ryl.* IV 623; *ChLA* XIX 687; *P. Oxy.* LV 3821; *P. Abinn.* 31; *P. Berl. Sarisch.* 11; *P. Amh.* II 145; *P. Oxy.* LVI 3857; *P. Oxy.* VIII 1162; P. Oxy. XXXI 2603; *P. Nag Hamm.* 78;

(xi) fourth-fifth century AD: *P. Oxy.* XVIII 2193; *SB* III 7269 and *P. Köln* II 112.

No division has been made between official and private recommendation letters. A majority of the letters are introductions. Some 15 letters can be identified as having a Christian background. However, I do not agree with Luijendijk 2008, p. 103-104 and 107-108, who holds the opinion that Christian letters of introduction have certain features that make them a subgroup within the genre. Undoubtedly, the Christian letters have insufficient distinctive features to separate them from other recommendation letters.

[4] Ps.-Demetr. *Typ. epist.* 2: Ὁ δὲ συστατικός, ὃν ὑπὲρ ἄλλου πρὸς ἄλλον γράφομεν ἔπαινον συγκαταπλέκοντες ἅμα καὶ τοὺς πρότερον ἠγνοημένους λέγοντες ὡς ἐγνωσμένους οὕτως. — "The commendatory type, which we write on behalf of one person to another, mixing in praise, at the same time also speaking of those who had previously been unacquainted as though they were (now) acquainted" (translation Malherbe); *Ps.-Lib. Epist. Char.* 8: Συστατικὴ δι' ἧς συνιστῶμέν τινα παρά τινι. ἡ δ' αὐτὴ καὶ παραθετικὴ καλεῖται. — "The commending style is that in which we commend someone to someone. It is also called the introductory style" (translation Malherbe).

[5] Mratschek 2015, p. 136: "Recommendation letters by their nature would establish a complex social relationship involving three participants: the recommendee, the author and the recipient of the letter. The interaction involving these three determines the outcome of the recommendation."

hierarchical or mental distance between a recommendee and an addressee. Such letter was often transformational, in that the recommendation primarily intended to change the recommendee's status. Also, it is an instrument that exhibits asymmetries of power and knowledge, and it permits communication in a mediated way with a person who was usually more powerful than the recommendee himself. Inasmuch a recommendation contains the evocation of the recommendee's character or some personal detail, such a letter can be considered biographical.[6] Finally, it could also serve to establish a person's identity.[7] A recommendation letter was a flexible instrument that could easily be adapted to different circumstances.[8]

Recommendations can be distinguished according to the aim they want to achieve: introduction, endorsement, or intervention. However, these three broad categories sometimes overlap. For the sake of clarity, I will briefly touch upon them. As for the introduction, the purpose of such a letter was to introduce someone in a place where he is unknown to others, that is, to present and to bring him to the attention of the addressee and, if necessary, to ask for protection. Such a letter was meant to facilitate one's approach to an important figure that "controlled resources that the recommendee wanted or needed."[9] A second and more limited category contains those letters that aim to endorse someone as worthy of or competent for a certain position or office.[10] In antiquity, recommendations coming from an influential person were the best-known procedure for appointments.[11] A third group — and this is the

---

[6] TRAPP 2006, p. 339.

[7] COTTON 1981, p. 6.

[8] On the one hand, recommendations on papyrus and likewise several letters of Synesius or Symmachus are rather short and unembellished documents whose length do not exceed three paragraphs, on the other hand the request of Paulinus of Nola for a ship-owner (*Ep.* 49), filling an entire scroll, is in length equal to a *libellus.*

[9] VERBOVEN 2002, p. 296.

[10] In the absence of a more objective system of examinations and promotions or an evaluation against universally recognised criteria, appointments were inevitably secured through patronage. See PEDERSEN 1975, p. 180.

[11] LIEBESCHUETZ 1972, p. 194: "The government had to be informed in some way about the candidates for governmental posts, and in the absence of a system of examinations, patronage in the field of appointments is inevitable." Yet, Augustine refused to write such letters during his bishopric. See CHADWICK 2009, p. 66: "There was one practice normally expected of bishops which he declined to perform, namely to write references or letters of commendation to powerful patrons to fix appointments for people."

category this paper will focus on — are the letters which ask for assistance, help or support; generally speaking, these are intervention letters.[12]

At first sight, it might seem rather strange to range an intervention among the recommendation letter. Yet, four arguments are in favour of including this kind of letter. Firstly, in several cases these intervention letters cannot be clearly dissociated from mere introduction letters, since the letter writer appealed to the recommendee's friendship in both categories. Numerous recommendation letters request protection or patronage from a more powerful person. A second argument is provided by Book 13 of Cicero's letters *ad Familiares*. This collection consists of letters that were grouped into one book because they all (except one) have a recommendation in common. Likewise, more than one letter[13] in this collection asked for support or assistance. Thirdly, none of the extant ancient letter manuals identify the letter requesting aid or support as a separate letter type, nor do they discuss any letter type (other than the

[12] For a description of a recommendation, see also MARIEN 2018, p. 186-188, and MARIEN 2019, p. 106-108. Recent literature has examined the ancient recommendation letter from different perspectives. Not only did it consider the formal features of such a document or explore themes that are common to several letter writers, it also revealed specific functions and uses of this kind of letter and highlighted that the recommendation was an instrument in a letter writer's network. It would lead too far to list all of the publications that treat these major strands of research. However, the following works can be cited as relevant for a specific author or aspect. KIM (1972) investigated the integral elements that constituted a recommendation letter. COTTON (1984 and 1985) highlighted the formal aspects of Cicero' s recommendation letter. REES (2007) argued that on the one hand, the recommendations of Pliny and Fronto display a remarkably continuity in the form from Cicero, but on the other hand, these letters are markedly influenced by epideictic rhetoric. CABOURET (2011) pointed out that Libanius easily adapted the set pattern of recommendation letters into highly personalised documents. It was shown by DENIAUX (2011) that recommendation letters could be used in a judicial context, as an instrument to influence a judge or a testimony of someone's character. The issue how Symmachus' recommendation letters were part of the late antique Roman betrothal practice, was investigated by SOGNO (2010). LLEWELYN (1989) focused on recommendation letters used in a specifically Christian context. VERBOVEN (2002) studied such letters in the framework of economical interests and activities. This list does not allow for an exhaustive and complete overview. Moreover, some of the issues have been discussed more within the framework of ancient epistolography than at the level of an ancient recommendation letter.

[13] Examples are *Epp.* 11, 14, 28, 61 and 66.

commendatory type)[14] that has to do with a third person (i.e. in addition to the writer and the addressee). By contrast, all of the other epistolary types concern direct relationships between the writer and addressee. Thus, an intervention letter on behalf of a third person would not have fitted into this last group. Finally, Augustine made a clear link between help and recommendation, as in *Ep.* 212 he described the recommendation letter as symbolic of a helping hand.[15]

Before embarking on a discussion of judicial intervention in recommendation letters, it is necessary to briefly explain this concept. Judicial intervention is an intercession that could occur at any moment of the legal procedure on behalf of one of the litigants.[16] Such an intervention could take many forms: it could aim to support one of the parties in a trial, to influence the judge, to change the nature of the case, to avoid a judge from exercising his jurisdiction or to grant a request provided by procedural law. According to the quality of the litigants or the nature of the case, the lawsuits were conducted before different jurisdictions.[17]

[14] See n. 4.

[15] *Honorabiles Dei famulas,* (...) *Venerationi tuae in Christi dilectione commendo et tamquam mea manu per hanc epistolam trado consolandas, et in omnibus adiuvandas, quae utilitas earum vel necessitas postulat* — "I commend to your Reverence in Christ the honourable servants of God (...) By this letter, as by my own hand, I entrust them to you to be consoled and helped in every way, according as their interest or necessity requires" (translation Parsons).

[16] Contrary to modern western democracies, which are based on the separation of three branches of government, such an intercession in the course of justice was not considered improper or illegal.

[17] The jurisdictions are: (i) Governor: As a rule in Late Antiquity, a governor would render verdicts in both civil and criminal cases, except for some minor cases. (ii) The urban prefect was competent for cases in Rome and Constantinople; (iii) Also by the end of the fourth century and beginning of the early fifth century, bishops were allowed to hear civil cases in the *episcopalis audientia* (bishop's court). HARRIES 2001, p. 194: "He was clearly not strictly a *iudex*, in a secular juridical sense: he was not obliged to use Roman, or any other system of law; his judgements, even in 'civil' disputes, could not be enforced by any form of state authority, and the range of formal sanctions available to him was limited." And (iv) special administrative court for some professional categories, see JONES 1964, I, p. 484: "There was a luxuriant growth of special courts, which handled particular. categories of cases, usually of an administrative character, or cases in which the parties, or one of them usually the defendant, belonged to a privileged group. Some of the regular courts also possessed special jurisdictions outside their normal competence. It was an old principle of Roman government that magistrates possessed jurisdiction in disputes arising out of their sphere of administration. (...) These special courts handled particular

The discussion of a representative selection of Latin and Greek letters by epistolographers of the fourth-sixth century AD will show that the above-mentioned judicial elements are largely present in recommendation letters of Late Antiquity. The analysis starts with a discussion of a sixth-century papyrus from the archive of Dioscorus, followed by examples from the main figures of fourth-early fifth-century epistolography: Augustine, Symmachus, Gregory of Nazianzus, Basil, Synesius and finally Libanius.

1. PAPYRUS LETTER *SB* IV 7438 (TM 18048)

If Procopius[18] is to be believed, who said that the emperor as the supreme judge was more accessible than ever before, even for the humblest ones, the Justinian period might have constituted the heyday of petitions and requests addressed to the emperor.[19] To a certain extent, the rise of private petitioning in late antique Egypt has to be seen in relation to the decline of civil procedure exercised by state authorities.[20]

It is against this background that a dossier of four papyri from the archive of Dioscorus has to be considered. These documents concern a demand for a double payment of taxes, addressed to the village of Aphrodito. The dispute arose when Dioscorus' father Apollos, who was πρωτοκωμήτης of Aphrodito, died (end 546/beginning 547). Apparently, Theodosius, a local powerful figure, had taken advantage of Apollos' death to misappropriate a large tax payment by the village Aphrodito. As a result, the administration requested a second tax payment, since the authorities had not received any contribution. Probably in 548, Dioscorus, with other villagers, went for a first time to Constantinople to

categories of cases, usually of an administrative character (for example tax matters) or cases in which one of the parties belonged to a privileged group (for example disciplinary jurisdiction over officials)."

[18] Procop., *Arc.* 13,1.

[19] ZUCKERMAN 2004, p. 80.

[20] ZUCKERMAN 2004, p. 90, points to the "*grave déclin*" of the judicial system. However, SIMON 1971, p. 645-649, does not accept the thesis that "state litigation was absent and private petitioning paramount for the settlement of private disputes." He has a far more nuanced view on the so-called collapse of the judicial system.

plead his case with the emperor.[21] Subsequently, an imperial rescript (*P. Cair. Masp.* I 67029, TM 18993, a draft version)[22] was issued that ordered the *dux* and the *praeses* to take action in relation to the tax claim.[23] Probably prior to the audience with the emperor, Dioscorus managed to have a letter sent by the *curator* of the *domus divina* (κουράτωρ τῆς θείας οἰκίας) to the *dux Thebaidos* requesting to seek an early arrangement with Theodosius (*SB* VI 9102, TM 17848).[24] In the same period, but presumably later than the imperial rescript, the *dux* received an intervention (*SB* IV 7438) in favour of Dioscorus.[25] In all likelihood, the reason for this intervention was that until then the *dux* had not been very keen on executing the rescript. Yet, it seems that the overall efforts were not sufficient, as the intrigues continued and the villagers saw themselves constrained to appeal to the emperor once again, which resulted in another imperial rescript three years later.[26] Accordingly, in 551 Dioscorus secured a second imperial ordinance asking the competent official to do his duty and that "proper effect shall be given to the divine letter about this question which has been given to the suppliant and that he or rather his village shall not be deprived year after year of what is due to them"[27] (*P. Cair. Masp.* I 67024/67025, TM 18988 and 18989, both preserved in draft version).[28]

The intervention letter *SB* IV 7438 was addressed to the *dux Thebaidos* and, according to the most recent literature, written in autumn 548.[29] The reason why I do not consider this letter a petition, but an intervention, is that this papyrus clearly shows that a third party is requested

[21] ZUCKERMAN 2004, p. 77: "Il est, en revanche, certain qu'au temps du faits étudies plus loin le village d'Aphroditè n'a plus son ancien protecteur, le comte Ammônios, ni un autre patron sur place. Les villageois sont alors obligés de chercher la justice au loin dans la capitale impériale."

[22] AZZARELLO 2012, p. 88-89. FOURNET 1999, p. 318, n. 410, dates this imperial rescript to a date a little later than 31 August 548.

[23] At that moment the village of Aphrodito had *autopragia*.

[24] SALOMON 1948; PALME 2008, p. 206; AZZARELLO 2012, p. 82-88.

[25] PESTMAN & DAVID 1990, p. 275 dates this letter to 551.

[26] SALOMON 1948, p. 106.

[27] *P. Cair. Masp.* I 67024, l. 17-22. For the translation, see HUNT & EDGAR 1932-1941, II, p. 101.

[28] SALOMON 1948, p. 104; AZZARELLO 2012, p. 94-97. PALME 2008, p. 207: "The tone in this document is more forceful in comparison to the first rescript."

[29] AZZARELLO 2012, p. 83, n. 250.

— on behalf of the aggrieved party — to find a solution for the dispute. Most probably, Dioscorus approached the author of the intervention letter[30] and asked him to intervene on his (i.e. Dioscorus') behalf.

After a brief description of the problems Dioscorus had been confronted with, the letter writer points out that Dioscorus already received an imperial rescript:[31] (...) ἱκέτης τε γενόμενος τοῦ εὐσεβ(εστάτου) δεσπότου θείων ἔτυχεν συλλαβῶν πρὸς τὴν ὑμετέραν φιλανθρωπείαν (*SB* IV 7438, l. 4-6).[32]

But seemingly this imperial rescript was not enough for the letter writer, since he deems that the support given by the addressee is the only way that can advance Dioscorus' case: μίαν ταύτην αὐτῷ βοήθειαν ἀσφαλῆ καλῶς ὑπολαβὼν τὴν ἐκ τῆς ὑμετέρας δικαιοσύνης ἐπικουρίαν (...) (*SB* IV 7438, l. 6-7).[33] For this reason, he requests the addressee to intervene: (...) ταύτης δεῖται τυχεῖν παρ' ὑμῶν καὶ τὴν ἐπιστολὴν ὑπὲρ τούτων ᾔτησεν πρὸς ὑμᾶς (*SB* IV 7438, l. 8-9).[34]

The word μίαν emphatically put at the beginning of the phrase (l. 6) is meant to emphasise the addressee's ability to assist. The same line of reasoning is continued in the next phrase, where he underscores the addressee's custom to assist others: οἶδα δέ, ὅτι καὶ τῆς ἐμῆς αἰτήσεως χωρὶς αὐτῷ τε καὶ τοῖς ἄλλοις ἅπασιν τὰ δίκαια δίδωσιν ἡ ὑμετέρα ὑπεροχή (*SB* IV 7438, l. 9-11).[35] Finally, the letter writer hopes that his intervention will be beneficial for the recommendee and the addressee will be rewarded accordingly: ὥστε κἀμὲ χρήσιμον αὐτῷ φανῆναι καὶ ὑμᾶς πολλῷ πλείονα τὸν ἀπὸ τοῦ δεσπότου θεοῦ μισθὸν ἀπολαβεῖν (*SB* IV 7438, l. 12-13).[36] The stress on the addressee's ability to assist and the

---

[30] The question of who might have been the writer of this letter, will be discussed later in this chapter.

[31] This is *P. Cair. Masp.* I 67029.

[32] "(...) having made supplication to our pious master, he obtained a divine letter addressed to your Clemency" (translation Hunt and Edgar slightly modified).

[33] "Rightly conceiving that his only sure help lies in the support of your justice (...)" (translation Hunt and Edgar).

[34] "(...) he seeks to obtain this support from you and he has asked for this letter to you about his case" (translation Hunt and Edgar).

[35] "I know that without any request from me your eminence deals justice both to him and all others" (translation Hunt and Edgar).

[36] "(...) so that I may appear to have been of service to him and you again may receive a much increased reward from the lord God" (translation Hunt and Edgar).

ensuing benefits have to be seen as a subtle pressure by the letter writer, since any lack of action by the addressee would automatically be regarded in this respect as wrong.

The above-discussed themes (difficult situation of the recommendee as a ground for an intervention, assistance expected from the addressee, the recommendation being useful for the recommendee and the increased status for the addressee) are themes that frequently appear in late antique recommendations.[37] Moreover, the tone in this letter is neither familiar, nor commanding.[38] Such a tone, which is normally adopted in recommendation letters, points to the absence of any direct hierarchical relationship.[39] Therefore, *SB* IV 7438 can safely be described as a recommendation letter.

The imperial rescript of 548 (*P. Cair. Masp.* I 67029) gives an interesting indication on the precise role of the recommendation letter. This rescript instructed (θεσπίζο(?)]μ̣εν) the addressee, the *dux*,[40] to investigate the facts such as they were reported to the emperor ([ἐξ]ετάσαι τὰ εἰς ἡμᾶς ἀνηνεγμένα). He had to find out whether the facts corresponded to reality (εἰ ταῦτα λάβοι[τε] τ̣ῇ [ἀ]λ̣ηθείᾳ συμβαί̣ν̣[ει]ν) (*P. Cair. Masp.* I 67029, l. 13-15). An imperial rescript only gets executory power, after

[37] A few examples from recommendation letters of other epistolographers: (i) difficult situation of the recommendee: Lib. *Epp.* 885, 3 and 1336, 1; Symm. *Epp.* IV, 67, 1 and V, 41, 1; Bas. *Epp.* 86 and 147; Greg. Naz. *Ep.* 14; Syn. *Epp.* 34 and 131 (ii) addressee's ability to assist: Lib. *Epp.* 538, 3 and 559, 4; Symm. *Epp.* I, 72 and III, 35; Bas. *Ep.* 31; Syn. *Epp.* 75 and 102 (iii) recommendation being useful for the addressee/recommendee: Lib. *Epp.* 557, 6 and 978, 3; Bas. *Epp.* 15 and 272; Greg. Naz. *Epp.* 105, 2 and 129, 5; Syn. *Epp.* 99, 4-5 and 116, 3 (iv) enhanced status for the addressee: Lib. *Epp.* 804, 5 and 847, 4; Bas. *Ep.* 18, 4-7; Greg. Naz. *Epp.* 146, 5 and 199, 5; Syn. *Epp.* 18, 4-7 and 119, 1-2. The last two themes are clearly absent from Symmachus' recommendation letters. When a letter writer mentions that a recommendation can be useful for the adressee, or provide him an enhanced status, he stresses the future result that will ensue from the recommendation. Frequently, Symmachus, however, bases his argument on the current, existing important qualities of the addressee, as if the status of the latter was high enough and, accordingly, an increase was therefore not needed.

[38] A clear example of a commanding tone is *SB* VI 9102 sent out by the *curator* of the *domus divina* to the *dux*. Accordingly, a hierarchical relationship between the *curator* of the *domus divina* and the *dux* can safely be assumed.

[39] However, I do not share FOURNET's view (2015, p. 258) that the content and the tone of this letter point to a low-ranking individual ("un personnage bien subalterne").

[40] ZUCKERMAN 2004, p. 84: "Le rôle de l'empereur se borne à dire le droit et à désigner le juge."

the *dux* conducted a lawsuit in presence of both parties.[41] The words τὴν ἐκ τῆς ὑμετέρας δικαιοσύνης ἐπικουρίαν (*SB* IV 7438, l. 11)[42] in the recommendation letter indicate that a trial had actually started. Consequently, this intervention has to be seen as a support written by a third person to the office holder who would judge the lawsuit.[43] Accordingly, there is no reason to doubt that the letter for Dioscorus was written in the framework of the current litigation.[44]

I also assume, contrary to recent research,[45] that the letter has actually been sent out. I do not see any reason why Dioscorus considered this letter unuseful. The intervention fits well the chain of documents that were written for this case between 548 and 551. In the course of four years Dioscorus and the other villagers undertook many attempts to thwart the double payment of taxes. However, these attempts resulted to be ineffective, because the influence of the opponent Theodosius was such that a lawsuit and even two imperial rescripts could not undo the double taxation.[46]

Finally, who wrote this intervention? Older literature took the view that the letter originated from a high official of central government,

---

[41] ZUCKERMAN 2004, p. 83-84: "Les recrits impériaux n'ont donc force exécutoire qu'après un procès mené par le duc en bonne et due forme, en présence des deux parties."

[42] "the support of your justice" (translation Hunt and Edgar).

[43] BERKES 2017 concluded that "Die Identifikation des dux von SB IV 7438 bleibt somit unklar."

[44] Recommendation letters written to judges are also found in late antique epistolographers. Examples are (i) August. *Ep.* 116 (discussed *infra*); (ii) Greg. Naz. *Ep.* 146 (discussed *infra*) and (iii) Syn. *Ep.* 42 (discussed *infra*). As for Libanius, the instances are: a) procedure at first instance: (i) (*Ep.* 163 (presumably, discussed *infra*) (ii) (*Ep.* 165 (doubtful); (iii) *Ep.* 214 (discussed *infra*); (iv) *Ep.* 604 (presumably); (v) *Ep.* 831; (vi) *Ep.* 1145; (vii) *Ep.* 1169; (viii) *Epp.* 1208 and 1273 and (ix) *Ep.* 1511 — b) appeal: (i) *Ep.* 220 (discussed *infra*).

[45] ZUCKERMAN 2004, p. 84-85: "La lettre n'a pas été livrée à son destinataire sans doute parce que Dioscore s'est aperçu qu'elle ne lui serait d'aucune utilité." See also PALME 2008, p. 207, n. 17.

[46] FOURNET 2015, p. 255 : "Si le système antique accordait à tout sujet libre le privilège d'accès direct auprès des autorités dans le cadre de la procédure de pétition, en cas de blocage au niveau local, le sujet pouvait en référer à l'autorité suprême, en l'occurrence l'empereur, et ce privilège se transformait alors pour les provinciaux désireux d'obtenir la décision écrite du prince en une odyssée longue et parsemée d'ébuches que rien n'illustre mieux que le dossier constantinopolitain des archives de Dioscore d'Aphrodité."

hierarchically superior to the *dux*.[47] Later research theorised that the language used in this document does not fit such a profile.[48] I prefer to consider the question of the authorship from the perspective of the addressee of a recommendation letter. Such an addressee generally had the same status in society as the letter writer, and belonged to his network. Therefore, without being able to give a more precise identification, I suggest that the letter was written not by a high official of the central government in Constantinople, but by another influential person who knew the *dux* quite well, as he belonged to the first-order zone of his network.[49]

2. Letters by Augustine

In the first decades of the fifth century AD, a certain Faventius, Augustine's tenant farmer in Paratianis,[50] had been arrested for reasons that are not explained. On different occasions Augustine intervened for him. In total, Augustine sent seven letters: four letters that have been preserved (*Epp.* 113-116 dating to 409/423) and three others which are referred to in letters 113 to 115. This table provides an overview of the differents letters and interventions (including indirect interventions).

ADDRESSEE	FIRST INTERVENTION	SECOND INTERVENTION
Cresconius → Florentinus (indirect intervention)	Referred to in *Ep.* 113	*Ep.* 113
Florentinus	Referred to in *Ep.* 114	*Ep.* 114
Fortunatus → Generosus (indirect intervention)	Referred to in *Ep.* 115	*Ep.* 115 + referred to in *Ep.* 116
Generosus	*Ep.* 116	

[47] MARTIN 1929, p. 100 and SALOMON 1948, p. 98: *praefectus praetorio Orientis*.

[48] ZUCKERMAN 2004, p. 84: "Un tel langage est inconcevable dans une lettre du préfet du prétoire, surtout lorsqu'il s'adresse à un duc, son subordonné hiérarchique."

[49] This theoretical analysis is mainly based on the insights of Boissevain (see BOISSEVAIN 1974). The social relationships in which an individual ("the central person" — *ego*) is embedded can be viewed as a network. Those whom *ego* knows personally form the first-order zone. The first-order persons are also in contact with others ("the second zone") who are unknown to the central person, but with whom he could come into contact via members of his first-order zone.

[50] A small city in the province of *Africa Proconsularis*.

In addition, Augustine asks that the provisions of a procedure law be applied to Faventius. This law can be found in the chapter on the transfer of accused persons of the *Codex Theodosianus* (*Cod. Theod.* 9.2.6), issued in 409. It allowed an accused person to be questioned by the local (town) authorities. He then could remain under light custody for 30 days in order to organise his affairs.[51] This option was open to whomever requested it.

The first letter (*Ep.* 113) is an indirect intervention, in which the addressee, Cresconius,[52] an official of the coast guards, is requested to intervene with Florentinus,[53] the officer who arrested Faventius, and ask him the application of this procedure law.[54] Florentinus is also the addressee of the subsequent letter (*Ep.* 114). Augustine has the intention to use the period of 30 days permitted by these provisions to reach an agreement with the opponent.[55] The letter explains that this is Augustine's second intervention with Cresconius (*iterum scribo*).

Augustine, when alluding to a previous intervention, does not refrain from putting some (subtle) pressure on Cresconius. Augustine skilfully draws him into the dispute, by holding him "responsible" for Augustine's hypothetical refusal to intervene.[56]

The subsequent letter (*Ep.* 114) is addressed to Florentinus. Augustine first explains that he had previously sent one of his diocesan priests with

---

[51] The *Codex Theodosianus* contains similar provisions dating to 380 (*Cod. Theod.* 9.2.3), to which this law refers. Moreover, the earlier rescript is repeated almost literally in the *Codex Justinianus* (*Cod. Just.* 9.3.2). Only *Cod. Theod.* 9.2.6 is cited by Augustine.

[52] Not mentioned in *PLRE* II.

[53] He was a member of staff of the *dux Africae*.

[54] *Rogo itaque Benignitatem tuam* (...) *hoc interim apud apparitorem qui eum tenet, petitionem meam adiuvare digneris, ut faciat quod Imperatoris leget praecipitur* (...) (*Ep.* 113) — "Therefore I ask your Benignity (...) to be so kind as to further my request to the arresting officer who is holding him, to do what is prescribed by imperial law" (translation Parsons).

[55] *Quorum dierum spatio, tua nobis annuente benevolentia, si eius causam amica disceptatione finire potuerimus, gratulabimur: si autem non potuerimus, inveniet eum exitus iudiciorum* (*Ep.* 113) — "If in that length of time, with the help of your Benevolence, we can reach an agreement on his case, by friendly discussion, we shall be thankful; if not, the verdict of the court will find him out" (translation Parsons).

[56] *Si ab ista causa dissimulavero, de qua tuae religioni ecce iterum scribo; non solum Eximietas tua,* (...), *merito me culpabit, et recte reprehendet* (*Ep.* 113) — "If I were to let drop the case about which I am writing to your Holiness this second time, not only your Excellency (...) would justly blame me and rightly reprove me" (translation Parsons).

a copy of the law to Florentinus, to whom the text had already been read aloud.[57] Later in this letter Augustine, who takes strong argument from his episcopal authority, directly intervenes with Florentinus, asking him in rather insisting terms to grant the provisions of the imperial law.[58]

The subsequent letter (*Ep.* 115) is another example of an indirect intervention. In this long letter Augustine asks his colleague Fortunatus,[59] bishop of Cirta, to approach Generosus,[60] the governor of Numidia before whom Faventius is to appear.[61] Generosus was thus the judge of the case. The passage proves that Augustine had previously approached the governor, but apparently in vain.

Augustine's intercession in the judicial procedure is expressed in strong, unambiguous terms. The letter writer not only asks the hearing of the case to be (provisionally) cancelled, but also the procedural provisions to be observed.[62] In the first half of this letter Augustine highlighted what he had already undertaken in favour of Faventius (see also *Epp.* 113 and 114). He specifically informs that he had requested the aforementioned

[57] *Quamvis ergo iam per fratrem et compresbyterum meum Coelestinum miserim legem (...) quae lex, sicut mihi memoratus presbyter renuntiavit, tuae religioni recitata est* (*Ep.* 114) — "I sent a copy of the law by my brother and fellow priest Caelestinus (...). The abovementioned priest brought me back word that this law had been read aloud to your Reverence" (translation Parsons).

[58] *Tamen etiam nunc eam cum his litteris identidem misi; non terrens, sed rogans, et pro homine humane, et episcopali misericordia (...) intercedens (...) ut et hoc existimationi tuae et petitioni meae praestare digneris, et quod lex Imperatoris iubet (...)* (*Ep.* 114) — "However, I am now sending it again in this letter, not to threaten you, but to ask you as a man of feeling, exercising the mercy expected of a bishop and to intercede with you (...) that you would kindly grant this favour (...) and not refuse to do, at my prayer and intercession, what the law of the emperor commands (...)" (translation Parsons).

[59] *PCBE*, I, p. 494-496.

[60] *PLRE* II, p. 501, Generosus 1.

[61] *(...) peto Sanctitatem tuam, (...) ut honorabili nobisque carissimo Consulari digneris tradere litteras meas, et has ei legere; quia bis eamdem causam insinuare necessarium non esse arbitratus sum* (*Ep.* 115) — "(...) I beg your Holiness (...) to be so kind as to take my letter to the honourable governor and read it to him, because I do not think it necessary to go into detail on the same case twice" (translation Parsons).

[62] *Et eius causae differat audientiam, quoniam nescio utrum in ea nocens an innocens sit. Et quod circa eumdem leges non servatae sunt, ut sic raperetur, neque ut ab Imperatore praeceptum est (...)* (*Ep.* 115) — "Ask him to put off the hearing of the case, since I do not know whether he is guilty or innocent. And ask him not to make light of the fact that the laws were not observed in regard to the man, since he was carried off in that manner and not taken, as the emperor prescribed (...)" (translation Parsons).

law to be applied to his recommendee.[63] Augustine's focus on previous actions is meant to lend more support and credibility to his case.

Finally, in letter 116, Augustine intervenes a second time with Generosus, but now, contrary to the previous letter, he directly approaches the governor.[64] He subtly reminds his addressee that he also wrote an intervention for this case (*Ep.* 115) to his colleague bishop Fortunatus.[65] Probably, by reminding that intervention, Augustine not only wants to underscore the seriousness of Faventius' case, but also to exert some influence on his addressee.

Three conclusions emerge from the comparison of these letters. The first has to do with the access to legal knowledge. Augustine, eagerly seeking the enforcement of the procedure law, provided on at least four occasions the addressee with a copy of the provisions of the law. Augustine apparently had a written copy of the text of the provisions, since several legal terms that appear in the law, are also found in the letters 113, 114 and 115, in which the provisions are summarised or paraphrased.[66] Moreover, both the law and the different citations follow the same line of reasoning. Since on some occasions, Augustine provided his addressee with a copy of the text, while in other letters, he summarised the content of the law, legal information was specialised knowledge

[63] *Alio die misi litteras, petens ut ei concederetur quod iussit in causis talibus Imperato* (*Ep.* 115) — "On the next day I sent a letter requesting for Faventius the privilege which the emperor prescribed in such cases" (translation Parsons).

[64] *Et profecto facies quod non solum integrum, verum etiam christianum iudicem decet* (*Ep.* 116) — "Doubtless, you will do what an upright judge, not to say a Christian one, ought to do (...)" (translation Parsons).

[65] *Sed nunc quid in civitate* (...), *factum sit, cum ex litteris quas ad venerabilem fratrem et coepiscopum meum Fortunatum dedi,* (...) (*Ep.* 116) — "But now, when your Excellency finds out what happened in the city (...), from the letter which I have given to my reverend brother and fellow bishop, Fortunatus (...)" (translation Parsons).

[66] (i) *municipalibus actis interrogentur* (*Cod. Theod.* 9.2.6); *apud acta municipalia interrogari faciat* (*Ep.* 113); *ad gesta municipalia perducantur* (*Ep.* 114); *ut actis municipalibus interrogarentur* (*Ep.* 115) — (ii) *XXX diebus sibi concessis* (*Cod. Theod.* 9.2.6); *dies triginta concedi* (*Ep.* 113); *triginta dies* (*Ep.* 114); *triginta dies agere* (*Ep.* 115) — (iii) *sub moderata et diligenti custodia* (...) *in civitate residere* (*Cod. Theod.* 9.2.6); *sub moderata custodia in ea civitate in qua detentus est* (*Ep.* 113); *triginta dies in ea civitate ubi tenentur, agere sub moderata custodia* (*Ep.* 114); *in ea civitate sub custodia moderata* (*Ep.* 115) — (iv) *propter ordinationem domus propriae parandosque sibi sumptus* (*Cod. Theod.* 9.2.6); *ut sua ordinet, sumptusque provideat* (*Ep.* 113); *ad parandos sibi fructus, vel rem suam, sicut necesse fuerit, ordinandam* (*Ep.* 114); *ut rem suam ordinent vel praeparent sumptus* (*Ep.* 115).

which was not easily accessible, even for holders of a high (secular) office.[67]

Secondly, the letters provide indications of how Augustine used his network to advance the interests of Faventius. Not only the governor of Numidia but also the arresting officer, who both had effective power in this dispute,[68] were approached in two ways, by a direct intervention and by an indirect intervention, that is through a third person who probably belonged to the network of the main figure. Moreover, in these letters he exerts a subtle pressure on the addressee, by referring to previous interventions.

This leads us to the third conclusion. Surprisingly, in three out of the four cases the first letter that Augustine wrote to his addressee has not come down to us. The very fact that Augustine addressed seven letters to four different addressees, and at least on four occasions asked for the enforcement of the law on legal procedure, suggests that Augustine's attempts were eventually not fruitful. Apparently, the epistolographer had to face a powerful opponent who had his own means of persuasion, by spending a large amount of money on this lawsuit.[69] Against the background of a powerful opponent, the fact that (only) four letters are extant, has probably its relevance. Augustine, when he was reviewing his literary corpus in later years,[70] knew of course how this dispute had evolved. With only four (and not seven) letters being preserved, Augustine did not run (too) many risks of being seen as weak and lacking effective influence.

---

[67] See also JONES 1964, I, p. 474: "In the fourth-fifth century AD there was not only no collection available to the general public, the legal profession, or the courts themselves, and no authoritative record existed at all of what laws had been promulgated."

[68] Or at least were considered by Augustine of having it.

[69] *Habet enim causam cum homine pecuniosissimo, quamvis iudicis integritas fama clarissima praedicetur. Ne quid tamen apud Officium pecunia praevaleat* (...) (*Ep.* 115) — "Although the judge has the highest reputation for honesty, he has to deal with a very rich man. So, to prevent his money from influencing the court (...)" (translation Parsons).

[70] EBBELER 2017, p. 240-241: "In the final years of his life, Augustine began to review and redact his literary corpus. (...) There is not firm evidence to support claims that Augustine ordered his correspondence or otherwise created a comprehensive letter collection during his lifetime, though it is widely assumed that he did some editorial work when he read through the letters in the late 420s."

3. Letters by Symmachus

Symmachus wrote *Epistulae* VII, 108 and 109 (both dating to 398-401) on behalf of Caecilianus,[71] who had left the office of *praefectus annonae*. They are addressed to the brothers Patruinus (*Ep.* 108)[72] and Petronius (*Ep.* 109),[73] both influential figures in the palatial administration. Symmachus states that, in spite of previous agreements, Caecilianus faces a second trial,[74] probably in a special administrative court.

By approaching two persons who were connected to each other, Symmachus aimed at increasing the recommendee's chances. In both letters Symmachus asks to intervene in the course of justice.[75] Also, in *Ep.* VII, 109 the letter writer explicitly mentions the addressee's brother. By appealing to Petronius' sense of honour not to be second to his brother, he wants to put some additional pressure on the addressee.[76] Patruinus was probably the judge who would examine the recommendee, since it was Petronius who was advised to emulate his brother.

According to Jean-Pierre Callu, the French editor of Symmachus' correspondance, *Epp.* VII, 108 and 109 have to be seen in relation to a previous lawsuit for which Symmachus wrote recommendation letter *Ep.* III, 36 (396-397).[77] Symmachus had previously asked Patruinus to intervene

---

[71] *PLRE* II, p. 244-245, Caecilianus 1.

[72] *PLRE* II, p. 843-844.

[73] *PLRE* II, p. 862, Petronius 1.

[74] (...) *filius meus Caecilianus denuo ad incerta litis adtrahitur* (*Ep.* VII, 108) — "Again, my son is drawn into the uncertainties of a trial", and (*eorum qui*) (...) *finem iurgii secunda lite commutant* (*Ep.* VII, 109) — "(those who) change the end of a dispute by a second trial."

[75] *Hoc tantum de sancto animo tuo inpetratum volo, ut iisdem viribus, quibus pro eo luctamina prima sedasti, repetitae medearis iniuriae* (...) (*Ep.* VII, 108) — "Only do I want to obtain from your dedication that with the same vigour as you settled the first contest in his favour, you will remedy an injustice that is repeated", and *Nam reducitur in longinqua iudicia, quibus facile, si suffragium tuleris, eruetur* (*Ep.* VII, 109) — "He is indeed facing long disputes, from which he will be easily pulled out, if you should give him your support."

[76] *Est enim in te atque fratre portus omnium, quos fortuita sollicitant* (*Ep.* VII, 109) — "Since you and your brother are the haven of those who are afflicted by misfortune."

[77] Callu 1972-2002, III, p. 101, n. 1. See also Bruggisser 1987, and Ebbeler 2007, p. 236, n. 37.

in the same dispute.[78] Manifestly, Patruinus' intercession[79] turned out to be succesful at that moment.[80]

Ep. III, 36 is a peculiar case of judicial intervention, as it concerns the question whether the judge has jurisdiction to decide a dispute. It emerges from this letter that a pecuniary lawsuit had been launched against Caecilanus when holding the office of *praefectus annonae*. The adversary had brought the case before bishop Ambrosius, who, according to the practice of the *episcopalis audientia*, had competence to decide disputes among Christians.[81]

Symmachus, however, tried to protect the interests of his recommendee by pleading the inadmissibility of the case and refuting the competence of the judge. He therefore theorised that this case has to be brought before the secular judge:[82] "He virtually warns Ambrosius to avoid exercising his episcopal jurisdiction in a matter affecting his client."[83] Symmachus highlighted "that Ambrose did not usually

[78] According to *Cod. Theod.* 2.9.1 (*Litigia sententiis vel transactionibus terminata non sinimus restaurari* — "We do not allow litigation to be revived if it has been terminated by judicial decision or by compromise" (translation Pharr)), Caecilianus should not be judged twice for the same offence. This principle also known as "*ne bis in idem*", is still very important today, as it is almost universally included in the domestic laws of modern States.

[79] *PLRE* II, p. 843: "he (*sc.* Patruinus) had helped once before, but his brother had not, perhaps because he was absent in Spain."

[80] (*iisdem viribus, quibus*) *pro eo luctamina prima sedasti* (...) (*Ep.* VII, 108) — "(with the same vigour as) you settled the first contest in his favour."

[81] The *episcopalis audientia* had its origin in St. Paul's exhortation to resolve issues within the community (*I Cor.* 6.1-8). SIRKS 2013, p. 79: "Basically the *episcopalis audientia* concerns a way of deciding a dispute, next to the official way of entering the official hierarchy of courts." See also MCLYNN 1994, p. 269: "The ill-defined scope of a bishop's judicial activity left much to the inclinations (and stature) of the individual prelate."

[82] *Sunt leges, sunt tribunalia, sunt magistratus, quibus litigator utatur salva conscientia tua* (*Ep.* III, 36) — "There are laws, courts and magistrates at the disposal of a litigant, without your conscience being affected."

[83] BARNES 1992, p. 10. MCLYNN 1994, p. 269: "The invitation was forcefully put. Symmachus reminded the bishop of the adequacy of the apparatus of secular justice."

adjudicate lawsuits involving money and advised the bishop to refuse the case"[84].[85]

Modern lawyers would call this issue a case of *forum shopping*: the practice adopted by litigants to have their legal case heard in the court that is thought most likely to provide them a favourable judgement.[86]

This discussion leads us to the conclusion that Symmachus would promote his recommendee's interests by (simultaneously) approaching two influential figures for the same case. In this vein, he used different strategies to influence his addressee. Symmachus subtly manipulated one of the addressees by appealing to his sense of honour. In *Ep.* III, 36 the letter writer clearly attempted to shift the balance of power in his own favour, as he asserted that the *episcopalis audientia* does not apply in the case of his recommendee.

4. Letters by Gregory of Nazianzus

Epistulae 146, 147 and 148 were written in 383 in favour of Nicobulus, a nephew of the epistolographer. Nicobulus is charged for an offence committed by his slaves. The first letter is adressed to Olympius,[87] governor of *Cappadocia Secunda*, who was the judge of the case, while his

---

[84] EBBELER 2007, p. 236, n. 37. MCLYNN 1994, p. 271-272: "Ambrose's *De Officiis* allows one exemption (pecuniary lawsuits) from the clergyman's primary responsability to provide justice. Perhaps Symmachus who was presented to posterity as the keeper of Cicero's shrine was invited by his peers to offer an opinion upon this somewhat presomptuous reworking of the deity's masterpiece (i.e. Cicero's *De Officiis*) and took the opportunity to store up a few telling quotations for use against the author."

[85] *Negavi te solere recipere in tuam curam pecuniarias actiones* (*Ep.* III, 36) — "I denied that it is your custom to accept pecuniary lawsuits into your concern."

[86] See also HUMFRESS 2007b, p. 162: "Given the state of our evidence it is difficult to make any definitive statements about how episcopal 'legal' jurisdiction was in fact understood at any given time, by any particular individual or group. Nonetheless, we do know that some late Roman litigants (perhaps guided by the advice of advocates and/or *iurisconsulti*) attempted to 'forum-shop', for example, by pleading *praescriptio fori* as a jurisdictional 'dodge'; that some challenged a bishop's authority to act as a *iudex datus* or as an arbitrator in their case; and that others attempted to frame persuasive appeals from episcopal *sententiae* (...)."

[87] *PLRE* I, p. 646, Olympius 10.

assessor Asterius[88] received recommendation letters 147 and 148.[89] The governor is thus approached in two ways, directly and through a subordinate.[90] In both letters he argues it is incongruous that Nicobolus has to pay for the faults of his slaves, while he himself is completely innocent.[91]

---

[88] *PLRE* I, p. 119, Asterius 4.

[89] According to GALLAY 1964-1967, II, p. 39, n. 3 and p. 154-155, n. 1 to page 39, after the division of the province into two separate entities, Cappadocia Prima and Cappodocia Secunda in 382, Olympius became governor of Cappadocia Prima and Asterius, governor of Cappodocia Secunda.

[90] Examples of interventions jointly written to a governor and his assessor or another member of staff, are also found in Libanius: (i) Lib. *Epp.* 68 and 91 (Themistius 1) versus 52, 67 and 90 (Clearchus 1); (ii) *Epp.* 101 (Modestus 2) versus 102 (Urbanus 3); (iii) *Epp.* 214 (Priscianus 1) versus 215 (Ammianus 3); (iv) *Epp.* 1145 (Domninus 2) versus 1146 (Theodotus 0); (v) *Epp.* 1200 (Domitianus 4) versus 1201 (Euethius 1); (vi) *Epp.* 1530 (Domninus 2) versus 1531 (Hermogenes 5). The numerals refer to the corresponding entries in *PLRE.* I suggest that the reason for a joint intervention was that a governor of a province was probably inundated with recommendations and requests, as he was the nearest (or the least distant) and, consequently, the most approachable representative of imperial power for local communities. Approaching the governor (or any other holder of an influential office) in an effective way would, thus, be a challenging task. The result of it could not be assured in advance. In order to be sure that the case was given all necessary attention, a similar intervention was also sent to a member of the governor's staff. See also SALLER 1982, p. 164 who describes the situation in the Principate: "(...) from the time a governor took up office he faced a barrage of requests to take orators, friends of friends, local notables etc. in his *amicitia.* The requests came from every quarter, from the emperor down to humbler friends (...)." The governor in Late Antiquity presumably faced similar challenges. Insights from papyrology also point to this important work volume, see KELLY 2011, p. 112 and n. 152: "The petitions received by the prefect during a particular *conventus* session could run into the hundreds, or even thousands. It is hardly realistic to expect the prefect and his rather limited staff to deal with each case promptly and personally. (...) *P. Yale* I 61 (AD 208-210, TM 13738) mentions that 1,804 petitions addressed to the prefect governor during the conventus in a little over two days." Yet, the administrative reforms of the fourth century AD resulted in an ever increasing encroachment of the central level on the authority of a provincial governor. SLOOTJES 2006, p. 25: "First, by breaking up the larger provinces, the novel system of dioceses and prefectures, and the creation of separate military commanders (*duces*), Diocletian diminished the status of provincial governors. Consequently, a governor was no longer the highest Roman authority in a province, but other Roman officials — with more power than the governor, and able to interfere with his business — became a permanent presence throughout the provinces."

[91] Ἀλλ᾽ οὐκ οἶδα εἴ σοι παραστήσεται δίκαιον ὑπὲρ ἄλλων ἁμαρτημάτων ἐν ἄλλοις ἀπαιτεῖσθαι δίκην, καὶ τούτων ἀλλοτρίων, καὶ οὐδὲ ἑκουσίων (...) (*Ep.* 146.5) — "I do

In *Ep.* 146 Gregory aks the governor to be a benevolent judge.[92] He attempts to give a more solemn character to the case, presenting it as a choice between good and evil. By putting the case on a higher level, Gregory appealed to Olympius' conscience and, in this way, gave him not much leeway. The aim of this rhetorical device was to force the addressee to take a decision in Nicobulus' favour. It is, however, doubtful whether it had the aimed effect.

Moreover, it seems that Gregory's position lacked credibility, as he had previously defended Nicobulus' opponent.[93] Manifestly, he was aware of it, since he eagerly tried, starting from a hypothesis *ex absurdo*, to justify his defence of Nicobulus.[94] The overall impression is that Gregory struggled to make his point.

The next letter is an indirect intervention in which he asks the assessor to intercede with the governor.[95] Apparently, the aim of Gregory's intervention was to prevent the case from getting a criminal (public) character, also because the epistolographer clearly considered it a private affair.[96] Maybe Gregory deemed that the trial being heard as a criminal (public)

---

not know whether it would appear just to you if he has to pay for the faults of others, faults that are foreign to him and are even not voluntary (...)?" and Ἀλλὰ τί τοῦτο πρὸς τοὺς δεσπότας, οἳ μηδενὸς τῶν γεγενημένων κεκοινωνήκασιν; ἢ τίς ὁ λόγος, ὑπὲρ τῶν ἀλλοτρίων ἁμαρτημάτων ἐν ἄλλοις ἀπαιτεῖσθαι δίκην (...) (*Ep.* 147.6) — "But what has it to do with the masters, who have not taken any part in what happened? And what is the reason that he should pay for the faults of others (...)?"

[92] (...) φιλάνθρωπον σεαυτὸν παράσχου τοῖς κινουμένοις κριτήν, ὡς οὐκ ἀνθρώποις μόνον δικάζων σήμερον, ἀλλὰ καὶ ἀρετῇ καὶ κακίᾳ· (*Ep.* 146.7) — "Present yourself as a benevolent judge for those who are disturbed, since today you do not only judge between persons, but also between virtue and vice."

[93] Αἰσχύνομαι γὰρ κατηγορεῖν ἐπὶ τῆς σῆς ὀρθότητος οὗ πρώην ὑπερεμάχουν (*Ep.* 146.4) — "I am ashamed at defending before your Rightness the man for which I lately fought."

[94] Ἔστω καὶ δικαιότατος ἀνθρώπων ὁ νῦν ἡμῖν πολεμῶν (*Ep.* 146.4) — "Let us assume that Nicobulus is the worst of everyone, whose sole offence is to be regarded with jealousy because of us (...)."

[95] Τοῦτον ὑπὸ τὰς σὰς τίθεμεν χεῖρας, καὶ διὰ τῶν σῶν ταῖς τοῦ ἄρχοντος (*Ep.* 147.3) — "This man, we hand him over into your hands, and through you into the governor's hands."

[96] GALLAY 1964-1967, II, p. 40, n. 1: ἢ τίς ὁ λόγος, ὑπὲρ τῶν ἀλλοτρίων ἁμαρτημάτων ἐν ἄλλοις ἀπαιτεῖσθαι δίκην καὶ νῦν τῶν δημοσίων φροντίζειν, ἡνίκα λυπεῖ τὸ ἴδιον; (*Ep.* 147.6) — "What is the reason that one is punished for mistakes of the other, and public interest is now considered, when the opponent troubles private interests?"

case would bring negative publicity to Nicobulus, and thus diminish the chances for a positive outcome. Nicobulus would run less risk, if the case could be treated as a private affair.

Yet, the letter to Asterius seems to have been to no effect and, thus, in *Ep.* 148 Gregory repeats his request in rather insisting terms, by advancing arguments that deal more with the addressee himself than with Nicobulus.[97] Gregory also hints that it was thanks to him that others had previously received favours from Asterius, hence insinuating in guarded terms that it might be fitting for the latter to also grant this request.[98]

At first sight it might seem surprising that Asterius, and not Olympius, was approached by Gregory for a second time.[99] As Gregory had already approached the governor for several (other) cases, he could not expect his addressee to accede to every request. Therefore, he had to carefully consider how he would phrase this intervention. It was important not to endanger this and future cases.[100] Gregory's "hesitating" attitude might also point to the fact that his status was not wholly unchallenged. Assumingly, Gregory's posture has to been seen against the background of his position in Cappadocia after his (humiliating) return from Constantinople.[101] Another element was, as explained earlier, that

---

[97] Καὶ χρῆσαι πάσῃ τῇ φιλίᾳ καὶ τῇ συνέσει καὶ τῷ δύνασθαι σὺν Θεῷ περὶ τὰ ἡμέτερα πράγματα (*Ep.* 148.5) — "Use with God's help all your friendship, intelligence and power on our behalf."

[98] (…) τὰς μὲν ἄλλας χάριτας ἄλλοι δι' ἡμῶν ἐλάμβανον, ταύτης δὲ ἡμεῖς χρῄζομεν ὑπὲρ ἡμῶν αὐτῶν (…) (*Ep.* 148.6) — "Others received the other favours through us, we need this favour for ourselves."

[99] McLynn 2014, p. 48: "In his collected correspondence Gregory included thirteen letters addressed to Olympius; all of these relate to the latter's term of office, which ran roughly from mid-382 to mid-383. Most of the letters are intercessions."

[100] Gregory might have had this in mind in *Ep.* 146.1: Τοῦτο ἦν ὅπερ ἔλεγον (…) ὅτι δέδοικα μὴ κενώσω τὸ φιλάνθρωπον ὑμῶν ἐν τοῖς ἀλλοτρίοις — "This was what I used to say (…) that I feared to empty your humanity in other's cases."

[101] McLynn 2001, p. 193: "After the humilating loss of his position in the capital, Gregory faced the very difficult task of constructing a commensurate (or at least compensating) authority at home, independently of the ecclesiastical hierarchy." However, Van Dam 2002, p. 85 assumes that "once back in Cappadocia, Gregory resumed his standing as a prominent local notable. Not only was he a landowner, and the scion of a prominent family, but he was a former bishop of Constantinople. He corresponded with a wide range of imperial magistrates, and he still received an invitation to attend a council directly from the Emperor Theodosius."

Gregory's current intervention was negatively tainted by his recent defence of Nicobulus' opponent. It is for these reasons that the letter writer considered it preferable to approach Asterius, all the more so since this channel had already proved its efficiency (see *Ep.* 148, 6).[102]

The discussion of these letters brings us to three conclusions. Firstly, in order to be on the safe side and to maximalise his chances, Gregory simultaneously approached the two office holders who dealt with Nicobulus' case. Secondly, with regard to the letters to Asterius (*Epp.* 147 and 148), it is clear that, after a first and unsuccessful attempt, the letter writer by advancing stronger arguments, attempted to increase the pressure in the second letter. Gregory plainly intended to convince Asterius to have the petition granted. Finally, the letter to the governor Olympius shows that when a letter writer would write multiple interventions (on behalf of different persons), it could lead to a "conflict of interest" which, however, did not prevent Gregory from acting.[103]

5. Letters by Basil

Epistulae 177 and 178 are both short interventions, dating to 374, in favour of Eusebius, bishop of Samosata,[104] and addressed to Sophronius,[105] *magister officiorum* and Aburgius,[106] probably *quaestor sacri palatii* or *comes rerum privatarum*.[107] Regional or local links must have had some

---

[102] In *Ep.* 147.3 Gregory hints at his previous interventions that turned out to be succesful; apparently they occurred in more serious cases: (…) πάνυ δεινὸν νομίζοντες τοὺς μὲν ἄλλους καὶ τῶν μεγίστων ἐγκλημάτων ἐλευθεροῦν δι' ἡμῶν, (…) — "We considered a very strange thing that whilst our intervention cleared others from the most serious accusations (…)." This (partly) contradicts McLynn 2014, p. 56: "There is no indication, significantly, that Gregory had known Asterius before Olympius' term."

[103] It is interesting to draw a parallel with modern law practice: in many countries law practitioners have the statutory obligation, when acting on behalf of their clients, to avoid any conflict of interest that might have occurred from previous cases.

[104] He was a close friend of Basil. Eusebius held the bishopric from 361 till approximately 379.

[105] *PLRE* I, p. 847-848, Sophronius 3.

[106] *PLRE* I, p. 960.

[107] Both addressees head the list of officials to whom Basil addressed most recommendation letters (see Treucker 1981, p. 405).

importance in this case, as the letter writer and the two addressees are all natives of Caesarea.

The letters have the same line of reasoning. First, Basil underscores the addressee's willingness and ability to assist others:[108] He then underlines the special qualities of his recommendee.[109] Finally, he counts that the addressee's support for this trial will eventually unveil the truth.[110] According to Philip Rousseau, the letters may allude to the treason trials initiated at Antioch by the emperor Valens.[111] Neither intervention indicates that the addressee was the judge of the trial. On the contrary, it is likely that Basil sought the support of Sophronius and Aburgius in order to influence the decision of the judge and, by doing so, to obtain a favourable outcome for Eusebius.

However, the short length, the lack of specific features and the similar structure suggest that the documents can be considered as ordinary, day-to-day letters, and, therefore, have to be distinguished from more individualised letters, which were of particular interest for the letter

---

[108] Καταλέγειν μὲν πάντας τοὺς δἰ ἡμᾶς εὐεργετηθέντας παρὰ τῆς σῆς μεγαλονοίας οὐ ῥᾴδιον (*Ep.* 177.1-2) — "To reckon up all those who have received kindness at your excellency's hand, for my sake, is no easy task" (translation Deferrari), and Πολλοὺς οἶδα πολλάκις συστήσας τῇ τιμιότητί σου καὶ γενόμενος ἐπὶ μεγίστων καιρῶν χρήσιμος ἱκανῶς τοῖς καταπονουμένοις (*Ep.* 178.1-3) — "I know that I have often recommended many persons to your excellency, and so in serious emergencies have been very useful to friends in distress" (translation Deferrari).

[109] Δικαιότατος δὲ πάντων καὶ ὁ νῦν προσαγόμενος διὰ τοῦ γράμματος ἡμῶν τυγχάνει, ὁ αἰδεσιμώτατος ἀδελφὸς Εὐσέβιος (…) (*Ep.* 177.6-7) — "But most worthy of all happens to be the one now being introduced to you through our letter, our most reverend brother Eusebius (…)" (translation Deferrari), and Οὐ μὴν τιμιώτερόν γε ἐμοὶ οὐδ' ὑπὲρ μειζόνων ἀγωνιζόμενον οἶδα πρότερον παραπέμψας τῇ κοσμιότητί σου τοῦ ποθεινοτάτου υἱοῦ Εὐσεβίου (*Ep.* 178.3-6) — "But no man more honoured in my eyes or fighting for more important things, have I ever before, I know, sent to your Decorum than our most beloved son Eusebius" (translation Deferrari).

[110] παρακαλοῦμεν, (…) προστῆναι αὐτοῦ μετὰ τῆς ἀληθείας. ἔχει γὰρ οὐ μικρὰν συμμαχίαν τὴν ἀπὸ τοῦ δικαίου (*Ep.* 177.10-14) — "Therefore we urge you (…) and in company with the truth to defend him. For he has no mean alliance in having justice on his side" (translation Deferrari), and (…) ἀλλὰ τυχεῖν δικαστηρίου, καὶ εἰς ἐξέτασιν αὐτοῦ τὸν βίον ἀχθῆναι. ῥᾷστα γὰρ οὕτω καὶ ἡ συκοφαντία φανερὰ γενήσεται (…) (*Ep.* 178.14-15) — "On the contrary, he should obtain a trial, and his life should be subjected to examination. For in this way the calumny will very easily become manifest (…)" (translation Deferrari).

[111] ROUSSEAU 1994, p. 159, n. 107.

writer.[112] The epistolary features discussed above suggest that Basil simultaneously tried his chances with two different addressees. Consequently, based on the features of *Epp.* 177 and 178, it seems plausible that at the moment when Gregory wrote these interventions,[113] the case did not hold particular interest for him and/or, for some specific reasons, he did not want to engage himself too fully.[114] Maybe this cannot be seen apart from the fact that Sophronius and Aburgius were the officials to whom Basil addressed most recommendation letters.[115]

6. Letters by Synesius

Two interesting letters (*Epp.* 42 and 47, probably dating to 411) expound how victims of a theft of wine jars had to take legal action, as they were confronted with an opponent (the thief) who vigorously tried, apparently by exploiting some legal loopholes,[116] to retain possession of the stolen goods. The victims tried — through Synesius — to intervene in the course of justice. Each intervention occurred at a different stage in the judicial procedure.

Ep. 42 in favour of Asphalius,[117] a relative of Synesius was probably written after Synesius became bishop in spring 411. The letter is addressed to the judge in this case, Cledonius,[118] governor of Pentapolis. Synesius

[112] In that case, the letter writer wants to give a personal touch to his letter by taking the individual merits or qualities of the recommendee into account. The stress on the individual merits and, in addition, a more stylistically elaborate letter would underscore the importance that the letter writer attaches to this particular recommendation.

[113] Some casual remarks actually suggest that epistolographers drew distinctions between those who requested a recommendation letter. The comments in August. *Ep.* 28.1; Symm. *Ep.* II, 82 and Bas. *Ep.* 37 highlight that the letter writer's approach to a request could vary in relation to the degree of importance that the request had for him.

[114] However, this hypothesis partly contradicts Schor 2014, p. 310-311. The author stresses the importance of Basil's Nicene partisanship, among which was bishop Eusebius of Samosata.

[115] Treucker 1981, p. 411 gives the list of the most frequent addressees.

[116] In *Ep.* 47.3 the offender is described as (…) τὴν διὰ τῶν νόμων ἐπὶ τοὺς νόμους ἐλθεῖν — "(…) to use the law against the law" (translation Fitzgerald). I assume that τὴν refers to ὁδόν (see LSJ, p. 1199, which explains that ὁδός is often omitted).

[117] *PLRE* II, 170.

[118] *PLRE* II, 302.

asks the governor to judge in favour of Asphalius, and consequently, that the stolen objects be restituted to the owner.[119]

The second letter, *Ep.* 47, was written to Theotimus,[120] a well-known "wandering poet".[121] This document states that the thief, who was condemned to restitute the wine jars to the owner, Martyrius.[122], was seriously thinking about lodging an appeal with Anthemius,[123] *praefectus praetorio Orientis.*[124] Synesius, trying to cross the plans of his opponent, requested Theotimus to intervene with Troilus,[125] a famous rhetor in Constantinople and advisor to Anthemius.[126] In this letter Synesius exerted some pressure on the addressee by holding him responsible for finding a solution.[127] It emerges from this letter that since Synesius was able to approach the *praefectus praetorio Orientis*, he had a network that reached to the highest power circles.[128] Other letters suggest that this network was quite effective.[129]

---

[119] ἐπανίτω τοίνυν Ἀσφάλιος εἰς τὸ δεσπότης εἶναι τῶν κεραμίων τῇ τοῦ πατρὸς διαθήκῃ προσλαβὼν τὴν ἀπόφασιν (*Ep.* 42.2) — "Let Asphalius come again into possession of his wine jars in peace, receiving a decision of the court in accordance with his father's will" (translation Fitzgerald slighty modified).

[120] *PLRE* II, 1111.

[121] CAMERON 1965, *passim.*

[122] Not mentioned in *PLRE.*

[123] *PLRE* II, Anthemius 1, p. 93-95.

[124] παρὰ δὲ Ἀνθεμίου καλῶς ἂν ἔχοι τὸ μὴ κακόν τι λαβεῖν, εἰ Πέτρος αὐτόν, ὥσπερ ἠπείλησεν, ἀπαιτήσειεν (*Ep.* 47.3) — "Only do I hope that he will not encounter any evil at the hands of Anthemius, to whom Peter threatens to appeal" (translation Fitzgerald slightly modified). JONES 1964, p. 481: "The imperial appellate jurisdiction was radically reorganised by Constantine, who regularly delegated it not only to the praetorian prefects (...)."

[125] *PLRE* II, Troilus 1, p. 1128: "His knowledge and skill in politics — πολιτικὴ φρόνησις — rivalled Anthemius' own."

[126] ἀλλ' ἵνα μὴ γένηται τοῦτο, δέομαι σοῦ τε αὐτοῦ καὶ διὰ σοῦ τοῦ θαυμασίου ἀνδρὸς καὶ φιλοσόφου Τρωΐλου, κωλύσατε τὸν ἀλιτήριον ἄνθρωπον τὴν διὰ τῶν νόμων ἐπὶ τοὺς νόμους ἐλθεῖν (*Ep.* 47.3) — "To prevent this, I beg of you, and I make this request, through you, to the renowned and wise Troilus to make it impossible for such a sinful creature as this to use the law against the law" (translation Fitzgerald slightly modified).

[127] τὸ δὲ πῶς ἂν συκοφάντης ἀνακοπείη οὐκ ἐμὸν εὑρεῖν, ἀλλὰ σόν (...) (*Ep.* 47.4) — "It is not my task, but yours to answer the question how this humbug can be cut short."

[128] As the power behind Arcadius' throne, Anthemius was the most powerful person in the East.

[129] There was actually a communication channel between Synesius and Anthemius. In the same year (411) Synesius wrote not only a recommendation to Troilus, advisor to

7. Letters by Libanius

Libanius' letter collection provides some fine examples of how the letter writer, by approaching the judge or other influential officials, tried to hold sway on a court's decision. The first letter (*Ep.* 163) (359/360) is a manifest judicial intervention on behalf of the governor Tryphonianus, *consularis Syriae*, addressed to Modestus,[130] who was *comes Orientis*.[131] The *consularis Syriae* had his residence in Antioch, where Libanius worked. "The governor's troubles stemmed from the difficulties of tax collection for which payment he was personally responsible."[132] An enquiry into his financial conduct as governor was launched by Ursulus,[133] *comes sacrarum largitionum*.[134] Accordingly, the *comes* imposed the governor a heavy fine in gold.[135] Libanius, who hints at his own limited power, asks Modestus to use his influence in this case.[136] More specifically, he insists that the governor's fine be acquitted.[137] The judicial intervention is repeated at the end of the letter,[138] indicating that Libanius was confident that

Anthemius, for Martyrius (*Ep.* 91), but also a letter to Theotimus (*Ep.* 49) in which he praises the addressee and, in the same vein, Anthemius. This document also learns us that Theotimus previously wrote panegyrics in favour of Anthemius. For a contrary opinion about Synesius' contacts in the capital, see LIEBESCHUETZ 1986, p. 189-190.

[130] *PLRE* I, p. 605-608, Domitius Modestus 2.

[131] JONES 1964, I, p. 364: "Under the diocesan system, the *comes Orientis* exercised a general supervision over the administration of his provinces."

[132] NORMAN 1992, II, p. 43, n. b.

[133] *PLRE* I, p. 988, Ursulus 1.

[134] (...) περιέσχε νέφος ἀρθὲν ἐκ τῶν Οὐρσουάλου χειρῶν (*Ep.* 163.2) — "(...) he found himself in the middle of a storm raised by the agency of Ursulus" (translation Norman).

[135] As Tryphonianus was accused of financial offences, he might have been judged by a special administrative court.

[136] (...) σὺ δὲ παρ' ᾧ τι πλέον μεθ' ἡμῶν μὲν συνάλγησον, μόνος δὲ ἐπικούρησον χρηστός τε φαινόμενος καὶ τῇ δυνάμει χρώμενος (*Ep.* 163.4) — "You (...) must feel the same feeling of outrage as I do; show yourself a good fellow, use your influence and be his sole source of assistance" (translation Norman).

[137] ἔστω δὲ (...) τῆς χάριτος δεύτερον δὲ τὸ λῦσαι τὴν ἐπικειμένην ζημίαν (*Ep.* 163.5) — "(...) next, relieve him of the penalty imposed upon him." (translation Norman).

[138] ἀλλ' ἐννοήσας τε ὅθεν ἡ καταδίκη καὶ τὸ πρᾶγμα μεμψάμενος καὶ τὸ τῆς ζημίας μέγεθος (*Ep.* 163.7) — "But consider the source of the verdict and disapprove of the case and the amount of the fine" (translation Norman).

Modestus would accede to his request, the more so as earlier in the letter he pointed to Modestus' efficiency and influence.[139]

A second example are three letters (*Epp.* 214, 215 and 220 dating to approximately 359) in favour of Calliopius,[140] who was probably assessor of the governor of Euphratensis and who was prosecuted for his official conduct.[141] Being native of Antioch, the office holder was a fellow citizen of Libanius. The letters are addressed to Priscianus,[142] governor of *Euphratensis* (*Ep.* 214), Ammianus,[143] possibly *assessor* of the governor of *Euphratensis* (*Ep.* 215),[144] and Modestus,[145] *comes Orientis* (*Ep.* 220).

In *Ep.* 214 Libanius highlights that he is bound to Calliopius by the same origin. I hold the view that Libanius here refers to his sojourn in Constantinople which he has in common with Calliopius.[146] It is quite likely that Priscianus would immediately understand why Libanius made a reference to Constantinople.[147] He also underscores that Calliopius had

---

139 οὐδὲ γὰρ ἃ πράττεις καθημέραν τῶν ῥεόντων ἐστίν, (...). μὴ οὖν θαυμάσῃς, εἰ (...) ἀπαιτῇ παρὰ τῶν ἐκεῖνα ὁρώντων ἕτερα ἐκείνοις ἐοικότα (*Ep.* 163.6) — "(...) your daily activities show no irresolution (...). Do not be surprised (...) if you are called upon again by those who have seen it happen (*i.e.* surmounting any impasse) to do the like once more" (translation Norman).

140 *PLRE* I, p. 174-175, Calliopius 2.

141 BRADBURY 2004, p. 104.

142 *PLRE* I, p. 727, Priscianus 1. Calliopius was *assessor* of Probatius (see *PLRE* I, p. 733, Probatius 1), the immediate predecessor of Priscianus.

143 *PLRE* I, p. 54, Ammianus 3.

144 See BRADBURY 2004, p. 160. However, according to *PLRE* I, *s.v.* "Ammianus 3 held a position of influence, but no office."

145 *PLRE* I, p. 605-608, Domitius Modestus 2.

146 εἰ πολίτῃ δίκαιον βοηθεῖν, διπλοῦν τοῦτο νυνὶ γίγνεται τὸ δίκαιον. εἴτε γὰρ Ἀντιοχεὺς ὁ Καλλιόπιος καλοῖτο, δεῖ δή που με συμμαχεῖν· εἴτ' ἀπὸ τῆς μείζονος, ἐγγέγραμμαι παρ' αὐτοῖς, ὥστε καὶ ταύτῃ βοηθητέον (*Ep.* 214.1) — "If it is just to help a fellow citizen, then it is now two times just. For if Calliopius might be called Antiochene, then I have to be an ally, and if he comes from a bigger city, then I am registered among its citizens, so that I have to help him on that account." According to *PLRE* I, p. 174-175, Calliopius 2, the words ἀπὸ τῆς μείζονος ("from a bigger city") mean that the recommendee became senator of Constantinople before 360. However, I hold that ἀπὸ τῆς μείζονος has to be read in relation to ἐγγέγραμμαι παρ' αὐτοῖς ("I am registered among its citizens"). Then, it refers to Calliopius as Libanius' assistant-teacher in Constantinople.

147 In 359 Priscianus was summoned to court with prospects of office. The next year he became governor of *Euphratensis* (see *PLRE* I, p. 727, Priscianus 1). In this way, Libanius wants to suggest that a sojourn in Constantinople can be favourable to someone's career. Maybe Libanius also hints at his own stint in the capital.

chosen for a subordinate position.[148] The letter writer reckons that he is probably more successful by underscoring the inferior role of Calliopius, as as *assessor* (in comparison to a governor), since such a situation does not constitute any threat to the current position of Priscianus. Libanius places reliance on Priscianus to obtain execution of the imperial rescript that was favourable to Calliopius.[149] This clear petition to Priscianus also suggests that Libanius did not rule out that the addressee would disregard the imperial despatch.

Libanius points out in the very beginning of *Ep.* 215 that Ammianus acceeded to his previous requests, thus creating the expectation that the current favour will also be granted by him.[150] Libanius points to his own lack of influence, and, by association, Ammianus' effective power.[151] This lack of influence is probably a rhetorical pose, as Libanius threatens to directly write to the *comes Orientis*, if the current intervention turns out to be of no avail.[152] Probably, Libanius did not exclude that the verdict

---

[148] τοῦ δὲ καὶ τοῦτο ἐπηνεῖτο, ὅτι πλείω λαμβάνειν ἐξὸν ἠσπάζετο τοὔλαττον. (*Ep.* 214.2) — "He was also praised for the fact that he welcomed the lesser, while he could take the greater."

[149] πάντα δ' ἂν γένοιτο τῆς σῆς φρενός τε καὶ ῥώμης, τῆς μὲν ἀνευρισκούσης πόρον, τῆς δὲ ἐπὶ τὸ πέρας ἰούσης (*Ep.* 214.4) — "Everything might depend on your intelligence and influence, your intelligence will find a way how to obtain it, your influence will proceed until the end." Previously Libanius had obtained an imperial rescript that was favourable to Calliopius: μᾶλλον δέ, οὐ πάντα δυσχερῆ· τῇ γὰρ ἀληθείᾳ προσέθετο βασιλεὺς καὶ λύει τὴν ταραχήν (*Ep.* 214.3) — "Rather, not everything is in trouble, since the Emperor took the side of the truth and has made an end to the turmoil." Of course 'truth' does not mean the objective reality here, but Calliopius' version of the facts.

[150] οὔτ' ἐγώ σε χάριν αἰτῶν καινόν τι ποιῶ σύ τε τὰ σαυτοῦ μιμήσῃ, τὴν χάριν εἰ καταθεῖο· πολλὰ γὰρ ἐγὼ μὲν ᾔτησα, σὺ δὲ δέδωκας (*Ep.* 215.1) — "Neither am I doing anything new in requesting a favour of you, and you'll imitate your usual conduct if you should grant the favour, since I've asked for many things and you've granted them" (translation Bradbury). Possibly, this is the first extant letter written to Ammianus. In total, Libanius wrote seven letters to this addressee. Five out of them date to 365 (see also Bradbury 2004, p. 160, n. 99).

[151] ἐχω δὲ βοηθεῖν οὐ τῇ ἐμαυτοῦ δυνάμει, ἀλλὰ τῇ σῇ. χρῶμαι δὲ αὐτῇ κατὰ τὴν φιλίαν. ὅρα δέ, ὅπως σε ἀκριβέστερον ἑτέρων οἶδα (*Ep.* 215.2) — "I can't assist him through my own influence, but I can through yours, and I'm making use of that in accordance with friendship. So see to it that I judge you more scrupulous than other people" (translation Bradbury).

[152] καὶ παῦε τῶν κακῶν ὁπόσα ἔξεστί σοι καὶ δεῖξον ἡμῖν ὡς οὐδὲν ἔλαττον ἐσχήκαμεν ἢ εἰ γράφειν εἴχομεν τῷ τῆς γνώσεως κυρίῳ (*Ep.* 215.4) — "(...) and put a stop to whichever of the evils you can and demonstrate to me that I've achieved no less than if I were

would not be favourable to Calliopius in first instance, and, as a result, considered the possibility to lodge an appeal at an higher level.

Indeed, the letters to the governor and his assessor did not produce the results that Libanius had hoped for, as Calliopius had not been cleared of the charges. An appeal against the governor's verdict was then launched with the *comes Orientis* who would conduct the investigation.[153] In the letter to Modestus (*Ep.* 220).[154] Libanius asks his addressee who was known as a harsh judge,[155] to adopt a lenient attitude towards Calliopius.[156] It is beyond any doubt for the letter writer that Calliopius is completely innocent, because — as Libanius affirms — he did not commit any offence.[157] Also, Libanius describes his request as a normal one.[158] This small phrase emphatically put before the proper request, points more to the letter writer's expectations than it corresponds to reality. That Libanius does actually not expect Modestus to have a mild disposition towards Calliopius, is proven by a final prayer to Zeus Meilichius, the "mild Zeus", that Modestus be propitious to the recommendee.[159]

---

to write to the man in charge of the investigation" (translation Bradbury). Γνώσις specifically means a judicial investigation see LSJ, γνώσις, I.

[153] SLOOTJES 2006, p. 33:"If provincials disagreed with the verdict of a governor, they could appeal, both in civil and in criminal cases, to the Vicar or the Praetorian Prefect (...)." The province of *Euphratensis* lies within the jurisdiction of the *comes Orientis.*

[154] *Ep.* 220 remains silent about the previous recommendation letters. It was probably not in Calliopius' interest to mention these interventions, since they were not successful. It is not known how much time elapsed between *Epp.* 214-215 and *Ep.* 220. It is, however, not at all impossible that Modestus was already cognisant of Libanius' interventions, before he received *Ep.* 220.

[155] BRADBURY 2004, p. 108.

[156] δεῖξαι αὐτῷ τὸ ὄμμα ἐπὶ τῆς δίκης ἥμερον (*Ep.* 220.2) — "(...) to show him a kindly gaze at the trial" (translation Bradbury).

[157] καὶ ἐγὼ τοίνυν οἶδα μὲν ἀκριβῶς ὡς οὔτε μικρὸν οὔτε μεῖζον ἀδικεῖ Καλλιόπιος οὑτοσί (*Ep.* 220.2) — "Now, I know perfectly well that this Calliopius commits no crime, either great or small" (translation Bradbury).

[158] δέομαι δέ σου τὸ κοινὸν δὴ τοῦτο (...) (*Ep.* 220.2) — "I make this very normal request of you (...)" (translation Bradbury). Libanius probably meant that it is normal to ask for some mildness.

[159] It is interesting to note how many words in this short prayer belong to the semantic field of gentleness: Μειλίχιε, ἡμερώτερε, ἵλεων and indirectly σαυτῷ προσόμοιον (*Ep.* 220.3).

What was the outcome of this trial at appellate level, can only be guessed. As Calliopius became governor of *Macedonia* in 362, it seems that the court case did not impact too much his further career.[160]

A last, interesting letter is *Ep.* 394 (dating to 355), written to a certain Arabius.[161] Litigant in a lawsuit he had to appear in court before Apellio,[162] the governor of Bithynia. Being native of Antioch, the latter was a fellow citizen of Libanius. The *praefectus praetorio Orientis* Strategius Musonianus[163] had appointed Apellio as judge in this lawsuit.[164] Previously Libanius had approached Musonianus for this case.[165] In veiled terms, Libanius affirms to Arabius that Musonianus had made sure that the judge would be on Arabius' side. This letter repeats what Musonianus had previously asked Libanius to do (ἐκέλευσε γράψαι). The last sentence — a carefully crafted passage — suggests that, therefore, Arabius has nothing to fear from the judge.[166] He thus stresses that in both cases (either he is guilty or not guilty) the outcome for Arabius will be positive. The reason for this artful rendering might be that Libanius preferred the truth to be "read between the lines", as he considered that a too open support might be prejudicial to Arabius' interests. Strictly speaking, *Ep.*

[160] Probably in the months subsequent to the trial, Calliopius fell out of imperial grace. As a result, he had to abide this uncomfortable situation until his career perspectives were finally improving. This explains why it was only in 362 that he could only take up another (and more prestigious) office.

[161] *PLRE* I, p. 92.

[162] *PLRE* I, p. 80.

[163] *PLRE* I, p. 611-612.

[164] Τοῦτον γὰρ ἀπέδειξέ σοι δικαστὴν ὁ γενναῖος Στρατήγιος (*Ep.* 394.1) — "The noble Strategius appointed him as a judge for you."

[165] μαθὼν δὲ παρ' ἡμῶν, ὅστις εἴης πρὸς ἡμᾶς, ἐκέλευσε γράψαι, καὶ ὑπήκουσα ἄσμενος νομίζων ἔσεσθαι καὶ σοὶ καὶ τοῖς σοῖς καταφυγὴν τὴν Ἀπελλίωνος γνώμην (*Ep.* 394.2) — "When he (Musonianus) learned from us how was your tie with us, he ordered me to write (to you) and I gladly complied with it, as I thought that the judgement of Apellio would be a refuge for you and your relatives."

[166] περὶ δὲ τῆς δίκης ὡδί σε χρὴ φρονεῖν· εἰ μὲν ἀδικεῖς, οὐδεὶς οὕτως αἰδέσιμος τῷ δικαστῇ, δι' ὃν οὐ δώσεις δίκην· εἰ δὲ παρὰ σοὶ τοῦ δικαίου τὸ μέρος, οὐδεὶς οὕτω σοι δυσμενὴς δυνατός, δι' ὃν οὐ λήψῃ δίκην (*Ep.* 394.3) — "With regard to the trial, you have to understand it in this way: if you are guilty, nobody holds the judge, thanks to whom you will not be punished, in such an awe; if you are right, nobody who is hostile to you, has such a power that you will not receive satisfaction."

394 is not an intervention but a letter confirming that the necessary actions in favour of the recommendee have been taken.[167]

What can be seen from this letters, is that Libanius, just as other late antique epistolographers, used his influence to intervene at various stages of the judicial procedure. Also, when Libanius considered it necessary, he approached more than one person, in order to increase the recommendee's chances.

Conclusion

SB IV 7438 shares several characteristics with recommendation letters from late antique epistolographers. They demonstrate that a judicial intervention was a wide-spread practice in Late Antiquity, since letter writers frequently sent a recommendation with the aim to intervene in a dispute and thus to influence justice. Both *SB* IV 7438 and the late antique recommendations prove that a letter writer could directly approach the judge of the case, as he probably belonged to the letter writer's network.

The intervention could take many forms: the letter writer could support one of the litigant parties, the intercession could also deal with the nature of the case, the competence of the judge or provisions from procedural law. Not only courts of first instance, but also appellate courts could be subject to intervention.

In addition, letter writers regularly approached more than one office holder for the same case, as they considered the power or influence of only one official not sufficient for the intervention to be effective. Also, they used some rhetorical strategies to increase the pressure on the addressee: letter writers referred to a previous intervention (written either by the epistolographer himself or by one of his friends/relatives), or stressed the addressee's ability to assist, or shifted the responsibility to the addressee. On the other hand, short letters lacking any specific feature would imply that the letter writer did not want to engage himself too much. As Gregory's epistolary activity in 382-383 suggests, the effectiveness

[167] Contra LIEBESCHUETZ 1972, p. 195 and *PLRE* I, p. 80, who both consider the document a recommendation letter.

of a particular recommendation might also be influenced by previous letters written by the same epistolographer.

Moreover, it is difficult to gauge to which extent legal knowledge played a (determining) role in the settlement of a dispute. At any rate, Augustine's letters suggest that legal information was not easily accessible.

Finally, the letters give an interesting glimpse of the machinery behind the judicial scene. On the one hand, the letters inform us about the manoeuvres of the intervening party, on the other hand they provide an insight into the actions that the opponent undertook (or intended to undertake), especially — as it emerges from *SB* IV 7438 and other documents pertaining to the same dossier — when the opponent could sway a lot of influence. Often one party acted in reaction to the other party. More in particular, the dossier of Dioscorus indicates that a dispute could last over a certain lapse of time, out of which the intervention letter confers us a particular snapshot.

ROMAN ELEMENTS OF RELIGIOUS DISPUTE RESOLUTIONS IN THE THEODOSIAN AGE*

Luise Marion FRENKEL
(Universidade de São Paulo)

Abstract: In the fourth and fifth centuries, the suitability for dispute resolution of religious leaders such as Christian bishops is mentioned in a range of texts, from discourses highlighting it to rulings circumscribing episcopal legal jurisdiction. These signal their practice of dispute resolution and the relevance of the religious authority of the arbiter. However, these identities are seldom mentioned in legal papyri. Also, the collective decision-making processes described with Roman legal features in the literature and the vast written material to which it refers are not reflected in the papyri. This chapter contextualizes the legal narrative argument inherent to the making of both literary sources and documentary papyri of dispute resolution in the discursive strategies used in Roman legislation, thereby addressing the use and purpose of writings in late antique Egypt. It shows that behind the rhetorical "norm", the organization of the networking in the religious "parallel states", their stability and especially their autonomy in the fourth and fifth centuries were significantly linked to Roman order and thereby cultural fragmentation predominated over regional isolation.

INTRODUCTION

The expectation that bishops should be normal citizens of particular moral and ethical authority, literate, apt orators, and knowledgeable

* The research leading to this study has received the generous support of St Edmund's College (Cambridge), the fellowships at the research group 'Religious individualisation in historical perspective' at the Max Weber Centre for Advanced Cultural and Social Studies, University of Erfurt, funded by the Deutsche Forschungsgemeinschaft (2016-2018) and the University of São Paulo, which granted leaves to pursue research abroad out of term and to take part in the conference in Leuven where these results were first presented. I thank Sofie WAEBENS and Katelijn VANDORPE for their support, and Geoffrey GREATREX, Bernard PALME and the reviewers for insightful comments.

about the administration of their provinces, whose interests they had to defend and advance in all that pertained to Christian life developed gradually and later than the few relevant documents and literary sources suggest. From the sixth century on, there is growing evidence that the society and administration expected them to deal with the internal jurisdiction of their dioceses, and therefore to adjudicate cases on Christian matters, which included, for example, property not only of the church but also of those in holy orders, as well as disturbances provoked by the spread of corrupting ideas. A bishop's decision on such matters was, in principle, only valid for those under his jurisdiction, that is, the Christians in his province. By the seventh century, they are frequently attested being eligible in their provinces as adjudicators, mediators and arbiters, especially if they were known to have legal experience, at least for those who recognized their episcopal authority.[1]

The relevance of the late antique imperial laws on *episcopalis audientia* and the medieval engagement with them decisively shaped the balance between church and state in the Christian world, especially in the West.[2] The interpretation of the laws and of their actual regional implementation are intrinsically connected to the debate about the extent and religious character of Constantine's reforms.[3] His public stance on the validity of bishops' arbitration did not legally endorse an existing practice, but represented a project of an alternative regional court, less corrupt than the governor's. Often dismissed as a well-meant mistake by a naïve

[1] On the issues of the very few papyri that allude to the ecclesiastic rank of the arbiter and suggests that his authority was recognised by the parties see RAPP 2005, p. 242-252 and HARRIES 1999, p. 191-211. See also HUMFRESS 2011 and COOPER 2011, p. 332. ABRAMS REBILLARD 2013, p. 203-204, and SLOOTJES 2011, p. 108, analyse passages which portray Gregory of Nazianzus and Gregory Thaumaturgus, respectively, taking on the responsibilities of a governor.

[2] See FRAKES 2001, p. 207-211. For an overview of the relevant passages and insights of the traditional interpretation, see MAZZA 2015. On the dating of the current text of *Sirmondian Constitution* 1 see VESSEY 2010, p. 195-197. Bearing in mind surveys such as METZGER 2013, p. 27-30, the harmonising interpretation of the literary sources is exemplified by KLEIN 2008, p. 35-40, but further texts minimise their accuracy, as discussed by HARRIES 2011, p. 368-369. See also WIENAND 2012, p. 418-420, and SCHMELZ 2014.

[3] See CORCORAN 2015, p. 86-88, BRYEN 2013, p. 315, and LENSKI 2016, p. 198-199, 335, who despite the evidence in VESSEY 2010, sides with the arguments in HUCK 2003 and HUCK 2008, not considering the compelling analysis in SIRKS 2013 on the falsification of *Sirm.* 1.

legislator, it was part of the rhetorical construction of a (Christian) legislative narrative of a pious and merciful emperor, which is also present in his rulings on reporting acclamations. They project the image of an emperor with an open ear to collective unanimous complaints.[4] A bishop did not have full jurisdiction and could not issue an enforceable sentence against the wish of one party, but he had arbitration. The law made episcopal identity apposite to his rulings, and he had to live up to the expectations about bishops and arbiters.[5]

The decision of groups claimed universal validity by being convincingly cast as a consensus of a representative body, such as a synod in the case of bishops. In the handing over of records of social control, such as univocal voicing of collective opinion and acclamations, the responsibility for arbitration shifted from individuals respected by a group to the association. The narrative representation of the dispute was decisive for the recognition of its resolution.[6] The arbitration could be expressed in a number of formats, from rumor and oratory to letters and, ultimately, synodical proceedings. Therefore, not only papyri, but also literary texts about dispute resolution which refer to the religious identity of the protagonists have been considered evidence of the authority of religious leaders to issue enforceable sentences on financial, moral, liturgical and theological issues.

In the context of the dynamics between Theodosian administrative and religious processes of institutionalization, the literary sources of dispute resolutions in which the religious identity matters for the resolution cannot be corroborated. This will be discussed in the first section, before turning to the at best highly tenuous evidence offered by contemporary fourth- and fifth-century papyri. It is also argued that both this material and the textual evidence have didactic and epideictic dimensions which were decisive for their survival.[7]

4 See DILLON 2012, chapter 5, nuancing the effectiveness of imperial legislation or synodical decisions in defining administrative and episcopal powers of adjudication; also see WEISWEILER 2017, p. 164, and on an earlier use of legislation for communicative purposes, see SCHMIDT-HOFNER 2015, p. 98.

5 See UHALDE 2012, p. 777-778, HARRIES 1999, HUCK 2003, p. 80-81, COOPER 2011, p. 342, CONNOLLY 2010, p. 10-12, and SIRKS 2013.

6 See STOLTE 2001, p. 172-173.

7 See PALACIOS 2009 and HUMFRESS 2013b.

1. (Institutionalized?) episcopal dispute resolution

Are the *Sacrorum Conciliorum Nova Amplissima Collectio* and the philologically improved and growing *Acta conciliorum oecumenicorum* series trustworthy accounts of what happened in the early councils and of proceedings of Christian dispute resolution? For most historians and classicists, the answer is obviously positive.[8] They fit well with the expectation that in the mid-fifth century churches were hierarchical institutions with full-time positions and shared patterns for religious, civil, political and military rituals. The modern editions by Mansi, Schwartz e.a. contributed to give to the patterns attested in the Cyrillian *acta* of their sessions in Ephesus in 431 a foundational status and a teleological perspective to its seeming replication in the documentation of the Councils of Ephesus 449 and Chalcedon 451, as if it had worked to start with and then become standard. Complaints of forgery in the *acta* of Ephesus 449, the disputed or ignored authority of councils such as Ephesus 431 and Chalcedon during the fifth century,[9] and the ongoing variety of conciliar proceedings and documentation in the sixth and seventh centuries[10] clearly show that the format of the Cyrillian sessions in 431 was not a widely acknowledged valid pattern that lent itself authority.

Even with these caveats it seems natural to identify the proceedings contained in these editions with the writings sent by synods or their members, such as mentioned for example in the letter of the Cyrillians to the emperors,[11] and to take it for granted that fifth-century synods and councils were like courts and hearings following institutionalized traditions, issuing proceedings and other texts which convey reliable historical information about the period and preserve exact words, opinions, and practices. The narratives in the *acta* do not reflect the events straightforwardly, and the function of the proceedings as written object is not clear.[12] The product of their later redaction gives the impression of

---

[8] It is, for example, mentioned in Ando 2012, p. 229 and Weckwerth 2010, p. 4-5. See however Frenkel 2017, and Fournet 2010a.

[9] See Bevan 2016, p. 271-279 and Price & Graumann 2020, p. 84.

[10] See Lamberz 2016, p. XVI-XIX, van Minnen 2006 and Humfress 2016.

[11] *Relatio Cyrillianorum ad Theodosium et Valentinianum imperatores* (CPG 8697), Collectio Vaticana 81, ACO, I, 1/3, p. 3-5.

[12] Stenography was an argument for the accuracy and truthfulness, *ergo*, reliability and authority, of the (edited) text of proceedings, dialogues, meetings, and all references to it

having been written down as evidence, testimony and proof. Accepting it is to misunderstand the nature of the late antique collections and codices from which ultimately depend the Latin or Greek medieval or Byzantine sources of the printed editions, with proceedings, synodical letters and canons juxtaposed to an array of documents sometimes only vaguely related to the proceedings.[13]

Like most sources of Roman Law, these texts were not made *ad hoc* but "followed tried and tested formulae in which every word was fixed",[14] not because proceedings were stiff, but for the sake of the authority of the record.[15] At the stage of compilation, in being attached to other documents or bound in codices, the texts assumed their current shape, absorbing and crafting information about written proofs where it was or could be presumed to have been available.[16] Written proof of collective resolution of disputes are as numerous in the literature as they are rare in the papyri or other support an Egyptian or south European scribe would be handling,[17] Instead of such material evidence most remaining

cannot be proved. See PALME 2015, p. 5, n. 6, YIFTACH-FIRANKO 2014, p. 7, COLES 1966, p. 17, 36. For the compilers of the Syriac hagiographical *Life of Barsauma*, personal sealing of a document by the emperor was also relevant and plausible, betraying their limited knowledge of Theodosian legal practice. See CORCORAN 2016. See also RÜPKE & DEGELMANN 2015 and MOSCOVITZ 2003.

[13] See, for example, HUMFRESS 2007a, DUNN 2015 and HARRIES 2016. On the range of writings that can be called legal commentaries, see BRYEN 2013, p. 358, and KROPPENBERG 2016.

[14] WOLF 2015, p. 64.

[15] See BRANDES 2014 and WHITBY 2013.

[16] The transformations of the format at their redaction and compilation correspond to a shift away from epigraphic monumentalisation of Roman Law. The reading aloud gained more relevance and greater attention was given to the production of manuscript copies, attested in Roman legislation and especially in hagiographic and Rabbinic literature on the respect due to the reading of imperial communications. See ROWE 2014, p. 299-300, and FRENKEL 2020, p. 169-171. They affect the content by the mechanisms of decontextualisation and recontextualisation intrinsic to processes of entextualisation and textualisation, which have received significant attention in communication theory and anthropological studies. Especially the former is relevant, with minor adaptations, to the legal writings of late antique Egypt. See URBAN 1996 and MORALES 2016, p. 70.

[17] For example, the carefully packed wicker basket of tablets from Puteoli or the monastic archives. See WOLF 2015, p. 74, JAKAB 2013, p. 128-130, ADAMS 2016, p. 210-220, MANTOVANI 2016, p. 28-29, HAENSCH 2013, LAMBERZ 2010, PALME 2009 and BAGNALL 2009, p. 51. On the monastic dossiers of Deir el-Naqlun, Bawit, Wadi Sarga, and Deir el-Bala'izah, see WEGNER 2017, p. 10-11.

texts are bound in codices, such as *Parisinus latinus* 8907 or the presumed prototype of codex *Ambrosianus* 235 D51 Sup., and have gained an aura of precious remains.[18]

Parisinus latinus 8907, a fifth-century copy of the Acts of the Council of Aquileia of 381, is a key piece of evidence, since the 'Arian *scholia*' it contains are probably Maximinus' autograph marginal notes. He undertook a defense of Palladius on two fronts, addressing the flaws in the theological argumentation and in the written evidence. For that, he adduced what ought to have been or should be presented to counter those proceedings.[19] It is not a script for a retrial, such as Chalcedon was in relation to Ephesus 449, but a scholarly engagement.[20] It establishes a dialogue, as known from the polemical literature in the form of refutations of florilegia and mostly fictitious dialogues.[21] Paraphrasing Joseph Georg Wolf on the literature of this period,[22] and calling 'Christian jurists' those in charge of writing documents such as the synodical *acta*, the texts now considered evidence for Christian dispute resolution were a scholarly literature, written by Christian jurists for Christian jurists. Even when they drew their material from practice, this is not conclusive about the actual application of dispute resolution by those whose authority derived from their Christian religious or ecclesial position, or about its effectiveness in everyday life. Quite the contrary. The *scholia* show the engagement with the actions, sayings and ideas which could be linked to the characters, whose social position or memory could be attacked or defended.

---

18 See TETZ 1990, p. 84-86.

19 See MCLYNN 1996 and with care TESTA 2013. See also BAMMEL 1984 and especially GRYSON 1984.

20 On late antique Christian scholarship see GRAFTON & WILLIAMS 2006, p. 206, LÖSSL & WATT 2011 and CHITWOOD 2017, p. 152-162. See also HAENSCH 2013, STOLTE 2014, p. 65-66, PALME 2015 and HEZSER 2002, p. 173-178.

21 See CAMERON 1991, HEZSER 2007, VAN NUFFELEN 2014, MACÉ 2015, GRAUMANN 2015. On *catenæ*, see BANDT forthcoming.

22 See WOLF 2015, p. 61.

1.1. *Written proofs*

In 449, several bishops met in Ephesus for a synod under imperial auspices. At one point, Dioscorus, bishop of Alexandria, invited three bishops to report the proceedings against Ibas of Edessa which they had witnessed. In the *acta*, in its Syriac translation,[23] this is followed by one discourse as if by all three together, describing the deposition of a complaint against him, accepted despite the absence of witnesses, hindered by the distance to Edessa. The bishops had commanded the clerics of Edessa to swear on the Scriptures not to keep anything back about the many things circulating in that city. The complaints were, so the bishops say, the denunciations of all those named in the proceedings, which the emperor had also accepted, since they were acclamations and they had written proof that the hyparch had reported them. Since the emperor had accepted the witnesses, the record should be read. They had already deposed Daniel of Harran against whom accusations had also been made. Ibas, so their narrative goes, had then published writings, which were at hand at the sessions, and the three bishops suggested that these should be used to decide. Finally, the three bishops claim that, since they had presented all this written material, they could not be accused of having kept anything back. In the *acta* this is followed by the intervention of Cyrus of Aphrodisias, who proposed that the matters concerning Ibas should be finished first, and that if the assembly saw it fitting, the records (ὑπομνήματα) should be read. After this narrative connector, a reader of the *acta* of 449 finds a letter of the hyparch, excusing, with reference to duty, the disturbing content which is embedded in a dramatic scene in which he is seized by a crowd and taken to witness the protests of an even larger crowd.[24] Finally, the reader finds the popular acclamations against Ibas in April 449 embedded in all these layers which reinforce the uniqueness and reliability of that piece of writing.

The passage from the *acta* of 449 epitomizes the abundant references to written proofs, the ability of upright characters to have them readily available and, therefore, the profusion of material apparently archived by the holders of imperial and ecclesiastic jurisdiction in major sees. However, letters and canon lists, florilegia and statements of faith were types

---

[23] FLEMMING e.a. 1917, p. 14-55.

[24] On this scene and the presumed social context of the acclamations, see RAMMELT 2013. On acclamations in conciliar proceedings, see FRENKEL 2016 and FORNESS 2020.

of texts with which Christians registered the decisions, but not the proceedings, of their dispute resolutions. *Acta* provided written proof of the decision-making procedures in dispute resolutions adequate to be assessed and upheld by criteria which went beyond the religious and ecclesial values acknowledged by the parties. Their development of the discursive strategies of the fourth- and fifth-centuries synodical and conciliar *acta* shows that the 'rhetorical norms' that lent validity to the claims of the narratives about Christian dispute resolutions and other individual or collective proceedings which issued enforceable sentences were flexible.[25]

The authority and reliability of narratives on liturgies, calendars and proceedings came partially from making rituals seem like realizations of endorsed traditions even when the accounts had no referent in reality.[26] Traditions developed orally too, influencing and adapting to the texts which in their turn reflect the circumstances of redaction and transmission. In this regard, scholarship on Christian arbitration can draw important insights from Rabbinic writings of dispute resolutions, with which it can be correlated in many respects and for which the preliminary and parallel existence of oral narratives is clearer.[27] They too show features of Roman jurisdiction, legislation and dispute resolution and the influence of Roman rhetoric, without — with a few exceptions — having from the start envisaged Roman scrutiny. The trustworthiness of the author and of the represented characters contributed too, being informed by their previous reputation and the content of the texts or passages in them, nuancing them. Their acceptance depended on this combination.

1.2. *An army of experts?*

An army of expert stenographers, scribes and editors would have had to be at the disposal of the bishops on a daily basis, to register and copy *ad hoc* petitions and reports if all was as well documented in late antique sees as implied in Cyril's letters on the *aitia* of the controversy with Nestorius,[28] and as portrayed in the reports from Edessa. Probably closer

[25] See GRAUMANN 2020, p. 20-22 and CAMPLANI 2018, p. 253-265.

[26] On the narrative as an inextricable element of the legal system of the Roman Empire, and the 'legal' character of didactic elements, see BRYEN 2014, p. 352-355.

[27] See WIMPFHEIMER 2011, chapter 3.

[28] See GRAUMANN 2004, p. 228, and WESSEL 2004, p. 76-78.

to the actual use and purpose of writings are narratives which cast them not as documents but as pamphlets, as seen in a sequence of denunciations and petitions of the Nestorian controversy.

Like Cyril's prequel narrative of monks upset with the ideas in Nestorius' writings which were circulating in Egypt, after the council of Ephesus 431, a monk Vitalis[29] addressed Theodotus of Ancyra, a Cyrillian, with analogous complaints against spreading ideas and writings of a bishop, Eutherius of Tyana, who, though deposed in 432 by Nestorius' successor, remained for several years in his see with local support. Now, against Theodotus, John of Antioch wrote to the *praefectus praetorio orientis* Antiochus Chuzon, requesting measures to curb his slander.[30] The internal narrative of these texts may point to written proofs, but suggests by itself that only few copies circulated, possibly as the hypothetical anchor of the oral transmission from which it cannot be dissociated.

John of Antioch's letter differs in its matter-of-fact style without trope-like motifs such as generic monks' complaints and the promise of written proofs. His is not a literary text offering a historiography also or primarily to the implied public of the edited text, as in the case of Cyril, who at the start of the controversy, also was writing to the imperial administration. John resorted to the *praefectus* responsible for the region, with whom he had both political and religious affinities, asking for intercession at the imperial court if he could not solve the issue alone. The relevant imperial authority to deal with tensions across provincial boundaries, as in Cyril's protests against Nestorius of Constantinople, was the imperial court. Thus, Cyril's and John of Antioch's letters requesting the endorsement of only their synod and the formal condemnation of at least the leaders of the other party were addressed to Theodosius II. He had to be persuaded of the validity of the case and moved to convert it into formal measures.

The success of a search for endorsement was more obvious if the resulting imperial measure reflected the terms of the request, which had

---

[29] *Pars, <epistulae> Theodoti Ancyrae ad Vitalem monachum Cappadocem* (CPG 6130), Collectio Casinensis 289, ACO I, 4, p. 212, 10-19.

[30] *Epistula Iohannis Antiocheni ad Antiochum praef. praet.* (CPG 8764), Collectio Casinensis 127, ACO I, 4, p. 79-80. On Maximian's deposition of Eutherius, the involvement of imperial and Christian leaders in failed attempts to enthrone a successor and his exile, see FRENKEL 2015, p. 87-88, and on John of Antioch's letter, see ead. 2014, p. 263-266.

therefore to be expressed with imperial rhetoric.[31] A narrative of dispute resolution would then seem a valid precedent, possibly for unregulated cases. Thus, such accounts are historiographically causative of subsequent developments, but the nexus is generally not historical. Complaints uttered by monks, if possible voicing unisonous discourses or even acclamations, and the promise of written proofs were discursive strategies which gave weight to accusations, but were ultimately only rhetoric. Its persuasiveness relied on the reputation of the writer and the credibility of his account of imperial involvement in the controversy built on a number of pieces of narratives that created a chain of events and portraits.

The letters contributed to the image attached to their authors and characters. They associate John with elite and erudite legal experts, and Cyril with the 'common' Christian. Having gradually become the 'received' version with narratives taken to register real events, the Cyrillian account informed decisively modern perception of the motivations and actions of the others. Organised with hindsight, the collections seem aligned with post-433 Theodosian imperial rhetoric, reflecting its reception in Justinianic and later agendas.[32] However, in the fifth and sixth centuries, the Cyrillian account coexisted with written and oral stories which were equally retrospective accounts and redacted with full awareness of the outcome. For example, the *Bazaar of Heracleides* presented an alternative etiology of the council, describing it as Cyril's plot, historiographically creating a mesh of causative relations in which the main protagonists are office holders in the Roman or Christian administration.[33]

It is now widely accepted that papyri of dispute resolution may but need not have been preserved because of their legal function, but rather as historiographical, hagiographical or didactic literature, possibly relying on oral traditions.[34] Such a cultural and religious value of proceedings of dispute resolution can be seen also in literary texts. For example, the late

---

[31] See HARRIES 2013, p. 61, and compare with similar conclusions from epigraphical sources in KOKKINIA 2014, p. 193. Petitioners instructing the officials are discussed by CONNOLLY 2010, p. 113.

[32] See PRICE & GRAUMANN 2020, p. 5-15, showing that the earliest possible dates for the Latin and Greek collections are the sixth and seventh centuries, respectively.

[33] See BEVAN 2016, p. 310-330.

[34] See PAPACONSTANTINOU 2020, p. 19-21, RICHTER 2005, p. 254-258, and SCHENKE 2016, p. 511.

antique transmission of Origen's works shows the redaction of unhistorical legal proceedings and the contribution of narratives of dispute resolution to the development of his reputation. While the evidence for third and fourth-century copying of his works is very small, the *spuria* are literary texts which point to the reduced demands on factuality. For example, in the sixth or seventh-century Tura and Egerton papyri,[35] the scene of the *Disputation between Origen and Heraclides* is set with a paragraph claiming that all bishops had made their remarks and put forward their questions about Heraclides' profession of faith. After a couple of pages of brief exchanges, the fiction drops and Origen's monologues allow longer expositions. The theological content was decisive for the copying, as in the case of the Arian *scholia* in *Parisinus latinus* 8907 of the Acts of Aquileia, or collections of letters by the like of Theodoret and Maximus.[36]

The Tura papyri attest to the scholarly engagement with Origen's works even after repeated condemnation of his writings.[37] The scribe registered his controversial reputation in the dialogue between main matter and marginalia, with a cautious and ambiguous note on his eminence and orthodoxy.[38] However, the partisan or antagonistic public could also draw important biographical information about Origen from the narrative content. Alongside oral traditions, the papyri and other writings contributed to the construction of Origen's legacy, and his status as archetype arbiter in dispute resolutions. Whether authored, authentic or spurious, they were didactic, mingling narrative information about the characters with particulars about the ideas being discussed which could help to convince the readership or audience to accept them as part of their received opinion about the characters.

The next session shows how fourth- and fifth-century documentary papyri on legal matters also could serve as material and narrative token, shaping the reputation of known characters or being instructive on the handling and writing of legal scenarios. It argues that insofar as the papyri

[35] See YUEN-COLLINGRIDGE 2010.

[36] See SCHOR 2017 and JANKOWIAK & BOOTH 2015.

[37] On the tenuous evidence of widespread acceptance of the condemnation see, for example, PERCZEL 2015, p. 227-230.

[38] On the annotation on the lower margin of Cairo, Egyptian Museum inv. no. JdE 88747 + 88748 (TM 62347), p. 8, see YUEN-COLLINGRIDGE 2010, p. 44.

had a didactic function on methodology, it was not for carrying out dispute resolutions that might be referred to the imperial administration, but for writing about them.[39] The narrative context in them is as apposite to late antique legal practice of bishops in Egypt or elsewhere as Quintilian and Ps-Quintilian *Declamationes* were to imperial Roman jurisdiction and arbitration. The atemporal scenario with discursive and legal information from all times concocted in them depended literarily on received opinions about the works and lives of the authors and characters, contributing to shape them further.[40]

2. Christian and episcopal identity in papyri of dispute resolutions

From the fourth century on, a growing proportion of the presbyters and especially of the bishops counted among the 'elders' and other affluent well-educated men involved in dispute resolutions leading to the social dynamics well attested in Coptic papyri and Syriac manuscripts from the sixth century on. This reflected the consolidation of the expectation that it was fitting that bishops should keep such moral, ethical and religious qualities which would have made them prime candidates as arbiters.[41] However, this is poorly attested in the fourth- and fifth-century material, in which the values advanced in ancient literary works are hardly present in the narratives, and the characters rather challenge modern expectations.[42]

If from the sixth century on a considerable number of documents illustrate bishops as mediators in conflicts of their flock, especially in largely rural areas with many villages, some small towns, no city of higher

---

[39] On similar aspects of Rabbinic texts and the oral development of the traditions, see Hezser 1998, Simon-Shoshan 2012, p. 97-99, and Fraade 2014, p. 348-349, and the case-study in Ilan 2012, p. 266-267.

[40] On chronological and regional variation in processes of textualisation and interaction with Roman law, see Fishman 2011, p. 45-50, and Novick 2013.

[41] For example, the fourth-century *P. Oxy.* VI 903 (TM 33342), on which see Bryen 2013, p. 105-108, 273-274. On *P. Lond.* I 77 (TM 39851) as an example of the papyri providing growing evidence of illiteracy in Greek, see Richter 2014, p. 139.

[42] The narratives are described and analysed by Harries 1999, p. 181-185, and Rapp 2005. Bryen 2013 and Schmelz 2014 discuss several further literary and legal tropes.

administrative status and a considerable presence of Christian leaders or institutions — as was the case in West-Thebes[43] —, relatively few references to the Christian and episcopal identity of the arbiters can be found in earlier papyri. These are usually embedded in complex and idiosyncratic scenarios, which suggests that the religious identity of the arbiter was not a trope, rather, linked to the situations which can be interpreted as being of internal jurisdiction or informal dispute resolution. However, even then the ecclesiastical identity of one or more of the protagonists is not at the centre of his decision-making authority. Moreover, the implementation and validity of the decisions is not clear.

It is the case of *P. Lips.* I 43 (TM 33702), from Hermopolis, which describes a dispute about property between a nun and tenants on which a bishop Plousianos issues an order. According to the text, the bishop's authority justifies (morally) the nun's access to property, and (fiscally) the tenant's relinquishing it. It also casts the virtues of Plousianos, who follows a judgment of Solomon.

Even if the religious identity of the arbiter or court influenced the choice of dispute resolution, 'religious identity' was not (yet) part of the repertory of 'forms' of Roman legal documents and therefore not conducive to the argument. Rather, it could unnecessarily introduce conflicts with legislation. Thus, the invisibility in the 'sources' of Christian identity, which cannot be taken for granted in the religiously very diverse context, ought to be related to the nature and purpose of the writings. Since legal papyri were largely purpose-driven, complex underlying narratives which point to redaction and edition suggest that these papyri were envisaged for further legal or not purposes,[44] such as written evidence of a precedent, epideictic or didactic texts.[45] Even then, references to religious identity are not prominent, possibly because they would not be lifelike.

For example, *SB* III 7033 (TM 17370) contains details of the dispute involving four clerics of a church, which the deacon Theophilus raised and won against his bishop Cyrus and his brothers, two priests. The

---

[43] See BERKES 2017a, p. 195-200.

[44] See HARRIES 1999, p. 70-77.

[45] On papyrus as (material) token of an honour, lastingly conveyed by the texts on the *laudandus*'s merits, actions, or relation to powerful and erudite people, see KRUSE 2013, p. 322-324, FRENKEL 2016, p. 205-209.

papyrus confirms that bishops could, *qua* private persons, be the object of suits and denunciations, and not only be antagonized by cities and religious groups *qua* bishops.[46] By its narrative, the papyrus was a material (and written) proof of a proceeding lest any party, for example, anyone on behalf of the bishop, should attempt to take Theophilus, the winning accuser, to court. The last lines describe the penalty to be exacted on anyone disputing that the agreement ended the dispute. They echo the threats to guarantee the integrity of curse-tablets and magical written objects.[47]

The moral authority of Cyrus would have been harmed by the arbitration since the suit was not kept among the interested parties but was to a smaller or greater extent public. Countering this, the narrative casts him in an ambiguous light, since it also details that he made up for any harm incurred by generously refunding the third parties who had unknowingly become illicit owners of a large number of quite luxurious garments of which they had been deprived in the course of the dispute. In a reception of this papyrus beyond the court case which may have led to its creation, a late antique reader or audience, probably unacquainted with the protagonists, would get from this small novel a moral tale about ecclesiastic hierarchy and the fallible nature of bishops and what they could do to remedy cases of mismanagement and corruption, which were frequent in accusations recurrently placed in the mouth of the people.[48] The narrative would be a warning especially for endowed readerships that financial misconduct might elicit popular dissatisfaction that could lead to the deposition of a religious authority, here typified by the bishop. It challenges the literary ideals of bishops as ideal arbiters or holders of full jurisdiction, by ascribing to Cyrus moral and civic faults. In legal proceedings presented to the imperial administration, such accusations

---

[46] On violence against bishops, see SIZGORICH 2009, p. 132-143, SARRIS e.a. 2011, p. 72-75, DRAKE 2013, VAN NUFFELEN & HILKENS 2013, and various chapters in MAYER & NEIL 2013 and HILLNER e.a. 2016, by Fournier, Dunn and especially by Allen.

[47] See GORDON 2015, 149 and MEYER 2004, 101.

[48] See, for example, RAMMELT 2013, WIEMER 2014 and MATTHEIS 2014 on the accusations of mismanagement of ecclesiastic property and of improper behaviour against Ibas, his brother Eusebius and an Eulogius in the acclamations in Edessa in 449. On the identity of the 'people' and the identification with traditions, see ZUCKERMAN 2000, p. 78, 87.

were weightier than, for example, theological denunciations.[49] However, even when denigrating a particular bishop, the papyrus was not reducing the scope of episcopal authority or suitability to arbitrate, quite the contrary. Snapping it from the (particular) aim of invective for the (generic) interest of bishops, it was reinforcing the notion that money and violence should arguably not even be of concern to Christian religious authorities, an idea which was gaining prominence in the institutionalized church, regardless of the ongoing religious and social diversity, and the economic relevance of many sees and monasteries.[50]

Faults of character are present in most of the papyri attesting episcopal dispute resolution. They are particularly prominent in the lively narrative of the violence of *P. Lond.* inv. no. 2217 (TM 35117).[51] Challenging readers to reconstruct the underlying dispute, the papyri could instruct, reinforcing a conventional narrative and rhetorical turns of phrases, useful in epideictic discourses or in documents addressed to the Roman administration, probably more than in actual dispute resolution, for which matter-of-fact texts, such as John of Antioch's or Isidore of Pellusium's letters, sufficed.

Concluding remarks

The analysis of the representative examples above showed that narratives of dispute resolution within religious groups allegedly written during the Theodosian Age contain scenes, turns of phrases and expressions characteristic of contemporary accounts of Roman legal procedure. They point to religious hierarchies similar to Roman structures of authority, and associate an increased awareness of Roman institutions and regulations with a monk's, bishop's or rabbi's greater authority to arbitrate.

---

[49] Faults of character are prominent in the synodical sentence of deposition of Nestorius (ACO, I, 1/2, 54), for example. On the idealising *topos* of what the provincials wished of an arbiter, and the prestige associated to the role, see MEYER 2006, p. 178-180.

[50] See GAUTHIER 2000, VOLPE 2007 and BLAUDEAU 2009.

[51] *SB* IV 7449 (TM 35117) denounces a monk to Apa Theodorus, bishop of Oxyrhynchus, and is signed by a relative of the monk. The narrative is unfolded in RAPP 2005, p. 247-248, and provides evidence for the analysis of the plural legal system of Roman Egypt in BRYEN 2013, p. 141, 315.

The prominence given in Christian polemical literature to documents, stenography or letter writing and to a habit of having miscellaneous problems in the diocese being brought to its attention is not paralleled in the juristic papyri, nor are the numerous mentions of varied written proofs reflected in the material and archaeological evidence.

Insofar as Cyril's and John of Antioch's letters are not only the result of authorial or posthumous later edition, they show the authors using shared 'discursive norms' that make their arguments relevant for imperial authority to deal with them and reusable as written proofs that could stand the scrutiny of Roman (or Persian) legal practice. A part of that paid heed to the on-going late antique cultural fragmentation which instead of leading to regional isolation envisaged, at least on a narrative level, the possibility of being taken to the attention of central political or legislative courts. Religious dispute resolution was not 'out' of the Roman legal environment, but 'in', as one of many in the bazaar that was not self-contained, but determined case by case, moment by moment, with the alternative of resorting to a Roman Empire always ready at hand, so that it was often convenient to have it expressed in the ways acknowledged by the Roman legal and administrative structures.[52] That required an expertise which was projected textually in the engagement with scholarly works, such as the thematic codices drawing from various sources, including narratives of disputes and dispute resolutions, such as the letters and proceedings of conciliar *acta*. The 'norms' were, however, the same also from Christian perspectives and thus narratives apparently made 'for the administration' were or became 'for internal use'.

The statements or stories told about Origen, Cyril, Nestorius and Theodorus[53] were once considered reliable information about them. The autographs, such as the Arian *scholia*, point towards a literary activity akin to the redaction of legal codes as political endeavors which were locally rewritten. In the practice and, sometimes, on the paper, they created for 'internal use' texts which convincingly seemed to be written proofs, such as the *Sirmondian Constitution* 1, of 331/3 in Visigoth or after 506 Merovingian Gaul, and the fictitious narrative of the Coptic Acts of Ephesus 431, in later Greek or Coptic Egypt, which, like the 'sources' on

[52] See HUMFRESS 2013a, p. 240, ANDO 2015, p. 55, BRYEN 2016, p. 20-21, WEISWEILER 2017, p. 164-166. TUORI 2007, p. 41-43 and DOHRMANN 2015 discuss relevant test cases.

[53] Bishop Apa Theodorus in papyrus *SB* IV 7449.

Origen of *P. Egert.* 2 (TM 62337), show the ongoing relevance of the Roman legal rhetoric in the narrative expression of Christian dispute resolution. Legal papyri and stories of dispute resolution reflect the growing use of durable media to convey narratives and practices showing regional differences, possible by the cultural diversity which gradually became fragmentation when the engagement with a common denominator, in the form of imperial rhetoric and Roman Law, abated. During the Theodosian period, the use of Latin or Greek for legal documents, and the communication across the empire attested in letters, spread of writings, travel, exile and migration prevents attributing the production of the diverse and sometimes irreconcilable cultural expressions of dispute resolution to regional isolation.

HOLY MEN, ROMAN LEGAL PRACTICE, AND SOCIAL MEMORY IN LATE ANTIQUE EGYPT

Nicholas VENABLE
(University of Chicago)

Abstract: The Christianization of Egypt generated significant social change, such as conflict between Christians and non-Christians as well as the emergence of monks and clergy as new figures of authority. However, when Egyptian clerics handled legal disputes, they frequently acted through Roman officials or used methods of reproducing social memory originating in Roman legal practice. This chapter examines evidence for the involvement of clergy in legal disputes in both Coptic hagiography, such as the *Life of Shenoute* and *Panegyric of Macarius of Tkow*, and Late Antique papyrus documents, such as letters and petitions addressed to monks and *dialysis* documents where they served as arbiters. Using these two different types of evidence will allow the chapter to address this historical problem at the level of both discourse and practice. Egyptian holy men often conceded to Roman officials a legitimate monopoly over the authorization of social violence, and they acknowledged Roman document forms and methods of memory reproduction as legitimate mechanisms for producing social knowledge, even in polemical texts where the motives of Roman magistrates were called into question. This appeal to particular Roman norms highlights effects of the Roman imperial legal regime in Egypt that lasted into the eighth century.

INTRODUCTION

> This lawless transgressor, Ammonius, drank a sea of wine in the night season, toward morning, and descended upon me in those hours with the son of Penson and his servant. They left me no resemblance of myself, neither foot nor hand being without some disfigurement. I beseech you...[1]

A scholar of Roman Egypt might read this text and assume that it represents an excerpt from an AD first- or second-century petition to an imperial official with the power to pass judgment enforceable under

[1] *O. Mich. Copt.* 4, l. 12-23 (TM 84284). WORRELL 1942 translation.

Roman law. Indeed, it could easily be one of the 135 petitions translated in an appendix to Ari Bryen's monograph on *Violence in Roman Egypt.* Its familiar rhetoric describes a defendant who is violent and intoxicated, a "lawless transgressor" who is a threat to the proper functioning of the imperial order. The plaintiff's description of his own physical injuries parallels what Bryen called "a discourse of wounded bodies, and in particular, bodies with wounds that were publicly visible".[2] This is precisely the sort of language consonant with the self-definition of Roman rule as being responsive to such accusations of injustice and to claims based on the abstract rights held by its citizens.

However, this is not a translation of a first-century Greek papyrus addressed to the prefect of Egypt. Rather, it is a Coptic ostracon addressed to an ecclesiastic, dated to the seventh century on the basis of paleography. In this century, Byzantine imperial control of Egypt became extremely tenuous for a few decades, and was eventually destroyed by Persian and later Islamic conquerors. Unlike a first-century petition, this later petition is prefaced by florid, pious language incorporating tropes from the epistolary books of the New Testament to which I will return when I examine it more closely later in this chapter. But despite the decline of the Byzantine imperial administration between AD 400 and 700 and the sharp drop in the number of petitions submitted to imperial officials during this time,[3] the language and basic form of this letter still resembles that of earlier Roman petitions. It represents only one example of how the language and forms of Roman law were invoked as late as the ninth century in the literary and documentary sources of Late Antique Egypt.

This chapter argues that the social prestige of Roman legal forms and practices in Egypt persisted beyond the decline of imperial rule, as reflected by the ways in which Christian clergy and monastics resolved legal disputes in Egypt during the fifth and sixth centuries AD. I will focus especially on a corpus of saints' lives written in the period after the Council of Chalcedon and the subsequent enforcement of its doctrinal position, which caused significant theological conflict between religious communities in Egypt, as well as conflict between monophysite Christians and imperial officials accused of corruption and heresy.

---

[2] BRYEN 2013, p. 120.

[3] KELLY 2011, p. 23-24.

I begin by charting the continued use of Roman legal practices in a corpus of hagiography written in reaction to the Council of Chalcedon.[4] At the level of discourse, even those religious texts composed in monophysite monasteries continued to acknowledge the legitimacy of Roman practices for recording legal agreements, producing social knowledge, and conducting and recording legal proceedings — even as other texts produced in these monasteries criticized imperial officials. I then examine the documentary evidence for the involvement of clergy and monks in petitions and arbitration in this period. By considering this evidence in conjunction with existing studies of petitioning in Roman Egypt, I demonstrate that Egyptian clergy inserted themselves into the legal institutions of Late Antique Egypt, while still respecting the logic of those institutions and the rights of imperial subjects to seek recourse through these legal processes. The persistence of Roman legal forms in the discourse and practice of Late Antique Egyptian Christianity suggests that Roman legal institutions continued to represent the dominant cultural archetype for dispute resolution. Furthermore, the consistent recourse of monks and clergy to the structure of Greco-Roman legal documents suggests that they considered Roman forms to be the legitimate mechanisms for producing this kind of social knowledge.

1. Hagiographical corpus

The late-fourth/early fifth-century hagiographical fragment *Life of Aaron* depicts an episode that resembles the informal forms of arbitration recorded in documentary papyri. Like *Vitae* quoted later in this chapter, it was composed in a monastic context.[5] The episode involves a dispute over a debt owed by a poor man to a rich man. The poor man comes to Aaron saying:

> There is a certain rich man in my city whom I owe ten *obeli*, and I cannot get the money to pay him. I have begged him, "Be patient with me and I will repay you." But he would not agree to this and has seized me for what I owe him. He wants to take from me my vineyard which I inherited from my parents and from which I make a small profit, enough for my poor

[4] For a general introduction to this corpus, see JOHNSON 1986, p. 216-234.

[5] VIVIAN 1993, p. 54.

> children and me to live on. I am paying him the interest I owe him. I beg you, your Holiness, to send a message to him to ease up on me, for someone from his household told me, "He's going to press you for the principal and haul you (into court) so he can take away your vineyard." (ϥⲛⲁⲧ ⲁⲛⲁⲅⲕⲏ ⲉⲣⲟⲕ ⲉⲧⲃⲉ ⲡⲕⲁⲓⲫⲁⲗⲓⲟⲛ (= κεφάλαιον) ϥⲛⲁⲧⲣⲕ̄ϩⲱϣ[6] ⲛⲅ̄ⲁⲡⲟⲧⲁⲥⲥⲉ (= ἀποτάσσω) ⲙⲡⲉⲕⲙⲁ ⲛ ⲉⲗⲟⲟⲗⲉ) But I believe if you were to send a message he would not refuse to listen to you.[7]

The poor man initially asks Aaron to petition the rich man on his behalf, asking him twice to "send a message", a form of intervention similar to that practiced by other holy men. Since it is the rich man's threat of legal action that prompts the poor man to turn to Aaron, he appears not to be anticipating an in-person arbitration, but to expect Aaron to act as a protector of the poor from oppression through the legal system, like other holy men of this period.

The rich man is subsequently struck blind and comes to Aaron for help, allowing the holy man to arbitrate in person between the two. While the fragment does not record the usual statement that both parties would abide by the decision of the arbiter, this constraint is effectively imposed by the suggestion that the rich man risks lifelong blindness if he does not reconcile himself with the poor man. The episode continues:

> The holy man said to him, "If you show mercy to the poor man, Christ himself will heal you." The rich man called one of those who had come with him, and he took the loan agreement from him and gave it to the righteous man Abba Aaron. (ⲁϥⲙⲟⲩⲧⲉ ⲉⲟⲩⲁ ⲛ̄ⲛⲉⲧⲙⲟⲟϣⲉ ⲛⲙ̄ⲙⲁϥ ⲁϥϫⲓ ⲙⲡⲉⲕⲣⲁⲙⲙⲁⲧⲟⲛ (= γραμματεῖον) ⲛ̄ⲧⲟⲟⲧϥ̄ ⲁϥⲧⲁⲁϥ ⲙⲡⲇⲓⲕⲁⲓⲟⲥ ⲁⲡⲁ ϩⲁⲣⲟⲛ) The holy man Abba Aaron said to him "[If you give wages to the poor man]/in this world, God will give you your wages in the world to come."[8]

Aaron then made the sign of the cross over his eyes and instructed him to wash his face in faith. The rich man was healed immediately:

> The rich man rose and prostrated himself before the holy man Abba Aaron, giving thanks both to God and to Abba Aaron because he could see. The holy one gave the loan agreement to the poor man (ⲁϥϯ ⲙ̄ⲡⲉⲕⲣⲁⲙⲙⲁⲧⲟⲛ ⲙ̄ⲡⲣⲱⲙⲉ ⲛ̄ϩⲏⲕⲉ) and commanded him saying, "You too are to be merciful to your neighbor, as mercy has been shown to you. … Do not

---

[6] "Will require thy capital", CRUM 1939, p. 740.

[7] VIVIAN 1993 translation, p. 126.

[8] *Ibidem*, p. 128.

> be like that worthless servant whose master forgave a debt of many talents. He went and squeezed his fellow-servant for the little bit he owed him. No, be like the wise servant who doubled his talent."[9]

This in-person resolution of a dispute over a debt resembles the sort of arbitration that scholars identify as a fairly common means of informal dispute resolution under late Roman rule. However, the episode emphasizes certain formal elements of the Roman legal system that are not mentioned by parallel Christian episodes, such as the parable of the unforgiving servant[10] cited in this text. The text places emphasis on the loan document, ⲕⲣⲁⲙⲙⲁⲧⲟⲛ or Coptic for "bond, document, or contract", which is mentioned twice. Until this document was in the poor man's possession, there was no guarantee that the rich man would not take the dispute up legally and confiscate the poor man's vineyard. The transfer of the document shows that informal Christian arbitration was not seen as a replacement for the formal legal structures of the courts, since only handing over the document would ensure a lasting resolution for the dispute. The holy man's word alone could not bind the two parties; Apa Aaron also needed to ensure that the obligation had been erased within the realm of Egyptian notarial practice.

An episode from the fifth-century *Life of Longinus* likewise confirms the continued emphasis on the Roman legal practice of creating written legal instruments in hagiographies produced in monophysite monasteries after the Council of Chalcedon. In it, Longinus performs a miracle to recover a legal document lost by a grief-stricken family:

> I will also recount another wonder that God did through his servants. There was a man from the surrounding countryside there who had a noble son whom he had raised to adulthood from a child. There was a woman named Flavia who entrusted a document (ⲁⲥϭⲟⲓⲗⲉ ⲙ̄ⲟⲩⲕⲣⲁⲙⲁⲧⲓⲟⲛ) to the parents of that youth, which they gave to their son to protect (ⲉⲧⲣⲉϥⲥⲕⲉⲡⲁⲍⲉ = σκεπάζω). When the youth died suddenly, his parents did not know where the document was. That woman, Flavia, went to recover her deposit (ⲧⲉⲥⲡⲁⲣⲁⲑⲏⲕⲏ = παραθήκη), that is, the document (ⲡⲉⲕⲣⲁⲙⲙⲁⲧⲓⲟⲛ) that she had entrusted to them. When they were at a loss regarding it and could not find it because they did not know where

[9] *Ibidem*, p. 128-129.

[10] Matthew 18:21-35.

> the young man had put it, with great anger she threatened that she would make them her slaves if they did not restore her document to her.[11]

Although the *Vita* does not specify the legal relationship between Flavia and the parents of the deceased boy, its vocabulary suggests that it may have involved a deposit held in trust, since the text uses the Coptic verb ⲁⲥϭⲟⲓⲗⲉ which means "to deposit or entrust" and later the Greek loanword ⲡⲁⲣⲁⲑⲏⲕⲏ, which is a "deposit". Flavia is unlikely to have had any lawful way to enslave the parents, though they may have been subject to penalties for losing a legal document held in trust. It is more likely that Flavia, who is described as the "wife of a rich man" later in the text, threatened extra-legal recriminations against them for losing an important legal document. The parents were so distressed by Flavia's threats that they left their son unburied and traveled to Apa Longinus, whom they begged to reveal where their son had hidden the document. Apa Longinus returned with the parents to their house, and raised their son from the dead so that they could ask him where the document was, after which he "lay down again", presumably once again dead. This somewhat bizarre episode conveys the great value placed on properly composed legal instruments enforceable in Roman courts, even in a text that otherwise displays hostility towards the imperial administration. The rare Greek loanword παραθήκη[12] may even indicate that the author himself was familiar with Byzantine Greek legal documents.

The *Life of Shenoute*, the famous fifth-century abbot, represents an evocative instance of an Egyptian holy man aligning himself with the Roman legal principle that only designated secular magistrates may adjudicate capital crimes. Shenoute's monastic federation became a center of monophysite monasticism in the aftermath of the Council of Chalcedon. While the core of his *Life* was probably composed by his successor Besa, most scholars agree that it was augmented over time by encomia pronounced on the anniversary of his death, with the text reaching its most extended form in the seventh century.[13] This text exists in multiple forms, but this paper will focus on the Bohairic Coptic edition. This Bohairic *Life* was most likely an abridged version of a longer text, an Arabic

[11] VIVIAN 1999, p. 14.

[12] FÖRSTER 2002 does not record any uses of this word in published Coptic documentary texts.

[13] LOPEZ 2013, p. 135-137.

translation of which survives, which records more conflict between Shenoute and local (possibly Chalcedonian) clergy and the patriarchs of Alexandria.[14] The Arabic translation, which appears to have been addressed to Shenoute's monastic federation, also depicts him prosecuting pagans more aggressively than does the Coptic text.[15]

While the greater part of Shenoute's *Life* concerns his involvement with the monastic foundation, personal asceticism, and ministry to the poor, there is one episode that provides insight into the attitudes of Late Antique monasteries towards the enforcement of law by Roman magistrates. It involves a man who came to Shenoute after murdering a traveler in order to rob him of his gold pouch. He found that the pouch contained only a single gold coin and came to Shenoute, fearing for the fate of his soul. Before he is allowed to explain his circumstances, Shenoute stipulates the following condition: "If you will obey me in what I shall say to you, you will see me; if you will not obey me, you will not look upon my face." The man said, "I will obey you, my lord and father, in all that you command me."[16] This promise is significant because of its formal similarity to the typical binding promise to obey the arbiter's ruling. With this framework in place, Shenoute instructs the man to turn himself over to the authorities:

> Do not stay here, but get up quickly and go into the city of Smin, where you will find the duke (ⲇⲟⲩⲝ). He has come south down the river and is being greeted by his people. Some thieves who robbed an eminent man of the city of Smin will be handed over to him and he will be incensed with them. You too must go and join the thieves, and they will say to the duke: "He is here with us." The duke will ask you: "Is this true?" Say to him: "It is true," and he will therefore kill you with the others. You will then enter into the eternal life of God. The man left immediately and did just as the holy [Apa Shenoute] had told him, and the duke cut off his head with the rest of the thieves. In this way the mercy of God came upon him, just as my father told us.[17]

At least four significant observations arise from this passage. Firstly, even though the hagiography as a whole adheres to an Anti-Chalcedonian literary setting, the holy man does not do what one might expect on the

[14] LUBOMIERSKI 2008, p. 94. But see BELL 1983, p. 4-5.
[15] LUBOMIERSKI 2008, p. 94.
[16] *Life of Shenoute*, BELL 1983 translation, p. 46. LEIPOLDT & CRUM 1896, p. 15.
[17] BELL 1983, p. 47.

basis of Peter Brown's characterization of the late antique holy man[18] and pass judgment himself on the murderer. Despite his status as a holy man, Shenoute holds back from exacting a penalty. His choice is consistent with the evidence from the papyri and imperial codifications concerning the episcopal courts, which had to rely on secular magistrates to enforce their legal decisions. With respect to imperial policy, Leslie Dossey notes that "Emperors jealously reserved the use of force to secular (preferably imperial) officials ... Constantine's successors tried to prevent bishops from judging criminal and civil suits that were likely to involve corporal punishment."[19] This passage suggests that the ideology of imperial legislation permeated even the very different rhetorical context of hagiography. Shenoute does not kill the man himself or order one of his followers to do it. Instead, he relies on the court of a secular magistrate, in this case a military commander, whom the text refers to as a ⲇⲟⲩⲝ and is most likely the *dux Thebaidis*. In other words, Shenoute admits that this military official has a legitimate monopoly on authorized violence in the form of a legal execution within his Egyptian community.

Second, while Shenoute's resolution is portrayed as satisfying the requirements for divine justice, it conflicts with the Roman objectives of fair law enforcement, since the murderer's conviction rests on two separate instances of false testimony that cause him to be executed for a crime that he did not commit. From this perspective, the holy man could be viewed as coopting the Roman system of law enforcement. To the extent that the imperial magistrate is concerned with the uniform and fair enforcement of law and the holy man with divine justice, the two figures are acting at cross-purposes. Third, this coopting of the Roman legal system is accomplished in part through miraculous intervention. Shenoute predicts both the trial in Smin and the fact that the thieves will lie about the murderer being complicit in their crime. The narrative implies that God approved of this method of administering divine justice and permitted Shenoute to coopt the Roman legal system for divine purposes. Fourth, the immediately preceding point brings to mind the Christological elements of this episode. According to Christian theology, Jesus' execution represents the ultimate coopting of the Roman legal system for divine purposes. In this episode, the murderer is executed with

---

18 BROWN 1971.

19 DOSSEY 2001, p. 98-99.

thieves as Jesus was, and he in some sense takes on the sin of another as he is executed for a crime that he did not commit in order to restore the ultimate balance of divine justice.

This instance of secular authorities acting as unwitting agents of divine justice illustrates the very different concerns of Christian figures and the Roman authorities. But despite its subversive elements, the hagiography does conform to the Roman principle that only imperial magistrates can adjudicate capital criminal cases like this one, and enforce their decisions through legitimate violence. Shenoute does not claim for himself the authority to execute the thief, despite his divine insight and the thief's full confession, but instead relinquishes it to the secular Roman magistrate.

The early sixth-century *Panegyric on Macarius, Bishop of Tkow* contains the strongest anti-Chalcedonian polemic of the texts that I cite in this chapter, and its depiction of holy men represented the greatest threat to imperial political authority. Macarius was a contemporary of Shenoute, and Tkow, or Antaeopolis, was not far from Shenoute's White monastery.[20] Furthermore, the *Panegyric*, firmly rooted in its monophysite context of literary production, links the two figures by relating that Shenoute received a vision that designated Macarius as the champion of orthodoxy who would fight in the then-elderly Shenoute's place on behalf of the Coptic-speaking church at the Council of Chalcedon.[21] As part of a larger description of temple destruction and the extirpation of paganism, one episode describes a particularly heinous group of pagans apprehended by unnamed secular authorities while performing child sacrifices:

> One day they waylaid them performing these lawless acts (ⲉⲩⲉⲓⲣⲉ ⲛ̄ⲧⲉⲓⲁⲛⲟⲙⲓⲁ) by slaying the little children and pouring out their blood upon the altar of their god, Kothos. They seized some of them and handed them over to the tribunal. They interrogated them orally, and they confessed the truth without torture (ⲁⲩϭⲱⲡⲉ ⲛ̄ϩⲟⲉⲓⲛⲉ ⲉⲃⲟⲗ ⲛ̄ϩⲏⲧⲟⲩ ⲁⲩⲧⲁⲁⲩ ⲉⲧⲉⲡⲣⲉⲧⲁⲛⲓⲁ̄. ⲁⲩⲉⲝⲉⲧⲁⲍⲉ ⲙ̄ⲙⲟⲟⲩ ϩⲙⲡϣⲁϫⲉ. ⲁⲩϩⲟⲙⲟⲗⲟⲅⲓ ⲭⲱⲣⲓⲥ ⲃⲁⲥⲁⲛⲟⲥ), saying "We call to the children of the Christians and deceive them and give them something to eat. And we take them to hidden places and pour their blood upon the altar and take out their intestines and stretch their sinews for our harps and we sing to

[20] LOPEZ 2013, p. 109.

[21] JOHNSON 1991, V, p. 1492-1494.

> our gods on them. But we burn the rest of their bodies and reduce them to ashes. And everywhere where we realize there is treasure, we take a little of their ashes and put them upon it. And we sing on our harps with the little children's intestines for strings. The treasure comes to light at once, and we take what we want." And those men gave large sums of money to those who had seized them in order to be set free, for the leaders of that district were money-lovers (ⲁⲩϯ ⲛ̅ϩⲉⲛⲛⲟϭ ⲛ̅ⲭⲣⲏⲙⲁ ϣⲁⲛⲧⲟⲩⲛⲟⲩϩⲙ̅: ⲉⲡⲉⲓⲇⲏ ϩⲛ̅ⲙⲁⲓⲭⲣⲏⲙⲁⲛⲉ ⲛⲁⲣⲭⲱⲛ ⲧⲏⲣⲟⲩ ⲙ̅ⲡⲧⲁϣ ⲉⲧⲙ̅ⲙⲁⲩ).[22]

The passage evinces Christian hostility against pagans, using language obviously calculated to inspire the reader's outrage, and alleging that the secular authorities were too corrupt to administer justice. But despite its evident hostility to the corrupt magistrates, the Coptic text mirrors the language of petitions in civil and administrative law. The text states that the pagans were performing a "lawless act", ⲛ̅ⲧⲉⲓⲁⲛⲟⲙⲓⲁ, echoing language used throughout the Roman period, even in documents that do not otherwise display an extensive knowledge of Roman law. Alleged offenders were often described as ἄνομος or "lawless" in cases of civil law, especially those involving compensation for injury. At the same time, the text combines this language of petition with a persistent political theme within these hagiographical texts, that the magistrates could not be trusted to prosecute pagans because of their corruption and connection to the Chalcedonian imperial administration.[23] Despite the alleged corruption of secular officials and the charge that the magistrates were money-lovers, ϩⲛ̅ⲙⲁⲓⲭⲣⲏⲙⲁⲛⲉ ⲛⲁⲣⲭⲱⲛ, the hagiography nevertheless adopts language familiar from earlier Roman petitions as the legitimate way for the holy man to describe injustice and lawlessness within his community.

It is curious that the text invokes the conceit of the first person testimony collected "without torture", even though such a testimony would hardly have been necessary in reality. The pagans could simply have paid off the magistrates and continued in their infanticidal ways; recording

---

[22] JOHNSON 1980 translation, p. 22-23.

[23] For instance, the *Life of Shenoute* laments the fact that pagans were able to sacrifice and openly practice their cult on the mountain of Abydos. The text claims that they were able to do this because the local officials were corrupt: "Since the governors (ⲛⲁⲣⲭⲱ̅ⲛ) ruling (ⲉⲧⲁⲣⲭⲉⲓ) at that time were greedy (ⲙⲁⲓⲭⲣⲏ̅ⲙⲁ̅), they turned a blind eye at them, and because of the cash, the pagans had begun to speak openly (ⲙ̅ⲡⲁⲣⲣⲏ̅ⲥⲓⲁⲍⲉ)." ULJAS 2012, p. 9 and 12.

an official testimony would have been contrary to the magistrates' purposes. But from a literary point of view, the testimony, which was all the more credible because it was extracted without torture, provides the necessary substance for the petition it resembles in being bracketed by the appropriate conventional language. In adopting the language of petitions, the *Panegyric* reveals ideological affinities to Shenoute's own writings. Ariel Lopez argues that his *Discourses* and *Letters* "can be considered a long, single-minded, and ultimately successful petition" as they attempted, through appeals to the emperor and his representatives, to denounce the oppression of the poor by the rich.[24] Furthermore, Shenoute characterized his enemies using language identical to that of the *Panegyric*: "*Anomia*, that is, lawlessness, is what defines his enemies in Panopolis."[25] This rhetoric exemplifies what Lopez characterizes as Shenoute's "loyal opposition", that is, ultimate loyalty to the emperor and his laws balanced against strident opposition to the injustice perpetuated by the local elite and the "corrupt, deficient enforcement of the law that makes his intervention necessary."[26] The *Panegyric*'s adoption of this language and the device of the testimony suggests a similar attitude. Even if the *Panegyric*'s forceful anti-Chalcedonian polemic fails to express confidence in imperial officials, the language and ideology of Roman law still permeates its discussion of law and justice.

This literary form may serve to justify what follows. Macarius goes with some of his disciples to confront the pagans, who chain him up within their temple and are preparing to sacrifice him when God delivers him and destroys the temple through the agency of Besa, Shenoute's successor at Atripe. Macarius and Besa enter the neighboring village together, investing Macarius' actions with God's divine deliverance and with the symbolic sanction of Shenoute's legacy through the physical presence of his successor. Macarius confronts the leader of the pagan community, and throws him onto a fire alive, along with his idols, with the orthodox Christians of the village looking on and singing psalms.

Here, the holy man takes both components of the legal process, adjudication and enforcement, into his own hands. The reader is prepared for this startling conclusion by the earlier quotation of the pagans'

---

[24] Lopez 2013, p. 35.

[25] *Ibidem*, p. 40.

[26] *Ibidem*, p. 40 and 159.

confession in the form of a testimony. By echoing the form of a written court transcript, the text suggests they underwent a legal process that helps to justify what was in fact a summary execution. A holy man assuming this role would have done so in direct competition with Roman secular magistrates. Even if the magistrates were not themselves corrupt, as is alleged, they might have been hesitant to prosecute pagans who were prominent members of the community, especially if they were merely engaged in regular pagan worship rather than something as dramatic as child sacrifice.[27] In their efforts to suppress pagan worship aggressively while using the language and forms of legal institutions, the holy men would have represented a pressing threat to the secular order. There was clearly some place for informal arbitration before holy men, and possibly even adjudication, as long as state magistrates still served as the enforcers of the law, but when a holy man assumed the position of judge and executioner he could expect at best uneasy toleration on the part of secular authorities, and at worst outright conflict or retaliation. Despite this potential *political* conflict, the holy man still couched his claims to legitimacy in administering justice in the language and forms of Roman legal discourse.

*

* *

The literary texts treated here offer some insight into the actual legal practices of monks and holy men. It is likely that some monks petitioned magistrates on behalf of the downtrodden and others conducted arbitration "in the shadow of the law", assuring the proper transfer of legal documents to prevent subsequent litigation. The next section of this chapter provides further documentary evidence supporting these practices. The theme that has emerged so far is the presence of the language and institutions of Roman law in these texts as a matter of intellectual history and what it reveals about fifth and sixth-century Coptic Thebaid monasteries. Whereas Lopez argues that Shenoute is unique among Egyptian monks in terms of the political and economic role that he played in his community, these texts depict other monks and minor

[27] David FRANKFURTER offers convincing arguments for why hagiographies in general, and this text in particular, cannot be used as accurate sources for the specific practices of non-Christian cult in Late Antiquity: see FRANKFURTER 2006, p. 17-22.

bishops acting in similarly proactive ways within the legal systems of their communities, while linking them to Shenoute at times, especially in the domain of idol and temple destruction.

The common veneration of Shenoute does not, however, sufficiently explain the prevalence of the language and institutions of Roman law in these texts. The strong presence of Roman legal discourse within these accounts reveals that these monastic communities conceptualized or commemorated these actions not as a new form of divine justice, divorced from the legal structures that preceded it, but instead as practices couched in terms of Roman legal discourse. Even where the authors sought to distinguish Christian figures from Roman magistrates, as in the case of the *Panegyric of Macarius*, they still retained the vocabulary and structures of Roman law as a discourse that conferred legitimacy and delineated just action.

2. Documentary evidence

Numerous instances of Late Antique Egyptian monks and clergy submitting and receiving petitions and mediating legal disputes exist in extant documentary papyri. For the purposes of this chapter, I will focus on four examples: a document recording the results of an arbitration, a letter discussing arbitration, and two petitions submitted to clergy that exhibit language and structure shared with earlier petitions to Roman secular authorities.

P. Münch. I 14 (TM 15322) is a *dialysis* or arbitration agreement from AD 594 that provides documentary evidence for the involvement of Egyptian clergy in dispute resolution. *Dialysis* agreements recorded the decision of an arbiter or panel of arbiters that both parties of a legal dispute had agreed on beforehand. They sometimes included a history of prior conflict that preceded the decision to submit the dispute to arbitration as well as several clauses regarding its enforcement, sometimes including previously agreed upon financial penalties. In the period following AD 400, the number of petitions in extant papyri decreases rapidly while *dialysis* agreements begin to appear.[28] Individual examples of

[28] Kelly 2011, p. 23-24.

these agreements have received extensive scholarly attention,[29] but there has been no comprehensive study of all Greek and Coptic examples of this type of document of the sort necessary to trace the networks of social authority that allowed this kind of legal instrument to function. For the purposes of my research, I focus in particular on the presence of Coptic monks and clergy as arbiters and witnesses in these documents. *P. Münch.* I 14 provides an illustrative example of how these documents combined the social authority of Christian clergy with the notarial forms of Roman law.

The legal case at issue in this papyrus is complicated: the entire text is 111 lines and includes a number of complex clauses employing the florid language common in documents of this period. The plaintiffs, who are brothers-in-law, each brought a suit against the other before the *vicarius* of Hermonthis[30] for violating a prior arbitration agreement. Patermouthis sued Ioannes because the latter had brought a previous suite over an inheritance dispute that had resulted in Patermouthis being fined 7 *solidi*, even though that inheritance dispute was recorded as being resolved in *dialysis* agreements (ἔγγραφοι διαλύσεις) that both men had signed.[31] In response to Patermouthis' charge, Ioannes responded that he had only revisited the inheritance dispute because Patermouthis (who was married to Ioannes' sister) had prevented Ioannes' mother from giving him money that she owed to him as a result of a dispute over her house that had been arbitrated by Paeion, a local lawyer.[32]

In the passage relevant to Christian arbitration, the text abruptly shifts to explain that the two parties settled the issue via the arbitration of a priest, instead of awaiting the results of litigation:

> ...καὶ πολλῶν
> ὅσων λεχθέντων καὶ ἀντιλεχθέντων μεταξὺ ἀλλήλων ἔδοξεν κατὰ κοινὴν

[29] GAGOS & VAN MINNEN 1994.

[30] The term βικάριος very generally means a representative and was consequently used in Late Antiquity to designate a range of individuals who had civil responsibilities or jurisdiction, see GUTSFELD 2006. In this particular context, he seems to have been a subordinate of the τοποτηρητής in Hermopolis who held civil and military jurisdiction, see HAGEDORN 1986, p. 160-161.

[31] *P. Münch.* I 14, l. 15-25.

[32] *P. Münch.* I 14, l. 25-30.

συναίνεσιν ἀπαντῆσαι αὐτοὺς εἰς δίαιταν παρὰ Σερῆυ τῷ εὐλαβεστάτῳ πρεσβυτέρῳ τῆς ἁγίας ἐκκλησίας Ὄμβων εὑρεθέντι κατὰ τύχην ἐν ταύτῃ τῇ Συηνιτῶν. *vac.* ? καὶ δὴ γενόμενοι παρὰ τῇ αὐτοῦ θεοφιλείᾳ ἑκάτερον μέρος ἀνέθετο αὐτῷ τὰς ἑαυτοῦ δικαιολογίας, ὅστις ἀκροασάμενος τῶν μεταξὺ αὐτῶν ἀμφιβαλλομένων, διελθὼν δὲ καὶ τὰς διαλύσεις τὰς προενεχθείσας παρὰ Πατερμο(υ)θίο(υ) γενομένας εἰς αὐτὸν καὶ Κακὸ τὴν αὐτοῦ γαμετὴν παρὰ Ἰωάννου τοῦ προειρημένο(υ), οὐ μὴν ἀλλὰ καὶ ἐφειδὼν τὴν ἐπίκρισιν τὴν δοθεῖσαν Ἰωάννῃ καὶ τῇ μητρὶ αὐτοῦ παρὰ τοῦ αὐτοῦ λογιωτάτου γραμματικοῦ ἕνεκεν τῆς ὑποθέσεως τῆς οἰκίας, δι᾽ ἧς ἐπέκρινεν καὶ συνεῖδεν δοθῆναι Ἰωάννῃ παρὰ τῆς μητρὸς αὐτοῦ νομίσματα τέσσερα, καὶ αὐτοῦ Ἰωάννου \ἐπιμείναντος/ καὶ λέγοντος, ὡς ἐμποδισθεὶς παρὰ Πατερμουθίου το(ῦ) εἰρημένο(υ) λαβεῖν παρὰ τῆς μητρὸς αὐτο(ῦ) τὰ αὐτὰ νομίσματα τέσσερα ᾐτιάσατο αὐτόν, συνεῖδεν καὶ ἐπέκρινεν ὁ προειρημένος θεοφιλέστατος διαιτητής, ὥστε πρὸ παντὸς λόγου καταβαλεῖν Ἰωάννην τὸν προλελεγμένον ἐπὶ Πατερμοῦθιν χρυσο(ῦ) νομίσματα πέντε ὑπὲρ ἧς ἔλεγεν δεδόσθαι ζημίας

And after they had said and argued much with each other, they decided by common accord to appear for arbitration before Sereu, the most reverent priest of the holy church of Omboi, who happened to be found in the city of the Syenians. And then, when they came before his Godbelovedness, each side prepared for him his own pleas of justification. He, when he had listed to what was in dispute between them, and when he had also gone through the settlements brought forward by Patermouthis which had been made for him and his wife Kako by the said Ioannes, and when, moreover, he had also examined the arbitration award given to Ioannes and his mother by the same most learned lawyer on account of the case of the house, in which he awarded and decided that four *solidi* be given to Ioannes by his mother and since Ioannes himself persisted and said that he charged him because he had been hindered by the said Patermouthis from receiving from his mother the same four *solidi*, the aforesaid most-beloved-of-God arbitrator decided and arbitrated that above all the said Ioannes should tender to Patermouthis five gold *solidi*, for the penalty which he said had been given.[33]

The text then goes on to describe at length the process by which both parties accepted the settlement in which Ioannes would pay Patermouthis one *solidus* once a previous arbitration award was taken into account. It also includes an elaborate quitclaim, several security and penalty clauses, and the signatures of seven witnesses.

This case demonstrates how the initial resolution of a dispute through arbitration could be revisited in the formal court setting, where the violation of these arbitration awards constituted grounds for ligation and the documents themselves were used as evidence. Furthermore, this document illustrates how the imperial state power was felt in legal disputes, even at this late date at the end of the sixth century. In the two extensive security clauses at the end of the document, each party agreed not to contest the arbitration in the future through a variety of legal means, including through "imperial pronouncements [θείων βέρβων]" or "an imperial rescript [θείας ἀδνουτατίωνος]".[34] However unlikely it was in a dispute over comparatively modest sums, the perceived possibility of an imperial intervention on behalf of one of the plaintiffs is expressed in this security clause. The clause indicates an awareness of imperial legal authority at the level of imagination and discourse, even as it tries to block an intervention through a contractual clause. The document as a whole exhibits the tendency of Byzantine legal prose to employ a string of similar words in order to make a legal claim more secure. One example of this is in the opening lines, which state, "This acknowledgement of settlements is drawn up and made as the termination of all criticism and accusation and liability and inculpation and inquiry and altercation [by Patermouthis and Ioannes]."[35] This ornate prose style persists throughout the document and can be observed in many other contracts and legal documents from this period.

This text is incredibly rich, but for the purposes of this excerpt I will emphasize three facts from the underlying legal situation. First, the legal

---

[33] *P. Münch.* I 14, l. 30-46. PORTEN e.a. 2011 translation.

[34] *P. Münch.* I 14, l. 71 and 85.

[35] *P. Münch.* I 14, l. 6-8: ταύτην τίθενται καὶ ποιοῦνται τὴν ὁμολογίαν τῶν διαλύσεων ἀναιρετικὴν οὖσαν πάσης μέμψεως καὶ ἀγωγῆς καὶ ἐνοχῆς καὶ ἐγκλήσεως καὶ ζητήσεως καὶ ἀμφισβητήσεως.

adversaries appear to have selected Sereu as an arbiter in part based on his status as a priest. Georg Schmelz notes that they were not members of his congregation, as he was from Omboi and only in Syene "by chance"; therefore, "his spiritual authority [alone] gives sufficient grounds for his competence as an arbiter."[36]

Second, the text records how the arbitration proceeded. Sereu heard oral arguments prepared by each side, and also examined the written legal instruments upon which they based their respective cases, such as the previous arbitration agreement awarded to Ioannes. These documents were crucial to the proceedings, forming an important evidentiary basis for Sereu's eventual decision.

Finally, while the litigants trusted in the spiritual authority of the priest to reach a just resolution of their dispute, they did not trust in this same spiritual authority to enforce that outcome or record the results of the arbitration and the history of the case. They instead preferred an extensive agreement drawn up by a professional scribe with a dizzying array of clauses waiving the right to future suits and establishing penalties for cases of non-compliance. Crucially, this written Roman legal instrument was perceived as the legitimate mechanism for recording knowledge within the community, even in a dispute in which a priest was trusted more than a secular judge to reach a just outcome.

Evidence for arbitration by Egyptian monks and clergy exists in papyri of many other genres beyond arbitration agreements, including letters, petitions, and reports of proceedings. Furthermore, as *P. Münch.* I 14 demonstrates, the individuals who served as arbiters did not necessarily rely on institutional adjudicatory authority granted to them by the church, such as the bishop's *episcopalis audientia*. Priests, deacons, and monastics often served as arbiters simply by virtue of their prestige and social prominence, as the sixth or seventh century letter *BGU* I 103 (TM 37124) suggests:

Recto

† ἐπιδὴ [*l.* ἐπειδὴ] οἱ ἀδελφοὶ τοῦ μακαρίου Ἐνὼχ ἦλθαν πρὸς ἡμᾶς λέγοντες

ὅτι δικασθῆναι θέλωμεν [*l.* θέλομεν] μετὰ τὴς γυνεκὸς [*l.* γυναικὸς] ἑαυτοῦ, καταξήωσον [*l.* καταξίωσον]

[36] Schmelz 2014, p. 526.

οὖν ἡ ὑμετέρα θεωφελία [*l.* θεοφιλία], ἐὰν αὐθεντίσεις [*l.* αὐθεντήσῃς] τω [*l.* τὸ] πρᾶγμα καὶ λάβις [*l.* λάβῃς]
αὐτοὺς ἐν τῇ πόλει, καὶ ἀπαλλαγοῦσιν [*l.* ἀπαλλαγῶσιν] πρὸς ἀλλίλους [*l.* ἀλλήλους], εἰ δὲ μή γε,
καταξήωσον [*l.* καταξίωσον] τούτους παρασκευάσε [*l.* παρασκευάσαι] ἀμφοτέρους ἐλθῆν [*l.* ἐλθεῖν] ἐνταῦθ[α]
καὶ τούτους παρασκευάσωμεν αὐτοὺς ἀπαλλαγῖνε [*l.* ἀπαλλαγῆναι] κατὰ των [*l.* τὸν] τοῦ δι-
κέου [*l.* δι|καίου] καὶ κατὰ τω [*l.* τὸ] ἔθος τοῦ κτίματος [*l.* κτήματος]. ἀλλὰ μὴ ὑπερθῖ [*l.* ὑπερθῇ] ἡ ὑμετέρα εὐλάβια [*l.* εὐλάβεια]
πατριδιαθεσιν τούτους ἐκπέμψε [*l.* ἐκπέμψαι], εἰ δὲ πάλιν αὐθεντῖς [*l.* αὐθεντεῖς] καὶ
λαμβάνις [*l.* λαμβάνεις] αὐτοὺς ἐν τῇ πόλει, καλὸς [*l.* καλῶς], ὅτι γὰρ μέτριοί εἰσιν καὶ δημόσια
συντελοῦσιν ἁγιωτάτωι πατρί. †

Verso

τῷ ἁγιωτ(ά)τ(ῳ) πατρ(ὶ) ἄββᾳ Σερῖνος [*l.* Σερίνῳ] ἀρχιμανδρ(ίτῃ) † Ἀβραὰμ Ἀρωω[...]
μίζ(ων)[*l.* μείζ(ων)] Πιναρά(χθεως) .[.....]

Since the brothers of the deceased Enoch came to us saying "We wish to have our case with his [Enoch's] wife decided in court," so then, your divine grace, if you assume authority over the matter and receive them in the city, see to it [that it be decided] and let them be reconciled towards one another. But if not, be so good as to have both parties come here and let us induce them to reconcile themselves according to the just outcome and custom regarding an estate. But so that your reverence not delay and exclude them from their inheritance, if you do exercise authority and receive them in the city, [it happens] rightly, for they are reasonable and contribute public gifts for (their) most holy father.
To the most holy father Abba Serenus archimandrite. Abraam Aroo... headman of Pinarachthis.[37]

As the text on the verso makes clear, this letter is addressed to an individual named Serenus, whom we know to be an abbot of a monastery based on his honorific "ἄββᾳ" and his designation as an "ἀρχιμανδρ(ίτῃ)".[38] Here again, some choice exists about where the two parties will have their case arbitrated: it can be heard by Serenus the abbot or Abraam, who is probably a village headman based on his designation as

[37] *BGU* I 103. My translation.

[38] The latter term often designates abbots of large monasteries, see DELATTRE 2007, p. 67.

"μείζ(ων)". Abraam attempts to refer the case to Serenus and does not explicitly state his reasons for doing so. He might have thought that Serenus' position within the community would help bring about a lasting settlement that both parties would respect. However, Abraam also gives Serenus the option of referring the arbitration back to him. The relatively rare verb used for Serenus acting as arbiter, αὐθεντίζω or αὐθεντέω in lines 3 and 8, is simultaneously recalling two different uses of the word in this one instance. Words from this root are frequently used in documentary papyri to mean "authentic", "warranted", or "authoritative" with reference to documents or officials. At the same time, the verb form also has a specifically Christian register, concerning the exercise of a priest's authority over his congregation. For instance, it is controversial among New Testament scholars due to its occurrence in a passage on the role of women in the church in Second Timothy.[39] Despite this controversy, we can say that the verb seems to refer to the exercise of pastoral authority, power, or rights in other patristic Greek and Byzantine contexts in which it is used.

The brothers and widow of Enoch do not appear to be monastics under Serenus' supervision, since they are not designated as such and would have to travel to another, unnamed, city where Serenus is in order for him to be able to hear their case. Either Serenus or Abraam would be judging these villagers on the basis of their social authority within their communities. In fact, Abraam explicitly states that he would decide the case according to the custom regarding estates "ἔθος τοῦ κτήματος" in his village. This term is not specific enough for us to understand the substantive legal standards that Abraam or Serenus would make use of, and we do not know what the evidentiary basis of their decision would be. This sort of information is less likely to be preserved in letters than in more formal legal documents like arbitration agreements or reports of proceedings. Nevertheless, this letter provides clear evidence of a monastic abbot serving as an arbiter in a secular inheritance dispute of the sort commonly found in *dialysis* documents. This provides further documentary evidence of monastic leaders serving as arbiters that we have also seen in the Coptic *Lives* of Longinus and Shenoute of Atripe. The literary depictions of monastics engaging in arbitrations are historically plausible,

---

[39] 1 Timothy 2:12. See, e.g., KNIGHT 1984 and PAYNE 2009, p. 361-398, for two competing interpretations of this passage.

and thus we should take all the more seriously the legal standards and values articulated in these Coptic *Vitae.*

By the late fifth century, formal petitions submitted to bishops and other clergy began to appear. These petitions drew extensively on the structure, language, and tropes of first through third-century petitions. They are contemporaneous with the hagiographic texts discussed in the first part of this chapter, and their adoption of Roman legal forms in a religious setting accords with the respect for Roman legal language evident in the literary sources. Leaving aside the legal and ecclesiastical institutions that invested bishops with the authority to respond to these petitions for the purposes of this chapter, I discuss the formal similarities between a fifth-century petition and comparable documents from earlier periods of Roman rule in Egypt. These resemblances demonstrate that the forms of Roman legal practice attained a level of social prestige that contributed to their appropriation in Christian institutional contexts.

One of the most extensive early papyrological examples of a formal petition to a bishop is the late fifth-century document addressed to Theodore, bishop of Oxyrhynchos, by Aurelia Nonna:

> τῷ ἁγιωτάτῳ καὶ [εὐσε]β(εστάτῳ) ἄπα Θεοδώρῳ ἐπισκ(όπῳ) τῆς λαμπρᾶς καὶ λαμ[προτ]άτης Ὀξυρυγχιτῶν πόλεως παρὰ Αὐρηλίας Νόννα[ς] ἀ̣πὸ κώμ(ης) Σπανίας τοῦ Ὀξυρυγχ(ίτου) νομο̣ῦ̣. Ἀλύπιος μονάζων ὁρμώμενος ἀπὸ τῆς ἡμετέρας κώμης ἀδελφιδοῦ[ς] ἡμέτερος τυγχάνων τὴν ἐμὴν θυγατέρα μικκη [*l.* μικκὴ<ν>] ἠθέλησεν δοῦναι Ἀπαείωνι συγγενεῖ πάλιν ἡμετέρῳ. τοῦτο δὲ ποιῆσαι ἐσπούδασαν <οἱ> ἡμέτερα πράγματα ἔχοντες καὶ μὴ θέλοντες, ταῦτά μοι ἀποκαταστ̣ῆσαι. ἐπὶ [*l.* ἐπεὶ] τοίνυν Θ̣ε . . ἥ μου θυγάτηρ ἐκείνῳ <οὐ(?)> βούλεται συνάπτεσθαι, π[αρὰ] τ̣ὸ σχῆμ[α] δὲ διαπραττόμενος ὁ μονάζων πληγάς μοι ἐ̣π̣ήγαγεν καὶ τὴν ἐ̣σ̣θῆτά μου διέρηξεν [*l.* διέρ<ρ>ηξεν] καὶ ἀχρίαν [*l.* ἀχρείαν] ἀπέδιξεν [*l.* ἀπέδειξεν], τούτου [χάρ]ι̣ν̣ παρακαλῶ σου τὴν ἁγιοσύνην [*l.* ἁγιωσύνην] κατελεῆσαί με καὶ κελεῦσαι αὐτὸν ἐνεχθῆναι καὶ τύπο̣ν̣ με δέχεσθαι τὸν τῇ σῇ ἁγιοσύνῃ [*l.* ἁγιωσύνῃ] παριστάμενον, ἁγιώτατε ἐπίσκοπε κύριε.
> (Hand 2) † Α̣ὐ̣ρ̣[η]λ̣ί[α Νόννα ἐπιδ]ε̣δωκα.

To the most holy and most pious Apa Theodore, bishop of the illustrious and most illustrious city of the Oxyrhynchites, from Aurelia Nonna of the village of Spania of the Oxyrhynchite nome. Alypios, a monk, native of our village, who is our nephew, desired to give (in marriage) my little daughter to Apaion, also a relative of ours. And the administrators of our estate, who are unwilling to restore it to me, were eager to do this. Since therefore The[…], my daughter, (does not?) wish to marry him, and acting in defiance of his cloth, the monk beat me and tore my clothing and ruined it, therefore I beg your holiness to have compassion upon me and order him

> to be brought (before you), and for me to receive whatever decision you shall approve of, my lord, most holy bishop. I, Aurelia Nonna, have presented this petition.[40]

The letter does not indicate whether Theodore occupied a supervisory position over Alypios within the ecclesiastical hierarchy. But even if he did, this is not a case of church discipline, but rather a secular case centering on a family dispute and physical abuse.[41] This document adopts the exact form of petitions submitted to judicial and military officers, naming the addressee in the dative with his respective titles and place of residence, as well as the plaintiff in the genitive following the preposition παρά, the plaintiff's place of residence, a *narratio* of the violent incident, the precise request for the legal proceedings desired, and the signature of the plaintiff in the form "NN ἐπιδέδωκα". The formal similarities to earlier petitions are so strong that Bryen included this petition in his appendix of translations of petitions concerning violence,[42] though he acknowledges that there are questions in the scholarship about the exact nature of a bishop's jurisdiction.[43]

The *narratio* contains elements familiar from petitions from earlier periods as well as indications that the official being addressed is an ecclesiastical one. It also invokes what Bryen calls the "discourse of wounded bodies".[44] Aurelia Nonna explains that Alypios physically abused her and destroyed her property when trying to force the marriage of her daughter. The mention of "πληγάς" or "blows" is common in petitions that describe violence, and this term recurs frequently in the petitions Bryen studies. The mention of the torn cloak is also consistent with the language of earlier petitions, since a record of material damage would help cement the financial obligation that the defendant owed to the plaintiff if the petition was successful. It is also possible to render the phrase "καὶ ἀχρίαν [*l.* ἀχρείαν] ἀπέδιξεν [*l.* ἀπέδειξεν]" as "making me appear helpless", as Bryen does in his translation of this document.[45] This is an interesting possibility, as it would speak unambiguously to Aurelia Nonna's status and how this incident has caused her to lose face in the

[40] *SB* IV 7449 (TM 35117). SCHMELZ 2014 translation.
[41] SCHMELZ 2014, p. 527.
[42] BRYEN 2013, p. 277-278.
[43] *Ibidem*, p. 315 n. 55.
[44] *Ibidem*, p. 120.
[45] *Ibidem*, p. 277.

community. However, I have preferred the translation "ruined it" for this clause, because I believe ἐσθῆτα to be the more likely antecedent for ἀχρείαν than an implied ἐγώ.

The assertion that Alypios "acted in defiance of his cloth", or "π[αρὰ] τ̣ὸ σχῆμ[α] δὲ διαπραττόμενος", was probably intended to erode any natural sympathy Theodore might have toward someone with a monastic title by explicitly questioning his suitability for that position. The need for this sort of attack arose in conjunction with the use of ecclesiastical and monastic titles as symbols of prestige on legal documents. In a petition that otherwise mimicks the rhetoric of petitions to secular officials, the attack on Alypios' conduct as a monk derives from the new institutional context of the monastery and its effect on legal practice.

The second petition to an ecclesiastic is the seventh-century Coptic ostracon cited at the start of this paper. Unfortunately, neither the name nor the title of the addressee has survived. The text reads as follows:

> † ϣⲟⲣⲡ̅ ⲙⲉⲛ ϯⲡⲣⲟⲥⲕ/ ⲁⲩⲱ ϯϣⲓⲛⲉ ⲉⲧⲉⲕⲁⲅⲁⲡⲏ ⲉⲧⲥⲙⲁⲙⲁⲧ [*l.* ⲥⲙⲁⲙⲁⲁⲧ] ⲧⲁⲓ ⲛ̅ⲧⲁⲛⲉⲓⲃⲉ ⲙⲙⲟⲥ ⲛ̅ⲑⲉ ⲉϣⲁⲣⲉ ⲡⲕⲁϩ ⲕⲱϣⲧ [*l.* ϭⲱϣⲧ] ⲉⲃⲟⲗ ϩⲏⲧⲥ ⲙ̅ⲡϩⲟⲟⲩ ⲡϫⲟⲉⲓⲥ ⲡⲉⲧⲥⲟⲁⲛ [*l.* ⲥⲟⲟⲩⲛ] ϫⲉ ⲁⲓⲟⲩⲱϣ ⲉⲥϩⲁⲓ ⲛⲧⲁⲡⲣⲟⲥⲕⲩ/ ⲛⲁⲕ ⲙ̅ⲡⲣⲱϣⲉ ⲛ̅ϩⲟⲡ/ ⲙ̅ⲡⲉ ⲡϩⲟⲡϩⲡ̅ ⲕⲁⲁⲧ ⲙ̅ⲛ̅ ⲡⲡⲉⲓⲣⲁⲥⲙⲟⲥ ⲡⲗⲏⲛ ⲉⲥϫⲉ ⲧⲛ̅ⲉⲓⲣⲉ ⲁⲛ ⲙ̅ⲡⲁⲓ ⲡ̅ⲛⲟⲩⲧⲉ ⲡⲉⲧⲥⲟⲟⲩⲛ ϫⲉ ⲡⲉⲕⲣⲡⲙⲉⲩ [*l.* ⲙⲉⲉⲩⲉ] ⲗⲟ ⲁⲛ ϩⲙ ⲡⲉⲛϩⲏⲧ ⲛⲧⲉⲩϣⲏ ⲁⲩⲱ ⲡⲉϩⲟⲟⲩ· ϯⲧⲁⲙⲟ ⲛ̅ ⲛ̅ⲧⲉⲕⲙⲛⲧ̅ⲙⲁⲓⲛⲟⲩⲧⲉ ϫⲉ ⲁ ⲡⲉⲓ ⲡⲁⲣⲁⲃⲁⲧⲏⲥ ⲙ̅ⲡⲁⲣⲁⲛⲟⲥ [*l.* ⲡⲁⲣⲁⲛⲟⲙⲟⲥ] ϫⲉ ⲁⲙⲙⲱⲛⲓⲟⲥ ⲥⲟⲩ ⲟⲩⲉⲓⲟⲙ̅ ⲛ̅ⲏⲣⲡ ⲙ̅ⲡϩⲓⲣⲟⲩϩⲉ ⲛⲧⲁⲧ ⲡⲉ ϩⲟⲟⲩ ⲁϥⲉⲓ ⲉϩⲣⲁⲓ ⲉⲣⲟⲓ ⲛ̅ⲛⲉⲩ ⲛⲟⲟⲩⲉ ⲉⲧⲙ̅ⲙⲁⲁⲩ ⲙⲛ̅ ⲡϣⲓⲛ ⲡⲉⲛⲥⲟⲛ ⲙⲛ̅ ⲡⲉϥϩⲙ̅ϩⲁⲗ ⲙ̅ⲡⲟⲩⲕⲱ ϩⲓⲕⲱⲛ ϩⲓⲱⲧ ⲟⲩⲧⲉ ⲟⲩⲣⲏⲧⲉ ⲟⲩⲧⲉ ϭϫ [*l.* ϭⲓϫ] ⲉⲙⲛ̅ⲧⲁϥ ⲗⲁⲩⲉ ⲛ̅ϩⲱⲃ. ϯⲡⲁⲣⲁⲕⲁⲗⲉⲓ ⲟⲩⲛ ⲛ̅. [ⲙⲟ]ⲧⲛ ⲉⲧⲣⲁ ⲡ. ..ⲙⲟ..

> First I do homage and I enquire after your blessed love which we have thirsted after as the earth looks toward the day. It is the Lord who knows I have wished to write and do homage to you often enough. Excitement and temptation have not left me. But, if we have not done this, it is God that knows that thought of you has not ceased in our heart by night and by day. I inform your Piety that this lawless transgressor, Ammonius, drank a sea of wine in the night season, toward morning, and descended upon me in those hours with the son of Penson and his servant. They left me no resemblance of myself, neither foot nor hand being without some disfigurement. I beseech you moreover to let me...[46]

---

[46] *O. Mich. Copt.* 4. WORRELL 1942 translation.

This document obviously does not follow the structure of Roman-period petitions as closely as does *SB* IV 7449. This divergence probably stems in part from the fact that it was written in Coptic and thus followed the conventions of Coptic epistles, which had been in circulation for centuries, whereas Coptic legal documents were just beginning to appear in this period.[47] For example, the petition opens with language characteristic of salutations in Coptic correspondence: "ϯπροcκ/ ⲁⲩⲱ ϯϣⲓⲛⲉ ⲉⲧⲉⲕⲁⲅⲁⲡⲏ ⲉⲧⲥⲙⲁⲙⲁⲧ." It is clear that a pastoral relationship existed between the unknown addressee and the author of the petition. The plaintiff refers to an earlier confession of the temptation from which he suffers, saying that the "disturbance" or "excitement", "ⲡϩⲟⲡϩⲡ̄", and the "temptation" or "trial", "ⲡⲡⲉⲓⲣⲁⲥⲙⲟⲥ", have not left him. Nevertheless, he still asserts his strong spiritual connection to the addressee: "God knows that thought of you has not ceased in our heart by night and day" or "ⲡ̄ⲛⲟⲩⲧⲉ ⲡⲉⲧⲥⲟⲟⲩⲛ ϫⲉ ⲡⲉⲕⲣⲡⲙⲉⲩ ⲗⲟ ⲁⲛ ϩⲙ ⲡⲉⲛϩⲏⲧ ⲛ ⲧⲉⲩϣⲏ ⲁⲩⲱ ⲡⲉϩⲟⲟⲩ." This rhetoric is fairly typical of correspondence between two Coptic Christians who have a pastoral relationship, but in this case it serves to introduce a petition.

The narrative of the assault carried out by Ammonius in *O. Mich. Copt.* 4 contains several elements seen in earlier petitions. Ammonius is described as a "lawless transgressor" or "ⲡⲁⲣⲁⲃⲁⲧⲏⲥ ⲙ̄ⲡⲁⲣⲁⲛⲟⲥ [*l.* ⲡⲁⲣⲁⲛⲟⲙⲟⲥ]". He has transgressed the normal bounds of civilized, Christian society and has incurred an obligation to the plaintiff by mistreating him. Furthermore, the author of the petition denigrates Ammonius' character by stating that he was very drunk during the attack, thereby asserting that Ammonius does not comport himself as a Christian should. The statement that Ammonius and his accomplices left the plaintiff "no resemblance of myself, neither foot nor hand being without some disfigurement" or "ⲙ̄ⲡⲟⲩⲕⲱ ϩⲓⲕⲱⲛ ϩⲓⲱⲧ ⲟⲩⲧⲉ ⲟⲩⲣⲏⲧⲉ ⲟⲩⲧⲉ ϭϫ [*l.* ϭⲓϫ] ⲉⲙⲛ̄ⲧⲁϥ ⲗⲁⲩⲉ ⲛ̄ϩⲱⲃ" again taps into the "discourse of wounded bodies" that Ari Bryen has shown to have permeated the petitions of the Roman period. Even as this petition exemplifies the formal Christian characteristics of a Coptic letter, the narration of Ammonius' attack draws on the rhetoric of a Roman petition by invoking obligations incurred.

---

[47] On the first Coptic legal documents, see FOURNET 2010b.

CONCLUSION

The involvement of Christian clerics in the practice of law in fifth and sixth century Egypt laid the foundations for the monastic legal culture that would dominate Coptic society in the seventh and eighth centuries. Even as the increased spiritual prestige and authority of monks and clergy created new *loci* of power, the social prestige of Roman law assured that its language and forms would still confer legitimacy in administering justice. This was true both at the level of discourse, as Coptic hagiographies reaffirmed the legitimacy of Roman practices for producing transcripts of legal proceedings, and at the level of practice, as legal documents show clerics serving as arbiters in their respective communities, making decisions that were recorded using the elaborate rhetoric of Byzantine legal documents.

Petitions to bishops and clergy invoked the narrative *topoi* of petitions from earlier periods while simultaneously appealing to new figures of authority within Christian communities. Both literary and documentary evidence for the practice of law in this period draw on the rhetorical style and theological content of the Christian writings that came to permeate the Egyptian context. The social prestige of Roman law in Christian documents, as well as the gradual adaptation of legal institutions to include Christian elements, would persist as monasteries became central to the practice of Roman law in Egypt in the seventh and eighth centuries.

BIBLIOGRAPHY

ABRAMS REBILLARD 2013: S. ABRAMS REBILLARD, 'The Speech Act of Swearing: Gregory of Nazianzus's Oath in *Poema* 2.1.2 in Context', *JECS* 21/2 (2013), p. 177-207.

ADAMS 2013: C. ADAMS, 'War and Society in the Roman Empire', in: B. CAMPBELL & L.A. TRITLE (eds.), *The Oxford Handbook of Warfare in the Classical World*, Oxford 2013, p. 261-276.

ADAMS 2016: J.N. ADAMS, *An Anthology of Informal Latin, 200 BC-AD 900: Fifty Texts with Translations and Linguistic Commentary*, Cambridge 2016.

AGUIZY 1996: O. EL-AGUIZY, 'Two New Demotic Temple Oaths on Ostraca', *BIFAO* 96 (1996), p. 1-11.

ALLAM 1991: S. ALLAM, 'Egyptian Law Courts in Pharaonic and Hellenistic Times', *JEA* 77 (1991), p. 109-127.

ALLAM 2008: S. ALLAM, 'Regarding the *Eisagogeus* at Ptolemaic Law Courts', *Journal of Egyptian History* 1/1 (2008), p. 3-19.

ALSTON 1994: R. ALSTON, 'Violence and Social Control in Roman Egypt', in: A. BÜLOW-JACOBSEN (ed.), *Proceedings of the 20th International Congress of Papyrologists. Copenhagen, 23-29 August 1992*, Copenhagen 1994, p. 517-521.

ALSTON 1995: R. ALSTON, *Soldier and Society in Roman Egypt: A Social History*, London & New York 1995.

AMMAR 1954: H. AMMAR, *Growing up in an Egyptian village, Silwa, Province of Aswan*, London 1954.

ANAGNOSTOU-CANAS 1984: B. ANAGNOSTOU-CANAS, 'La femme devant la justice provinciale dans l'Égypte romaine', *RHD* 62 (1984), p. 337-360.

ANAGNOSTOU-CANAS 1991: B. ANAGNOSTOU-CANAS, *Juge et sentence dans l'Égypte romaine* (Études de Philosophie et d'Histoire du Droit 6), Paris 1991.

ANAGNOSTOU-CANAS 2000: B. ANAGNOSTOU-CANAS, 'La documentation judiciaire pénale dans l'Égypte romaine', *Mélanges de l'École française de Rome. Antiquité* 112/2 (2000), p. 753-779.

ANDO 2000: C. ANDO, *Imperial Ideology and Provincial Loyalty in the Roman Empire* (Classics and Contemporary Thought 6), Berkeley 2000.

ANDO 2012: C. ANDO, *Imperial Rome AD 193 to 284: The Critical Century* (Edinburgh History of Ancient Rome), Edinburgh 2012.

ANDO 2015: C. ANDO, *Roman Social Imaginaries: Language and Thought in Contexts of Empire* (Robson Classical Lectures), Toronto 2015.

ARLT & MONSON 2010: C. ARLT & A. MONSON, 'Rules of an Egyptian Religious Association from the Early Second Century BCE', in: H. KNUF, C. LEITZ & D. VON RECKLINGHAUSEN (eds.), *Honi soit qui mal y pense. Studien zum pharaonischen, griechisch-römischen und spätantiken Ägypten zu*

Ehren von Heinz-Josef Thissen (Orientalia Lovaniensia Analecta 194), Leuven 2010, p. 113-122.

ARNAOUTOGLOU 1995: I. ARNAOUTOGLOU, 'Marital Disputes in Greco-Roman Egypt', *JJP* 25 (1995), p. 11-28.

ASSMANN 1992: J. ASSMANN, 'When Justice Fails: Jurisdiction and Imprecation in Ancient Egypt and the Near East', *JEA* 79 (1992), p. 149-172.

AST 2001: R. AST, 'Tziper, not Q. Iper', *ZPE* 137 (2001), p. 229-230.

AUBERT 1995: J.-J. AUBERT, 'Policing the Countryside: Soldiers and Civilians in Egyptian Villages in the Third and Fourth Centuries A.D.', in: Y. LE BOHEC (ed.), *La hiérarchie de l'armée romaine sous le Haut-Empire. Actes du Congrès de Lyon (15-18 septembre 1994)*, Paris 1995, p. 257-265.

AUSTIN 2006: M. AUSTIN, *The Hellenistic World from Alexander to the Roman Conquest*, 2nd ed., Cambridge 2006.

AZZARELLO 2012: G. AZZARELLO, *Il dossier della "domus divina" in Egitto*, Berlin 2012.

BAETENS 2014: G. BAETENS, 'Demotic Petitioning', *JJP* 44 (2014), p. 29-69.

BAETENS 2020a: G. BAETENS, *A Survey of Petitions and Related Documents from Ptolemaic Egypt* (Trismegistos Online Publications, Special Series, V), Revised 2017 diss., KU Leuven, Leuven 2020.

BAETENS 2020b: G. BAETENS, 'An Embalmer's Dispute in Hypsele/Shashotep', *AfP* 66/2 (2020), p. 273-312.

BAETENS & CLARYSSE 2016: G. BAETENS & W. CLARYSSE, 'A Quarrel at the Beer Shop of Little Memphis and a Murder', *AfP* 62/2 (2016), p. 396-404.

BAETENS & DEPAUW 2015: G. BAETENS & M. DEPAUW, 'The Legal Advice of Totoes in the Siut Archive (P. BM 10591 Verso, Col. I-III)', *JEA* 101 (2015), p. 197-215.

BAGNALL 1982: R.S. BAGNALL, 'The Population of Theadelphia in the Fourth Century', *Bulletin de la Société d'Archéologie Copte* 24 (1982), p. 35-57.

BAGNALL 1987: R.S. BAGNALL, 'Church, State and Divorce in Late Roman Egypt', in: K.-L. SELIG & R. SOMERVILLE (eds.), *Florilegium Columbianum: Essays in Honor of Paul Oskar Kristeller*, New York 1987, p. 41-61.

BAGNALL 1989: R.S. BAGNALL, 'Official and Private Violence in Roman Egypt', *BASP* 26 (1989), p. 201-216.

BAGNALL 1993: R.S. BAGNALL, *Egypt in Late Antiquity*, Princeton 1993.

BAGNALL 2006: R.S. BAGNALL, 'The People of the Roman Fayum', in: M.L. BIERBRIER (ed.), *Portraits and Masks: Burial Customs in Roman Egypt*, London 1997, p. 7-15 (reprinted in R.S. BAGNALL, *Hellenistic and Roman Egypt: Sources and Approaches*, Aldershot & Burlington (Vt.) 2006, Chapter XIV).

BAGNALL 2009: R.S. BAGNALL, *Early Christian Books in Egypt*, Princeton (N.J.) 2009.

BAGNALL 2011: R.S. BAGNALL, *Everyday Writing in the Graeco-Roman East*, Berkeley (Ca.), Los Angeles & London 2011.

BAGNALL & CRIBIORE 2006: R.S. BAGNALL & R. CRIBIORE, *Women's Letters from Ancient Egypt. 300 B.C.-A.D. 800*, Ann Arbor 2006.

BAGNALL & DEROW 1981: R.S. BAGNALL & P. DEROW, *Greek Historical Documents: The Hellenistic Period*, Chicago 1981.

BAGNALL & DEROW 2004: R.S. BAGNALL & P. DEROW, *The Hellenistic Period: Historical Sources in Translation* (Blackwell Sourcebooks in Ancient History), Malden (MA) & Oxford 2004.

BAGNALL & FRIER 2006: R.S. BAGNALL & B. FRIER, *The Demography of Roman Egypt*, revised ed., Cambridge 2006.

BAGNALL & WORP 2004: R.S. BAGNALL & K. WORP, *Chronological Systems of Byzantine Egypt*, 2nd ed., Leiden 2004.

BAINES 1987: J. BAINES, 'Practical Religion and Piety', *JEA* 73 (1987), p. 79-98.

BAINES & LACOVARA 2002: J. BAINES & P. LACOVARA, 'Burial and the Dead in Ancient Egyptian Society: Respect, Formalism, Neglect', *JSA* 2 (2002), p. 5-36.

BALAMOSHEV 2011: C. BALAMOSHEV, 'ΑΠΟΤΥΜΠΑΝΙΣΜΟΣ: Just Death by Exposing on the Plank?', *JJP* 41 (2011), p. 15-33.

BALDWIN 1963: B. BALDWIN, 'Crime and Criminals in Graeco-Roman Egypt', *Aegyptus* 43 (1963), p. 256-263.

BAMMEL 1984: C.P.H. BAMMEL, 'Products of Fifth-Century Scriptoria Preserving Conventions Used by Rufinus of Aquileia', *JTS* 35 (1984), p. 347-393.

BANAJI 2001: J. BANAJI, *Agrarian Change in Late Antiquity: Gold, Labour, and Aristocratic Dominance*, Oxford 2001.

BANDT forthcoming: C. BANDT, 'Kompilator oder Komponist: Ein Einblick in die Arbeit der Psalmenkatenisten', in: H. AMIRAV, E. FIORI & C. MARKSCHIES (eds.), *The Systematization of Knowledge in Late Antiquity: Catenae, Florilegae and Related Collections* (Late Antique History and Religion), Leuven forthcoming.

BARBANTANI 2010: S. BARBANTANI, 'Idéologie royale et littérature de cour dans l'Égypte Lagide', in: I. SAVALLI-LESTRADE & I. COGITORE (eds.), *Des rois au prince: Pratiques du pouvoir monarchique dans l'Orient hellénistique et romain*, Stendhal 2010, p. 227-251.

BARNES 1992: T.D. BARNES, 'Augustine, Symmachus, and Ambrose', in: J. MCWILLIAM (ed.), *Augustine: From Rhetor to Theologian*, Waterloo (Ont.) 1992, p. 7-13.

BARNES 2013: J. BARNES, *Cultivating the Nile: The Everyday Politics of Water in Egypt*, Durham (NC) 2014.

BARNS 1949: J. BARNS, 'The Nevill Papyrus: A Late Ramesside Letter to an Oracle', *JEA* 35 (1949), p. 69-71.

BAUSCHATZ 2007: J. BAUSCHATZ, 'Police Corruption in Ptolemaic Egypt', *CJ* 103/1 (2007), p. 13-39.

BAUSCHATZ 2013: J. BAUSCHATZ, *Law and Enforcement in Ptolemaic Egypt*, Cambridge & New York 2013.

BEAUCAMP 1992: J. BEAUCAMP, *Le statut de la femme à Byzance (4e-7e siècle). II. Les pratiques sociales*, Paris 1992.

BEGASS 2018: C. BEGASS, *Die Senatsaristokratie des oströmischen Reiches, ca. 457-518: Prosopographische und sozialgeschichtliche Untersuchungen*, Munich 2018.

BELL 1983: D. BELL (trans.), *The Life of Shenoute*, Kalamazoo 1983.

BELL 1917: H.I. BELL, 'The Byzantine Servile State', *JEA* 4 (1917), p. 86-106.

BELL 1944: H.I. BELL, 'An Egyptian Village in the Age of Justinian', *JHS* 64 (1944), p. 21-36.

BELL 2013: P.N. BELL, *Social Conflict in the Age of Justinian. Its Nature, Management, and Mediation*, Oxford 2013.

BELLO Y VILLARINO 2021: J.-M. BELLO Y VILLARINO, 'Measuring Corruption: A Critical Analysis of the Existing Datasets and their Suitability for Diachronic Transnational Research', *Social Indicators Research* 157/3 (2021), p. 709-747.

BENCIVENNI 2003: A. BENCIVENNI, *Progetti di riforme costituzionali nelle epigrafi greche dei secoli IV-II a.C.* (Tarsie. Studi di Antichistica 1), Bologna 2003.

BERGER 1953: A. BERGER, *Encyclopedic Dictionary of Roman Law* (Transactions of the American Philosophical Society 43/2), Philadelphia 1953.

BERKES 2017a: L. BERKES, *Dorfverwaltung und Dorfgemeinschaft in Ägypten von Diokletian zu den Abbasiden* (Philippika 104), Wiesbaden 2017.

BERKES 2017b: L. BERKES, 'SB IV 7438', *Tyche* 32 (2017), p. 253-254.

BERKES & HAUG 2016: L. BERKES & B. HAUG, 'Villages, Requisitions, and Tax Districts: Two Greek Lists from the Eighth-Century Fayyum', *BASP* 53 (2016), p. 189-222.

BERTHELOT 2015: H. BERTHELOT, 'De l'épistolaire au lapidaire: la publication des décisions lagides à Cyrène', in: Laboratoire ERAMA, *Les mises en scène de l'autorité dans l'Antiquité*, Nancy & Paris 2015, p. 215-227.

BEVAN 2016: G.A. BEVAN, *The New Judas: The Case of Nestorius in Ecclesiastical Politics, 428-451 CE* (Late Antique History and Religion 13), Leuven 2016.

BIERBRIER 2012: M.L. BIERBRIER, *Who Was Who in Egyptology*, 4th rev. ed., London 2012.

BIEZUNSKA-MALOWIST 1974: I. BIEZUNSKA-MALOWIST, *L'esclavage dans l'Égypte gréco-romaine. Première partie: période ptolémaïque*, Wrocław, Warsaw, Krakow & Gdańsk 1974.

BINGEN 1991: J. BINGEN, 'Notables hermopolitains et onomastique féminine', *CE* 66 (1991), p. 324-329.

BLAUDEAU 2009: P. BLAUDEAU, 'Puissance ecclésiale, puissance sociale: le siège alexandrin au prisme du Code Théodosien et des constitutions sirmondiennes', in: J.-J. AUBERT & P. BLANCHARD (eds.), *Droit, religion et société dans le Code Théodosien. Troisièmes Journées d'Étude sur le Code Théodosien (Neuchâtel, 15-17 février 2007)* (Université de Neuchâtel, Recueil de travaux publiés par la Faculté des Lettres et Sciences Humaines 55), Geneva 2009, p. 87-110.

BOAK 1937: A.E.R. BOAK, 'The Organization of Gilds in Greco-Roman Egypt', *TAPhA* 68 (1937), p. 212-220.

BOISSEVAIN 1974: J. BOISSEVAIN, *Friends of Friends: Networks, Manipulators and Coalitions*, New York 1974.

BONNEAU 1993: D. BONNEAU, *Le régime administratif de l'eau du Nil dans l'Égypte grecque, romaine et byzantine*, Leiden 1993.

BOURRIAU 1979: J. BOURRIAU, 'Museum Acquisitions, 1977: Egyptian Antiquities Acquired in 1977 by Museums in the United Kingdom', *JEA* 65 (1979), p. 151-155.

BOWERSOCK 1925: G.W. BOWERSOCK, 'Agesilaos', in: *Xenophon*, vol. VII: *Scripta minora* (Loeb Classical Library), Cambridge (MA) 1925.

BOYAVAL 1974: B. BOYAVAL, 'Une malédiction pour viol de sépulture', *ZPE* 14 (1974), p. 71-73.

BRADBURY 2004: S. BRADBURY, *Selected Letters of Libanius from the Age of Constantius and Julian*, Liverpool 2004.

BRANDES 2014: W. BRANDES, '*Damnatio* für die Ewigkeit – zur Entwicklung der Anathematismen auf Konzilien des 7. Jahrhunderts', in: S. SCHOLZ, G. SCHWEDLER & K.-M. SPRENGER (eds.), *Damnatio in memoria: Deformation und Gegenkonstruktionen in der Geschichte* (Zürcher Beiträge zur Geschichtswissenschaft 4), Cologne 2014, p. 265-277.

BRANSBOURG 2016: G. BRANSBOURG, 'Capital in the Sixth Century. The Dynamics of Tax and Estate in Roman Egypt', *Journal of Late Antiquity* 9/2 (2016), p. 305-414.

BRENNAN & PETTIT 2004: G. BRENNAN & P. PETTIT, *The Economy of Esteem*, Oxford 2004.

BRESCIANI 1994: E. BRESCIANI, 'Nuovi statuti demotici di 'Confraternite' dalla necropoli dei coccodrilli a Tebtynis (P. Vogl. demot. Inv. 77 et Inv. 78)', *EVO* 17 (1994), p. 46-67.

BRINK 2014: L. BRINK, *Soldiers in Luke-Acts* (Wissenschaftliche Untersuchungen zum Neuen Testament 2. Reihe 362), Tübingen 2014.

BROOKS 2016: G. BROOKS, *Criminology of Corruption: Theoretical Approaches*, Basingstoke 2016.

BROUX 2015: Y. BROUX, *Double Names and Elite Strategy in Roman Egypt* (Studia Hellenistica 54), Leuven 2015.

BROWN 1971: P. BROWN, 'The Rise and Function of the Holy Man in Late Antiquity', *JRS* 61 (1971), p. 80-101.

BRUGGISSER 1987: P. BRUGGISSER, '*Orator disertissimus*: À propos d'une lettre de Symmaque à Ambroise', *Hermes* 115 (1987), p. 106-115.

BRUNSCH 1982-83: W. BRUNSCH, 'Acht Holztafeln aus dem Britischen Museum, London', *Orientalia Suecana* 31-32 (1982-83), p. 33-42.

BRYEN 2013: A.Z. BRYEN, *Violence in Roman Egypt. A Study in Legal Interpretation* (Empire and After), Philadelphia 2013.

BRYEN 2014: A.Z. BRYEN, 'Law in Many Pieces', *CPh* 109/4 (2014), p. 346-365.

BRYEN 2016: A.Z. BRYEN, 'When Law Goes off the Rails, or, *Aggadah* among the *iurisprudentes*', *Critical Analysis of Law* 3/1 (2016), p. 9-29.

BUCHBERGER 1991: H. BUCHBERGER, 'Ḥtp an Ipw-rs.ti – Der Brief auf dem Gefäß München ÄS 4313', *SAK* 18 (1991), p. 49-87.

BURKES 1999: S. BURKES, *Death in Qoheleth and Egyptian Biographies of the Late Period*, Atlanta 1999.

BURMIL 2003: S. BURMIL, 'Landscape and Water in the Oases of Egypt's Western Desert', *Landscape Research* 28/4 (2003), p. 427-440.

BURT 2005: R. BURT, *Brokerage and Closure: An Introduction to Social Capital*, Oxford 2005.

BUTZER 1976: K. BUTZER, *Early Hydraulic Civilization in Egypt*, Chicago 1976.

CABOURET 2011: B. CABOURET, 'Art, technique et fonctions de la lettre de recommendation chez Libanios', in: J. DESMULLIEZ, C. HOËT-VAN CAUWENBERGHE & J.-C. JOLIVET (eds.), *L'étude des correspondances dans le monde romain de l'Antiquité classique à l'Antiquité tardive: permanences et mutations*, Villeneuve-d'Ascq 2011, p. 191-208.

CALLU 1972-2002: J.P. CALLU, *Symmaque. Correspondance*, Paris 1972-2002.

CAMERON 1965: A. CAMERON, 'Wandering Poets: A Literary Movement in Byzantine Egypt', *Historia* 14 (1965), p. 470-509.

CAMERON 1991: A. CAMERON, *Christianity and the Rhetoric of Empire: The Development of Christian Discourse* (Sather Classical Lectures 55), Berkeley 1991.

CAMPAGNO 2006: M. CAMPAGNO, 'Judicial Practices, Kinship and the State in "The Contending of Horus and Seth"', *ZÄS* 133 (2006), p. 20-33.

CAMPAGNO 2009: M. CAMPAGNO, 'Parentesco y Estado en los conflictos entre Horus y Seth', in: D.A. BARREYRA FRACAROLI & G. del OLMO LETE (eds.), *Reconstruyendo el Pasado Remoto. Estudios sobre el Próximo Oriente Antiguo en homenaje a Jorge R. Silva Castillo* (Aula Orientalis Suppl. 25), Sabadell 2009, p. 31-43.

CAMPBELL 1994: B. CAMPBELL, *The Roman Army, 31 BC – AD 337: A Sourcebook* (Routledge Sourcebooks for the Ancient World), London 1994.

CAMPLANI 2018: A. CAMPLANI, 'Setting a Bishopric/Arranging an Archive: Traces of Archival Activity in the Bishopric of Alexandria and Antioch', in: A. BAUSI, C. BROCKMANN, M. FRIEDRICH & S. KIENITZ (eds.), *Manuscripts and Archives: Comparative Views on Record-Keeping* (Studies in Manuscript Cultures 11), Berlin 2018, p. 231-272.

CANTARELLA 2005: E. CANTARELLA, 'Children and Divorce in Roman Law', in: K. MUSTAKALLIO & J. HANSKA (eds.), *Hoping for Continuity: Childhood, Education and Death in Antiquity and in the Middle Ages* (Acta Instituti Romani Finlandiae 33), Rome 2005, p. 33-48.

CASTIGLIONE 2017: D. CASTIGLIONE, 'Social Learning and the Bonds of Self-governing Communities', in: F. SABETTI & D. CASTIGLIONE (eds.), *Institutional Diversity in Self-Governing Societies: The Bloomington School and Beyond*, New York 2016, p. 129-156.

CECCONI 1994: G.A. CECCONI, *Governo imperiale e élites dirigenti nell'Italia tardoantica. Problemi di storia politico-amministrativa 270–476 d.C.* (Bibliotheca di Athenaeum 24), Como 1994.

ČERNÝ & GARDINER 1957: J. ČERNÝ & A.H. GARDINER, *Hieratic Ostraca*, Volume I, Oxford 1957.

CHADWICK 2009: H. CHADWICK, *Augustine of Hippo. A Life*, Oxford 2009.

CHAMPLIN 1991: E. CHAMPLIN, *Final Judgments. Duty and Emotion in Roman Wills 200 BC - AD 250*, Berkeley 1991.

CHAUVEAU 2001: M. CHAUVEAU, 'Les *qanāts* dans les ostraca de Manāwīr', in: P. BRIANT (ed.), *Irrigation et drainage dans l'antiquité: qanāts et canalisations souterraines en Iran, en Égypte et en Grèce*, Paris 2001, p. 137-142.

CHITWOOD 2017: Z. CHITWOOD, *Byzantine Legal Culture and the Roman Legal Tradition, 867-1056*, Cambridge & New York 2017.

CLARK 1990: D.S. CLARK, 'Civil Litigation Trends in Europe and Latin America since 1945: The Advantage of Intracountry Comparisons', *Law & Society Review* 24/2 (1990), p. 549-569.

CLARKE & MALCOLM 2016: A. CLARKE & R. MALCOLM, 'The Role of Property in Water Regulation: Locating Communal and Regulatory Property Rights on the Property Rights Spectrum', in: C. GODT (ed.), *Regulatory Property Rights: The Transforming Notion of Property in Transnational Business Regulation*, Leiden 2016, p. 121-140.

CLARYSSE 1990: W. CLARYSSE, 'Ptolémées et temples', in: D. VALBELLE (ed.), *Le décret de Memphis*, Paris 1990.

CLARYSSE 2001: W. CLARYSSE, 'Use and Abuse of Beer and Wine in Graeco-Roman Egypt', in: K. GEUS & K. ZIMMERMANN (eds.), *Punica – Libyca – Ptolemaica. Festschrift für Werner Huß, zum 65. Geburtstag dargebracht von Schülern, Freunden und Kollegen* (Orientalia Lovaniensia Analecta 104), Leuven 2001, p. 159-166.

CLARYSSE 2008: W. CLARYSSE, 'Graeco-Roman Oxyrhyncha, a Village in the Arsinoite Nome', in: S. LIPPERT & M. SCHENTULEIT (eds.), *Graeco-Roman Fayum. Texts and Archaeology*, Wiesbaden 2008, p. 55-73.

CLARYSSE 2009: W. CLARYSSE, 'Notes on Papyri', *ZPE* 168 (2009), p. 243-246.

CLARYSSE 2010: W. CLARYSSE, 'Bilingual Papyrological Archives', in: A. PAPACONSTANTINOU (ed.), *The Multilingual Experience in Egypt, from the Ptolemies to the 'Abbasids*, Farnham 2010, p. 47-72.

COLEMAN 1988: J.S. COLEMAN, 'Social Capital in the Creation of Human Capital', *American Journal of Sociology* 94 (1988), supplement, p. S95-S120.

COLES 1966: R.A. COLES, *Reports of Proceedings in Papyri* (Papyrologica Bruxellensia 4), Brussels 1966.

CONNOLLY 2010: S. CONNOLLY, *Lives Behind the Laws: The World of the* Codex Hermogenianus, Bloomington & Indianapolis 2010.

COOPER 1974: R.S. COOPER, *Ibn Mammātī's Rules for the Ministries: Translation with Commentary of the Qawānin al-Dawāwīn*, unpubl. diss., UC Berkeley, Berkeley 1974.

COOPER 2011: K. COOPER, 'Christianity, Private Power, and the Law from Decius to Constantine: The Minimalist View', *JECS* 19/3 (2011), p. 327-343.

CORCORAN 1996: S. CORCORAN, *The Empire of the Tetrarchs: Imperial Pronouncements and Government AD 284-324*, Oxford 1996.

CORCORAN 2015: S. CORCORAN, 'From Unholy Madness to Right-mindedness: Or How to Legislate for Religious Conformity from Decius to Justinian', in: A. PAPACONSTANTINOU, N. MCLYNN & D.L. SCHWARTZ (eds.), *Conversion in Late Antiquity: Christianity, Islam, and Beyond. Papers from the*

Andrew W. Mellon Foundation Sawyer Seminar, University of Oxford, 2009-2010, Farnham (Surrey) 2015, p. 67-94.

CORCORAN 2016: S. CORCORAN, 'The Emperors and the Monk Barsauma at Ephesus and Chalcedon', in: *2. Internationaler Workshop 'Law and Lawmaking in the Acts of the Ecumenical Councils'*, Bamberg 2016, unpublished.

COSME 2020: P. COSME, 'Les rapports entre soldats et paysans en Phrygie au Haut-Empire (27 avant J.-C.-235 après J.-C.)', in: M. ROUX (ed.), *La présence militaire dans les campagnes aux époques hellénistique et romaine: chance ou fatalité pour les communautés rurales?*, Perpignan 2020, p. 119-139.

COTTON 1981: H.M. COTTON, *Documentary Letters of Recommendation in Latin from the Roman Empire*, Königstein 1981.

COTTON 1984: H.M. COTTON, 'Greek and Latin Epistolary Formulae: Some Light on Cicero's Letter Writing', *AJPh* 105 (1984), p. 409-425.

COTTON 1985: H.M. COTTON, '*Mirificum Genus Commendationis*: Cicero and the Latin Letter of Recommendation', *AJPh* 106 (1985), p. 328-334.

COWEY & MARESCH 2001: J.M.S. COWEY & K. MARESCH, *Urkunden des Politeuma der Juden von Herakleopolis (144/3-133/2 v. Chr.) (P.Polit. Iud.)*, Wiesbaden 2001.

CRAWFORD 1978: D.J. CRAWFORD, 'The Good Official of Ptolemaic Egypt', in: H. MAEHLER & V.M. STROCKA (eds.), *Das ptolemäische Ägypten. Akten des internationalen Symposions 27.–29. September 1976 in Berlin*, Mainz 1978, p. 195-202.

CRAWFORD 1988: S. CRAWFORD, *Mayordomo: Chronicle of an Acequia in Northern New Mexico*, Albuquerque 1988.

CROOK & STONE 1967: J. CROOK & R. STONE, 'The Oppressor's Wrong, the Proud Man's Contumely?', *CR* 17 (1967), p. 83-86.

CRUM 1939: W. CRUM, *A Coptic Dictionary*, Oxford 1939.

DANIEL & MALTOMINI 1990-92: R.W. DANIEL & F. MALTOMINI, *Supplementum Magicum*, 2 vol., Opladen 1990-92.

DANIEL e.a. 1986: R.W. DANIEL, M. GRONEWALD & H.-J. THISSEN, *Griechische und demotische Papyri der Universitätsbibliothek Freiburg*, Bonn 1986.

DAVID 2010: A. DAVID, *The Legal Register of Ramesside Private Law Instruments*, Wiesbaden 2010.

DAVIES 1969: R.W. DAVIES, 'Joining the Roman Army', *BJ* 169 (1969), p. 208-232 (reprinted in D.J. BREEZE & V.A. MAXFIELD (eds.), *Service in the Roman Army*, Edinburgh 1989, p. 175-185).

DAVIES 1973: R.W. DAVIES, 'The Investigation of Some Crimes in Roman Egypt', *AncSoc* 4 (1973), p. 199-212 (reprinted in D.J. BREEZE & V.A. MAXFIELD (eds.), *Service in the Roman Army*, Edinburgh 1989, p. 175-185).

DAVIES 2002: S. DAVIES, 'The Organization, Administration and Functioning of the Sacred Animal Cults at North Saqqara as Revealed by the Demotic Papyrus from the Site', in: K. RYHOLT (ed.), *Acts of the Seventh International Conference of Demotic Studies*, Copenhagen 2002, p. 77-84.

DE CENIVAL 1972: F. DE CENIVAL, *Les associations religieuses en Égypte d'après les documents démotiques* (Bibliothèque d'Étude 46), Cairo 1972.

DEFERRARI 1922-34: R.J. DEFERRARI, *St. Basil. The Letters*, Cambridge 1922-1934.

DEFLEM 2015: M. DEFLEM, 'Deviance and Social Control', in: E. GOODE (ed.), *The Handbook of Deviance*, Malden (MA) 2015, p. 30-44.

DELATTRE 2007: A. DELATTRE, *Papyrus coptes et grecs du monastère d'apa Apollô de Baouît conservés aux Musées Royaux d'Art et d'Histoire de Bruxelles*, Brussels 2007.

DEMONT 2006: P. DEMONT, 'Hubris, «outrage», «anomie» et «démesure» de Gernet à Fisher', in: P. BRILLET-DUBOIS & E. PARMENTIER (eds.), *Φιλολογία. Mélanges offerts à Michel Casevitz*, Lyon & Paris 2006, p. 347-359.

DENIAUX 2011: E. DENIAUX, 'Lettres de recommendation et pratiques judiciaires à l'époque de Cicéron', in: J. DESMULLIEZ, C. HOËT-VAN CAUWENBERGHE & J.-C. JOLIVET (eds.), *L'étude des correspondances dans le monde romain de l'Antiquité classique à l'Antiquité tardive: permanences et mutations*, Villeneuve-d'Ascq 2011, p. 181-190.

DEPAUW 2006: M. DEPAUW, *The Demotic Letter. A Study of Epistolographic Scribal Traditions against Their Intra- and Intercultural Background* (Demotische Studien 14), Sommerhausen 2006.

DERDA 1991: T. DERDA, 'Necropolis Workers in Graeco-Roman Egypt', *JJP* 21 (1991), p. 13-36.

DEVAUCHELLE 1997: D. DEVAUCHELLE, 'Les serments à la porte de Djêmé', *RdE* 48 (1997), p. 260-263.

DI BITONTO 1968: A. DI BITONTO, 'Le petizioni ai funzionari nel periodo tolemaico', *Aegyptus* 48 (1968), p. 53-107.

DILLON 2012: N. DILLON, *The Justice of Constantine: Law, Communication, and Control* (Law and Society in the Ancient World), Ann Arbor 2012.

DOGAER 2015: N. DOGAER, 'Egyptian Names Derived from Foreign Elements: Innovation in Egyptian Onomastic Practice after the Roman Conquest', *CE* 90/2 (2015), p. 360-370.

DOHRMANN 2015: N.B. DOHRMANN, 'Can "Law" Be Private? The Mixed Message of Rabbinic Oral Law', in: C. ANDO & J. RÜPKE (eds.), *Public and Private in Ancient Mediterranean Law and Religion* (Religionsgeschichtliche Versuche und Vorarbeiten 65), Berlin & Boston 2015, p. 187-216.

DOLGANOV 2018: A. DOLGANOV, *Empire of Law: Legal Culture and Imperial Rule in the Roman Province of Egypt*, diss., Princeton University, Princeton 2018.

DOLGANOV 2020: A. DOLGANOV, '*Nutricula causidicorum.* Legal Practitioners in Roman North Africa', in: K. CZAIKOWSKI & B. ECKHARDT (eds.), *Law in the Roman Provinces*, Oxford 2020, p. 358-416.

DONCHEV & UJHELYI 2014: D. DONCHEV & G. UJHELYI, 'What Do Corruption Indexes Measure?', *Economics and Politics* 26/2 (2014), p. 309-331.

DONNAT 2007: S. DONNAT, 'Contacts with the Dead in Pharaonic Egypt: Ritual Relationships and Dead Classification', Manuscript published on www.academia.edu (https://www.academia.edu/8304758/Contacts_with_the_dead_in_Pharaonic_Egypt_Ritual_relationships_and_dead_classification).

DONNAT 2010: S. DONNAT, 'Written Pleas to the Invisible World: Texts as Media between Living and Dead in Pharaonic Egypt', in: A. STORCH (ed.), *Perception of the Invisible: Religion, Historical Semantics and the Role of Perceptive Verbs*, Cologne 2010, p. 51-80.

DONNAT 2014: S. DONNAT, *Écrire à ses morts: Enquête sur un usage rituel de l'écrit dans l'Égypte pharaonique*, Grenoble 2014.

DOSSEY 2001: L. DOSSEY, 'Judicial Violence and the Ecclesiastical Courts in Late Antique North Africa', in: R. MATHISEN (ed.), *Law, Society, and Authority in Late Antiquity*, Oxford 2001, p. 98-114.

DOSSEY 2010: L. DOSSEY, *Peasant and Empire in Christian North Africa*, Berkeley 2010.

DRAKE 2006: H.A. DRAKE (ed.), *Violence in Late Antiquity. Perceptions and Practices*, Aldershot 2006.

DRAKE 2013: H.A. DRAKE, 'Monotheism and Violence', *Journal of Late Antiquity* 6/2 (2013), p. 251-263.

DUNAND & ZIVIE-COCHE 1991: FR. DUNAND & C. ZIVIE-COCHE, *Dieux et hommes en Égypte*, Paris 1991.

DUNN 2015: G. DUNN, 'The Emergence of Papal Decretals: The Evidence of Zosimus of Rome', in: G. GREATREX, H. ELTON & L. MCMAHON (eds.), *Shifting Genres in Late Antiquity*, Farnham (Surrey) 2015, p. 81-92.

EBBELER 2007: J.V. EBBELER, 'Religious Identity and the Politics of Patronage: Symmachus and Augustine', *Historia* 56 (2007), p. 230-242.

EBBELER 2017: J.V. EBBELER, 'The Letter Collection of Augustine of Hippo', in: C. SOGNO, B.K. STORIN & E.J. WATTS (eds.), *Late Antique Letter Collections: A Critical Introduction and Reference Guide*, Oakland 2017, p. 239-253.

EICH 2015: P. EICH, 'The Common Denominator. Late Roman Imperial Bureaucracy from a Comparative Perspective', in: W. SCHEIDEL (ed.), *State Power in Ancient China and Rome* (Oxford Studies in Early Empires), Oxford 2015, p. 90-149.

ENDREFFY 2009: K. ENDREFFY, 'Reason for Despair: Notes on Some Demotic Letters to Thoth', in: B.S. EL-SHARKAWY (ed.), *The Horizon Studies in Egyptology in Honour of M.A. Nur el-Din (10-12 April 2007)*, Cairo 2009, p. 241-251.

ENDREFFY 2010: K. ENDREFFY, 'Business with Gods: The Role of Bargaining in Demotic Letters to Gods and Graeco-Roman Judicial Prayers', in: A. HUDECZ & M. PETRIK (eds.), *Commerce and Economy in Ancient Egypt. Proceedings of the Third International Congress for Young Egyptologists, 25-27 September 2009, Budapest* (BAR International Series 2131), Oxford 2010, p. 49-54.

EVANS-GRUBBS 1999: J. EVANS-GRUBBS, *Law and Family in Late Antiquity: The Emperor Constantine's Marriage Legislation*, Oxford 1999.

EVANS-GRUBBS 2002: J. EVANS-GRUBBS, *Women and the Law in the Roman Empire: A Sourcebook on Marriage, Divorce and Widowhood*, London & New York 2002.

EYRE 2004: Ch. EYRE, 'Judgement to the Satisfaction of All', in: *La fonction de juger. Égypte ancienne et Mésopotamie = Droit et Cultures. Revue semestrielle d'anthropologie et d'histoire* 47/1 (2004), p. 91-107.

FARAONE 2011: C.A. FARAONE, 'Curses, Crime Detection and Conflict Resolution at the Festival of Demeter Thesmophoros', *JHS* 131 (2011), p. 25-44.

FARAONE e.a. 2005: C.A. FARAONE, B. GARNAND & C. LÓPEZ-RUIZ, 'Micah's Mother (Judg. 17:1-4) and a Curse from Carthage (KAI 89): Canaanite Precedents for Greek and Latin Curses against Thieves?', *JNES* 64/3 (2005), p. 161-186.

FARAONE & RIFE 2007: C.A. FARAONE & J.L. RIFE, 'A Greek Curse against a Thief from the Koutsongila Cemetery at Roman Kenchreai', *ZPE* 160 (2007), p. 141-157.

FARBER 1979: J.J. FARBER, 'The Cyropaedia and Hellenistic Kingship', *AJPh* 100 (1979), p. 497-514.

FAULKNER 1955: R.O. FAULKNER, 'The Installation of the Vizier', *JEA* 41 (1955), p. 18-29.

FEISSEL & GASCOU 2004: D. FEISSEL & J. GASCOU (eds.), *La pétition à Byzance* (Centre de recherche d'Histoire et Civilisation de Byzance. Monographies 14), Paris 2004.

FISHER 1992: N.R.E. FISHER, *Hybris: A Study in the Values of Honour and Shame in Ancient Greece*, Warminster 1992.

FISCHER-BOVET 2014: C. FISCHER-BOVET, *Army and Society in Ptolemaic Egypt*, Cambridge 2014.

FISHMAN 2011: T. FISHMAN, *Becoming the People of the Talmud: Oral Torah as Written Tradition in Medieval Jewish Cultures* (Jewish Culture and Contexts), Philadelphia 2011.

FITZENREITER 2013: M. FITZENREITER, *Tierkulte im pharaonischen Ägypten*, Munich 2013.

FITZGERALD 1926: A. FITZGERALD, *The Letters of Synesius of Cyrene*, London 1926.

FLEMMING e.a. 1917: J.P.G. FLEMMING, G. HOFFMANN & H. LIETZMANN (eds.), *Akten der Ephesinischen Synode vom Jahre 449: syrisch mit deutscher Übersetzung und Anmerkungen* (Abhandlungen der Königlichen Gesellschaft der Wissenschaften zu Göttingen. Philologisch-historische Klasse. Neue Folge XV 1), Berlin 1917.

FORNESS 2020: P.M. FORNESS, 'Representing Lay Involvement in the Christological Controversies', in: W. BRANDES, A. HASSE-UNGEHEUER & H. LEPPIN (eds.), *Konzilien und kanonisches Recht in Spätantike und frühem Mittelalter: Aspekte konziliarer Entscheidungsfindung* (Forschungen zur byzantinischen Rechtsgeschichte – Neue Folge, 2), Berlin & Boston 2020, p. 57-80.

FÖRSTER 2002: H. FÖRSTER, *Wörterbuch der griechischen Wörter in den koptischen dokumentarischen Texten*, Berlin 2002.

FOURNET 1999: J.-L. FOURNET, *Hellénisme dans l'Égypte du VIe siècle. La bibliothèque et l'œuvre de Dioscore d'Aphrodité* (Mémoires publiés par les membres de l'Institut français d'archéologie orientale 115/1), 2 vol., Cairo 1999.

FOURNET 2000: J.-L. FOURNET, 'Le système des intermédiaires dans les reçus fiscaux byzantins et ses implications chronologiques sur le dossier de Dioscore d'Aphrodité', *AfP* 46/2 (2000), p. 233-248.

FOURNET 2003: J.-L. FOURNET, 'Between Literary Tradition and Cultural Change. The Poetic and Documentary Production of Dioscorus of Aphrodite', in: A.A. MACDONALD, M.W. TWOMEY & G.J. REININK (eds.), *Learned Antiquity: Scholarship and Society in the Near East, the Greco-Roman World, and the Early Medieval West*, Leuven 2003, p. 101-114.

FOURNET 2004: J.-L. FOURNET, 'Entre document et littérature. La pétition dans l'Antiquité tardive', in: D. FEISSEL & J. GASCOU (eds.), *La pétition à Byzance*, Paris 2004, p. 61-74.

FOURNET 2008: J.-L. FOURNET (ed.), *Les archives de Dioscore d'Aphrodité cent ans après leur découverte. Histoire et culture dans l'Égypte byzantine. Actes du colloque de Strasbourg 8-10 décembre 2005* (Études d'archéologie et d'histoire ancienne), Paris 2008.

FOURNET 2010a: J.-L. FOURNET, 'Les petitions des Acta Conciliorum Oecumenicorum comparées à celles de la documentation papyrologique (V^e^-VIe s.)', in: C. GASTGEBER (ed.), *Quellen zur byzantinischen Rechtspraxis: Aspekte der Textüberlieferung, Paläographie und Diplomatik. Akten des internationalen Symposiums, Wien, 5.-7.11.2007* (Veröffentlichungen zur Byzanzforschung 25), Vienna 2010, p. 61-80.

FOURNET 2010b: J.-L. FOURNET, 'Sur les premiers documents juridiques coptes', in: A. BOUD'HORS & C. LOUIS (eds.), *Études coptes XI. Treizième journée d'études (Marseille, 7-9 juin 2007)* (Cahiers de la Bibliothèque copte 17), Paris 2010, p. 125-137.

FOURNET 2015: J.-L. FOURNET, 'Des villageois en quête de lettres officielles. Le cas des pétitionnaires d'Aphrodité (Égypte, VIe s. ap. J.-C.)', in: S. PROCHÁZKA, L. REINFANDT & S. TOST (eds.), *Official Epistolography and the Language(s) of Power. Proceedings of the First International Conference of the Research Network "Imperium & Officium. Comparative Studies in Bureaucracy and Officialdom," Vienna, 10–12 November 2010* (Pap.Vind. 8), Vienna 2015, p. 255-266.

FOURNET & GASCOU 2002: J.-L. FOURNET & J. GASCOU, 'Moines pachômiens et batellerie', in: C. DÉCOBERT (ed.), *Alexandrie médiévale 2* (Études Alexandrines 8), Cairo 2002, p. 23-45.

FOURNET & GASCOU 2004: J.-L. FOURNET & J. GASCOU, 'Liste des pétitions sur papyrus des Ve–VIIe siècles', in: D. FEISSEL & J. GASCOU (eds.), *La pétition à Byzance*, Paris 2004, p. 141-196.

FRAADE 2014: S. FRAADE, 'Response to Azzan Yadin-Israel on Rabbinic Polysemy: Do They "Preach" What They Practice?', *Association for Jewish Studies Review* 38/2 (2014), p. 1-57.

FRAKES 1994: R.M. FRAKES, 'Late Roman Justice and the Origin of the *Defensor Civitatis*', *CJ* 89/4 (1994), p. 337-348.

FRAKES 2001: R.M. FRAKES, Contra potentium iniurias*: The* Defensor Civitatis *and Late Roman Justice* (Münchener Beiträge zur Papyrusforschung und antiken Rechtsgeschichte 90), Munich 2001.

FRANKFURTER 1998: D. FRANKFURTER, *Religion in Roman Egypt: Assimilation and Resistance*, Princeton 1998.

FRANKFURTER 2000: D. FRANKFURTER, 'A Plea to a Local God for a Husband's Attentions', in: R. VALANTASIS (ed.), *Religions of Late Antiquity in Practice*, Princeton 2000, p. 230-231.

FRANKFURTER 2006: D. FRANKFURTER, 'Hagiography and the Reconstruction of Local Religion in Late Antique Egypt: Memories, Inventions and Landscapes', in: J. DIJKSTRA & M. VAN DIJK (eds.), *The Encroaching Desert: Egyptian Hagiography and the Medieval West*, Leiden 2006, p. 13-37.

FRANKFURTER 2018: D. FRANKFURTER, '"It is Esrmpe Who Appeals!" Place, Object, and Performance in a Quest for Pregnancy in Roman Egypt', in: M. AHUVIA & A.G. KOCAR (eds.), *Placing Ancient Texts: The Rhetorical and Ritual Use of Space*, Tübingen 2018, p. 181-196.

FRASER 1972: P.M. FRASER, *Ptolemaic Alexandria*, 3 vol., Oxford 1972.

FREDERIKSEN 1967: M.W. FREDERIKSEN, 'Review of J. M. Kelly, *Roman Litigation*', *JRS* 57 (1967), p. 254-256.

FRENKEL 2014: L.M. FRENKEL, '"Dear Prefect, Stop the Ill Rumour!" – John of Antioch's Tactics to Counter Cyrillian Propaganda After the Council of Ephesus I', in: A. BRENT, M. LUDLOW & M. VINZENT (eds.), *Studia Patristica. Vol. LXXII – Including Papers Presented at the Fourth British Patristics Conference, at the University of Exeter, 5-7 September 2012* (Studia Patristica 72), Leuven 2014, p. 257-267.

FRENKEL 2015: L.M. FRENKEL, *Theodotus of Ancyra's Homilies and the Council of Ephesus (431)* (Studia Patristica Supplements 4), Leuven 2015.

FRENKEL 2016: L.M. FRENKEL, 'Individual Christian Voices in the Narratives of Late Antique Acclamations', *RRE* 2/2 (2016), p. 196-226.

FRENKEL 2017: L.M. FRENKEL, 'Procedural Similarities Between Fourth- and Fifth-Century Christian Synods and the Roman Senates: Myth, Politics or Cultural Identity?', in: M. VINZENT (ed.), *Studia Patristica Vol. XCII – Papers presented at the Seventeenth International Conference on Patristic Studies held in Oxford 2015. Volume 18: Liturgica and Tractatus symboli-Orientalia* (Studia Patristica 92), Leuven 2017, p. 293-302.

FRENKEL 2020: L.M. FRENKEL, 'Historiographic Narratives on the Authority of Imperial Writings in Christian Polemics', in: H.A.G. HOUGHTON, M.L. DAVIES & M. VINZENT (eds.), *Studia Patristica Vol. C – Including Papers Presented at the Sixth British Patristics Conference, Birmingham, 5-7 September 2016* (Studia Patristica 100), Leuven 2020, p. 165-172.

FUHRMANN 2012: C.J. FUHRMANN, *Policing the Roman Empire: Soldiers, Administration, and Public Order*, Oxford 2012.

GABRIELSEN 1994: V. GABRIELSEN, 'The Rhodian Associations Honouring Dionysodoros from Alexandria', *C&M* 45 (1994), p. 137-160.

GABRIELSEN 2016: V. GABRIELSEN, 'Be Faithful and Prosper: Associations, Trust and the Economy of Security', in: K. DROSS-KRÜPE, S. FÖLLINGER & K. RUFFING (eds.), *Antike Wirtschaft und ihre kulturelle Prägung – The Cultural Shaping of the Ancient Economy*, Wiesbaden 2016, p. 87-111.

GABRIELSEN & PAGANINI 2021: V. GABRIELSEN & M.C.D. PAGANINI (eds.), *Private Associations in the Ancient Greek World: Regulations and the Creation of Group Identity*, Cambridge 2021.

GAGOS & VAN MINNEN 1994: T. GAGOS & P. VAN MINNEN, *Settling a Dispute: Toward a Legal Anthropology of Late Antique Egypt*, Ann Arbor 1994.

GAGOS e.a 1992: T. GAGOS, L. KOENEN & B.E. MCNELLEN, 'A First Century Archive from Oxyrhynchos or Oxyrhynchite Loan Contracts and Egyptian Marriage', in: J.J. JOHNSON (ed.), *Life in a Multi-cultural Society: Egypt from Cambyses to Constantine and Beyond* (Studies in Ancient Oriental Civilization 51), Chicago 1992, p. 181-208.

GALANTER 1983: M. GALANTER, 'Reading the Landscape of Disputes: What We Know and Don't Know (and Think We Know) about Our Allegedly Contentious and Litigious Society', *UCLA Law Review* 31 (1983), p. 4-71.

GALLAY 1964-1967: P. GALLAY, *Saint Grégoire de Nazianze. Correspondance*, Paris 1964-1967.

GALLAZZI 1985: C. GALLAZZI, 'Supplica ad Atena su un ostrakon da Esna', *ZPE* 61 (1985), p. 101-109.

GARDINER 1930: A.H. GARDINER, 'A New Letter to the Dead', *JEA* 16/1-2 (1930), p. 19-22.

GARDINER & SETHE 1928: A.H. GARDINER & K. SETHE, *Egyptian Letters to the Dead, Mainly from the Old and Middle Kingdoms*, London 1928.

GARNSEY 1970: P.D.A. GARNSEY, *Social Status and Legal Privilege in the Roman Empire*, Oxford 1970.

GASCOU 2008: J. GASCOU, 'Justice d'Athéna en Égypte romaine', in: F.A.J. HOOGENDIJK & B.P. MUHS (eds.), *Sixty-Five Papyrological Texts Presented to Klaas A. Worp on the Occasion of his 65th Birthday* (Pap.Lugd.Bat. 33), Leiden 2008, p. 29-39.

GAUTHIER 2000: N. GAUTHIER, 'Le réseau de pouvoirs de l'évêque dans le Gaule du haut Moyen-Âge', in: G.P. BROGIOLO, N. GAUTHIER & N. CHRISTIE (eds.), *Towns and Their Territories between Late Antiquity and the Early Middle Ages* (Transformation of the Roman World 9), Leiden 2000, p. 173-208.

GEHRKE 1982: H.-J. GEHRKE, 'Der siegreiche König: Überlegungen zur hellenistischen Monarchie', *AKG* 64 (1982), p. 247-277.

GELZER 1909: M. GELZER, *Studien zur byzantinischen Verwaltung Ägyptens* (Leipziger historische Abhandlungen 13), Leipzig 1909.

GELZER 1913: M. GELZER, 'Altes und Neues aus der byzantinisch-ägyptischen Verwaltungsmisere, vornehmlich im Zeitalter Justinians', *AfP* 5 (1913), p. 346-377.

GERACI 1979: G. GERACI, 'Per una storia dell'amministrazione fiscale nell'Egitto del VI secolo d. C. Dioskoros e l'autopragia di Aphrodito', in: J. BINGEN & G. NACHTERGAEL (eds.), *Actes du XVe Congrès Internationale de Papyrologie* (Papyrologica Bruxellensia 19), vol. 4, Brussels 1979, p. 195-205.

GIBBS 2011: M. GIBBS, 'Trade Associations in Roman Egypt: Their Raison d'Être', *AncSoc* 41 (2011), p. 291-315.

GIBBS 2015: M. GIBBS, 'The Trade Associations of Ptolemaic Egypt: Definition, Organization and Their Relationship with the State', in: V. GABRIELSEN & C.A. THOMSEN (eds.), *Private Associations and the Public Sphere: Proceedings of a Symposium Held at the Royal Danish Academy of Sciences and Letters, 9-11 September 2010* (Scientia Danica. Series H, Humanistica, 8 vol. 9), Copenhagen 2015, p. 241-268.

GOFF 2005: M.J. GOFF, 'Hellenistic Instruction in Palestine and Egypt: Ben Sira and Papyrus Insinger', *JSJ* 36 (2005), p. 147-172.

GOLDBRUNNER 2006: S. GOLDBRUNNER, *Der verblendete Gelehrte: Der erste Setna-Roman (P. Kairo 30646): Umschrift, Übersetzung und Glossar* (Demotische Studien 13), Sommerhausen 2006.

GORDON 2015: R. GORDON, 'Showing the Gods the Way: Curse-tablets as Deictic Persuasion', *RRE* 1/2 (2015), p. 148-180.

GORRE & WACKENIER 2020: G. GORRE & S. WACKENIER (eds.), *Quand la fortune du royaume ne dépend pas de la vertu du Prince. Un renforcement de la monarchie lagide de Ptolemée VI à Ptolemée X (169-88 av. J.-C.)?* (Studia Hellenistica 59), Leuven 2020.

GOUDRIAAN 1988: K. GOUDRIAAN, *Ethnicity in Ptolemaic Egypt*, Amsterdam 1988.

GOZZOLI 2006: R.B. GOZZOLI, *The Writing of History in Ancient Egypt during the First Millennium BC (ca. 1070-180 BC). Trends and Perspectives*, London 2006.

GRADENWITZ, PREISIGKE & SPIEGELBERG 1912: O. GRADENWITZ, F. PREISIGKE & W. SPIEGELBERG, *Ein Erbstreit aus dem ptolemäischen Ägypten: griechische und demotische Papyri der Wissenschaftlichen Gesellschaft zu Strassburg i. Els*, Strassburg 1912.

GRAFTON & WILLIAMS 2006: A. GRAFTON & M.H. WILLIAMS, *Christianity and the Transformation of the Book: Origen, Eusebius, and the Library of Caesarea*, Cambridge (Mass.) 2006.

GRAUMANN 2004: T. GRAUMANN, 'Distribution of Texts and Communication: Networks in the Nestorian Controversy', in: *Comunicazione e ricezione del documento cristiano in epoca tardoantica: XXXII Incontro di studiosi dell' antichità cristiana: Roma, 8-10 maggio 2003* (Studia Ephemerides Augustinianum 90), Rome 2004, p. 227-238.

GRAUMANN 2015: T. GRAUMANN, 'Altkirchliche Synoden zwischen theologischer Disputation und rechtlichem Disput', in: C. DARTMANN, A.N. PIETSCH & S. STECKEL (eds.), *Ecclesia disputans. Die Konfliktpraxis vormoderner Synoden zwischen Religion und Politik* (Historische Zeitschrift. Beihefte N.F. 67), Berlin & Boston 2015, p. 35-60.

GRAUMANN 2020: T. GRAUMANN, 'Die Verschriftlichung synodaler Entscheidungen', in: W. BRANDES, A. HASSE-UNGEHEUER & H. LEPPIN (eds.), *Konzilien und kanonisches Recht in Spätantike und frühem Mittelalter: Aspekte konziliarer Entscheidungsfindung* (Forschungen zur byzantinischen Rechtsgeschichte – Neue Folge, 2), Berlin & Boston 2020, p. 1-24.

GREY 2011: C. GREY, *Constructing Communities in the Late Roman Countryside*, Cambridge 2011.

Grieshammer 1975: R. Grieshammer, 'Briefe an Tote', *LÄ* I, col. 863-870.

Grotkamp 2014: N. Grotkamp, 'The Ptolemaic *Dikasterion*', in: A. Lanni & M. Gagarin (eds.), *Symposion 2013: Vorträge zur griechische und hellenistische Rechtsgeschichte (Cambridge MA, 26.08.2013 - 29.08.2013)* (Akten der Gesellschaft für griechische und hellenistische Rechtsgeschichte 24), Vienna 2014, p. 347-360.

Grotkamp 2018: N. Grotkamp, *Rechtsschutz im hellenistischen Ägypten*, Munich 2018.

Gruen 1996: E.S. Gruen, 'Hellenistic Kingship: Puzzles, Problems and Possibilities', in: P. Bilde, T. Engberg-Pedersen, L. Hannestad & J. Zahle (eds.), *Aspects of Hellenistic Kingship*, Cambridge 1996, p. 116-125.

Grünewald 1999: T. Grünewald, *Räuber, Rebellen, Rivalen, Rächer. Studien zu Latrones im Römischen Reich* (Forschungen zur antiken Sklaverei 31), Stuttgart 1999.

Gryson 1984: R. Gryson, 'Origine et composition des «scolies ariennes» du manuscrit Paris, B.N., lat. 8907', *RHT* 14 (1984), p. 369-375.

Guilmot 1966: M. Guilmot, 'Les lettres aux morts dans l'Égypte ancienne', *RHR* 170 (1966), p. 1-27.

Gutsfeld 2006: A. Gutsfeld, 'Vicarius', in: H. Cancik & H. Schneider (eds.), *Brill's New Pauly*, consulted online on 19 October 2017 <https://doi.org/10.1163/1574-9347_bnp_e12203980>, Leiden 2006.

Habermann 1997: W. Habermann, 'Aspekte des Bewässerungswesens im kaiserzeitlichen Ägypten. I: Die 'Erklärungen für nicht-überflutetes Land' (Abrochia-Deklarationen)', in: K. Ruffing & B. Tenger (eds.), *Miscellanea oeconomica. Studien zur antiken Wirtschaftsgeschichte. H. Winkel zum 65. Geb.*, St. Katharinen 1997, p. 213-283.

Haensch 1997: R. Haensch, 'Zur Konventsordnung in Aegyptus und den übrigen Provinzen des römischen Reiches', in: B. Kramer e.a. (eds.), *Akten des 21. internationalen Papyrologenkongresses Berlin, 13.-19.8.1995*, Stuttgart & Leipzig 1997, vol. 1, p. 320-391.

Haensch 2013: R. Haensch, 'Die Statthalterarchive der Spätantike', in: M. Faraguna (ed.), *Archives and Archival Documents in Ancient Societies. Trieste 30 September-1 October 2011* (Legal Documents in Ancient Societies 4), Trieste 2013, p. 333-349.

Haensch 2015: R. Haensch, 'From Free to Fee? Judicial Fees and Other Litigation Costs during the High Empire and Late Antiquity', in: D. Kehoe, D. Ratzan & U. Yiftach (eds.), *Law and Transaction Costs in the Ancient Economy*, Ann Arbor 2015, p. 253-272.

Haensch 2016: R. Haensch (ed.), *Recht haben und Recht bekommen im Imperium Romanum. Das Gerichtswesen der römischen Kaiserzeit und seine dokumentarische Evidenz. Ausgewählte Beiträge einer Serie von drei Konferenzen an der Villa Vigoni in den Jahren 2010 bis 2012* (JJP Suppl. 24), Warsaw 2016.

Häge 1968: G. Häge, *Ehegüterrechtliche Verhältnisse in den griechischen Papyri Ägyptens bis Diokletian*, Cologne & Graz 1968.

HAGEDORN 1986: D. HAGEDORN (ed.), *Byzantinische Papyri der Bayerischen Staatsbibliothek München*, 2nd ed., Stuttgart 1986.

HAGEN 2012: F. HAGEN, *An Ancient Egyptian Literary Text in Context: The Instruction of Ptahhotep* (Orientalia Lovaniensia Analecta 218), Leuven 2012.

HALEY 1991: J.O. HALEY, *Authority without Power. Law and the Japanese Paradox*, New York 1991.

HARARI 2014: Y.N. HARARI, *Sapiens: A Brief History of Humankind*, London 2014.

HARDIN 1968: G. HARDIN, 'The Tragedy of the Commons', *Science* 162/3859 (1968), p. 1243-1248.

HARDY 1931: E.R. HARDY, *The Large Estates of Byzantine Egypt* (Studies in History, Economics and Public Law 354), New York 1931.

HARPER 2017: K. HARPER, *The Fate of Rome: Climate, Disease, and the End of an Empire*, Princeton 2017.

HARRAUER & PINTAUDI 2012: H. HARRAUER & R. PINTAUDI, 'Mein Haus ist leer!: Enteuxis gegen die eigene Frau. P.Vindob. Barbara Inv. 34', *Aegyptus* 92 (2012), p. 3-12.

HARRIES 1999: J.D. HARRIES, *Law and Empire in Late Antiquity*, Cambridge 1999.

HARRIES 2001a: J.D HARRIES, *Law and Empire in Late Antiquity*, rev. ed., Cambridge 2001.

HARRIES 2001b: J.D. HARRIES, 'Resolving Disputes. The Frontiers of Law in Late Antiquity', in: R.W. MATHISEN (ed.), *Law, Society, and Authority in Late Antiquity*, Oxford 2001, p. 68-82.

HARRIES 2011: J.D. HARRIES, 'Superfluous Verbiage?: Rhetoric and Law in the Age of Constantine and Julian', *JECS* 19/3 (2011), p. 345-374.

HARRIES 2013: J.D. HARRIES, 'Roman Law from City State to World Empire', in: J. DUINDAM, J.D. HARRIES, C. HUMFRESS & H. NIMROD (eds.), *Law and Empire: Ideas, Practices, Actors* (Rulers & Elites 3), Leiden 2013, p. 45-61.

HARRIES 2016: J.D. HARRIES, 'Legal Education and Training of Lawyers', in: P.J. DU PLESSIS, C. ANDO & K. TUORI (eds.), *The Oxford Handbook of Roman Law and Society*, Oxford 2016, p. 151-163.

HARRINGTON 2013: N. HARRINGTON, *Living with the Dead: Ancestor Worship and Mortuary Ritual in Ancient Egypt*, Oxford 2013.

HAUBEN 2016: H. HAUBEN, 'The Ptolemaic Ordinance of 118 BC on the Jurisdiction of Royal and Egyptian Courts', *Przeglad Historyczny* 107 (2016), p. 441-470.

HAUG 2017: B. HAUG, '360 Days of Summer: Experiencing the Fluvial in Egypt's Fayyum', in: T. FRANCONI (ed.), *Fluvial Landscapes in the Roman World* (JRA Supplement 104), Portsmouth 2017, p. 139-158.

HAUKEN 1998: T. HAUKEN, *Petition and Response. An Epigraphic Study of Petitions to Roman Emperors, 181–249* (Monographs from the Norwegian Institute at Athens 2), Bergen 1998.

HAUKEN & MALAY 2009: T. HAUKEN & H. MALAY, 'A New Edict of Hadrian from the Province of Asia Setting Regulations for Requisitioned Transport', in: R. HAENSCH (ed.), *Selbstdarstellung und Kommunikation: Die Veröffentlichung staatlicher Urkunden auf Stein und Bronze in der Römischen Welt*, Munich 2009, p. 327-348.

HAWKINS 2016: C. HAWKINS, *Roman Artisans and the Urban Economy*, Cambridge 2016.

HAZZARD 2000: R.A. HAZZARD, *Imagination of a Monarchy: Studies in Ptolemaic Propaganda*, Toronto 2000.

HELMIS 1986: A. HELMIS, *Crime et châtiment dans l'Égypte ptolémaïque: recherches sur l'autonomie d'un modèle pénal*, unpubl. diss., Université Paris X Nanterre, Paris 1986.

HENGSTL 1997: J. HENGSTL, 'Petita in Petitionen gräko-ägyptischer Papyri', in: G. THÜR & I. VÉLISSAROPOULOS-KARAKOSTAS (eds.), *Symposion 1995: Vorträge zur griechischen und hellenistischen Rechtsgeschichte* (Akten der Gesellschaft für griechische und hellenistische Rechtsgeschichte 11), Cologne 1997, p. 265-289.

HENGSTL 2002: J. HENGSTL, 'Zum rechtlichen Sprachgebrauch in Petitionen der Ptolemäerzeit', in: *Antike Rechte und Gesellschaft. Festschrift für Panayotis Dimakis*, Athens 2002, p. 213-228.

HEZSER 1998: C. HEZSER, 'The Codification of Legal Knowledge in Late Antiquity: The Talmud Yerushalmi and Roman Law Codes', in: P. SCHÄFER (ed.), *The Talmud Yerushalmi and Graeco-Roman Culture, I* (Texte und Studien zum antiken Judentum 71), Tübingen 1998, p. 581-642.

HEZSER 2002: C. HEZSER, 'The Mishnah and Ancient Book Production', in: A.J. AVERY-PECK & J. NEUSNER (eds.), *The Mishnah in Contemporary Perspective* (Handbuch der Orientalistik. Erste Abteilung, Nahe und der Mittlere Osten 65), Leiden 2002, p. 167-192.

HEZSER 2007: C. HEZSER, 'Roman Law and Rabbinic Legal Composition', in: C.E. FONROBERT & M.S. JAFFEE (eds.), *The Cambridge Companion to the Talmud and Rabbinic Literature*, Cambridge 2007, p. 144-163.

HILLNER e.a. 2016: J. HILLNER, J. ULRICH & J. ENGBERG (eds.), *Clerical Exile in Late Antiquity* (Early Christianity in the Context of Antiquity 17), Frankfurt am Main 2016.

HIRATA 2008: A. HIRATA, 'Die Generalklausel zur Hybris in den alexandrinischen Dikaiomata', *ZRG* 125 (2008), p. 675-681.

HIRATA 2010: A. HIRATA, 'Die alexandrinischen Dikaiomata als Quelle der historischen Rechtsvergleichung', in: M. LANG, H. BARTA & R. ROLLINGER (eds.), *Staatsverträge, Völkerrecht und Diplomatie im Alten Orient und in der griechisch-römischen Antike*, Wiesbaden 2010, p. 39-50.

HIRSCHFELD 1892: O. HIRSCHFELD, 'Die ägyptische Polizei der römischen Kaiserzeit nach Papyrusurkunden', *Sitzungsberichte der Königlich Preussischen Akademie der Wissenschaften zu Berlin* 1892/II (1892), p. 815-824.

HMIC 2020: HER MAJESTY'S INSPECTORATE OF CONSTABULARY (HMIC), *State of Policing: The Annual Assessment of Policing in England and Wales 2019*, London 2020.

HOBSON 1993: D.W. HOBSON, 'The Impact of Law on Village Life in Roman Egypt', in: B.H. HALPERN & D.W. HOBSON (eds.), *Law, Politics and Society in the Ancient Mediterranean World*, Sheffield 1993, p. 193-219.

HODGKINSON, CAPUTO & MCINTYRE 2019: T. HODGKINSON, T. CAPUTO & M.L. MCINTYRE, 'Beyond Crime Rates and Community Surveys: A New Approach to Police Accountability and Performance Measurement', *Crime Science* 8/13 (2019), p. 1-7.

HODGSON 2006: S. HODGSON, *Modern Water Rights: Theory and Practice* (FAO Legislative Study 92), Rome 2006.

HÖLBL 2015: G. HÖLBL, 'Zur Bautätigkeit der Ptolemäer in Ägypten', in: W. SEIPEL (ed.), *Ägypten: die letzten Pharaonen*, Leoben & Regensburg 2015, p. 109-117.

HOLMES 2015: L. HOLMES, *Corruption: A Very Short Introduction*, Oxford 2015.

HONIGMAN 2003: S. HONIGMAN, 'Politeumata and Ethnicity in Ptolemaic and Roman Egypt', *AncSoc* 33 (2003), p. 61-102.

HONIGMAN 2016: S. HONIGMAN, 'The Ptolemaic and Roman Definitions of Social Categories and the Evolution of Judean Communal Identity in Egypt', in: Y. FURSTENBERG (ed.), *Jewish and Christian Communal Identities in the Roman World*, Leiden & Boston 2016, p. 25-74.

HUCHTHAUSEN 1973: L. HUCHTHAUSEN, 'Soldaten des 3. Jahrhunderts u. Z. als Korrespondenten der kaiserlichen Kanzlei', in: *Altertumswissenschaft mit Zukunft: Dem Wirken Werner Hartkes gewidmet*, Berlin 1973, p. 17-51.

HUCHTHAUSEN 1974: L. HUCHTHAUSEN, 'Herkunft und ökonomische Stellung weiblicher Adressaten von Reskripten des *Codex Iustinianus* (2. und 3. Jh. u. Z.)', *Klio* 54 (1974), p. 199-228.

HUCHTHAUSEN 1976: L. HUCHTHAUSEN, 'Zu kaiserlichen Reskripten an weibliche Adressaten aus der Zeit Diokletians (284-305 u. Z.)', *Klio* 58 (1976), p. 55-85.

HUCHTHAUSEN 1992: L. HUCHTHAUSEN, *Frauen fragen den Kaiser: Eine soziologische Studie über das 3. Jh. n. Chr.*, Konstanz 1992.

HUCK 2003: O. HUCK, 'À propos de CTh 1,27,1 et CSirm 1. Sur deux textes controversés relatifs à l'*episcopalis audientia* constantinienne', *ZRG* 120/1 (2003), p. 78-105.

HUCK 2008: O. HUCK, 'La «création» de l'*audientia episcopalis* par Constantin', in: J.-N. GUINOT & F. RICHARD (eds.), *Empire chrétien et église aux IV*[e] *et V*[e] *siècles: intégration ou concordat, le témoignage du Code Théodosien: actes du colloque international (Lyon, 6, 7 et 8 Octobre 2005)*, Paris 2008, p. 285-305.

HUE-ARCÉ 2017a: C. HUE-ARCÉ, 'Violence against Women in Graeco-Roman Egypt: The Contribution of Demotic Documents', in: U. MATIĆ & B. JENSEN (eds.), *Archaeologies of Gender and Violence*, Oxford 2017, p. 133-150.

HUE-ARCÉ 2017b: C. HUE-ARCÉ, 'Hiérarchies socio-professionnelles et violence interpersonnelle dans l'Égypte du Nouvel Empire et d'époque hellénistique', *Archimède. Archéologie et histoire ancienne* 4 (2017), p. 174-183.

HUE-ARCÉ 2019: C. HUE-ARCÉ, '"This Oath Is a True Oath": Family Involvement in the Demotic Temple Oaths', in: F. NAETHER (ed.), *New Approaches*

in Demotic Studies. Acts of the 13th International Conference of Demotic Studies (ZÄS, Beihefte 10), Berlin 2019, p. 123-134.
HUE-ARCÉ 2020: C. HUE-ARCÉ, *La violence interpersonnelle en Égypte au Nouvel Empire et à l'époque gréco-romaine*, Wallasey 2020.
HUEBNER 2013: S. HUEBNER, *The Family in Roman Egypt: A Comparative Approach to Intergenerational Solidarity and Conflict*, Cambridge 2013.
HUGHES 1958: G.R. HUGHES, 'A Demotic Letter to Thoth', *JNES* 17/1 (1958), p. 1-12.
HUGHES 1968: G.R. HUGHES, 'A Demotic Plea to Thoth in the Library of G. Michaelides', *JEA* 54 (1968), p. 176-182.
HUGHES 1969: G.R. HUGHES, 'The Cruel Father. A Demotic Papyrus in the Library of G. Michaelides', in: G.E. KADISH (ed.), *Studies in Honor of John A. Wilson* (Studies in Ancient Oriental Civilization 35), Chicago 1969, p. 43-54.
HUMFRESS 2007a: C. HUMFRESS, 'Judging by the Book: Christian Codices and Late Antique Legal Culture', in: W.E. KLINGSHIRN & L. SAFRAN (eds.), *The Early Christian Book* (Catholic University of America Studies in Early Christianity), Washington D.C. 2007, p. 141-158.
HUMFRESS 2007b: C. HUMFRESS, *Orthodoxy and the Courts in Late Antiquity*, Oxford 2007.
HUMFRESS 2011: C. HUMFRESS, 'Bishops and Law Courts in Late Antiquity: How (Not) to Make Sense of the Legal Evidence', *JECS* 19/3 (2011), p. 375-400.
HUMFRESS 2013a: C. HUMFRESS, 'Thinking Through Legal Pluralism: 'Forum Shopping' in the Later Roman Empire', in: J. DUINDAM, J.D. HARRIES, C. HUMFRESS & H. NIMROD (eds.), *Law and Empire: Ideas, Practices, Actors* (Rulers & Elites 3), Leiden 2013, p. 225-250.
HUMFRESS 2013b: C. HUMFRESS, 'Law's Empire: Roman Universalism and Legal Practice', in: P.J. DU PLESSIS (ed.), *New Frontiers: Law and Society in the Roman World*, Edinburgh 2013, p. 73-101.
HUMFRESS 2016: C. HUMFRESS, 'Ordering Divine Knowledge in Late Roman Legal Discourse', in: M. KAHLOS (ed.), *Emperors and the Divine – Rome and its Influence* (COLLeGIUM: Studies Across Disciplines in the Humanities and Social Sciences 20), Helsinki 2016, p. 160-176.
HUNT & EDGAR 1932-1941: A.S. HUNT & C.C. EDGAR (eds. & trans.), *Select Papyri* (Loeb Classical Library), London 1932-1941.
HUSS 1980: W. HUSS, 'Staat und Ethos nach den Vorstellungen eines Ptolemäischen Dioiketes des 3. Jh. Bemerkungen zu P. Tebt. III 1, 703', *AfP* 27 (1980), p. 67-77.
HUSS 2001: W. HUSS, *Ägypten in hellenistischer Zeit, 332-30 v. Chr.*, Munich 2001.
HUSS 2011: W. HUSS, *Die Verwaltung des ptolemaiischen Reichs*, Munich 2011.
HUSSELMAN, BOAK & EDGERTON 1944: E.M. HUSSELMAN, A.E.R. BOAK & W.F. EDGERTON, *Papyri from Tebtunis. Part II* (Michigan Papyri 5), Ann Arbor 1944.

IBRAHIM & IBRAHIM 2003: F.N. IBRAHIM & B. IBRAHIM, *Egypt: An Economic Geography*, London 2003.

ILAN 2012: T. ILAN, 'Babatha the Killer-wife: Literature, Folk Religion and Documentary Papyri', in: K.-P. ADAM, F. AVEMARIE, N. WAZANA & D. FELSCH (eds.), *Law and Narrative in the Bible and in Neighbouring Ancient Cultures* (Forschungen zum Alten Testament 2. Reihe 54), Tübingen 2012, p. 263-278.

ISAAC 1991: B. ISAAC, 'The Roman Army in Judaea: Police Duties and Taxation', in V.A. MAXFIELD & M.J. DOBSON (eds.), *Roman Frontier Studies 1989*, Exeter 1991, p. 455-461.

JACKSON & BRADFORD 2010: J. JACKSON & B. BRADFORD, 'Measuring Public Confidence in the Police: Is the PSA23 Target Fit for Purpose?', *Policing: A Journal of Policy and Practice* 4 (2010), p. 241-248.

JAKAB 2013: É. JAKAB, 'Financial Transactions by Women in Puteoli', in: P.J. DU PLESSIS (ed.), *New Frontiers: Law and Society in the Roman World*, Edinburgh 2013, p. 123-150.

JANKOWIAK & BOOTH 2015: M. JANKOWIAK & P. BOOTH, 'A New Date-List of the Works of Maximus the Confessor', in: B. NEIL & P. ALLEN (eds.), *The Oxford Handbook of Maximus the Confessor*, Oxford 2015, p. 19-83.

JASNOW 2001: R. JASNOW, '"And Pharaoh Laughed." Reflections on Humor in Setne 1 and Late Period Egyptian Literature', *Enchoria* 27 (2001), p. 62-81.

JASNOW & VITTMANN 1992/93: R. JASNOW & G. VITTMANN, 'An Abnormal Hieratic Letter to the Dead (P. Brooklyn 37.1799 E)', *Enchoria* 19/20 (1992/93), p. 23-40.

JAY 2016: J. JAY, *Orality and Literacy in Demotic Tales* (Culture and History of the Ancient Near East 81), Leiden 2016.

JOHNSON 1980: D. JOHNSON (ed. and trans.), *A Panegyric of Macarius, Bishop of Tkow* (Corpus Scriptorum Christianorum Orientalium 415-416), Leuven 1980.

JOHNSON 1986: D. JOHNSON, 'Anti-Chalcedonian Polemics in Coptic Texts, 451-641', in: B. PEARSON & J. GOEHRING (eds.), *The Roots of Egyptian Christianity*, Philadelphia 1986, p. 216-234.

JOHNSON 1987: J.H. JOHNSON, 'Ptolemaic Bureaucracy from an Egyptian Point of View', in: M. GIBSON & R. BIGGS (eds.), *The Organization of Power: Aspects of Administration in the Ancient, Medieval and Ottoman Middle East, a Symposium Held at the University of Chicago, Spring, 1983* (Studies in Ancient Oriental Civilization 46), Chicago 1987, p. 141-149.

JOHNSON 1991: D. JOHNSON, 'Macarius of Tkow', in: A. ATIYA (ed.), *The Coptic Encyclopedia*, New York 1991, vol. 5, p. 1492-1494.

JOHNSON 1994: J.H. JOHNSON, '"Annuity Contracts" and Marriage', in: D.P. SILVERMAN (ed.), *For His Ka Offered in Memory of Klaus Baer* (Studies in Ancient Oriental Civilization 55), Chicago 1994, p. 113-132.

JONES 1964: A.H.M. JONES, *The Later Roman Empire, 284–602: A Social, Economic and Administrative Survey*, 2 vol., Oxford 1964.

JORDAN 1993: T.E. JORDAN, '"L'Homme Moyen": Estimating the Quality of Life for British Adults, 1815-1914, an Index', *Social Indicators Research* 29 (1993), p. 183-203.

JORDAN 1996: T.E. JORDAN, 'A Weighted Index of Quality of Life for Irish Children: 1841, 1851, and 1861', *Social Indicators Research* 37 (1996), p. 47-73.

JORDAN 2009: T.E. JORDAN, 'Source, Method and Surmise: Quality of Life in History', *Social Indicators Research* 94 (2009), p. 227-239.

JORDAN 2010: T.E. JORDAN, 'Quality of Family Life and Mortality in Seventeenth Century Dublin', *Social Indicators Research* 98 (2010), p. 251-263.

KAGAN 1981: L. KAGAN, *Lawsuits and Litigants in Castile: 1500-1700*, Chapel Hill (NC) 1981.

KANAVOU & PAPATHOMAS 2016: N. KANAVOU & A. PAPATHOMAS, 'An Alexandrian Murder Case Revisited (P. Philammon = BGU IV 1024 pp. 6.3-8.21)', *ZPE* 200 (2016), p. 453-469.

KANTOR 2012: G. KANTOR, 'Review of Kelly, *Petitions, Litigation, and Social Control in Roman Egypt*', *BMCR* 2012.02.47, Bryn Mawr 2012 (available online: https://bmcr.brynmawr.edu/2012/2012.02.47/).

KAPLONY-HECKEL 1963: U. KAPLONY-HECKEL, *Die demotischen Tempeleide* (Ägyptologische Abhandlungen 6), Wiesbaden 1963.

KAPLONY-HECKEL 1968: U. KAPLONY-HECKEL, 'Die demotischen Tempeleide der Berliner Papyrussammlung', *Forschungen und Berichte* 10 (1968), p. 133-184.

KAPLONY-HECKEL 1994: U. KAPLONY-HECKEL, 'Sowahr der Stier von Medamod lebt! Über die Ortsgötter in den Tempel-Eiden', in: C. EYRE, A. LEAHY & L. MONTAGNO LEAHY (eds.), *Studies in the Culture and Heritage of Ancient Egypt in Honor of A.F. Shore* (EES Occasional Publications 11), London 1994, p. 149-159.

KARKOWSKI & WINNICKI 1983: J. KARKOWSKI & J.K. WINNICKI, 'Amenhotep, Son of Hapu and Imhotep at Deir el-Bahari – Some Reconsiderations', *MDAIK* 39 (1983), p. 93-105.

KATZOFF 1972: R. KATZOFF, 'Precedents in the Courts of Roman Egypt', *ZRG* 89 (1972), p. 256-292.

KAYSER 2013: F. KAYSER, 'Les communautés ethniques du type *politeuma* dans l'Égypte hellénistique', in: F. DELRIEUX & O. MARIAUD (eds.), *Communautés nouvelles dans l'antiquité grecque. Mouvements, intégrations et représentations* (Sociétés, Religions, Politiques 24), Chambéry 2013, p. 126-158.

KEENAN 1975: J.G. KEENAN, 'On Law and Society in Late Roman Egypt', *ZPE* 17 (1975), p. 237-250.

KEENAN 1985: J.G. KEENAN, 'Village Shepherds and Social Tension in Byzantine Egypt', *YClS* 28 (1985), p. 245-259.

KEENAN 1989: J.G. KEENAN, 'Roman Criminal Law in a Berlin Papyrus Codex (BGU IV 1024–1027)', *AfP* 35 (1989), p. 15-23.

KEENAN 1993: J.G. KEENAN, 'Papyrology and Byzantine Historiography', *BASP* 30 (1993), p. 137-144.

KEENAN 2001: J.G. KEENAN, '"Die Binnenwanderung" in Byzantine Egypt', *GRBS* 42 (2001), p. 57-82.

KEENAN 2008: J.G. KEENAN, '"Tormented Voices". *P.Cair.Masp.* I 67002', in: J.-L. FOURNET (ed.), *Les archives de Dioscore d'Aphrodité cent ans après leur découverte. Histoire et culture dans l'Égypte byzantine. Actes du colloque de*

Strasbourg 8-10 décembre 2005 (Études d'archéologie et d'histoire ancienne), Paris 2008, p. 171-180.

KEENAN 2014: J.G. KEENAN, 'Criminal Procedure in the Roman Period', in: J.G. KEENAN, J.G. MANNING & U. YIFTACH-FIRANKO (eds.), *Law and Legal Practice in Egypt from Alexander to the Arab Conquest: A Selection of Papyrological Sources in Translation, with Introductions and Commentary*, Cambridge 2014, p. 502-517.

KEENAN, MANNING & YIFTACH-FIRANKO 2014: J.G. KEENAN, J.G. MANNING & U. YIFTACH-FIRANKO (eds.), *Law and Legal Practice in Egypt from Alexander to the Arab Conquest: A Selection of Papyrological Sources in Translation, with Introductions and Commentary*, Cambridge 2014.

KEHOE 2008: D. KEHOE, 'Economics and the Law of Water Rights in the Roman Empire', in: E. HERMON (ed.), *Vers une gestion intégrée de l'eau dans l'Empire romain. Actes du Colloque International, Université Laval, Octobre 2006*, Rome 2008, p. 243-252.

KELLY 1966: J.M. KELLY, *Roman Litigation*, Oxford 1966.

KELLY 2011: B. KELLY, *Petitions, Litigation, and Social Control in Roman Egypt* (Oxford Studies in Ancient Documents), Oxford 2011.

KELLY 2021: B. KELLY, '"Access to Justice": Die soziale Reichweite gerichtlicher Konfliktregulierung', in: N. GROTKAMP & A. SEELENTAG (eds.), *Handbuch zur Geschichte der Konfliktlösung in Europa, Band 1: Konfliktlösung in der Antike*, Berlin 2021, p. 13-25.

KESSLER 2003: D. KESSLER, 'Tierische Missverständnisse: Grundsätzliches zu Fragen des Tierkultes', in: M. FITZENREITER (ed.), *Tierkulte im pharaonischen Ägypten und im Kulturvergleich*, Berlin 2003, p. 33-67.

KIM 1972: C.-H. KIM, *Form and Structure of the Familiar Greek Letter of Recommendation*, Missoula 1972.

KLEIN 2008: R. KLEIN, *Zum Verhältnis von Staat und Kirche in der Spätantike: Studien zu politischen, sozialen und wirtschaftlichen Fragen* (Tria corda 3), Tübingen 2008.

KNIGHT 1984: G. KNIGHT, 'ΑΥΘΕΝΤΕΩ in Reference to Women in 1 Timothy 2.12', *NTS* 30 (1984), p. 143-157.

KOCKELMANN 2014: H. KOCKELMANN, 'Lesestoffe? Leinen als Träger altägyptischer Texte', in: J.F. QUACK & D.C. LUFT (eds.), *Erscheinungsformen und Handhabungen Heiliger Schriften*, Berlin 2014, p. 79-109.

KOKKINIA 2014: C. KOKKINIA, 'Rome, Ephesos, and the Ephesian Harbor: A Case Study in Official Rhetoric', in: A. KOLB (ed.), *Infrastruktur und Herrschaftsorganisation im Imperium Romanum: Herrschaftsstrukturen und Herrschaftspraxis III. Akten der Tagung in Zürich 19.-20.10.2012*, Berlin 2014, p. 180-196.

KOTSIFOU 2016: C. KOTSIFOU, 'Prayers and Petitions for Justice: Despair and the Crossing of Boundaries between Religion and Law', *Tyche* 31 (2016), p. 167-199.

KOVELMAN 1991: A.B. KOVELMAN, 'From Logos to Myth. Egyptian Petitions of the 5th-7th Centuries', *BASP* 28 (1991), p. 135-152.

KRAMER & SÁNCHEZ-MORENO ELLART 2017: B. KRAMER & C. SÁNCHEZ-MORENO, *Neue Quellen zum Prozessrecht der Ptolemäerzeit. Gerichtsakten aus der Trierer Papyrussamlung (P. Trier I)* (Archiv für Papyrusforschung und verwandte Gebiete Beihefte 36), Berlin 2017.

KRAUSE 2011: J.U. KRAUSE, 'Children in the Roman Family and Beyond', in: M. PEACHIN (ed.), *The Oxford Handbook of Social Relations in the Roman World*, Oxford 2011, p. 623-642.

KROPPENBERG 2016: I. KROPPENBERG, 'Codex Theodosianus Revisited – Plädoyer für eine Geschichte der juridischen Form', in: S. DUSIL, G. SCHWEDLER & R. SCHWITTER (eds.), *Exzerpieren-Kompilieren-Tradieren: Transformationen des Wissens zwischen Spätantike und Frühmittelalter* (Millennium Studies 64), Berlin & Boston 2016, p. 71-84.

KRUSE 2013: T. KRUSE, 'Bevölkerungskontrolle, Statuszugang und Archivpraxis im römischen Ägypten', in: M. FARAGUNA (ed.), *Archives and Archival Documents in Ancient Societies. Trieste 30 September-1 October 2011* (Legal Documents in Ancient Societies 4), Trieste 2013, p. 307-330.

KRUSE 2015: T. KRUSE, 'Ethnic *Koina* and *Politeumata* in Ptolemaic Egypt', in: V. GABRIELSEN & C.A. THOMSEN (eds.), *Private Associations and the Public Sphere: Proceedings of a Symposium Held at the Royal Danish Academy of Sciences and Letters, 9-11 September 2010* (Scientia Danica. Series H, Humanistica, 8 vol. 9), Copenhagen 2015, p. 270-300.

KUMAMURA 2017: W. KUMAMURA, 'The Early Ottoman Rural Government System and its Development in View of Water Administration', in: S. CONERMANN & S. GÜL (eds.), *The Mamluk-Ottoman Transition: Continuity and Change in Egypt and Bilad al-Sham in the Sixteenth Century*, Göttingen 2017, p. 87-114.

LAMBERZ 2010: E. LAMBERZ, 'Die Akten des Nicaenum II in der kanonistischen Überlieferung', in: C. VON GASTGEBER (ed.), *Quellen zur byzantinischen Rechtspraxis: Aspekte der Textüberlieferung, Paläographie und Diplomatik. Akten des internationalen Symposiums, Wien, 5.-7.11.2007* (Denkschriften der Österreichische Akademie der Wissenschaften. Philosophisch-Historische Klasse 413), Wien 2010, p. 81-88.

LAMBERZ 2016: E. LAMBERZ (ed.), *Pars 3: Concilii Actiones VI-VII. Tarasii et synodi epistulae. Epiphanii sermo laudatorius. Canones. Tarasii epistulae post synodum scriptae. Appendix Graeca* (Acta conciliorum oecumenicorum: Series Secunda, III: Concilium Universale Nicaenum Secundum), Berlin & Boston 2016.

LANGELLOTTI 2016: M. LANGELLOTTI, 'Professional Associations and the State in Roman Egypt: The Case of First-Century Tebtunis', *CE* 91 (2016), p. 111-134.

LAZARIDIS 2016: N. LAZARIDIS, 'Different Parallels, Different Interpretations: Reading Parallels Between Ancient Egyptian and Greek Works of Literature', in: I. RUTHERFORD (ed.), *Greco-Roman Interactions*, Oxford 2016, p. 187-207.

LEGRAS 2012: B. LEGRAS, 'Le pouvoir des Ptolémées: singularité égyptienne ou normalité hellénistique', in: C.-G. SCHWENTZEL & E. SANTINELLI-FOLTZ (eds.), *La puissance royal: image et pouvoir de l'antiquité au Moyen Âge*, Rennes 2012, p. 73-83.

LEGRAS 2019: B. LEGRAS, 'Policymakers in a Changing World', in: K. VANDORPE (ed.), *A Companion to Greco-Roman and Late Antique Egypt*, Hoboken (NJ) 2019, p. 139-146.

LEIPOLDT & CRUM 1896: J. LEIPOLDT & W. CRUM, *Sinuthii archimandritae vita et opera omnia*, Paris 1896.

LEITHY 2003: H. EL-LEITHY, 'Letters to the Dead in Ancient and Modern Egypt', in: Z. HAWASS & L.P. BROCK (eds.), *Egyptology at the Dawn of the Twenty-first Century: Proceedings of the Eighth International Congress of Egyptologists, Cairo, 2000*, Cairo 2003, vol. 1, p. 304-313.

LENSKI 2016: N.E. LENSKI, *Constantine and the Cities: Imperial Authority and Civic Politics* (Empire and After), Philadelphia 2016.

LEWIS 1981: N. LEWIS, 'The Prefect's Conventus: Proceedings and Procedures', *BASP* 18 (1981), p. 119-129.

LEWIS 1982: N. LEWIS, '*Aphairesis* in Athenian Law and Custom', in: J.M. MÉLÈZE-MODRZEJEWSKI & D. LIEBS (eds.), *Symposion 1977: Vorträge zur griechischen und hellenistischen Rechtsgeschichte (Chantilly, 1.-4. Juni 1977)*, Cologne 1982, p. 161-178.

LICHTHEIM 1983: M. LICHTHEIM, *Late Egyptian Wisdom Literature in the International Context: A Study of Demotic Instructions*, Göttingen 1983.

LIEBESCHUETZ 1972: J.H.W.G. LIEBESCHUETZ, *Antioch: City and Imperial Administration in the Later Roman Empire*, Oxford 1972.

LIEBESCHUETZ 1986: J.H.W.G. LIEBESCHUETZ, 'Why Did Synesius Become Bishop of Ptolemais?', *Byzantion* 56 (1986), p. 180-195.

LIEBESCHUETZ 2001: J.H.W.G. LIEBESCHUETZ, *Decline and Fall of the Roman City*, Oxford 2001.

LIPPERT 2012: S.L. LIPPERT, *Einführung in die altägyptische Rechtsgeschichte*, 2nd ed., Berlin 2012.

LLEWELYN 1989: S.R. LLEWELYN, 'Christian Letters of Recommendation', in: G.H.R. HORSLEY & S.R. LLEWELYN (eds.), *New Documents Illustrating Early Christianity: A Review of the Greek Inscriptions and Papyri Published 1984-85*, North Ryde 1989, p. 169-172.

LOFTUS 2000: A. LOFTUS, 'A Textile Factory in the Third Century BC Memphis: Labor, Capital and Private Enterprise in the Zenon Archive', in: D. CARDON & M. FEUGÈRE (eds.), *Archéologie des textiles des origines au Ve siècle*, Montagnac 2000, p. 173-186.

LOPEZ 2013: A. LOPEZ, *Shenoute of Atripe and the Uses of Poverty*, Berkeley 2013.

LÖSSL & WATT 2011: J. LÖSSL & J.W. WATT (eds.), *Interpreting the Bible and Aristotle in Late Antiquity: The Alexandrian Commentary Tradition between Rome and Baghdad*, Farnham (Surrey) 2011.

LOVE 2020: E.O.D. LOVE, 'The Literary vs The Literal: The Narration of Magical Practices, Texts, and Their Practitioners in Setne I and II Compared with the So-called Demotic and Greek Magical Papyri', in: F. NAETHER (ed.), *Cult Practices in Ancient Literatures: Egyptian, Near Eastern and Graeco-*

Roman Narratives in a Cross-Cultural Perspective. Proceedings of a Workshop at the Institute for the Study of the Ancient World, New York, May 16-17, 2016 (ISAW Papers 18), online publication, 2020 (http://hdl.handle.net/2333.1/hmgqnw66).

LOVE forthoming: E.O.D. LOVE, *Petitioning Osiris: The Old Coptic Schmidt Papyrus and Curse of Artemisia in Context among the Letters to Gods from Egypt*, forthcoming.

LUBOMIERSKI 2008: N. LUBOMIERSKI, 'The Coptic Life of Shenoute', in: G. GABRA & H. TAKLA (eds.), *Christianity and Monasticism in Upper Egypt*, Cairo 2008, p. 91-99.

LÜDDECKENS 1971: E. LÜDDECKENS, 'Frühdemotische Inschrift eines Tongefäßes in Berlin', *Enchoria* 1 (1971), p. 1-8.

LUIJENDIJK 2008: A.M. LUIJENDIJK, *Greetings in the Lord: Early Christians and the Oxyrhynchus Papyri*, Cambridge 2008.

MACCOULL 1988: L.S.B. MACCOULL, *Dioscorus of Aphrodito. His Work and His World*, Berkeley 1988.

MACDONALD e.a. 2003: A.A. MACDONALD, M.W. TWOMEY & G. REININK (eds.), *Learned Antiquity. Scholarship and Society in the Near East, the Greco-Roman World and the Early Medieval West* (Groningen Studies in Cultural Change 5), Leuven 2003.

MACÉ 2015: C. MACÉ, 'Pseudo-Césaire, Anastase, Pseudo-Athanase: quelques réflexions sur les collections de Questions-et-Réponses dans la littérature grecque chrétienne', *SHS Web of Conferences* 22/4 (2015) (DOI: 10.1051/shsconf/20152200004).

MACMULLEN 1988: R. MACMULLEN, *Corruption and the Decline of Rome*, New York 1988.

MAIRS 2012: R. MAIRS, 'Interpreters and Translators in Hellenistic and Roman Egypt', in: P. SCHUBERT (ed.), *Actes du 26e Congrès International de Papyrologie, Genève, 16-21 août 2010*, Geneva 2012, p. 457-462.

MAIRS & MARTIN 2008/9: R. MAIRS & C.J. MARTIN, 'A Bilingual 'Sale' of Liturgies from the Archive of the Theban Choachytes: P. Berlin 5507, P. Berlin 3098 and P. Leiden 413', *Enchoria* 31 (2008/9), p. 22-67.

MALHERBE 1988: A.J. MALHERBE, *Ancient Epistolary Theorists*, Atlanta 1988.

MALININE 1962: M. MALININE, 'Une lettre démotique à Aménothès fils de Hapou', *RdE* 4 (1962), p. 37-43.

MANNING 2003: J.G. MANNING, *Land and Power in Ptolemaic Egypt. The Structure of Land Tenure*, Cambridge 2003.

MANNING 2010: J.G. MANNING, *The Last Pharaohs: Egypt under the Ptolemies, 305-30 BC*, Princeton 2010.

MANNING 2012: J.G. MANNING, 'The Representation of Justice in Ancient Egypt', *Yale Journal of Law and Humanities* 24/1 (2012), p. 111-118.

MANTOVANI 2016: D. MANTOVANI, 'More than Codes: Roman Ways of Organising and Giving Access to Legal Information', in: P.J. DU PLESSIS, C. ANDO & K. TUORI (eds.), *The Oxford Handbook of Roman Law and Society*, Oxford 2016, p. 23-42.

MARIEN 2018: B. MARIEN, 'Symmachus as an Active Power Broker: What Do His Recommendation Letters Reveal about the Writer's Network?', *RhM* 161 (2018), p. 184-235.

MARIEN 2019: B. MARIEN, 'Symmachus' Epistolary Influence: The Rehabiliation of Nicomachus Flavianus through Recommendation Letters', in: K.C. CHODA, M.S. DE LEEUW & F. SCHULZ (eds.), *Gaining and Losing Imperial Favour in Late Antiquity*, Leiden 2019, p. 105-124.

MARTIN forthcoming: C.J. MARTIN, 'The Demotic Legal Manuals – or Codes – or Coutumiers – or Commentaries – or Case Law? Does Modern Terminology Help or Hinder Us in Interpreting These Texts?', *RIDA*.

MARTIN 2007: M.J. MARTIN, 'Writing Divine Speech: Greek Transliterations of Near Eastern Languages in the Hellenistic East', in: C. COOPER (ed.), *Politics of Orality*, Leiden & Boston, p. 251-276.

MARTIN 1929: V. MARTIN, 'A Letter from Constantinople', *JEA* 15 (1929), p. 96-102.

MASSA 2018: V. MASSA, *Temple Oaths in Ptolemaic Egypt. A Study at the Crossroads of Law, Ethics and Religion*, unpubl. diss., Leiden University, Leiden 2018.

MATTHA 1976: G. MATTHA, *The Demotic Legal Code of Hermopolis West* (Bibliothèque d'étude 45), Cairo 1976.

MATTHEIS 2014: M. MATTHEIS, *Der Kampf ums Ritual: Diskurs und Praxis traditioneller Rituale in der Spätantike* (Geschichte 4), Düsseldorf 2014.

MAYER & NEIL 2013: W. MAYER & B. NEIL (eds.), *Religious Conflict from Early Christianity to the Rise of Islam* (Arbeiten zur Kirchengeschichte 121), Berlin 2013.

MAZZA 1995: R. MAZZA, 'Ricerche sul pagarca nell'Egitto tardoantico e bizantino', *Aegyptus* 75 (1995), p. 169-242.

MAZZA 2015: M. MAZZA, 'L'autorità della legge e la cristianizzazione dell'impero: qualche (breve) considerazione sul libro XVI del Teodosiano', in: U. ROBERTO & L. MECELLA (eds.), *Governare e riformare l'impero al momento della sua divisione: Oriente, Occidente, Illirico* (Collection de l'École Française de Rome 507), Rome 2015, p. 103-124.

MCCORMICK e.a. 2012: M. MCCORMICK, U. BÜNTGEN, M. CANE, E.R. COOK, K. HARPER, P. HUYBERS, T. LITT, S.W. MANNING, P.A. MAYEWSKI, A.F.M. MORE, K. NICOLUSSI & W. TEGEL, 'Climate Change during and after the Roman Empire: Reconstructing the Past from Scientific and Historical Evidence', *Journal of Interdisciplinary History* 43/2 (2012), p. 169-220.

MCDOWELL 1993: A.G. MCDOWELL, *Hieratic Ostraca in the Hunterian Museum, Glasgow: The Colin Campbell Ostraca*, Oxford 1993.

MCGING 1998: B.C. MCGING, 'Bandits, Real and Imagined, in Greco-Roman Egypt', *BASP* 35 (1998), p. 159-183.

MCLYNN 1994: N.B. MCLYNN, *Ambrose of Milan: Church and Court in a Christian Capital*, Berkeley 1994.

MCLYNN 1996: N.B. MCLYNN, 'From Palladius to Maximinus: Passing the Arian Torch', *JECS* 4/4 (1996), p. 477-493.

McLynn 2001: N.B. McLynn, 'Gregory Nazianzen's Basil: The Literary Construction of a Christian Friendship', in: M.F. Wiles & J. Yarnold (eds.), *Studia Patristica* vol. 37, Leuven 2001, p. 178-193.

McLynn 2014: N.B. McLynn, 'Gregory's Governors: *Paideia* and Patronage in Cappadocia', in: L. Van Hoof & P. Van Nuffelen (eds.), *Literature and Society in the Fourth Century AD: Performing Paideia, Constructing the Present, Presenting the Self*, Leiden 2014, p. 48-67.

Mehanna e.a. 1984: S. Mehanna, R. Huntington & R. Antonius, *Irrigation and Society in Rural Egypt* (Cairo Papers in Social Science 7, Monograph 4), Cairo 1984.

Mehari e.a. 2007: A. Mehari, F. van Steenbergen & B. Schultz, 'Water Rights and Rules, and Management in Spate Irrigation Systems in Eritrea, Yemen and Pakistan', in: B. van Koppen, M. Giordano & J. Butterworth (eds.), *Community-based Water Law and Water Resource Management* (Comprehensive Assessment of Water Management in Agriculture 5), Cambridge (Mass.) 2007, p. 114-129.

Meinzen-Dick & Nkonya 2007: R. Meinzen-Dick & L. Nkonya, 'Understanding Legal Pluralism in Water and Land Rights: Lessons from Africa and Asia', in: B. van Koppen, M. Giordano & J. Butterworth (eds.), *Community-based Water Law and Water Resource Management* (Comprehensive Assessment of Water Management in Agriculture 5), Cambridge (Mass.) 2007, p. 12-27.

Mélèze-Modrzejewski 1952: J. Mélèze-Modrzejewski, 'Private Arbitration in the Law of Greco-Roman Egypt', *JJP* 6 (1952), p. 239-256.

Mélèze-Modrzejewski 1959: J. Mélèze-Modrzejewski, 'La notion d'injustice dans les papyrus grecs', *Iura* 10 (1959), p. 67-85.

Mélèze-Modrzejewski 1984: J. Mélèze-Modrzejewski, 'La structure juridique du marriage', in: E. Bresciani (ed.), *Scritti in Onore di O. Montevecchi*, Bologna 1984, p. 231-258.

Mélèze-Modrzejewski 1995: J. Mélèze-Modrzejewski, 'Law and Justice in Ptolemaic Egypt', in: M.J. Geller & H. Maehler (eds.), *Legal Documents of the Hellenistic World*, London 1995, p. 1-19.

Mélèze-Modrzejewski 2011: J. Mélèze-Modrzejewski, *Droit et justice dans le monde grec et hellénistique* (JJP Suppl. 10), Warsaw 2011.

Mélèze-Modrzejewski 2014a: J. Mélèze-Modrzejewski, *Loi et coutume dans l'Égypte grecque et romaine: les facteurs de formation du droit en Égypte d'Alexandre le Grand à la conquête arabe* (JJP Suppl. 21), Warsaw 2014.

Mélèze-Modrzejewski 2014b: J. Mélèze-Modrzejewski, 'Ptolemaic Justice', in: J.G. Keenan, J.G. Manning & U. Yiftach-Firanko (eds.), *Law and Legal Practice in Egypt from Alexander to the Arab Conquest: A Selection of Papyrological Sources in Translation, with Introductions and Commentary*, Cambridge 2014, p. 470-482.

Metzger 2013: E. Metzger, 'An Outline of Roman Civil Procedure', *Roman Legal Tradition* 9 (2013), p. 1-30.

Meyer 2004: E.A. Meyer, *Legitimacy and Law in the Roman World.* Tabulae *in Roman Belief and Practice*, Cambridge 2004.

MEYER 2006: E.A. MEYER, 'The Justice of the Roman Governor and the Performance of Prestige', in: A. KOLB (ed.), *Infrastruktur und Herrschaftsorganisation im Imperium Romanum: Herrschaftsstrukturen und Herrschaftspraxis III. Akten der Tagung in Zürich 18.-20.10.2004*, Berlin 2006, p. 167-180.

MEYER & SMITH 1994: M. MEYER & R. SMITH, *Ancient Christian Magic: Coptic Texts of Ritual Power*, San Francisco 1994.

MIGAHID 1986: A.G. MIGAHID, *Demotische Briefe an Götter von der Spät- bis zur Römerzeit: ein Beitrag zur Kenntnis des religiösen Brauchtums im alten Ägypten*, 2 vol., Würzburg 1986.

MIGAHID & VITTMANN 2003: A.G. MIGAHID & G. VITTMANN, 'Zwei weitere frühdemotische Briefe an Thot', *RdE* 54 (2003), p. 47-59.

MIGLIARDI ZINGALE 2007: L. MIGLIARDI ZINGALE, 'Catene di costituzioni imperiali nelle fonti papirologiche: brevi riflessioni', in: *Atti dell'Accademia Romanistica Constantiniana. XVI convegno internazionale in onore di Manuel J. García Garrido*, Napoli 2007, p. 423-434.

MILLAR 1992: F.G.B. MILLAR, *The Emperor in the Roman World*, 2nd ed., London 1992.

MITCHELL 1976: S. MITCHELL, 'Requisitioned Transport in the Roman Empire: A New Inscription from Pisidia', *JRS* 66 (1976), p. 106-131.

MITTHOF 2008: F. MITTHOF, 'Das Dioskoros-Archiv und die militärischen Reformen Justinians in der Thebais', in: J.-L. FOURNET (ed.), *Les archives de Dioscore d'Aphrodité cent ans après leur découverte. Histoire et culture dans l'Égypte byzantine. Actes du colloque de Strasbourg 8-10 décembre 2005* (Études d'archéologie et d'histoire ancienne), Paris 2008, p. 248-259.

MONSON 2006: A. MONSON, 'The Ethics and Economics of Ptolemaic Religious Associations', *AncSoc* 36 (2006), p. 221-238.

MONSON 2007: A. MONSON, 'Private Associations in the Ptolemaic Fayyum: The Evidence of Demotic Accounts', in: M. CAPASSO & P. DAVOLI (eds.), *New Archaeological and Papyrological Researches in Fayyum. Proceedings of the International Meeting of Egyptology and Papyrology (Lecce, June 8th-10th 2005)* (Papyrologia Lupiensia 14), Galatina 2007, p. 178-196.

MONTSERRAT 1996: D. MONTSERRAT, *Sex and Society in Graeco-Roman Egypt*, London & New York 1996.

MOOREN 1975: L. MOOREN, *The Aulic Titulature in Ptolemaic Egypt: Introduction and Prosopography*, Brussels 1975.

MORALES 2016: A.J. MORALES, 'From Voice to Papyrus to Wall: Verschriftung and Verschriftlichung in the Old Kingdom Pyramid Texts', in: M. HILGERT (ed.), *Understanding Material Text Cultures: A Multidisciplinary View* (Materiale Textkulturen 9), Berlin & Boston 2016, p. 69-130.

MORRIS 1981: L.R.B. MORRIS, 'Reflections of Citizen Attitudes in Petitions from Roman Oxyrhynchus', in: R.S. BAGNALL e.a. (eds.), *Proceedings of the Sixteenth International Congress of Papyrology, New York 24-31 July 1980*, Chico (CA) 1981, p. 363-370.

MOSCOVITZ 2003: L. MOSCOVITZ, 'Legal Fictions in Rabbinic Law and Roman Law: Some Comparative Observations', in: C. HEZSER (ed.), *Rabbinic Law*

in Its Roman and Near Eastern Context (Texts and Studies in Ancient Judaism 97), Tübingen 2003, p. 105-132.
MRATSCHEK 2015: S. MRATSCHEK, 'A Living Relic for the Vicar of Rome: Strategies of Visualization in a Civil Case', in: L. VAN HOOF & P. VAN NUFFELEN (eds.), *Literature and Society in the Fourth Century AD: Performing Paideia, Constructing the Present, Presenting the Self*, Leiden 2015, p. 134-156.
MUHS 2001: B.P. MUHS, 'Membership in Private Associations in Ptolemaic Tebtunis', *JESHO* 44/1 (2001), p. 1-21.
MUHS 2005: B.P. MUHS, 'The Girls Next Door. Marriage Patterns among the Mortuary Priests in Early Ptolemaic Thebes', *JJP* 35 (2005), p. 169-194.
MULDREW 1993: C. MULDREW, 'Credit and the Courts: Debt Litigation in a Seventeenth-Century Urban Community', *Economic History Review* 46 (1993), p. 23-38.
MURRAY 1971: O. MURRAY, *Περὶ βασιλείας: Studies in the Justification of Monarchic Power in the Hellenistic World*, unpubl. diss., Oxford University, Oxford 1971.
MUSZYNSKI 1977: M. MUSZYNSKI, 'Les associations religieuses en Égypte d'après les sources hiéroglyphiques, démotiques et grecques', *OLP* 8 (1977), p. 145-174.
NADER & TODD 1978: L. NADER & H. TODD, *The Disputing Process: Law in Ten Societies*, New York 1978.
NIPPEL 1995: W. NIPPEL, *Public Order in Ancient Rome*, Cambridge 1995.
NORLIN 2009: G. NORLIN, 'To Nicocles', in: *Isocrates*, vol. I (Loeb Classical Library), Cambridge (MA) 2009.
NORMAN 1992: A.F. NORMAN, *Libanius. Autobiography and Selected Letters*, Cambridge 1992.
NOVICK 2013: T. NOVICK, 'Greenblatt and the Blatt: New Perspectives on the Nature and Reception of the Bavli', *Jewish Quarterly Review* 103/2 (2013), p. 259-270.
OGILVIE 2004: S. OGILVIE, 'The Use and Abuse of Trust: Social Capital and Its Deployment by Early Modern Guilds', *CESifo Working Paper no. 1302* (2004); also published in *Jahrbuch für Wirtschaftsgeschichte*, 2005 (1), p. 15-52 (available online: http://www.cesifo-group.de/w/krlsrcrj).
OMITOWOJU 2002: R. OMITOWOJU, *Rape and the Politics of Consent in Classical Athens*, Cambridge 2002.
OSING 1998: J. OSING, *Hieratische Papyri aus Tebtunis I*, Copenhagen 1998.
OSTROM 1990: E. OSTROM, *Governing the Commons: The Evolution of Institutions for Collective Action*, Cambridge 1990.
OSTROM 1998: E. OSTROM, 'A Behavioral Approach to the Rational Choice Theory of Collective Action (Presidential Address, American Political Science Association, 1997)', *The American Political Science Review* 92/1 (1998), p. 1-22.
OSTROM 1999: E. OSTROM, 'Coping with Tragedies of the Commons', *Annual Review of Political Science* 2 (1999), p. 493-535.
OSTROM 2002: E. OSTROM, 'How Farmer Managed Irrigation Systems Build Social Capital to Outperform Agency Managed Systems That Rely Primarily

on Physical Capital', in: P. PRADHAN & U. GAUTAM (eds.), *Farmer Managed Irrigation Systems in the Changed Context*, Kathmandu 2002, p. 15-65.

OSTROM & GARDNER 1993: E. OSTROM & R. GARDNER, 'Coping with Asymmetries in the Commons: Self-Governing Irrigation Systems Can Work', *The Journal of Economic Perspectives* 7/4 (1993), p. 93-112.

OSTROOT & SNYDER 1996: N. OSTROOT & W. SNYDER, 'The Quality of Life in Historical Perspective. France: 1695-1990', *Social Indicators Research* 38 (1996), p. 109-128.

PAGANINI 2016: M.C.D. PAGANINI, 'Decisional Practices of Private Associations in Ptolemaic and Early Roman Egypt', in: T. DERDA, A. ŁAJTAR & J. URBANIK (eds.), *Proceedings of the 27th International Congress of Papyrology, Warsaw, 29 July – 3 August 2013* (JJP Suppl. 28), Warsaw 2016, p. 1889-1901.

PAGANINI 2017: M.C.D. PAGANINI, 'Greek and Egyptian Associations in Egypt: Fact or Fiction?', in: B. CHRUBASIK & D. KING (eds.), *Hellenism and the Local Communities of the Eastern Mediterranean, 400 BCE-250 CE*, Oxford 2017, p. 131-154.

PALACIOS 2009: J.L.C. PALACIOS, 'La utilidad política y social del vocabulario religioso en la legislación del Teodosiano', in: J.-J. AUBERT & P. BLANCHARD (eds.), *Droit, religion et société dans le Code Théodosien. Troisièmes Journées d'Étude sur le Code Théodosien (Neuchâtel, 15-17 février 2007)* (Université de Neuchâtel, Recueil de travaux publiés par la Faculté des Lettres et Sciences Humaines 55), Geneva 2009, p. 129-146.

PALME 1999a: B. PALME, 'Pflichten und Risiken des Bürgen in byzantinischen Gestellungsbürgschaften', in: G. THÜR & F.J. FERNÁNDEZ NIETO (eds.), *Symposion 1999. Vorträge zur griechischen und hellenistischen Rechtsgeschichte, Pazo de Mariñán, La Coruña, 6.–9. September 1999* (Akten der Gesellschaft für griechische und hellenistische Rechtsgeschichte 14), Cologne 2003, p. 531-555.

PALME 1999b: B. PALME, 'Die *officia* der Statthalter in der Spätantike. Forschungsstand und Perspektiven', *Antiquité Tardive* 7 (1999), p. 85-133.

PALME 2007: B. PALME, 'The Imperial Presence. Government and Army', in: R.S. BAGNALL (ed.), *Egypt in the Byzantine World 300-700*, Cambridge 2007, p. 244-270.

PALME 2008: B. PALME, 'Dioskoros und die staatlichen Autoritäten', in: J.-L. FOURNET (ed.), *Les archives de Dioscore d'Aphrodité cent ans après leur découverte. Histoire et culture dans l'Égypte byzantine. Actes du colloque de Strasbourg 8-10 décembre 2005* (Études d'archéologie et d'histoire ancienne), Paris 2008, p. 203-222.

PALME 2009: B. PALME, 'The Range of Documentary Texts: Types and Categories', in: R.S. BAGNALL (ed.), *The Oxford Handbook of Papyrology*, Oxford 2009, p. 358-394.

PALME 2013: B. PALME, 'Staat und Gesellschaft des spätantiken Ägypten im Spiegel der Papyri', *JJP* 43 (2013), p. 95-133.

PALME 2014: B. PALME, 'Roman Litigation: Reports of Court Proceedings', in: J.G. KEENAN, J.G. MANNING & U. YIFTACH-FIRANKO (eds.), *Law and Legal*

Practice in Egypt from Alexander to the Arab Conquest: A Selection of Papyrological Sources in Translation, with Introductions and Commentary, Cambridge 2014, p. 482-502.

PALME 2015: B. PALME, 'Die bilinguen Prozessprotokolle und die Reform der Amtsjournale im spätantiken Ägypten', in: A.L.M. GAGARIN (ed.), *Symposion 2013: Vorträge zur griechischen und hellenistischen Rechtsgeschichte (Cambridge MA, 26.-29. August 2013)* (Akten der Gesellschaft für Griechische und Hellenistische Rechtsgeschichte 24), Vienna 2015, p. 401-427.

PALME 2016: B. PALME, 'Eingaben an Militärs im spätantiken Ägypten', in: R. HAENSCH (ed.), *Recht haben und Recht bekommen im Imperium Romanum: Das Gerichtswesen der römischen Kaiserzeit und seine dokumentarische Evidenz. Ausgewählte Beiträge einer Serie von drei Konferenzen an der Villa Vigoni in den Jahren 2010 bis 2012* (JJP Suppl. 24), Warsaw 2016, p. 457-482.

PALME forthcoming: B. PALME, 'Emotional Strategies in Petitions of Dioscorus of Aphroditê', in: C. KOTSIFOU (ed.), *Emotional Display, Persuasion, and Rhetoric in the Papyri*, forthcoming.

PAPACONSTANTINOU 2020: A. PAPACONSTANTINOU, 'Hagiography in the Archives: Real-Life Miracles and the Sacred Economy in Eighth-Century Egypt', in: V. DÉROCHE, B. WARD-PERKINS & R. WIŚNIEWSKI (eds.), *Culte des saints et littérature hagiographique* (Centre de recherche d'Histoire et Civilisation de Byzance, Monographies 55), Leuven 2020, p. 55-75.

PAPAKONSTANTINOU 2008: Z. PAPAKONSTANTINOU, *Lawmaking and Adjudication in Archaic Greece*, London 2008.

PARASSOGLOU 1978: G. PARASSOGLOU, *The Archive of Aurelius Sakaon: Papers of an Egyptian Farmer in the Last Century of Theadelphia*, Bonn 1978.

PARKINSON 1991: R. PARKINSON, *The Tale of the Eloquent Peasant*, Oxford 1991.

PARSONS 1965-1981: W. PARSONS, *St. Augustine. Letters*, Washington D.C. 1965-1981.

PAYNE 2009: P. PAYNE, *Man and Woman, One in Christ: An Exegetical and Theological Study of Paul's Letters*, Grand Rapids 2009.

PEACHIN 2007: M. PEACHIN, 'Petition to a Centurion from the NYU Papyrus Collection and the Question of Informal Adjudication Performed by Soldiers', in: A.J.B. SIRKS & K.A. WORP (eds.), *Papyri in Memory of P.J. Sijpesteijn* (Amercian Studies in Papyrology 40), Oakville 2007, p. 79-97.

PEDERSEN 1975: F.S. PEDERSEN, 'On Professional Qualifications for Public Posts in Late Antiquity', *C&M* 31 (1975), p. 161-213.

PERCZEL 2015: I. PERCZEL, 'Saint Maximus on the Lord's Prayer: An Inquiry into His Relationship to the Origenist Tradition', in: A. LÉVY, P. ANNALA, O. HALLAMAA, T. LANKILA & D. KALEY (eds.), *The Architecture of the Cosmos. St Maximus the Confessor: New Perspectives* (Schriften der Luther-Agricola-Gesellschaft 69), Helsinki 2015, p. 221-278.

PESTMAN 1961: P.W. PESTMAN, *Marriage and Matrimonial Property in Ancient Egypt. A Contribution to Establishing the Legal Position of the Woman*, Leiden 1961.

PESTMAN 1969: P.W. PESTMAN, 'The Law of Succession in Ancient Egypt', in: J. BRUGMAN e.a. (eds.), *Essays on Oriental Laws of Succession*, Leiden 1969, p. 58-77.

PESTMAN 1993: P.W. PESTMAN, *The Archive of the Theban Choachytes (Second century BC): A Survey of the Demotic and Greek Papyri contained in the Archive* (Studia Demotica 2), Leuven 1993.

PESTMAN & DAVID 1990: P.W. PESTMAN & M. DAVID, *The New Papyrological Primer*, Leiden 1990.

PESTMAN e.a. 1981: P.W. PESTMAN e.a., *A Guide to the Zenon Archive* (Pap.Lugd. Bat. 21), 2 vol., Leiden 1981.

PHANG 2001: S.E. PHANG, *The Marriage of Roman Soldiers (13 B.C.–A.D. 235): Law and Family in the Imperial Army* (Columbia Studies in the Classical Tradition 24), Leiden 2001.

PHARR 1952: C. PHARR, *The Theodosian Code and Novels and the Sirmondian Constitutions*, Princeton 1952.

PIANKOFF & CLÈRE 1934: A. PIANKOFF & J.J. CLÈRE, 'A Letter to the Dead on a Bowl in the Louvre', *JEA* 20 (1934), p. 157-169.

PLATER 2001: C. PLATER, 'Aspects of the Interaction between the Living and the Dead', unpubl. diss., University of Liverpool, Liverpool 2001.

PLESCIA 1970: J. PLESCIA, *The Oath and Perjury in Ancient Greece*, Tallahassee 1970.

PORTEN e.a. 2011: B. PORTEN, J. FARBER, C. MARTIN, G. VITTMANN, L. MACCOULL, & S. CLACKSON (eds.), *The Elephantine Papyri in English: Three Millennia of Cross-Cultural Continuity and Change*, Atlanta 2011.

PRATT 2012: T.C. PRATT (ed.), *Advancing Quantitative Methods in Criminology and Criminal Justice*, Oxford 2012.

PRÉAUX 1939: C. PRÉAUX, *L'économie royale des Lagides*, Brussels 1939.

PREISENDANZ 1928-31: K. PREISENDANZ, *Papyri Graecae Magicae: Die griechischen Zauberpapyri*, 2 vol., Berlin & Leipzig 1928-31.

PRICE 1995a: D. PRICE, 'Water Theft in Egypt's Fayoum Oasis: Emics, Etics, and the Illegal', in: M.F. MURPHY & M. MARGOLIS (eds.), *Science, Materialism and the Study of Culture*, Gainesville 1995, p. 96-110.

PRICE 1995b: D. PRICE, 'The Cultural Effects of Conveyance Loss in Gravity-Fed Irrigation Systems', *Ethnology* 34/4 (1995), p. 273-291.

PRICE & GRAUMANN 2020: R. PRICE & T. GRAUMANN, *The Council of Ephesus of 431: Documents and Proceedings* (Translated Texts for Historians 72), Liverpool 2020.

QUACK 2002: J.F. QUACK, 'Zur Chronologie der Demotischen Weisheitsliteratur', in: K. RYHOLT (ed.), *Acts of the Seventh International Conference of Demotic Studies*, Copenhagen 2002, p. 329-342.

QUACK 2009: J.F. QUACK, *Einführung in die altägyptische Literaturgeschichte III, die demotische und gräko-ägyptische Literatur* (Einführungen und Quellentexte zur Ägyptologie 3), 2nd ed., Berlin 2009.

QUACK 2011: J.F. QUACK, 'Das Diktum Tutu über die Eingabe an Numenios', in: A. JÖRDENS & J.F. QUACK (eds.), *Ägypten zwischen innerem Zwist und äußerem Druck. Die Zeit Ptolemaios' VI. bis VIII.* (Philippika 45), Wiesbaden 2011, p. 268-275.

QUAEGEBEUR 1983: J. QUAEGEBEUR, 'Twee laategyptische teksten rond dierenverering. Stèle Ny Carlsberg Glyptotheek 1681 en Papyrus BM 10845', in: K.R. VEENHOF (ed.), *Schrijvend Verleden: Documenten uit het Oude Nabije Oosten, Vertaald en Toegelicht*, Leiden 1983, p. 263-276.

QUAEGEBEUR 1993: J. QUAEGEBEUR, 'La justice à la porte des temples et le toponyme Premit', in: C. CANNUYER & J.-M. KRUCHTEN (eds.), *Individu, société et spiritualité dans l'Égypte pharaonique et copte. Mélanges égyptologiques offerts au Professeur Aristide Théodoridès*, Ath, Brussels & Mons 1993, p. 201-220.

RAMMELT 2013: C. RAMMELT, 'Christologische Positionierung als religiöses Alltagsgeschäft in Edessa?', in: P. EICH & E. FABER (eds.), *Religiöser Alltag in der Spätantike* (Potsdamer Altertumswissenschaftliche Beiträge 44), Stuttgart 2013, p. 127-144.

RAPOPORT 2018: Y. RAPOPORT, *Rural Economy and Tribal Society in Islamic Egypt: A Study of al-Nābulusī's* 'Villages of the Fayyum' (The Medieval Countryside 19), Turnhout 2018.

RAPOPORT & SHAHAR 2018: Y. RAPOPORT & I. SHAHAR (eds. and trans.), *The Villages of the Fayyum: A Thirteenth-Century Register of Rural, Islamic Egypt* (The Medieval Countryside 18), Turnhout 2018.

RAPP 2005: C. RAPP, *Holy Bishops in Late Antiquity. The Nature of Christian Leadership in an Age of Transition*, Berkeley 2005.

RATHBONE 1991: D. RATHBONE, *Economic Rationalism and Rural Society in Third-Century A.D. Egypt: The Heroninos Archive and the Appianus Estate*, Cambridge 1991.

RAY 1975: J.D. RAY, 'Papyrus Carlsberg 67: A Healing-Prayer from the Fayûm', *JEA* 61 (1975), p. 181-188.

RAY 1976: J.D. RAY, *The Archive of Hor*, London 1976.

RAY 1994: J.D. RAY, 'How Demotic is Demotic?', *EVO* 17 (1994), p. 251-265.

RAY 2005a: J.D. RAY, 'An Inscribed Linen Plea from the Sacred Animal Necropolis, North Saqqara', *JEA* 91 (2005), p. 171-179.

RAY 2005b: J.D. RAY, *Demotic Papyri and Ostraca from Qasr Ibrim*, London 2005.

RAY & MARTIN 2011: J.D. RAY & C. MARTIN, *Texts from the Baboon and Falcon Galleries: Demotic, Hieroglyphic and Greek Inscriptions from the Sacred Animal Necropolis, North Saqqara*, London 2011.

RAY & MARTIN 2013: J.D. RAY & C. MARTIN, *Demotic Ostraca and Other Inscriptions from the Sacred Animal Necropolis, North Saqqara*, London 2013.

REES 2007: R. REES, 'Letters of Recommendation and the Rhetoric of Praise', in: R. MORELLO & A.D. MORRISON (eds.), *Ancient Letters: Classical and Late Antique Epistolography*, New York 2007, p. 149-168.

RÉMONDON 1968: R. RÉMONDON, 'Soldats de Byzance d'après un papyrus trouvé à Edfou', *Recherches de Papyrologie* 1 (1961), p. 41-93.

REVILLOUT 1883: E. REVILLOUT, 'Le requête d'un esclave', *REgypt* 3 (1883), p. 125.

REVILLOUT 1888: E. REVILLOUT, 'Les papiers administratifs du Sérapéum et l'organisation sacerdotale en Égypte', *REgypt* 5 (1888), p. 31-61.

REYMOND 1972: E.A. REYMOND, 'Two Demotic Memoranda', *JEA* 58 (1972), p. 254-267.

RHEINSTEIN 1954: M. RHEINSTEIN (ed.), *Max Weber on Law in Economy and Society*, New York 1954.

RICHTER 2005: T.S. RICHTER, 'What's in a Story? Cultural Narratology and Coptic Child Donation Documents', *JJP* 35 (2005), p. 237-264.

RICHTER 2014: T.S. RICHTER, 'Greek and Coptic in the Byzantine Era', in: J.G. KEENAN, J. MANNING & U. YIFTACH-FIRANKO (eds.), *Law and Legal Practice in Egypt from Alexander to the Arab Conquest: A Selection of Papyrological Sources in Translation, with Introductions and Commentary*, Cambridge 2014, p. 134-144.

RIESS 2012: W. RIESS, *Performing Interpersonal Violence. Court, Curse and Comedy in Fourth-Century BCE Athens*, Berlin & Boston 2012.

RITNER 1993: R.K. RITNER, *The Mechanics of Ancient Egyptian Magical Practice*, Chicago 1993.

ROBERTS 1979: S. ROBERTS, *Order and Dispute: An Introduction to Legal Anthropology*, Oxford 1979.

ROEBUCK 2001: D. ROEBUCK, *Ancient Greek Arbitration*, Oxford 2001.

RÖMER 2013: C. RÖMER, 'Why Did the Villages in the Themistou Meris Die in the 4th Century CE? New Ideas about an Old Problem', in: C. ARLT & M. STADLER (eds.), *Das Fayyûm in Hellenismus und Kaiserzeit. Fallstudien zu multikulturellem Leben in der Antike*, Wiesbaden 2003, p. 169-179.

ROQUET 2016: G. ROQUET, '"Mon Papyrus de Tehneh": Provenance du texte vieux-copte Carl Schmidt d'après les manuscrits de Pierre Lacau', in: P. COLLOMBERT, D. LEFÈVRE, S. POLIS & J. WINAND (eds.), *Aere Perennius: Mélanges égyptologiques en l'honneur de Pascal Vernus* (Orientalia Lovaniensia Analecta 242), Leuven 2016, p. 663-676.

ROUSSEAU 1994: P. ROUSSEAU, *Basil of Caesarea*, Berkeley 1994.

ROWE 2014: G. ROWE, 'Laws, Lawmaking, and Legal Documents', in C. BRUUN & J. EDMONDSON (eds.), *The Oxford Handbook of Roman Epigraphy* (Oxford Handbooks), Oxford 2014, p. 299-318.

ROWLANDSON 1998: J. ROWLANDSON, *Women and Society in Greek and Roman Egypt: A Sourcebook*, Cambridge 1998.

ROWLANDSON 2013: J. ROWLANDSON, 'Dissing the Egyptians: Legal, Ethnic, and Cultural Identities in Roman Egypt', in: K. LOMAS, A. GARDNER & E. HERRING (eds.), *Creating Ethnicities and Identities in the Roman World* (BICS Supplement 120), London 2013, p. 213-247.

RUFFINI 2008a: G.R. RUFFINI, *Social Networks in Byzantine Egypt*, Cambridge 2008.

RUFFINI 2008b: G.R. RUFFINI, 'Factions and Social Distance in Sixth-Century Aphrodito', in: J.-L. FOURNET (ed.), *Les archives de Dioscore d'Aphrodité cent ans après leur découverte. Histoire et culture dans l'Égypte byzantine. Actes du colloque de Strasbourg 8-10 décembre 2005* (Études d'archéologie et d'histoire ancienne), Paris 2008, p. 157-170.

RUFFINI 2011: G.R. RUFFINI, *A Prosopography of Byzantine Aphrodito* (American Studies in Papyrology 50), Durham 2011.

RUFFINI 2013: G.R. RUFFINI, 'Review of B. Kelly, *Petitions, Litigation, and Social Control in Roman Egypt*', *Topoi* 18 (2013), p. 603-611.

RÜPKE & DEGELMANN 2015: J. RÜPKE & C. DEGELMANN, 'Narratives as a Lens into Lived Ancient Religion, Individual Agency and Collective Identity', *RRE* 1/3 (2015), p. 289-296.

RUPPRECHT 1993: H.A. RUPPRECHT, 'Hybris. Anmerkungen zu einem Delikt in den Papyri der ptolemäischen und römischen Zeit', in: S. BUCHHOLZ (ed.), *Überlieferung, Bewahrung und Gestaltung in der rechtsgeschichtlichen Forschung*, Paderborn 1993, p. 269-275.

RUPPRECHT 1998: H.A. RUPPRECHT, 'Marriage Contract Regulations and Documentary Practice in the Greek Papyri', *SCI* 17 (1998), p. 60-76.

RYHOLT 2015: K. RYHOLT, 'A Self-Dedication Addressed to Anubis', in: R. NYORD & K. RYHOLT (eds.), *Lotus and Laurel: Studies on Egyptian Language and Religion in Honour of Paul John Frandsen*, Copenhagen 2015, p. 329-350.

RYHOLT 2018: K. RYHOLT, 'Two Self-Dedications Addressed to Isis-Nephersais of Euhemeria', in: C.J. MARTIN, F.A.J. HOGENDIJK & K. DONKER VAN HEEL (eds.), *Hieratic, Demotic and Greek Studies and Text Editions. Of Making Many Books There is No End: Festschrift in Honour of Sven P. Vleeming* (Pap.Lugd.Bat. 34), Leiden & Boston 2018, p. 205-218.

SADĀT 1979: A. EL-SADĀT, *In Search of Identity*, New York 1979.

SALLER 1980: R.P. SALLER, 'Promotion and Patronage in Equestrian Careers', *JRS* 70 (1980), p. 44-63.

SALLER 1982: R.P. SALLER, *Personal Patronage under the Early Empire*, Cambridge 1982.

SALLER 1984: R.P. SALLER, 'Roman Dowry and the Devolution of Property in the Principate', *CQ* 34/1 (1984), p. 195-205.

SALOMON 1948: R.G. SALOMON, 'A Papyrus from Constantinople (Hamburg Inv. No. 410)', *JEA* 34 (1948), p. 98-108.

SAMBIN 1992: C. SAMBIN, 'Les portes de Médamoud du musée de Lyon', *BIFAO* 92 (1992), p. 147-187.

SAMUEL 1993: A.E. SAMUEL, 'The Ptolemies and the Ideology of Kingship', in: P. GREEN (ed.), *Hellenistic History and Culture*, Berkeley 1993, p. 168-191.

SAN NICOLÒ 1972: M. SAN NICOLÒ, *Ägyptisches Vereinswesen zur Zeit der Ptolemäer und Römer* (Münchener Beiträge zur Papyrusforschung und antiken Rechtsgeschichte 2), 2 vol., 2nd ed., Munich 1972.

SÄNGER 2011: P. SÄNGER, 'Das Sicherheitswesen im römischen Ägypten nach den Papyri', in: M. REITER & R. SCHIAVONE (eds.), *Gefährliches Pflaster: Kriminalität im römischen Reich* (Xantener Berichte 21), Mainz am Rhein 2011, p. 241-253.

SÄNGER 2014: P. SÄNGER, 'The *Politeuma* in the Hellenistic World (Third to First Century B.C.): A Form of Organisation to Integrate Minorities', in: J. DAHLVIK, C. REINPRECHT & W. SIEVERS (eds.), *Migration und Integra-*

tion – Wissenschaftliche Perspektiven aus Österreich (Jahrbuch 2/2013), Göttingen 2014, p. 51-68.

SÄNGER 2019: P. SÄNGER, *Die ptolemäische Organisationsform Politeuma. Ein Herrschaftsinstrument zugunsten jüdischer und anderer hellenischer Gemeinschaften*, Tübingen 2019.

SÄNGER 2019: P. SÄNGER, 'Anständig oder korrupt? Eine kritische Einschätzung des gut dokumentierten Sicherheitswesens im griechisch-römischen Ägypten', in: CH. BACHHIESL, M. HANDY, P. MAURITSCH & W. PETERMANDL (eds.), *Gier, Korruption und Machtmissbrauch in der Antike* (Antike Kultur und Geschichte 20), Vienna 2019, p. 321-333.

SARRIS 2006: P. SARRIS, *Economy and Society in the Age of Justinian*, Cambridge 2006.

SARRIS e.a. 2011: P. SARRIS, M.D. SANTO & P. BOOTH (eds.), *An Age of Saints?: Power, Conflict, and Dissent in Early Medieval Christianity* (Brill's Series on the Early Middle Ages 20), Leiden 2011.

SATO 1997: T. SATO, *State and Rural Society in Medieval Islam: Sultans, Muqta's and Fellahun*, Leiden 1997.

SATZINGER 1975: H. SATZINGER, 'The Old Coptic Schmidt Papyrus', *JARCE* 12 (1975), p. 37-50.

SATZINGER 1984: H. SATZINGER, 'Die altkoptischen Texte als Zeugnisse der Beziehungen zwischen Ägyptern und Griechen', in: P. NAGEL (ed.), *Graeco-Coptica: Griechen und Kopten im byzantinischen Ägypten*, Halle (Saale) 1984, p. 137-146.

SAYED 1984: R. EL-SAYED, 'Deux statues inédites du musée de Caire', *BIFAO* 84 (1984), p. 127-153.

SCHARR 1919: E. SCHARR, *Xenophon's Staats- und Gesellschaftideal und seine Zeit*, Halle 1919.

SCHAUB 2014: E. SCHAUB, *Studien zur Lebenssituation der Bevölkerung Ägyptens als Ursache der Revolten unter römischer Herrschaft, 30 v. Chr. bis 300 n. Chr.* (Pharos. Studien zur griechisch-römischen Antike 31), Rahden 2014.

SCHEIDEL 2001: W. SCHEIDEL, 'Progress and Problems in Roman Demography', in: W. SCHEIDEL (ed.), *Debating Roman Demography*, Leiden, Boston & Cologne 2006, p. 1-81.

SCHENKE 2016: G. SCHENKE, 'The Healing Shrines of St. Phoibammon: Evidence of Cult Activity in Coptic Legal Documents', *ZAC* 20 (2016), p. 496-523.

SCHMELZ 2014: G. SCHMELZ, 'Clerics as Arbiters in Christian Egypt', in: J.G. KEENAN, J. MANNING & U. YIFTACH-FIRANKO (eds.), *Law and Legal Practice in Egypt from Alexander to the Arab Conquest: A Selection of Papyrological Sources in Translation, with Introductions and Commentary*, Cambridge 2014, p. 517-529.

SCHMIDT-HOFNER 2015: S. SCHMIDT-HOFNER. 'Ostentatious Legislation: Law and Dynastic Change, AD 364-365', in: J. WIENAND (ed.), *Contested Monarchy: Integrating the Roman Empire in the Fourth Century AD*, Oxford 2015, p. 379-404.

SCHOR 2014: A.M. SCHOR, 'Becoming Bishop in the Letters of Basil and Synesius: Tracing Patterns of Social Signaling Across Two Full Epistolary Collections', *JLA* 7 (2014), p. 298-328.

SCHOR 2017: A.M. SCHOR, 'The Letter Collection of Theodoret of Cyrrhus', in: C. SOGNO, B.K. STORIN & E.J. WATTS (eds.), *Late Antique Letter Collections: A Critical Introduction and Reference Guide*, Berkeley 2017, p. 269-285.

SCHORN 2016: S. SCHORN, 'Das Idealbild des Beambten in den Papyri der ptolemäischen Zeit', in: K. DROSS-KRÜPE, S. FÖLLINGER & K. RUFFING (eds.), *Antike Wirtschaft und ihre kulturelle Prägung (2000 v.Chr. – 500 n. Chr.)*, Wiesbaden 2016, p. 131-161.

SCHUBART 1937: W. SCHUBART, 'Das hellenistische Königsideal nach Inschriften und Papyri', *AfP* 12 (1937), p. 1-26.

SCHUBERT 2005: P. SCHUBERT, 'BGU I 361 et P.Gen. inv. 69: retour sur l'encre rouge', *AfP* 51 (2005), p. 228-252.

SCHULLER 1982: W. SCHULLER, 'Prinzipien des spätantiken Beamtentums', in: W. SCHULLER (ed.), *Korruption im Altertum. Konstanzer Symposium, Oktober 1979*, Munich 1982, p. 201-208.

SCOTT 2008: A. SCOTT, *The Evolution of Resource Property Rights*, Oxford 2008.

SEIDL 1929: E. SEIDL, *Der Eid im ptolemäischen Recht*, Munich 1929.

SEIDL 1962: E. SEIDL, *Ptolemäische Rechtsgeschichte*, 2nd ed., Glückstadt 1962.

SEIDL 1966: E. SEIDL, 'Die Gottesentscheidungen der Saiten- und Perserzeit', in: A.E. SAMUEL (ed.), *Essays in Honor of C. Bradford Welles* (American Studies in Papyrology 1), New Haven 1966, p. 59-65.

SEIDL 1967: E. SEIDL, 'Der Prozeß Chrateanch gegen Tefhape im Jahre 170 v. Chr.', *Zeitschrift für vergleichende Rechtswissenschaft* 69 (1967), p. 96-117.

SEIDL 1975: E. SEIDL, 'Zur Vorgeschichte der *actio rerum amotarum*', *ZRG* 92 (1975), p. 234-238.

SHARQĀWĪ 1968: A. AL-R. AL-SHARQĀWĪ, *Al-Arḍ*, 3rd ed., Cairo 1968.

SHORE & SMITH 1959: A.F. SHORE & H.S. SMITH, 'Two Unpublished Demotic Documents from the Asyut Archive', *JEA* 45 (1959), p. 52-60.

SIJPESTEIJN 2014: P. SIJPESTEIJN, *Shaping a Muslim State: The World of a Mid-Eighth-Century Egyptian Official*, Oxford 2014.

SIMON 1971: D. SIMON, 'Zur Zivilgerichtsbarkeit im spätbyzantinischen Ägypten', *RIDA* 18 (1971), p. 623-657.

SIMON-SHOSHAN 2012: M. SIMON-SHOSHAN, *Stories of the Law: Narrative Discourse and the Construction of Authority in the Mishnah*, New York 2012.

SIMPSON 1966: W.K. SIMPSON, 'The Letter to the Dead from the Tomb of Meru (N 3737) at Nag' ed-Deir', *JEA* 52 (1966), p. 39-52.

SIMPSON 1970: W.K. SIMPSON, 'A Late Old Kingdom Letter to the Dead from Nag' Ed-Deir N 3500', *JEA* 56 (1970), p. 58-64.

SIMPSON 1973: W.K. SIMPSON, *The Literature of Ancient Egypt*, New Haven & London 1973.

SIMPSON 1981: W.K. SIMPSON, 'The Memphite Epistolary Formula on a Jar Stand of the First Intermediate Period from Naga ed-Deir', in: W.K. SIMPON & W.M. DAVIS (eds.), *Studies in Ancient Egypt, the Aegean, and the Sudan:*

Essays in Honor of Dows Dunham on the Occasion of his 90th Birthday, June I, 1980, Boston 1981, p. 173-179.

SIMPSON e.a. 2003: W.K. SIMPSON e.a. (eds.), *The Literature of Ancient Egypt*, 3rd ed., New Haven 2003.

SINCLAIR 1951: T.A. SINCLAIR, *A History of Greek Political Thought*, London 1951.

SIRKS 2013: A.J.B. SIRKS, 'The *episcopalis audientia* in Late Antiquity (L'*episcopalis audientia* dans l'antiquité tardive)', *Droit et cultures* 65 (2013), p. 79-88.

SIZGORICH 2009: T. SIZGORICH, *Violence and Belief in Late Antiquity: Militant Devotion in Christianity and Islam* (Divinations), Philadelphia 2009.

SKALTSA 2016: S. SKALTSA, '"Housing" Private Associations in Hellenistic Athens: Three Case-Studies for a Place to Meet and Worship the Gods', in: O. RODRÍGUEZ GUTIÉRREZ, N. TRAN & B. SOLER HUERTAS (eds.), *Los espacios de reunión de las asociaciones romanas. Diálogos desde la arqueología y la historia, en homenaje a Bertrand Goffaux*, Sevilla 2016, p. 79-92.

SLOOTJES 2006: D. SLOOTJES, *The Governor and His Subjects in the Later Roman Empire*, Boston 2006.

SLOOTJES 2011: D. SLOOTJES, 'Bishops and their Position of Power in the Late Third Century CE: The Cases of Gregory Thaumaturgus and Paul of Samosata', *Journal of Late Antiquity* 4/1 (2011), p. 100-115.

SMITH 1995: H.S. SMITH, 'Marriage and the Family in Ancient Egypt. I. Marriage and Family Law', in: M.J. GELLER & H. MAEHLER (eds.), *Legal Documents of the Hellenistic World*, London 1995, p. 46-57.

SMITH 2002: H.S. SMITH, 'The Saqqara Papyri: Oracle Questions, Pleas and Letters', in: K. RYHOLT (ed.), *Acts of the Seventh International Conference of Demotic Studies: Copenhagen, 23-27 August 1999*, Copenhagen 2002, p. 367-375.

SMITH 2018: M. SMITH, 'A Further Demotic Source of Evidence for the Expulsion of Antiochus IV from Egypt: O. Hor. 3 verso, lines 7-25', in: C.J. MARTIN, F.A.J. HOOGENDIJK & K. DONKER VAN HEEL (eds.), *Hieratic, Demotic and Greek Studies and Text Editions. Of Making Many Books There is No End: Festschrift in Honour of Sven P. Vleeming* (Pap.Lugd.Bat. 34), Leiden 2018, p. 219-227.

SMITH, ANDREWS & DAVIES 2011: H.S. SMITH, C.A.R. ANDREWS & S. DAVIES, *The Sacred Animal Necropolis at North Saqqara: The Mother of Apis Inscriptions*, 2 vol., London 2011.

SMITH & DAVIES 2014: H.S. SMITH & S. DAVIES, 'Demotic Papyri from the Sacred Animal Necropolis at North Saqqara. Pleas, Oracle Questions and Documents Referring to Mummies', in: M. DEPAUW & Y. BROUX (eds.), *Acts of the Tenth International Congress of Demotic Studies, Leuven, 26-30 August 2008* (Orientalia Lovaniensia Analecta 231), Leuven 2014, p. 263-317.

SOGNO 2010: C. SOGNO, 'Roman Matchmaking', in: S. MCGILL, C. SOGNO & E.J. WATTS (eds.), *From the Tetrarchs to the Theodosians: Later Roman History and Culture, 284-450 CE*, Cambridge 2010, p. 55-71.

SPIEGELBERG 1904-32: W. SPIEGELBERG, *Die demotischen Denkmäler*, 3 vol., Leipzig 1904-32.

SPIEGELBERG 1917: W. SPIEGELBERG, 'Briefe der 21. Dynastie aus el-Hiba', *ZÄS* 53 (1917), p. 1-30.

SPIERENBURG 2004: P. SPIERENBURG, 'Social Control and History: An Introduction', in: H. ROODENBURG (ed.), *Social Control in Europe* I, Colombus 2004, p. 1-22.

STERN 2015: M. STERN, 'Der Pagarch und die Organisation des öffentlichen Sicherheitswesens im byzantinischen Ägypten', *Tyche* 30 (2015), p. 119-144.

STERN 2020: M. STERN, 'Local Magnates, but Mobile. Elite Dynamics in Byzantine Provinces', in E. GAROSI, S.R. HUEBNER, I. MARTHOT-SANTANIELLO, M. MÜLLER, S. SCHMIDT & M. STERN (eds.), *Living the End of Antiquity. Individual Histories from Byzantine to Islamic Egypt*, Berlin 2020, p. 33-48.

STOLK 2011: J. STOLK, *Archives from Cartonnage: The Dossier of Lamiske*, unpubl. MA diss., KU Leuven, Leuven 2011.

STOLTE 2001: B.H. STOLTE, 'The Impact of Roman Law in Egypt and the Near East in the Third Century AD: The Documentary Evidence. Some Considerations in the Margin of the Euphrates Papyri (P.Euphr.)', in: L. DE BLOIS (ed.), *Administration, Prosopography and Appointment Policies in the Roman Empire: Proceedings of the First Workshop of the International Network Impact of Empire (Roman Empire, 27 B.C.-A.D. 406), Leiden, June 28-July 1, 2000* (Impact of Empire 1), Amsterdam 2001, p. 167-179.

STOLTE 2014: B.H. STOLTE, 'Codification in Byzantium: From Justinian I to Leo VI', in: J. HUDSON & A.R. LÓPEZ (eds.), *Diverging Paths? The Shapes of Power and Institutions in Medieval Christendom and Islam* (Medieval Mediterranean 101), Leiden 2014, p. 59-74.

TAUBENSCHLAG 1944: R.S. TAUBENSCHLAG, *The Law of Greco-Roman Egypt in the Light of the Papyri 332 B.C.-640 A.D.*, New York 1944.

TAUBENSCHLAG 1955: R.S. TAUBENSCHLAG, *The Law of Greco-Roman Egypt in the Light of the Papyri, 332 B.C.-640 A.D.*, 2nd ed., Warsaw 1955.

TCHERIKOVER 1945: V. TCHERIKOVER, *The Jews in Egypt in the Hellenistic-Roman Age in the Light of the Papyri*, Jerusalem 1945.

TESTA 2013: R.L. TESTA, '«inter christianos etiam gentilitatis cultores sed et veteris legis studiosi audientiae sint adhibendi»: The Impact of Theological Controversies on the Intellectual Life of Late Antiquity', *Adamantius* 19 (2013), p. 276-289.

TETZ 1990: M. TETZ, 'Eine asketische Ermunterung zur Standhaftigkeit aus der Zeit der Maximinischen Verfolgung (311/313)', *ZNTW* 81/1 (1990), p. 79-102.

THISSEN 2002: H.-J. THISSEN, 'Achmim und die demotische Literatur', in: A. EGBERTS, B.P. MUHS & J. VAN DER VLIET (eds.), *Perspectives on Panopolis* (Pap.Lugd.Bat. 31), Leiden 2002, p. 249-260.

THOMAS 1975: J.D. THOMAS, *The Epistrategos in Ptolemaic and Roman Egypt.* Part 1. *The Ptolemaic Epistrategos* (Pap.Col. 6), Opladen 1975.

THOMPSON 1934: H. THOMPSON, *A Family Archive from Siut, from Papyri in the British Museum, Including an Account of a Trial Before the Laocritae in the Year B.C. 170*, Oxford 1934.

THOMPSON 1938: H. THOMPSON, 'Self-Dedications', in: *Actes du Ve Congrès International de Papyrologie, Oxford, 30 août-3 septembre 1937*, Brussels 1938, p. 497-504.
THOMPSON 1941: H. THOMPSON, 'Two Demotic Self-Dedications', *JEA* 26 (1941), p. 68-78.
THOMPSON 1999: D.J. THOMPSON, '"When Egypt Divorced Itself": Ptolemaic *Tarache* and the *Elpis* of Harchonesis', in: A. LEAHY & J. TAIT (eds.), *Studies on Ancient Egypt in Honour of H.S. Smith* (EES Occasional Publications 13), London 1999, p. 322-326.
THOMPSON 2011: D.J. THOMPSON, 'Ethnic Minorities in Hellenistic Egypt', in: O.M. VAN NIJF & R. ALSTON (eds.), *Political Culture in the Greek City after the Classical Age*, Leuven 2011, p. 101-117.
THOMPSON 2012: D.J. THOMPSON, *Memphis under the Ptolemies*, 2nd ed., Princeton & Oxford 2012.
THONEMANN 2016: P. THONEMANN, *The Hellenistic Age*, Oxford 2016.
TILLY 2005: C. TILLY, *Trust and Rule*, Cambridge 2005.
TORALLAS TOVAR 2006: S. TORALLAS TOVAR, 'Violence in the Process of Arrest and Imprisonment in Late Antique Egypt', in: H.A. DRAKE (ed.), *Violence in Late Antiquity. Perceptions and Practices*, Aldershot 2006, p. 101-110.
TRAPP 2006: M.B. TRAPP, 'Biography in Letters: Biography and Letters', in: B. MCGING & J. MOSSMAN (eds.), *The Limits of Ancient Biography*, Swansea 2006, p. 335-350.
TRAUNECKER 1992: Cl. TRAUNECKER, *Coptos. Hommes et dieux sur le parvis de Geb* (Orientalia Lovaniensia Analecta 43), Leuven 1992.
TRAUNECKER 1997: Cl. TRAUNECKER, 'L'appel au divin: la crainte des dieux et les serments de temple', in: J.-G. HEINTZ (ed.), *Oracles et prophéties dans l'antiquité. Actes du colloque de Strasbourg, 15-17 juin 1995* (Université des Sciences Humaines de Strasbourg. Travaux du Centre de recherche sur le Proche-Orient et la Grèce antiques 15), Paris 1997, p. 35-54.
TREGGIARI 1991a: S. TREGGIARI, 'Divorce Roman Style: Ease and Frequency', in: B. RAWSON (ed.), *Divorce and Children in Ancient Rome*, Oxford 1991, p. 31-46.
TREGGIARI 1991b: S. TREGGIARI, *Roman Marriage: Iusti Coniuges from the Time of Cicero to the Time of Ulpian*, Oxford & New York 1991.
TREUCKER 1981: B. TREUCKER, 'A Note on Basil's Letters of Recommendation', in: P.J. FEDWICK (ed.), *Basil of Caesarea, Christian, Humanist, Ascetic: A Sixteen-Hundredth Anniversary Symposium*, Toronto 1981, p. 405-410.
TROCHE 2018: J. TROCHE, 'Letters to the Dead', in: J. DIELEMAN & W. WENDRICH (eds.), *UCLA Encyclopedia of Egyptology*, online publication, Los Angeles 2018 (available online: https://escholarship.org/uc/item/6bh8w50t).
TUORI 2007: K. TUORI, 'Legal Pluralism and the Roman Empires', in: J.W. CAIRNS & P.J. DU PLESSIS (eds.), *Beyond Dogmatics: Law and Society in the Roman World* (Edinburgh Studies in Law 3), Edinburgh 2007, p. 39-52.
TURPIN 1991: W. TURPIN, 'Imperial Subscriptions and the Administration of Justice', *JRS* 81 (1991), p. 101-118.

UHALDE 2012: K. UHALDE, 'Justice and Equality', in: S.F. JOHNSON (ed.), *The Oxford Handbook of Late Antiquity*, Oxford 2012, p. 764-788.

ULJAS 2012: S. ULJAS, 'Cambridge Leaves of Moses of Abydos', *Le Muséon* 125 (2012), p. 1-33.

URBAN 1996: G. URBAN, 'Entextualization, Replication, and Power', in: M. SILVERSTEIN (ed.), *Natural Histories of Discourse*, Chicago 1996, p. 21-44.

URBANIK 2007: J. URBANIK, 'Compromesso o processo? Alternativa risoluzione dei conflitti e tutela dei diritti nella prassi della tarda antichità', in: E. CANTARELLA, I. MELÈZE-MODRZEJEWSKI & C. THÜR (eds.), *Symposion 2005. Vorträge zur griechischen und hellenistischen Rechtsgeschichte*, Vienna 2007, p. 377-400.

URBANIK 2014: J. URBANIK, '4.2. Divorce', in: J. KEENAN, J.G. MANNING & U. YIFTACK-FIRANKO (eds.), *Law and Legal Practice in Egypt from Alexander to the Arab Conquest: A Selection of Papyrological Sources in Translation, with Introductions and Commentary*, Cambridge 2014, p. 154-175.

UYTTERHOEVEN 2009: I. UYTTERHOEVEN, *Hawara in the Graeco-Roman Period. Life and Death in a Fayum Village* (Orientalia Lovaniensia Analecta 174), Leuven 2009.

VAN DAM 2002: R. VAN DAM, *Kingdom of Snow: Roman Rule and Greek Culture in Cappadocia*, Philadelphia 2002.

VAN MEETEREN 2006: A. VAN MEETEREN, *Op Hoop van Akkoord: Instrumenteel Forumgebruik bij Geschilbeslechting in Leiden in de Zeventiende Eeuw*, Hilversum 2006.

VAN MINNEN 1995: P. VAN MINNEN, 'Deserted Villages: Two Late Antique Town Sites in Egypt', *BASP* 32 (1995), p. 41-56.

VAN MINNEN 2003: P. VAN MINNEN, 'Dioscorus and the Law', in: A.A. MACDONALD, N.W. TWOMEY & G.J. REININK (eds.), *Learned Antiquity: Scholarship and Society in the Near East, the Greco-Roman World and the Early Medieval West*, Leuven 2003, p. 115-133.

VAN MINNEN 2006: P. VAN MINNEN, 'Saving History? Egyptian Hagiography in Its Space and Time', in: J.H. DIJKSTRA & M. VAN DIJK (eds.), *The Encroaching Desert: Egyptian Hagiography and the Medieval West*, Leiden 2006, p. 57-92.

VAN MINNEN 2013: P. VAN MINNEN, 'Review of B. Kelly, *Petitions, Litigation, and Social Control in Roman Egypt*', *Gnomon* 85 (2013), p. 718-722.

VAN MINNEN 2014: P. VAN MINNEN, 'Review of A.Z. Bryen, *Violence in Roman Egypt: A Study in Legal Interpretation*', *BASP* 51 (2014), p. 265-268.

VAN NUFFELEN 2014: P. VAN NUFFELEN, 'The End of Open Competition? Religious Disputation in Late Antiquity', in: P. VAN NUFFELEN & D. ENGELS (eds.), *Religion and Competition in Antiquity* (Collection Latomus 343), Brussels 2014, p. 149-172.

VAN NUFFELEN & HILKENS 2013: P. VAN NUFFELEN & A. HILKENS, 'Recruitment and Conflict in Sixth-Century Antioch: A Micro-Study of Select Letters 6, 1, 5 of Severus of Antioch', *ZAC* 17/3 (2013), p. 560-575.

VAN STEENBERGEN 1997: F. VAN STEENBERGEN, 'Understanding the Sociology of Spate Irrigation: Cases from Balochistan', *Journal of Arid Environments* 35/2 (1997), p. 349-365.

VANDERHEYDEN 2012: L. VANDERHEYDEN, 'Les lettres coptes des archives de Dioscore d'Aphroditê', in: P. SCHUBERT (ed.), *Actes du 26e Congrès International de Papyrologie, Genève, 16-21 août 2010*, Geneva 2012, p. 793-799.

VANDIER 1961/62: J. VANDIER, *Le papyrus Jumilhac*, Paris 1961/62.

VANDORPE 1995: K. VANDORPE, 'City of Many a Gate, Harbour for Many a Rebel. Historical and Topographical Outline of Greco-Roman Thebes', in: S.P. VLEEMING (ed.), *Hundred-Gated Thebes. Acts of a Colloquium on Thebes and the Theban Area in the Graeco-Roman Period* (Pap.Lugd.Bat. 27), Leiden 1995, p. 203-239.

VANDORPE 2013: K. VANDORPE, 'A Happiness Index for Antiquity? Hellenistic Egypt as a Case-study', in: S. BUSSI (ed.), *Egitto dai faraoni agli arabi. Atti del Convegno 'Egitto: amministrazione, economia, società, cultura dai Faraoni agli Arabi' (Milano, Università degli studi, 7-9 gennaio 2013)*, Pisa & Rome 2013, p. 91-104.

VANDORPE 2019: K. VANDORPE (ed.), *A Companion to Greco-Roman and Late Antique Egypt*, Hoboken (NJ) 2019.

VANDORPE & VLEEMING 2017: K. VANDORPE & S.P. VLEEMING, *The Erbstreit Papyri. A Bilingual Dossier from Pathyris of the Second Century BC* (Studia Demotica 13), Leuven 2017.

VANDORPE & WAEBENS 2010: K. VANDORPE & S. WAEBENS, *Reconstructing Pathyris' Archives. A Multicultural Community in Hellenistic Egypt* (Collectanea Hellenistica 3), Brussels 2010.

VARGA 2021: D. VARGA, 'The Cult of the Bull at Medamud in the Ptolemaic Period', in: Ch. THIERS (ed.), *Documents de Théologies Thébaines Tardives* (*D3T* 4) (CEN*i*M 27), Montpellier 2021, p. 163-184

VARISCO 1983: D.M. VARISCO, 'Sayl and Ghayl: The Ecology of Water Allocation in Yemen', *Human Ecology* 11/4 (1983), p. 365-383.

VEÏSSE 2004: A.-E. VEÏSSE, *Les "révoltes égyptiennes": Recherches sur les troubles intérieurs en Égypte du règne de Ptolémée III à la conquête romaine* (Studia Hellenistica 41), Leuven 2004.

VÉLISSAROPOULOS 1981: J. VÉLISSAROPOULOS, *Alexandrinoi nomoi. Politike autonomia kai nomike autoteleia tes ptolemaikes Alexandreias*, Athens 1981.

VENTICINQUE 2010: P.F. VENTICINQUE, 'Family Affairs: Guild Regulations and Family Relationships in Roman Egypt', *GRBS* 50 (2010), p. 273-294.

VENTICINQUE 2015: P.F. VENTICINQUE, 'Courting the Associations: Cooperation, Conflict and Interaction in Roman Egypt', in: V. GABRIELSEN & C.A. THOMSEN (eds.), *Private Associations and the Public Sphere: Proceedings of a Symposium Held at the Royal Danish Academy of Sciences and Letters, 9-11 September 2010* (Scientia Danica. Series H, Humanistica, 8 vol. 9), Copenhagen 2015, p. 314-340.

VENTICINQUE 2016: P.F. VENTICINQUE, *Honor among Thieves. Craftsmen, Merchants, and Associations in Roman and Late Roman Egypt*, Ann Arbor 2016.

VERBOVEN 2002: K. VERBOVEN, *The Economy of Friends: Economic Aspects of* Amicitia *and Patronage in the Late Republic*, Brussels 2002.

VERHOEVEN 2003: U. VERHOEVEN, 'Post ins Jenseits – Formular und Funktion altägyptischer Briefe an Tote', in: A. WAGNER (ed.), *Bote und Brief – Sprach-*

liche Systeme der Informationsübermittlung im Spannungsfeld von Mündlichkeit und Schriftlichkeit, Frankfurt am Main 2003, p. 31-51.

VÉRILHAC & VIAL 1998: A.M. VÉRILHAC & C. VIAL, *Le mariage grec du VIe siècle av. J.-C. à l'époque d'Auguste* (BCH Suppl. 32), Athens 1998.

VERMEESCH 2015a: G. VERMEESCH, 'Reflections on the Relative Accessibility of Law Courts in Early Modern Europe', *Crime, History and Societies* 19 (2015), p. 53-76.

VERMEESCH 2015b: G. VERMEESCH, 'The Social Composition of Plaintiffs and Defendants in the Peacemaker Court, Leiden, 1750-54', *Social History* 40 (2015), p. 208-229.

VERSNEL 1991: H.S. VERSNEL, 'Beyond Cursing: The Appeal to Justice in Judicial Prayers', in: C.A. FARAONE & D. OBBINK (eds.), *Magika Hiera Ancient Greek Magic and Religion*, New York & Oxford 1991, p. 60-106.

VERSNEL 2002: H.S. VERSNEL, 'Writing Mortals and Reading Gods. Appeal to the Gods as a Dual Strategy in Social Control', in: D. COHEN & E. MÜLLER-LUCKNER (eds.), *Demokratie, Recht und soziale Kontrolle im klassischen Athen*, Munich 2002, p. 37-76.

VERSNEL 2010: H.S. VERSNEL, 'Prayers for Justice, East and West: New Finds and Publications since 1990', in: H.S. VERSNEL, D. FRANKFURTER & J. HAND (eds.), *Magical Practice in the Latin West: Papers from the International Conference Held at the University of Zaragoza, 30 Sept.-1 Oct. 2005*, Leiden 2010, p. 275-354.

VESSEY 2010: M. VESSEY, 'The Origins of the *Collectio Sirmondiana*: A New Look at the Evidence', in: J. HARRIES & I.N. WOOD (eds.), *The Theodosian Code*, 2nd ed., Ithaca (N.Y.) 2010, p. 178-199.

VINSON 2008: S. VINSON, 'Through a Woman's Eyes, and in a Woman's Voice: Ihweret as Focalizor in the *First Tale of Setne Khaemwas*', in: P. MCKECHNIE & Ph. GUILLAUME (eds.), *Ptolemy II Philadelphus and His World*, Leiden 2008, p. 303-351.

VINSON 2011: S. VINSON, 'Strictly Tabubue: The Legacy of an Ancient Egyptian Femme Fatale', *KMT: A Modern Journal of Ancient Egypt* 22/3 (2011), p. 46-57.

VINSON 2018: S. VINSON, *The Craft of a Good Scribe. History, Narrative and Meaning in the First Tale of Setne Khaemwas*, Leiden 2018.

VITTMANN 1991: G. VITTMANN, 'Eine demotische Erwähnung des Ibi?', *Enchoria* 18 (1991), p. 123-128.

VITTMANN 1995: G. VITTMANN, 'Zwei demotische Briefe an den Gott Thot', *Enchoria* 22 (1995), p. 169-181.

VITTMANN 1998: G. VITTMANN, *Der demotische Papyrus Rylands 9* (Ägypten und Altes Testament 38), Wiesbaden 1998.

VITTMANN 2011: G. VITTMANN, 'Eine Urkunde mit den Satzungen eines Kultvereins', in: F. FEDER, L. LORENZ & G. VITTMANN (eds.), *Von Theben nach Giza. Festmiszellen für Stefan Grünert zum 65. Geburtstag*, Göttingen 2011, p. 169-179.

VIVIAN 1993: T. VIVIAN (trans.), *Histories of the Monks of Upper Egypt and the Life of Onnophrius*, Kalamazoo 1993.

VIVIAN 1999: T. VIVIAN, 'Humility and Resistance in Late Antique Egypt: The Life of Longinus', *Coptic Church Review* 20/1 (1999), p. 2-30.

VLEEMING 1989: S.P. VLEEMING, 'Strijd om het Erfdeel van Tefhapi', in: P.W. PESTMAN (ed.), *Familiearchieven uit het land van Pharao*, Zutphen 1989, p. 30-45.

VLEEMING 1994: S.P. VLEEMING, *Ostraka Varia: Tax Receipts and Legal Documents on Demotic, Greek, and Greek-Demotic Ostraka, Chiefly of the Early Ptolemaic Period, from Various Collections* (Pap.Lugd.Bat. 26), Leiden 1994.

VLEEMING 1995: S.P. VLEEMING, 'The Office of a Choachyte in the Theban Area', in: S.P. VLEEMING (ed.), *Hundred-Gated Thebes. Acts of the Colloquium on Thebes and the Theban Area in the Graeco-Roman Period* (Pap. Lugd.Bat. 27), Leiden, New York & Cologne 1995, p. 241-255.

VOLPE 2007: G. VOLPE, 'Il ruolo dei vescovi nei processi di trasformazione del paesaggio urbano e rurale', in: G.P. BROGIOLO & A.C. AMAU (eds.), *Archeologia e società tra Tardo Antico e Alto Medioevo: 12° Seminario sul tardo antico e l'alto Medioevo, Padova, 29 settembre-1 ottobre 2005* (Documenti di archeologia 44), Mantua 2007, p. 85-106.

WALBANK 2002: F.W. WALBANK, 'The Idea of Decline in Polybius', reprinted in *Polybius, Rome and the Hellenistic World. Essays and Reflections*, Cambridge 2002, p. 193-211.

WECKWERTH 2010: A. WECKWERTH, *Ablauf, Organisation und Selbstverständnis westlicher antiker Synoden im Spiegel ihrer Akten* (Jahrbuch für Antike und Christentum. Ergänzungsband, Kleine Reihe 5), Münster 2010.

WEGNER 2017: J. WEGNER, *Monastic Communities in Context: Social and Economic Interrelations of Monastic Institutions and Laymen in Middle Egypt (6th–8th centuries)*, unpubl. diss., University of Warsaw, Warsaw 2017.

WEISWEILER 2012: J. WEISWEILER, 'From Equality to Asymmetry. Honorific Statues, Imperial Power, and Senatorial Identity in Late-Antique Rome', *JRA* 25 (2012), p. 319-350.

WEISWEILER 2014: J. WEISWEILER, 'Review of L. Dossey, *Peasant and Empire in Christian North Africa*, Berkeley 2010 and C. Grey, *Constructing Communities in the Late Roman Countryside*, Cambridge 2011', *JRS* 104 (2014), p. 350-352.

WEISWEILER 2017: J. WEISWEILER, 'Populist Despotism and Infrastructural Power in the Later Roman Empire', in: C. ANDO & S. RICHARDSON (eds.), *Ancient States and Infrastructural Power: Europe, Asia, and America*, Philadelphia 2017, p. 149-178.

WENTE 1975/76: E.F. WENTE, 'A Misplaced Letter to the Dead', *OLP* 6/7 (1975/76), p. 595-600.

WESSEL 2004: S. WESSEL, *Cyril of Alexandria and the Nestorian Controversy: The Making of a Saint and of a Heretic* (Oxford Early Christian Studies), Oxford 2004.

WHITBY 2013: M. WHITBY, 'Writing in Greek: Classicism and Compilation, Interaction and Transformation', in: C. KELLY (ed.), *Theodosius II: Rethinking the Roman Empire in Late Antiquity* (Cambridge Classical Studies), Cambridge 2013, p. 195-218.

WHITE 1986: J.L. WHITE, *Light from Ancient Letters*, Philadelphia 1986.

WHITEHORNE 1984: J.E.G. WHITEHORNE, 'Tryphon's Second Marriage', in: *Atti del XVII Congresso Internationale di Papirologia*, Naples 1984, vol. 2, p. 1267-1274.

WHITEHORNE 2003: J.E.G. WHITEHORNE, 'Strategus, Centurion, or Neither: *BGU* I 321 and 322 (= *M.Chrest.* 114 and 124) and their Duplicates', *BASP* 40 (2003), p. 201-211.

WICKHAM 2005: C. WICKHAM, *Framing the Early Middle Ages. Europe and the Mediterranean 400-800*, Oxford 2005.

WIEMER 2014: H.-U. WIEMER. 'Akklamationen im spätrömischen Reich', *AKG* 86/1 (2004), p. 27-74.

WIENAND 2012: J. WIENAND, *Der Kaiser als Sieger: Metamorphosen triumphaler Herrschaft unter Constantin I*, Berlin 2012.

WILCKEN 1927: U. WILCKEN, *Urkunden der Ptolemäerzeit (ältere Funde)*, Berlin 1927.

WILSON 1948: J.A. WILSON, 'The Oath in Ancient Egypt', *JNES* 7 (1948), p. 129-156.

WILSON 2014: A.I. WILSON, 'Quantifying Roman Economic Performance by Means of Proxies: Pitfalls and Potential', in: F. DE CALLATAŸ (ed.), *Quantifying the Greco-Roman Economy and Beyond* (Pragmateiai 27), Bari 2014, p. 147-167.

WIMPFHEIMER 2011: B.S. WIMPFHEIMER, *Narrating the Law: A Poetics of Talmudic Legal Stories* (Divinations), Philadelphia 2011.

WITTENBURG 1990: A. WITTENBURG, *Il testamento di Epikteta*, Trieste 1990.

WOJTCZAK 2012: M. WOJTCZAK, 'Settlement of Claims as a Way of Dispute Resolution in the Light of P. Petra IV 39 – A Legal Commentary', *JJP* 42 (2012), p. 353-380.

WOJTCZAK 2016: M. WOJTCZAK, 'Legal Aspects of Dispute Resolution in Late Antiquity. The Case of P. Mich. XIII 659', *JJP* 46 (2016), p. 275-308.

WOLF 2015: J.G. WOLF, 'Documents in Roman Practice', in: D. JOHNSTON (ed.), *The Cambridge Companion to Roman Law*, Cambridge 2015, p. 61-84.

WOLFF 1960: H.-J. WOLFF, 'Plurality of Laws in Ptolemaic Egypt', *Revue Internationale des Droits de l'Antiquité* 7 (1960), p. 191-223.

WOLFF 1970: H.J. WOLFF, *Das Justizwesen der Ptolemäer* (Münchener Beiträge zur Papyrusforschung und antiken Rechtsgeschichte 44), 2nd ed., Munich 1970.

WOLFF 2020: C. WOLFF, 'La présence militaire dans les campagnes à l'époque romaine: chance ou fatalité pour les communautés rurales? Que disent les sources littéraires?', in: M. ROUX (ed.), *La présence militaire dans les campagnes aux époques hellénistique et romaine: chance ou fatalité pour les communautés rurales?*, Perpignan 2020, p. 13-28.

WOLLSCHLÄGER 1990: C. WOLLSCHLÄGER, 'Civil Litigation and Modernization: The Work of the Municipal Courts of Bremen, Germany, in Five Centuries, 1549-1984', *Law and Society Review* 24/2 (1990), p. 261-282.

WORRELL 1942: W.H. WORRELL, *Coptic Texts in the University of Michigan Collection*, Ann Arbor 1942.

Wörrle 2015: M. Wörrle, 'Die ptolemäische Garnison auf der Burg von Limyra im Licht einer neuen Inschrift', in: B. Beck-Brandt e.a. (eds.), *Turm und Tor, Siedlungsstrukturen in Lykien und benachbarten Kulturlandschaften*, Vienna 2015, p. 291-304.
Wuttmann 2001: M. Wuttmann, 'Les *qanāts* de 'Ayn-Manāwīr (oasis de Kharga, Égypte)', in: P. Briant (ed.), *Irrigation et drainage dans l'antiquité: qanāts et canalisations souterraines en Iran, en Égypte et en Grèce*, Paris 2001, p. 109-136.
Wyns 2016: V. Wyns, *Happiness and State in Ptolemaic Egypt* (Lecture delivered at the 28th International Congress of Papyrology), Barcelona 1-6 August 2016.
Wyns 2017: V. Wyns, 'The State Ideology of the Ptolemies: Origins and Influences', *CE* 92 (2017), p. 137-174.
Wyns 2018: V. Wyns, 'Happiness in the Kingdom of the Cleopatras: Examining Government Influence on Quality of Life in Hellenistic Egypt (332-30 BC)', *Historical Sociology* 2 (2018), p. 9-26.
Wyns 2019: V. Wyns, *"Everything Managed in the Best Way": Government Investments and Well-Being in Ptolemaic Egypt (332-30 BC)*, unpubl. diss., KU Leuven, Leuven 2019.
Wysocki 1985: Z. Wysocki, 'The Discovery and Reintegration of Two Niches in the East Chamber of the Queen. Hatshepsut's Main Sanctuary at Deir el-Bahari', in: P. Posener-Kriéger (ed.), *Mélanges Gamal Eddin Mokhtar*, 2 vol., Cairo 1985, p. 361-370.
Yiftach-Firanko 2001: U. Yiftach-Firanko, 'Was There a 'Divorce Procedure' among Greeks in Early Roman Egypt?', in M. Manfredi, I. Andorlini & G. Menci (eds.), *Atti del XXII Congresso Internazionale di Papirologia, Firenze, 23-29 agosto 1998*, Firenze 2001, vol. 2, p. 1331-1339.
Yiftach-Firanko 2003: U. Yiftach-Firanko, *Marriage and Marital Arrangements: A History of the Greek Marriage Document in Egypt 4th century BC-4th Century CE*, Munich 2003.
Yiftach-Firanko 2009: U. Yiftach-Firanko, 'Law in Graeco-Roman Egypt: Hellenization, Fusion, Romanization', in: R.S. Bagnall (ed.), *The Oxford Handbook of Papyrology*, Oxford 2009, p. 541-557.
Yiftach-Firanko 2014: U. Yiftach-Firanko, 'The Genesis of Byzantine Bilingual Reports of Proceedings: A Response to Bernhard Palme', in: M. Gagarin & A. Lanni (eds.), *Symposion 2013 – Vorträge zur griechischen und hellenistischen Rechtsgeschichte (Cambridge MA, 26.-29. August 2013)* (Akten der Gesellschaft für griechische und hellenistische Rechtsgeschichte 24), Vienna 2014, p. 429-438.
Yiftach 2015: U. Yiftach, 'The *Grammatikon*: Some Considerations on the Feeing Policies of Legal Documents in the Ptolemaic and Roman Periods', in: D. Kehoe e.a. (eds.), *Law and Transaction Costs in the Ancient Economy*, Ann Arbor 2015, p. 162-180.
Yuen-Collingridge 2010: R. Yuen-Collingridge, 'Hunting for Origen in Unidentified Papyri: The Case of P.Egerton 2 (= inv. 3)', in: T.J. Kraus &

T. NICKLAS (eds.), *Early Christian Manuscripts: Examples of Applied Method and Approach* (Texts and Editions for New Testament Study 5), Leiden & Boston 2010, p. 39-58.

ZAGHLOUL 1985: EL-H.O.M. ZAGHLOUL, *Frühdemotische Urkunden aus Hermupolis*, Cairo 1985.

ZAUZICH 1992/93: K.-Th. ZAUZICH, 'Paläographische Herausforderungen I', *Enchoria* 19/20 (1992/93), p. 165-179.

ZAUZICH 2000: K.-Th. ZAUZICH, 'Die demotischen Orakelfragen', in: P.J. FRANDSEN & K. RYHOLT (eds.), *A Miscellany of Demotic Texts and Studies*, Copenhagen 2000, p. 1-25.

ZICHE 2006: H. ZICHE, 'Making Late Roman Taxpayers Pay. Imperial Government Strategies and Practice', in: H.A. DRAKE (ed.), *Violence in Late Antiquity. Perceptions and Practices*, Aldershot 2006, p. 125-134.

ZUCKERMAN 2000: C. ZUCKERMAN, 'Le cirque, l'argent et le peuple. À propos d'une inscription du Bas-Empire', *REB* 58 (2000), p. 69-96.

ZUCKERMAN 2004: C. ZUCKERMAN, 'Les deux Dioscore d'Aphroditè ou les limites de la pétition', in: D. FEISSEL & J. GASCOU (eds.), *La pétition à Byzance* (Centre de recherche d'Histoire et Civilisation de Byzance. Monographies 14), Paris 2004, p. 75-92.

INDEX LOCORUM

1. Ostraca & papyri, tablets, linen, inscriptions (Hieratic, Demotic, Greek, Coptic; editions and/or inventory numbers)

2. Ancient literature, legal, episcopal and hagiographic sources

3. Medieval documents

STUDIA HELLENISTICA
(available volumes)

14. Goffinet, É., *L'utilisation d'Origène dans le Commentaire des psaumes de Saint Hilaire de Poitiers*. 1965, XXI-174 p. 12 EURO
15. Denis, A.-M., *Les thèmes de connaissance dans le Document de Damas*. 1967, XXV-245 p. 13 EURO
19. Olshausen, E., *Prosopographie der hellenistischen Königsgesandten*, Teil 1: *Von Triparadeisos bis Pydna*. 1974, XXVI-375 p. 30 EURO
20. Peremans, W., Van 't Dack, E., *Prosopographia Ptolemaica, VII: Index nominum*, par L. De Meulemeester-Swinnen et H. Hauben. 1975, 408 p. 45 EURO
21. Peremans, W., Van 't Dack, E., *Prosopographia Ptolemaica, VIII: Addenda et corrigenda aux volumes I (1950) et II (1952)*, par L. Mooren et W. Swinnen. 1975, 251 p. 22 EURO
22. Devijver, H., *De Aegypto et Exercitu Romano sive Prosopographia Militiarum Equestrium quae ab Augusto ad Gallienum seu statione seu origine ad Aegyptum pertinebant*. 1975, 128 p. 9 EURO
25. Peremans, W., Van 't Dack, E., *Prosopographia Ptolemaica, IX: Addenda et corrigenda au volume III (1956)*, par W. Clarysse. 1981, XX-285 p. 36 EURO
28. Mehl, A., *Seleukos Nikator und sein Reich. Teil 1: Seleukos' Leben und die Entwicklung seiner Machtposition*. 1986, XVI-351 p. 54 EURO
29. Van 't Dack, E., *Ptolemaica selecta. Études sur l'armée et l'administration lagides*. 1988, XXVIII-409 p. 60 EURO
30. Verdin, H., Schepens, G., De Keyser, E. (eds.), *Purposes of History. Studies in Greek Historiography from the 4th to the 2nd Centuries B.C. Proceedings of the International Colloquium Leuven, 24-26 May 1988*. 1990, XXX-385 p. 68 EURO
32. Van der Stockt, L. (ed.), *Plutarchea Lovaniensia. A Miscellany of Essays on Plutarch*. 1996, XIV-328 p. 55 EURO
33. Osborne, M.J., Byrne, S.G., *The Foreign Residents of Athens. An Annex to the Lexicon of Greek Personal Names, Attica*. 1996, XXXVIII-423 p. 63 EURO
35. Bollansée, J., *Hermippos of Smyrna and his Biographical Writings. A Reappraisal*. 1999, XXXVI-256 p. 30 EURO
36. Mooren, L. (ed.), *Politics, Administration and Society in the Hellenistic and Roman World. Proceedings of the International Colloquium Bertinoro, 19-24 July 1997*. 2000, XXII-514 p. 97 EURO
38. Clarysse, W., Hauben, H., Mooren, L., Vandorpe, K., *Prosopographia Ptolemaica, X:* La'da, C.A., *Foreign Ethnics in Hellenistic Egypt*. 2002, XLVI-384 p. 85 EURO

39. Ridley, R.T., *The Emperor's Retrospect. Augustus' Res Gestae in Epigraphy, Historiography and Commentary*. 2003, XXVI-252 p. 70 EURO
40. Byrne, S.G., *Roman Citizens of Athens*. 2003, XXXIV-566 p. 80 EURO
41. Véïsse, A-E., *Les «Révoltes Égyptiennes». Recherches sur les troubles intérieurs en Égypte du Règne de Ptolémée III à la conquête Romaine*. 2004, XVI-298 p. 70 EURO
42. Schepens, G., Bollansée, J. (eds.), *The Shadow of Polybius. Intertextuality as a Research Tool in Greek Historiography. Proceedings of the International Colloquium Leuven, 21-22 September 2001*. 2005, XIV-345 p. 65 EURO
43. Mueller, K., *Settlements of the Ptolemies. City Foundations and New Settlement in the Hellenistic World*. 2006, XVII-249 p. 59 EURO
44. Verboven, K., Vandorpe, K., Chankowski, V. (eds.), *Pistoi dia tèn technèn. Bankers, Loans and Archives in the Ancient World. Studies in Honour of Raymond Bogaert*. 2008, XLVIII-482 p. 84 EURO
45. Gorre, G., *Les relations du clergé égyptien et des Lagides d'après les sources privées*. 2009, LVIII-641 p. 105 EURO
46. Bravo, B., *La Chronique d'Apollodore et le Pseudo-Skymnos. Érudition antiquaire et littérature géographique dans la seconde moitié du IIe siècle av. J.-C.* 2009, XXIV-268 p. 70 EURO
47. Haegemans, K., *Imperial Authority and Dissent. The Roman Empire in AD 235-238*. 2010, LXIV-276 p. 70 EURO
48. Van Nuffelen, P. (ed.), *Faces of Hellenism. Studies in the History of the Eastern Mediterranean (4th Century B.C. – 5th Century A.D.)*. 2009, X-342 p. 62 EURO
49. Legras, B., *Les reclus grecs du Sarapieion de Memphis. Une enquête sur l'hellénisme égyptien*. 2011, XIII-320 p. 72 EURO
50. Schäfer, D., *Makedonische Pharaonen und hieroglyphische Stelen. Historische Untersuchungen zur Satrapenstele und verwandten Denkmälern*. 2011, XLVI-323 p. 72 EURO
51. Iossif, P.P., Chankowski, A.S., Lorber, C.C. (eds.), *More than Men, Less than Gods: Studies on Royal Cult and Imperial Worship. Proceedings of the International Colloquium organized by the Belgian School at Athens (November 1-2, 2007)*. 2011, XVIII-735 p. 97 EURO
52. Bennett, C., *Alexandria and the Moon. An Investigation into the Lunar Macedonian Calendar of Ptolemaic Egypt*. 2011, XXXVI-276 p. 68 EURO
53. Hauben, H., Meeus, A. (eds.), *The Age of the Successors and the Creation of the Hellenistic Kingdoms (323-276 B.C.)*. 2014, XVI-733 p. 105 EURO
54. Broux, Y., *Double Names and Elite Stategy in Roman Egypt*. 2015, X-317 p. 94 EURO
55. Coussement, S., *'Because I Am Greek'. Polyonymy as an Expression of Ethnicity in Ptolemaic Egypt*. 2016, XX-429 p. 98 EURO
56. Caneva, S.G., *From Alexander to the Theoi Adelphoi. Foundation and Legitimation of a Dynasty*. 2016, XVI-289 p. 94 EURO

57. Engels, D., *Benefactors, Kings, Rulers. Studies on the Seleukid Empire between East and West.* 2017, XIV-603 p. 110 EURO
58. Hau, L.I., Meeus, A., Sheridan, B. (eds.), *Diodoros of Sicily. Historiographical Theory and Practice in the Bibliotheke.* 2018, X-612 p. 115 EURO
59. Gorre, G., Wackenier, S. (eds.), *Quand la fortune du royaume ne dépend pas de la vertu du prince : Un renforcement de la monarchie lagide de Ptolémée VI à Ptolémée X (169-88 av. J.-C.)?.* 2020, VIII-192 p. 68 EURO
60. Fernoux, H., Gangloff, A., Guerber, É., *La gloire de Rhodes au Ier siècle de notre ère (à partir du Discours aux Rhodiens de Dion de Pruse).* 2021, X-341 p. 88 EURO
61. Chaufray, M.-P., *La fonction du lésônis dans les temples égyptiens de l'époque saïte à l'époque ptolémaïque.* 2023, XXX-510 p. 155 EURO

PRINTED ON PERMANENT PAPER • IMPRIME SUR PAPIER PERMANENT • GEDRUKT OP DUURZAAM PAPIER - ISO 9706
N.V. PEETERS S.A., WAROTSTRAAT 50, B-3020 HERENT